This modern text is designed to prepare you for your future professional career. While theories, ideas, techniques, and data are dynamic, the information contained in this volume will provide you a quick and useful reference as well as a guide for future learning for many years to come. Your familiarity with the contents of this book will make it an important volume in your professional library.

EX LIBRIS

Compensation

Compensation

George T. Milkovich
Cornell University

Jerry M. Newman
State University of New York—Buffalo

1987   Second Edition
BUSINESS PUBLICATIONS, INC. Plano, Texas 75075

ISBN 0-256-03709-4

Library of Congress Catalog Card No. 86-72247

Printed in the United States of America

2 3 4 5 6 7 8 9 0 DO 4 3 2 1 0 9 8 7

Preface

Compensation is a fascinating subject. Everyone suspects it is determined without apparent justice. No one is indifferent to the subject, particularly when their own pay is being discussed. In addition to this inherent fascination, we are in a period when traditional approaches to pay determination are increasingly challenged and scrutinized.

Faced with serious economic pressures to improve productivity, boost the quality of products and services, and control labor costs, as well as social pressures from shifting employee expectations and continued government regulations, managers are reexamining their approaches to pay determination. They need to better understand how to design and manage the compensation their employees receive. As a result traditional, often bureaucratic, approaches are being reexamined. In some instances different approaches, some new and some simply old goods in new wrappings, are being tried. Often the current approach is retained but becomes better understood and managed after being reexamined.

This process of creative reexamination is both a boon and a source of frustration for compensation managers. On the positive side, compensation managers have the opportunity to make decisions that dramatically affect their organizations. Pay decisions can be integrated into the entire strategic management process. Compensation policies can facilitate effective work behaviors, support equitable treatment of employees, and accomplish organization objectives.

These opportunities can also be a source of frustration. Very simply, compensation management can no longer be managed from a limited approach. Pursuit of the single correct technique is futile. Multiple answers are more or less viable depending on the characteristics of both the organization and its environment.

About this Edition

The design of this book is largely based on four strategic choices involved in managing compensation systems. As the compensation model in Chapter 1 illustrates, these strategic choices include concerns for internal consistency (internal equity), external competitiveness (external equity), employee contributions (employee equity), and the process of administration. Four sections in this book examine each of these strategic decisions and discuss the major compensation issues requiring resolution. These discussions are placed in the context of related theories, research, and state-of-the-art practices that can guide compensation decision making.

Additional chapters of this book cover employee benefits, government's influences on compensation, pay discrimination, and unions' role in pay administration. These are topics of continuing importance. First, costs of employee benefits have escalated rapidly, and employers are taking significant steps to contain these costs by modifying benefit programs. Employees are also increasingly able to choose various benefits tailored to their individual circumstances. Next, the government's role is considered in terms of its direct and indirect effects on pay. Directly, government is a regulator of pay decisions through legislation and the courts (e.g., minimum wage, pay discrimination, and comparable worth). Indirectly, through its fiscal and monetary policies (e.g., tax laws and stimulating the economy), the government affects the supply and demand for labor and, hence, compensation decisions. The changing yet critical role unions play in compensation management is also examined in a separate chapter and throughout the book.

This book undertakes three central tasks. The first is to examine the current theory and research related to managing compensation. This analysis is supported by extensive up-to-date references in each chapter.

The second task is to examine the changing state of compensation practice. Here we draw upon practices actually used by wide variety of employers and consulting firms. These practices illustrate new developments as well as the established approaches to compensation decisions.

Finally, this book provides an opportunity for you to develop your own decision-making skills through a series of exercises based on actual experiences. These exercises emphasize using concepts and techniques. A workbook with more extensive cases and computer applications is also available. Completing these exercises will help you develop skills readily transferable to future jobs and assignments.

Acknowledgments

We relied on the contributions of many people in the preparation of this book. We owe a special, continuing debt of gratitude to our students. In the classroom they motivate and challenge us, and as returning managers with compensation experience, they try mightily to keep our work relevant.

Compensation professionals in many different organizations shared their ideas and practices with us for the first edition and we would like to acknowledge them again. Our appreciation goes to Steve Kumagai (Control Data Corporation), David Ness (Metronics), Ronald Page (Control Data Corporation),

George Schmidt (Citibank), and David Wessinger (Organization Resources Counselors).

We would also like to acknowledge those academic colleagues who helped us with the first edition. Detailed comments by George Bohlander (Arizona State University), Chris Berger (Purdue University), John Fossum (University of Minnesota), and Sara Rynes (Cornell University) were particularly useful. Michael Gold's (Cornell University) and Cynthia Fukami's (University of Denver) comments strengthened the first edition. David Belcher (San Diego State) influenced the thinking of many compensation professionals, including us.

We appreciate the contributions of the many compensation professionals who shared their ideas and practices with us for this second edition. Some commented on early drafts of chapters; others shared details about particular problems and projects. While we cannot hope to recognize all of them, a few who went beyond the call of duty include:

Harold Bell	J. C. Penney
Al Bellak	Hay Associates
Brian Cartwright	General Motors Corporation
Don Finn	J. C. Penney
Ron Hansen	3M
Wes Leibtag	IBM
Dan Lesch	Honeywell Corporation
Ray Olsen	TRW
Walt Read	IBM
Ken Ross	AT&T
James Urbas	Borg Warner
Steve Wolf	Kerr-McGee

One compensation professional's efforts stand out—we owe a special debt of gratitude to Nathan Winstanley of the Rochester Institute of Technology. His crisp comments and criticisms—written on backs of envelopes, all manner of notepads, lecture notes, textbook margins, and the like—were absolutely invaluable. His suggestions for improving this book, if not always followed, are greatly appreciated.

Several academic colleagues were helpful in the preparation of this book. The detailed comments of the following were especially appreciated:

Ronald A. Ash	University of Kansas
David B. Balkin	Louisiana State University—Baton Rouge
Renae Broderick	University of California—Los Angeles
Robert Cardy	State University of New York—Buffalo
Michael D. Crino	Clemson University
James C. Hodgetts	Memphis State University

Gregory S. Hundley	University of Oregon
John G. Kilgour	California State University
Frank Krzystofiak	State University of New York—Buffalo
Bonnie Rabin	Cornell University
Robert Risley	Cornell University
Sara Rynes	Cornell University
Vida Scarpello	University of Georgia
Donald P. Schwab	University of Wisconsin
Susan Schwozhau	State University of New York—Buffalo
Thomas H. Stone	University of Iowa

Gloria deBajar of Cornell University developed the glossary and offered particularly helpful comments.

Our deans, Robert Doherty (Cornell) and Joe Alutto (SUNY—Buffalo), continue to provide supportive work climates, for which we thank them. Manuscript preparation by Josephine Churey and Hilde Rogers was always thorough and timely.

Contributions of Sarah Milkovich and Terrie, Erinn, and Kelly Newman to the authors' quality of work life is unparalleled.

We owe a continuing and special debt to Carolyn Milkovich. Her administrative, editing, and motivational talents continue to be of inestimable value.

George T. Milkovich
Jerry M. Newman

Contents

Part 3
Employee Contributions: Determining Individual Pay *266*

Chapter 1

Strategic Issues and the Pay Model

Think of an employer, any employer—from Burlington Northern Railroad to Ralph's Pretty Good Groceries—and consider the array of wages paid. Burlington Northern's wages differ for different jobs ranging from locomotive engineers, to laborers on maintenance-of-way gangs, accountants, traffic clerks, and nurses. Similarly, Ralph's pays checkout clerks, produce department managers, and butchers.[1]

Why do some employers pay more (or less) than other employers? Why are different jobs within the same organization paid differently? And why do different workers doing the same job for the same employer receive different pay?

---

[1] Garrison Keillor, *Lake Wobegon Days* (New York: Viking Press, 1985).

1

How are these decisions made and who is involved in making them? What are the consequences of these decisions for both the employer and the employee? These questions were so interesting to Mary Lemons, a Denver nurse, that she took her employer, the city of Denver, to court, alleging that it was illegal to pay Denver's tree trimmers (all men) more than its nurses (mostly women).[2] Compensation, whether it's your own or someone else's, is a fascinating topic.

Compensation professionals are immersed in one of society's greatest challenges: the efficient and equitable distribution of the returns for work. As already noted, compensation decisions are many and varied. They include how much to pay people who perform both similar and different types of work; whether to use pay to recognize variations in individual employees' experience and/or performance; and how to allocate pay between cash and benefits and services. Such basic decisions must be made by every employer, no matter how large or small. Further, these decisions must be consistent both with society's changing values about what constitutes fair and equitable pay and with government legislation and regulations. Consequently, decisions about compensating people for the work they perform are increasingly complex, as are the skills required to make those decisions.

This book is about the management of compensation—the decisions that go into paying employees; the concepts and research underlying those decisions; the alternative techniques used to help make decisions; and the objectives obtained. Its purpose is to give you the background required to make these pay decisions. Let us start with what is meant by compensation.

COMPENSATION IN CONTEMPORARY SOCIETY

Perceptions of compensation vary. Some in *society* may see it as a measure of equity and justice. Others may see high pay as a cause of U.S. firms' inability to meet foreign competition. Still others may see it as an underlying cause of tax increases. For example, a comparison of 1984 median weekly earnings of fully employed women ($268, or 66 percent) with that of men ($404) highlights apparent inequities in pay decisions, which many consider an indication of discrimination against women.[3] To consumers, the fact that production workers in South Korea earn, on average, 11 percent ($1.29) of their U.S. counterparts' hourly pay ($12.26) is the root of U.S. manufacturing competitive problems.[4] Some voters also see compensation as the cause of increased taxes (wages for teachers and public employees) and inflation (wage settlements negotiated by

---

[2] *Lemons* v. *City and County of Denver,* 620 F.2d 228 (1980).

[3] "The Wage Gap," in *Comparable Worth: An Analysis and Recommendations,* a Report of the United States Commission on Civil Rights, June 1985; June O'Neill, "The Trend in the Male-Female Wage Gap in the United States," *Journal of Labor Statistics* 3 (1985), pp. S91–S116.

[4] Joyanna Moy, "Recent Trends in Unemployment and the Labor Force, 10 Countries," *Monthly Labor Review,* August 1985, pp. 9–22; and "Sky-High U.S. Wages May Hurt Competitive Stance," *Compensation and Benefits Review,* November–December 1985, pp. 4–5.

unions). Public policymakers and legislators may view income differences as guides for adjusting entitlements and transfer payments (social security, aid to dependent children, and the like).

In contrast to the societal perspectives, *employees* may see compensation as a return for services rendered or as a reward for satisfactory or meritorious work. Compensation to some reflects the value of their personal skills and abilities, or the return for the education and training they have acquired. The pay individuals receive for the work they perform is usually the major source of personal income and hence a vital determinant of an individual's economic and social well-being.

Managers also have a stake in compensation; they view it from two perspectives. First, it is a *major expense.* Studies show that in many enterprises labor costs account for more than 50 percent of total costs.[5] Among some industries, such as service or public employment, this figure is even higher. Recent studies report that labor costs as a percent of total costs vary even among individual firms within one industry. This has led some to conclude that compensation practices can offer some firms a competitive advantage in their industry.[6]

In addition to viewing compensation as an expense, a manager will also view it as a possible *influence on employee work attitudes and behaviors.*[7] Compensation may affect an individual's decision to apply for a job, to work productively, to organize a union, to take the employer to court, or even to undertake more training for a new job. This potential to influence employees' work attitudes and behaviors is an important rationale for ensuring that compensation is managed fairly and equitably. These contrasting perspectives of compensation—societal, individual, and managerial, each with different stakes in compensation decisions—can account for the relevance of the topic. But these perspectives can also cause confusion if not everyone is talking about the same thing. So let's define what we mean by compensation.

FORMS OF PAY

Compensation, or pay (the words are used interchangeably in this book), is defined in the following terms:

> **Compensation** refers to all forms of financial returns and tangible services and benefits employees receive as part of an employment relationship.

---

[5]Ira T. Kay and Martin Leshner, *Human Resource Costs and Business Strategy: Striving for Competitive Advantage in the Pharmaceutical Industry* (New York: The Hay Group, 1986).

[6]Ibid.

[7]Edward E. Lawler III, *Pay and Organizational Development* (Reading, Mass.: Addison-Wesley Publishing, 1981).

EXHIBIT 1.1
Forms of Compensation

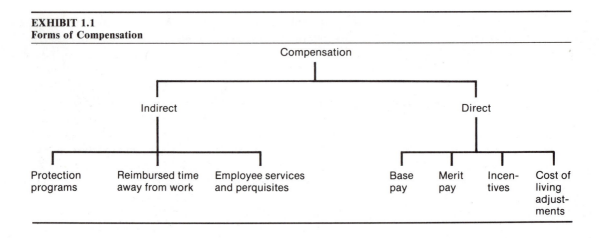

Exhibit 1.1 shows the variety of forms of compensation. Pay may be received directly in the form of cash (e.g., wages, merit increases, incentives, cost-of-living adjustments) or indirectly through benefits and services (e.g., pensions, health insurance, time off). This definition excludes other forms of rewards or returns that employees may receive, such as promotions, verbal recognition for outstanding work behaviors, feelings of accomplishment, and the like. Such factors may be thought of as part of an organization's "total reward system" and should be coordinated with compensation wherever possible.[8]

Programs that distribute compensation to employees can be designed in an unlimited number of ways, and a single employer typically will use more than one program. These pay delivery programs typically fall into four forms: base wage, merit pay, incentives, and employee services and benefits.

Base wage is the basic cash compensation that an employer pays for the work performed. Base wage tends to reflect the value of the work itself and generally ignores differences in contribution attributable to individual employees. For example, the base wage for a word processor's work may be $8 an hour, but some individual operators may receive more because of their experience and/or performance. Some pay systems set base wage as a function of the skill or education an employee possesses; examples include engineers, scientists, and craft workers. Periodic adjustments to base wages may be made on the basis of changes in the overall cost of living or inflation, changes in what other employers are paying for the same jobs, or changes in experience/performance/ skill of employees.

---

[8]We thank Chris Berger and Bill Whitely for this comment. Readers interested in a broader perspective of reward systems in organization can turn to M. A. Von Glinow, "Reward Strategies for Attracting, Evaluating and Retaining Professionals," *Human Resource Management,* Summer 1985, pp. 191–206; or L. L. Cummings, "Compensation, Culture, and Motivation: A Systems Perspective," *Organizational Dynamics,* Winter 1984, pp. 33–44.

A distinction is often made between salary and wage, with *salary* referring to pay for those workers who are exempt from regulations of the Fair Labor Standards Act, and hence do not receive overtime pay.[9] Managers and professionals usually fit this category. We refer to such employees as "exempts." Their pay would be calculated at an annual or monthly rate rather than hourly, because hours worked do not need to be recorded. In contrast, workers who are covered by overtime and reporting provisions of the Fair Labor Standards Act—"nonexempts"—usually have their pay calculated at an hourly rate referred to as a *wage*. Some employers, such as Hewlett-Packard and IBM, label all base pay as salary in an attempt to support a management philosophy that all employees are working as a team, rather than being divided into salaried and wage earners.

Merit pay rewards past work behaviors and accomplishments. It is often given as lump-sum payments or as increments to the base pay. Merit programs are commonly designed to pay different amounts (often at different times) depending on the level of performance. Thus, outstanding performers may receive a 10 to 12 percent merit increase nine months after their last increase, whereas a satisfactory performer may receive, say, a 6 to 8 percent increase after 12 to 15 months.

Note that merit pay is defined as *rewards*. A reward is given for meritorious performance. A *return* is given in exchange for something of value. Students of compensation do not always make a distinction between rewards and returns. Some refer to all pay as "rewards." Yet few employees would see all of their compensation as a "reward." Rather, they are more likely to describe it as a *return* received in exchange for labor and services given to an employer.

What difference does the distinction between reward and return make? As we will see later, differences in employee and employer perceptions about pay and pay increases may influence the effectiveness of the pay program. These differences in perception are one reason for the ineffectiveness of many "merit pay" programs.

Incentives also tie pay directly to performance. Incentives may be long or short term, and can be tied to the performance by an individual employee, a team of employees, a total business unit, or even some combination of individual, team, and unit. Usually very specific performance standards are used in short-term incentive programs. For example, Allstate Insurance agents who write $1 million worth of new insurance policies by March 1 win a trip to Aruba. At General Motors, an increase in yearly profits results in an average incentive payment of $640 per employee.[10] Performance results may be defined as cost

---

[9]The Fair Labor Standards Act is discussed in Chapter 13.

[10]U.S. Department of Labor, "Wage Highlights," *Current Wage Developments* 37, no. 5 (March 1985), p. 3. See also "Developments in Industrial Relations," *Monthly Labor Review,* December 1984, pp. 46–49, 54; and Harry C. Katz, "The GM–UAW Sellout," *Personnel,* January 1985, pp. 16–24.

savings, volume produced, quality standards met, revenues, returns on investments, or increased profits; the possibilities are endless.

Long-term incentives are intended to focus employee efforts on longer range (multiyear) results. Top managers or professionals are often offered long-term incentives (e.g., stock ownership, bonuses) to focus on long-term organizational objectives such as return on investment, market share, return on net assets, and the like.[11]

Incentives and merit pay differ. While both may influence performance, incentives do so by offering pay as an inducement. Merit, on the other hand, is a reward that recognizes outstanding past performance. The distinction is a matter of timing. Incentive systems are offered prior to the actual performance. Sales commissions are an example; an auto sales agent knows the commission on a Cadillac versus that on a Chevy prior to making the sale. Merit pay, on the other hand, typically is not communicated beforehand, and the amount of money to fund merit increases is usually not known very far in advance.

Merit and incentives are clearly related. Insofar as employees begin to anticipate their merit pay, it acts as an incentive to induce performance. Thus, anticipated rewards become incentives. Merit is typically based on individual performance; incentives may be based on the performance of an individual, team, or unit.

Employee services and benefits are the programs that include a wide array of alternative pay forms ranging from time away from work (vacations, jury duty), services (drug counseling, financial planning, cafeteria support), and protection (medical care, life insurance, and pensions). Because the cost of providing these services and benefits has been rising (for example, employers pay nearly half the nation's health care bills, and health care expenditures have increased at rates in excess of the overall inflation rate every year since 1970), they have become an increasingly important form of pay.[12] Many employers now manage benefits as closely as they manage direct compensation.[13]

These four pay forms make up the total compensation package paid to employees. The compensation professional is responsible for designing and managing all elements of pay—total compensation. We turn now to a pay model

---

[11]Bruce R. Ellig, *Executive Compensation—A Total Pay Perspective* (New York: McGraw Hill, 1982), pp. 219–66; Tom Patten, *Pay: Employee Compensation and Incentive Plans* (New York: Free Press, 1977); Jude T. Rich and John A. Larson, "Why Some Long-Term Incentives Fail," *Compensation Review,* First Quarter 1984, pp. 26–38; Michael J. Walters and Peter T. Chingos, *Accountants' Handbook Executive Compensation* (New York: Peat, Marwick, Mitchell & Co., 1980).

[12]Leonard Marlnaccio, "Managing the Health Care Dollar," *Compensation and Benefits Management,* Winter 1985, pp. 169–74.

[13]R. E. Herzlinger, "How Companies Tackle Health Care Costs, Parts I, II, & III," *Harvard Business Review,* July–August 1985, pp. 68–81, September–October 1985, pp. 108–20, and November–December 1985, pp. 72–87.

which will serve as both a framework for examining current pay systems and a guide for much of this work.

A PAY MODEL

The pay model shown in Exhibit 1.2 contains three basic components: (1) the policies that form the foundations of the compensation system; (2) the techniques that make up much of the mechanics or technology of compensation management; and (3) the compensation objectives. Each of these components and the relationships among them are discussed in turn.

Compensation Objectives

Pay systems are designed and managed to achieve certain objectives. The basic objectives, shown at the right side of the model, include efficiency, equity, and compliance with laws and regulations. These objectives in the model are broadly conceived. The *efficiency* objective is typically stated more specifically: (1) improving productivity and (2) controlling labor costs. Often these two can be found in an employer's statement of pay objectives, such as "to facilitate orga-

EXHIBIT 1.2
A Pay Model

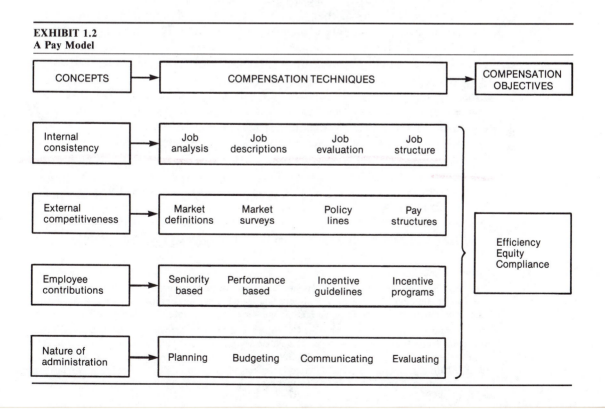

nization performance, to cost effectively attract and retain competent employees and to reward employee contributions and performance."[14]

Equity is a fundamental theme in pay systems. Statements such as "fair treatment for all employees" or "a fair day's pay for a fair day's work" reflect a concern for equity. Thus, the equity objective attempts to ensure fair pay treatment for all participants in the employment relationships. The equity objective focuses on designing pay systems that recognize both employee *contributions* (e.g., offering higher pay for greater performance or greater experience or training) and employee *needs* (e.g., providing a "living wage," or health care insurance).

Procedural equity, often overlooked by compensation researchers, is concerned with the processes used to make decisions about pay.[15] It suggests that the way a pay decision is made may be as important to employees as are the results of the decision. As an objective for a pay system, procedural equity helps ensure that employees, managers, and other relevant parties have a voice in the design of pay plans and an opportunity to voice any dissatisfaction with the pay received.

Compliance, as a pay objective, involves conforming to various federal and state compensation laws and regulations. As these laws and regulations change, pay systems often need to be adjusted to ensure continued compliance.

There are probably as many statements of pay objectives as there are employers. In fact, some highly diversified firms, such as TRW and Dart-Kraft Industries, which compete in multiple lines of businesses, have different pay objectives for different business units. Examples of Honeywell's and Hewlett-Packard's pay objectives are shown in Exhibit 1.3. Both sets of objectives emphasize high-quality and innovative performance (productivity), competitiveness (costs), ability to attract and retain quality people (productivity), and equity (employee communications, openness, and understanding).

Establishing pay objectives involves several important decisions because these objectives serve several purposes. First, objectives shape the design of the pay system. Consider the employer whose objective is to reward outstanding individual performance. That objective will determine the pay policy (e.g., pay for performance) as well as the elements of pay plans (e.g., merit and/or incentives). Another employer may decide the primary objective of the pay system is to attract and retain competent, highly skilled employees. This employer may

---

[14]Some writers distinguish between efficiency and effectiveness in organizations. Efficiency focuses on operational concerns such as improving productivity in operations, whereas effectiveness focuses on overall organization performance. The terms are used interchangeably in this text.

[15]Jerald Greenberg and Ronald L. Cohen, eds., *Equity and Justice in Social Behavior* (New York: Academic Press, 1982); also see G. L. Leventhal, "What Should Be Done with Equity Theory?" in *Social Exchange Theory,* ed. K. Gergen, M. Greenberg, and R. Willis (New York: Plenum Press, 1980); and Robert Folger and Jerald Greenberg, "Procedural Justice: An Interpretive Analysis of Personal Systems," in *Research in Personnel and Human Resources Management,* vol. 3, ed. K. Rowland and G. Ferris, (Greenwich, Conn.: Jai Press, 1985), pp. 141–83.

EXHIBIT 1.3
Comparison of Pay System Objectives

Hewlett-Packard

At Hewlett-Packard, our pay program is designed to be innovative, competitive, and equitable so that H-P will continue to attract and retain creative and enthusiastic people who will contribute to H-P's continuing success.

> Your pay has been established to reflect the company's policy of "paying among the leaders."
>
> Your pay will accurately reflect your sustained relative contribution to your unit, division, and H-P.
>
> Your pay system will be open and understandable. You are encouraged to discuss the pay process with your supervisor.

Honeywell

To attract the best person available for each Honeywell job.

To encourage growth both on an individual basis and as a participant on a work team.

To recognize the importance of high-quality work performance and to reward it accordingly.

To encourage a career-long commitment to Honeywell.

---

decide that performance is best influenced through other personnel practices such as job enrichment or team building techniques. A pay system with these objectives may stress market competitiveness and relatively high base salaries. The point is that different objectives may result in the design of different pay systems.

Besides affecting the mechanics of pay systems, objectives serve as the standards against which the success of the pay system is evaluated. If the pay objective is to attract and retain a highly competent staff, yet skilled employees are leaving to take higher paying jobs at other employers, the pay system may not be performing effectively. While there may be many nonpay reasons for turnover (or even if there is a desirable level of turnover), objectives serve as a standard for evaluating the effectiveness of a pay system.

The Four Basic Policy Decisions

The pay model in Exhibit 1.2 rests on four basic policies that any employer must consider in compensation management. The four policy decisions shown on the left side of the pay model include (1) internal consistency, (2) external competitiveness, (3) individual contributions, and (4) the nature of the administration of the pay system. These policies form the four building blocks, the foundation on which pay systems are designed and administered. These policies also serve as guidelines within which pay is managed to accomplish the system's objectives.

Internal consistency. Internal consistency, often called internal equity, refers to comparisons among jobs or skill levels *inside* a single organization. The focus is on comparing jobs and skills in terms of their relative contributions to the organization's objectives. How, for example, does the work of the word processor compare with the work of the computer operator, the programmer, and the systems analyst? Does one job require more skill or experience than another? Is the output from one job valued more than the output from another? Internal consistency becomes a factor in determining the pay rates both for employees doing equal work and for those doing dissimilar work. In fact, determining what is an equitable difference in pay for people performing different work is one of the key issues in compensation management.

But internal consistency goes beyond the same treatment. It incorporates concerns for the fairness of pay. Internal equity has two dimensions:

1. The relative similarities and differences in the content of the work or skills required.
2. The relative contribution of the work or skills to the organization's objectives.

The content of one set of tasks and behaviors (a job) is either equal to or different from another set of tasks and behaviors. A job's relative worth is based on its differing work content and its differing contribution to achieving the objectives of the organization. For example, the contribution of a systems analyst who designs a new inventory or production control system is typically considered to be greater than that of the programmer of the system.

A policy that emphasizes internal consistency may affect all three basic compensation objectives. Equity and compliance with legislation are directly affected, while efficiency is affected more indirectly. Pay relationships that are internally consistent are based on the content of the work or skills required and the relative contribution of the work to the organization's overall objectives. As we shall see in Part 1 of the text, equitable pay relationships within the organization directly affect employee decisions to stay (retention), to invest in additional skills (training), or to seek greater responsibility and higher skills (promotion). By motivating increased training and greater responsibility, pay relationships indirectly affect the efficiency of the work force and hence the effectiveness of the total organization.

All employers must decide the relative importance of internal consistency (equity) in their pay systems. If it is very important, then resources will be allocated to support this policy. For example, employers who emphasize internal consistency in pay will have relatively elaborate techniques included in their pay systems (e.g., job analysis and job evaluation) designed to assess internal consistency.

External competitiveness. External competitiveness refers to how an employer positions its pay relative to what competitors are paying. How much do other employers pay accountants, and how much do we wish to pay accountants in comparison to what other employers would pay them? All employers make decisions regarding the external competitiveness of their pay, and in doing so they have several policy options. Some employers may set their pay levels higher than their competition, hoping to attract the best applicants. Of course, this assumes that someone is able to identify and hire the "best" from the pool of applicants. Another employer may offer lower base pay but greater opportunity to work overtime or better benefits than those offered by other employers. Or pay and benefits may be lower, but job security may be higher. The policy regarding external competitiveness has a twofold effect on objectives: (1) to ensure that the pay rates are sufficient to attract and retain employees—if employees do not perceive their pay as equitable in comparison to what other organizations are offering for similar work, they may be more likely to leave—and (2) to control labor costs so that the organization's prices of products or services can remain competitive. So external competitiveness directly affects both the efficiency and equity objectives. And it must do so in a way that complies with relevant legislation. Employers who place relatively greater emphasis on external competitiveness may be likely to match or exceed job offers that employees receive from competing firms and may allocate more resources to surveying competitors' pay practices.

Employee contributions. The policy on employee contributions refers to the relative emphasis placed on the performance and/or seniority of people doing the same job or possessing the same job skills. Should all such employees receive the same pay? Or should one programmer be paid differently from another if one has better performance and/or greater seniority? Or should a more productive team of employees be paid more than less productive teams? The degree of emphasis to be placed on performance and/or seniority is an important policy in the design and administration of pay since it may have a direct effect on employees' attitudes and work behaviors and hence on improving efficiency and achieving equity. Employers with strong pay for performance policies are more likely to design more elaborate incentive and merit schemes as part of their pay systems.

Nature of administration. Policies regarding the nature of the administration of the pay system is the last building block in our model. While it is possible to design a system that incorporates internal consistency, external competitiveness, and employee contributions, the system will not achieve its objectives unless it is administered properly. The greatest system design in the world is useless without competent administration. Administration involves planning the elements of pay that should be included in the pay system (e.g., base pay, short-term and long-term incentives), evaluating how the pay system is operating, communicating with employees, and judging whether the system is achieving its objectives. Are we able to attract skilled workers? Can we keep them? Do our employees feel our system is fair? Do they understand what factors are considered in setting their pay? Do they agree that these factors are important? Do employees have channels for raising questions and voicing complaints about their pay? How do the better performing firms, with better financial returns and larger shares of the market, pay their employees? Are the systems used by these firms different from those used by less successful firms? How does our labor cost per unit produced compare to that of our competitors? Such information is necessary to tune or redesign the system, to adjust to changes, and to highlight potential areas for further investigation.

Balancing Consistency, Competitiveness, Contributions, and Administration

The balance or relative emphasis among the four basic policies is a key decision to be made in any employer's compensation strategy. Does it ever make sense to emphasize one policy concern over another? For example, some firms emphasize an integrated approach to all human resource management, and internal consistency of pay becomes part of that strategy. Other firms tend to emphasize external competitiveness of pay and to place less emphasis on internal consistency. Sometimes it makes sense to emphasize external competitiveness because the relationship of an employer's pay level to a competitor's pay level directly affects the ability to attract a competent work force, to control labor costs, and hence to compete with products or services. Yet, ignoring internal consistency and employee contributions may increase an employer's vulnerability to lawsuits and may decrease employee satisfaction. If the person next to me is doing the same job but is paid more than I am, there had better be a good reason for this differential. Internal pay differences can affect employees' willingness to accept a promotion, pay satisfaction, absenteeism, turnover, and interest in unionization.

Thus, all four—internal consistency, external competitiveness, employee contributions, and the nature of administration—are critical in the management of pay systems; achieving the desired balance among them is an important part of compensation management. The policies determined for compensation should be consistent and reinforce the overall approach taken to managing human resources.

Pay Techniques

The remaining portion of the model in Exhibit 1.2 shows the pay techniques. The exhibit provides only an overview since techniques are the topic of much of the rest of the book. Techniques tie the four basic policies to the pay objectives. Internal consistency is typically established through a sequence of techniques starting with job analysis. Job analysis collects and then evaluates information about jobs. Based on these evaluations, a job structure is built. A job structure depicts relationships among jobs inside an organization, based on work content and the jobs' relative contributions to achieving the organization's objectives. The goal is to establish a job structure that is internally equitable, because this is related to the equity of the pay system and will affect employee attitudes and behaviors as well as the organization's regulatory compliance.

External competitiveness is established by setting the organization's pay level in comparison with what the competition pays for similar work. But who precisely is the "competition"? The pay level is determined by defining the relevant labor markets in which the employer competes, conducting surveys to find out what other employers pay, and using that information in conjunction with the organization's policy decisions to generate a pay structure. The pay structure influences how efficiently the organization is able to attract and retain a competent work force and to control its labor costs.

The relative emphasis on employee contributions is established through performance and/or seniority based increases, incentive plans, and salary increase guidelines. If an organization decides to pay employees on the basis of performance, it must have some way to evaluate employee performance, and must adjust pay on the basis of that evaluation. Many organizations (and union agreements) decide to pay on the basis of years of service, and so attempt to retain an experienced work force. These practices are all intended to have a significant effect on employee attitudes and behaviors, in particular the decisions to join, to stay, and to perform effectively.

Uncounted variations of these pay techniques exist; many are examined in this book. Such variations arise from the multitude of strategies organizations adopt to accomplish their objectives. A few surveys have studied differences in compensation policies and techniques among firms.[16] While no single comprehensive analysis of the four major policy decisions has been reported, it seems clear that the variations in compensation approaches arise from differences in the environments and natures of organizations and in the objectives they are trying to achieve with pay. Such variations may also arrive from the various strategies organizations adopt to accomplish their objectives.

STRATEGIC ISSUES

So far our discussion has highlighted the major perspectives of compensation and the basic components of the pay model. Upcoming chapters will discuss the particulars of various techniques. But examining and dissecting techniques is so

---

[16]David B. Balkin and Luis R. Gomez-Mejia, "Compensation Practices in the High Technology Industry," *Personnel Administrator* 30, no. 6 (June 1985), pp. 111–23; Fred K. Foulkes, *Personnel Policies in Large Nonunion Companies* (Englewood Cliffs, N.J.: Prentice-Hall, 1980); T. Mahoney, B. Rosen, and S. Rynes, "Comparable Worth: Perspectives of Compensation Managers," *Compensation Review* 16, no. 4 (1984), pp. 30–31. Several of the leading consulting firms also survey pay practices of firms. For example, see Peat, Marwick, Mitchell & Co., *Compensation Strategies in the New England High Technology Industry 1985;* and Hay Associates, *1985 Hay Compensation Conference Proceedings* (New York: The Hay Group, 1985).

seductive that the mechanics of doing so become the focus, the ends in themselves for some compensation specialists. All too often, traditional pay systems seem to have been designed in response to some historical but long-forgotten situation or purpose. Questions such as "So what does this technique do for (to) us?" "How does this help achieve pay objectives?" and "Why bother with this technique?" are not asked.

So before proceeding to the particulars of pay systems, let us pause to consider some major strategic issues related to pay. The issues to which we will pay special attention include matching compensation to the organization's strategic conditions, its culture and values, the needs of its employees, and its union/management relationship.

The Pay System and the Organization's Strategic Conditions

All pay systems have a purpose. Answer the question, "For what do we want to pay?" and you'll begin to specify the objectives of the pay system. Some are clearly identified, as in our pay model; others must be inferred from the actions of employers. A currently popular prescription found in almost every professor's textbook and consultant's report is for compensation managers to tailor their systems to support the organization's strategic conditions.[17]

The notion is seductive.[18] The reasons offered seem persuasive. They are based on contingency notions. That is, differences in a firm's strategies should

[17]Jay Schuster, *Management Compensation in High Technology Companies* (Lexington, Mass.: Lexington Books, 1984); Jay Schuster, "Compensation Plan Design," *Management Review,* May 1985, pp. 21–25; Ellig, *Executive Compensation—A Total Pay Perspective,* see especially, chap. 2 and pp. 14–15; Jude T. Rich, "Strategic Incentives," *1980 National Conference Proceedings* (Scottsdale, Ariz.: American Compensation Association, 1981), pp. 90–96; D. Balkin and L. Gomez-Mejia, "Toward a Contingency Theory of Compensation Strategy," University of Florida, Gainesville, Fla., working paper, 1986; Stephen J. Carroll, "Business Strategies and Compensation Systems," University of Maryland, College Park, Md., working paper, 1986; Jerry Newman, "Selecting Incentive Plans to Complement Organizational Strategy," State University of New York, Buffalo, N.Y., working paper, 1986; L. Gomez-Mejia and D. Balkin, "Determinants of R&D Compensation Strategies in the High Tech Industry," University of Florida, Gainesville, Fla., working paper, 1986; G. Milkovich, "Compensation Systems in High Technology Companies," paper presented at *Conference on Human Resources in High Technology Firms,* UCLA, June 1985; Nancy F. Napier and Mark Smith, "Product Diversification, Performance Criteria, and Compensation at the Corporate Manager Level," paper presented at the *4th Annual Strategic Management Conference,* Philadelphia, Pa., October 1984; R. Broderick, "Report to the American Compensation Association: Study of Pay Policies and Business Strategies," (Scottsdale, Ariz.: American Compensation Association, 1985); and James Salscheider, "Devising Pay Strategies for Diversified Companies," *Compensation Review,* Second Quarter 1981, pp. 15–24. Two older references that raise issues that are still relevant include Malcom S. Salter, "Tailor Incentive Compensation to Strategy," *Harvard Business Review,* March–April 1973, pp. 94–102; and J. R. Galbraith and D. A. Nathanson, *Strategy Implementation: The Role of Structure and Process* (St. Paul, Minn.: West Publishing, 1978).

[18]George T. Milkovich and William Glueck, *Personnel/Human Resource Management: A Diagnostic Approach,* 4th ed. (Plano, Tx.: Business Publications, 1985); and Newman, "Selecting Incentive Plans."

be supported by corresponding differences in personnel policies, including compensation policies. The underlying premise is that the greater the congruency, or "fit," between the organization conditions and the compensation system, the more effective the organization. Further, different pay system designs should be aligned with changes in strategic conditions.

Strategy refers to the fundamental direction of the organization. Strategies guide the deployment of all resources, including compensation. U.S. Steel's $6 billion acquisition of Marathon Oil reflects a new strategic direction for that company. After the acquisition, less than 40 percent of U.S. Steel's total revenues came from basic steel operations. Another example is J. C. Penney marketing the Halston product line. Penney's worked hard to establish a reputation for providing good value for the price of its merchandise. This strategy was aimed at "middle America." But a new strategy seeks to adjust Penney's image and also to attract a more affluent shopper. The Halston contract is part of this new strategy. These decisions by U.S. Steel and J. C. Penney reflect fundamental changes in direction. Organization resources—financial, capital, and human—will need to be deployed in a manner consistent with these new directions.

Compensation systems need to be designed to reinforce the strategies adopted by these organizations. To assure a maximum return on its investment in the Halston fashion line, Penney's has begun to design incentives tied to sales targets for that product.

Strategic decisions are also evident in governmental and public not-for-profit organizations. Examples include a university's desire for a winning football team, or a regional symphony orchestra's attempt to gain national recognition. Pay programs should also be tailored to facilitate the strategic directions of these organizations. The orchestra can offer a renowned conductor a share of the revenues gained from recording sales, or the university may increase funding for the coaching staff through a cut of the gate for that particular sport.

In the compensation field, the strategic concept that has received the most attention is organization life cycles.[19] Based on biological growth curves, the basic premise underlying life cycles is that organizations emerge, grow, mature, and eventually decline.

As shown in Exhibit 1.4, different combinations of pay are designed to fit with different strategic conditions. Exhibit 1.4 shows six strategic stages ranging from start-up through decline and renewal. In the example, business units just starting up are described as having a limited, closely related set of products and are exploring their markets. Cash flow problems are common at this stage, earnings and revenues are low, and the human resource objective is to attract and retain key contributors and encourage innovation. Computer software and

---

[19]Ellig, *Executive Compensation;* Gomez–Mejia and Balkin, "Determinants of R&D Compensation Strategies."

EXHIBIT 1.4
Pay Tailored to Strategic Conditions: An Illustration

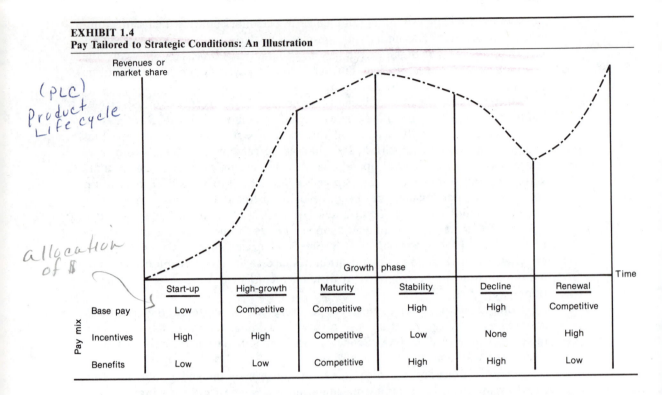

(PLC)
Product
Life cycle

allocation
of $

	Start-up	High-growth	Maturity	Stability	Decline	Renewal
Base pay	Low	Competitive	Competitive	High	High	Competitive
Incentives	High	High	Competitive	Low	None	High
Benefits	Low	Low	Competitive	High	High	Low

genetic engineering firms are recent examples of these new ventures. The mix of pay forms in the example is a relatively low base pay (to conserve cash), strong emphasis on incentive pay (to emphasize unit and individual performance and to share the results of growth), and low benefits (to control costs). Contrast this with a unit in the mature stage. Its product line is now diversified; revenues and earnings are stronger; and the main human resource management focus is on consistency of programs within the organization and on the need to control costs and encourage more efficient operations. The mix of pay forms typically aligned with this stage includes greater emphasis on base pay, short-term incentives, and competitive benefits.

Organization life cycles and the associated pay programs shown in Exhibit 1.4 oversimplify the real world.[20] All business units do not go through all stages. Units may be divested, others acquired. Labor market competition may preclude offering low benefits or base salaries. And many companies have a variety of products at different stages, which makes it difficult to characterize any single unit as being in any one stage. One objective of management ought to be

[20]For an elaboration of the notion of strategic pay, especially the use of life cycles, see Milkovich, "Compensation Systems in High Technology Companies."

to prevent a decline. Furthermore, even if an organization was clearly in one stage, very little is known about what compensation mix corresponds to it, or whether the compensation mix and the stage affect each other.

The common view is that business strategy should affect the design of pay systems. But it can also be argued that historical pay decisions can affect subsequent business strategies. In some cases, efforts to adapt pay systems to shifts in strategic conditions are hindered by existing pay policies and techniques.

Compensation professionals should recognize that pay systems can be tailored to an organization's strategic conditions. In highly decentralized organizations, this can even mean that different subunits may adopt different pay systems. It is also important to recognize that existing pay systems can affect the success of shifts in an organization strategy.

The Pay System and the Organization's Culture and Values

Not only are pay programs related to strategic conditions, they are also related to the organization's culture and values. The notions of cultures and values are complex.[21] But the values underlying an employer's treatment of its employees can be reflected in its pay system. Some employers articulate their philosophies regarding pay, such as those for Hewlett-Packard and Honeywell, which are shown in Exhibit 1.5. These philosophies give us a sense of how these two firms treat employees and serve as guides for their pay systems. Note that Honeywell's philosophic principles (number 4) reflect its decentralized approach in which each business unit is responsible for its own pay system.

Pay is just one of many systems that make up an organization; its design is also partially influenced by how it fits with the other structures and systems in the organization.[22] A highly centralized and confidential pay system, controlled by a few people in a corporate unit, will not, according to this view, operate effectively in a highly decentralized and open organization.[23] Unfortunately, little research has been done directly on the relationship between pay systems and the culture and values of an organization.[24]

The importance of congruency between pay programs and other management processes can be shown with examples of recruiting, hiring, and promoting. The pay linked with a job offer or a promotion must be sufficient to induce acceptance. Some employers do not maintain significant pay differences between manufacturing workers (such as assemblers or inspectors) and their

---

[21]Harrison M. Trice and Janice M. Beyer, "Studying Organizational Cultures through Rites and Ceremonials," *Academy of Management Review,* October 1984, pp. 653–69.

[22]Lawler, *Pay and Organizational Development.*

[23]Ibid.

[24]Sam Gould and Larry E. Penley, "Career Strategies and Salary Progression: A Study of Their Relationships in a Municipal Bureaucracy," *Organizational Behavior and Human Performance* 34 (1984), pp. 244–65.

EXHIBIT 1.5
Comparisons of Pay System Philosophies

Hewlett-Packard's Pay Philosophy

Philosophy of Leadership

Hewlett-Packard's pay philosophy serves as a base for its pay objectives. The major elements of H-P's pay philosophy can be summarized as follows:

"At Hewlett-Packard, we believe in paying people at rates that place us among the leading companies in the country or region from which we attract our people. Our merit pay system uses salary curves derived from these competitive data.

"Your salary position within these curves is determined by your sustained contribution to the company, its customers and shareholders relative to the contributions of others at H-P doing the same or a similar job."

Honeywell's Pay Philosophy

Honeywell is one company, made up of many different businesses. These businesses are united by a common set of values and by common technologies. Yet they differ in respect to their products and services, size, customers, locations, and competitors.

The company's pay philosophy reflects who Honeywell is—both its diversity and its unit. It allows each individual business to design pay systems responding to that business's own requirements. It also means that each system must contain certain assurances of Honeywell employment. These assurances are expressed in four basic pay principles.

Pay Principles

In support of these objectives, four basic pay principles also apply to all Honeywell pay systems.

First, pay must be fully competitive in the market, as defined by each business.

Second, each individual's pay must be fair in relationship to the pay other employees receive within the same Honeywell business.

Third, pay must be communicated. That communication must explain general pay principles, the specific pay system applicable, and the process used to determine individual pay levels under that system.

Fourth, each Honeywell business has the basic responsibility for establishing and maintaining its own pay system.

---

first-line supervisors. Lack of an adequate pay increase diminishes the incentive for employees to take the training required to be a supervisor or to accept the promotion to supervisor. The situation is reversed for many engineering and research jobs, where the pay for managerial positions induces people to leave engineering and research positions.

For compensation professionals, the key point to remember is that pay coexists with other structures in the organization. An effective pay system cannot be designed without taking into account the nature of the organization, its climate, and its values.

The Pay System and Employee Needs

Within some legally imposed limits, compensation can be delivered to employees in various forms already identified. The allocation of compensation among these pay forms to emphasize performance, seniority, entitlements, or the long versus short term can be tailored to the pay objectives of the organization. It can also be tailored to the needs of the individual employees.

The simple fact that employees differ is too easily and too often overlooked in designing pay systems. Individual employees join the organization, make investment decisions, design new products, assemble components, and judge the quality of results. Individual employees receive the pay. Opsahl and Dunnette were among the first to observe that a major limitation of contemporary pay systems is the degree to which individual attitudes and preferences are ignored.[25] Other researchers agree.[26] Older, highly paid workers may wish to defer taxes by putting their pay into retirement funds, while younger employees may have high cash needs to buy a house, support a family, or finance an education. Dual career couples who are overinsured medically may prefer to use more of their combined pay for child care, automobile insurance, financial counseling, or other benefits.

Short of letting all employees specify their own pay form (a choice that would meet with Internal Revenue Service disapproval and be a headache to administer), pay systems can be designed to permit employee choices. Flexible benefit plans are examples, and many employers have adopted them.[27]

The Pay System and Unions

The fourth strategic issue involves adapting the pay system to the nature of the union-management relationship. Strategies for dealing with unions vary widely. The federal government declared a strike by the air traffic controllers illegal and dissolved their union. The governor of Minnesota sent troops to Austin, Minnesota, to restore order when a strike involving Hormel and local meatpackers threatened to turn violent. Eastern Air Lines' lack of accord with its unions forced a last-ditch sale to Texas Air, in order to stave off bankruptcy. In spite of these highly publicized events, hundreds of union contracts are negotiated each year with little fanfare or rancor.

Union influence on the design and administration of pay systems is significant. Not only do unions affect pay rates and pay forms, they appear to affect the way compensation decisions are made. Freedman and Kochan conclude that

---

[25]R. L. Opsahl and M. D. Dunnette, "The Role of Financial Compensation in Industrial Motivation," *Psychological Bulletin* 66 (1966), pp. 94–118; Edward E. Lawler III, *Pay and Organizational Effectiveness* (New York: McGraw-Hill, 1971).

[26]Research on this topic dates to the 1970s. See, for example, Lawler, *Pay and Organization Effectiveness;* George T. Milkovich and Michael Delaney, "A Note on Cafeteria Pay Plans," *Industrial Relations,* February 1975, pp. 112–16; B. N. Fragner, "Employees' 'Cafeteria' Offers Insurance Options," *Harvard Business Review* 53 (1975), pp. 2–4; E. E. Lawler and J. R. Hackman, "The Impact of Employee Participation in the Development of Pay Incentive Plans: A Field Experiment," *Journal of Applied Psychology* 53 (1969), pp. 467–71.

[27]For an extensive discussion of flexible benefit programs, see Chapters 11 and 12.

a high degree of centralization of decision making exists in collective bargaining.[28] Even where the bargaining was conducted at plant level, only 20 percent of the firms gave responsibility to formulate pay proposals to plant level management. Corporate staffs typically undertook the drafting and submission of pay proposals. Consequently the very existence of a union seems to affect the degree of centralization that management adopts.

Union preferences for different forms of pay (e.g., cost-of-living adjustments, improved health care) and their concern with job security also affect pay system design. Historically, the allocation between wages and benefits was greatly affected by unions.[29] Unionized workers still have a greater percentage of their total compensation allocated to benefits than do nonunion workers. Solnick found unionization associated with 24 percent higher levels of pension expenditures and 46 percent higher insurance expenditures.[30] More recent evidence suggests that the differentials are declining.[31]

Recent competitive pressure, particularly from foreign manufacturers, has affected the pay rates and forms that unions seem willing to negotiate.[32] Employers point to data, such as those shown in Exhibit 1.6, to argue for changes in existing pay systems. In 1985, hourly compensation for production workers in West Germany was 85 percent of that for the U.S. worker, while a South Korean received only 11 percent of the U.S. average wage. Caution should be exercised in interpreting these data, because government-provided benefits (e.g., health care and large layoff awards in West Germany) are not included. International wage comparisons also seem to vary considerably. For example, a recent study issued by Japan's Labor Ministry reports that a Japanese factory worker makes the equivalent of $1,872 a month, some 12 percent more than the $1,671 earned by a U.S. worker.[33] Currency fluctuations play a substantial role here. Nevertheless, in response to these kinds of pressures and to layoffs among

---

[28]Audrey Freedman, *Managing Labor Relations: Organization, Objectives, and Results* (New York: The Conference Board, 1979); Thomas A. Kochan, *Collective Bargaining and Industrial Relations* (Homewood, Ill.: Richard D. Irwin, 1980).

[29]John A. Fossum, *Labor Relations* (Plano, Tex.: Business Publications, 1985); Richard B. Freeman and James Medoff, *What Do Unions Do?* (New York: Basic Books, 1984).

[30]Loren Solnick, "Unionism and Fringe Benefit Expenditures," *Industrial Relations* 17, no. 1 (1978), pp. 102–7.

[31]William T. Dickens and Kevin Lang, *Labor Market Segmentation and the Union Wage Premium* (Cambridge, Mass.: NBER working paper 1883), April 1986.

[32]Daniel J. B. Mitchell, *Union versus Nonunion Wage Norm Shifts* (Los Angeles: UCLA working paper 91), September 1985; Daniel J. B. Mitchell, "Shifting Norms in Wage Determination," *Brookings Papers on Economic Activity* 2, 1985; and Thomas A. Kochan, Robert B. McKersie, and Harry C. Katz, "U.S. Industrial Relations in Transition: A Summary Report," in *Proceedings of the Thirty-Seventh Annual Meeting,* ed. Barbara Dennis (Madison, Wis.: Industrial Relations Research Association, 1985), pp. 261–76.

[33]"Labor Costs: The Japanese Are Taking Their Lumps," *Business Week,* August 1, 1986, p. 6.

EXHIBIT 1.6
Worldwide Comparative Wage Costs *(hourly compensation for production workers in manufacturing, 1972–1983)** *

	1972	Percent of United States	1980	Percent of United States	1983	Percent of United States
United States	$6.35		$ 9.89		$12.26	
West Germany	6.19	97%	12.33	122%	10.41	85%
Japan	3.05	48	5.61	57	6.20	51
Brazil	1.13	18	1.70	17	1.68	14
South Korea	.36	06	1.08	11	1.29	11

Note: Figures converted to U.S. dollars at average exchange rate for listed year.
*Excludes benefits.
Source: U.S. Department of Labor, October 1984.

their members, many unions have accepted wage concessions, one-time lump sum increases which are not rolled into base pay, two-tier pay structures, and health care deductibles.

In addition to affecting forms of pay, unions also play a role in administering pay. Most negotiated contracts specify pay intervals, minimum rates, and the basis for movement through a wage range. Some employers adopt the maintenance of union-free status as an objective of its pay system. Such systems usually are based on policies that include strong external competitiveness, internally consistent pay treatment to avoid feelings of inequitable treatment, emphasis on performance, and a fair and open administration of the compensation system. These policies often translate into rates that are at or above those for the market, merit pay or an all-salaried work force, and great emphasis on communicating pay and benefit programs and on attitude surveys to monitor employee reactions.

BOOK PLAN

Compensation is such a broad and compelling topic that several books could be devoted to it. The focus of this book will be on the design and management of compensation systems. To aid in understanding how and why pay systems work, a pay model has been presented. This model, which emphasizes the key policies, techniques, and objectives of pay systems, also provides the structure for much of the book.

Policy decisions form the crucial foundations of any pay systems. The pay model identifies four basic policy decisions; the first three sections of the book examine each in detail. The first, internal consistency (Part 1, Chapters 2 through 5), examines pay relationships among jobs within a single organization. What are the pay relationships among jobs and skills within the organization? What are the relative contributions of each job toward achieving the organization's goals? The linkage of pay decisions with the strategic and operating objectives of the organization, the need to establish internal equity, and the importance of ensuring the work relatedness of pay decisions are examined. Job analysis and job evaluation are the main techniques for achieving internally consistent pay. Developments and innovations in these techniques, some of them flowing from research efforts and some from organizations' responses to challenges they face, are discussed.

Part 2 (Chapters 6 and 7) examines external competitiveness—the competitive pay relationships among organizations—and analyzes the influence of market conditions, setting pay policies to reflect these conditions, and tailoring those pay policies to strategic objectives. Techniques include conducting pay surveys; updating survey data; establishing pay policy lines; and determining pay rates, ranges, and structures. Once again, related theoretical, research, and programmatic developments are reviewed.

Once the compensation rates and structures are established, other issues emerge. How much should we pay each individual employee? How much and how often should a person's pay be increased and on what basis? Should employees be paid based on experience, seniority, or performance? Should pay increases be contingent on the unit's or the employee's performance? These are examples of employee contributions, the third building block in the model (Part 3, Chapters 8, 9, and 10). Approaches which deliver pay to individual employees are designed with employee knowledge, skills, abilities, needs, preferences, performance, and seniority, as well as the presence or absence of unions, in mind. Recent theoretical and research developments related to motivational effects of pay, goal setting, and performance evaluation are examined in the light of the pay decisions which must be made by employers and in light of the current state of pay practices.

Part 4 covers employee services and benefits (Chapters 11 and 12). While only two chapters are devoted to employee benefits, this does not imply that the design and management of benefits is unimportant. The opposite is true. Benefits have become so critical that a separate book is required. All we do here is discuss the major benefit forms, the issues involved in designing and administering the benefit program, and how to tie benefits to the organization's strategic directions.

The government's role in compensation is examined in Part 5, Chapters 14 and 15. The government affects compensation through its purchase of goods and services and its employment of a sizable segment of the work force. Additionally, pay practices must comply with legislation and court interpretations.

Managing the compensation system (Part 6, Chapters 15 through 17) includes planning, budgeting, evaluating, communicating, and providing for the special needs of certain groups (e.g., sales representatives, executives, unions).

Even though the book is divided into sections that are reflected in the pay model, that does not mean that pay policies and decisions are necessarily so discrete. All the basic policy decisions are interrelated, and together they form a major system designed to influence organization performance and employee behaviors. Throughout the book our intention is to examine alternative approaches. Rarely is there a single "correct" approach; rather, alternative approaches exist or can be designed. The one most likely to be effective depends on the circumstances. We hope that this book will help you become better informed about these options and how to design new ones. Whether as an employee, a compensation manager, or an interested member of society, you should be able to assess effectiveness of compensation approaches and equity of pay systems.

SUMMARY

The model presented in this chapter provides a structure for understanding compensation systems. The three main components of the model include the objectives of the pay system, the policy decisions that provide the system's foundation, and the techniques that link policies and objectives. The following sections of the book examine in turn each of the four policy decisions—internal consistency, external competitiveness, employee contributions, and the nature of administration—as well as the techniques, new directions, and related research.

Two questions should constantly be in the minds of compensation professionals and readers of this text. First, "Why do it this way?" There is rarely one "correct" way to design a system or pay an individual. Organizations, people, and circumstances are too varied. But a well-trained compensation specialist can select or design a suitable approach.

Second, "So what?" What does this technique do for us? How does it help achieve our organization goals? If good answers are not apparent, there is no point to the technique. Adapting the pay system to meet the needs of the employees and to help achieve the goals of the organization is what this book is all about.

The basic premise of this book is that compensation systems can have a profound impact on a variety of individuals and objectives. Yet too often, traditional pay systems seem to have been designed in response to some historical but long-forgotten problem. The practices continue, but the logic underlying them is not always clear or even relevant.

REVIEW QUESTIONS

1. How do differing perspectives affect our perceptions of compensation?
2. What rewards can an employer provide that are not part of the compensation system?
3. Describe and distinguish among the major forms of pay.
4. What can a pay system do for an organization? For an employee?
5. How may the pay system be tied to organization strategy?
6. Under what circumstances would one of the three basic pay policies be emphasized relative to the other two? Try to think of a separate example for each basic pay policy.

Chapter 1
Compensation Applications

Case 1   Strategy and Pay Systems at Cigna

A *Wall Street Journal* description of problems at Cigna Corporation is reprinted below. The article describes the corporate culture at INA and Connecticut General before their merger, as well as problems that have developed since their merger into Cigna Corporation.

1. About what pay issues should Cigna be concerned?
2. If you were an outside compensation consultant, what would you recommend?
3. Discuss the concepts of external competitiveness, internal consistency, and employee contributions and how they relate to Cigna.

Merger of Two Insurers into Cigna Corp. Brings Discord, Layoffs, and Profit Drop

by Daniel Hertzerg

When Connecticut General Corp. and INA Corp. tied the knot in the nation's biggest financial services merger last year, the two insurers vowed to live happily ever after.

But a cartoon that soon circulated around INA's headquarters here suggested a rockier marriage. It showed two armies advancing on one another. One was a disciplined phalanx of Roman legionnaires, with "CG"—for Connecticut General—on their shields. The other was a ragtag band of barbarians waving clubs and axes and led by a figure clearly resembling INA's chairman, Ralph S. Saul. One barbarian was asking another: "Isn't it time we got our act together?"

From the start, Connecticut General and INA hailed their combination, in a $4.3 billion swap of stock, as a "merger of equals." The companies were of similar size—each with revenue exceeding $5 billion—though they came from different sides of the insurance business. When the new financial services giant named Cigna Corp. started up on March 31, 1982, the top corporate jobs were carefully apportioned, five to INA's executives, four to Connecticut General's. And, in a highly unusual arrangement, "co-chief executive officers"—one from each company—were named to run Cigna.

Considerable Discord

Little more than a year later, the cartoon seems prophetic. Bliss hasn't reigned. Officials from Connecticut General's disciplined ranks have gained control of Cigna. INA's president has left, and the system of dual chief executives has been discarded. Now, there's only one, Robert D. Kilpatrick, Connecticut General's 59-year-old former president. Moreover, the announcement about two chief executives apparently was a sham; there was private agreement before the merger that Mr. Kilpatrick would lead the merged company.

Cigna's problems haven't been limited to turmoil in the executive suite. The huge insurer's earnings have been disappointing, it has ordered extensive layoffs, and its stock has taken a beating despite the bull market on Wall Street.

As much as any of the recent jumbo-sized mergers, Cigna's problems show that top executives at many companies are right in worrying that a merger may cost them their jobs, notwithstanding any fine-sounding assurances. Even when the companies are of equal size, one soon edges out the other. "There's no question that Connecticut General people have overwhelmed the INA people," says Donald E. Franz, Jr., a securities analyst at Smith Barney, Harris Upham & Co.

Penchant for Planning

Cigna illustrates other difficulties. B. P. Russell, the chairman of Xerox Corp.'s Crum & Forster insurance unit, says Cigna is "a fine outfit, but they've got all sorts of problems because they're trying to put together two insurance operations, and they've got two of everything." Especially tough is melding two top managements with different styles, different "corporate cultures." To people outside the industry, all insurers may seem cut from the same gray cloth. But INA and Connecticut General were run very differently, executives at both companies agree.

At Connecticut General, a disciplined, deliberate management style is epitomized by what employees call "The Process." In this companywide planning program, managers meet individually with 2,000 employees to set up specific, written goals to advance the company's master plan. Each employee is then subject to periodic review.

"The planning goes so far down in the organization that everyone can identify with their part of the plan," says an admirer at another insurer. However, an ex-executive complains that the employees "tend to put on blinders. Once you got the plan, the plan is what you achieve. You don't see other opportunities."

At INA, the style was more freewheeling. "Smart risk taking," not management skills, were at a premium, says Andrew M. Rouse, A Cigna executive vice president who came from INA. Adds one former Cigna executive: "At INA, anyone could speak his mind. When we came together with the CG people, they were accustomed to everything being within The Plan."

The differences stem partly from the two companies' different businesses. Connecticut General was a leading writer of group life and health insurance and group pensions. In life insurance, a company insider says, "You never really need to rush because things move too slowly." INA, in contrast, mainly wrote property and casualty insurance, where unpredictable events and boom-and-bust cycles prevail.

Other Differences

The two managements had other important differences. Connecticut General's top executives generally spent years rising through its ranks. Mr. Kilpatrick, its 6-foot, 5-inch, president, started there as a trainee in 1954. Several key INA officials, in contrast, came from outside the insurance business, arriving in the mid-1970s to revitalize the company. INA's chairman, Mr. Saul, was a former president of the American Stock Exchange, and Richard M. Burdge, another top INA executive, had been chief operating officer of the Amex.

"CG people are stayers; INA people are recent comers, and therefore goers," a Connecticut General insider says.

Even the two corporate headquarters differ. Connecticut General sits on an isolated, wooded tract in Bloomfield, Connecticut, a 15-minute drive from Hartford. A paternalistic employer, it buses workers from Hartford and provides them with a store and bowling alley in Bloomfield. INA, in Philadelphia, pays less attention to corporate niceties. "In a big city, you expect people to take care of themselves," Mr. Rouse says.

The merger almost immediately got off to a rocky start. Three weeks after the start-up, Cigna's top officials warned a group of Wall Street securities analysts that their profit estimates were too high. Cigna's stock plunged, eventually dropping 40 percent. Operating profit in 1982 fell 26 percent to $490.1 million, or $6.38 a share, from $658 million, or $8.51 a share, in 1981 (calculated as if the companies were combined that year).

More Bad News

Earlier this week, there was further bad news. Cigna said it expects to report a 25 percent decline in operating earnings for the second quarter, and on Wednesday Cigna's stock plunged $4.75 a share on the New York Stock Exchange to $42.75, well below its all-time high of $55.375 in April 1982.

Company officials blame the disappointing earnings on a "brutal" property-casualty insurance market—a situation, insiders note, that inevitably has reduced the influence of former INA officials. Cigna has responded to its poor earnings with tough steps. In a move that stunned the industry, it slashed 2,000 jobs from its payroll last year and vowed to drop 2,000 more by 1984 in a $100 million cost-cutting campaign.

Rumors of management tensions cropped up quickly, too. They centered on John R. Cox, the 49-year-old former president of INA, who became an executive vice president of INA and the head of Cigna's property-casualty operations, and Wilson H. Taylor, a 40-year-old former senior vice president of Connecticut General, who became Cigna's chief financial officer. In June 1982, the two men appeared together at a hastily convened securities-analyst meeting in an attempt to dispel the talk of a rift.

But by last January, the Connecticut General takeover of the executive suite had become obvious, analysts say. Cigna announced that Mr. Kilpatrick would become the sole chief executive. Mr. Saul remained chairman but relinquished both his title of cochief executive and day-to-day control of Cigna's operations.

Necessary Maneuver?

The 60-year-old Mr. Saul says that before the merger, he told directors of both companies that he planned to withdraw from active management within two years. Agrees Mr. Kilpatrick: "There was no question who was going to be chief executive officer." Mr. Saul defends the deceptive announcement about dual chief executives. "I don't think we could have done the merger without it," he comments.

Once Mr. Saul reduced his role, "Kilpatrick began to set the tone for the company," says Mr. Cox, adding, "People like myself weren't accustomed to that planned, structured approach." The next month, Mr. Cox said he was leaving, and Mr. Taylor was picked to replace him as the property-casualty chief. Officials say Mr. Cox isn't suffering financially, that he held $1 million of INA stock at the time of the merger and also had a "golden parachute" with generous severance provisions.

*****

Mr. Kilpatrick calls reports of turmoil at Cigna exaggerated. "The coming-together of these two companies to make Cigna has been one of the most orderly mergers of its size," he contends. "The we-they attitude has disappeared entirely," and executive turnover has been "very minimal," he adds.

INA executives now head Cigna's investment operations and run its planning and legal affairs. After some hesitation, the company also chose Philadelphia for its headquarters. But officials from Connecticut General run Cigna's biggest money-making units, including employee benefits and financial services, plus property-casualty.

In light of the weak second-quarter earnings, Mr. Kilpatrick has reversed his earlier prediction of higher profits for this year; now he expects operating earnings to be "moderately below" 1982's, a spokesman said yesterday. Some analysts believe that it may take three to five years before the full benefits of the merger are realized.

Chiding Critics

Mr. Saul chides the analysts and the press for asking too much too soon of the new company. "Here we take a very bold, long-term step," he says, "yet we're expected to produce short-term results."

Cigna's future may hinge on developments in the insurance industry. Many insurers think that the workplace will become an important distribution point for property-casualty insurance. Big corporations may offer group automobile and homeowners insurance as employee benefits, much as they currently do with group life and health insurance. This blend of employee benefits and property-casualty insurance would suit Cigna remarkably well.

Meanwhile, some INA alumni say they welcome Connecticut General's disciplined management style. For example, Mr. Rouse, now a Cigna executive vice president, says a giant company like Cigna "has got to put more emphasis on what CG was stronger at"—management skills. The true picture, he adds, is a lot more complicated than Roman legions versus barbarians. "A cartoon always deals in hyperbole," he says.

Case 2   *Merging Pay Systems*

Students will take the roles of Connie Jensen, former compensation director at Connecticut General, Inez Taylor, former compensation director at INA Corporation, and a three-member compensation committee at the new Cigna Corporation. Using the information in *The Wall Street Journal* article that is part of the first case (Strategy and Pay Systems at Cigna), Connie and Inez will present brief reports. Both Connie and Inez believe that a compensation system should be tailored to an organization's culture and strategy. For this case, we will assume that the compensation systems that each of them managed before the merger were well suited to their particular organization. INA's compensation system was tailored to INA's strategies and culture; Connecticut General's compensation system was tailored to Connecticut General's strategies and culture.

Connie and Inez will each make a recommendation for a compensation system at Cigna, based in part on their previous experience. Based on these presentations and discussions among themselves, the members of the compensation committee will make a recommendation on how to proceed at Cigna. They should address the following questions:

1. Can any elements from the previous system at INA and Connecticut General be incorporated into a pay system at Cigna?
2. What process can be used to design a new compensation system?
3. Who should be involved in the process?
4. What might be the objectives of the new compensation system?

Part 1

Internal Consistency: Determining the Structure

Exxon employs a chief executive officer, chemical engineers, plant managers, nurses, market analysts, laboratory technicians, financial planners, hydraulic mechanics, accountants, guards, oil tanker captains, sailors, word processors, and so on. How is pay determined for these different jobs? This question and the techniques employed to answer it lie at the heart of compensation management. Is the financial planner worth more than the accountant, or the mechanic more than the word processor? How much more? What procedures are used to set pay rates and who does it? How important are the characteristics of the employee—knowledge, skills, abilities, or experience? How important are the characteristics of the work, the conditions under which it is done, or the value of what is produced? What about the employer's financial condition, or employee and union preferences?

These questions can be examined within the framework introduced in Chapter 1 and shown again in Exhibit I.1. This part of the book examines the first basic policy issue (internal consistency) and the pay structure. In Chapter 2, the policy of internal consistency is considered. Chapter 3 discusses various approaches to assess the similarities and differences in work content (job and skill analysis). Chapters 4 and 5 scrutinize job evaluation, which assesses the relative content or value of the work performed.

EXHIBIT I.1
The Pay Model

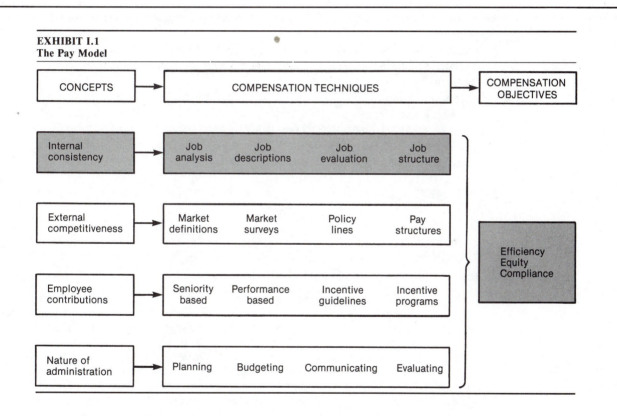

Chapter 2

Internal Consistency and the Structure

Chapter Outline
INTERNAL CONSISTENCY AND THE PAY MODEL
FACTORS INFLUENCING INTERNAL STRUCTURES
    Societal Factors
    Economic Factors
    Organizational Factors
EMPLOYEE ACCEPTANCE: THE KEY TEST
CONSEQUENCES OF INTERNAL PAY STRUCTURES
    Pay Structures and Work Behaviors
    Pay Structures and Pay Satisfaction
SUMMARY

For the kingdom of heaven is like a householder who went out early in the morning to hire laborers for his vineyard. And having agreed with the laborers for a denarius a day, he sent them into his vineyard. And about the third hour, he went out and saw others standing . . . idle; and he said to them, "Go you also into the vineyard, and I will give you whatever is just." And again he went out about the sixth, and about the ninth hour, and did as before. . . . But about the eleventh hour he went out and found others . . . and he said to them, "Go you also into the vineyard." When evening came, the owner said to his steward, "Call the laborers, and pay them their wages, beginning from the last even to the first." When they of the eleventh hour came, they received each a denarius. . . . When the first in their turn came . . . they also received each his denarius. . . . They began to murmur against the householder, saying, "These last have worked a single hour, and thou hast put them on a level with us, who have borne the burden of the day's heat." But answering them, he said, "Friend, I do thee no injustice; take what is thine and go."[1]

---

[1]Matthew, chap. 20, verses 1–16, of the New Testament.

St. Matthew's parable raises age-old questions about internal consistency and pay structures within a single organization. Clearly the laborers in the vineyard felt that those "who have borne the burden of the day's heat" should be paid more, perhaps because they had contributed more to the householder's economic benefit. According to the laborers, the criteria on which to base "fair pay" are two: the value of contributions and the time worked. Differences in pay could also be based on a third criterion, an individual's needs, without regard to differences in the work performed.[2] Contemporary compensation practices, reflecting prevalent opinion in Western society, typically include the value of the work performed in determining pay structures. Consequently, designers of pay structures must be able to recognize similarities and differences in the value of various kinds of work and contributions and must do so through procedures acceptable to the parties involved. This chapter examines the policy of internal consistency in pay structures and its consequences.

INTERNAL CONSISTENCY AND THE PAY MODEL

Two basic policy issues—internal consistency and pay structures—need to be clarified.

> **Internal consistency refers to the pay relationships among jobs or skill levels within a *single* organization. It focuses attention on employee and management acceptance of those relationships.**

> **Pay structure refers to the array of pay rates for different jobs within a single organization. It focuses attention on differential compensation paid for work or skills of unequal worth.**

Internal consistency is one of the basic compensation policies any employer must confront when managing employee compensation. It involves establishing equal pay for jobs of equal worth and acceptable pay differentials for jobs of unequal worth. Pay differentials make up the pay structure. Pay structures, designed to be internally consistent, typically pay more for jobs which require greater qualifications to perform, which must be performed under less desirable working conditions, and/or whose output is more valued.

But internal consistency involves more than just the same treatment. Often called internal equity, it includes the fairness of the pay structure and the proce-

---

[2]For an excellent history of the different standards for pay, see N. Arnold Tolles, *Origins of Modern Wage Theories* (Englewood Cliffs, N.J.: Prentice-Hall, 1964).

dures used to establish it. Thus, compensation professionals must design procedures and establish pay structures that are acceptable to employees and managers and are in compliance with laws and regulations.

Why bother with a policy that emphasizes internal equity? How do internally equitable rates help operating managers achieve their objectives? And what are the potential consequences of pay structures that are not internally equitable? A policy that emphasizes the internal consistency of a pay structure focuses attention on the link between employee perceptions and work behaviors. Recall the typical objectives of pay systems shown in Exhibit I.1. Important among them are employee decisions to join, to stay, or to leave the organization, and to invest in additional training. Pay differences among different jobs influence some of these decisions. Properly designed pay structures may facilitate employee decisions to stay with an organization, to undertake the necessary training, and to gain the required experience to obtain promotions and the accompanying higher pay. Consequently, pay structures can be an important management tool.

Considering their importance, it is surprising that so little is known about employee perceptions of the equity of pay differentials among jobs. Equity, like beauty, may be in the eye of the beholder. For example, little research has been reported on whether different employee groups (older versus younger, line versus staff, men versus women, engineers versus personnel specialists, crafts versus office and clerical) hold different ideas about what constitutes fair pay differences among jobs.[3] Mahoney asked business students and compensation administrators to assign pay levels to organization charts (Exhibit 2.1).[4] One of the jobs was already assigned a pay rate to anchor the responses. The object of the study was to determine if different groups would assign similar pay differentials. He found that business students and administrators did assign similar differentials. On the basis of his findings, Mahoney suggests that a compensation differential of approximately 30 percent is considered appropriate for the higher of two managerial organization levels and that the hierarchical level in the organization is the key determinant of judgments of equitable pay for managers.[5]

Some research suggests that women have lower pay expectations and lower expectation about future pay than similarly qualified men. For example, two studies have reported substantial differences in the pay expectations of male

[3]David W. Belcher, "Pay Equity or Pay Fairness?" *Compensation Review,* Second Quarter 1979, pp. 31–37; Jerald Greenberg and Suzy N. Ornstein, "High Status Job Title as Compensation for Underpayment: A Test of Equity Theory," *Journal of Applied Psychology* 68, no. 2 (1983), pp. 285–97.

[4]Thomas A. Mahoney, "Organizational Hierarchy and Position Worth," *Academy of Management Journal,* December 1979, pp. 726–37.

[5]Thomas A. Mahoney, *Compensation and Reward Perspectives* (Homewood, Ill.: Richard D. Irwin, 1979), p. 171.

EXHIBIT 2.1

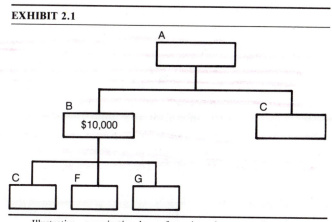

Illustrative organizational configuration from questionnaire, J. L. Kuethe and Bernard Levenson, "Conceptions of Organizational Worth," *The American Journal of Sociology,* November 1964, pp. 342–48. © The University of Chicago Press, 1964.

and female M.B.A. students, with women reporting lower career entry and career peak pay expectations than similarly qualified men.[6]

But judgments about equitable differentials are probably a function of a lot of things, including, apparently, the organization culture. For example, Rosow reports that as work is made more democratic, and as more employees are involved in decision making, salaries and benefits are made more equal; that is, the size of differentials narrows.[7] Jaques asserts the existence of *societal-wide norms* of equitable pay.[8] He believes that most people would assign approximately the same pay differentials to various levels of work, based on commonly held feelings of fairness in pay. While research, limited though it is, lends support to the existence of pay norms among *similar* groups of employees (such as business students and administrators), little evidence supports Jaques's idea of universally held norms across a highly complex society. And the number of lawsuits over what constitutes pay equity would seem to indicate that substantial disagreement exists in contemporary society.

---

[6]S. M. Freedman, "The Effects of Subordinate Sex, Pay Equity and Strength of Demand on Compensation Decisions," *Sex Roles* 5 (1979), pp. 649–58; B. Major and E. Konan, "An Investigation of Sex Differences in Pay Expectations and Their Possible Causes," *Academy of Management Journal,* in press; B. Major, V. Vanderslie, and D. McFarlein, "Effects of Pay Expected on Pay Received: The Conformatory Nature of Initial Expectations," *Journal of Applied Social Psychology* 14, no. 5 (1984), pp. 399–412.

[7]Jerome M. Rosow, *The Organization in the Decade Ahead,* conference sponsored by Work in America Institute, Scarsdale, N.Y., March 3–5, 1986.

[8]Elliot Jaques, *Equitable Payment* (New York: John Wiley & Sons, 1961).

Procedural equity and internal consistency policy. A policy that emphasizes internal consistency also focuses attention on the procedures used to establish the structure. Procedural equity is the perceived fairness, to all relevant parties, of the process used to design the pay structure.[9] Some even assert that the procedures used are more important than the resulting pay structure; that employees and managers are more willing to accept inconsistent pay differentials if they feel the way they were obtained was fair.[10] Little research exists on this issue; however, proponents of the importance of internal consistency state that procedures are more likely to be perceived as fair if they are consistently applied to all employees involved, if employee participation and/or representation is included, and if the data used are accurate.

Distinction between employee contributions and internal consistency policy. Note the distinction between employee contribution (what *I* am worth in this job) and internal consistency (what this *job* is worth to the organization, no matter who does it). Internal consistency refers primarily to the relationships among *jobs* rather than among *individuals*. The comparison is *not* over pay differences between two individuals; the worth of the work itself is determined with little regard to the individuals who are doing it. For example, a word processor may be paid $9.50 per hour whether the employee doing the job holds a Ph.D. or is a vocational school graduate.

Separating internal consistency concerns from employee contribution and individual pay clearly oversimplifies the real world. In some jobs, particularly those with great responsibility and discretion, distinguishing the worth of the job from the individual doing it is extremely difficult. A vice president whose job is designed around the qualifications and experiences of the individual performing it is one example.

Some organizations have extended this concept to manufacturing and assembly work. In these firms pay structures are based directly on the employees' skills, rather than the job performed. TRW, for example, has applied such skill-based approaches in several plants. So while a policy of internal consistency deals primarily with *job relationships, irrespective of who is in the job,* equitable pay structures can sometimes be based directly on the skills of employees, irrespective of the jobs to which they may be assigned.[11]

---

[9]Gerald Greenberg and Ronald Cohen, eds., *Equity and Justice in Social Behavior* (New York: Academic Press, 1982); also see Jane Giacobbe, "An Examination of the Relationship between Perceived Justice of State Impasse Procedures and Perceived Equity of Teacher Pay," Ph.D. thesis, Cornell University, Ithaca, N.Y.; 1986.

[10]J. Thibaut and L. Walker, *Procedural Justice: A Psychological Analysis* (New York: John Wiley & Sons, 1975); and G. S. Leventhal, "What Should Be Done with Equity Theory?" in *Social Exchange,* ed. K. J. Gergen, M. S. Greenberg, and R. H. Willis (New York: Plenum Press, 1980).

[11]E. E. Lawler III and G. E. Ledford, Jr., "Skill-Based Pay: A Concept That's Catching On," *Compensation and Benefits Review,* September 1985, pp. 54–61.

EXHIBIT 2.2
Factors Influencing Pay Structures

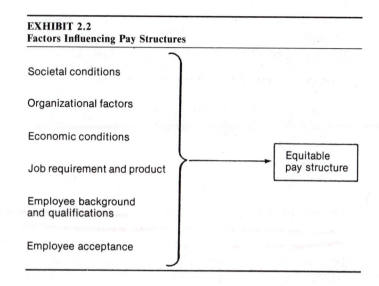

Societal conditions

Organizational factors

Economic conditions

Job requirement and product

Employee background
and qualifications

Employee acceptance

→ Equitable
pay structure

   Comparisons of pay structures across organizations reveal significant differences. Mahoney points out that in some organizations the highest paid job may receive 100 times the compensation of the lowest paid job.[12] In other organizations the differences are considerably less (9 or 10 times). Schaeffer also reports differences in pay structures across organizations.[13] These observed differences raise questions about the design of internal pay structures. What factors influence or determine these structures? What are the consequences of different structures? Each of these is considered in turn.

FACTORS INFLUENCING INTERNAL PAY STRUCTURES

   A variety of factors influence the internal structures within a single organization. Some of the major ones are shown in Exhibit 2.2. They include societal norms and customs; the culture, technology, policies, and objectives of a particular organization; the economic conditions in which the organization operates; and the particular characteristics of the jobs and the employees involved. The confluence of these pressures influences the design of pay structures.

Societal Factors

The role that societal conditions have played historically can be traced in various theories rationalizing pay differences.[14] These theories draw upon concepts

---

   [12]Mahoney, *Compensation and Reward Perspectives.*

   [13]Ruth Schaeffer, "Comparing Staffing Patterns, *Management Review,* July 1976, pp. 41–47.

   [14]See Tolles, *Origins of Wage Theory;* also see Greenberg and Cohen, eds., *Equity and Justice in Social Behavior.*

from philosophy, sociology, economics, and psychology. Matthew's parable, for example, reveals an egalitarian policy: "the last even to the first," regardless of employee qualifications, working conditions, or hours worked. Apparently such a policy was less acceptable to the workers, since they are reported to have murmured against it.

Another approach to pay structures, the *just wage doctrine,* is attributed to attempts by 13th-century artisans and craftsmen to take advantage of economic pressures. Nobles and landholders had bid up the prevailing wages of skilled artisans, who were in relatively short supply. The church and state responded by proclaiming a schedule of "just wages." "Just" wages tended to reflect that society's class structure and were consistent with the prevailing notions of birth rights. Economic and market forces were explicitly denied as appropriate determinants of pay structures. Hence, some early "compensation specialists" employed concepts such as *societal norms, custom,* and *tradition* to design and justify pay structures. Present day manifestation of the just wage doctrine can be seen in debates over minimum wage legislation and comparable worth, which also argue against the appropriateness of market forces for determining pay structures.

Economic Factors

"Just wage" may have been a useful theory when the majority of people lived in feudal societies in which wages played little role. But by the end of the 19th century, for the first time, the majority of people came to depend on wages for their livelihood. Clearly, the just wage concept preserved a privileged position in society for landowners and other small groups, including some skilled craftsmen. But the new commercial system developing in the 18th century, in Adam Smith's view, had the potential to make nations wealthy and also improve the welfare of the ordinary workers—if it would be allowed to operate unfettered by the customs and regulations of the past, including just wage. Smith advocated allowing supply and demand be the main factors in setting wages. He ascribed to labor both exchange and use values. *Exchange value* is the price of labor (the wage) determined in a competitive market; in other words, labor's worth (price) is whatever the buyer and seller agree on. *Use value,* on the other hand, is the value or price ascribed to the use or consumption of labor in the production of goods or services. Exchange value is analogous to external competitiveness, whereas use value is related to internal equity.

But Smith did not address the issue of *how* supply and demand regulate wages. Ricardo, a 19th century businessman-turned-economist, addressed the issue of labor supply. Accompanying the Industrial Revolution was a tremendous population surge and widespread poverty as people left the countryside for city life; this poverty contrasted sharply with the rising profits of employers. Observing these trends, theorists assumed the supply of labor would constantly expand until there was just a bare minimum of subsistence for everyone. Ricardo theorized that the wages of labor would always just equal the amount necessary to buy the goods the worker needed in order to live at a subsistence level. Any deviation from this equilibrium, for example, a wage increase, would bring about population changes that would reestablish the equilibrium, again at the subsistence level. This became known as the "iron law of wages."

On this foundation, Karl Marx built his theory of surplus value.[15] Under capitalism, he said, wages will always be based on exchange value and will provide only a subsistent wage. But labor's use value is higher than its exchange value. The difference between exchange and use value produces a surplus which is being pocketed by the employer, when it should be paid to the worker, according to Marx.

These early theorists concentrated on the supply of labor to explain wages. But by the last half of the 19th century, wages began to rise, and so new theories were required. Emphasis shifted to the demand for labor, and theorists argued that employers will pay a wage to a unit of labor that equals that unit's use value.[16] Unless a worker can produce a value equal to the value received in wages, it will not be worthwhile for the employer to hire that worker. This is the marginal productivity theory of wages. It says that work is compensated proportionately to its contribution to satisfying desires or the organization's production objectives. Accordingly, differences in compensation reflect differences in contributions associated with different jobs. In this view, jobs are compensated on the basis of worth to the employing organization, the volume of production or output associated with the job, and the net revenue accruing to the organization from sale of the output. The marginalist theories assert that one job is paid more or less than another because of differences in productivity of the job and/or differences in consumer valuation of the output. Differences in productivity may be attributed to three factors: (1) *the employee* (e.g., knowledge, skill, abilities, effort); (2) *the job* (e.g., technology, capital investment); and (3) *the match* between the employee's qualifications and the job requirements. Hence, differences in productivity may provide a rationale for the internal job structure. These views underlie many contemporary compensation practices.

The internal structure is also affected by other economic factors. Pay differences may reflect difficulties in recruiting and retaining employees for different jobs. University professors of accounting and engineering who command higher salaries than do professors of history or Serbo-Croatian are examples.

Some explanations of differences in pay among jobs within a single organization combine both sociological and economic factors. Relative pay differences at one particular time may be attributed to temporary economic conditions, such as a shortage of electrical engineers or computer specialists. These

---

[15]R. C. Tucker, ed., *The Marx-Engels Reader,* 2nd ed. (New York: W. W. Norton, 1978).

[16]Allan M. Cartter, *Theory of Wages and Employment* (Homewood, Ill.: Richard D. Irwin, 1959).

differences may become accepted as "just" or customary, and any restructuring of them may be resisted as disruptive of the relationships within the organization. Examples can be found in the auto and steel companies where certain craft jobs receive relatively higher pay than other work, or within municipalities where fire fighters' pay is tied to that of police officers.

Organizational Factors

The effects of many economic and organizational factors are combined in the notion of *internal labor markets*.[17] As depicted in Exhibit 2.3, internal labor markets refer to the rules and procedures that serve to regulate the allocation of employees among different jobs within a single organization. Individuals tend to be recruited and hired only for specific "entry jobs" and are later allocated (promoted or transferred) to other jobs. Because the employer competes in the external market for people to fill these jobs, pay for entry jobs tends to be tied to the external market. It must be set high enough to attract a qualified pool of job applicants. In contrast, pay for nonentry jobs (those staffed internally via transfer and promotions) tends to be more influenced by the organization's culture and norms and less by external economic conditions.[18] In other words, external economic factors are dominant influences on pay for entry jobs, but the differentials for nonentry jobs tend to reflect the organization's culture and traditions.

Expanding on this theme, Thurow asserts that internally equitable pay structures must also be designed to be congruent with the progression of jobs, or *career paths,* within an organization.[19] Greater pay is required for higher level jobs in order to encourage employees to undertake the necessary training and gain the required experience to attain these jobs.

Other organizational factors also influence the design of pay structures. The technology employed is one of the factors.[20] Technology used in producing

---

[17]Mark Granovetter, "Labor Mobility, Internal Markets, and Job Matching: A Comparison of the Sociological and the Economic Approaches," *Research in Social Stratification and Mobility* 5 (1986), pp. 222–27; Peter Doeringer and Michael J. Piore, *Internal Labor Markets and Manpower Analysis* (Lexington, Mass.: Heath-Lexington Books, 1971); and ed. Paul Osterman, *Internal Labor Markets* (Cambridge, Mass.: MIT Press, 1984).

[18]David Pierson, "Labor Market Influences on Entry vs. Non-Entry Wages," *Nebraska Journal of Economics and Business,* Summer 1983, pp. 7–18; and Marc Wallace and Charles Fay, "Job Evaluation and Comparable Worth: Compensation Theory Basis for Modeling Job Worth," *Proceedings, Academy of Management,* 1981, pp. 296–300.

[19]Lester C. Thurow, *Generating Inequality: Mechanisms of Distribution in the U.S. Economy* (New York: Basic Books, 1975).

[20]M. Roznowski and C. Hulin, "Influences of Functional Speciality and Job Technology on Employees' Perceptual and Affective Responses to their Jobs," *Organizational Behavior and Human Decision Processes* 36 (1985), pp. 196–208; Jay Turk, "Determination of Job Characteristics of Automated Process Operators as a Function of Technology and Managerial Choice," Ph.D. thesis, Cornell University, Ithaca, N.Y., June 1986.

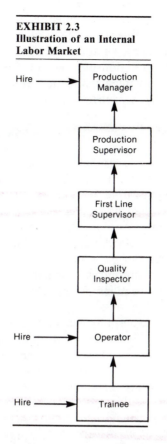

EXHIBIT 2.3
Illustration of an Internal
Labor Market

goods and services influences organizational structures, functional specialties, work teams, and departments. Technology influences the work to be performed and the skills required to perform it.

The organization's human resource policy is another influence. A policy in some organizations dictates using pay as an incentive to induce employees to apply for higher level positions (e.g., machinists to first-line supervisors), while in other organizations, offering "management status" is considered a sufficient inducement, and little or no pay differential is offered. If pay differentials are designated as a key mechanism to encourage employees to accept greater responsibilities, then the pay structure must be designed to facilitate those decisions.

Mahoney points out that all of these explanations of pay structures have some validity and "in fact, likely are interrelated in the explanation of any specific pay structure."[21] In other words, some pay differentials may have been

---

[21]Mahoney, *Compensation and Reward Perspectives*.

initiated in response to economic factors such as shortages of qualified persons. Over time, the differential associated with the skill became accepted as equitable and customary; efforts to change it were resisted as inequitable and destructive of social relationships within the organization. Thus, the compensation structures within organizations established for economic reasons may be maintained for other reasons.[22]

EMPLOYEE ACCEPTANCE: THE KEY TEST

In a classic article on pay structures, Livernash asserts that employees desire "fair" compensation.[23] He states that employees judge the fairness of their pay through comparisons with the compensation paid other jobs related in some fashion to their own jobs. Such interrelated jobs he called *job clusters.* Accordingly, the central criterion for assessing the internal pay structure is its *acceptability to the employees involved.* Effectiveness of the pay structure depends on employee acceptance. Other factors (societal and organizational) also influence employee acceptance. Thurow agrees, "workers' views about what constitutes an 'equitable' wage structure have an important role to play in the determination of wages."[24]

Since employee judgments about pay structures are so important, we need to understand how employees make these judgments. Exhibit 2.4 shows the main determinants of whether an employee is likely to perceive pay for a job as being equitable. The model, adapted from the distributive justice and inequity models, shows that employees' judgments about equity are based on comparisons.[25] A pay structure will be perceived as equitable or inequitable depending on whether the pay for Job A compared to its requirements (education, experience), the work performed (task, behaviors, working conditions), and the value of contributions (to organization objectives and/or consumers) is congruent with the pay for Job B relative to its requirements, work performed, contribution, and so on, through all jobs in the structure.

---

[22]Ibid.

[23]E. Robert Livernash, "The Internal Wage Structure," in *New Concepts in Wage Determination,* ed. George W. Taylor and Frank C. Pierson (New York: McGraw-Hill, 1957), pp. 143–72.

[24]Thurow, *Generating Inequality.*

[25]The first three references listed are classics on this topic. G. C. Homans, *Social Behavior: Its Elementary Forms* (New York: Harcourt Brace Jovanovich, 1961); M. Patchen, *The Choice of Wage Comparisons* (Englewood Cliffs, N.J.: Prentice-Hall, 1961); J. S. Adams, "Inequity in Social Exchange," in *Advances in Experimental Social Psychology,* Vol. 2, ed. L. Berkowitz (New York: Academic Press, 1965), pp. 267–99. Also see Allan Nash, *Managerial Compensation* (Scarsdale, N.Y.: Work in America Institute, 1980); F. S. Hills, "The Relevant Other in Pay Comparisons," *Industrial Relations* 19 (1980), pp. 345–51; P. S. Goodman, "An Examination of Referents Used in the Evaluation of Pay," *Organizational Behavior and Human Performance* 12 (1974), pp. 170–95; and V. Scarpello and J. P. Campbell, "Job Satisfaction: Are All the Parts There?" *Personnel Psychology* 36 (1983), pp. 577–600.

EXHIBIT 2.4
Perceived Equity of a Pay Structure

$$\frac{\text{Pay}_A}{Q_A, W_A, P_A} \quad \begin{array}{c} \text{compared} \\ \text{to} \end{array} \quad \frac{\text{Pay}_B}{Q_B, W_B, P_B} \quad \begin{array}{c} \text{compared} \\ \text{to} \end{array} \quad \frac{\text{Pay}_C}{Q_C, W_C, P_C} \ \text{etc.}$$

where

Q = Qualifications.
W = Work performed.
P = Product value.

Very little research addresses the question of what factors influence employee perceptions of the equity or fairness of the pay structure among different jobs.[26] Most of the equity research examines perceptions of individual pay relative to pay received by other individuals on the same job (a topic discussed in Part 3, Employee Contributions). But the emphasis in this chapter is on factors influencing differential payment for the work itself rather than the attributes of individuals. The distinction is an important one. It assumes that a job's worth is derived from the value of the work performed. Hence, procedures to establish internal pay structures focus on the actual content of the work and its requirements (assessed through job analysis) and the work's value to the organization (assessed through job evaluation).

CONSEQUENCES OF INTERNAL PAY STRUCTURES

But why worry about the internal pay structure at all? Why not simply pay employees what it takes to get them to take a job and to stay? Why not simply let external market forces determine wages? The answers can be found in several situations. One is the presence of unique jobs that reflect organizational idiosyncracies. For example, the School of Veterinary Medicine at Cornell University has installed "windows" in the stomachs of several cows to study the animals' digestive processes. Laboratory technicians help install these windows and perform other exotic duties. Without similar jobs at other employers, it is difficult to determine the appropriate wage for such jobs. Other, more common illustrations of unique jobs may be found under titles such as "administrative assistant" or "research associate." The specific content of these jobs will vary with the technologies employed, the manner in which a supervisor has designed the job, the skills and experiences of the particular incumbent, and so on. The pay for these unique jobs is typically set through comparison of the work with other internal jobs. So the existing internal wage structure provides a basis for arriving at a wage for unique jobs.

---

[26]Belcher, "Pay Equity or Fairness?"; Giacobbe, "Examination of Relationship between Perceived Justice."

It is also possible that some jobs are valued by a specific organization more or less than the rates reflected for that job in the market. For example, top-notch compensation specialists or accountants may have greater value to a compensation or accounting consulting firm than to heavy manufacturing companies such as Caterpillar. The consulting firm may pay greater-than-market rates for the greater contribution of the particular job to organization goals. Other examples of policies which emphasize internal structure over market-determined external competitiveness can be found among public employers that have granted salary increases to clerical jobs held predominantly by women. The city of San Jose's agreement with the American Federation of State, County, and Municipal Employees to raise the pay for office and clerical jobs relative to the pay for other city jobs is a case in point.[27]

Pay Structures and Work Behaviors

In the compensation literature, the pay structure is said to be related to everything from employee performance to strikes.[28] Exhibit 2.5 suggests some of the consequences of pay structures. Several writers argue that employees' judgments about the fairness of the pay structure affect their work behaviors.[29] Some of those views have been discussed already. Livernash, for example, asserts that departures from an acceptable wage structure will occasion turnover, grievances, and diminished motivation of workers.[30] Jaques argues that if fair differentials among jobs are not paid, individuals may harbor ill will toward the employer, resist change, change employment if possible, become depressed, and "lack that zest and enthusiasm which makes for high efficiency and personal satisfaction in work."[31]

More recently, Frank argues that pay structures have value in themselves and hence influence employee behaviors.[32] Employees, according to Frank, value the status attached to their relative position in a pay structure. Consequently, they make trade-offs between the value of the status in their current pay structure and the value of pay for a new job and its status in the pay structure. Using the analogy of a big fish in a little pond, Frank argues that pay structures can influence employees "choosing the right pond." Employees may forgo changing ponds (organizations with new pay structures) if their status (relative

---

[27]*Background Material on the San Jose Situation,* available from Comparable Worth Project, 488 41st Street, Oakland, CA 94609; and *Pay Equity: A Union Issue for the 1980's,* American Federation of State, County, and Municipal Employees, 1625 L Street N.W., Washington, D.C. 20036.

[28]Allen Nash and Stephen Carroll, *The Management of Compensation* (Monterey, Calif.: Brooks/Cole Publishing, 1975).

[29]Livernash, "Internal Wage Structure"; Jaques, *Equitable Payment;* and Mahoney, *Compensation and Reward Perspectives.*

[30]Livernash, "Internal Wage Structure."

[31]Jaques, *Equitable Payment,* p. 123.

[32]Robert H. Frank, *Choosing the Right Pond* (New York: Oxford University Press, 1985).

EXHIBIT 2.5
Some Consequences of Pay Structures

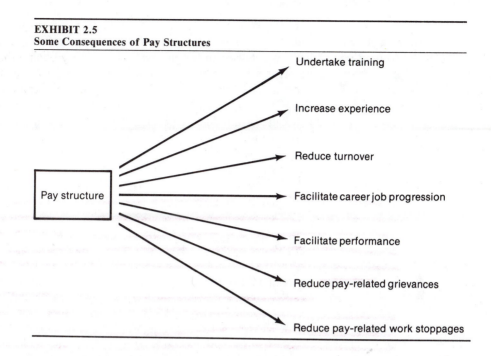

Pay structure
- Undertake training
- Increase experience
- Reduce turnover
- Facilitate career job progression
- Facilitate performance
- Reduce pay-related grievances
- Reduce pay-related work stoppages

---

position) in the current pay structure has greater value than the increased pay for the new job and its status.

Pay structures also imply future rewards in a career, and hence influence both the attractiveness of current employment and decisions to stay or leave. Pay structures may induce employees to increase their human capital by undertaking the training and obtaining the experience required for promotions. Human capital theorists suggest that pay differentials serve as inducements for employees to invest in acquiring added knowledge, skills, and experience. Workers do not bring fully developed job skills into the labor market. After obtaining an entry job, skills are acquired either formally or informally through on-the-job training. The incentive to acquire these skills is the pay differentials among jobs requiring varying skill levels. According to this view, a computer design engineering job should pay more than a programming job. Without that pay difference, individuals are less likely to go through the education (and forgone earnings while in school) required. Similar logic can be applied to differentials to encourage employees to undertake more responsibilities (pay differentials between supervisors and production workers). This point is consistent with Lazear's research, which concludes that wage differentials within organizations induce employees to remain with the organization and increase their experience and training.[33]

---

[33]Edward P. Lazear, "Severance Pay, Pensions, and Efficient Mobility," Working Paper No. 854, National Bureau of Economic Research, Cambridge, Mass., February 1982.

Mahoney observes, "The structure of compensation differentials within the organization influences dissatisfaction and the desire to leave but does not appear to be particularly relevant in the motivation of desired behavior within the organization . . . [it] is a necessary but not sufficient, condition for the motivation of task performance."[34] He asserts that equity of the structure does not appear to contribute to *job* satisfaction, but it contributes to *pay* satisfaction. Let us examine the question of pay satisfaction and its relationship to pay structures in greater detail.

Pay Structures and Pay Satisfaction

Pay satisfaction, as defined by Lawler, is a function of the discrepancy between two perceptions.[35] The first is how much pay employees feel they *should receive*, and the second is how much pay they feel they *do receive*. If these two perceptions are equal, an employee is said to experience pay satisfaction; if a discrepancy exists, then the employee feels dissatisfaction with pay.

Heneman states that "use of the term 'pay satisfaction' is a bit of a misnomer."[36] He argues that pay satisfaction needs to be considered in terms similar to the four basic policy areas used in the pay model: satisfaction with the pay structure (internal consistency), with the pay level (external consistency), with the pay level (external competitiveness), with individual pay (employee contribution), and with the administration of the pay system. Dyer and Theriault's study found that perceived adequacy of pay administration was an important aspect of pay satisfaction.[37]

Recognizing that satisfaction may be linked to each of the basic policies and its techniques has important implications for the management of compensation. It permits better analysis of specific aspects of the compensation system

---

[34]Mahoney, *Compensation and Reward Perspectives,* p. 202.

[35]Lawler, *Pay and Organization Development.* Also see Stephan J. Motowidlo, "Relationship between Self-Related Performance and Pay Satisfaction among Sales Representatives," *Journal of Applied Psychology* 2 (1982), pp. 209–13; Stephan J. Motowidlo, "Predicting Sales Turnover from Pay Satisfaction and Expectation," *Journal of Applied Psychology* 68 (1983), pp. 484–89.

[36]R. A. Ash, G. P. Dreher, and R. D. Bretz, "A Note on the Dimensionality and Stability of the Pay Satisfaction Questionnaire," working paper, University of Kansas, Lawrence, Kans., 1986; G. F. Dreher, "Predicting the Salary Satisfaction of Exempt Employees," *Personnel Psychology* 34 (1981), pp. 579–89; Herbert G. Heneman III, "Pay Satisfaction," *Research in Personnel and Human Resources Management,* Vol. 3, eds. K. M. Rowland and G. R. Ferris (Greenwich, Conn.: JAI Press, 1985), pp. 115–39; also see H. G. Heneman III and D. P. Schwab, "Work and Rewards Theory," in *ASPA Handbook of Personnel and Industrial Relations,* eds. D. Yoder and H. G. Heneman, Jr. (Washington, D.C.: Bureau of National Affairs, 1979), pp. 6(1)–6(22).

[37]L. Dyer and R. Theriault, "The Determinants of Pay Satisfaction," *Journal of Applied Psychology* 61 (1976), pp. 596–604; and Nan Weiner, "Determinants and Behavioral Consequence of Pay Satisfaction: A Comparison of Two Models," *Personnel Psychology* 33 (Winter 1980), pp. 741–57.

and employee attitudes toward them. Lowering the external competitive position of pay may affect the satisfaction with the pay level, but should leave attitudes toward the pay structure unchanged.

Despite the fact that a great deal of research has been conducted relating to pay satisfaction and dissatisfaction, very little research has been directed toward understanding the consequences of *pay differences for different jobs*. Consequently, there are few theories or views that relate employees' judgments about the *equity of pay structures* to their work behaviors.

Based on two reviews of the pay satisfaction research, Lawler and Heneman glean the following general findings:[38]

1. Pay satisfaction was found to be significantly predictive of both absenteeism and turnover, though the strength of the relationships is moderate.
2. The greater the pay dissatisfaction, the greater the likelihood of voting for a union, going on strike, and filing grievances.
3. Pay satisfaction is a function of how much pay is received, how much others are perceived to receive (e.g., perceived pay structures), and perceptions of what should have been received.
4. Pay satisfaction can influence job satisfaction.
5. The stronger causal tendency is that of *performance causing pay satisfaction, rather than pay satisfaction causing performance.* Interestingly, pay satisfaction will be related to performance only when pay is based on performance—an issue to which we will return in our discussion of performance-based pay systems in later chapters.

What does the pay satisfaction/dissatisfaction literature tell us about designing pay structures? The answer is not much. Most of the studies fail to distinguish among internal pay structures, external market comparisons, individual pay, and how the pay is administered. Consequently, few of them offer much guidance in designing compensation systems.

SUMMARY

This chapter discusses at length what is meant by a pay policy that emphasizes internal consistency and how it affects employees, managers, and employers. Internal consistency refers to the pay relationships among jobs within a single organization. While the potential consequences of internal pay structures are vital to organizations and individuals, little guidance has emerged from research concerning employee perceptions of internal pay structure. Jaques posits the existence of society-wide norms of equitable pay structures, but little research supports this.

Pay structures—the array of pay rates for different jobs within an organization—are shaped by societal, economic, and organizational factors. Employ-

---

[38]Heneman, "Pay Satisfaction"; Lawler, *Pay and Organizational Development*.

ees judge a structure to be equitable on the basis of comparisons. The "ratio" of a job's relative pay to its relative requirements, work performed, and value of that performance is compared to the "ratio" for other jobs in the structure. Congruent ratios are felt to be equitable. Acceptance by employees of the relative pay differentials is the key test of an equitable pay structure.

Keep in mind that these comparisons focus on the jobs themselves, and not on the individuals doing the jobs. Thus, personal characteristics such as seniority or experience do not enter into the judgment here and are not discussed until a later section of this book. The emphasis here is on jobs, and the next chapter discusses the analysis of jobs with an eye toward determining an equitable structure.

REVIEW QUESTIONS

1. Why should internal consistency be part of the foundation for the compensation system?
2. Discuss the factors that influence internal equity and pay structures. Based on your own experience, which ones do you think are the most important?
3. Does it always make sense to distinguish the worth of the job from the worth of the individual?
4. What is the "just wage" doctrine? Can you think of any present-day applications?
5. Explain how internal labor markets work.
6. What factors are thought to go into employees' judgments of fairness of pay?

Chapter *3*
Job Analysis

**APPENDIX A: EXAMPLE OF CONVENTIONAL JOB ANALYSIS
  QUESTIONNAIRE**
APPENDIX B: COMPUTER-GENERATED JOB DESCRIPTION

Three workers sit in front of computer display terminals, all of them nimbly pushing keys. But each of them is doing a different job. Modern technology has made it possible for a stockbroker, a word processor, and a telephone operator to all perform very different jobs using the same tool, the computer terminal. If pay for these jobs is to be based on what work is performed, some way to discover what work employees actually do is needed. Observation is not enough. Some way to identify the differences and similarities among jobs is needed.

What is required, then, is information that will help ensure that compensation decisions are firmly based on identifiable similarities and differences in the work. Collecting and interpreting information about jobs is known as job analysis. Job analysis can be defined as:

> **The systematic process of collecting and making certain judgments about all of the important information related to the nature of a specific job.**

Recall from earlier chapters that the concern for internal consistency is one of the building blocks in our compensation model. Recognizing similarities and differences among jobs is an important aspect of achieving internal consistency. The basic premise underlying job analysis is that jobs are more likely to be described, differentiated, and valued fairly if accurate information about them is available. Exhibit 3.1 shows that job analysis provides the underlying information for preparing job descriptions and evaluating jobs; it is a prerequisite for describing and valuing work and therefore is highly related to the equity and efficiency of the pay system.

Exhibit 3.1 also calls out the major decisions in designing a job analysis: (1) For what purpose are we collecting job information? (2) What information should be collected? (3) What methods should be used? (4) To what extent should the various parties be involved? (5) How useful for compensation purposes are the results?

EXHIBIT 3.1
Determining the Internal Job Structure

Internal relationships among jobs within the organization	→	Job Analysis	→	Job Descriptions	→	Job Evaluation	→	Job Structure
		Collecting information and making judgments about the nature of a specific job		Summary reports that identify, define, and describe the job as it is actually performed		Comparison of jobs within an organization		An ordering of jobs based on their content or relative value

Some Major Issues in Job Analysis
- Analysis for what purpose
- What information to collect
- How to collect information
- Who should be involved
- Usefulness of results

WHY PERFORM JOB ANALYSIS?

There are a number of reasons why an organization may perform job analysis.[1] They range from concerns for productivity and consistent treatment of employees to more specific uses in compensation and other personnel systems.

Productivity

Varieties of job analysis were used in early factory systems to improve the flow of work and increase productivity through efficient job design.[2] Typically this meant specifying precise actions to be taken, for example, lifting 50-pound pig iron ingots from molds to flatbed railcars, or fastening links to drive chains for use in automobile transmissions. The design of jobs focused on establishing productivity standards and specifying the skills necessary to achieve them. Contemporary use of job analysis continues to include job design and the identification of qualifications used in recruiting, placement, or training. Optimizing

---

[1] Particularly valuable sources of information on job analysis definitions and methods are U.S. Department of Labor, Manpower Administration, *Handbook for Analyzing Jobs* (Washington, D.C.: U.S. Government Printing Office, 1972); S. A. Fine and W. W. Wiley, *An Introduction to Functional Job Analysis,* monograph no. 4 (Kalamazoo, Mich.: W. E. Upjohn Institute for Employment Research, 1971); E. J. McCormick, "Job and Task Analysis," in *Handbook of Industrial and Organizational Psychology,* ed. M. D. Dunnette (Chicago: Rand McNally, 1976), pp. 651–96; E. J. McCormick, *Job Analysis: Methods and Applications* (New York: AMACOM, 1979); and Stephen E. Bemis, Ann Holt Belenky, and Dee Ann Soder, *Job Analysis: An Effective Management Tool* (Washington, D.C.: Bureau of National Affairs, 1983).

[2] J. R. Hackman and G. R. Oldham, *Work Redesign* (Reading, Mass.: Addison-Wesley Publishing, 1980).

the match between skills possessed by workers and requirements of the job remains basic in productivity management.

Internal Consistency

Compared to the days of the early factory, many organizations have become more complex and diverse. TRW, for example, operates in multiple and unrelated lines of business. Their products range from zippers for Levi's jeans to electronic guidance systems for the military. The products and technologies involved require widely diverse jobs and skills. Even firms in a single line of business, like Apple Computer, Inc. or American Airlines, Inc., require widely diverse tasks to be performed. However, such firms still have concerns about ensuring consistent treatment of employees across various locations. While the responsibility for collecting job information may be decentralized to specific business units or individual locations, collected information that is comparable helps to locate discrepant treatment of employees and to evaluate differences in work arrangements across different locations.

For most people, the pay attached to their job is a matter of stunning importance. If the number of discrimination and pay-related lawsuits is any index, then employees are increasingly willing to challenge the logic or fairness of their employer's pay decisions. Faced with this challenge, pay decisions must be shown to be based on work-related logic and administered fairly. If an employer is not consistent in its treatment of employees or cannot demonstrate the work-related logic of its pay, then it will be hard-pressed to defend itself. While job analysis is not legally required, the data collected helps managers construct a work-related rationale to defend their decisions and assists their efforts to communicate that rationale to employees.

Lacy concludes a review of EEO court decisions dealing with job analysis by observing:

> A well-done job analysis is an important step in both complying with and defending against actions brought under these laws. This may seem axiomatic. . . . To a great many employers, unfortunately, it does not appear to be clear. Until these employers understand the implications of job analysis to equal employment opportunity, they will be "aiming in the dark."[3]

Compensation

There are two critical uses for job analysis in compensation: (1) to establish job similarities and differences in the content of the jobs and (2) to help establish an internally equitable job structure. If jobs have equal content, then in all likelihood the pay established for them will be equal. If, on the other hand, the

---

[3]John Lacy, "Job Evaluation and EEO," *Employee Relations Law Journal* 7, no. 3 (1979), pp. 210–17.

EXHIBIT 3.2
Personnel Functions, Job Analysis Information, and Results

	Job Analysis		
Function	*Information*		*Result*
Recruitment and selection	Required skills, abilities, and experience	→	Selection and promotion standards
Training and development	Tasks, behaviors	→	Training programs
Performance appraisal	Behavior standards or expected results	→	Performance appraisal criteria
Job design and organization development	Tasks, expected results	→	Organization structure
Compensation	Tasks, abilities, skills, behaviors	→	Similarities and differences in the work; job descriptions

---

job contents differ, then those differences are part of the rationale for paying them differently. Additional data, such as market rates and skills required to perform the jobs, are also considered before any pay structure is determined.

Any process designed to collect job data for determining pay rates needs to ensure that sufficient detail about the actual work performed is collected and that the methods employed can withstand challenges from both inside and outside the organization. The data collected through job analysis becomes one of the key supports of an equitable pay structure. If the support is weak, the structure is vulnerable to challenge.

Additional Applications of Job Analysis Data

Pay decisions are only one of many possible uses of job analysis data. Potential applications are found in every major personnel function.[4] Exhibit 3.2 illustrates the type of job analysis data needed in various functions. For example, job analysis is used to identify the skills and experience required to perform a job, thereby clarifying hiring and promotion standards. Training programs may be designed with job analysis data; jobs may be redesigned based on it. In per-

---

[4]R. A. Ash, E. L. Levine, and F. Sistrunk, "The Role of Jobs and Job-Based Methods in Personnel and Human Resources Management," *Research in Personnel and Human Resources Management* 1 (1983), pp. 45–84; Duane Thompson and Toni Thompson, "Court Standards for Job Analysis in Test Validation," *Personnel Psychology* 35 (1982), pp. 865–74; also see George T. Milkovich and William Glueck, *Personnel/Human Resource Management: A Diagnostic Approach,* 4th ed., chap. 4. (Plano, Tex.: Business Publications, 1985).

formance evaluation, both employees and supervisors look to the required behaviors and results expected in a job to help assess performance.

Rather than conducting a separate analysis for each application, some writers argue that a single, omnibus method can be designed to capture sufficient data for all (or most) uses.[5] Several employers, including J. C. Penney, Hewlett-Packard, 3M, and Nationwide Insurance, have gone so far as to design such methods.[6] To date, their implementation focuses on one or two uses (e.g., compensation and training); wider application seems to be limited by lack of acceptance of the results by employees and managers, questions about the usefulness of the data collected, and the significant expense involved.

Employee and manager acceptance of data collected is important and easily overlooked.[7] For example, the analyst may feel behavioral descriptions adequately describe a job (e.g., coordinate advertising campaigns with marketing group plans), while the jobholders may feel that greater emphasis on the scope of contacts (e.g., works with outside clients, prepares reports for vice president of marketing) or the financial responsibility (e.g., budgetary control and approvals) more accurately describe the job. No matter how well the rest of the compensation system is designed and administered, if jobholders are dissatisfied with the initial data collected, they are less likely to feel satisfied with the resulting structure.

With respect to the usefulness of the data, different personnel functions require different types of work-related data. For example, job design focuses on how differences in the job structure and content affect satisfaction and performance.[8] Different data are required for recruitment and selection decisions,

---

[5] Ronald C. Page, "The Use of Job Content Information for Compensation and Reward Systems," paper presented at Academy of Management Meetings, August 1982; Debra Suhadolnik, Clark Miller, Ronald Page, *FOCAS Job Analysis/Evaluation System* (Minneapolis, Minn.: Control Data Business Advisors, 1986).

[6] J. C. Penney General Management Position Questionnaire (New York: J. C. Penney Company, 1985); Management Position Description (Palo Alto, Calif.: Hewlett-Packard, 1983); 3M Management Position Description Questionnaire (St. Paul, Minn.: 3M, 1985); Superior Oil Job Analysis Questionnaire (Houston, Tex.: Superior Oil Company, 1982).

[7] Luis R. Gomez-Mejia, Ronald C. Page, and Walter W. Tornow, "A Comparison of the Practical Utility of Traditional, Statistical, and Hybrid Job Evaluation Approaches," *Academy of Management Journal* 25, no. 4 (1982), pp. 790–809.

[8] Hackman and Oldham, *Work Redesign;* R. W. Griffen, A. Welsh, and G. Moorhead, "Perceived Task Characteristics and Employee Performance: A Literature Review," *Academy of Management Review* 6 (1981), pp. 655–64; J. M. Nicholas, "The Comparative Impact of Organizational Developments on Hard Criteria Measures," *Academy of Management Review* 7 (1982), pp. 531–42; R. W. Griffen, *Task Design, an Integrative Approach* (Glenview, Ill.: Scott, Foresman, 1982), pp. 14–24; C. Pinder, *Work Motivation: Theory, Issues, and Application* (Glenview, Ill.: Scott, Foresman, 1984); David A. Nadler, J. Richard Hackman, and E. E. Lawler III, *Managing Organizational Behavior* (Boston: Little, Brown, 1979); Ramon J. Aldag, Steve H. Barr, and Arthur P. Brief, "Measurement of Perceived Task Characteristics," *Psychological Bulletin* 90, no. 3 (1981), pp. 413–31.

where the specific skills and abilities required to perform the work are of interest.[9] It remains an unanswered question whether a single omnibus job analysis procedure can collect data to accommodate so many diverse uses. With the aid of computers, it has become feasible to collect and analyze vast amounts of work-related data. The key issue for compensation professionals is still to ensure that the data collected serve the purpose of the compensation decision makers and are acceptable to the employees involved. As the flowchart in Exhibit 3.1 indicates, collecting job information is only an interim step, not an end in itself.

WHAT DATA TO COLLECT?

Recommendations on the types of data to collect can range from the job title (clerk typist I, administrative assistant) to the frequency with which specific tasks (i.e., answer the phone or open the mail) are performed.[10] There are lists upon lists of suggested data to be gathered during job analysis. Exhibit 3.3 is typical.

Identification. Data that identify a job include its title, the number of people in the organization who hold this job, and the department where the job is located. For managerial jobs, statistics on the size of the budget under the control of this job, the number (and job titles) of people supervised, and reporting relationships with other managers at both higher and lower organization levels are frequently included, also.

Functional Job Analysis

The U.S. Department of Labor's work on job analysis may be the strongest single influence on job analysis practice in the United States.[11] Certainly anyone contemplating undertaking job analysis for the first time would be well advised to consult the *Handbook for Analyzing Jobs.*

Developed in the 1930s, the original Department of Labor (DOL) methodology categorized data to be collected as (1) actual work performed and (2)

---

[9]Robert M. Guion, "Recruiting, Selection, and Job Placement," in *Handbook of Industrial and Organizational Psychology,* ed. Marvin D. Dunnette (Chicago: Rand McNally, 1976); D. P. Schwab, "Recruiting and Organization Participation," in *Personnel Management,* ed. K. M. Rowland and G. R. Ferris (Boston: Allyn & Bacon, 1982), pp. 105–30.

[10]Sidney Gael, *Job Analysis* (San Francisco: Jossey-Bass, 1983); Bemis, Belenky, and Soder, *Job Analysis: An Effective Management Tool;* Jesse T. Cantrill, "Collecting Job Content Information through Questionnaires," and Thomas S. Roy, Jr., "Collecting Data through Interviews and Observations," both in *Handbook of Wage and Salary Administration,* 2nd ed., ed. Milton L. Rock (New York: McGraw-Hill, 1984).

[11]U.S. Department of Labor, *Handbook for Analyzing Jobs.*

EXHIBIT 3.3
Typical Data Collected for Job Analysis

Job content/context factors

Duties	Reporting relationships
Functions	Communications network
Tasks	Output (e.g., reports, analyses)
Activities	Working conditions
Performance criteria	Time allocation
Critical incidents	Resource responsibility
Organizational level	Roles (e.g., negotiator, monitor, leader)

Worker characteristics

Professional/technical knowledge	Managerial skills
Prior experience	Bargaining skills
Manual skills	Leadership skills
Verbal skills	Consulting skills
Written skills	Human relations skills
Quantitative skills	Aptitudes
Mechanical skills	Values
Conceptual skills	Style

Work characteristics

Risk or exposure	Dependence/independence
Constraints	Pattern or cycle
Choices	Time pressure
Conflicting demands	Fragmentation
Origin of activities	Sustained attention
Expected/unexpected	Time orientation (short or long)

Interpersonal relationships

Internal	External
Boss	Suppliers
Other superiors	Customers
Peers	Regulatory
Subordinates	Consultants
Other juniors	Professional/industry
	Community
	Union/employee group

Source: Howard Risher, "Job Analysis: A Management Perspective," *Employee Relations Law Journal* 4, no. 4 (Spring 1979), pp. 535–51. © *Employee Relations Law Journal*, 22 West 21st Street, New York, NY 10010. Reprinted with permission of the publisher.

worker traits or characteristics. It further refined work performed into three categories.[12]

1. Worker functions: What the worker does in relationship to *data, people,* and *things.*
2. Work fields: The methods and techniques employed.
3. Products and services: The materials, products, subject matter, and/or services that result.

---

[12]U.S. Civil Service Commission, *Job Analysis: Developing and Documenting Data* (Washington, D.C.: Bureau of Intergovernmental Personnel Programs, 1973).

For each of these three categories of data, a list of classes was developed. For example, data, people, and things were further refined into 24 worker functions (e.g., computing data differs from copying it). Work fields, defined into 39 subfields, include both "method" verbs (e.g., pouring) and the equipment used to carry out the action (e.g., steel cauldron). An analyst is trained to distinguish the two types of verbs: Method verbs are all action verbs, while the verbs in worker functions are descriptive and encompass a broader activity. Products and services include 375 different categories of results from the job. Finally, worker traits were refined into (1) training time, (2) aptitudes, (3) temperament, (4) interests, and (5) physical demands and environmental conditions.

Fine modified the DOL's methodology to place greater emphasis on the worker functions and relate those functions to the goals and objectives of the organization.[13] His work resulted in Functional Job Analysis (FJA), which is widely used in the public sector. While few private-sector employers use it, their practices reflect its influence.

The DOL's two basic categories, actual work performed and worker traits, provide the basis for much of current research on quantifying the job analysis process. However, most researchers subdivide worker traits into two groups, one concerned with the worker's behavior on the job, and the other with the underlying abilities required to make such behavior possible.

So we essentially have three categories of information to consider: work data (what tasks are done), worker data (what behaviors occur), and ability data (what abilities underlie the behaviors and task performance).[14] These categories can be confusing because they all look at the same thing—a worker doing a job—and take different approaches to describe what is happening. Perhaps some examples will clarify the differences.

Work or Task Data

Work data involve the elemental units of work, subparts of a job called tasks, with emphasis on the purpose of each task. An excerpt from a job analysis questionnaire that collects task data is shown in Exhibit 3.4. While the aspect of work being considered here is "communication," note how the inventory describes communication in terms of actual tasks; for example, "read technical publications" and "consult with co-workers." The other distinguishing characteristic is the emphasis on output, or objective of the task; for example, "read technical publications to keep current on industry" and "consult with co-workers

---

[13]Sidney Fine, *Functional Job Analysis Scales: A Desk Aid* (Kalamazoo, Mich.: Upjohn Institute for Employment Research, 1973); Fine and Wiley, *Introduction to Functional Job Analysis.*

[14]Ron Ash, "Job Elements for Task Clusters: Arguments for Using Multi-Methodological Approaches to Job Analysis and a Demonstration of their Utility," *Public Personnel Management Journal,* June 1982, pp. 80–90.

EXHIBIT 3.4
Job Analysis Questionnaire *(excerpt)*

SECTION II: TASK INVENTORY

STEP I	STEP II

STEP II — TIME SPENT

Compared to all other tasks performed on your present job.

Rating scale (1–9):
- 1 = Extremely small compared to other tasks
- 2 = Very small compared to other tasks
- 3 = Small compared to other tasks
- 4 = Slightly smaller than other tasks
- 5 = About average compared to other tasks
- 6 = Slightly larger than other tasks
- 7 = Larger than other tasks
- 8 = Very large compared to other tasks
- 9 = Extremely large compared to other tasks

STEP I — Do perform / Do not perform

1. Review all subduties and tasks.
2. Mark "Do Perform" for all subduties and tasks you perform in your current job and "Do Not Perform" for all subduties and tasks you do not perform in your current job.
3. At the end of the inventory, in the space provided, write in any unlisted tasks that you perform.

Prepare data.
411. Write test data for keypunch operators.
412. Prepare data entry instructions or data.

Enter and transmit data.
413. Enter data using terminal.
414. Transmit data between computer systems via teleprocessing (e.g., cyberlink, remote batch facility, etc.).

Perform keypunch activities.
415. Keypunch data.
416. Verify punched data.
417. Edit data file to correct input errors.
418. Write batches to tape, stats, and backups.
419. Reproduce and/or produce punched cards to correct errors, replace damaged cards, or add information.
420. Operate tab equipment.

PERFORM COMMUNICATIONS ACTIVITIES

Obtain technical information.
421. Read technical publications about competitive products.
422. Read technical publications to keep current on industry.
423. Attend required, recommended, or job-related courses and/or seminars.
424. Study existing operating systems/programs to gain/maintain familiarity with them.
425. Perform literature searches necessary to the development of products.
426. Communicate with system software group to see how their recent changes impact current projects.
427. Study and evaluate state-of-the-art techniques to remain competitive and/or lead the field.
428. Attend industry standards meetings.

Exchange technical information.
429. Interface with coders to verify that the software design is being implemented as specified.
430. Consult with co-workers to exchange ideas and techniques.
431. Consult with members of other technical groups within the company to exchange new ideas and techniques.
432. Interface with support consultants or organizations to clarify software design or courseware content.
433. Attend meetings to review project status.
434. Attend team meetings to review implementation strategies.
435. Discuss department plans and objectives with manager.

to exchange ideas and techniques". Task data reveal the actual work performed and its purpose or outcome.[15]

Worker or Behavioral Data

This data approach describes jobs in terms of the behaviors that occur. Exhibit 3.5 shows such behavioral observations, again concerned with "communications." This time, the questions focus on verbs that describe the human behavior (e.g., advising, negotiating, persuading). Exhibit 3.5 is from the Position Analysis Questionnaire (PAQ), developed by McCormick and his associates.[16] The PAQ groups work information into seven basic factors: information input, mental processes, work output, relationships with other persons, job context, other job characteristics, and general dimensions. With the PAQ, similarities and differences among jobs are described in terms of these seven general processes, rather than in terms of specific aspects unique to each job.[17] The communications behavior in Exhibit 3.5 is part of the "relationships with other persons" factor. Let us compare the PAQ's approach to communications to the task inventory's approach. Item 105 on the PAQ: "nonroutine information exchange (the giving and/or receiving of *job-related* information of a nonroutine

---

[15]Ramon J. Aldag, Steve H. Barr, and Arthur P. Brief, "Measurement of Perceived Task Characteristics," *Psychological Bulletin* 90, no. 3 (1981), pp. 415–31; Page, "The Use of Job Content Information."

[16]Much of the developmental and early applicatons of the PAQ was done in the 1960s and 1970s. See, for example, Ernest J. McCormick, "Job Information: Its Development and Applications," in *Handbook of Personnel and Industrial Relations,* ed. D. Yoder and H. G. Heneman, Jr. (Washington, D.C.: Bureau of National Affairs, 1979); McCormick, *Job Analysis* (New York: AMACOM, 1979); McCormick, "Job and Task Analysis," in *Handbook of Industrial and Organizational Psychology,* ed. M.D. Dunnette (Chicago: Rand McNally, 1979); McCormick, *The Development, Analysis, and Experimental Application of Worker-Oriented Job Variables* (Washington, D.C.: Office of Naval Research Report, Department of the Navy, 1964); E. J. McCormick, J. W. Cunningham, and G. C. Gordon, "Job Dimensions Based on Factorial Analyses of Worker-Oriented Job Variables," *Personnel Psychology* 20 (1967), pp. 417–30; E. J. McCormick, R. H. Finn, and C. D. Scheips, "Patterns of Job Requirements," *Journal of Applied Psychology* 41 (1957), pp. 358–65; E. J. McCormick, P. R. Jeanneret, and R. C. Mecham, *The Development and Background of the Position Analysis Questionnaire (PAQ)* (West Lafayette, Ind.: Occupational Research Center, Purdue University, 1969); McCormick et al., *A Study of Job Characteristics and Job Dimensions as Based on the Position Analysis Questionnaire* (West Lafayette, Ind.: Occupational Research Center, Purdue University, 1969); P. R. Jeanneret and R. C. Mecham, "A Study of Job Characteristics and Job Dimensions as Based on the Position Analysis Questionnaire (PAQ)," *Journal of Applied Psychology* 56 (1972), pp. 347–68; R. C. Mecham and E. J. McCormick, *The Rated Attribute Requirements of Job Elements in the Position Analysis Questionnaire* (West Lafayette, Ind.: Occupational Research Center, Purdue University, 1969); Mecham et al., *The Use of Data Based on the Position Analysis Questionnaire* (West Lafayette, Ind.: Occupational Research Center, Purdue University, 1969). The PAQ is distributed by the University Book Store, 360 West State St., West Lafayette, Ind. 47906.

[17]R. C. Mecham, E. J. McCormick, and P. R. Jeanneret, *Technical Manual for the Position Analysis Questionnaire (PAQ) System* (Logan, Utah: PAQ Services, 1977).

EXHIBIT 3.5
Job Analysis Questionnaire *(excerpt)*

Section 4   Relationships with Other Persons

This section deals with different aspects of
interaction between people involved in various
kinds of work.

Code Importance to this Job (1)	
N	Does not apply
1	Very minor
2	Low
3	Average
4	High
5	Extreme

4.1   Communications

Rate the following in terms of how *important* the activity is to the completion of the job. Some jobs
may involve several or all of the items in this section.

4.1.1   Oral (communicating by speaking)

99 ____ Advising (dealing with individuals in order to counsel and/or guide them with regard to
problems that may be resolved by legal, financial, scientific, technical, clinical, spiritual,
and/or other professional principles)

100 ____ Negotiating (dealing with others in order to reach an agreement or solution, for example,
labor bargaining, diplomatic relations, etc.)

101 ____ Persuading (dealing with others in order to influence them toward some action or point of
view, for example, selling, political campaigning, etc.)

102 ____ Instructing (the teaching of knowledge or skills, in either an informal or a formal manner,
to others, for example, a public school teacher, a machinist teaching an apprentice, etc.)

103 ____ Interviewing (conducting interviews directed toward some specific objective, for
example, interviewing job applicants, census taking, etc.)

104 ____ Routine information exchange: job related (the giving and/or receiving of *job-related*
information of a routine nature, for example, ticket agent, taxicab dispatcher,
receptionist, etc.)

105 ____ Nonroutine information exchange (the giving and/or receiving of *job-related*
information of a nonroutine or unusual nature, for example, professional committee
meetings, engineers discussing new product design, etc.)

106 ____ Public speaking (making speeches or formal presentations before relatively large
audiences, for example, political addresses, radio/TV broadcasting, delivering a sermon,
etc.)

4.1.2   Written (communicating by written/printed material)

107 ____ Writing (for example, writing or dictating letters, reports, etc., writing copy for ads,
writing newspaper articles, etc.; do *not* include transcribing activities described in item
4.3, but only activities in which the incumbent creates the written material)

4.1.3   Other Communications

108 ____ Signaling (communicating by some type of signal, for example, hand signals, semaphore,
whistles, horns, bells, lights, etc.)

109 ____ Code communications (telegraph, cryptography, etc.)

Source: E. J. McCormick, P. R. Jeanneret, and R. C. Mecham, *Position Analysis Questionnaire,* copyright ©
1969 by Purdue Research Foundation, West Lafayette, Indiana 47907. Reprinted with permission.

or unusual nature, for example, professional committee meetings, engineers discussing new product design, etc.)" is probably similar to item 430 on the task inventory: "consult with co-workers to exchange ideas and techniques." Both are getting at the same aspect of work, by different approaches. But lest you think the previous task inventory (Exhibit 3.4) offers the beauty of simplicity, note that item 431 lists "consult with members of other technical groups . . . to exchange new ideas and techniques" and item 432 lists "interface with support consultants to clarify . . . design." In fact, the task inventory from which Exhibit 3.4 is excerpted contains 250 items and covers only systems analyst jobs, whereas the work behavior data in Exhibit 3.5 is from an inventory of 194 items, whose developers claim it can be used to analyze *all* jobs. Consequently, new task-based questions need to be designed for each new set of jobs, whereas behaviors, at least as defined in the PAQ, may be applied across all jobs. However, some evidence suggests that the PAQ's seven functions are simply too generally defined for pay purposes.[18] These functions seem to emphasize similarities in the jobs and are less sensitive to differences.

Abilities Data

Abilities data capture the knowledge and skill a worker must possess for satisfactory job performance. A taxonomy developed by Fleishman includes (1) psychomotor abilities, (2) physical proficiency abilities, and (3) cognitive abilities, and forms the foundation for ability-based job analysis.[19] Ross and others at AT&T, in conjunction with the Communication Workers of America and other unions, have developed a set of 16 abilities required in nonmanagerial work at AT&T, shown in Exhibit 3.6.[20] "Expression" and "comprehension," their first two factors, probably correspond most closely to the communication aspect we looked at with task data and worker data. Exhibit 3.7 shows part of how AT&T measures "expression" and "comprehension" abilities required on the job. Note that the behavioral descriptors used to anchor the scales for oral compre-

[18]E. T. Cornelius III, T. J. Carron, and M. M. Collins, "Job Analysis Models and Job Classification," *Personnel Psychology* 32 (1979), pp. 693–708; also see R. W. Lissitz, J. L. Mendoza, C. J. Huberty, and V. H. Markos, "Some Ideas on a Methodology for Determining Job Similarities/Differences," *Personnel Psychology* 32 (1979); and JoAnn Lee and Jorge L. Mendoza, "A Comparison of Techniques which Test for Job Difference," *Personnel Psychology* 34 (1981), pp. 731–48.

[19]E. A. Fleishman, *Structure and Measurement of Physical Fitness* (Englewood Cliffs, N.J.: Prentice-Hall, 1964); Fleishman, "Toward a Taxonomy of Human Performance," *American Psychologist* 30 (1975), pp. 1017–32; Fleishman, "Evaluating Physical Abilities Required by Jobs," *The Personal Administrator* 24 (1979), pp. 82–92; and Fleishman, "On the Relation between Abilities, Learning, and Human Performance," *American Psychologist* 27 (1972), pp. 1017–32.

[20]Ken Ross, "Occupational Job Evaluation Study," unpublished report (Basking Ridge, N.J., AT&T, 1983); and Ronnie J. Straw and Lorel E. Foged, "The Limits of Job Evaluation to Achieve Comparable Worth," paper presented at Atlantic Economic Conference, Montreal, Canada, October 11–14, 1984.

EXHIBIT 3.6
AT&T—CWA Job Analysis Factors: Knowledge/Abilities/Skill-Based

---

1. *Expression* is speaking and/or writing in words, sentences, or numbers so others will understand. It is measured in terms of the complexity of the information being expressed as well as the comprehension ability of the receiver of the information.

2. *Comprehension* is understanding spoken and/or written words, sentences, or numbers. It is measured in terms of the complexity of the information being received as well as the quality of the information being received.

3. *Fact Finding* is obtaining or selecting pertinent information through observation, research, or questioning. It includes organizing and combining different pieces of information into meaningful order to identify a problem. It does not include the application of this information to solve the problem. An unknown is the key element in fact finding.

4. *Systems Reasoning* is making decisions that involve the selection and application of appropriate business resources or usage of relevant facts to solve identified problems or to achieve a desired result. This is based on knowledge and understanding of products and services, materials, policies, practices and procedures.

5. *Mathematics* is the selection and application of mathematical methods or procedures to solve problems or to achieve desired results. These systems range from basic arithmetic computations to the most complex statistical techniques or other applications such as occur in physics or engineering problems.

6. *Adaptability* is the need to adapt one's behavior to changing or unusual circumstances to achieve a desired result. This includes changes in personal interactions or work situations.

7. *Persuasion* is influencing the behaviors or actions of others. The changes in others' behaviors or actions may not be observed immediately.

8. *Mental Demand* is mental effort associated with attending to or performing a task in the presence of distractions or work frustrations. Distractions and work frustrations arise from boredom, overlapping demands, exacting deadlines and output standards, lack of latitude to adapt behavior, discouraging circumstances, repeated unsuccessful attempts, and nonemployee controlled work flow.

9. *Physical Demand* is physical effort associated with activities such as handling weights, repetition of work motions, maintenance of difficult work positions, or exposure to unpleasant surroundings.

10. *Safety Skills* measures the adherence to prescribed safety and personal security practices in the performance of tasks involving exposure to hazard or risk in the work environment.

11. *Electrical/Electronic Knowledge* is the knowledge and application of the principles of electricity, electronics, electronic logic, and integrated transmission technologies such as lasers and fiber optics. This includes understanding of circuits, their component parts and how they work together, and understanding the output from devices or meters that register or display information related to these systems.

12. *Mechanical Knowledge* is the knowledge and application of principles of how mechanical equipment such as gears, pulleys, motors, and hydraulics works. It includes the operation, repair or maintenance of systems. It *does not* include knowledge of tools and their uses.

13. *Tools and Uses* is the knowledge, appropriate selection and application of hand tools, office machines, mechanical and electrical tools (test sets). This does not include keyboard devices.

14. *Graphics* is reading, interpreting and/or preparing graphic representations of information such as maps, plans, drawings, blueprints, diagrams, and timing/flow charts. It includes the preparation of visual artwork.

15. *Coding* is reading and/or writing and interpreting coded information. Codes may be identified by the fact that the ideas or concepts they represent may be translated, expanded, or expressed in English.

16. *Keyboard Skills* is the operation of keyboard devices such as typewriters, data terminals, calculators, and operator equipment.

EXHIBIT 3.7

WRITTEN COMPREHENSION

This is the ability to understand written sentences and paragraphs.

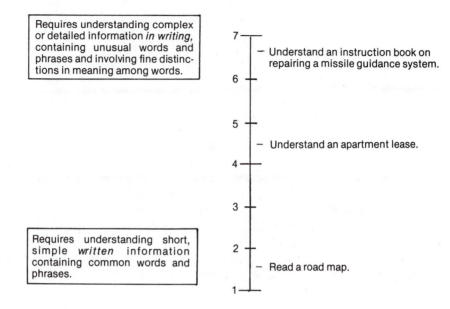

Requires understanding complex or detailed information *in writing*, containing unusual words and phrases and involving fine distinctions in meaning among words.

7 — Understand an instruction book on repairing a missile guidance system.

6

5 — Understand an apartment lease.

4

3

Requires understanding short, simple *written* information containing common words and phrases.

2 — Read a road map.

1

ORAL COMPREHENSION

This is the ability to understand spoken English words and sentences.

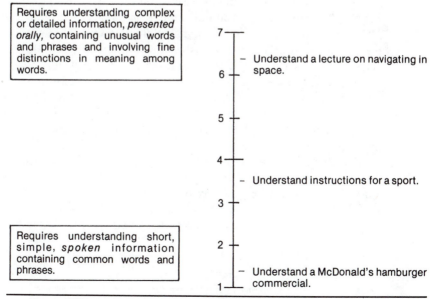

Requires understanding complex or detailed information, *presented orally*, containing unusual words and phrases and involving fine distinctions in meaning among words.

7 — Understand a lecture on navigating in space.

6

5

4 — Understand instructions for a sport.

3

Requires understanding short, simple, *spoken* information containing common words and phrases.

2

1 — Understand a McDonald's hamburger commercial.

Source: AT&T.

hension (e.g., "understand a McDonald's hamburger commercial," "understand instructions for a sport," and "understand a lecture on navigating in space") are not work-specific but are drawn from daily life outside of the job. Work-specific illustrations could also be used to anchor these scales.

While "communication" scales, shown in Exhibits 3.4, 3.5, and 3.7, were used to illustrate the shades of differences in task, behavior, and ability data, these three represent different views of work. Work data, worker data, and ability data vary in the way they describe a job. Thus, it is not surprising that varying approaches to job analysis may yield different results. Cornelius, Carron, and Collins examined seven foreman jobs in a chemical processing plant using all three types of job analysis data.[21] Using the same statistical procedures on all three data sets, they found that different data sets yielded different results. In other words, the type of data collected will affect the results. Their research provides sound advice for the compensation professional: The purpose of the analysis dictates the nature of the data to collect. Thus, if you intend to design training programs, according to Exhibit 3.2, you'll need to collect task and behavioral data. If it's an equitable pay structure you need to develop, then all three types of data may be useful. Other research has identified another factor that affects the results of job analysis: the level of analysis.

Level of Analysis

The nature of the data collected can be considered in terms of a hierarchy, shown in Exhibit 3.8. Some of the levels in the hierarchy are the same as the types of data we just discussed. Employee attributes (abilities) and task elements are examples. In the hierarchy, tasks represent a grouping of elements or behaviors into a basic accomplishment or duty. For example, elements such as "gathering time cards and using calculators to multiply hours worked by hourly wage" are combined into a task called "calculating employee wages for time cards." Moving up the hierarchy, tasks are grouped into positions, which constitute different individuals performing the same group of tasks in a particular organization. In the illustration in Exhibit 3.8 there are three positions (individuals) as Bookkeeper I (job in firm A). Jobs similar across several firms (Bookkeeper, Accounting Clerk, Teller) are in turn considered to belong to an occupation. The occupation, at the most general level of analysis, could be grouped with other occupations into a job family. Such a family would involve computing, classifying, and recording numerical data, and may form a "computing and account/recording job family."

What does all this have to do with making pay decisions? First, the types of data collected at each level may differ. You have already seen the distinction

---

[21]Cornelius, Carron, and Collins, "Job Analysis Models;" and Jack E. Smith and Milton D. Hakel, "Convergence among Data Sources, Response Bias, and Reliability and Validity of a Structured Job Analysis Questionnaire," *Personnel Psychology* 32, no. 4 (1979), pp. 677–92.

EXHIBIT 3.8
Levels of Analysis

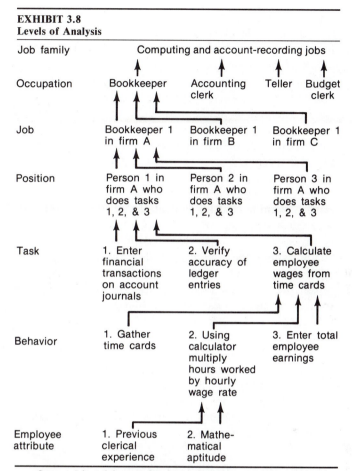

Job family	Computing and account-recording jobs
Occupation	Bookkeeper Accounting clerk Teller Budget clerk
Job	Bookkeeper 1 in firm A Bookkeeper 1 in firm B Bookkeeper 1 in firm C
Position	Person 1 in firm A who does tasks 1, 2, & 3 Person 2 in firm A who does tasks 1, 2, & 3 Person 3 in firm A who does tasks 1, 2, & 3
Task	1. Enter financial transactions on account journals 2. Verify accuracy of ledger entries 3. Calculate employee wages from time cards
Behavior	1. Gather time cards 2. Using calculator multiply hours worked by hourly wage rate 3. Enter total employee earnings
Employee attribute	1. Previous clerical experience 2. Mathematical aptitude

Source: Adapted from K. Pearlman, "Job Families: A Review and Discussion of their Implications for Personnel Selection," *Psychological Bulletin* 87 (1980), pp. 1–28. Copyright 1980 by the American Psychological Association. Adapted by permission of the author.

---

among task, worker, and ability data. The task data yield a set of actual activities that can identify similarities and differences among jobs. Such data would not provide direct information on what abilities are required to perform the job; that may only be inferred. By contrast, a job description based on ability data, as used by AT&T, would identify similarities and differences on these factors, but little information on the tasks performed or the output or end result of a job.

Next, and perhaps more importantly, the level or unit of analysis chosen may influence the decision of whether the work is similar or dissimilar. At the occupation level, bookkeepers, tellers, and accounting clerks are considered to be similar; yet at levels below occupation (the job level, for example) these three are considered dissimilar. Hence, a critical decision in the design of job analysis is the level of analysis, which determines the specificity of the work information to be collected. An analogy might be looking at two grains of salt under a microscope versus looking at them as part of a serving of french fries. This is important because if job data suggest that jobs are similar, then the jobs must be paid equally; if jobs are different, they can be paid differently. The issue of whether or not jobs are substantially similar has been a main focus of a lot of discrimination litigation. In such cases the decision on whether or not the jobs are similar or different takes on financial meaning beyond concerns for internal consistency.

In practice, the level of analysis varies considerably. Some employers use aggregated levels (position or job) and ignore specific tasks and employee behavior, arguing that all the detailed data on tasks and behaviors are combined when deciding wage rates. They argue that the time and expense to collect data is unjustified, since the individual jobs are later grouped for pay purposes.

So where does this leave us? What data should be collected and what level of analysis should be used? There is no clear-cut answer. It depends on the situation, the resources available. But the more specific and detailed the data, the more likely it is to capture job differences and to more adequately describe the job content. Whether such detailed information is worth the expense involved depends on the circumstances. Clearly, detailed data may justify pay differences to a skeptical judge presiding over a pay discrimination suit. Yet, detailed job data often get combined in the name of flexibility for pay administration purposes, and separate jobs often get combined into more broadly defined jobs with generic titles and descriptions. This is done in an attempt to increase flexibility of work assignments without requiring a change in compensation to reassigned employees.

HOW CAN THE DATA BE COLLECTED?

After having decided on the purpose and the nature of the data, the next major decision is the method(s) of collecting it. A wide variety of methods exists; the most common ones are described in Exhibit 3.9. In this section we will combine these methods into two basic types: conventional and quantitative.

Conventional Methods

A common data collection method involves an analyst using a questionnaire to conduct a structured interview of job incumbents and supervisors.[22] The questionnaires and interviews are structured to achieve a uniform response format. The approach requires considerable involvement of employees and supervisors,

---

[22]For a more detailed description of conventional job analysis procedures, see U.S. Department of Labor, *Handbook for Analyzing Jobs.*

EXHIBIT 3.9
Data Collection Methods

Method	*Descriptions*	*Characteristics*
Questionnaire	Using standardized form, jobholders and/or supervisors describe the work. Data can be gathered either through mailed survey or through individual interview.	Variations include combining questionnaire with individual or group interview. As with all questionnaires, responses may be incomplete or difficult to interpret, a limitation minimized by combining with interviews. Standard format eases mathematical analysis. Interviews, however, may be time consuming, and become more difficult with workers at multiple locations.
Checklist	Jobholders and/or supervisors check items on a task inventory that apply to their particular job. Check list can be tailor-made or purchased.	Depends on recognition rather than recall. Cheap, easy to administer and analyze. However, care must be taken that all significant aspects of work are included in the list.
Diary	Jobholders record activities as they are performed.	Has the advantage of collecting data as events occur, but it is often difficult to obtain continuous and consistent entries. Obtained data is not in a standardized format.
Observation	Analyst records perceptions formed watching the work being done by one or more jobholders.	The absence of preconceived structures or artificial constraints can lead to richer data. Each job can be studied in any depth desired. However, validity and reliability of data can be a problem, and the relative emphasis of certain work aspects is dependent on the acuteness of the analyst's perceptions. Also, the observation of employee behavior by an analyst influences it.
Activity sampling	Observations are made at random intervals.	
Activity matrix	Respondents identify time spent in relation to tasks and products or services.	Data collected is amenable to quantitative analysis, and is highly adaptable to other human resource management needs; however, another job analysis procedure must be used initially to develop the matrix.
Critical incidents	Behaviorally oriented incidents describe key job behaviors. Analyst determines degree of each type of behavior present or absent in each job.	Analysis clearly based on concrete behavior. Scales require some expertise to develop.

which increases their understanding of the process, provides an opportunity to clarify their work relationships and expectations, and increases the likelihood that they will accept the results. Usually, an analyst translates the data collected to a summary job description sheet. Often, both incumbents and supervisors are given an opportunity to modify and approve the job description; this helps assure its acceptance. In some cases the preparation of these description sheets is left to the supervisors and incumbents, while the analyst role becomes one of trainer/facilitator. The analysts are trained (either formally or through trial and error) in verbal style and form to ensure that description sheets are uniform. Some trainers go so far as to specify "correct" verbs and adjectives to use.[23] A step-by-step procedure for conducting a conventional job analysis is shown in

---

[23]R. T. Henderson, *Compensation Management,* 4th ed. (Reston, Va.: Reston Publishing, 1985).

EXHIBIT 3.10
General Procedures for Conventional Job Analysis

Step	Things to Remember or Do
1. Develop preliminary job information	a. Review existing documents in order to develop an initial "big-picture" familiarity with the job: its main mission, its major duties or functions, work flow patterns. b. Prepare a preliminary list of duties which will serve as a framework for conducting the interviews. c. Make a note of major items which are unclear, or ambiguous or that need to be clarified during the data-gathering process.
2. Conduct initial tour of work site	a. The initial tour is designed to familiarize the job analyst with the work layout, the tools and equipment that are used, the general conditions of the workplace, and the mechanics associated with the end-to-end performance of major duties. b. The initial tour is particularly helpful in those jobs where a first-hand view of a complicated or unfamiliar piece of equipment saves the interviewee the thousand words required to describe the unfamiliar or technical. c. For continuity, it is recommended that the first level supervisor-interviewee be designated the guide for the job-site observations.
3. Conduct interviews	a. It is recommended that the first interview be conducted with the first-level supervisor who is considered to be in a better position than the jobholders to provide an overview of the job and how the major duties fit together. b. For scheduling purposes, it is recommended that no more than two interviews be conducted per day, each interview lasting no more than three hours.
Notes on selection of interviewees	a. The interviewees are considered subject matter experts by virtue of the fact that they perform the job (in the case of job incumbents) or are responsible for getting the job done (in the case of first-level supervisors). b. The job incumbent to be interviewed should represent the *typical* employee who is knowledgeable about the job (*not* the trainee who is just learning the ropes *nor* the outstanding member of the work unit). c. Whenever feasible, the interviewees should be selected with a view towards obtaining an appropriate race/sex mix.
4. Conduct second tour of work site	a. The second tour of the work site is designed to clarify, confirm, and otherwise refine the information developed in the interviews. b. As in the initial tour, it is recommended that the same first-level supervisor-interviewee conduct the second walk-through.
5. Consolidate job information	a. The consolidation phase of the job study involves piecing together into one coherent and comprehensive job description the data obtained from several sources: supervisor, jobholders, on-site tours, and written materials about the job. b. Past experience indicates that one minute of consolidation is required for every minute of interviewing. For planning purposes, at least 5 hours should be set aside for the consolidation phase. c. A subject matter expert should be accessible as a resource person to the job analyst during the consolidation phase. The supervisor-interviewee fills this role. d. Check your initial preliminary list of duties and questions—all must be answered or confirmed.
6. Verify job description	a. The verification phase involves bringing all the interviewees together for the purpose of determining if the consolidated job description is accurate and complete. b. The verification process is conducted in a group setting. Typed or legibly written copies of the job description (narrative description of the work setting *and* list of task statements) are distributed to the first-level supervisor and the job incumbent interviewees. c. Line by line, the job analyst goes through the entire job description and makes notes of any omissions, ambiguities, or needed clarifications. d. Collect all materials at the end of the verification meeting.

Exhibit 3.10, and Appendix A in this chapter contains a conventional job analysis questionnaire.

Conventional methods place considerable reliance on the analyst's abilities to understand the work performed and to translate it. Certain safeguards, such as multiple approvals (by supervisors and incumbents), may help minimize the difficulties inherent in translating the results of questionnaires and personal discussions into an accurate representation of the job.

In a review of job analysis, McCormick points out that "of the various deficiencies of conventional job analysis procedures, probably the sharpest criticism is that the typical essays of job activities *are not* adequately descriptive of the jobs in question." After granting the positive contribution of obtaining work-related data through conventional methods, he observes in an artful understatement, "They probably ha[ve] not generally benefited from . . . systematic, scientific approaches."[24]

Reducing subjectivity in job analysis is the primary goal of quantitative job analysis. The critical advantage of quantitative job analysis over conventional approaches is that quantitative analysis lends itself to statistical analysis, is documentable and quantifiable, and *may* be more objective. Additionally, a computerized job analysis may relieve much of the drudgery of collecting and translating job data.

Quantitative Methods

Inventories are the core of all quantitative job analysis. Inventories, illustrated in Exhibits 3.4, 3.5, and 3.7, are questionnaires in which tasks, behaviors, and abilities are listed. Each item is assessed, usually by both job incumbents and supervisors, in terms of time spent, importance to the overall job, and/or learning time.[25] The advantages of systematic assessment include the facts that decisions and results are documented, and that resulting data can be subjected to further statistical analysis.

Usually a compensation professional must decide whether to buy a commercially available, predeveloped inventory or to develop a quantitative inventory tailored for a specific organization. Not surprisingly, consulting firms

---

[24]McCormick, "Job and Task Analysis."

[25]J. E. Morsh, "Job Analysis in the United States Air Force," *Personnel Psychology* 17, no. 17 (1964), pp. 7–17; J. E. Morsh, M. Joyce Giorgia, and J. M. Madden, "A Job Analysis of a Complex Utilization Field—The R&D Management Officer," Personnel Research Laboratory, Aerospace Medical Division, Air Force Systems Command, 1965; J. N. Mosel, "The Domain of Worker Functions as a Partially Ordered Set," Paper presented at American Psychological Association Meetings, Philadelphia, 1963; and A. I. Siegel and D. G. Shultz, "Post-Training Performance Criterion Development and Application: A Comparative Multidimensional Scaling Analysis of the Task Performed by Naval Aviation Electronics Technicians at Two Job Levels" (Wayne, Pa.: Applied Psychological Services, 1964).

stand at the ready to offer predeveloped plans as well as the experience and analytical skills necessary to design a tailored one.[26]

Predeveloped Quantitative Inventories

Several quantitative inventories are available. Three are briefly discussed here; more details and other options may be found through the references.

Comprehensive Occupational Data Analysis Program (CODAP). Originally developed to aid the U.S. Air Force design training programs, CODAP is perhaps the earliest attempt to quantify job analysis. [27] The data are task oriented and cover over 200 Air Force specialties. The items are scaled in terms of the "average time spent" on each. While its use for pay administration is limited, the CODAP computer software, developed to analyze job analysis data, is available free to nonprofit organizations and can be used on pay-related job data.[28]

FOCAS. Control Data Business Advisors has developed an approach it markets as Flexible Occupation Analysis System (FOCAS).[29] While FOCAS is task based, it differs from other quantitative job analysis inventories in that separate questionnaires have been developed for several occupations (e.g., management, systems analysis, manufacturing, personnel, and others). All these questionnaires share a common core of task-based items; the approach is flexible, since unique items are added to the core for each unique occupation. Hewlett-Packard, 3M, and Nationwide Insurance are among the employers using some variation of FOCAS to help determine their pay structures.

Position Analysis Questionnaire. Without question the PAQ is the best-known and most generally used quantitative job analysis.[30] The PAQ has 194 items (Exhibit 3.5 is an example). As noted earlier, these items form seven basic

---

[26]Information on custom designed quantitative job analysis plans can be obtained from Control Data Business Advisors, 8200 34th Avenue South, Minneapolis, Minn.; Personnel Decisions Research Institute, Foshay Tower, Minneapolis, Minn.; Sibson & Co., Chicago, Ill., (and other locations); and Wyatt & Company, New York, Detroit, San Francisco (and other locations).

[27]R. E. Christal and J. J. Weissmuller, *New Comprehensive Occupational Data Analysis Programs* (*CODAP*) *for Analyzing Task Factor Information,* AHFRL Interim Professional Paper No. 7R-76-3, (Lackland Air Force Base, Tex.: Air Force Human Resources Laboratory, 1976); and M. H. Trattner, "Task Analysis in the Design of Three Concurrent Validity Studies of the Professional and Administrative Career Examination," *Personnel Psychology* 32 (1979), pp. 109–19.

[28]Contact the Personnel Research Division of the Human Resources Laboratory, Lackland Air Force Base, Texas.

[29]The address for Control Data Business Advisors is included in Note 26.

[30]Information on the PAQ is available from PAQ Services, P.O. Box 3337, Logan, UT 84321, (801) 752-5698.

factors and are scaled according to how important each item is in the total job. According to its developers, the PAQ can be used to analyze virtually any job or position, and can be completed by a typical employee without much special training.[31] However, its reading comprehension level is quite high and the instructions complex, making it difficult for some employees to complete it on their own.[32] Mecham and McCormick suggest that an analyst trained in its use could be used to assist employees in completing the inventory.[33] Compensation analysts may want to obtain a copy and try completing it themselves to get a feel for the questionnaire before they adopt it.[34]

Predeveloped inventories such as the CODAP, FOCAS, or PAQ offer the advantage of having been pretested, which avoids substantial expense and lead time required in inventory design. But a major limitation of most of these pre-developed plans is that they are not tailored to particular job families or organizations. Rather, most were developed to be applied across a wide variety of work in different organizations. Consequently, their questions may be too general to be useful in identifying differences in specific jobs.

Tailoring a Plan

Rather than adopting an existing inventory, some employers opt to tailor one to its specific work and conditions. Several consulting organizations market technical expertise to assist these employers.[35] So the choice is whether to purchase a predeveloped inventory or to custom-design one. While specific processes through which inventories are developed vary somewhat among consultants, all involve four basic steps.

Step 1: Generate items. An exhaustive list of tasks or worker traits relevant to the work is generated, typically through interviews with small groups of job incumbents and supervisors. The exact number of items generated for preliminary lists varies, depending on the nature of the jobs. Final lists may include over 600 items.

Tornow suggests that the following factors be considered when developing items.[36] Try to ensure:

---

[31]See Mecham, McCormick, and Jeanneret, *Technical Manual.*

[32]Ronald A. Ash and S. L. Edgell, "A Note on the Readability of the Position Analysis Questionnaire (PAQ)," *Journal of Applied Psychology* 60 (1975), pp. 765–66; John R. Roark and John H. Burnett, "Objective Methods of Job Analysis," in *Handbook of Wage and Salary Administration,* ed. Milton L. Rock (New York: McGraw-Hill, 1984).

[33]PAQ *Technical Manual.*

[34]See address for the PAQ given in Note 16.

[35]See addresses in Note 26.

[36]Walter W. Tornow, "An Integrated Personnel Approach to Job Analysis and Job Evaluation," Paper presented at Conference on Job Analysis, Institute of Industrial Relations, University of California, Berkeley, February 1979.

- Item content covers the entire domain of tasks/activities/behaviors of the jobs under analysis.
- Items are able to discriminate among jobs which are known to be different.
- Items are not so general as to apply to all positions equally, yet not so specific as to apply to only one job.
- Items permit a quantifiable response format.

Once a preliminary list of items is generated, it is usually culled for duplicate or overlapping items. Usually this process reduces the items to between 200 and 300. An additional set of interviews may be required to ensure that the final list adequately covers the domain of the work.

Step 2: Determine the scaling format.[37] Scaling formats usually include the frequency, importance, and learning time required. Other scales could include consequences of errors, and difficulty.

Step 3: Pilot the preliminary inventory. Once the inventory is generated and scaled, it is administered to a group of jobs whose contents and requirements are relatively unambiguous and accepted by all the parties involved. The purpose of the pilot is to determine if the inventory does identify similarities and differences in work of known characteristics. The pilot also provides the analyst with feedback on a variety of factors, such as how "user friendly" it is, the time required to complete it, and the reactions of incumbents to how adequately the items capture all the aspects of the work. Most pilots include provisions for open-ended responses to write in information that may have been omitted in the item list.

Step 4: Analyze and feed back results. A primary advantage of quantitative job analysis over conventional methods is that the data are amenable to statistical analysis. The increased availability of statistical software packages capable of analyzing such data has led to new techniques for determining similarities and differences in work. The Comprehensive Occupational Data Analysis Program (CODAP) is an example. However, the software is not particularly flexible to other settings and has not been improved as frequently as commercially available software. Alternatives are noted in references in this chapter.

Results of analysis are usually fed back to supervisors and jobholders in profiles and narrative descriptions. Exhibit 3.11 is a comparison of factor profiles for four systems analysis jobs analyzed with Control Data Business Advisors FOCAS. The four jobs of programmer aide, associate programmer, senior program analyst, and consultant have all been analyzed using the same task inventory. The varying profiles result from the different ways the same questions were answered for the four different jobs. Supervisors are supposed to analyze these profiles to determine if they make sense (e.g., programmer aide does fewer design tasks than the other three jobs). Presumably, if the profile fails to make sense to supervisors, they take corrective actions.

---

[37]Also see John Gaito, "Measurement Scales and Statistics: Resurgence of an Old Misconception," *Psychological Bulletin* 87, no. 3 (1980), pp. 564–67.

EXHIBIT 3.11
Comparison of Duty Profiles for Software Jobs

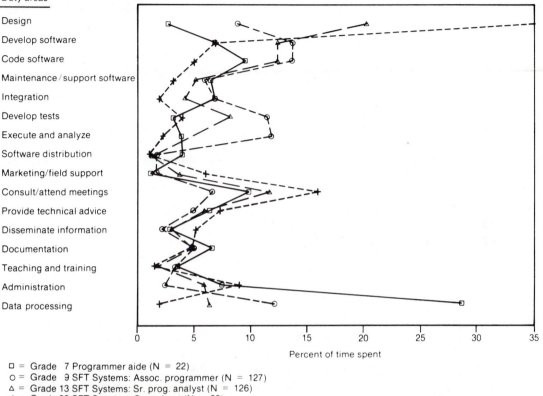

Duty areas

Design
Develop software
Code software
Maintenance / support software
Integration
Develop tests
Execute and analyze
Software distribution
Marketing/field support
Consult/attend meetings
Provide technical advice
Disseminate information
Documentation
Teaching and training
Administration
Data processing

Percent of time spent

□ = Grade 7 Programmer aide (N = 22)
○ = Grade 9 SFT Systems: Assoc. programmer (N = 127)
△ = Grade 13 SFT Systems: Sr. prog. analyst (N = 126)
+ = Grade 38 SFT Systems: Consultant (N = 30)

Job Descriptions

No matter what job analysis technique is used, the information collected usually requires translating and summarizing into the standard format of a job description. A job description should identify, define, and describe the job as it is being performed. As with job analysis, textbooks extol the multiple uses of job descriptions—in career development, replacement charting, performance evaluation, and employment planning, among others—and the question again arises whether a single format can usefully serve all these purposes.[38]

---

[38]Alfred R. Brandt, "Describing Hourly Jobs," in *Handbook of Wage and Salary Administration,* ed. Milton L. Rock (New York: McGraw-Hill, 1984).

The job description typically contains three sections, which roughly correspond with the purposes of identifying, defining, and describing the job. (See Exhibit 3.12 for an IBM job description of a compensation analyst.)

The interested reader may wish to turn to Appendix B to read a computer-generated job description used at 3M for a senior purchasing officer.

1. *Identify the job.* Good job titles will provide information and will not obfuscate. Job families may have similar titles, but titles should be consistent

---

EXHIBIT 3.12
Exempt Position Classification

Identification

Job Title: Senior Compensation Analyst   Job Code and Level: 4130-54
                                                          Division: 01

Summary

Responsible for counseling and providing an assigned broad area of management* with the information necessary for the proper and equitable administration of salaries and classification of employees. Perform salary forecasts, job evaluation, and special salary studies, including salary equity; interpret and advise management regarding additional compensation instructions and, as required, perform analysis of salary survey data. Receives only general managerial directions.

Responsibilities and duties

1. Regularly counsel and advise all levels of management on the proper administration of the merit increase program (pay-for-performance).
2. Administer the exempt and nonexempt evaluation plans through the review and analysis of job responsibilities and interpretation of the evaluation plans. Contact counterparts in division and other locations to make job comparisons.
3. Review and process salary increases, promotions, and reclassifications of all levels of employees. Prepare analyses and rationale, make recommendations, and obtain approval of upper management in accordance with salary guidelines.
4. Review with employment/placement personnel and recommend salary offers and classification for new hires and/or transfers.
5. Perform a lead role in the development of the salary forecast and various complex salary studies (pay-for-performance tests, peer group comparisons, etc.). Develop and recommend programs to achieve salary equity. Track actuals through the year to ensure salary objectives are being met. Recommend corrective programs where necessary.
6. As required, review, analyze, and prepare data relating outside salary survey statistics and comparison, COL trend data, per diem survey, and so on.
7. Interpret additional compensation policies giving appropriate recommendation to management.
8. Conduct training programs on salary administration and make salary presentations to management groups.
9. Assume additional responsibilities as assigned.

---

*Frequently involves difficult contacts on controversial evaluations and salary administration matters.

with work level; similar sounding titles at different levels can be confusing. The job may be further identified by number of incumbents, whether or not it is exempt from the Fair Labor Standards Act, where it is located (department, work site), and job number, if any is used.

2. *Define the job.* This summary section reflects the purpose of the job, why the job exists, and how it fits in with other jobs and with overall organization objectives. End results which flow from the satisfactory performance of this job are typically included.

3. *Describe the job.* What are the major duties of this jobholder? What specific work is performed? How closely supervised is this job; how much discretion does jobholder enjoy; what controls limit the actions of the jobholder? The training and experience required for the job may also be included.

Managerial job descriptions differ from nonmanagerial in several important ways. First, financial and organizational data are needed in order to locate a job in the hierarchy. So the "defining" section may be two parts, with one containing information on what positions and departments are supervised and what functions are the responsibility of this position; and another part containing the number of people directly and indirectly supervised, the department budget, and payroll.

The managerial job description describes major duties by listing the organization objectives that lie in this position's control (e.g., "interpret additional compensation policies giving appropriate recommendation to management").

The purpose of job descriptions is to facilitate decisions on the relationships among jobs, so the descriptions must clearly differentiate similar jobs. Details on how to write job descriptions, including specific definitions of verbs, are available.[39] They caution against vague terms (e.g., "many" or "relatively easy") or those with a variety of meanings (e.g., "takes care of" or "handles"). Enough detail is needed to permit evaluation of the job; anything additional is extraneous for compensation purposes and may discourage use of the information. The most crucial attribute of a good job description is that it be *accurate*. As suggested earlier, one way to encourage accuracy is to require both jobholder and supervisor to sign an approval of the proposed description.

In addition to compensation decisions, accurate job descriptions can affect union/management relations. For example, disputes may arise if workers feel they are performing work that is specified in a higher level, higher paid job. Or union jurisdictional disputes may arise if work is described in such a way that it may fall within more than one union's jurisdiction. Many problems can be

---

[39]Henderson, in *Compensation Management,* lists eight pages of definitions of "action words."

avoided or at least minimized by careful writing. Problems can also arise if job descriptions are not kept current or are not changed if the jobs change. Changes in technology, physical location, product line, strategic direction, and even key personnel can precipitate job changes. A difficulty here is that the compensation department may not always find out about job changes. Supervisors may not be aware of the importance of current, accurate job descriptions and of their responsibility in ensuring accurate descriptions. The point is that management should be aware of the potential disharmony and loss of flexibility if job descriptions are not accurate, readable, and meaningful. The purpose of job descriptions is to provide part of the justification for judgments on compensation. Good job descriptions can reduce the amount of subjectivity in these judgments.

WHO IS INVOLVED IN JOB ANALYSIS?

New York State employs approximately 175,000 people, 30 of whom are job analysts. These analysts receive about 4,500 requests for job analysis and reclassification annually. General Mills Corporation includes job analysis tasks as part of its compensation specialist job, while TRW deemphasizes job analysis altogether. Some employers view the job analyst as an entry-level position and adopt the "learn by doing" approach: Analyzing work provides a thorough introduction to the company, and after 6 to 12 months the analyst is ready for a new job assignment. In spite of real world practice, most textbook writers continue to insist that the analysis should be done by someone who is thoroughly familiar with the organization, its work flow, and its policies and objectives.

Who Collects the Data?

The choice of who collects the data is usually among an analyst, the supervisors, and/or the jobholders. Some firms require the supervisor to perform the analysis, since supervisors are assumed to be knowledgeable, and their involvement may help increase their understanding of exactly what their subordinates do and help them gain acceptance of subordinates. Obvious shortcomings of this arrangement include the possibility of limited knowledge of the actual tasks, skills, and behaviors required on the job. The writers' experience suggests that the employees actually performing the work need to be involved in the analysis process as a way to ensure accuracy and acceptability of any pay structures based on it. But not everyone agrees; Brandt says job descriptions written by job incumbents are unsatisfactory because they don't use the proper words to facilitate comparisons among jobs. He even argues against incumbent approval of a proposed job description, saying this is a prerogative of management. But research results suggest that the involvement of multiple parties as well as mutual "sign-offs" by the supervisor and jobholders are likely to increase the usefulness of the data.[40]

Regardless of who collects the data, some training in the process seems to be a requirement. In the absence of more research, publicly available materials from the Department of Labor may be of value in developing training programs.

Who Provides the Data?

The decision on the source of the data (jobholders, the supervisors, and/or an analyst) hinges on how to ensure consistent, accurate, and acceptable data. Expertise about the work resides with the jobholders and the supervisors; hence they are the principle sources. For key managerial/professional jobs, supervisors "two levels above" have also been suggested as valuable sources since they may have a more cosmic view on how jobs fit into the overall organization. In other instances, subordinates and coordinates (employees in other jobs that interface with the job under study) are also involved. Obviously the greater the involvement, the more time-consuming and expensive the process. The use of coordinates and subordinates seems to be limited to situations in which disagreements over reporting relationships or work domain occur.

One research and development company ran into an interesting problem when it sought to obtain agreement among engineers and their supervisors on what were the engineers' responsibilities. Engineers were wonderfully and capably assuming responsibilities far beyond those assigned by their supervisors. What supervisor would be so foolish as to tell a group of high-performing engineers that what they were doing was not required? The requirement for engineer approval of their job descriptions was dropped, and the widespread discrepancy between job requirements and actual performance was noted. This contradicts the dictum to describe the job as it is actually performed.

One study of the PAQ concluded that alternative sources of data didn't seem to make any difference in the way jobs were described.[41] Supervisors, job-

[40]Charles A. O'Reilly III and David F. Caldwell, "The Impact of Normative Social Influence and Cohesiveness on Task Perceptions and Attitudes: A Social Information Processing Approach," Working paper, University of California, Berkeley, July 1982; D. Caldwell and C. A. O'Reilly III, "Task Perceptions and Job Satisfaction: A Question of Causality," *Journal of Applied Psychology* 67, no. 3 (1982), pp. 361–69; Kenneth N. Wexley and Stanley B. Silverman, "An Examination of Differences between Managerial Effectiveness and Response Patterns on a Structured Job Analysis Questionnaire," *Journal of Applied Psychology* 63, no. 5 (1978), pp. 646–49; Charles O'Reilly, G. N. Parlette, and J. Blum, "Perceptual Measures of Task Characteristics: The Biasing Effects of Differing Frames of Reference and Job Attitudes," *Academy of Management Journal* 123, no. 1 (1980), pp. 118–31; Dunham, "The Measurement of Dimensionality;" C. O'Reilly and D. Caldwell, "Informational Influence as a Determinant of Task Characteristics and Job Satisfaction," *Journal of Applied Psychology* 64 (1979), pp. 157–65.

[41]Smith and Hakel, "Convergence among Data Sources."

holders, analysts, and college students who only had read a description of the work all responded similarly to the PAQ. However, because the PAQ is designed to cover all jobs, there will always be a high number of "does not apply" responses for a specific job. Cornelius, DeNisi, and Blencoe demonstrate that eliminating the "does not apply" items results in experts and trained analysts being the best sources of job information.[42]

Finally, Henderson points out the need for the support of top management. They must also be alerted to the cost and time-consuming nature of job analysis.[43]

- Does top management understand what is involved in performing job analysis?
- Have all time and cost considerations been explored? Are they understood and approved?
- Is it understood that changes may be recommended as a result of the analysis? Has the potential nature of these changes been discussed prior to undertaking job analysis?

The vital importance of employee and operating management involvement has been repeatedly emphasized. This involvement may take several forms, ranging from active participation in describing their own and/or subordinates' work to serving on compensation task forces or committees directly responsible for the design and development of job analysis procedures. Even for those employees not directly involved, the compensation professional should keep them informed as to the purposes and progress of all the activity. Employees will guess at the purpose of this work, and it seems only sound compensation practice to help make it an educated guess.

IS JOB ANALYSIS USEFUL?

Job analysis procedures, whether conventional or quantitative, involve a high degree of judgment. It is important to consider the comparative usefulness of job analysis methods, particularly in terms of their reliability, validity, acceptability, and costs.

Reliability

Reliability is the consistency of the results obtained. Are the results (whether the work is similar or dissimilar) the same regardless of who is involved (supervisors, incumbents, analysts, consultants) and what methods are used?

---

[42]Edwin T. Cornelius III, Angelo S. DeNisi, and Allyn Blencoe, "Expert and Naive Raters Using the PAQ? Does it Matter?" *Personnel Psychology* 37 (1984), pp. 453–64.

[43]Henderson, *Compensation Management.*

Several studies have compared employee-supervisor agreement of work content.[44] They present a mixed picture of the reliability of job analysis. Employees and supervisors often differ in how they view the distribution of time among tasks, the skills required to perform the work, and the difficulties of the tasks performed. Different analysts using the same quantitative methods on the same jobs tend to get the same results. However, O'Reilly and Caldwell found that "one's frame of reference, as represented by factors such as past experiences, present jobs, and expectations, may result in different perceptions and definitions of the same work."[45] For example, employees who have been on the job a long time may change it by adopting shortcuts and new routines. So the employees' and supervisors' backgrounds (as well as the analysts') may influence the results.

Conventional job analysis does not usually lend itself to formal reliability analysis because of the narrative and unstructured output.[46] This imprecision and obscure structure makes reliability a serious issue for conventional methods. But even quantitative methods have problems. The high reliability measures attributed to the PAQ, for example, are probably the result of inadequate statistical analysis.[47] The high number of "does not exist (as part of this job)" responses may yield false statistics that paint an overly optimistic picture of the questionnaire's reliability. With such mixed results, it is important to ensure that whatever method is adopted, it should be used independently by several people (analysts, supervisors, subordinates), and any differences should be investigated and resolved.[48] Consistent (reliable) job information does not necessarily mean that it is accurate, comprehensive, or free from bias. To find out if the results are accurate, we need to consider its validity.

---

[44]Paul R. Sackett, Edwin T. Cornelius III, and Theodore J. Carron, "A Comparison of Global Judgment vs. Task-Oriented Approaches to Job Classification," *Personnel Psychology* 34 (1981), pp. 791–804. Other examples of earlier studies include H. H. Meyer, "Comparison of Foreman and General Foreman Conceptions of the Foreman's Job Responsibility," *Personnel Psychology* 12 (1959), pp. 445–52; A. P. O'Reilly, "Skill Requirements: Supervisor-Subordinate Conflict," *Personnel Psychology* 26 (1973), pp. 75–80; J. T. Hazel, J. M. Madden, and R. E. Christal, "Agreement between Worker-Supervisor Descriptions of the Worker's Job," *Journal of Industrial Psychology* 2 (1964), pp. 71–79; and R. Likert, *New Patterns of Management* (New York: McGraw-Hill, 1961).

[45]O'Reilly and Caldwell, "Impact of Normative Social Influence."

[46]George T. Milkovich and Charles J. Cogill, "Measurement as an Issue in Analysis and Evaluation of Jobs," in *Handbook of Wage and Salary Administration,* ed. Milton L. Rock (New York: McGraw-Hill, 1984).

[47]Roark and Burnett, "Objective Methods of Job Analysis."; and Cornelius, DeNisi, and Blencoe, "Expert and Naive Raters Using the PAQ?" For an example of the statistical analysis on PAQ results, see R. D. Arvey, S. E. Maxwell, R. L. Gutenberg, and C. Camp, "Detecting Job Differences: A Monte Carlo Study," *Personnel Psychology* 34 (1981), pp. 709–30.

[48]Ash, "Job Elements for Task Clusters."

Validity

Research on how to estimate the validity of job analysis is particularly difficult, since there is almost no way of showing the extent to which the results are accurate portraits of the work. The most promising approach may be to examine the convergence of results among multiple sources of job data (analysts, incumbents, supervisors) and multiple methods. A common approach to attempt to increase accuracy of job analysis is to require the job holder and the manager to mutually "sign off" on the results. While getting the parties to mutually sign off on the results may reflect their acceptance, it may also reflect their desire to get rid of the analyst and get back to performing the job rather than analyzing it.

Acceptability

Employee acceptability of data collected is important and easily overlooked. The acceptability of the results of job analysis by the employees and managers remains a critical test. No matter how well the rest of the compensation system is administered, if jobholders are dissatisfied with the initial data collected and the process for collecting it, they are not likely to feel the results are internally equitable.

Conventional job analysis is not always well accepted by the parties involved because of its potential for subjectivity. One writer says, "We all know the classic procedures. One (worker) watched and noted the actions of another . . . at work on (the) job. The actions of both are biased, and the resulting information varied with the wind, especially the political wind."[49] But the acceptability of quantitative job analysis is also mixed. Gomez-Mejia reported that Control Data's Executive Position Questionnaire, developed over a four-year period, ran into several problems, which led most managers to refuse to use it.[50] Among the problems faced were:

1. Employee/manager understanding. The statistical methods used were difficult to understand, so many managers were unable to communicate the results to employees. Consequently, an antagonistic climate was created and the credibility of the system deteriorated.
2. Behaviorally oriented versus "scope" data. Analyzing work in terms of work behaviors, omitting "scope" data (e.g., size of budgets, total payroll, contribution to organization objectives) caused managers to feel that the questionnaire did not accurately analyze their jobs.

---

[49]E. M. Ramras, "Discussion," in *Proceedings of 19, Division of Military Psychology Symposium: Collecting, Analyzing, and Reporting Information Describing Jobs and Occupations,* 77th Annual Convention of the American Psychological Association, Lackland Air Force Base, Tex., September 1969, pp. 75–76.

[50]Gomez-Mejia, Page, and Tornow, "A Comparison of the Practical Utility of Traditional, Statistical, and Hybrid Job Evaluation Approaches."

3. Abstract and ambiguous factors. The data collected (e.g., analyze subordinates' weaknesses and strengths) were perceived to be too abstract and ambiguous. Results were considered too subjective and open to personal interpretation.

Practicality

Researchers recognize the necessity of judging the usefulness of job analysis methods according to the purpose of the analysis. Cornelius, Carron, and Collins suggest that for compensation purposes, those methods that compare jobs in terms of level of responsibility, training, working conditions, and work hazards may be most useful.[51]

The trade-off between results versus cost points out the need for an additional evaluation index that Ash and Levine call "practicality."[52] It includes such factors as costs and versatility (i.e., uses for various personnel decisions). In one study using this framework, Levine, Ash, Hall, and Sistrunk had 93 experienced job analysts evaluate seven job analysis methods on their utility for 11 different organization purposes and on 11 practicality indicators.[53] Their results, shown in Exhibit 3.13, showed that the seven job analysis methods were rated differently for effectiveness and practicality across all 22 purposes and indicators. The PAQ and CODAP were among those rated highest for the purpose of job evaluation (i.e., job structures), in spite of CODAP's original development for training needs analysis. While this study is based only on perception of analysts rather than on evaluation of the actual uses of different methods, the authors concluded that combining methods is preferable to using one method alone. Reliance on a combination of methods is a common theme in the research literature on job analysis. The usefulness of the results obtained is probably the most important criterion on which to judge alternative approaches to job analysis. If there is a need for uniform job data at many locations, does the method provide it? Can the method provide documentable evidence of the work relatedness of the pay structure? Does it adequately assess the subtle differences among jobs unique to our organization? Are both the typist and the vice president of marketing convinced that it fairly describes their jobs? These challenges to job analysis provide criteria to judge a method's usefulness.

---

[51]Cornelius, Carron, and Collins, "Job Analysis Models and Job Classification."

[52]Ronald A. Ash and Edward L. Levine, "A Framework for Evaluating Job Analysis Methods," *Personnel* 57, no. 6 (November–December 1980), pp. 53–59; E. L. Levine, R. A. Ash, and N. Bennett, "Exploratory Comparative Study of Four Job Analysis Methods," *Journal of Applied Psychology* 65 (1980), pp. 524–35; and R. A. Ash, E. L. Levine, and F. Sistrunk, "The Role of Jobs and Job Based Methods in Personnel and Human Resources Management," *Research in Personnel and Human Resources Management* 1 (1983), pp. 45–84.

[53]Edward L. Levine, Ronald A. Ash, Hardy Hall, and Frank Sistrunk, "Evaluation of Job Analysis Methods by Experienced Job Analysts," *Academy of Management Journal* 26, no. 2 (1983), pp. 339–48.

EXHIBIT 3.13
Effectiveness Ratings of Seven Job Analysis Methods for Eleven Personnel Purposes *(Range = 1 to 5; 5 is high)*

	Job Analysis Methods					
Purposes	*Ability Requirements Scales*	*Position Analysis Questionnaire*	*Critical Incident Technique*	*Task Inventory/ CODAP*	*Functional Job Analysis*	*Job Elements Method*
Job description	2.15	2.86	2.59	4.20	4.07	2.66
Job classification	2.61	3.67	2.19	4.18	3.81	2.73
Job evaluation	2.44	3.70	2.37	3.46	3.52	2.72
Job design	2.28	2.99	2.52	3.72	3.64	2.59
Personnel requirements/ specification	3.51	3.36	2.86	3.19	3.58	3.64
Performance appraisal	2.75	2.72	3.91	3.24	3.58	3.07
Worker training	2.78	2.76	3.42	3.65	3.63	3.33
Worker mobility	2.47	2.78	2.20	3.34	3.07	2.62
Efficiency/safety	1.90	2.46	3.08	2.79	2.81	2.30
Manpower/workforce planning	2.32	2.83	2.24	3.41	3.11	2.60
Legal quasilegal requirements	2.44	3.03	2.66	3.67	3.38	2.79

Ratings of Seven Job Analysis Methods for Eleven Practicality Concerns

Practicality Concerns						
Occupational versatility/ suitability	3.61	3.82	3.86	4.13	4.06	3.58
Standardization	3.40	4.28	1.99	3.97	3.54	2.88
Respondent/user acceptability	3.00	3.12	3.19	3.43	3.44	3.16
Amount of job analyst training required*	3.00	2.78	3.04	2.39	2.57	2.68
Operational	3.09	4.20	3.42	4.04	3.85	3.52
Sample size†	2.51	3.53	3.04	2.08	3.26	3.16
Off-the-shelf	3.27	4.51	2.43	2.98	3.28	3.03
Reliability	3.10	3.84	2.67	4.05	3.49	2.93
Cost‡	3.23	3.29	2.57	2.29	2.80	2.96
Quality of outcome	2.61	3.17	2.74	3.63	3.53	2.76
Time of completion§	3.36	3.43	2.17	1.93	2.57	2.93

*The higher the rating the less training required.
†The higher the rating the fewer respondents required.
‡The higher the rating the lower the cost.
§The higher the rating the less time required for completion.
Source: Adapted from E. L. Levine, R. A. Ash, H. Hall, and F. Sistrunk, "Evaluation of Job Analysis Methods by Experienced Job Analysts," *Academy of Management Journal* 26, no. 2 (1983), pp. 339–48.

There is very little data publicly available on costs of various approaches to job analysis.[54] Our own experience with custom designed quantitative job analysis plans suggests direct costs of between $250,000 and $500,000 for consulting and development expertise, at least one personnel professional's time for one

---

[54]Frank Krzystofiak, Jerry M. Newman, and Gary Anderson, "A Quantified Approach to Measurement of Job Content: Procedures and Payoffs," *Personnel Psychology,* Summer 1979, pp. 341–57.

year, and about 24 months from design through installation. Gambordella and Alvord report on an installation of CODAP. Requirements included a full-time project director who combined managerial and communications skills with a personal background, knowledge of the work in the organization, and knowledge of data management and computer principles; three to seven job analysts, and a system analyst.[55] For one task inventory, an inexperienced project staff required 44 weeks to move from defining the scope of the inventory and identifying job families to production of management reports. So considerable time and money are required for any job analysis, with or without computer assistance. Efforts to improve the data collection procedures and minimize the expense and effort involved need to continue. By comparison, the PAQ or conventional job analysis is relatively inexpensive.

The practical utility of quantitative job analysis, with its relatively complex procedures and analysis, remains in doubt for many organizations. Some advocates get so taken with their statistics and computers that they ignore the role that human judgment must continue to play in job analysis. As Dunnette states,

> I wish to emphasize the central role played in all these procedures by human judgment. I know of no methodology, statistical technique or objective measurement that can negate the importance of, nor supplement, rational judgment as an important element in the process of deriving behavior and task information about jobs and of using that information to develop or justify human resources programs.[56]

Quantitative and more systematic approaches to job analysis do not remove the judgment; they only permit us to become more systematic in the way we make it.

INDIVIDUAL-BASED SYSTEMS

An underlying premise throughout this chapter has been that *jobs* are the basic unit of analysis used to determine the pay structure; hence job analysis is required. But many employers choose not to use job analysis. Some of them adopt a policy of discounting the importance of internal consistency of the pay structure, deciding instead to set pay for jobs based directly on "market" rates and letting the resulting pay relationships among jobs be an afterthought. Termed *market pricing,* this approach does not completely ignore pay differentials between jobs, but its policy is to weigh "whatever pay rate it takes to get people to join and stay with us" much more heavily. The market pricing approach is examined more closely in Chapters 6 and 7.

---

[55]J. J. N. Gambordella and W. G. Alvord, "Ti-CODAP: A Computerized Method of Job Analysis for Personnel Management," Prince Georges County, Maryland, April 1980.

[56]M. D. Dunnette, L. M. Hough, and R. L. Rosse, "Task and Job Taxonomies as a Basis for Identifying Labor Supply Sources and Evaluating Employment Qualifications," in *Affirmative Action Planning,* ed. George T. Milkovich and Lee Dyer (New York: Human Resource Planning Society, 1979), pp. 37–51.

EXHIBIT 3.14
Knowledge-Based Compared to Job-Based Plans

	Job Based	*Knowledge Based*
Pay structure	Based on job performed	Based on skills possessed by the employee
Managers' focus	Job carries wage Employee linked to job	Employee carries wage Employee linked to skill
Employee focus	Job promotion to earn greater pay	Skill acquisition to earn greater pay
Procedures required	Assess job content Value jobs	Assess skills Value skills
Advantages	Pay based on value of work performed	Flexibility Reduced work force
Limitations	Potential personnel bureaucracy Inflexibilities	Potential personnel bureaucracy Cost controls

Other employers emphasize internal consistency in their pay structures, based on the individual employee rather than job characteristics. Such approaches are not new, though they are receiving increased attention. Let us examine a few of these situations.

Knowledge-Based Pay Systems

Under knowledge-based pay systems, individual employees are paid for the work-related skills they possess rather than for the specific job they are performing.[57] Knowledge-based pay is also referred to as skill-based pay. Under such a system at a Borg Warner facility, an employee may be qualified to operate both a complex auto transmission chain assembly machine and a forklift. If the plant manager needs the forklift operated, the employee is assigned to drive it but is paid at the higher assembly operator rate. Under this plan, a starting rate is typically set below the starting rate paid by other employers in the area. Pay increases are earned by learning and demonstrating mastery of various work-related skills. Once a skill is mastered, pay is immediately increased, and the employee may be rotated to jobs requiring that skill when necessary.

Exhibit 3.14 contrasts job- versus knowledge-based systems. Under a knowledge-based approach, pay is based on the highest work-related skills em-

---

[57]Henry Tosi and Lisa Tosi, "Knowledge Based Pay: Some Propositions and Guides to Effective Use," Working paper, University of Florida, Gainesville, Fla., 1984; and Edward J. Lawler and Gerald E. Ledford, Jr., "Skill-Based Pay: A Concept That's Catching On," *Compensation and Benefits Review,* January-February 1986, pp. 54–61; and N. Gupta, G. D. Jenkins, Jr., and W. P. Curington, "Paying for Knowledge: Myths and Realities," *National Productivity Review,* Spring 1986, pp. 107–23.

ployees possess (e.g., what they *can* do) rather than on the specific job performed (e.g., what they *are* doing). Under the job-based approach, the wage is assigned to the job, and employees move in and out of the job. Under a knowledge-based approach, the wage is assigned to an employee regardless of the job performed. Hence, managers focus on controlling the pay rates assigned to jobs and on the need to allocate employees among various jobs. In contrast, under a knowledge-based plan, employees carry both the wage and a set of skills. The manager has the flexibility to reassign individual employees to any tasks as long as the employees have the required skills and are paid at the rate of the highest skill possessed. Note the shift in employee focus under a knowledge-based plan. Pay increases are earned by demonstrating mastery of additional skills rather than by getting promoted to a higher pay job. Knowledge-based systems reward acquisition of additional work-related skills, whether or not those skills are used on the present job.

Advocates point to more flexible and better trained work forces as one of the key advantages of knowledge-based plans.[58] For them, knowledge-based pay is part of a philosophy of managing human resources that emphasizes teamwork and flexibility. Many plant managers also claim that the ability to freely reassign employees within the plant substantially reduces the number of employees required. They claim that the smaller work force required more than offsets the higher average wage paid under a knowledge-based system (i.e., as more workers qualify for highest paid skills the facility's average wage will increase).

Beyond advocates' testimonials and claims from plant managers, more rigorous examination of the effects of knowledge-based pay is required. Greater flexibility can be achieved by other actions. And all pay schemes, including those based on skills, can become bureaucratic burdens. Examples include the craft's master-journeyman-apprentice system or the elementary-secondary schoolteachers' pay plans (both knowledge-based schemes). Both have become heavily procedure ridden and inflexible. The recent knowledge-based plans are not inherently free of "creeping" bureaucracy. Some plans now have instituted "holding rates" for employees that have demonstrated mastery of a high paying skill for which there is no vacancy. Other plans have begun to develop elaborate peer review boards to assess skill mastery. Finally, it is feasible that two employees doing equal work could be earning different pay due to differences in their skill levels. Undoubtedly some employees and their lawyers will want to test the legality of that practice if women or minorities receive the lower pay.

What are the implications for job analysis of skill-based pay? Paying people on the basis of the knowledge they possess or the tasks they *can* do rather than the jobs they actually do does not negate the need for analysis. Rather, it

---

[58]Edward E. Lawler III, "The New Pay," in *Current Issues in Human Resource Management,* ed. Sara L. Rynes and George T. Milkovich (Plano, Tex.: Business Publications, 1986); and Gupta, Jenkins, and Curington, "Paying for Knowledge."

shifts the emphasis from analyzing job content to analyzing the skills required to adequately perform specified tasks. Thus, some form of skill or knowledge analysis, perhaps analogous to the AT&T approach discussed earlier, may be required.

Managers

The content of many jobs is a function of the person doing the job. For example, John Scully was a highly regarded marketing executive at PepsiCo when Apple Computer hired him. The price of Apple's stock immediately rose as a result of Scully's joining the firm. No one expected Mr. Scully to perform exactly the same marketing tasks that his predecessor had done; indeed, everyone assumed Scully would use his unique skills in whatever way he felt was to Apple's advantage. Mr. Scully did just that: He soon became their chief executive officer. The point is that in certain jobs, it is difficult to separate the job from the person doing it. In fact the person's unique attributes may shape the job. The top jobs in almost any organization seem to be designed more around the talents and experience of the individuals involved, rather than any rigidly defined duties and responsibilities. This is not to say that internal consistency is not important in executive compensation; the pecking order gets pretty intense. But job analysis plays a smaller role in establishing internal consistency. Executive pay is discussed in greater detail in Chapter 16, Compensation of Special Groups.

Professionals

Scientists and engineers are another group of employees where pay is often individual rather than job based. Often work varies as a function of the project to which the engineer or scientist is assigned. Many projects require a great deal of cooperation and teamwork, and the chief engineer may assign employees to projects on the basis of the characteristics of the particular projects and the technical skills of each person. As we discuss in Chapter 16, many organizations choose to pay such employees on the basis of the type of degree each individual possesses (e.g., B.S. in chemistry, or Ph.D. in electrical engineering) and the number of years since earning the last degree. Job analysis has little role to play here.

SUMMARY

Fairness of the pay structure within an organization is one of the hallmarks of a sound compensation system. The compensation professional faces several decisions during the process of designing an equitable pay structure. One of the first is a policy decision—how much to emphasize the importance of an internally consistent and equitable pay structure. Some emphasize market pricing over internal consistency. Whatever the choice, it needs to support the organization's overall human resource strategy.

Next, the compensation professional must decide whether job and/or individual employee characteristics will be the basic unit of analysis supporting the pay structure. This is followed by deciding what data need to be collected, what method(s) will be used to collect it, and who should be involved in the process.

A key test of an equitable pay structure is acceptance of results by managers and employees. The best way to ensure acceptance of job analysis results is to involve employees as well as supervisors in the process. At the minimum, all employees should be informed of purposes and progress of the activity.

If almost everyone agrees about the importance of job analysis for equitable compensation, does that mean everyone does it? Of course not. Unfortunately, job analysis can be tedious and time-consuming. Often the job is given to newly hired compensation analysts, ostensibly to help them learn the organization, but perhaps there's also a hint of "rites of passage" in such assignments.

This completes our discussion of job analysis. The next step is to take the resulting job descriptions and evaluate the jobs according to their contributions to the organization goals. This is the subject of the next chapters.

REVIEW QUESTIONS

1. What does job analysis have to do with internal consistency?
2. Describe the major decisions in designing job analysis.
3. Distinguish between task data and worker data.
4. What is the critical advantage of quantitative job analysis over conventional approaches? Why is this important?
5. What are some noncompensation uses of job analysis information? Would the same data serve all needs?
6. What are the basic steps in developing a quantitative job analysis?

Appendix A

Example of Conventional Job Analysis Questionnaire
(next three pages)

Job Analysis Report

Date __2-23-86__

Job Analyst __C. Davis__

1. Job Title __Executive Secretary__

2. Department __General Headquarters__

3. No. incumbents __2__   Interviewed __2__

4. Relation to other jobs:

   Promotion: From __Secretary-D__   To __Executive Secretary__

   Transfer: From __Administrative Assistant__   To __Executive Secretary__

   Supervision received __From President and/or Chairman of the Board.__

   __Works under minimal supervision.__

   Supervision given __Regularly to other clerical personnel.__

5. Summary of Job:

   Personal Secretary to President and/or Chairman of the Board. Performs variety of secretarial and clerical duties including transcribing dictation, filing, routing mail, as well as answering telephone and written inquiries. Exercises discretion in handling confidential and specialized information, screening telephone calls and letters, arranging meetings, and handling inquiries during superior's absence.

6. Equipment used: Typewriter, word processor, dictaphone and telephone.

Working conditions:

   Hazards (list): N/A

   Work space and quarters: Office environment

Noise exposure: None

Lighting: Good

Temperature: Regulated office environment

Miscellaneous: —

Job training:

A.   Required experience: (include other jobs)
     Four years of secretarial-stenographic experience or the equivalent.

B.   Outside educational courses:

	Time in semesters/quarters
Vocational courses: Typing, stenography	2 semesters
High school courses: Graduate	6-8 semesters
College courses:	None
Continuing education required:	None

C.   In-house training courses:

	Time in months
Courses: Basic and Advanced Word Processing	1/2 month

Task Statement Worksheet

Task Statement: Opens and organizes mail addressed to superior.

1.   Equipment used   —

2.   Knowledge required   Must be well versed on superior's responsibilities, how superior's job fits into overall organization.

3.   Skills required   —

4.   Abilities required   Discretion. Organization skills.

5. Time spent and frequency of task performance (hourly, daily, monthly)
   Time varies by assignment. Weekly frequency.

6. Level of difficulty/consequence of error
   Relatively difficult, little effect of error.

Task Statement: Establishes, maintains, and revises files.

1. Equipment used Typewriter, word processor.

2. Knowledge required Understanding of organization and responsibilities of superior.

3. Skills required Typing and word processing, filing.

4. Abilities required Ability to organize and categorize information.

5. Time spent and frequency of task performance (hourly, daily, monthly)
   One hour spent daily.

6. Level of difficulty/consequence of error Relatively easy, but moderate to serious consequences if information mishandled.

Appendix B

Computer-Generated Job Description
(next six pages)

NAME:	SMITH, A. B.
EMPLOYEE NUMBER:	0012343
POSITION:	SENIOR PURCHASING OFFICER-ENGI
FUNCTIONAL AREA:	ADMINISTRATION/DISTRIBUTION

DATE COMPLETED:	1/27/87
SUPERVISOR:	R. C. JONES
SUPERVISOR'S TITLE:	MANAGING DIRECTOR
PERCENT OF JOB TAPPED:	80%

I. Accountability

A. HUMAN RESOURCES

The jobholder has management responsibility for **4** employees.

    3.0 (**75%**) of these are in Job Groups 1–5.
    1.0 (**25%**) of these are in Job Groups 6–10.

0.0 subordinate(s) report(s) directly to the jobholder and **0** worker(s) report(s) to him/her on a dotted line basis.
The highest direct subordinate reporting to this person as a(n) **BUYER**, Grade **6.**
The jobholder works approximately **15** days a year in locations other than his/her home location.

B. FINANCIAL RESPONSIBILITIES

For the current fiscal year, the jobholder has responsibility for an annual operating budget of $250,000.
He/she has direct management responsibility for annual sales totaling $0.

II. Primary Responsibilities and Activities

A. SUPERVISING & CONTROLLING

20% of the jobholder's time is spent Supervising subordinates, and it is considered **a very important** part of the position.
15% of his/her time is spent on Controlling activities, and these are considered to be **a very important** aspect of the position.
The most significant activities concerning Supervising & Controlling are:

Significance	Activity
CRUCIAL	Interacts face-to-face with subordinates on an almost daily basis.
CRUCIAL	Reviews subordinates' work almost continually.
SUBSTANTIAL	Makes use of assigned administrative or technical staff.
SUBSTANTIAL	Assigns priorities for others on no less than a quarterly basis.
SUBSTANTIAL	Develops subordinates for improved job performance and future responsibility.
SUBSTANTIAL	Reviews subordinates' work methods for possible increases in productivity.
SUBSTANTIAL	Motivates subordinates to change or improve performance.
SUBSTANTIAL	Maintains a smooth working relationship among various individuals who need to work cooperatively.
MODERATE	Monitors progress of geog. sep. orgs. toward objec. and adjusts activs. as necessary to reach them.
MODERATE	Analyzes subordinates' weaknesses and training needs.
MODERATE	Conducts regular performance reviews with subordinates.
MODERATE	Monitors subordinates' progress toward objec. of unit and adjusts activ. as necessary to reach them.
MODERATE	Delegates work, assigns responsibility to subordinates, and establishes appropriate controls.

MODERATE	Analyzes at least monthly the effectiveness of operations.
MINOR	Guides subordinates on technical aspects of the job.
MINOR	Provides complete instructions to subordinates when giving assignments.
MINOR	Forecasts manpower requirements.
MINOR	Reviews and if necessary revises budget allocations.
MINOR	Develops evaluation criteria that serve to measure progress and effectiveness of the operation.

B. MONITORING BUSINESS INDICATORS

0–2% of the jobholder's time is spent Monitoring Business Indicators, and it is considered **an unimportant** function of this position. The most significant activities for this aspect of the position are Monitoring:

Significance	Activity
SUBSTANTIAL	Price trends in the industry.
MODERATE	Events occuring outside the company which have an impact on your functional area.
MINOR	Proposed legislation that might affect 3M.
MINOR	International business and economic trends.
MINOR	Economic trends which may affect 3M's business.

C. CONSULTING & INNOVATING

5% of the jobholder's time is spent Consulting, and it is considered **a moderately important** part of this position. The most significant activities relating to Consulting & Innovating for this position are:

Significance	Activity
SUBSTANTIAL	Frequently crosses over organ. lines of authority to consult on problems in other organ. areas.
SUBSTANTIAL	Serves as a specialist and is recognized in 3M as such.
MODERATE	Anticipate new or changed demands for products, services, or technologies.
MODERATE	Does a considerable amount of job-related reading on a regular basis.
MODERATE	Knows how to ask key questions on subject matters that he/she is not intimately familiar with.
MINOR	Applies advanced principles, theories, and concepts in more than one recognized field.
MINOR	Prepares reports on complex matters so people without knowledge of the subject can understand them.
MINOR	Brainstorms to address unique problems.
MINOR	Offers constructive criticism about policies or decisions formulated by higher management.

D. ADMINISTRATION

10% of the jobholder's time is spent Administering, and it is considered **an important** function of this position. The most significant Administration activities for this position are:

Significance	Activity
CRUCIAL	Works in pressure situations, such as increased workload periods, to meet tight deadlines.
CRUCIAL	Handles a great deal of routine paperwork.
SUBSTANTIAL	Frequently is required to react to unexpected events.
MODERATE	Documents and files important details for future reference.

MINOR   Meets a heavy schedule of appointments each day.
MINOR   Prepares speeches, briefings, or presentations.
MINOR   Switches strategies rapidly to achieve an objective.
MINOR   Works with a normal schedule which has a regular cycle of specific deadlines.
MINOR   Drafts position papers, policy letters, contracts, etc.
MINOR   Tracks project activities closely and ensures, where appropriate, that follow-up is made.

E. COORDINATING

20% of this jobholder's time is spent Coordinating, and it is considered a very important part of this position.
The most significant Coordinating activities for this position are:

Significance	Activity
SUBSTANTIAL	Sounds out many different people before making major decisions.
SUBSTANTIAL	Works with other individuals/groups not under his/her direct supervision to solve problems.
SUBSTANTIAL	Coordinates with other departments to meet previously established plans.
MODERATE	Is aware of conflict between executive-level management personnel.
MODERATE	Is aware of the aims and plans of other divisions/subsidiaries.
MODERATE	Motivates others who are not subordinates to produce desired results.
MODERATE	Provides information required by other department to achieve their objectives.
MINOR	Negotiates for limited organizational resources.
MINOR	Coordinates the efforts of others over whom he/she has no direct authority.
MINOR	Acts as mediator in the solution of deadlocks or problems between key individuals in depts/divs.
MINOR	Works to increase cooperation among different departments/divisions.
MINOR	Makes formal presentations to higher management.

F. REPRESENTING

20% of the jobholder's time is spent Representing 3M, and it is considered an extremely important function of the position.
The position's most significant activities relating to Representing are:

Significance	Activity
MODERATE	Responds to complaints or questions submitted by other offices, employees or persons outside the company.
MINOR	Negotiates with individuals/groups whose goals may often be contrary to those of 3M.

G. PLANNING & ORGANIZING

0.2% of the jobholder's time is spent on Long-range Planning, and it is considered an unimportant aspect of this position.
10% of the jobholder's time is spent on Planning and Organizing, and it is considered a moderately important part of this position.
Significant Planning and Organizing activities, broken down by the nature of the decision-making role, are:

APPROVAL: Authority to approve without review by superiors.

CRUCIAL	Revising planning schedules to ensure project completion.
SUBSTANTIAL	Allocating and scheduling resources to ensure that they will be available when needed.
SUBSTANTIAL	Determining implementation methods for meeting operational objectives established by others.

SHARED APPROVAL: Share authority for decisions with others, but without review by superiors.
MINOR   Making additions to headcount that are within the approved budget.
MINOR   Hiring an individual for an approved position.

PRIMARY RECOMMENDATION: Provide superiors with their sole or primary input for decisions.
MINOR   Determining reductions in employee headcount, should this become necessary.

III. Internal & External Contacts

PURPOSE OF CONTACT

A. <u>INTERNAL CONTACTS</u>

INTERNAL CONTACTS	SHARE INFORMATION regarding activities or decisions	INFLUENCE OTHERS to act in a manner consistent with my objectives.	DIRECT and/or integrate the plans, activities or decisions of others.
Senior manager	MODERATE	MINOR	
Other manager	MODERATE	MODERATE	.
Supervisor	MODERATE	MODERATE	MODERATE
Professional/admin. employees	MODERATE	MODERATE	MODERATE
Jr. clerical and secretarial employs	MINOR	MODERATE	MODERATE

B. **EXTERNAL CONTACTS**

EXTERNAL CONTACTS	PROVIDE INFORMATION or promote the organization or its product/services	SELL products/services	NEGOTIATE contracts, settlements, etc.
Senior Representatives of major suppliers	MODERATE		CRUCIAL
Employees of suppliers who admin. the delivery of parts or services	MODERATE		MODERATE

IV. KNOW-HOW

A. **LEVEL OF KNOWLEDGE**

To perform the position requirements, the jobholder regularly uses Know-How from the following content areas, at the level of knowledge shown:

LEVEL 1: Sufficient familiarity to COMMUNICATE with individuals in this content area	LEVEL 2: Sufficient knowledge to SOLVE BASIC PROBS. by applying 3M policies/procedures related to this area	LEVEL 3: Thorough knowledge of basic principles to SOLVE COMPLEX PROBS. when policies/procedures are not clear	LEVEL 4: Thorough KNOWLEDGE OF ADVANCED PRINCIPLES to solve complex problems	LEVEL 5: Thorough knowledge of advanced principles + DEVELOP NEW ADVANCEMENTS in area to solve unique, complex probs.
Production Process & Indus. Eng. Plant Engineering Architectural/Civil Elec. Instrumentation Mathematics/Statistics Data Processing Transportation Personnel	Mechanical Finance/Accounting Distribution	Law/Contracts	Purchasing	

B. EDUCATION AND EXPERIENCE

For each knowledge content area, the jobholder has the following amounts of on-the-job experience and formal education that contribute to proficient accomplishment of the position's responsibilities:

KNOW-HOW AREA	YEARS OF EXPERIENCE	AMOUNT OF FORMAL EDUCATION
Production	1	
Process & Indus. Eng.	1	
Plant Engineering	1	
Architectural/Civil	1	
Mechanical	5	Post-secondary level, vocational, or business qualifications
Elec. Instrumentation	1	
Mathematics/Statistics	2	
Finance/Accounting	2	First-level university degree (BA, BSC, or equivalent)
Data Processing	1	
Law/Contracts	3	
Distribution	2	
Purchasing	5	First-level university degree (BA, BSC, or equivalent)
Transportation	1	
Personnel	1	

Chapter *4*

Job Evaluation: Perspectives and Design

"When I use a word," Humpty Dumpty said in rather a scornful tone, "it means just what I choose it to mean—nothing more or less."

"The question is," said Alice, "whether you *can* make words mean so many different things."

"The question is," said Humpty Dumpty, "which is to be master—that is all."[1]

Were Humpty Dumpty and Alice discussing job evaluation? Some managers may think so. People have differing perspectives on the purpose of job evaluation and differing opinions about its value. This chapter discusses these various perspectives on job evaluation and some of the key decisions in the process. Chapter 5 continues the discussion. Establishing the purposes and choosing among alternative methods of job evaluation are discussed here. Evaluating the process and involving affected employees are discussed in the next chapter.

Designing a pay structure involves setting the pay for each job relative to other jobs within a single employer. By law, pay must be equal for equal work; pay differentials may be established for dissimilar work. Job evaluation helps develop and maintain pay structures by comparing the similarities and differences in the content and value of jobs. When properly designed and administered, job evaluation can help ensure that pay structures are internally consistent and acceptable to the parties involved. In this chapter we will examine how job evaluation helps ensure a policy that emphasizes internal consistency.[2]

JOB EVALUATION AND THE PAY MODEL

Recall from our model on page 31 the techniques typically used to design internal pay structures. The results of job analysis serve as input for evaluating jobs and establishing a job structure. Job evaluation involves the systematic evaluation of the job descriptions that result from job analysis. The evaluation is based on many factors: content of the work, value of the work to the organization, the culture of the workplace, and external market forces. This potential to blend internal and external market forces represents both a major contribution of job evaluation and a source of controversy. This will become evident as we discuss the variety of definitions and decisions that surround job evaluation.

DIFFERING PERSPECTIVES

Perspectives on job evaluation are as diverse as the blind men's elephants. The differences in perspectives revolve around three basic issues: (1) the distinction

---

[1]Lewis Carroll, *Through the Looking Glass* (Chicago: Classic Press, 1969).

[2]T. J. Atchison and D. W. Belcher, "Equity, Rewards and Compensation Administration," *Personnel Administration* 34, no. 2 (1971), pp. 32–46.

between classifications and hierarchies, (2) the distinction between a job's content and its value, and (3) the view that job evaluation may simultaneously include aspects of measurement as well as negotiation and rationalization.

Classifications and Hierarchies

Historically, job evaluation was conceived in the public sector as a device for classifying rather than valuing jobs. As part of attempts in the 1880s to reform abuses in government hiring and pay practices, jobs were classified according to their work content. As early as 1912, the city of Chicago adopted a system of job classification.[3] Personnel decisions were to be based on the content of the work as assessed through job evaluation, rather than on who you voted for or who you knew. Obviously, job evaluation was not a cure for such practices. It did, however, help group jobs according to similarities and differences in their content. Similar jobs are slotted into the same group or class.

In addition to classifying jobs, job evaluation may be used in the design of an organization pay structure. Pay structures, as defined in Chapter 2, are jobs ordered according to their relative content and/or value. Structure refers to a hierarchy of jobs, whereas classification refers to grouping jobs in terms of their similarities and differences. Thus, you could classify jobs into groups without arranging them in a hierarchy. Job evaluation can be designed to accomplish both a classification or a hierarchy.

Content and Value

Usually the end result of job evaluation is a structure—a hierarchy of jobs or groups of jobs in the organization. Perspectives vary on whether structures are based on comparing the jobs' content, on their value, or on some combination of both. Job content refers to the skills required, the degree of responsibilities

---

[3]E. Lanham, *Job Evaluation* (New York: McGraw-Hill, 1955). Also see Charles Walter Lytle, *Job Evaluation Methods* (New York: Ronald Press Company, 1954); Theodore R. Lawson, "How Much Is a Job Worth?" *Personnel* 43, no. 5 (September–October 1965), pp. 16–21; Labor Relations Associates, Job-Evaluation study report to city council, Moorhead, Minnesota, July 7, 1977; Bryan Livy, *Job Evalution: A Critical Review* (London, England: George Allen & Union Ltd., 1975); George Thomason, *Job Evaluation: Objectives and Methods* (London: Institute of Personnel Management, 1980); R. C. Smyth and M. J. Murphy, "Job Evaluation by the Point Plan," *Factor Management and Maintenance,* June 1946; Paul T. Stimmler, "The Job Evaluation Myth," *Personnel Journal,* November 1966, pp. 594–96; Douglas S. Sherwin, "The Job of Job Evaluation," *Harvard Business Review* 35 (1957), pp. 63–71; M. S. Viteles, "A Psychologist Looks at Job Evaluation," *Personnel,* May 1941; Herbert G. Zollitsch and Adolph Langsner, *Wage and Salary Administration* (Cincinnati, Ohio: South-Western Publishing Co., 1970); Howard Risher, *Job Evaluation Revisited,* (New York: William M. Mercer, Inc., 1982); Karl O. Mann, "Characteristics of Job Evaluation Programs," *Personnel Administration,* September/October 1965; R. F. Milkey, "Job Evaluation after 50 Years," *Public Personnel Review,* January 1960; Robert J. Neubauer, "Job Evaluation—The Mexican Encounter," *Personnel,* September/October 1978, pp. 52–56.

EXHIBIT 4.1
Perspectives on Job Evaluation

"the comparison of jobs by the use of formal and systematic procedures in order to determine the relative position of one job to another in a wage or salary hierarchy. The real object of comparison is the content of the job, not the rather imprecise notion of its 'value' to the organization."[a]

"We are not talking about worth in a metaphysical sense. Instead, we are talking about worth as defined in classification systems that already operate in large bureaucratic organizations."[b]

"should consider only the inherent characteristics and data of the job and *exclude extraneous factors* such as supply and demand of labor, local wage rates and geographic location"[c]

"the process in which the organization *finally assigns a worth to the job* and decides the related importance of one job to another"[d]

"the fundamental purpose is to establish a *mutually acceptable criterion of equity.*"[e]

"statistically establishing the relationships between wages paid for jobs and the content of these jobs. This is the specification of worth"[f]

"There is no single measure of job worth."[g]

"Job evaluation can and typically does accomplish a reasonable adaptation to internal and external forces."[h]

"is a method which helps to establish a justified rank order of jobs . . . it is *only one of the starting points for establishing the relative differentiation of wage rates*"[i]

---

[a]David W. Belcher, *Compensation Administration,* 3rd ed. (Englewood Cliffs, N.J.: Prentice-Hall, 1974), p. 88.

[b]Ronnie J. Steinberg, "Identifying Wage Discrimination and Implementing Pay Equity Adjustments," in *Comparable Worth: Issue for the 80's,* vol. 1 (Washington, D.C.: U.S. Civil Rights Commission, 1985).

[c]J. D. Dunn and Frank M. Rachel, *Wage and Salary Administration: Total Compensation Systems* (New York: McGraw-Hill, 1971).

[d]Richard I. Henderson, *Compensation Management: Rewarding Performance in the Modern Organization* (Reston, Va.: Reston Publishing, 1976), p. 149

[e]William Gombert, *A Trade Union Analysis of Time Study,* 2nd ed. (Englewood Cliffs, N.J.: Prentice-Hall, 1955).

[f]Steinberg, "Identifying Wage Discrimination."

[g]Harold D. Janes, "Union Views on Job Evaluation, 1971 vs. 1978," *Personnel Journal,* February 1979, pp. 80–85; and John Zalusky, "Job Evaluation: An Uneven World," *AFL–CIO American Federationist,* April 1981, pp. 13–18.

[h]E. Robert Livernash, "Internal Wage Structure," in *New Concepts in Wage Determination,* ed. George W. Taylor and Frank C. Pierson (New York: McGraw-Hill, 1957).

[i]Eugene J. Benge, *Job Evaluation and Merit Rating* (New York: National Foremen's Institute, Inc., 1946).

---

assumed, and so on. The relative value of jobs refers to their relative contributions to organization goals, to their external market rates, or to some other agreed upon rates.[4]

Note the various shadings of perspectives of job evaluation in Exhibit 4.1. Some say that job evaluation "considers only the inherent characteristics and

---

[4]Thomas A. Mahoney, *Compensation and Reward Perspectives* (Homewood, Ill.: Richard D. Irwin, 1979); Lester Thurow, *Generating Inequality* (New York: Basic Books, 1975); E. Robert Livernash, "Internal Wage Structure," in *New Concepts in Wage Determination,* ed. George W. Taylor and Frank C. Pierson (New York: McGraw-Hill, 1957); also see C. Kerr and L. Fisher, "Effect of Environment and Administration on Job Evaluation," *Harvard Business Review,* May 1950, pp. 77–96.

data of jobs"[5] or "the real object of comparison is the content of job not the rather imprecise notion of 'value'."[6] Others see job evaluation as "the process in which the organization finally assigns worth to the job"[7] or "there is general agreement that the objective of job evaluation is to produce an acceptable pay structure."[8]

When the structure is based on the comparison of job content, some argue that it reflects relative value.[9] For them there is no practical difference between content and value. The job structure derived from comparing the content of different jobs becomes the structure for determining the pay differences among the jobs. Thus: "The value of the jobs may be inferred by examining the variety and complexity of behaviors required by the job. The higher the variety and complexity the greater the 'contribution' of the job to the firm's viability and the more it should be compensated."[10]

This perspective of job evaluation overlooks the possibility that a structure based on comparing the relative content of jobs may differ from one based on relative value. This occurs, for example, when the relative value of the work performed is greater (or less) in one organization than in another. The value of a compensation specialist to a firm whose earnings are generated through sales of manufactured goods or engineering expertise may differ from the value of that specialist to a consulting firm whose revenues come through the sale of compensation expertise. The skills are similar, yet their relative value differs for each organization.

Linking Content with the External Labor Market

Pay structures also may differ if they are based on job evaluation that serves to link job content with the external market rates. Livernash observed, "The fundamental character of job evaluation is the integration of market wage rates

[5]J. D. Dunn and Frank M. Rachel, *Wage and Salary Administration: Total Compensation Systems* (New York: McGraw-Hill, 1971).

[6]David W. Belcher, *Compensation Administration,* 3rd ed. (Englewood Cliffs, N.J.: Prentice-Hall, 1974), p. 88.

[7]Richard I. Henderson, *Compensation Management: Rewarding Performance in the Modern Organization* (Reston, Va.: Reston Publishing, 1976), p. 149.

[8]F. Munson, "Four Fallacies for Wage and Salary Administrators," *Personnel* 40, no. 4 (1963), pp. 57–64.

[9]Alvin O. Bellak, "Comparable Worth: A Practitioner's View," in *Comparable Worth: Issue for the 80's,* vol. 1 (Washington, D.C.: U.S. Civil Rights Commission, 1985); and Ronnie J. Steinberg, "Identifying Wage Discrimination and Implementing Pay Equity Adjustments," in *Comparable Worth: Issue for the 80's,* vol. 1.

[10]David A. Pierson, Karen S. Koziara, and Russell E. Johannesson, "Equal Pay for Jobs of Comparable Worth: A Quantified Job Content Approach" (Philadelphia: Department of Industrial Relations and Organizational Behavior, Temple University, 1981).

and job content factors."[11] Schwab echoes Livernash: "As practiced, it [job evaluation] serves the important administrative function of linking external and internal labor markets. . . . No alternative procedure has been proposed that better performs this function."[12]

In their views, the job structure resulting from job evaluation does not completely reflect the job's relative value unless it incorporates external market influences. Consequently, certain aspects of job content (e.g., skills required, magnitude of responsibilities) take on value based on their relationship to market wages. Because higher skill levels or willingness to undertake greater responsibility usually commands higher wages in the labor market, then skill level and degree of responsibility become useful criteria in job evaluation for establishing differences in pay among jobs. If some aspect of job content, such as working conditions, were not related to wages paid in the external labor markets, then it would not be included in the job evaluation. Accordingly, since job content obtains value through the external market, it makes little sense to assert that content has an intrinsic value outside of its worth in the external market. It is job evaluation's role to integrate job content with external market forces.

But as you probably expect, another perspective on our elephant exists. Not everyone agrees that job evaluation's purpose is to link internal and external markets. Bellack, in describing the Hay job evaluation plan, states that the "measures are independent of the market and encourage rational determination of the basis for pricing of job content rather than automatic reaction to the forces that drove pay in the past."[13] For Bellack, job evaluation establishes the relative values of jobs based on their content and without reference to the external market. Bellack's view is that the structure (pay differences) among jobs can be established with job evaluation independent of a link to the market.

As you can see, job evaluation takes on many forms. In some cases it only classifies jobs, in others it helps establish a hierarchy. On the one hand it is a mechanism used to compare the relative content of jobs without reference to current or market-based rates. On the other hand, it serves as the link between market rates and the content of jobs. Various job evaluation plans have been designed based on all these perspectives.

Measurement and Rationalization

Job evaluation can take on the trappings of measurement (objective, numerical, generalizable, documented, and reliable), and it is also an administrative proce-

---

[11]E. Robert Livernash, *Comparable Worth Issues and Alternatives* (Washington, D.C.: Equal Employment Advisory Council, 1980).

[12]Donald P. Schwab, "Job Evaluation and Pay Setting: Concepts and Practices," in *Comparable Worth: Issues and Alternatives,* ed. E. Robert Livernash (Washington, D.C.: Equal Employment Advisory Council, 1980), pp. 49–77.

[13]Bellak, "Comparable Worth."

dure through which the parties can haggle over the relative worth of jobs—"the rules of the game."[14]

Viewed as a measurement instrument, job evaluation is judged according to technical standards. For example, to what extent is it free from error? Or how can the instrument be redesigned to reduce errors?

As an administrative procedure, job evaluation is a process used to help gain acceptance of pay difference among jobs.

Prior to the widespread use of job evaluation, employers in the 1930s and 1940s had complex and irrational pay structures—the legacy of decentralized and uncoordinated wage setting policies made permissable in an era of authoritarian and secretive managerial styles.[15] Pay differences were a major source of unrest among workers. American Steel and Wire, for example, had over 100,000 pay classifications.[16] According to Jacoby,

> employment and wage records were rarely kept before 1900; only the foreman knew with any accuracy how many workers were employed in his department and the rates they received. Foremen jealously guarded wage information, allowing them to play favorites by varying the day rate or assigning favored workers to jobs where piece rates were loose.[17]

To overcome these problems employers adopted job evaluation to help design and rationalize pay differences among jobs.

As an administrative procedure, job evaluation invites give and take. Consensus building often requires active discussion. Employees, union representatives, and managers may be involved in discussions about the pay differences among various jobs. Job evaluation even involves negotiations among managers of different units or functions within a single organization. So viewed as an administrative procedure, job evaluation is used for working out conflicts that inevitably arise about pay differences over time.

Some readers may conclude that job evaluation is no more than rationalization of a pay structure that is either negotiated by the parties or reflected in the external markets. Livernash comments on this view:

---

[14]George T. Milkovich, "Compensation, Equity, and Job Evaluation in the 1980's," *Proceedings of the Symposium on Job Evaluation and Equal Employment Opportunity* (New York: Industrial Relations Counselors, 1979); and George T. Milkovich and Charles J. Cogill, "Measurement as an Issue in Job Analysis and Job Evaluation," in *Handbook of Wage and Salary Management,* ed. Milton Rock (New York: McGraw-Hill, 1984). Also see Howard Risher, "Job Evaluation: Mystical or Statistical?" *Personnel* 55, no. 5 (September/October 1978), pp. 23–36; John Gaito, "Measurement Scales and Statistics: Resurgence of an Old Misconception," *Psychological Bulletin* 87, no. 3 (1980), pp. 564–67.

[15]Livernash, "Internal Wage Structure."

[16]Sanford M. Jacoby, "Development of Internal Labor Markets," in *Internal Labor Markets,* ed. P. Osterman (Cambridge, Mass.: MIT Press) 1984, pp. 23–70.

[17]Ibid., p. 26.

Job evaluation is not a rigid, objective, analytical procedure. Neither is it a meaningless process of rationalization. If a group of people with reasonable knowledge of certain jobs rate (evaluate) them, there will be frequent small differences of opinion, some major differences as well, but also a high degree of general agreement. The application of group judgment through the rating process normally produces an *improved pay structure,* but *extreme attitudes as to the accuracy of ratings are difficult to defend.*[18]

Culling through all of this, the following definition seems to include the nuances attributed to job evaluation.

> **Job evaluation is a systematic procedure designed to aid in establishing pay differentials among jobs within a single employer.**

MAJOR DECISIONS

The major decisions involved in the design and administration of job evaluation are depicted in Exhibit 4.2. They include: (1) determine the purpose(s) of job evaluation, (2) decide whether to use single or multiple plans, (3) choose among alternative approaches, (4) obtain the involvement of relevant parties, and (5) evaluate its usefulness. The first three of these decisions are discussed in this chapter; the remaining two are covered in the next.

EXHIBIT 4.2
Determining an Internally Consistent Job Structure

Internal Consistency:
Relationships → Job → Job → Job → Job
among jobs within   Analysis   Descriptions   Evaluation   Structure
the organization

Some Major Decisions in Job Evaluation
- Establish purpose of evaluation
- Decide whether to use single or multiple plans
- Choose among alternative approaches
- Obtain involvement of relevant parties
- Evaluate plan's usefulness

Establish the Purpose

Why bother with job evaluation? Because it aids in establishing a pay structure that is internally equitable to employees and consistent with the goals of the organization. The results of job evaluation should be relevant to managers who

---

[18]E. Robert Livernash, "The Internal Wage Structure," pp. 143–72.

will use them to help make pay decisions, and to employees whose pay rates they influence.

More specific purposes of job evaluation often include:

- Help foster equity by integrating pay with a job's contributions to the organization.
- Assist employees to adapt to organization changes by improving their understanding of job content and what is valued in their work.
- Establish a workable, agreed-upon pay structure.
- Simplify and rationalize the pay relationships among jobs, and reduce the role that chance, favoritism, and bias may play.
- Aid in setting pay for new, unique, or changing jobs.
- Provide an agreed-upon device to reduce and resolve disputes and grievances.
- Help ensure that the pay structure is consistent with the relationships among jobs, thereby supporting other human resource programs such as career planning, staffing, and training.

However, little empirical evidence exists that demonstrates the effects of formal job evaluation on these objectives.

Since they guide the design and administration of job evaluation, objectives need to be specified. But initially established objectives too often get lost in statistical procedures and in the bureaucracy which tends to sprout around the administration of job evaluation. Job evaluation sometimes seems to exist for its own sake, rather than as an aid to achieving the goals listed above.[19] So an organization is best served by initially establishing its objectives for the process, and using these objectives as a constant guide for its decisions.

Job evaluation emphasizes a systematic, rational assessment of jobs as a part of pay determination. Yet managers seem interested in job evaluation only when a pay problem exists—employee dissatisfaction, grievances, threats of unionization, or lawsuits. A more productive strategy is to anticipate or avoid potential challenges by ensuring an equitable and work-related pay structure.

Single versus Multiple Plans

Once the objectives of job evaluation are selected, then it is necessary to decide which jobs or job groups are going to be evaluated. Rarely will an employer evaluate all jobs in the organization at one time.[20] More typically, related groups of jobs, for example production, engineering, or marketing, will be concentrated on. Even when introducing job evaluation for the first time, it is usually applied to one occupation or subunit of the organization.

---

[19]Mike Burns, *Understanding Job Evaluation* (London: Institute of Personnel Management, 1978); Edwin F. Beal, "In Praise of Job Evaluation," *California Management Review,* Summer 1963, pp. 9–15.

[20]Bellak, "Comparable Worth."

Most employers design different job evaluation plans for different job families. They do so because they believe that the work content of various job families is too diverse to be adequately evaluated using the same plan. For example, production jobs may vary in terms of working conditions and the physical, manipulative skills required. But engineering and marketing jobs do not vary on these factors, nor are those factors particularly important in engineering or marketing work. Rather, other factors such as technical knowledge and skills and the degree of contacts with external customers may be relevant. These *compensable factors* are aspects of work that vary among jobs and may play an important role in establishing pay differences among jobs.

The point is that separate plans are typically used for production, engineering, marketing, managerial, office and clerical, and executive jobs within a single employer. The most common criteria for determining different job families include similar knowledge/skill/ability requirements, common licensing requirements, union jurisdictions, and career paths. Those who argue for multiple plans, each with unique compensable factors, claim that different job families have different and unique work characteristics. To design a single set of compensable factors capable of universal application, while technically feasible, would risk emphasizing generalized commonalities among jobs and minimizing uniqueness and dissimilarities. Accurately gauging the similarities and dissimilarities in jobs is critical to establish and justify pay differentials. Therefore, more than one plan is often used for adequate evaluation.

The decision about single versus multiple plans is important in the comparable worth controversy. The National Academy of Sciences' study committee on job evaluation and wage discrimination was divided on whether the jobs usually found within a single firm can be adequately evaluated by a single job evaluation or whether several plans are required to measure job characteristics adequately.[21] Remick argues that an operational definition of comparable worth hinges on the application of a single evaluation system across job families, both to rank order jobs and to set salaries.[22] Yet to define universal factors in such a way that they accurately evaluate all jobs within a single employer and at the same time remain acceptable to all parties imposes a great burden on a single job evaluation plan. The unresolved issue of comparable worth is examined in detail in the chapter on pay discrimination.

---

[21]Donald J. Treiman and Heidi J. Hartmann, eds., *Women, Work and Wages: Equal Pay for Jobs of Equal Value* (Washington, D.C.: National Academy Press, 1981); and D. Treiman, ed., *Job Evaluation: An Analytic Review,* Interim Report to the Equal Employment Opportunity Commission (Washington, D.C.; National Academy Press, 1981).

[22]Helen Remick, *Comparable Worth and Wage Discrimination* (Philadelphia: Temple University Press, 1984). See also Karin Allport, "Equal Pay for Equal Work? Of Course," *Across the Board* 17, no. 10 (October 1980); and James T. Brinks, "The Comparable Worth Issue: A Salary Administration Bombshell," *Personnel Administrator,* November 1981, pp. 37–40.

Rather than either universal factors or entirely unique factors for each job family, some employers, notable Hewett-Packard and Control Data, use a core set of common factors and another set of factors unique to particular occupational or functional areas (finance, manufacturing, software and systems, sales). These companies' experiences suggest that unique factors tailored to different job families are more likely to be both acceptable to employees and managers and easier to verify as work related than are generalized universal factors.

Choose among Job Evaluation Methods

Four fundamental job evaluation methods are in use: ranking, classification, factor comparison, and point plan. They can be distinguished by looking at (1) whether the evaluation is based on the whole job or specific factors, (2) whether jobs are evaluated against some standard or against each other, and (3) whether the evaluation is qualitative or quantitative. Of these, the key distinguishing feature is the degree of specificity of the standard with which the jobs are compared. Imagine a continuum of specificity, from ranking to classification to factor comparison to point plans. In ranking, the least specific job evaluation method, the whole job is compared against other whole jobs on some general notion of value or job content. This general notion may or may not be explicitly stated. In a classification method, the concepts of value or work content are divided into categories or classes, and jobs are slotted into these categories. In factor comparison and point plans, content and value are broken down into compensable factors, and jobs are evaluated by the degree of each factor the job possesses. Thus, these two methods are the most specific in that the standard for comparison is explicitly stated and even quantified.

Uncounted variations of these four methods exist. The following sections examine each of the methods and provide examples of some adaptations. All of the methods assume that the results of an accurate, thorough job analysis have been translated into readable, useful job descriptions and that the job families to be evaluated have been identified.

RANKING

Ranking simply involves ordering the job descriptions from highest to lowest based on a definition of value or contribution. It is the simplest, fastest, easiest to understand and explain to employees, and the least expensive job evaluation method, at least initially.

Two ways of ranking are usually considered: alternation ranking and paired comparison. Alternation ranking involves ordering the job descriptions alternately at each extreme. Exhibit 4.3 illustrates the method. Agreement is reached among evaluators on which job is the most valuable, then the least valuable. Evaluators alternate between the next most valued and next least valued, and so on, until all the jobs have been ordered. For example, evaluators agreed that

EXHIBIT 4.3
Alternation Ranking

Jobs		Rank
Number	Title	Most Valued
1	Millwright	Tool Maker
2	Shear Operator	Welder
-----3--------	Welder	Inspector
4	Punch Press Operator	
5	Silver Solderer	
6	Machine Operator	
7	Sub Assembler (Electronic)	
-----8--------	Packer	
9	Grinder (Rough)	
10	Unit Assembler	
11	Compressor Assembler	
----12--------	Janitor	
----13--------	Shipping & Receiving Clerk	
----14--------	Inspector	
15	Engine Lathe Operator	
16	Refrigeration Mechanic	
----17--------	Tool-Maker	
18	Sub Assembler (Mechanical)	Shipping & Receiving Clerk
19	Dip Tank Operator	Janitor
20	Spray Painter	Packer
		Least Valued

the job of tool maker was the most valued of the 20 jobs listed in the exhibit, and packer the least valued. Then they selected most and least valued from the 18 remaining jobs on the list.

The paired comparison method involves comparing all possible pairs of jobs under study. A simple way to do paired comparison is to set up a matrix, as shown in Exhibit 4.4. The two numbers that identify a cell location correspond to the two different jobs to be compared. The number of the higher ranked job is entered in the cell. For example, of jobs 1 and 2, 1 is ranked higher. Of jobs 1 and 3, 3 is ranked higher. When all comparisons have been completed, the job with the highest total number of "most valuable" rankings becomes the highest ranked job, and so on. In the exhibit, job 1 received 15 "most valuable" rankings; therefore we can assume that job 1 will be near the top of the job hierarchy. Some evidence suggests that the alternation ranking and paired

EXHIBIT 4.4
Paired Comparison Ranking

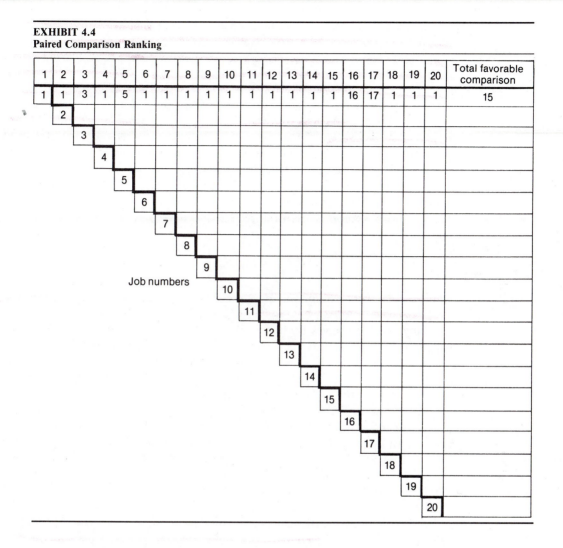

comparison methods are more reliable (produce similar results consistently) than simple ranking.[23]

If the ranking is performed by a committee, members may rank jobs separately and may then merge results into an "average" ranking. If wide disagreements exist, discussion of each member's rationale underlying the rankings usually obtains greater agreement.

[23]David J. Chesler, "Reliability and Comparability of Different Job Evaluation Systems," *Journal of Applied Psychology,* October 1948, pp. 465–75.

Ranking is seldom the recommended approach. The criteria or factors on which the jobs are ranked are usually so crudely defined (if they are specified at all) that the evaluations become subjective opinions that are difficult if not impossible to explain and justify in work-related terms. Further, evaluator(s) using this method must be knowledgeable about every single job under study. The numbers alone make this task formidable—50 jobs require 1,225 comparisons [(n) $(n - 1)/2$]; and as organizations change, it is difficult to remain knowledgeable about all jobs. Some organizations try to overcome this difficulty by ranking jobs within single departments and merging the results. However, without greater specification of the factors on which the rankings are based, merging ranks is a major problem. Even though ranking is simple, fast, and inexpensive, in the long term it may be more costly. Since the results are difficult to defend, costly solutions are often required to overcome the problems the ranking system has created.

CLASSIFICATION

The classification method involves slotting job descriptions into a series of classes that cover the range of jobs. Classes can be conceived as a series of carefully labeled shelves on a bookshelf. The labels are the class descriptions which serve as the standard against which the job descriptions are compared. Exhibit 4.5 lists the typical steps in the classification approach. Each class is described in such a way that it captures sufficient work detail and yet is general enough to cause little difficulty in slotting jobs.

Writing class descriptions can be troublesome when jobs from several occupations or job families are covered by a single plan. While greater specificity of class definition improves the reliability of evaluation, it also limits the variety of jobs that can easily be classfied. For example, class definitions written with sales jobs in mind may make it difficult to slot office or administrative jobs and vice versa. You can see the difficulty by examining the class definitions from the federal government's 18-class evaluation system, Exhibit 4.6.

The classes may further be labeled by the inclusion of benchmark jobs that fall into each class. Benchmark jobs are defined as reference points having the following characteristics:

- The contents are well known, relatively stable over time, and agreed upon by the employees involved.

EXHIBIT 4.5
Typical Steps in Classification System

1. Define classes.
2. Identify and slot benchmarks.
3. Prepare classification manual.
4. Apply system to nonbenchmark jobs.

EXHIBIT 4.6
Examples of General Schedule Descriptions for the Federal Government Job Classification Method

---

Grade General Schedule 1 includes all classes of positions the duties of which are to be performed, under immediate supervision, with little or no latitude for the exercise of independent judgment, (1) the simplest routine work in office, business, or fiscal operations, or (2) elementary work of a subordinate technical character in a professional, scientific, or technical field.

Grade-General Schedule 5 includes all classes of positions the duties of which are (1) to perform, under general supervision, difficult and responsible work in office, business, or fiscal administration, or comparable subordinate technical work in a professional, scientific, or technical field, requiring in either case (A) considerable training and supervisory or other experience, (B) broad working knowledge of a special subject matter or of office, laboratory, engineering, scientific, or other procedure and practice, and (C) the exercise of independent judgment in a limited field; (2) to perform, under immediate supervision, and with little opportunity for the exercise of independent judgment, simple and elementary work requiring professional, scientific, or technical training equivalent to that represented by graduation from a college or university of recognized standing but requiring little or no experience; or (3) to perform other work of equal importance, difficulty, and responsibility, and requiring comparable qualifications.

Grade-General Schedule 9 includes all classes of positions the duties of which are (1) to perform, under general supervision, very difficult and responsible work along special technical, supervisory, or administrative experience which has (A) demonstrated capacity for sound independent work, (B) thorough and fundamental knowledge of a special and complex subject matter, or of the profession, art, or science involved, and (C) considerable latitude for the exercise of independent judgment; (2) with considerable latitude for the exercise of independent judgment, to perform moderately difficult and responsible work, requiring (A) professional, scientific or technical training equivalent to that represented by graduation from a college or university of recognized standing, and (B) considerable additional professional, scientific, or technical training or experience which has demonstrated capacity for sound independent work; or (3) to perform other work of equal importance, difficulty, and responsibility, and requiring comparable qualifications.

Grade-General Schedule 13 includes all classes of positions the duties of which are (1) to perform, under administrative direction, with wide latitude for the exercise of independent judgment work of unusual difficulty and responsibility along special technical, supervisory, or administrative lines, requiring extended specialized, supervisory, or administrative training and experience which has demonstrated leadership and marked attainments; (2) to serve as assistant head of a major organization involving work of comparable level within a bureau; (3) to perform, under administrative direction, with wide latitude for the exercise of independent judgment, work of unusual difficulty and responsibility requiring extended professional, scientific, or technical training and experience which has demonstrated leadership and marked attainments in professional, scientific, or technical research, practice, or administration; or (4) to perform other work of equal importance, difficulty, and responsibility, and requiring comparable qualifications.

- The jobs are common across a number of different employers. They are not unique to a particular employer.
- They represent the entire range of jobs being evaluated.
- They are accepted in the external labor market for setting wages.

The point of using benchmark jobs is to anchor the comparisons for each job class. Anchoring the classes in this way has the advantage of illustrating the typical job in a class.

In practice, the job descriptions not only are compared to the standard class descriptions and benchmark jobs but also to each other, to insure that jobs within each class are more similar to each other than to adjacent classes.

The final result is a series of classes with a number of jobs in each. The jobs within each class are considered to be equal (similar) work and will be paid equally. Jobs in different classes should be dissimilar and may have different pay rates.

How Many Classes?

Class descriptions and the number of classes depend on tradition, range, and diversity of the job involved and on the career and promotion paths of the organization. Belcher suggests the "rule of thumb" that 7 to 14 classes will meet the needs of most organizations, a suggestion that seems more a matter of convention and experience than it is a matter of determining how many will best accomplish the pay system's objectives.[24] Some organizations have expanded their classes from 10 to 20; others have collapsed classes from 20 to 10; all seemed pleased with the results. Those adopting greater numbers of classes argue that employees favor frequent upgrading or promotions, and greater class numbers facilitate such moves. Those collapsing the number of classes argue that a proliferation of classes is difficult to explain or defend and become needless bureaucracy.

What is the appropriate number of classes? It depends. Variability and diversity in the work may call for many classes. Comparisons in the external market may be easier if the same number of classes as similar employers is adopted. The class descriptions, like job descriptions, are useful only when they are embedded in the actual work performed and when they capture meaningful similarities and differences among jobs to help ensure a workable and defensible pay structure.

The Federal Government's General Schedule

Classification, while more complex than ranking, is relatively inexpensive to develop and simple to install and understand. Probably the best known example is the Office of Personnel Management's General Schedule (GS), with 18 "grades" (classes).[25] Most jobs are in 15 grades; the top three have been combined into a "supergrade" which covers senior executives. Employees in these top three classes are eligible for bonuses and special stipends based on performance. Collapsing the top three classes into one "supergrade" provides flexibil-

---

[24]Belcher, *Compensation,* pp. 151–52. See also Paul A. Katz, "There IS Something New in Position Classification," *Defense Management Journal,* September 1978, pp. 16–19.

[25]The federal system utilizes the terms grades and classes differently than does this book. We have previously avoided referring to *job grades* because of possible confusion with *pay grades,* discussed in Chapter 7. However, the federal government refers to the results of its classification as grades, rather than classes. In the GS system a series of *classes* links jobs of similar work (e.g., clerk typist class I, clerk typist class II).

EXHIBIT 4.7
Factor Evaluation System: Nine Factors, with Subfactors

Knowledge required by the position
1. Nature or kind of knowledge and skills needed
2. How the knowledge and skills are used in doing the work

Supervisory controls
1. How the work is assigned
2. The employee's responsibility for carrying out the work
3. How the work is reviewed

Guidelines
1. The nature of guidelines for performing the work
2. The judgment needed to apply the guidelines or develop new guides

Complexity
1. The nature of the assignment
2. The difficulty in identifying what needs to be done
3. The difficulty and originality involved in performing the work

Scope and effect
1. The purpose of the work
2. The impact of the work product or service

Personal contacts

Purpose of contacts

Physical demands

Work environment

---

ity by making it easier to move people at this level among different agencies, in order to best utilize these particular employees' skills, and meet different agency needs. Several grade descriptions are given in Exhibit 4.6. The GS system is *not* based on related subject matter of work (e.g., finance systems analysis); rather, level of difficulty distinguishes the various classes.

The Federal Classification Act of 1923 provided an early impetus for job classification in the federal government. Classification and the job descriptions provided the basis for internal consistency that government employees demanded and a uniform job terminology, which allowed centralized financial control.[26] The argument at the time was that it made better, more efficient government a possibility. It also specified a standard of equal pay for equal work, over 40 years before legislation required such a standard in the private sector.

Subsequent classification acts further refined and expanded the use of the classification method at the federal level.

In 1975, a job evaluation and pay review task force released a report critical of federal classification practices. Specifically, it recommended the use of the same set of job factors to allocate all jobs and greater managerial participation. A Factor Evaluation System (FES) was installed in 1977, which uses nine factors to classify approximately 1 million nonsupervisory general schedule positions. These factors are listed in Exhibit 4.7. Using the plan, jobs as diverse as

---

[26]Paul A. Katz, "Specific Job Evaluation Systems: White Collar Jobs in the Federal Civil Service," in *Handbook of Wage and Salary Administration,* ed. Milton Rock (New York: McGraw-Hill, 1984), pp. 14/1–14/10; and Steven W. Hays and T. Zane Reeves, *Personnel Management in the Public Sector* (Boston: Allyn and Bacon, 1984).

work unit conservationist in the Agriculture Department, border patrol officer in Immigration, and account auditor in the Internal Revenue Service were placed in the same GS level. Each factor also receives point values that reflect the factor's importance in a job. The sum of the factor ratings equals the job's total worth. The Factor Evaluation System changes the original classification system to a hybrid of classification and point system evaluation. Under its use, managers have three potential comparisons to guide their evaluation of a job: the general class description, the factor comparisons, and the benchmark jobs that anchor each class.

The Factor Evaluation System is not the only job evaluation system within the federal government. The government's approach seems to be similar to that of private industry: pick and choose and adapt, according to specific needs. Many states and other governmental units use variations of the classification system, too. The references contain additional sources of information on public sector pay practices.[27]

In addition to public sector jobs, classification is applied to a wide variety of private sector jobs. Craft and assembly, as well as engineering and research jobs, are evaluated with it. High-technology and defense-related businesses have frequently developed four to six job classes for engineers.[28] However, the differences among classes in this setting are often more related to experience or "years-since-degree" than to differences in work done by the engineers.

Inherent Flexibility

Sufficient vagueness exists in many classification plans to permit what Patten calls "aggrandizing language" in the job descriptions.[29] A potential problem with the classification method is that it may degenerate into a title game. Usually

[27]Edward B. Shils, "A Perspective on Job Measurement," in *Handbook of Wage and Salary Administration,* ed. Milton Rock (New York: McGraw-Hill, 1984), pp. 8/1–8/14; Katz, "Specific Job Evaluation Systems," in *Job Evaluation and Pay Administration in the Public Sector,* ed. Harold Suskin, (Chicago: International Personnel Management Association, 1977); United Fund of Southeastern New England Position Classification and Salary Structure Guideline Manual, 1970; Donald F. Todd and Patrick M. Manning, "Job Evaluation Goes to School," *Personnel,* July–August 1974, pp. 53–59; Sigmund G. Ginsburg, "A Classification and Salary System for Professional Administrative Staff," *The Journal of the College and University Personnel Association,* Spring 1977, pp. 48–56; Gary Craver, "Survey of Job Evaluation Practices in State and County Governments," *Public Personnel Management* 6, no. 2 (March/April 1977), pp. 121–31; Robert L. Istnick, "New Dimensions for Position Evaluation," *ACA 1978 Regional Conference Proceedings* (Scottsdale, Ariz.: American Compensation Association, 1979); and Hays and Reeves, *Personnel Management in the Public Sector.*

[28]Robert B. Pursell, "R&D Job Evaluation and Compensation," *Compensation Review,* Second Quarter 1972, pp. 21–31; T. Atchinson, and W. French, "Pay Systems for Scientists and Engineers," *Industrial Relations* 7 (1967), pp. 44–56.

[29]Thomas H. Patten, Jr., *Pay Employee Compensation and Incentive Plans* (New York: Free Press, 1977).

each class has a title associated with it, often as part of the benchmark job. Managers may decide the classes to which they want the jobs assigned prior to any analysis, and then try to influence the classification by assigning an inflated title to the job. The potential for manipulating the results is inherent in the flexible nature of the classification system.

While not as vulnerable to legal and employee challenges as a ranking approach, classification plans do not offer much detailed, work-related rationale to justify pay differentials. This lack of work-related rationale may not be very compelling to a line manager whose immediate problem is getting a salary increase for a subordinate, but it takes on importance in an equal pay lawsuit or in reassuring disgruntled employees who feel their jobs are misvalued.

Finally, some employers are currently slashing the number of classes in their plans. There is speculation that the General Motors Saturn facilities in Spring Hill, Tennessee, will use about one to four job classes for all plant jobs.[30] Rather than use diverse job titles, all workers will be known as technicians or associates. The logic behind reducing classes and using universal titles is increased flexibility to overcome inefficient work rules. Yet some balance between complete flexibility and rules is required. Recall the earlier example, American Steel and Wire, where complete flexibility was given to supervisors and uncoordinated and irrational pay structures were the result. Removing inefficient bureaucracy is important, but some of the rules are necessary to help ensure that pay accomplishes the system's objectives.

FACTOR COMPARISON

In the factor comparison method, jobs are evaluated based on two criteria: (1) a set of compensable factors and (2) wages for a select set of jobs. Originated by Benge, Burk, and Hay, the method is more sophisticated than either the ranking or classification plans; however, its complexity often limits its usefulness.[31]

While several versions of factor comparison exist, the basic approach involves the following steps:

1. Conduct job analysis. As with all job evaluation methods, information about the jobs must be collected and job descriptions prepared. However, the factor comparison method differs from others in that it requires that jobs be analyzed and described in terms of the compensable factors used in the plan.

---

[30]Anne B. Fisher, "Behind All the Hype at GM's Saturn," *Fortune,* November 11, 1985, pp. 34–49.

[31]Eugene J. Benge, Samuel L. H. Burk, and Edward N. Hay, *Manual of Job Evaluation* (New York: Harper & Row, 1941). See also Eugene J. Benge, "Using Factor Methods to Measure Jobs," in *Handbook of Wage and Salary Administration,* ed. Milton R. Rock (New York: McGraw-Hill, 1972); Edward N. Hay, "Four Methods of Establishing Factor Scales in Factor Comparison Job Evaluation," *Personnel,* September 1946, pp. 115–24; Edward N. Hay, "Characteristics of Factor Comparison Job Evaluation," *Personnel* 22, no. 6 (1946), pp. 370–75.

EXHIBIT 4.8
Universal Factor Definitions Used in Factor Comparison Method

1. Mental requirements—either the possession of and/or the active application of the following:
   A. (Inherent) mental traits, such as intelligence, memory, reasoning, facility in verbal expression, ability to get along with people, and imagination.
   B. (Acquired) general education, such as grammar and arithmetic; or general information as to sports, world events, etc.
   C. (Acquired) specialized knowledge such as chemistry, engineering, accounting, advertising, etc.

2. Skill:
   A. (Acquired) facility in muscular coordination, as in operating machines, repetitive movements, careful coordinations, dexterity, assembling, sorting, etc.
   B. (Acquired) specific job knowledge necessary to the muscular coordination only; acquired by performance of the work and not to be confused with general education or specialized knowledge. It is very largely training in the interpretation of sensory impressions. Examples:
      (*1*) In operating an adding machine, the knowledge of *which key* to depress for a subtotal would be skill.
      (*2*) In automobile repair, the ability to determine the significance of a certain knock in the motor would be skill.
      (*3*) In hand-firing a boiler, the ability to determine from the appearance of the firebed how coal should be shoveled over the surface would be skill.

3. Physical requirements:
   A. Physical effort, as sitting, standing walking, climbing, pulling, lifting, etc.; both the amount exercised and the degree of the continuity should be taken into account.
   B. Physical status, as height, weight, strength and eyesight.

4. Responsibilities:
   A. For raw materials, processed materials, tools, equipment, and property.
   B. For money or negotiable securities.
   C. For profits or loss, savings or methods' improvement.
   D. For public contact.
   E. For records.
   F. For supervision.
      (*1*) Primarily the complexity of supervising *given* to subordinates; the number of subordinates is a secondary feature. Planning, direction, coordination, instruction, control, and approval characterize this kind of supervision.
      (*2*) Also, the degree of supervision *received*. If jobs A and B gave no supervision to subordinates, but A received much closer immediate supervision than B, then B would be entitled to a higher rating than A in the supervision factor.
         To summarize the four degrees of supervision:
         Highest degree—gives much—gets little
         High degree—gives much—gets much
         Low degree—gives none—gets little
         Lowest degree—gives none—gets much

5. Working conditions:
   A. Environmental influences, such as atmosphere, ventilation, illumination, noise, congestion, fellow workers, etc.
   B. Hazards—from the work or its surroundings.
   C. Hours.

Benge, Burk, and Hay prescribed five factors: mental requirements, skill requirements, physical factors, responsibility, and working conditions. Exhibit 4.8 contains definitions of these five factors. The developers consider these factors to be universal—able to evaluate all jobs in all organizations. However, there is some latitude in the specific definition of each factor among organizations.

Conducting job analysis on the basis of predetermined factors raises some questions. Should compensable factors be selected prior to job analysis? Or should job analysis and job descriptions be done, and then factors selected based on information gleaned in the analysis? If every job must be defined in terms of the five factors, then the *content* of the job analysis and job descriptions is controlled by these "universal" factors, and the decision on which factors to use necessarily comes before job analysis. But such an approach risks omitting aspects of the work unique to an organization and important to employees and managers. These five factors may not adequately capture the nature of the work. This risk can be reduced by first developing factors based on analysis of a representative sample of jobs, then applying the factors to all other jobs. In this way the factors are custom-tailored to particular occupations and organizations. Exhibit 4.9 is an example of a job description prepared for factor comparison evaluation.

2. Select benchmark jobs. The selection of benchmark jobs is critical since the entire method is based on them. Benchmark jobs (also called key jobs) serve as reference points. Earlier, we specified the following characteristics for a benchmark job:

- The contents are well known and agreed upon by the parties involved.
- The contents change very little over time.
- The current pay rates are generally acceptable and the differentials among the jobs are relatively stable.
- They are accepted in the external labor market for setting wages.

Another criterion is that the sample of benchmark jobs cover the entire range of jobs being evaluated (i.e., some from the top, middle, and low end of the range). If more than one job family is being evaluated, benchmarks are drawn from the top, middle, and low end of every included job family. But for factor comparison, the requirements for a benchmark job are even more specific: they must cover the entire range of each factor. For example, if a compensable factor is mental requirements, benchmark jobs must cover the full range of mental requirements that exists in the job group being evaluated. The exact number varies for benchmarks required; some rules of thumb have been suggested (15 to 25), but the number depends on the range and diversity of the work to be evaluated.

3. Rank benchmark jobs on each factor. Each benchmark job is ranked on each compensable factor (Exhibit 4.10). In our example, a job family consisting of six jobs is first ranked on mental requirements, then on experience, and so

EXHIBIT 4.9
Illustration of a Job Description Prepared for Factor Comparison

Job title ___Assistant Controller___   Dept. ___Controller___   Employee(s) Interviewed ___Edward Voight___

Duties (continue on other side if necessary)   Under supervision of controller, reconciles various controls with subsidiary and detail records. Assists in preparation of financial reports for use of management. Analyzes general ledger accounts to verify accuracy (payroll, pension, sales tax, returns, etc.) Helps compile annual financial reports. Occasionally makes special studies as assigned by controller.

Mental requirements	Skill requirements	Physical factors	Responsibilities	Supervision
C-4 Years education	Kind: SCHEDULE and coordinate clerical effort, dictation	— Sitting 95% — Standing 5% — Walking	Equipment Computer	Supervises 5 Persons Analysis:
XX Add and Subtract XX Multiply and divide XX Fractions and decimals		X Eyesight — Endurance — Lifting	Materials	RECEIVES None Some Much GIVES Much Some None
XX Accounting — Shorthand — Grammar — Other	Desirable prior experience: Accounting Background Systematizing	X Indoor — Outdoor — Unlocalized	Records Clerical and accounting,	Receives supervision from Controller
Job instructions: Graduate of accounting course	Time to develop average performance: 4 - 6 mos.	X Desk — Machine — Counter	Methods Suggests changes	Plans Work of clerks
	Prerequisite jobs: Accountant	Illumination: Excellent	Money Prepares cash requisition slips	Instructs Subordinates
— Meet distractions — Meet emergencies — Stand monotony XX Make decisions XX Analyze	X Repetitive — Varied	Atmosphere: Excellent	Savings Public contact	Approves Stationery requisitions Control devices:
— Patience X Tact — Superior memory	Sensory training — Sight — Hearing Operates computer & calculator	Hazards:	Confidential matters Payroll, financial statements Other	Highest job under: Chief accountant — Written instructions — Plans own time with supervision by controller

Receives: 3, 2, 1 / 6, X5, 4 / 9, 8, 7

Symbols: Use X to indicate;
XX to stress. P-preferred;
R-required; or show amount or %

Prepared by _____   J.R.B.   Date _3/10/71_   Approved by _____   T.W.

Adapted from E. J. Benge, "Using Factor Methods to Measure Jobs," in *Handbook of Wage and Salary Administration*, 2nd ed., ed. M. Rock (New York: McGraw-Hill, 1984), pp. 2–49.

EXHIBIT 4.10
Factor Comparison Method: Ranking Benchmark Jobs by Compensable Factor

	Benchmark Jobs	Mental Requirements	Experience/ Skills	Physical Factors	Supervision	Other Responsibilities
A.	Punch press operator	6	5	2	4	4
B.	Parts attendant	5	3	3	6	1
C.	Riveter	4	6	1	1	3
D.	Truck operator	3	1	6	5	6
E.	Machine operator	2	2	4	2	5
F.	Parts inspector	1	3	5	3	2

Note: Rank of 1 is high.

on. The approach differs from the ranking plan in that each job is ranked on *each factor* rather than as a "whole" job.

4. Allocate benchmark wages across factors. Once each benchmark is ranked on each factor, the next step is to allocate the wages paid for each benchmark to each factor. Essentially this is done by deciding how much of the wage rate for each benchmark job is associated with mental demand, how much with physical requirements, and so on across all compensable factors. This is done for each benchmark job and is usually based on the judgment of a compensation committee. For example, in Exhibit 4.11, of the $5.80 per hour paid to the punch press operator, the committee has decided that the job's mental requirements equal $.80, experience/skill is worth $.80, physical factors account for $2.40, supervision accounts for $1.10, and other responsibilities are worth $.70 an hour in this job. The total $5.80 is allocated among the compensable factors. This process is repeated for each of the benchmark jobs.

After the wage for each job is allocated among that job's compensable factors, the dollar amounts for each factor are ranked as shown in Exhibit 4.12. The job that has the highest wage allocation for mental requirements is ranked 1 on that factor, next highest is 2, and so on. Separate rankings are done for the wage allocation to each compensable factor. In the example in Exhibit 4.12, parts inspector has more of its wages allocated to mental demands than does any other job, and so it receives the highest rank for that factor.

EXHIBIT 4.11
Factor Comparison Methods: Allocation of Benchmark Job Wages Across Factors

	Benchmark Jobs	Current Wage Rate ($/hour)		Mental Requirements $		Experience/ Skills $		Physical Factors $		Supervision $		Other Responsibilities $
A.	Punch press operator	5.80	=	.80	+	.80	+	2.40	+	1.10	+	.70
B.	Parts attendant	9.60	=	2.15	+	2.35	+	1.90	+	.60	+	2.60
C.	Riveter	13.30	=	2.50	+	3.10	+	2.45	+	4.50	+	.75
D.	Truck operator	8.50	=	3.40	+	3.20	+	.60	+	.80	+	.50
E.	Machine operator	11.80	=	3.60	+	2.90	+	1.75	+	2.90	+	.65
F.	Parts inspector	11.40	=	4.50	+	2.20	+	1.20	+	2.50	+	1.10

EXHIBIT 4.12
Ranking Wage Allocations

		Factors								
		Mental Requirements		Experience/ Skills		Physical Factors		Supervision		Other Responsibilities	
	Benchmark Jobs	$	Rank	$	Rank	$	Rank	$	Rank	$	Rank
A.	Punch press operator	.80	6	.80	6	2.40	2	1.10	4	.70	4
B.	Parts attendant	2.15	5	2.35	4	1.90	3	.60	6	2.60	1
C.	Riveter	2.50	4	3.10	2	2.45	1	4.50	1	.75	3
D.	Truck operator	3.40	3	3.20	1	.60	6	.80	5	.50	6
E.	Machine operator	3.60	2	2.90	3	1.75	4	2.90	2	.65	5
F.	Parts inspector	4.50	1	2.20	5	1.20	5	2.50	3	1.10	2

Note: Rank of 1 is high.

We now have two sets of rankings, which are shown in Exhibit 4.13; the first ranking is based on comparisons of each benchmark job on each compensable factor (Exhibit 4.10). It reflects the relative presence of each factor among the benchmark jobs. The second ranking is based on the proportion of each job's wages that is attributed to each factor (Exhibit 4.12). The next step is to see how well the two rankings agree.

5. *Compare factor and wage allocation ranks.* The two rankings are judgments based on comparisons of compensable factors and wage distributions. They agree when each benchmark is assigned the same location in both ranks. If there is disagreement, the rationale for the wage allocations and factor rankings is reexamined. Both are judgments, so some slight "tuning" or adjustments may bring the rankings into line. The comparison of the two rankings is simply a cross-checking of judgments. If agreement cannot be achieved, then the job is no longer considered a benchmark and is removed. Possible explanations for lack of agreement in the two ranks may include union pressures or skill shortages in the external labor markets. Exhibit 4.13 reveals that the two rankings of benchmarks agree on all factors except experience/skills, and so the decisions that went into ranking this factor need to be reexamined. Perhaps the allocation of wages requires adjustment to bring the ranks into agreement.

EXHIBIT 4.13
Comparison of Factor and Wage Allocation Ranks

		Mental Requirements		Experience/ Skills		Physical Factors		Supervision		Other Responsibilities	
	Benchmark Jobs	Factor Rank	Wage Rank	Factor Rank	Wage Rank	Factor Rank	Wage Rank	Factor Rank	Wage Rank	Factor Rank	Wage Rank
A.	Punch press	6	6	5	6	2	2	4	4	4	4
B.	Parts attendant	5	5	3	4	3	3	6	6	1	1
C.	Riveter	4	4	6	2	1	1	1	1	3	3
D.	Truck operator	3	3	1	1	6	6	5	5	6	6
E.	Machine operator	2	2	2	3	4	4	2	2	5	5
F.	Parts inspector	1	1	3	5	5	5	3	3	2	2

EXHIBIT 4.14
Job Comparison Scale

$ Value	Mental requirements	Experience/ skills	Physical demands	Supervision	Other responsibilities
.00					
.20					
.40					Truck operator
.60			Truck operator	Parts attendant	Machine operator
					Punch press operator
					Riveter
.80	Punch press operator	Punch press operator		Truck operator	
1.00			STOCKER		STOCKER
.20			Parts inspector	Punch press operator	Parts inspector
.40	STOCKER			STOCKER	
				Parts inspector	
.60			Machine operator		
.80			Parts attendant		
2.00					
	Parts attendant				
.20		Parts inspector			
		Parts attendant			
.40			Punch press operator		
	Riveter		Riveter		
.60		STOCKER			Parts attendant
.80					
		Machine operator		Machine operator	
3.00		Riveter			
.20		Truck operator			
.40	Truck operator				
.60	Machine operator				
.80					
4.00					
.20					
.40					
	Parts inspector			Riveter	
.60					
.80					
5.00					

6. *Construct the job comparison scale.* Constructing a job comparison scale involves slotting benchmark jobs into a scale for each factor based on the amount of pay assigned to each factor. Such a scale is illustrated in Exhibit 4.14. Under mental requirements, the punch press operator is slotted at $.80, the parts attendant at $2.15, and so on. These slottings correspond to the wage allocations shown in Exhibit 4.11, as made by the compensation committee.

7. Apply the scale. The job comparison scale is the mechanism used to evaluate the remaining jobs. All the nonbenchmark jobs are now slotted into the scales under each factor at the dollar value thought to be appropriate. This is done by comparing the factors in the job descriptions of nonbenchmark jobs with the factors in the reference points. Consider nonbenchmark job parts stocker. The evaluator reads the stocker job description, examines the first compensable factor on the job comparison scale (mental requirements), and locates two benchmark jobs between which the mental requirements of the stocker job ranks. After examining the job descriptions for punch press operator and parts attendant, the stocker job might be judged to require greater mental demands than those required for the punch press operator but less than those for the parts attendant, and might be slotted at a rate of $1.40 for mental requirements. The same procedure is carried out for each of the other factors. To calculate the wage rate for each job, the dollar values assigned on the job comparison scale for all the factors are simply added. For the stocker job, the rate is $7.40 (mental requirements = $1.40, experience = $2.60, physical demands = $1.00, supervision = $1.40, and other responsibilities = $1.00).

Only about 10 percent of employers using formal job evaluations use the factor comparison approach.[32] The method is complex and difficult to explain, not only to dissatisfied employees but also to managers, equal employment opportunity agencies, or judges assessing the "fairness" of pay rates for jobs in lawsuits.

Not only are factor comparison plans difficult to explain, but the agreed-upon wage rates of the benchmark jobs are probably going to change. As they do, the relationships among the jobs may change, and the allocation of the wages among the factors must be readjusted. So continuous updating is required.

In spite of these difficulties, the factor comparison approach represents a significant change from simple ranking and classification. First, the criteria for evaluating jobs, the compensable factors, are made explicit. While some adaptations of the ranking method do specify compensable factors and some applications of classifications define the classes in terms of such factors, the factor comparison method requires that factors be more completely defined. Second, the use of existing wage rates of benchmark jobs as one of the criteria for designing and explaining the pay structure is unique. In a sense, factor comparison more systematically links external market forces with internal, work-related factors. Finally, in the factor comparison approach we see the use of a scale of degrees of worth (dollars) for each compensable factor in the job comparison scale. These three features—defining compensable factors, scaling the factors,

---

[32]Allan N. Nash and Stephen J. Carroll, Jr., *The Management of Compensation* (Belmont, Calif.: Wadsworth Publishing, 1975).

and linking an agreed-upon wage structure with the compensable factors—are the basic building blocks on which point plans are based. Point plans are probably the most common job evaluation method in use. We turn to point plans next.

POINT METHOD

Like factor comparison, designing a point system is rather complex and often requires outside assistance by consultants. But once designed, the plan is relatively simple to understand and administer. Point methods have three common characteristics: (1) compensable factors, with (2) factor degrees numerically scaled, and (3) weights reflecting the relative importance of each factor.

In point methods, each job's relative value, and hence its location in the pay structure, is determined by the total points assigned to it. A job's total point value is the sum of the numerical values for each degree of compensable factor that the job possesses. In the illustration in Exhibit 4.15 the point plan has four factors: skills required, effort required, responsibility, and working conditions. There are five degrees of each factor. In addition to factor definitions, the evaluator will be guided by benchmark jobs and/or written descriptions that illustrate each degree of every factor. Thus, the evaluator chooses a degree for each factor according to the correspondence between the job being evaluated and the benchmark jobs or descriptions for each factor scale.

Additionally, factors may be weighted. For example, in Exhibit 4.15, skills required carries a greater weight (40 percent of the total points) for this employer than does working conditions (10 percent of the total points). Thus a job's 240 total points may result from two degrees of skills required ($2 \times 40 = 80$), three each of effort required ($3 \times 30 = 90$) and responsibility ($3 \times 20 = 60$), and one of working conditions ($1 \times 10 = 10$); ($80 + 90 + 60 + 10 = 240$). Weighting reflects the relative value of a factor to an employer.

Once the total points for all jobs are computed and a hierarchy based on points established, then jobs are compared to each other to ensure that their relative locations in the hierarchy are acceptable.

EXHIBIT 4.15
Characteristics of the Point Method of Job Evaluation: Factors, Scaled Degrees, Weights

(3) Weights	(1) Factors	(2) Degrees				
40%	Skills required	1	2	3	4	5
30%	Effort required	1	2	3	4	5
20%	Responsibility	1	2	3	4	5
10%	Working conditions	1	2	3	4	5

DESIGNING THE POINT PLAN

Exhibit 4.16 illustrates the steps in the design of a point plan. As with all job evaluation plans, the first step is job analysis. The next steps are to choose the factors, scale them, and establish the factor weights. The end product of the design phase is a job evaluation plan that can be used to evaluate all other jobs.

EXHIBIT 4.16
Steps in Design of Point Job Evaluation

1. Conduct job analysis.
2. Choose compensable factors.
3. Establish factor scales.
4. Derive factor weights.
5. Prepare evaluation manual.
6. Apply to nonbenchmark jobs.

Conduct Job Analysis

Information about the jobs to be evaluated is the cornerstone of all job evaluation. While ideally, all jobs will be analyzed, the relevant work content—the behaviors, tasks performed, abilities/skills required, and so on—of a representative sample of jobs forms the basis for deriving compensable factors.

Choose Compensable Factors

Compensable factors play a pivotal role in the point method. In choosing factors, an organization must decide: "What factors are valued in these jobs? What factors will be paid for in this work?" Compensable factors should possess the following characteristics:

Work related. They must be demonstrably derived from the actual work performed. Some form of documentation (i.e., job descriptions, job analysis, employee and/or supervisory interviews) must support the factors. Factors that are embedded in a work-related logic can help withstand a variety of challenges to the pay structure. For example, managers often argue that the salaries of their subordinates are too low in comparison to other employees or that the salary offered to a job candidate is too low for the job. Union members may question their leaders about why one job is paid differently from another. Allegations of illegal pay discrimination may be raised. Line managers, union leaders, and compensation specialists must be able to explain differences in pay among jobs. Hence, differences in factors that are work related help provide that rationale. Properly selected factors may even diminish the likelihood of the challenges arising.

Acceptable to the parties. Acceptance of the pay structure by managers and employees is critical. This is also true of the compensable factors used to slot jobs into the pay structure. To achieve acceptance of the factors, all the relevant parties' viewpoints need to be considered.

An example illustrates the point. A senior manager refused to accept a job evaluation plan unless the factor "working conditions" was included. The compensation specialist demonstrated through statistical analysis that working conditions did not vary enough among 90 percent of the jobs under study to have a meaningful effect on the resulting pay structure; therefore the compensation specialist did not want "working conditions" included. The manager rejected this data, noting that the compensation professional had never seen the other 10 percent of the jobs (in the plant's foundry). The manager knew that working conditions were important to the foundry employees. To get the plan and pay decisions based on it accepted, the compensation specialist redesigned the plan to include working conditions.

Business-related. Compensable factors need to be consistent with the organization's culture and values, its business directions, and the nature of the work. Any changes in the organization or its directions may necessitate changing factors. For example, Burlington Northern recently revised its job evaluation plan to more accurately reflect the changing nature of the organization. One of the changes was to omit the factor "number of subordinates supervised." While many plans include a similar factor, Burlington Northern decided that a factor that values increases to staff may run counter to the objective of reducing work force size. While major changes in organizations are not daily occurrences, when they do occur the factors need to be reexamined to ensure that they are consistent with the new circumstances.

In addition to being work related, business related, and acceptable, compensable factors should have (4) the ability to differentiate among jobs. As part of differentiating among jobs, each factor must be (5) unique from other factors. If two factors overlap in what they assess in jobs, then that area of overlap will contribute disproportionately to total job points, which may bias the results. Factor descriptions must also possess (6) clarity of terminology so that all concerned can understand and relate to them.

Approaches to Choosing Factors

There are two basic ways to select and define factors: Adopt factors from an existing standard plan, or custom design a plan. In practice most applications fall between these two. Standard plans often are adjusted to meet the unique needs of a particular organization, and many custom-designed plans rely heavily on existing factors.

Adapting factors from existing plans. Although a wide variety of factors are used in standard existing plans, they tend to fall into four generic groups: skills required, effort required, responsibility, and working conditions. These four were used originally in the National Electrical Manufacturers Association

EXHIBIT 4.17
Comparisons of Definitions of Skill Required as a Compensable Factor

National Metal Trades Association	General Schedule (GS) System for Federal Government	Hay System	Cooperative Wage Study
Education. Trades training or knowledge required to perform the job. This job knowledge may be acquired either by formal education or by training on jobs of lesser degree.	*Knowledge required by the positions.* The nature and extent of information or facts which the workers must understand to do acceptable work (e.g., steps, procedures, practices, rules, policies, theories, principles, and concepts) and the nature and extent of the skills needed to apply those knowledges.	*Know-how.* The sum total of every kind of skill, however acquired, required for acceptable job performance. This sum total which comprises the over-all "savvy" has three dimensions—the requirements for: (a) Practical procedures, specialized techniques, and scientific disciplines.	*Employment training.* The mentality required to absorb training and exercise judgment for the satisfactory performance of the job. This mentality may be the result of native intelligence, and schooling or self study.
Training and experience. Appraises the length of time required by a person with the preemployment training to learn to produce work of required quality and quantity to justify continued employment.	*Supervisory controls.* The nature and extent of direct or indirect controls exercised by the supervisor, the employee's responsibility, and the review of completed work.	(b) Know-how of integrating and harmonizing the diversified functions involved in managerial situations occurring in operating, supporting, and administrative fields. This Know-how may be exercised consultatively (about management) as well as executively and involves in some combination the areas of organizing, planning, executing, controlling and evaluating.	*Employment training and experience.* The time required to learn how to do the job, producing work of acceptable quality and of sufficient quantity to justify continued employment. Consideration must be given to the necessary time spent on *directly related* work in addition to the necessary time spent on the job being classified.
Initiative and ingenuity. The independent action, use of judgment, the making of decisions and the amount of resourcefulness and planning the job requires based on the degree of the complexity of the work.	*Guidelines.* The nature of guidelines and the judgment needed to apply them. *Complexity.* The nature, number, variety, and intricacy of tasks, steps, processes, or methods in the work performed; the difficulty in identifying what needs to be done; and the difficulty and originality involved in performing the work.	(c) Active, practicing, face to face skills in the area of human relationships.	*Mental skill.* The mental ability, job knowledge, judgment and ingenuity required to visualize, reason through, and plan the details of a job without recourse to supervision. *Manual skill.* The physical or muscular ability and dexterity required in performing a given job including the use of tools, machines and equipment.

(NEMA) plan in the 1930s and are also included in the Equal Pay Act (1963) to define equal work.[33]

While most point plans tend to use these generic factors, the methods of operationalizing them vary. For example, the skill required factor, as defined in some widely used standard plans, is compared in Exhibit 14.17. Each of these plans was originally developed for application to different job families. Skill required may be defined as "trades training or knowledge required—length of time required in preemployment training" (National Metal Trades Association), or "the nature and extent of information or facts which workers must understand to do acceptable work" (GS System for federal government), or "know-how. The sum total of every kind of skill" (Hay Guide Charts), and so on. Thus, generic standard factor definitions provide sufficient flexibility to permit including nuances from each organization's unique circumstances. (A typical skill-based job evaluation plan using points is shown in Appendix B.)

Many of the early point plans, such as the National Metal Trades Association (NMTA), National Electrical Manufacturers Association (NEMA), and the Steel Plan, were developed for nonexempt manufacturing and/or office jobs.[34] Since then, point plans have also been applied to managerial and professional jobs. The Hay Guide Chart—Profile Method, used by 5,000 employers worldwide (130 of the 500 largest U.S. corporations), is perhaps the most widely used.[35] The three Hay factors—know how, problem solving, and accountability—and an example of the guide charts are included in Appendix A in this chapter. Hay Associates does not define their guide chart–profile method as a variation of the point method. A senior principal states, "As a practitioner of this method, I can state unequivocally that it was and is considered by its developers and chief proponents as a variation of the factor comparison method, not

[33]William Gomberg, *A Labor Union Manual on Job Evaluation* (Chicago: Roosevelt College, Labor Education Division, 1947).

[34] Helen Baker and John M. True, *The Operation of Job Evaluation Plans* (Princeton, N.J.: Princeton University, Industrial Relations Section, 1947); William Gomberg, "A Collective Bargaining Approach to Job Evaluation," *Labor and Nation,* November–December 1946, pp. 46–53; L. Cohen, "Union and Job Evaluation, *Personnel Journal,* May 1948, pp. 7–12; and Boris Shiskin, "Job Evaluation: What It Is and How It Works," *American Federationist,* July–September 1947, p. 213–22.

[35]Hay Associates, *The Guide Chart—Profile Method of Job Evaluation,* 1981. See also The Hay Group Annual Report, 1982; Edward N. Hay and Dale Purves, "A New Method of Job Evaluation," *Personnel,* July 1954, pp. 72–80; Edward N. Hay and Dale Purves, "The Profile Method of High-Level Job Evaluation," *Personnel,* September 1951, pp. 162–70; Edward N. Hay, "The Application of Weber's Law to Job Evaluation Estimates," *Journal of Applied Psychology* 34 (1950), pp. 102–4; Edward N. Hay, "Setting Salary Standards for Executive Jobs," *Personnel,* January/February 1958, pp. 18–21; Edward N. Hay, "Any Job Can be Measured by Its Know, Think, Do Elements," *Personnel Journal,* April 1958, pp. 24–30. See also *Management Job Evaluation Plan,* Human Resources Department, AT&T, July 1979.

the point plan."[36] For Hay, the distinction rests on the importance attached to comparing jobs one to another on each factor as well as on the total point scores each job receives. Whether it is a point or factor comparison is less important than recognizing that it is a widely used plan that combines characteristics of both methods. In the light of the Hay plan's wide acceptance, the three factors may have implicitly become "universally accepted" descriptors of managerial work.

Adapting factors from existing plans usually involves relying on the judgment of a task force or job evaluation committee. More often than not the committee is made up of key decision makers (or their representatives) from various functions (or units, such as finance, operations, engineering, and marketing).

In the early 1940s, union-management task forces were commonly used to jointly develop job evaluation plans. In 1944, the Cooperative Wage Study (CWS) undertaken by 12 steel companies and the United Steel Workers designed an industry-wide point plan (the Steel Plan). Joint union-management development of compensable factors has recently resurfaced; AT&T and the CWA, and Borg Warner and the machinists' union are two examples. Not only is increased employee acceptance of a jointly developed plan likely, but employees provide valuable expertise since they are usually the most knowledgeable about the actual work performed.

Once the committee is formed, the compensation specialist often presents a set of factors commonly used in various standard plans. The committee reviews the factors and adjusts the definitions until agreement is reached. The chosen factors represent aspects of the work that the organization values. Factors are chosen based on the criteria noted earlier: work relatedness, applicability, acceptability, ability to differentiate among jobs, and clarity of terminology.

Custom designed factors. While modifying factors "borrowed" from standard plans remains a common approach to choosing factors, several employers have custom designed their own plans. Approaches vary, but typically it begins with a task force or committee representing key figures from management. To identify compensable factors involves getting answers to two basic questions:

1. What in the nature of these jobs (work) should we value and pay for?
2. Based on our operating and strategic objections, what should we value and pay for in these jobs?

Generating compensable factors is based on the key managers' judgments regarding what should be valued in the work itself and in the context of the business objectives.

---

[36]Martin G. Wolf, "Review of Elizur, Dov, Job Evaluation: A Systematic Approach," in *Personnel Psychology,* June 1982, pp. 614–18. See also Marsh W. Bates, "New Horizons in Job Weighting Systems," Speech given to the Applied Workshop on New Developments in Job Analysis and Job Weighting in Wage and Salary Administration, University of Chicago, January 29, 1981.

An example illustrates the process. J. C. Penney is designing a new managerial job evaluation plan. The process used to generate compensable factors involved over 5,000 of the 15,000 managers whose jobs would eventually be covered by the plan in meetings (e.g., "focus groups") which generated suggested compensable factors. A compensation committee combined the lists of factors, refined the factor definitions, and eliminated duplicates and overlapping factors. In the end, six compensable factors were approved by top management (decision making, impact on the company's objectives, communications, supervision and management, knowledge requirements, and internal and external contacts). Two additional factors (stress and employee development) were eliminated because after further discussions with the top executive management, Penney's decided that these two factors were difficult to quantify and tended to be a function of the person, not the job (i.e., what I find "stressful," you may find "energizing"). Since the compensable factors were suggested by such a cross section of the managers, there's little question of their acceptability to those same managers when used to determine pay structures.

A similar process was reportedly used at Control Data Corporation. Rather than using managers, Control Data used 26 top personnel officials to identify compensable factors. Presumably, these officials knew what operating management and employees thought should be valued. In both the J. C. Penney and CDC cases the compensable factors were further defined in terms of specific and detailed items or questions (approximately 7 to 10 per factor).

Obviously, custom designing factors is time-consuming and expensive. The argument in favor of it rests on the premise that these factors are more likely to be work related, business related, and acceptable to the employees involved than would the jobs under study. The disadvantages are the expense and time involved.

Establish Factor Scales

Once the factors to be included in the plan are chosen, scales reflecting the different degrees within each factor are constructed. Each degree may also be anchored by the typical skills, tasks, and behaviors taken from benchmark jobs that illustrate each factor degree. Exhibit 4.18 shows NMTA's scaling for the factor of knowledge.

A major problem in determining degrees is to make each degree equidistant from the adjacent degrees (interval scaling). Belcher suggests the following criteria for determining degrees: (1) limit to the number necessary to distinguish among jobs; (2) use understandable terminology; (3) anchor degree definition with benchmark job titles; and (4) make it apparent how the degree applies to the job.[37] Using too many degrees makes it difficult for evaluators to accurately

---

[37]Belcher, *Compensation Administration*.

EXHIBIT 4.18
Illustration of a Compensable Factor from National Metal Trades Association

---

1. Knowledge

This factor measures the knowledge or equivalent training
required to perform the position duties.

1st Degree

Use of reading and writing, adding and subtracting of whole numbers; following of instructions; use of fixed gauges, direct reading instruments and similar devices; where interpretation is not required.

2nd Degree

Use of addition, subtraction, multiplication and division of numbers including decimals and fractions; simple use of formulas, charts, tables, drawings, specifications, schedules, wiring diagrams; use of adjustable measuring instruments; checking of reports, forms, records and comparable data; where interpretation is required.

3rd Degree

Use of mathematics together with the use of complicated drawings, specifications, charts, tables; various types of precision measuring instruments. Equivalent to 1 to 3 years applied trades training in a particular or specialized occupation.

4th Degree

Use of advanced trades mathematics, together with the use of complicated drawings, specifications, charts, tables, handbook formulas; all varieties of precision measuring instruments. Equivalent to complete accredited apprenticeship in a recognized trade, craft or occupation; or equivalent to a 2-year technical college education.

5th Degree

Use of higher mathematics involved in the application of engineering principles and the performance of related practical operations, together with a comprehensive knowledge of the theories and practices of mechanical, electrical, chemical, civil or like engineering field. Equivalent to complete 4 years of technical college or university education.

---

choose the appropriate degree and may result in a wide variance in total points assigned by different evaluators, which reduces the acceptability of the system.

Some plans employ two-dimensional grids to define degrees. For example, in the Hay Plan, degrees of the factor know-how are described by four levels of managerial know-how (limited, related, diverse, and comprehensive) and eight levels of technical know-how (ranging from professional mastery through elementary vocational). An evaluator may select among at least 32 ($=4 \times 8$) different combinations of managerial and technical know-how to evaluate a job.[38]

Derive Factor Weights

Once the degrees have been assigned, the factor weights must be determined. Exhibit 4.19 shows different weights assigned to factors in different point plans for managerial positions. For example, the National Electrical Manufacturers Association plan weights education at 17.5 percent; another employers associ-

---

[38]Actually, the different degrees of know-how are greater, since each of the subscales (technical and managerial) are further refined.

EXHIBIT 4.19
Factors and Weights: Point Plans, Managerial Jobs

Factors	NEMA	Employers' Association	Consultant	Trade Association	Appliance Manufacturer
Education	17.5	10.6	15.0	12.3	
Experience	29.0	16.0	9.0	19.0	10.1
Training			9.0		10.1
Complexity	14.5	10.6		12.3	
Mental skill			27.0	3.3	48.2
Responsibility for:					
Function		10.6	22.0		
Procedures		6.3			
Confidential data		4.2		3.3	
Assets		8.0			
Errors				11.0	11.6
Monetary responsibility	8.8				
Contacts	8.8	8.0	7.0	11.0	10.8
Working conditions	3.8	3.7	5.0	3.3	9.2
Hazards		7.0			
Type of supervision	8.8	7.5	3.0	11.0	
Extent of supervision	8.8	7.5	3.0	13.5	
Total	100.0	100.0	100.0	100.0	100.0

Source: David W. Belcher, *Compensation Administration* (Englewood Cliffs, N.J.: Prentice-Hall, 1974), p. 190.

ation weights it at 10.6 percent; a consultants' plan recommends 15.0 percent; and a trade association weights the same factor at 10.1 percent.

Factor weights are important since different weights reflect differences in importance attached to each factor by the employer.

There are two basic methods used to establish factor weights: committee judgment and statistical analysis. In the first, members of the compensation committee or, in some rare cases, groups of employees are asked to allocate 100 percent of value among the factors. Some structured decision process such as delphi or other nominal group technique may be used to facilitate consensus.[39] Using this approach, the weights reflect the decision makers' judgments about "what is the relative importance of each of the factors to the organization?" Different decision makers facing different circumstances may answer differently.

In the statistical approach, the weights are empirically derived in such a way as to correlate as closely as possible to a set of pay rates that is agreed upon by the parties involved.[40] Typically those rates are the agreed-upon pay structure for benchmark jobs. By statistically analyzing an agreed-upon pay

---

[39]Dov Elizur, *Job Evaluation: A Systematic Approach* (London: Gower Press, 1980); Dov Elizur, "The Scaling Method of Job Evaluation," *Compensation Review,* Third Quarter 1978, pp. 34–46; Dov Elizur and Louis Guttman, "The Structure of Attitudes toward Work and Technological Change within an Organization," *Administrative Science Quarterly* 21 (December 1976), pp. 611–21.

[40]Andre L. Delbecq, Andrew H. Van de Ven, and David H. Gustafson, *Group Techniques for Program Planning: A Guide to Nominal Group and Delphi Processes* (Glenview, Ill.: Scott, Foresman, 1975); and D. D. Robinson, O. W. Wahlstrom, and R. C. Mecham, "Comparison of Job

structure for benchmark jobs on the factor degrees assigned to each job, a set of weights is derived that will produce total job evaluation scores that will closely match the agreed-upon pay structure.

This statistical approach is not new. Edwards, and Otis and Leukart both used it in the 1940s.[41] More recently this approach has been used to establish weights for factors derived from quantitative job analysis procedures such as the Position Analysis Questionnaire and the Management Position Questionnaire.[42]

Choosing the criterion. The relative weights can reflect whatever criterion is specified. The choice of the criterion becomes a critical decision since the factor weights will be modeled to reproduce it. Most often the criterion has been wage rates for benchmark jobs. But many people object to this criterion, because they believe wage rates for clerical jobs have been artificially depressed due to historic sex discrimination.[43] Replicating the existing wage structure, they say, perpetuates this discrimination. Other possible criteria include a set of wage rates that have been negotiated with employees through collective bargaining. So the criterion may be either external (wage rates) or internal (negotiated rates). The same statistical procedure could be used to capture any pay structure agreeable to the parties involved. For example, the American Federation of State, County, and Municipal Employees negotiated equity pay adjustments for jobs held predominantly by women with the city of San Jose to satisfy a concern about comparable worth.[44] This new pay structure can be described

---

Evaluation Methods: A 'Policy-Capturing' Approach Using the PAQ," *Journal of Applied Psychology* 59, no. 5 (1974), pp. 633–37.

[41]Paul M. Edwards, "Statistical Methods in Job Evaluation," *Advanced Management,* December 1948, pp. 158–63; and J. L. Otis and R. H. Leukart, *Job Evaluation: A Basis for Sound Wage Administration* (Englewood Cliffs, N.J.: Prentice-Hall, 1954). See also Eugene J. Benge, "Statistical Study of a Job Evaluation Point System," *Modern Management,* April 1947, pp. 17–23.

[42]Jeffrey J. McHenry and M. D. Dunnette, "Development of a Computer-Assisted Management Job Analysis and Job Evaluation System for J. C. Penney," *Technical Report* 105 (Minneapolis: Personnel Decisions Research Institute, March 1986). The student case manual that accompanies this text, *Cases in Compensation* (Ithaca, N.Y.: Compensation, Box 4673; 1987) contains more detailed information on regression analysis. Also see Ernest J. McCormick, "Job and Task Analysis," in *Handbook of Industrial and Organizational Psychology,* ed. M. D. Dunnette (Chicago: Rand McNally, 1976); Walter Tornow and Patrick Pinto, "The Development of a Managerial Job Taxonomy: A System for Describing, Classifying, and Evaluating Executive Office Positions," *Journal of Applied Psychology* 61 (1976), pp. 410–18; and P. R. Jeanneret, "Equitable Job Evaluation and Classification with the PAQ," *Compensation Review,* First Quarter 1980, pp. 32–42.

[43]Donald J. Treiman, "Effect of Choice of Factors and Factor Weights in Job Evaluation," in *Comparable Worth and Wage Discrimination,* ed. H. Remick (Philadelphia: Temple University Press, 1984), pp. 79–89.

[44]Susan L. Josephs, "Equal Pay and Comparable Worth: Collective Bargaining Approaches," unpublished paper, Columbus: Ohio State University; Winn Newman, "Pay Equity Emerges as a Top Labor Issue in the 1980's," *Monthly Labor Review,* April 1982, pp. 49–51; and the MacNeill/Lehrer Report, "Wage Discrimination," Library #1287, Show #6047, New York: Educational Broadcasting Corporation, September 2, 1980.

statistically with an adjusted set of factor weights, and an adjusted job evaluation plan would be capable of reproducing the new pay structure.

The statistical approach is often labeled as *policy capturing* to contrast it with the committee judgment approach. Both approaches are "policy capturing"; only the policy or criterion captured may vary and the method used to capture that policy may vary (statistical versus judgmental).

Are factor weights even required? A recent study at AT&T and another at J. C. Penney raised that question when they found that their evaluations yielded an agreed-upon hierarchy of benchmark jobs without the use of factor weights.[45] The compensable factors, degrees, and specific skills required in the jobs are so richly defined in the AT&T and the J. C. Penney plans that the factors' relative importance is apparently captured without explicitly identifying weights.

Initial results of either the committee judgment or statistical approach for deriving factor weights may not lead to completely satisfactory results. The correspondence between the job evaluation results and the agreed-upon pay structure may not be sufficiently high. Several procedures are commonly used to increase this correspondence. First, the sample of benchmark jobs is often changed through adding or deleting key jobs. Second, the factor degree assigned to each key job may be adjusted. Third, the pay structure serving as criterion may be adjusted. And finally, the weighting scheme may be adjusted. Thus, a task force beginning with exactly the same factors and degrees could end up with very different job evaluation plans, depending on the specific benchmark jobs, the pay structure chosen as the criterion, and the method used to establish the weights. *How many factors?* A remaining issue to consider is how many factors should be included. We have already noted that factors must often be included to ensure the plan's acceptance. About 40 years ago Lawshe and others demonstrated that a few factors will yield practically the same results as many factors.[46] Some factors may have overlapping definitions and may fail to account for anything unique in the criterion chosen. In multifactor plans, three to five factors ex-

[45]Ken Ross, "Occupational Job Evaluation Study," unpublished report, Basking Ridge, New Jersey: AT&T, 1983. See also F. L. Schmidt, "The Relative Efficiency of Regression and Simple Unit Predictor Weights in Applied Differential Psychology," *Educational and Psychological Measurement* 31 (1971), pp. 699–713; *Your General Management Position Summary* (New York: J. C. Penney Company, 1986); and McHenry and Dunnette, "Development of a Computer-Assisted Management Job Analysis."

[46]C. H. Lawshe, Jr., "Studies in Job Evaluation. 2. The Adequacy of Abbreviated Point Ratings for Hourly-Paid Jobs in Three Industrial Plants," *Journal of Applied Psychology,* June 1945, pp. 177–84; C. H. Lawshe, Jr., and R. F. Wilson, "Studies in Job Evaluation. 6. The Reliability of Two Point Rating Systems," *Journal of Applied Psychology,* August 1947, pp. 355–65; and C. H. Lawshe, Jr., Edmund E. Dudek, and R. F. Wilson, "Studies in Job Evaluation. 7. A Factor Analysis of Two Point Rating Methods of Job Evaluation," *Journal of Applied Psychology,* 1948, pp. 118–29; Milton K. Davis and Joseph Tiffin, "Cross Validation of an Abbreviated Point Job Evaluation System," *Journal of Applied Psychology* 34, no. 4 (August 1950), pp. 225–28; and R. C. Rogers, "Analysis of Two Point-Rating Job Evaluation Plans," *Journal of Applied Psychology,* December 1946, pp. 579–85.

plained most of the variation in the job hierarchy. In a study conducted almost 20 years ago, a 21-factor plan produced the same job structure that could be generated using only 7 of the factors. Further, the jobs could be correctly slotted into classes using only three factors. Yet the company decided to keep the 21-factor plan because it was "accepted and doing the job."

SINGLE FACTOR SYSTEMS

Single factor job evaluation systems have been proposed by some researchers. They all appear to focus on measuring the amount of discretion an employee has in a job. The two most widely known are Jaques's Time Span of Discretion (TSD) and Arthur Young's Decision Banding.[47] In Time Span of Discretion, each job is comprised of tasks, and each task has an implicit or explicit time before its consequences become evident. Jaques defines TSD as "the longest period of time in completing an assigned task that employees are expected to exercise discretion with regard to the pace and quality of the work without managerial review."[48] According to Jaques, TSD is distinct from job evaluation in that it represents measurement (of time units) rather than subjective judgment.

The single factor used in the Decision Banding method is the decision making required on the job.[49] It identifies six types of decisions that may be required in a job; these range from defined decisions (the simplest) to policy decisions (the most complex) and are shown in Exhibit 4.20. Under the Decision

---

[47]Elliott Jaques, *Equitable Payment* (London: Heinemann, 1970); T. T. Paterson, *Job Evaluation,* Vol. 1 (London: Business Books Ltd., 1972); A. W. Charles, "Installing Single-Factor Job Evaluation," *Compensation Review,* First Quarter 1971, pp. 9–21; Jay R. Schuster, "Job Evaluation at Xerox: A Single Scale Replaces Four," *Personnel,* May/June 1966, pp. 15–23; Lee A. Chambliss, "Our Employees Evaluate Their Own Jobs," *Personnel Journal* 29, no. 4 (September 1950), pp. 141–42; Thomas J. Atchison, *A Comparison of the Time-Span of Discretion, A Classification Method of Job Evaluation and a Maturity Curve Plan as Methods of Establishing Pay Differentials for Scientists and Engineers Using Perceived Equity as a Criterion,* unpublished Doctoral Dissertation, Graduate School, University of Washington, Seattle, 1965; and T. T. Paterson, *Job Evaluation,* Vol. 2 (London: Camelot Press Ltd., 1972).

[48]Elliott Jaques, *Time Span Handbook* (London: Heinemann, 1964); Elliott Jaques, *Measurement of Responsibility* (London: Heinemann, 1972); and Elliott Jaques, "Taking Time Seriously in Evaluating Jobs," *Harvard Business Review,* September/October 1979, pp. 124–32. See also Michael E. Gordon, "An Evaluation of Jaques' Studies of Pay in the Light of Current Compensation Research," *Personnel Psychology* 4 (1969), pp. 369–89; Paul S. Goodman, "An Empirical Examination of Elliott Jaques' Concept of Time Span," *Human Relations* 20 (1967) pp. 155–70; T. O. Kvalseth and E. R. Crossman, "The Jaquesian Level-of-Work Estimators: A Systematic Formulation," *Organizational Human Performance* 11 (1974), pp. 303–15; J. M. M. Hill, "A Note on Time-Span and Economic Theory," *Human Relations,* November 1958, pp. 373–80.

[49]T. T. Paterson and T. M. Husband, "Decision-Making Responsibilities: Yardstick for Job Evaluation," *Compensation Review,* Second Quarter 1970, pp. 21–31; T. T. Paterson, "The Link between Pay and Decision-Making," *International Management,* December 1977, pp. 14–16; and N. H. Cuthbert and J. M. Paterson, "Job Evaluation: Some Recent Thinking and Its Place in an Investigation," *Personnel Management,* September 1966, pp. 152–62.

EXHIBIT 4.20
The Decision Band Method

Decision	Grade		Subgrade
Policy	11	Coordinating	1
Decisions that determine the scope, direction, and overall goals of the organization	10	Noncoordinating	3
	10		2
	10		1
Programming	9	Coordinating	2
	9		1
Decisions that result in programs to achieve the objectives established at Band F	8	Noncoordinating	3
	8		2
	8		1
Interpretive	7	Coordinating	2
	7		1
Decisions that translate the programs established at Band E into operational plans and schedules	6	Noncoordinating	3
	6		2
	6		1
Process	5	Coordinating	2
	5		1
Decisions concerned with the selection of a process for accomplishing the work	4	Noncoordinating	3
	4		2
	4		1
Operational	3	Coordinating	2
	3		1
Decisions on the carrying out of the operations of the selected process	2	Noncoordinating	3
	2		2
	2		1
Defined	1	Noncoordinating	3
Decisions on the manner and speed of performing the elements of an operation	1		2
	1		1

Typically 27 in total

EXHIBIT 4.21

BAND	GRADE	SUBGRADE	Job Description	
		*		ARTHUR YOUNG

JOB TITLE CONTROLLER	DEPARTMENT ACCOUNTING	JOB NO.

TITLE OF IMMEDIATE SUPERVISOR
VICE PRESIDENT, FINANCE

JOB SUMMARY

Maintains all accounting records and is responsible for developing, analyzing and interpreting statistical and accounting information for statutory and management purposes.

TASK LIST

TASK NO.	DESCRIPTION	FREQUENCY	BAND/GRADE
1.	Directs cost accounting, time-keeping, payroll and office service functions.	Daily 30%	D/6
2.	Develops and recommends inventory control procedures.	Monthly 5%	D/6
3.	Develops budgets and ensures adherence of user departments to budgeting guidelines.	Monthly 20%	D/6
4.	Interprets operating results of firm for senior management and recommends methods to reduce costs and improve profits.	Monthly 10%	D/6
5.	Acts as a liason with external auditors.	Annually	D/6
6.	Directs the preparation of quarterly and annual financial statements.	Quarterly Annually 15%	D/6
7.	Prepares and authorizes vouchers for payment by Treasurer's department.	Weekly 15%	C/4

ADDITIONAL NOTES OR COMMENTS

*This job would be graded Band D, Grade 6. Subgrade would be determined in relation to other D/6 jobs. As an example, if this job were assigned to the highest Subgrade in D/6, then the job would be denoted D/6-3.

APPROVED ON BEHALF OF JOB EVALUATION COMMITTEE	DATE

EXHIBIT 4.21 (*concluded*)

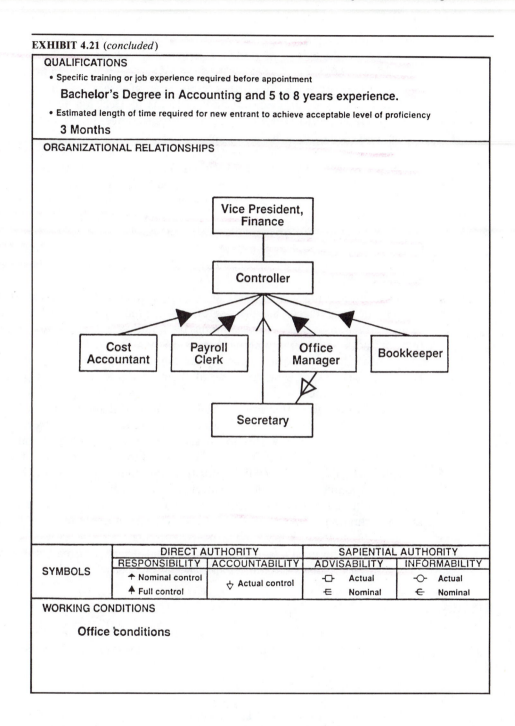

QUALIFICATIONS

• Specific training or job experience required before appointment

Bachelor's Degree in Accounting and 5 to 8 years experience.

• Estimated length of time required for new entrant to achieve acceptable level of proficiency

3 Months

ORGANIZATIONAL RELATIONSHIPS

	DIRECT AUTHORITY		SAPIENTIAL AUTHORITY	
SYMBOLS	RESPONSIBILITY	ACCOUNTABILITY	ADVISABILITY	INFORMABILITY
	⬆ Nominal control	⇩ Actual control	⊸⊐ Actual	⊸◯ Actual
	⬆ Full control		∈ Nominal	∈ Nominal

WORKING CONDITIONS

Office conditions

Banding approach, task statements obtained through job analysis are analyzed according to which type of decision each task involves. Each job is placed in the Decision Band that corresponds to the highest level of decision required for this job. There are similarities between time span of discretion (the longest period of time a task goes unreviewed) and decisions in Decision Banding. Both require an employee to exercise discretion. So discretion in the work appears to be the underlying factor in both plans.

The premise underlying these single factor approaches is that the job content or value construct is unidimensional. Elizur, for example, argues that job worth should be measured on the one dimension—freedom of action—which appears to be similar to both the discretion factor used by Jaques and the Decision Banding concept.[50] Elizur's research on over 4,500 jobs reveals that the freedom of action factor is made up of four other factors: freedom to change (e.g., to create), detail of instruction (e.g., general to detailed), supervision of the job (e.g., independent to detailed), and control over the job (e.g., periodic to permanent).

Perhaps the major complaint about single factor plans is from employees who are not convinced that one factor can adequately represent the entire domain of their jobs. Advocates counter by pointing out that the single factor (e.g., breadth of decision making) has component parts. Recall that acceptance of the procedure is critical in job evaluation. So employee confidence that the factors chosen insure wide coverage of their jobs is an important part to gain employee acceptance.

Finally, the job evaluation method chosen may shape the job analysis performed. Exhibit 4.21 shows a job description prepared using a Decision Banding approach. Notice how this job description, with its emphasis on decisions required in the job, differs from the one in Exhibit 4.9 and from those in the preceding chapters. These exhibits illustrate the interrelatedness of the steps involved in establishing a policy of internal consistency. For example, the information collected during job analysis needs to include data on the factors used in job evaluation. If you selected a Decision Banding approach or the Hay Plan (know-how, accountability, and problem solving) for evaluating jobs, you'd better collect the extent to which this factor(s) occurs in each job. So the job evaluation method chosen may shape the job analysis.

SUMMARY

The differences in pay among jobs within a single organization affect the ability of managers to achieve the objectives of the pay system. Together with job

---

[50]Dov Elizur, *Job Evaluation* (Hants, England: Gower Publishing, 1980) (Distributed in North America by Renouf/USA, Brookfield, Vt.); and Dov Elizur, "Facets of Work Values: A Structural Analysis of Work Outcomes," *Journal of Applied Psychology* 69, no. 3 (1984), pp. 379–89.

analysis, job evaluation techniques seek to ensure that the job structure is based on the content and relative contributions of the work.

Since its widespread use in the mid-1940s, job evaluation has evolved into many different forms and methods. Consequently, wide variations exist in its use and how it is perceived. This chapter discussed some of the many perceptions of job evaluation's role. No matter how job evaluation is designed, it should be tailored to the unique circumstances in each application.

At this point we have examined the alternative purposes of evaluation, whether to use single or multiple plans, and alternative job evaluation methods. In the next chapter we turn to ensuring the involvement of relevant parties, how to administer the plan once it has been designed, and evaluating its usefulness.

REVIEW QUESTIONS

1. What does job evaluation have to do with internal consistency?
2. What does job evaluation have to do with efficiency and equity?
3. Describe the major job evaluation decisions discussed so far.
4. Why are there so many definitions of job evaluation?
5. What are the pros and cons of using multiple evaluation plans within an organization?
6. Place the four basic job evaluation plans on a continuum of specificity, and discuss the major characteristics of each method.

Appendix A

The Hay Guide Chart—Profile Method of Position Evaluation (next five pages)

THE HAY GUIDE CHART

ILLUSTRATIVE

HAY GUIDE CHART—PROFILE METHOD
OF POSITION EVALUATION

INDUSTRIAL

Know-How DEFINITIONS

DEFINITION: Know-How is the sum total to every kind of skill, however acquired, required for acceptable job performance. This sum total which comprises the overall "savvy" has 3 dimensions — the requirements for:

1 Practical procedures, specialized techniques, and scientific disciplines.

2 Know-How of integrating and harmonizing the diversified functions involved in managerial situations occurring in operating, supporting, and administrative fields. This Know-How may be exercised consultatively (about management) as well as executively and involves in some combination the areas of organizing, planning, executing, controlling and evaluating.

3 Active, practicing, face-to-face skills in the area of human relationships (as defined at right).

MEASURING KNOW-HOW: Know-How has both scope (variety) and depth (thoroughness). Thus, a job may require some knowledge about a lot of things, or a lot of knowledge about a few things. The total Know-How is the combination of scope and depth. This comcept makes practical the comparison and weighing of the total Know-How content of different jobs in terms of: "How much knowledge about how many things."

3 **HUMAN RELATIONS SKILLS**

1. BASIC: Ordinary courtesy and effectiveness in dealing with others.

2. IMPORTANT: Understanding, influencing, and/or serving people are important, but not critical considerations.

3. CRITICAL: Alternative or combined skills in understanding, selecting, developing and motivating people are important in the highest degree.

KNOW-HOW

		MANAGERIAL KNOW-HOW											
		I. MINIMAL			II. RELATED			III. DIVERSE			IV. BROAD		
		1.	2.	3.	1.	2.	3.	1.	2.	3.	1.	2.	3.
A.	PRIMARY	50 57 57 66 66 76	57 66 76	66 76 87	66 76 87	76 87 100	87 100 115	87 100 115	100 115 132	115 132 152	115 132 152	132 152 175	152 175 200
B.	ELEMENTARY VOCATIONAL	66 76 87	76 87 100	87 100 115	87 100 115	100 115 132	115 132 152	115 132 152	132 152 175	152 175 200	152 175 200	175 200 230	200 230 264
C.	VOCATIONAL	87 100 115	100 115 132	115 132 152	115 132 152	132 152 175	152 175 200	152 175 200	175 200 230	200 230 264	200 230 264	230 264 304	264 304 350
D.	ADVANCED VOCATIONAL	115 132 152	132 152 175	(152) 175 200	152 175 200	175 200 230	200 230 264	200 230 264	230 264 304	264 304 350	264 304 350	304 350 400	350 400 460
E.	BASIC TECHNICAL-SPECIALIZED	152 175 200	175 200 230	200 230 264	200 230 264	230 264 304	264 304 350	264 304 350	304 350 400	350 400 460	350 400 460	400 460 528	460 528 608
F.	SEASONED TECHNICAL-SPECIALIZED	200 230 264	230 264 304	264 304 350	264 304 350	304 350 400	350 400 460	350 400 460	400 460 528	460 (528) 608	460 528 608	528 608 700	608 700 800
G.	TECHNICAL-SPECIALIZED MASTERY	(304) 350	304 350 400	350 400 460	350 400 460	400 460 528	460 528 608	460 528 608	528 608 700	608 (700)	608 700 800	700 800 920	800 920 1056
H.	PROFESSIONAL MASTERY	350 400 460	400 460 528	460 528 608	460 528 608	528 608 700	608 700 800	608 700 800	700 800 920	800 920 1056	800 920 1056	920 1056 1216	1056 1216 1400

KH	PS	AC	TOTAL
152			

SUPERVISOR KEY PUNCH

KH	PS	AC	TOTAL
304			

ACTUARIAL SPECIALIST
RESEARCH ASSOCIATE

KH	PS	AC	TOTAL
700			

AREA MANAGER

(Left vertical axis labels: PRACTICAL PROCEDURES — SPECIALIZED TECHNIQUES — SCIENTIFIC DISCIPLINES)

Problem Solving
DEFINITIONS

DEFINITION: Problem Solving is the original, "self-starting" thinking required by the job for analyzing, evaluating, creating, reasoning, arriving at and making conclusions. To the extent that thinking is circumscribed by standards, covered by precedents, or referred to others, Problem Solving is diminished, and the emphasis correspondingly is on Know-How.

Problem Solving has two dimensions:

1 The thinking environment in which the problems are solved.

2 The thinking challenge presented by the problem to be solved.

MEASURING PROBLEM SOLVING: Problem Solving measures the intensity of the mental process which employs Know-How to (1) identify, (2) define, and (3) resolve a problem. "You think with what you know." This is true of even the most creative work. The raw material of any thinking is knowledge of facts, principles and means; ideas are put together from something already there. Therefore, Problem Solving is treated as a percentage utilization of Know-How.

PROBLEM SOLVING

1 ⬇   2 ➡

	THINKING CHALLENGE					
	1. REPETITIVE	2. PATTERNED	3. INTERPOLATIVE	4. ADAPTIVE	5. UNCHARTED	
A. STRICT ROUTINE	10% 12%	14% 16%	19% 22%	25% 29%	33% 38%	A
B. ROUTINE	12% 14%	16% 19%	22% 25%	29% 33%	38% 43%	B
C. SEMI ROUTINE	14% 16%	19% 22%	25% 29%	33% 38%	43% 50%	C
D. STANDARDIZED	16% 19%	22% 25%	29% (33%)	38% 43%	50% 57%	D
E. CLEARLY DEFINED	19% 22%	25% 29%	33% 38%	43% 50%	57% 66%	E
F. BROADLY DEFINED	22% 25%	29% 33%	38% 43%	50% 57%	(66%) 76%	F
G. GENERALLY DEFINED	25% 29%	33% 38%	43% 50%	(57%) 66%	76% 87%	G
H. ABSTRACTLY DEFINED	29% 33%	38% 43%	50% 57%	66% 76%	87% 100%	H

KH	PS	AC	TOTAL
152	50		

SUPERVISOR KEY PUNCH

KH	PS	AC	TOTAL
304	200		

ACTUARIAL SPECIALIST
RESEARCH ASSOCIATE

KH	PS	AC	TOTAL
700	400		

AREA MANAGER

Accountability
DEFINITIONS

DEFINITION: Accountability is the answerability for action and for the consequences thereof. It is the measured effect of the job on end results. It has three dimensions in the **following order of importance.**

1 **FREEDOM TO ACT** — the degree of personal or procedural control and guidance as defined in the left-hand column of the chart.

2 **JOB IMPACT ON END RESULTS** — as defined at right.

3 **MAGNITUDE** — indicated by the general dollar size of the area(s) most clearly or primarily affected by the job.

2 **IMPACT OF JOB ON END RESULTS**

Indirect:

REMOTE: Informational, recording, or incidental services for use by others in relation to some important end result.

CONTRIBUTORY: Interpretive, advisory, or facilitating services for use by others in taking action.

Direct:

SHARED: Participating with others (except own subordinates and superiors), within or outside the organizational unit, in taking action.

PRIMARY: Controlling impact on end results, where shared accountability of others is subordinate.

ACCOUNTABILITY

1 ↓ **3** → **2** →

	(1) VERY SMALL OR INDETERMINATE				(2) SMALL				(3) MEDIUM				(4) L	
	R	C	S	P	R	C	S	P	R	C	S	P	R	C
A. PRESCRIBED	10	14	19	25	14	19	25	33	19	25	33	43	25	33
	12	16	22	29	16	22	29	38	22	29	38	50	29	38
	14	19	25	33	19	25	33	43	25	33	43	57	33	43
B. CONTROLLED	16	22	29	38	22	29	38	50	29	38	50	66	38	50
	19	25	33	43	25	33	43	57	33	43	57	76	43	57
	22	29	38	50	29	38	50	66	38	50	66	87	50	66
C. STANDARDIZED	25	33	43	57	33	43	57	76	43	57	76	100	57	76
	29	38	50	66	38	50	66	87	50	66	87	115	66	87
	33	43	57	76	43	57	76	100	57	76	100	132	76	100
D. GENERALLY REGULATED	38	50	66	87	50	66	87	115	66	87	115	152	87	115
	43	57	76	100	57	76	100	132	76	100	132	175	100	132
	50	66	87	115	66	87	115	152	87	115	152	200	115	152
E. DIRECTED	57	76	100	132	76	100	132	175	100	132	175	230	132	175
	66	87	115	152	87	115	152	200	115	152	200	264	152	200
	76	100	132	175	100	132	175	230	132	175	230	304	175	230
F. ORIENTED DIRECTION	87	115	152	200	115	152	200	264	152	200	264	350	200	264
	100	132	175	230	132	175	230	304	175	230	304	400	230	304
	115	152	200	264	152	200	264	350	200	264	350	460	264	350
G. BROAD GUIDANCE	132	175	230	304	175	230	304	400	230	304	400	528	304	400
	152	200	264	350	200	264	350	460	264	350	460	608	350	460
	175	230	304	400	230	304	400	528	304	400	528	700	400	528
H. STRATEGIC GUIDANCE	200	264	350	460	264	350	460	608	350	460	608	800	460	608
	230	304	400	528	304	400	528	700	400	528	700	920	528	700
	264	350	460	608	350	460	608	800	460	608	800	1056	608	800
I. GENERALLY UNGUIDED	304	400	528	700	400	528	700	920	528	700	920	1216	700	920
	350	460	608	800	460	608	800	1056	608	800	1056	1400	800	1056
	400	528	700	920	528	700	920	1216	700	920	1216	1600	920	1216

KH	PS	AC	TOTAL
152	50	66	268

SUPERVISOR KEY PUNCH

KH	PS	AC	TOTAL
304	200	115	619

ACTUARIAL SPECIALIST RESEARCH ASSOCIATE

KH	PS	AC	TOTAL
700	400	608	1708

AREA MANAGER

PROFILES CHECK EVALUATION JUDGEMENT

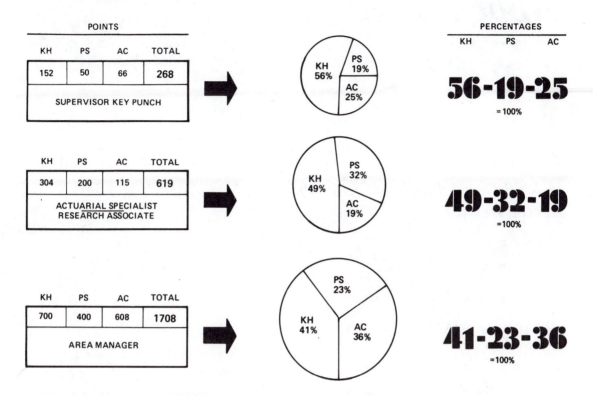

POINTS			
KH	PS	AC	TOTAL
152	50	66	268
SUPERVISOR KEY PUNCH			

KH 56%
PS 19%
AC 25%

PERCENTAGES		
KH	PS	AC

56-19-25
=100%

POINTS			
KH	PS	AC	TOTAL
304	200	115	619
ACTUARIAL SPECIALIST RESEARCH ASSOCIATE			

KH 49%
PS 32%
AC 19%

49-32-19
=100%

POINTS			
KH	PS	AC	TOTAL
700	400	608	1708
AREA MANAGER			

KH 41%
PS 23%
AC 36%

41-23-36
=100%

Appendix B

A Skill-Based Job Evaluation Plan for Manufacturing Jobs: Factor Definitions and Points

FACTOR 1: BASIC KNOWLEDGE

1st Degree (22 points)

Ability to read, write, add and subtract basic mathematics, interpret and complete simple instructions.

2nd Degree (47 points)

Knowledge of higher mathematical calculations such as basic decimal and fractional equations, ability to read and follow semicomplicated written instructions and to use basic measuring equipment.

3rd Degree (72 points)

Knowledge of a variety of manufacturing skills, specific training, work experience equivalent to trade school or high school, ability to read semicomplicated measuring equipment, graphics, technical or written reports.

4th Degree (111 points)

Extensive specific skills training in a specialized field; equivalent to one-two years of college or vocational (technical) training or master trade certificate.

FACTOR 2: ELECTRICAL/ELECTRONIC SKILLS

Application of the principles of electricity, electronics, electronic logic, and integrated transmission technologies such as lasers. This includes understanding of circuits, their component parts, and how they work together.

1st Degree (7 points)

Operational knowledge of electrical/electronic equipment without understanding the electrical/electronic principles on which the equipment operates.

2nd Degree (15 points)

Operational knowledge of electrical/electronic equipment with understanding the electrical/electronic principles on which the equipment operates.

3rd Degree (23 points)

Application of principles of electronic circuitry and appropriate wiring procedures.

4th Degree (37 points)

Application of principles of miniaturized electronic circuits and digital and analog transmission concepts.

FACTOR 3: MECHANICAL SKILLS

The application of mechanical knowledge of how/why mechanical equipment works. It includes the operation, repair, or maintenance of machinery/mechanical systems.

1st Degree (5 points)

This includes the use of basic mechanical ability to operate/adjust single or multiple pieces of mechanical or electromechanical equipment. It includes, but is not limited to, such elements as clearing jams and setting feed speeds and/or pressure changes.

2nd Degree (12 points)

This includes all elements of 1st Degree basic mechanical ability, with the exceptions that the incumbent is required to have the skills to perform preventive maintenance, disassemble/reassemble specific components, change tools, and the like.

3rd Degree (25 points)

Perform servicing and procedural repair activities on mechanical systems/machinery as the primary function.

4th Degree (31 points)

Apply advanced principles of mechanical skills to repair, rebuild, service to a close tolerance level of fit.

5th Degree (37 points)

Perform sophisticated diagnostic and repair activities on complex mechanical or electromechanical machinery/systems.

FACTOR 4: GRAPHICS

Reading, interpreting, and/or preparing graphic representations of information, such as maps, plans, drawings, blueprints, diagrams, schematics, and timing/flowcharts.

1st Degree (5 points)

Understand basic blueprints and/or prepare rough sketches.

2nd Degree (12 points)

Understand more complex blueprints and/or prepare simple graphic information.

3rd Degree (25 points)

Understand complex, technical graphic representations of information and/or prepare technical graphics.

4th Degree (31 points)

Prepare and/or interpret complex, technical graphic representations of a wide range of information.

5th Degree (37 points)

Develop, prepare, and/or interpret highly complex, sophisticated graphic representations.

FACTOR 5: MATHEMATICAL SKILLS

The selection and application of mathematical methods or procedures to solve problems or to achieve desired results.

1st Degree (8 points)

Simple arithmetic computations involving addition, subtraction, multiplication, or division.

2nd Degree (15 points)

Computations involving decimals, percentages, fractions, and/or basic statistics.

3rd Degree (23 points)

Computations involving algebra (e.g., solving for an unknown) or geometry (e.g., areas, volumes).

4th Degree (38 points)

Computations involving the use of trigonometry (properties of triangles and circles including sine, cosine, and tangent functions), logarithms and exponents, and advanced statistics.

FACTOR 6: COMMUNICATION/INTERPERSONAL SKILLS

This factor measures the scope and nature of relationships with others.

1st Degree (28 points)

Little or no contact with others. Relationships involve providing and/or receiving information or documents.

2nd Degree (56 points)

Some contact with others. Relationships often require explanation or interpretation of information.

3rd Degree (84 points)

Substantial contact with others. Relationships usually involve discussions with stakeholders or recommendations on issues regarding policies, programs, and so on. Impact is considerable and may be limited to individual departments/ programs.

4th Degree (140 points)

Extensive contact with others. Relationships usually include decisions in a broad sense and will affect several areas within the manufacturing unit.

FACTOR 7: SAFETY SKILLS

This factor measures the requirements for adherence to prescribed safety and personal security practices in the performance of required tasks. These safety and personal security practices are generally required to minimize exposure to hazard or risk in the work environment.

1st Degree (10 points)

Perform work in accordance with a few simple safety procedures to minimize potential for injury.

2nd Degree (40 points)

Perform work in accordance with several specific safety procedures to minimize potential for injury.

3rd Degree (80 points)

Perform work in accordance with a wide range of safety procedures to minimize some potential for injury.

4th Degree (100 points)

Perform work in a highly variable environment where safety principles and procedures need to be tailored to deal with unforeseen hazards to minimize high potential for serious injury.

FACTOR 8: DECISION MAKING/SUPERVISION REQUIRED

This factor measures the degree of decision making required without being checked by others, and the degree to which immediate supervisor is required to outline the procedures to be followed and/or the results to be attained on the job.

1st Degree (36 points)

Limited decision making by the incumbent. Progress of work is checked by others most of the time, and/or 60–90 percent of activities are defined by other than the incumbent.

2nd Degree (89 points)

Routine decision making based on specific criteria. Progress of work is often checked by others, and/or 40–60 percent of activities are defined by other than the incumbent.

3rd Degree (112 points)

Significant decision making based on established guidelines and experience. Progress of work is checked by others some of the time, and/or 25–40 percent of activities are defined by other than the incumbent.

4th Degree (180 points)

Extensive decision making based on broad policies, procedures, and guidelines. Progress of work is seldom checked by others, and/or less than 25 percent of activities are defined by other than the incumbent.

Chapter 5

Job Evaluation: Administration

American Telephone & Telegraph Co. for years had little competition in its business. Their local operating companies petitioned state commissions for rate changes which more often than not were not granted. Prices for phone services were calculated on some sense of "adequate return on investment." Profits generated by improved technology in long distance lines were used to hold down charges for local service. But antitrust lawsuits filed in the 1970s led to the breakup of AT&T in the 1980s. AT&T kept its long distance lines unit, its manufacturing unit (Western Electric), and its research arm (Bell Labs). They were integrated into two major business sections—regulated (long distance calls) and unregulated (information technologies, such as computers or switching equipment). Other subsidiaries and operating companies became completely separate business entities. For the first time, AT&T faced direct competition in both its regulated and unregulated businesses. The company became free to compete in the communications/information industry, and it transformed its basic business directions. Its objectives changed, and as a result, its compensation system also changed. For example, the management job evaluation plan at AT&T was redesigned to include compensable factors which more accurately reflect the new competitive environment. The company is asking, "What is it we want to pay for?" and it is getting a different set of answers than it did under its previous totally regulated environment. As a result of the changing business strategies and technological improvements, the work at nonmanagerial levels also has changed. More work involves information processing. Phones and other equipment are no longer owned, installed, and maintained by AT&T. Rather, the consumers now purchase and install such equipment. Even the telephone is changing. It is becoming a personal computer terminal that will be sold through phone stores and other retail outlets.

At the managerial level, the balance shifted from emphasis on government and public relations to increasing market share and profitability. While the job evaluation plans may retain a "skills required" factor, the nature of the required skills is being redefined and reweighted to reflect more accurately the changing environment, technologies, and strategies. At one newly created regional phone company, Bell South, the job evaluation plan was modified to reflect movement into new business ventures such as Hispanic yellow pages, automobile phones, and building services. So it is with other employers: the job evaluation system must be designed and administered in a manner consistent with the organizations' strategies and objectives.

We began our discussion of job evaluation in the previous chapter. Recall the major decisions already discussed: (1) determine the purpose of job evaluation, (2) decide whether to use a single or multiple plan, and (3) choose among job evaluation methods. The remaining decisions include: (4) ensure the involvement of relevant parties and (5) evaluate the plan's usefulness.

THE PARTIES INVOLVED IN JOB EVALUATION

Who should be involved in designing job evaluation? The choice is usually among compensation professionals, managers, and/or jobholders. If job evaluation is to be an aid to managers and if maximizing employee understanding and acceptance is an important objective, then all these groups need to be included.

Compensation/Job Evaluation Committees

A common approach to gaining acceptance and understanding of pay decisions is through use of a compensation (job evaluation) committee. Membership on these committees seems to vary among firms. All include representatives from key operating functions, and some even include nonmanagerial employees. In some cases the committee's role is only advisory; in others its approval may be required for all major changes.

The involvement of both operating managers and compensation professionals raises the potential for conflict due to their differing perspectives. For example, operating managers may wish to adjust the job title for a star performer, in order to exceed the maximum pay permitted for the present job title. The compensation specialist wishes to ensure that the policy of consistent treatment across the entire organization is followed and is aware of the difficulty caused by a title and pay change unconnected to a change in the actual work performed. Note the differences in focus. The manager has operating objectives to achieve, does not want to lose a key performer, and views compensation as a mechanism to help accomplish this. The compensation professional, on the other hand, focuses on ensuring that the system is managed consistently and is fairly applied throughout the organization.

Employee Participation

Employee participation in both the design and decisions involved in compensation is a key feature of what Lawler calls the "new pay."[1] He asserts that participation leads to increased trust, commitment, and perceptions of pay equity on the part of employees. Procedural equity, discussed in Chapter 2, is probably enhanced through this participation. Some research supports these contentions, but more is needed before we can be certain that the potential benefits from increased participation offset potential costs (time involved to reach consensus, potential problems caused by disrupting current perceptions, etc.).[2] Lawler and Hackman do report one study of a pay plan designed by a committee of employees and managers.[3] Within six months after the system went into

---

[1] E. E. Lawler III, "The New Pay," in *Current Issues in Human Resource Management,* ed. S. L. Rynes and G. T. Milkovich (Plano, Tex.: Business Publications, 1986).

[2] Jane Giacobbe, "An Examination of the Relationship between Perceived Justice of State Impasse Procedures and Perceived Equity of Teacher Pay," Ph.D. thesis, Cornell University, Ithaca, N.Y., 1986.

[3] Edward E. Lawler and J. Richard Hackman, "Impact of Employee Participation in the Development of Pay Incentive Plans: A Field Experiment," *Journal of Applied Psychology* 53, no. 6 (December 1969), pp. 467–71; D. E. Ewing, *Freedom Inside the Organization* (New York: E. P. Dutton, 1978); Carl F. Frost, John W. Wakely, and Robert A. Ruh, *The Scanlon Plan for Organization Development: Identity, Participation, and Equity* (East Lansing: Michigan State Press, 1974); E. E. Lawler, "Creating High Involvement Work Organizations," in *Perspectives on Organizational Behavior,* 2nd ed., ed. J. R. Hackman, E. E. Lawler, and L. W. Porter (New York: McGraw-Hill, 1982); K. C. Sheflen, E. E. Lawler, and J. R. Hackman, "Long-Term Impact of Employee Participation in the Development of Pay Incentive Plans: A Field Experiment Revisited," *Journal of Applied Psychology* 55 (1971), pp. 182–86; E. A. Locke and D. M. Schweiger, "Participation in Decision Making: One More Look," *Research in Organization Behavior* (Greenwich,

effect, significant improvements occurred in turnover and satisfaction with pay and administration. They attribute these improvements to employee participation.

To what extent should unions be involved? Management probably will find it advantageous to include union representation as a source of ideas and to help promote acceptance of the results. For example, both at AT&T and at a Borg-Warner facility, union-management task forces participated in the design of new job evaluation systems. Their roles involved mutual problem solving. Other union leaders feel that philosophical differences prevent their active participation in job evaluation.[4] They take the position that collective bargaining yields more equitable results than does job evaluation. In other cases, jobs are jointly evaluated by union and management representatives, and disagreements are submitted to an arbitrator. So the extent of union participation varies.

In 1971 and again in 1978, Janes surveyed the leaders of 38 unions representing over 7.2 million members.[5] While in 1971 the leadership viewed job evaluation as a threat to collective bargaining, by 1978 Janes identified a trend toward its acceptance. Leaders who oppose evaluation do so because they feel it is not understood by their members or because job descriptions on which evaluation is based may be poorly written. More recently a few leaders have advocated the adoption of job evaluation as a means of assessing comparable worth.[6] It appears that no single union perspective exists on the value of job evaluation, just as no single management perspective exists.

ADMINISTERING THE PLAN

Our previous chapter led us through the design of a job evaluation plan. The output of the design phase is a written manual to assist in applying the plan. The manual becomes the "yardstick" for the plan. It contains information on the job evaluation plan, including a description of the method used. If there are

---

Conn.: JAI Press, 1979); J. F. Carey, "Participative Job Evaluation," *Compensation Review,* Fourth Quarter 1977, pp. 29–38; and G. J. Jenkins, Jr., and E. E. Lawler III, "Impact of Employee Participation in Pay Plan Development," *Organizational Behavior and Human Performance* 28 (1981), pp. 111–28.

[4]Mike Burns, *Understanding Job Evaluation* (London: Institute of Personnel Management, 1978).

[5]Harold D. Janes, "Union Views on Job Evaluation, 1971 vs. 1978," *Personnel Journal,* February 1979, pp. 80–85; "Job Evaluation Plans," *Collective Bargaining Report,* June 1957, pp. 33–39.

[6]Winn Newman, "Pay Equity Emerges as a Top Labor Issue in the 1980s," *Monthly Labor Review,* April 1982, pp. 49–51; and Virginia Dean, Patti Roberts, Thomas Campanella, and John Henning, "Comparable Worth: Pros and Cons on a Controversial Issue," *California Public Employee Relations* 48 (March 1981), pp. 7–16; Lisa Portman, Joy Ann Grune, and Eve Johnson, "The Role of Labor," in *Comparable Worth and Wage Discrimination,* ed. H. Remick (Philadelphia: Temple University Press, 1984); and K. S. Koziara, "Comparable Worth: Organizational Dilemmas," *Monthly Labor Review,* December 1985, pp. 13–16.

compensable factors, these are defined in the manual, along with enough information to allow the user to recognize varying degrees of compensable factors. Information needs to be detailed enough to permit accurate and rapid evaluation of the bulk of jobs. Descriptions of all jobs are also often included.

Appeals/Review Procedures

No plan anticipates all situations. It is inevitable that some jobs will be incorrectly evaluated, or at least employees and managers may suspect incorrect evaluation. Consequently, the manual needs to contain review procedures to handle such cases and to help ensure procedural equity. Often the compensation specialist can handle most reviews, but sometimes the assistance of the compensation committee is required. Nevertheless a procedure for review should be developed and included in the manual to help ensure that employees can voice their questions and disagreements.

Training

Once the job evaluation manual is complete, those who will be applying the job evaluation methodology require training in its proper use, especially those evaluators who come from outside the personnel department.[7] These employees may also need background information on the entire pay system and how it is related to the overall strategies for managing human resources and the organization's objectives.

Evaluate Nonbenchmark Jobs

After evaluators are trained, the nonbenchmark jobs must be evaluated. (Benchmark jobs were already evaluated during the design phase.) In smaller firms, a personnel generalist may evaluate all the jobs alone. Larger firms may use their compensation committee. In committees, typically each member independently evaluates each job description.[8] These evaluations are then compared, with the evaluators explaining and defending their judgments if there is disagreement. If consensus does not emerge, employees with firsthand knowledge of the jobs may become part of the discussion. Eventually, a consensus about the job's proper evaluation emerges.

---

[7]Edward N. Hay, "Training the Evaluation Committee in Factor Comparison Job Evaluation," *Personnel,* July 1946, pp. 32–36.

[8]Harry Walter Daniels, "Winning Acceptance for the Job Evaluation Plan," *Personnel* 30, no. 1 (July 1953), pp. 30–33; Vincent S. Wilkins, "Seven Traps in Job Evaluation," *Management Review,* February 1961, pp. 120–29; G. K. Warner, "Using Salary Administration Committees Effectively," *Personnel Journal,* July/August 1961, pp. 116–18; Arthur H. Dick, "Job Evaluation's Role in Employee Relations," *Personnel Journal* 53, no. 3 (March 1974), pp. 176–79.

Approve and Communicate Results

When the evaluations are completed, approval by higher levels in the organization (e.g., vice president of human resources) is usually required. The particular approval process differs among organizations; Exhibit 5.1 is one example. The approval process serves as a control. It helps ensure that any changes that result from job evaluation are consistent with the rest of the organization's operations and directions.

The emphasis on employee and manager understanding and acceptance of the job evaluation requires that communications occur during the entire process. The goals of the system, the parties' roles in it, and the final results need to be explained.

Final Result: Structure

The final result of the administration phase is a hierarchy of jobs. This hierarchy translates the employers' internal consistency policy into practice. Exhibit 5.2 shows four hypothetical job structures within a single organization. These structures were obtained via different approaches to job evaluation. The jobs are arrayed in hierarchies within four basic functions: managerial, technical, manufacturing, and administration. The managerial structure was obtained via a point plan, technical and administrative jobs via two different classification plans, and the manufacturing hierarchy via a point system that was negotiated with the union. The point of Exhibit 5.2 is to illustrate the results of job evaluation: a job structure that should be consistent with the policy of internal consistency. The exhibit also illustrates that it is common for organizations to have multiple structures derived through multiple procedures. Consistency in such cases may be interpreted as consistency within each functional group or unit. While some employees in one job structure may wish to compare the procedures used in another structure versus their own, the underlying premise in the illustration and in practice is that internal equity (consistency) is most influ-

EXHIBIT 5.1
Job Evaluation Approval Process

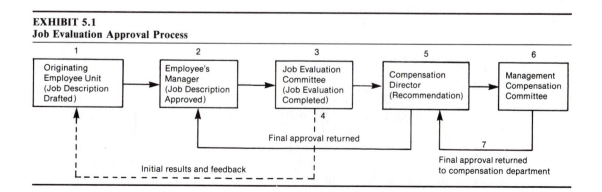

EXHIBIT 5.2
Resulting Job Structures

MANAGERIAL GROUP	TECHNICAL GROUP	MANUFACTURING GROUP	ADMINISTRATIVE GROUP
Vice Presidents		Assembler I Inspector I	Administrative Assistant
Division General Managers	Head/Chief Scientist	Packer	Principal Admin. Secretary
Managers	Senior Associate Scientist	Materials Handler Inspector II	Administrative Secretary
		Assembler II	Word Processor
Project Leaders	Associate Scientist	Drill Press Operator Grinder, Rough	
Supervisors	Scientist	Machinist I Coremaker	
	Technician		Clerk/Messenger

enced by fair and equitable treatment of employees doing similar work (other jobs in the same skill group) rather than dissimilar work. Some evidence supports this premise; however, little is known about the stability of such comparisons under different conditions.

Once the structure or structures are established, compensation managers must ensure that they remain equitable. This requires seeing that jobs which employees feel are incorrectly evaluated are reanalyzed and reevaluated (e.g., appeals/review procedures) and that new jobs or those that experience significant changes get submitted for evaluation.

EVALUATE JOB EVALUATION'S USEFULNESS

The usefulness of any management system is a function of how well it accomplishes its objectives. Job evaluation is no different; it needs to be judged in terms of its objectives. In the previous chapter we noted that pay structures are intended to influence a wide variety of employee behaviors, ranging from staying with an employer to investing in additional training and willingness to take on new assignments. Consequently, the structures obtained through job evaluation ought to be evaluated in terms of their ability to affect such decisions. Unfortunately, little of this type of evaluation seems to be done. More often than not, job structures are compared to what other employers are doing rather than to whether they aid employees and the organization.

On the other hand, the job evaluation procedures per se, rather than the structure obtained, have been subjected to extensive evaluation. In general, these efforts focus on job evaluation as a measurement device: its reliability, its validity, the costs included in design and implementation, and its compliance with laws and regulations. Ignored in these analyses has been research on the procedural equity of job evaluation. But let us review some of the work that has been reported.

Reliability: Consistency of Results

Job evaluation involves substantial judgment. Reliability refers to the consistency of results obtained from job evaluation conducted under different conditions. For example, to what extent do different job evaluators produce similar results? Few employers or consulting firms report the results of their studies. However, several research studies by academics have been reported.[9] These studies present a mixed picture; some report relatively high consistency (different evaluators assign the same jobs the same total point scores), while others report lower agreement on the values assigned to each specific compensable factor. Some evidence also reports that evaluators' background and training may

---

[9] Several studies on the reliability of job evaluation plans have been reported. Four reviews provide useful overviews: R. Arvey, "Potential Problems in Job Evaluation Methods and Processes," in *Compensation,* eds. L. Gomez-Mejia and D. Balkin (Englewood Cliffs, N.J.: Prentice-Hall, 1987); D. P. Schwab, "Job Evaluation and Pay Setting: Concepts and Practices," in *Comparable Worth: Issues and Alternatives,* ed. E. R. Livernash (Washington, D.C.: Equal Employment Advisory Council, 1980), pp. 49–78; R. J. Snelgar, "The Comparability of Job Evaluation Methods," *Personnel Psychology* 36 (1983), pp. 371–80; and R. M. Madigan, "Comparable Worth Judgments: A Measurement Properties Analysis," *Journal of Applied Psychology* 70 (1985), pp. 137–47. Other references include: G. Satter, "Method of Paired Comparisons and a Specification Scoring Key in the Evaluation of Jobs," *Journal of Applied Psychology* 33 (1949), 212–21; R. Richardson, *Fair Pay and Work: An Empirical Study of Fair Pay Perception and Time Span of Discretion* (Carbondale: Southern Illinois University Press, 1971); D. Doverspike and G. Barrett, "An Internal Bias Analysis of a Job Evaluation Instrument," *Journal of Applied Psychology* 69, no. 4 (1984), pp. 648–62; P. Ash, "The Reliability of Job Evaluation Rankings," *Journal of Applied Psychology* 32 (1948), pp. 313–20; D. J. Chesler, "Reliability and Comparability of Different Job Evaluation Systems," *Journal of Applied Psychology* 32 (1948), pp. 465–75; D. Doverspike, A. M. Carlisi, G. V. Barrett, and R. A. Alexander, "Generalizability Analysis of a Point-Method Job Evaluation Instrument," *Journal of Applied Psychology* 68 (1983), pp. 476–83; C. H. Anderson and D. B. Corts, *Development of a Framework for a Factor Ranking Benchmark System of Job Evaluation,* TS-73-3 (Washington, D.C.: U.S. Civil Service Commission, Personnel Research and Development Center, 1973); and R. D. Arvey, S. E. Maxwell, and L. M. Abraham, "Reliability Artifacts in Comparable Worth Procedures," *Journal of Applied Psychology* 70, no. 4 (1985), pp. 695–705.

affect consistency of the evaluations.[10] An evaluator's affiliation with union or management appears to have little effect on the consistency of the results.[11]

Using evaluators who are familiar with the jobs appears to enhance reliability.[12] This result lends support to the practice of involving employees in the evaluation process. One study reports that the job evaluation results obtained through a group consensus process were similar to those obtained by independent evaluators or an average of individual evaluator's results.[13] The group consensus process, a device widely used in practice, has each evaluator make a preliminary independent evaluation. Then, meeting as a job evaluation committee, they discuss their results until consensus emerges.

While all this research is interesting, it fails to address the key issue—to what extent does the degree of reliability of job evaluation influence pay decisions and employees' attitudes and work behaviors? Only one study has directly addressed this issue. In it, Madigan examined three different job evaluation plans: a guide chart method similar to the Hay Guide Charts presented in the appendix of the last chapter, the Position Analysis Questionnaire discussed in Chapter 3, and a custom-designed point plan using six factors (knowledge, experience, interpersonal skill, supervisory, decision making, and fiscal responsibilities).[14] He found that interrater evaluations (consistency among raters) was high and compared favorably to results of studies discussed above. However, when he examined the impact of the results from different plans on actual pay decisions, he found significant differences. For example, when different evaluators used the custom-designed point plan (the most reliable one), Madigan found that their pay recommendations for the jobs agreed in only 51 percent of jobs. The differences in results translated into a range of ± 160 evaluation

---

[10]Richard D. Arvey, Emily M. Passino, and John W. Lounsbury, "Job Analysis Results as Influenced by Sex of Incumbent and Sex of Analyst," *Journal of Applied Psychology* 62, no. 4 (1977), pp. 411–16; Carol T. Schreiber, "Job Evaluation and the Minority Issue." Paper presented at Industrial Relations Counselors Symposium, Atlanta, Georgia, September 1978, pp. 14–15; J. Goodman and J. Morgan, "Job Evaluation Without Sex Discrimination," *Personnel Management* 11, no. 10, October 1979, pp. 158–67; Catherine M. Meek, "Auditing Your Job Evaluation Plan—A Case Study," *EEO Today,* Spring 1979, pp. 21–27.

[11]C. H. Lawshe, Jr., and P. C. Farbo, "Studies in Job Evaluation: 8. The Reliability of an Abbreviated Job Evaluation System," *Journal of Applied Psychology* 33 (1949), pp. 158–66; Francis D. Harding, Joseph M. Madden, and Kenneth Colson, "Analysis of a Job Evaluation System," *Journal of Applied Psychology,* no. 5 (1960), pp. 354–57; F. G. Moore, "Statistical Problems in Job Evaluation," *Personnel,* September 1946, pp. 125–36; Marvin G. Dertien, "The Accuracy of Job Evaluation Plans," *Personnel Journal,* July 1981, pp. 566–70.

[12]J. M. Madden, "The Effect of Varying the Degree of Rater Familiarity in Job Evaluation," *Personnel Administrator* 25 (1962), pp. 42–45; R. E. Cristal and J. M. Madden, *Effect of Degree of Familiarity in Job Evaluation* (Lackland Air Force Base, Tex.: Personnel Laboratory, Wright Air Development Division, 1960).

[13]D. P. Schwab and H. G. Heneman III, "Assessment of a Consensus-Based Multiple Information Source Job Evaluation System," *Journal of Applied Psychology,* in press.

[14]Madigan, "Comparable Worth Judgments."

points, which meant significant differences in the pay for employees. Madigan points out that by traditional academic standards, the reliability of these three methods was acceptable. However, from a compensation manager's perspective, it is not. Madigan observes, "The assessment of potential error . . . in job evaluation must go beyond reliability estimates to include the estimates of impact on pay decisions."[15]

Validity: Which Method Does the Job?

The choice among ranking, classification, factor comparison, and point methods depends on the circumstances and objectives faced. Does it make any difference? Do the results obtained differ?

Validity refers to the degree to which a job evaluation method yields the desired results. The desired results can be measured several ways: (1) the hit rate (percentage of correct decisions it makes), (2) convergence (agreement with results obtained from other job evaluation plans), and (3) employee acceptance (employee and manager attitudes about the job evaluation process and the results).[16]

Hit rates: Agreement with predetermined benchmark structures. The hit rate approach focuses on the ability of the job evaluation plan to replicate a predetermined, agreed-upon job structure. The agreed-upon structure, as we discussed in the last chapter, can be based on several factors: the jobs' market rates, or a structure negotiated with a union or a management committee, or some combination of these. Exhibit 5.3 shows the hit rates for a hypothetical job evaluation plan. The agreed-upon structure has 49 benchmark jobs in it. This structure was derived through negotiation among managers serving on the job evaluation committee. The job evaluation plan results correctly placed only 14, or 29 percent, of the jobs into their current (agreed-upon) pay classes and comes within ± one pay class for 82 percent of the jobs in the agreed-upon structure. In a study conducted at Control Data Corporation, Gomez-Mejia, Page, and Tornow reported hit rates for six different plans ranging from 49 to 73 percent of the jobs classified within ± 1 class of their current, agreed-upon classes.[17] In another validation study Madigan and Hoover applied two job

---

[15]Ibid.

[16]Validity can also be reflected in the R^2 and standard error of estimate generated via regressing benchmark job's wages on compensable factors. R^2 alone is insufficient because it only reflects the strength of the relationship. The error terms are also important, since they reflect the precision with which job grade and pay decisions can be made. Hit rates, in a general sense, capture the R^2 and standard error information. For an early discussion of validation and job evaluation, see William M. Fox, "Purpose and Validity in Job Evaluation," *Personnel Journal* 41 (1962), pp. 432–37.

[17]L. R. Gomez-Mejia, R. C. Page, and W. W. Tornow, "A Comparison of the Practical Utility of Traditional, Statistical, and Hybrid Job Evaluation Approaches," *Academy of Management Journal* 25 (1982), pp. 790–809.

EXHIBIT 5.3
Illustration of Plan's Hit Rate as a Method to Judge the Validity of Job Evaluation Results

Job evaluation: Accuracy of job class estimated	Number of benchmark jobs	Hit rate (percent)
−2	5	10%
−1	11	23%
Correct evaluation	14	29%
+1	15	30%
+2	4	8%
	49	100%

The 23%, 29%, and 30% are bracketed together as — 82%

evaluation plans (a modification of the federal government's Factor Evaluation System discussed in Chapter 4 and the Position Analysis Questionnaire) to 206 job classes for the state of Michigan.[18] They reported rates ranging from 27 to 73 percent, depending on the scoring method used for the job evaluation plans.

Is a job evaluation plan valid (i.e., useful) if it can correctly place only one third of the jobs? As with so many questions in compensation, the answer is "it depends." It depends on the alternative approaches available, on the costs involved in designing and implementing these plans, and on the magnitude of errors involved in missing a "direct hit." If, for example, being within ±1 pay class translates into several hundred dollars in pay, then employees probably aren't going to express much confidence in the "validity" of this plan. If, on the other hand, the pay difference between ±1 class is not great *or* the plan's results are treated only as an estimate to be adjusted in the job evaluation committee, then its "validity" (usefulness) is more likely.

Convergence of results. Job evaluation plans can also be judged by the degree to which different plans yield similar results. The premise is that convergence of the results from independent methods increases the chances that the results, and hence the methods, are valid. Different results, on the other hand, point to lack of validity. For the best study to date on this issue, we again turn to Madigan's report of the results of three job evaluation plans (guide chart, PAQ, and point plan).[19] He concludes that the three methods generate different and inconsistent job structures. Further, he states that the measurement adequacy of the point, guide chart, and PAQ methods is open to serious question.

---

[18]R. M. Madigan and D. J. Hoover, "Effects of Alternative Job Evaluation Methods on Decisions Involving Pay Equity," *Academy of Management Journal,* March 1986, pp. 84–100.

[19]Madigan, "Comparable Worth Judgments;" also see Doverspike and Barrett, "Internal Bias Analysis," and Richardson, *Fair Pay.*

An employee could have received up to $427 per month more (or less), depending on the job evaluation method used.

These results are provocative. They are consistent with the proposition that job evaluation, as traditionally practiced and described in this and other textbooks, is not a measurement procedure. This is so because it fails to consistently exhibit properties of reliability and validity. However, it is important to maintain a proper perspective in interpreting these results. To date, the research has been limited to only a few employers. Further, few compensation professionals seem to consider job evaluation a measurement tool in the strict sense of that term. More often, it is viewed as a procedure to help rationalize an agreed-upon pay structure in terms of job and business-related factors. As such, it becomes a process of give and take, not some immutable yardstick. This perspective leads us to a third criteria used to judge the validity of a job evaluation plan: acceptance among the parties involved.

Acceptability. Acceptance by the employees and managers involved remains a key test of job evaluation. A recurring theme in this book is that the usefulness of pay techniques must include assessing employee and manager acceptance.

Several devices are used to assess and improve acceptability of job evaluation. An obvious one is the inclusion of a *formal appeals process,* discussed earlier. Employees who feel their jobs are incorrectly evaluated should be able to request reanalysis and reevaluation. Most firms respond to such requests from managers, but few extend the process to all employees, unless those employees are represented by unions who have negotiated a grievance process. They often justify this differential treatment on the basis of fears of being inundated with requests. Employers who open the appeals process to all employees theorize that jobholders are the ones most familiar with the work performed and the most sensitive to significant changes or misrepresentations. No matter what the outcome from the appeal, the results need to be explained in detail to anyone who requests reevaluation.

A second method of assessing acceptability is to include questions about it in *employee attitude surveys*. An example of questions directed to managers is shown in Exhibit 5.4. The questions assess perceptions of how useful job evaluation is as a management tool. In the illustration, managers in only one unit, marketing, considered the plan very useful.

Another method is to *audit* how the plan is being used based on a series of measures of use. Exhibit 5.5 lists examples of indexes used by various employers. These indexes range from the percentage of employees who understand the reasons for job evaluation to the percentage of jobs with current descriptions, to the rate of requests for reevaluation.

Costs

How costly is job evaluation? Two types of costs associated with job evaluation can be identified: (1) design and administration costs and (2) labor costs that

EXHIBIT 5.4
Managerial Perceived Usefulness of Job Evaluation

Acceptability dimensions	Unit	Percent indicating satisfied or better (0–100)	Mean rating (1 = lowest, 4 = highest)
1. Decisions and information derived from the system are based on objective, documentable information.	F		1.5
	E		1.9
	O		1.9
	M		3.6
2. The system provides accurate and reasonable evaluation of jobs.	F		2.0
	E		2.0
	O		1.8
	M		3.4
3. The system is easy to use (i.e., efficient in terms of the effort required of the incumbent and personnel for generating evaluation decisions).	F		2.1
	E		1.7
	O		2.3
	M		3.5
4. The system fosters consistent job decisions across the various operating organizations within the corporation.	F		1.6
	E		1.7
	O		2.1
	M		3.5
5. The system provides the diagnostic capability of identifying or explaining why a position was graded as it was.	F		1.1
	E		1.7
	O		1.7
	M		3.9
6. The job evaluation system has the acceptance of the incumbents who are evaluated.	F		1.5
	E		1.8
	O		1.4
	M		3.3
7. The job evaluation system has the acceptance of personnel professionals who use the system.	F		1.7
	E		1.8
	O		1.4
	M		3.5
8. The system provides information that can help insure that we are in compliance with equal pay guidelines.	F		1.1
	E		1.3
	O		2.1
	M		3.8
9. The system provides job analysis information that is applicable for other personnel functions (i.e., staffing, HRD, equal pay, etc.).	F		1.2
	E		1.4
	O		2.1
	M		3.7
10. Overall satisfaction with the system, all things considered.	F		1.5
	E		1.6
	O		1.2
	M		3.6

Key: F = Finance, E = Engineers, O = Operations, M = Marketing

Source: Adapted from L. Gomez-Mejia, R. Page, and W. Tornow, "A Comparison of the Practical Utility of Traditional, Statistical, and Hybrid Job Evaluation Approaches," *Academy of Management Journal* 25, no. 4 (December 1982), p. 805. Reprinted with permission.

EXHIBIT 5.5
Illustrations of Audit Indexes

A. Overall indicators.
   1. Ratio of numbers of current descriptions to numbers of employees.
   2. Number of job descriptions evaluated last year and previous year.
   3. Number of jobs evaluated per unit.
      (*a*) Newly created jobs.
      (*b*) Reevaluation of existing jobs.
B. Timeliness of job descriptions and evaluations.
   1. Percent of total jobs with current descriptions.
   2. Percentage of evaluation requests returned within 7 working days, within 14 working days.
   3. Percentage of reevaluation requests returned with changed (unchanged) evaluations.
C. Workability and acceptability of job evaluation.
   1. Percentage of employees (managers) surveyed who know the purposes of job evaluation.
   2. The numbers of employees who appeal their job's evaluation rating.
   3. The number of employees who receive explanations of the results of their reevaluation requests.

---

result from pay structure changes occasioned by job evaluation.[20] The labor cost effects will be unique for each application. Little recent data has been published on design and administration costs. Winstanley offers a rule of thumb of 1 to 3 percent of covered payroll.[21] Costs are another area where better data are needed. Recent experience suggests that costs can range from a few thousand dollars for a smaller organization to over $300,000 in consultant fees alone for major projects in firms like J. C. Penney, 3M, or TRW.

Gender Effects in Job Evaluation

Much attention has been directed at job evaluation as both a potential source of bias against women and as a mechanism to reduce bias.[22] Chapter 14 presents an extended discussion of pay discrimination and the use of job evaluation to establish a pay structure based on a policy of comparable worth. At this point we will discuss some of the studies of the effects of gender in job evaluation and then consider some recommendations offered to ensure bias-free job evaluation.

---

[20] David Belcher, *Compensation Administration* (Englewood Cliffs, N.J.: Prentice-Hall, 1974); H. S. Briggs, "Cost of Installing a Job Evaluation Plan," *Management Record* 12 (1951), pp. 422–23; C. W. Lytle, *Job Evaluation Methods* (New York: Ronald Press, 1954), pp. 34–35.

[21] Based on one of N. Winstanley's many welcome notes to us about the real world of compensation management.

[22] D. J. Treiman and H. I. Hartmann, eds., *Women, Work and Wages: Equal Pay for Jobs of Equal Value* (Washington, D.C.: National Academy of Sciences, 1981); H. Remick, *Comparable Worth and Wage Discrimination* (Philadelphia: Temple University Press, 1984); and R. G. Blumrosen, "Wage Discrimination, Job Segregation, and Title VII of the Civil Rights Act of 1964," *University of Michigan Journal of Law Reform* 12, no. 3 (1979), pp. 397–502.

It has been widely speculated that job evaluation is susceptible to gender bias. To date, three ways that job evaluation can be biased against women have been studied.[23] The first, direct bias, occurs if jobs held predominantly by women are undervalued relative to jobs held predominantly by men, simply because of the jobholder's gender. The evidence to date does not support the proposition that the gender of the jobholder influences the evaluation of the job. This evidence is drawn from several studies. Arvey, Passino, and Lounsbury found no effects when they varied the gender of jobholders using photographs and recorded voices.[24] They used the PAQ to evaluate the jobs. In another study, Grams and Schwab found no effects when they varied the gender of jobholders by simply telling evaluators that varying proportions of men and women performed the jobs.[25] They also used 103 compensation specialists as evaluators in another study and again found no evidence that the gender of the jobholder influenced the results of job evaluation.[26] This conclusion must be tempered by the evidence of gender effects in other studies not including job evaluation. For example, Krefting, Berger, and Wallace found evidence that the predominant gender of job incumbents (e.g., clerical jobs are predominantly occupied by women) influences managers' perception of the job's masculinity or femininity.[27]

The psychological literature identifies a common tendency to make stereotypical assumptions, usually to the detriment of women when compared to men.[28] Perhaps by calling out the job-related criteria for making judgments, job evaluation is able to avoid this bias.

---

[23]This discussion is adapted from D. Schwab and R. Grams, "Sex-Related Errors in Job Evaluation: A 'Real-World' Test," *Journal of Applied Psychology* 70, no. 3 (1985), pp. 533–59; and R. D. Arvey, "Sex Bias in Job Evaluation Procedures," Working paper, University of Minnesota, Minneapolis, June 1985.

[24]Arvey, Passino, and Lounsbury, "Job Analysis Results."

[25]R. Grams and D. Schwab, "An Investigation of Systematic Gender-Related Error in Job Evaluation," *Academy of Management Journal* 28, no. 2 (1985), pp. 279–90.

[26]Schwab and Grams, "Sex-Related Errors."

[27]L. A. Krefting, P. K. Berger, and M. J. Wallace, Jr., "The Contribution of Sex Distribution, Job Content, and Occupational Classification to Job Sextyping," *Journal of Vocational Behavior* 13 (1978), pp. 181–91; and L. A. Krefting, P. K. Berger, and M. J. Wallace, Jr., "Sextyping by Personnel Practitioners," Paper presented at Academy of Management national meetings, San Francisco, 1978.

[28]R. L. Dipboye, R. D. Arvey, and D. E. Terpstra, "Sex and Physical Attractiveness of Raters and Applicants as Determinants of Resume Evaluations," *Journal of Applied Psychology* 62 (1977), pp. 288–94; N. T. Feather and J. G. Simon, "Reactions to Male and Female Success and Failure in Sex-Linked Occupations: Impressions of Personality, Causal Attributions and Perceived Likelihood of Different Consequences," *Journal of Personality and Social Psychology* 31 (1975), pp. 20–31; B. Rosen and T. Jerdee, "Effects of Applicants' Sex and Difficulty of Job on Evaluations of Candidates for Managerial Positions," *Journal of Applied Psychology* 59 (1974), pp. 511–12; and G. Rose and T. Stone, "Why Good Job Performance May (Not) Be Rewarded: Sex Factors and Career Development," *Journal of Vocational Behavior* 12 (1978), pp. 197–207.

The second potential source of bias affects job evaluation indirectly, through the current wages paid for jobs. In this case, job evaluation results may be biased if the jobs held predominantly by women are incorrectly underpaid. Blumrosen, and Treiman and Hartmann argue that women's jobs are unfairly underpaid simply because women hold them.[29] If this is the case and if job evaluation is based on the current wages paid, then the job evaluation results simply mirror any bias in the current pay rates. Considering that many job evaluation plans are purposely structured to mirror the existing pay structure, it should not be surprising that the current wages for jobs influence the results of job evaluation. Grams and Schwab found that the pay rate reported for a job does indeed influence job evaluation results.[30] Theirs is the only reported study, but it offers strong evidence to support the proposition that pay rates influence job evaluation and the resulting job hierarchies. The implications of this evidence are important. Grams and Schwab observe that if, as some argue, current pay structures already reflect gender bias, then these biased pay structures could work indirectly through the job evaluation process to deflate the evaluation of jobs held primarily by women. They go on to assert that "biased pay rates may present problems for job evaluation regardless of whether the system is formally validated or not."[31]

The third possible source of gender bias in job evaluation flows from the gender of the individual evaluators. Some argue that male evaluators may be less favorably disposed toward jobs held predominantly by women. To date the research finds no evidence that the job evaluator's gender affects the results.

Remick makes several recommendations for ensuring that job evaluation plans are bias free.[32] Among them are:

1. Ensuring that the compensable factors and scales are defined to include the content of jobs held predominantly by women. For example, working conditions should include noise of office machines and the working conditions surrounding word processors.
2. Ensuring that factor weights are not consistently biased against jobs held predominantly by women. Are factors usually associated with these jobs al-

---

[29]Blumrosen, "Wage Discrimination"; and Treiman and Hartmann, *Women, Work and Wages.*

[30]Grams and Schwab, "Investigation of Systematic Gender-Related Error in Job Evaluation."

[31]Ibid.

[32] Remick, *Comparable Worth and Wage Discrimination*; Helen Remick, "Strategies for Creating Sound, Bias-Free Job Evaluation Plans," Paper presented at Industrial Relations Counselors, Inc., Symposium on Job Evaluation and EEO, September 15 and 17, 1978, Atlanta, Georgia. Also see David J. Thomsen, "Eliminating Pay Discrimination Caused by Job Evaluation," *Personnel,* September–October 1978, pp. 11–22; E. Miller, "Equal Pay for Comparable Work," *Personnel,* September–October 1979, pp. 14–32; Burton V. Dean, Arnold Reisman, and Joseph A. Svestka, "Job Evaluation Upholds Discrimination Suit," *Industrial Engineering* 3, no. 3 (March 1971), pp. 28–31; John Lacy, "Job Evaluation and EEO," *Employee Relations Law Journal* 7, no. 3 (1979), pp. 210–17.

ways given less weight? Remick cautions against assuming that if a job is held predominantly by women, it has low levels of such factors as decision making, fiscal responsibility, or skills required.

3.   Ensuring that the plan is applied in as bias-free a manner as feasible. This includes ensuring that the job descriptions are bias free, that incumbent names are excluded from the job evaluation process, and that women are trained as evaluators.

Some writers see job evaluation as the best friend of those who wish to combat pay discrimination. Bates and Vail argue that without a properly designed and applied system, "employers will face an almost insurmountable task in persuading the government that ill-defined or whimsical methods of determining differences in job content and pay are a business necessity."[33] On the other hand, some lawyers recommend that employers avoid job evaluation on the grounds that the results will lead to lawsuits.

A LOOK AT JOB EVALUATION PRACTICES

A recent survey of job evaluation practices reports the following results.[34]

Eighty-six percent of respondents reported using formal job evaluations for wage determination. A little more than half of the evaluation systems were developed with assistance from outside consultants, while 43 percent were developed by compensation specialists themselves.

On average, 87 percent of the workforce in each firm was covered by a job evaluation program. The use of multiple job evaluation programs was common (59 percent), especially in larger firms. The majority of job evaluation plans relied upon a judgmental weighting of compensable factors (59 percent), as opposed to weighting derived from statistical analysis (40 percent).

Microcomputers and job evaluation. Several compensation consulting firms offer computer-based job evaluation plans. Their software does everything from analyze the job analysis questions, provide computer-generated job descriptions, to predict the correct pay classes for each job. Some caution is required, however, as many firms are just now developing their software. In a survey of over 1,000 U.S. organizations, 76 percent of respondents currently are not using computer assistance in the job evaluation process.[35] However, ap-

---

[33]Marsh W. Bates and Richard G. Vail, "Job Evaluation and Equal Employment Opportunity: A Tool for Compliance—A Weapon for Defense," *Employee Relations Law Journal* 1, no. 4 (1984), pp. 535–46.

[34]Thomas Mahoney, Sara Rynes, and Benson Rosen, "Where Do Compensation Specialists Stand on Comparable Worth?" *Compensation Review* 16, no. 4 (1984), pp. 27–40.

[35]Fred Crandall, "Micro Computer Use on the Rise in Job Evaluation," *American Compensation Association News,* February 1986, p. 6. A full copy of the report is available from Sibson & Company, 101 N. Wacker Drive, Suite 705, Chicago, IL 60606.

proximately 30 percent said they are considering using some form of computer assistance. Complaints about job evaluation voiced by compensation professionals in the survey are that it takes too much time, it involves too many people to assure perceived equity, and the accuracy and objectivity of the results remain in question. The primary advantages seen for computer assistance in job evaluation include:

- Alleviation of the heavy paperwork and tremendous time saving.
- Marked increase in the accuracy of results.
- Creation of more detailed databases.
- Opportunity to conduct improved analysis.

But even with the assistance of computers, job evaluation remains a subjective process that involves substantial judgment. Computers may help reduce the bureaucratic burden that job evaluation often becomes, and it may even help make the process more systematic—but its subjective nature will remain.

SUMMARY

This section of the book started by examining pay structures within an organization. The importance to place on internal consistency in the pay structures was the basic policy issue addressed. We pointed out that the basic premise underlying a policy which emphasizes internal consistency is that equitable pay structures and the procedures used to manage them can influence employee attitudes and behaviors. Internal equity, the relationships among jobs within a single organization, is an important part of a policy of internal consistency. Equitable structures, acceptable to the parties involved, affect satisfaction with pay, the willingness to seek and accept promotions to more responsible jobs, and the propensity to remain with the employer, and they also reduce the incidence of pay-related grievances.

The techniques used to help establish internally consistent (equitable) structures typically include job analysis, job descriptions, and job evaluation. Although viewed by some as bureaucratic burdens, these techniques can aid in achieving the objectives of the pay system when they are properly designed and administered. Without them, our pay objective of equity is more difficult to achieve.

In response to challenges to traditional techniques, other approaches such as knowledge or skill-based systems and computer-assisted plans are being implemented. But no matter what mechanism is ultimately used, the purpose remains—to achieve pay structures that will help employees and employers achieve their objectives.

We have now finished the first part of the book. In it, you were introduced to compensation management, and the model that provides a framework for the book. Compensation management requires adapting the pay system to support the organization strategies, its culture, and the needs of individual employees. We examined the first basic policy issue—the emphasis to place on internal consistency of the pay structures. We discussed the techniques used to establish consistency, and its effects on compensation objectives. The next section of the book focuses on the second major policy issue in our pay model, external competitiveness.

REVIEW QUESTIONS

1. What are the pros and cons of having employees involved in compensation decisions?
2. Thinking back on the earlier chapters on job analysis and job evaluation, what forms can employee involvement take?
3. Where would such involvement be most effective? Easiest to attain?
4. If you were a compensation specialist, how would you recommend your company evaluate the usefulness of its job evaluation systems?
5. What are the sources of possible gender bias in job evaluation?
6. How can compensation specialists and employees insure that job evaluation plans are bias free?

Part 1
Compensation Applications

Case 1   Technet

You are the new compensation director at Technet, a manufacturer of business computer systems. Technet is a relatively young company but one which has grown exponentially over the past years, largely due to its reputation for technical innovation, but also as a result of its aggressive marketing techniques. These techniques have emphasized price advantage and on-time delivery while downplaying customer support and service.

All of this is now beginning to change. Technet is trying to consolidate and hold its market position and especially to improve its image and performance in the area of support and service. This means a number of changes in the organization. For the work force it is likely, over time, to mean tremendous shifts in the composition of jobs and skills. Technet management wants to retain most of its present work force, but recognizes that in order to do so employees will be required to redirect their careers from the old needs of Technet to the new. For example, there will be less emphasis on new computer design and manufacturing technical support, and more emphasis on effective servicing of systems and equipment already sold. Additionally, there will be added emphasis on developing additional business applications for existing equipment and in training customers in those applications. To stay employed, people will have to transist to new jobs, and management will need to identify instances where the transitions can logically be made. This process will be occurring for years to come.

All of this comes at a time when Technet management has decided to undertake a project to analyze and evaluate its jobs for compensation purposes. Tom Jones is responsible for accomplishing the project. He realizes some of the difficulties that might occur because of the fundamental changes going on. In discussions with the vice president for human resources, Andrea Dyer, he has presented—as a first step—the advantages and disadvantages of various job analysis data approaches: task oriented, worker oriented, and ability oriented. Andrea has asked Tom, based on that discussion, to prepare a one-page memo outlining the strengths and weaknesses of each of the options for the job analysis project at Technet, and to make a recommendation (along with his reasons) for the use of one of these approaches. Tom has completed his memo and is about to meet with Andrea to summarize his memo and make his recommendations.

Andrea Dyer did job analysis at Compugraphics before she joined Technet. She is of the opinion that a lot of time and effort went into a project that sat on the shelf. Compensation was set with little regard to the job analysis results. She will have to be convinced that Technet needs job analysis or that its results will be used if it is done.

Students will play the roles of Tom and Andrea in their meeting to discuss job analysis.

Case 2   Using the Hay Guide Chart

Using the Hay Guide Chart–Profile Method in Appendix A, Chapter 4, evaluate the job of Human Resources Consulting Associate. A job description is presented below.

JOB TITLE: HUMAN RESOURCES CONSULTING ASSOCIATE

Principal Duties

- Prepares variety of reports associated with labor relations in a major American industry.
- Collects data concerning wage rates, employee benefit information, and a variety of Bureau of Labor Statistics relevant to collective bargaining, and interprets this information for reports to senior executives.
- Maintains continuing communication with senior human resource executives and chief executive officers of major Fortune 500 companies.
- Works closely with president of consulting firm who has principal contacts with clients.
- Performs various analyses of corporate organization information related to human resource functions in major companies.
- Will develop appropriate training materials for use in presentations with senior executives on these matters.

Skills

- Must have thorough understanding of the employee relations collective bargaining process.

- Must be familiar with labor contracts and various aspects of a labor agreement.
- Must be facile with statistics and economic information used with reports.
- Must be able to communicate effectively and interpret complex data into meaningful and cogent executive reports.

Experience

- Three to five years of personnel and labor relations assignments.
- A graduate degree is desirable, preferably in business or a related discipline.

Case 3 *Sun State*

Sun State is enjoying economic growth. Tax revenues are up, but so is the work load for government employees. Recently there have been increasing complaints about pay. Some employees feel their salary is out of line in comparison to the amount received by other employees. As a first step, Sun State personnel director hired a summer intern to perform job analysis and write job descriptions. The results are shown below. Now, a job structure is needed.

1. Divide into teams of four to six students each. Each team should evaluate the eight jobs and prepare a job structure based on their evaluation.
2. Each team should describe the process the group went through to arrive at that job structure. Job evaluation techniques and compensable factors used should be described, and the reasons for selecting them should be stated.
3. Each team should give each job a title and put its job structure on the board. Comparisons can then be made among job structures of the various teams. Does the job evaluation method used appear to affect the results? Do compensable factors chosen affect the results? Does the process affect the results?

JOB A

Kind of Work

Highly responsible administrative work in directing a fiscal management program.

Difficulty and Responsibility of Work

Directs a large and complex fiscal management program in a large state department, agency, or institution. Provides technical and supervisory financial support to carry out policies and programs established by the department head. Serves as the chief liaison to activity managers to ensure coordination of their activities in planning with the accounting division. Maintains a close working relationship with the finance agency controller to ensure compliance with budgetary and financial planning requirements of the Department of Finance. Considerable latitude is granted employee in this class for developing, implementing, and administering financial methods and procedures. Typically reports to a high level department manager with work reviewed through periodic conferences and reports.

Principal Responsibilities

- Directs all accounting functions of the department, agency, or institution so that adequate financial records and fiscal controls are maintained.
- Provides supervisory and high professional skills for the financial operations of the department consistent with the appropriate state and federal laws and regulations so that state and federal funds are utilized and expanded in the most efficient and effective manner.
- Provides coordination with other state and federal agencies relating to financial matters so that the department head and agency controller are informed as to matters pertaining to policies, procedures, and programs which may have an effect on the financial operation of the department.
- Develops authorized department budgets and financial plans, goals, and objectives for review and approval by the agency controller and the department head so that maximum use will be made of financial resources.
- Consults with and advises the department head, managers, supervisors, and the agency controller on financial policies and procedures, organizational changes, and interpretation of financial data and reports to ensure efficient and effective fiscal management.

Essential Requirements of Work

Knowledge, skills, and abilities necessary for functioning at full productivity. (Those asterisked are also essential at entry.)

    Extensive knowledge of the department's accounting structure.

*   Extensive knowledge of accounting principles and practices.

    Extensive knowledge of federal government accounting, auditing, and reporting requirements.

    Thorough knowledge of the state's appropriation, budgetary, and accounting systems.

* Ability to direct a large fiscal program involving a considerable number of accounting professionals and technicians.

* Ability to develop and implement procedures to increase the efficiency and effectiveness of the fiscal program.

* Ability to independently carry out department objectives with only limited supervision.

* Ability to prepare and interpret complex fiscal records and reports, recognize problems, and effect solutions.

* Ability to coordinate the fiscal management program with the overall functions of the department.

* Ability to speak and write effectively.

* Ability to establish and maintain effective working relationships with managers, public, and other employees.

JOB B

Kind of Work

Difficult bookkeeping and clerical work in the maintenance of financial records.

Difficulty and Responsibility of Work

Keeps financial records where the accounts are relatively complex or assists higher level accountants and accounting technicians where the accounts are complex and extensive. Differentiated from the account clerk by the difficulty and complexity of the work, the greater use of initiative and independent judgment, and the greater specialized training required.

Receives direction from higher level accounting personnel in the form of a review of work for accuracy and completeness. In some cases, may provide lead work direction to account clerks or clerical personnel engaged in the bookkeeping operation. Prepares relatively simple reports, makes preliminary analyses of financial conditions for use by other employees, and implements minor procedural and transactional changes in the fiscal operation. As opposed to the accounting technician, however, emphasis is on bookkeeping procedures and the smooth transition of fiscal operations.

Principal Responsibilities

• Assists accountants or accounting technicians in a major department in a specific segment of the fiscal operation.

• Maintains the financial records of a moderate size department according to established procedures and makes adjustments to the records as directed.

- Prepares special analytical data for use by other accountants in preparing budget requests or other reports.
- Approves and processes travel, account, invoice, and claim documents for payment.
- Codes and records all receipts and disbursement of funds.
- Reviews encumbrance or liquidation documents for accuracy and conformity with procedures and expedites financial transactions.
- Accesses or inputs information to the statewide accounting system.
- Investigates errors or problems in the processing of fiscal transactions and recommends changes in procedures.
- Issues purchase orders.
- Provides lead work direction to other bookkeeping and clerical employees.
- Performs related work as required.

Essential Requirements of Work

Knowledge, skills, and abilities necessary for functioning at full productivity. (Those asterisked are also essential at entry.)

* Considerable knowledge of office procedures, methods, and equipment.
* Working knowledge of modern bookkeeping practices.
* Working knowledge of the State's appropriation, budgeting, and accounting system.
* Some knowledge of arithmetic and simple mathematics.
* Ability to do detailed and repetitive work with speed and accuracy.
* Ability to use a variety of office equipment.
* Ability to establish effective working relationships with the public and other employees.
* Ability to interpret bookkeeping records and documents and prepare information in summary form.
* Ability to understand fiscal procedural and transactional practices.

JOB C

Kind of Work

Highly difficult and responsible fiscal management and supervisory accounting work.

Difficulty and Responsibility of Work

Serves as section chief or top assistant to an accounting director or other high level fiscal management officer in a moderate or large size state department. Directs the activities of an accounting or fiscal management section consisting of several subsections or assists the supervisor with the supervision of a very large and complex accounting operation. Works closely with the chief fiscal officer in formulating fiscal policies and independently establishes new accounts in payroll procedures to accomplish the department's program. Considerable independence of action is granted the employee, with work reviewed through reports and conferences.

Principal Responsibilities

- Prepares and administers the department budget, confers with operating officials on projected needs, and devis es methods of adjusting budgets so that agency programs may be carried on efficiently and effectively.
- Provides technical accounting assistance and guidance to operational accounting units within a large or medium size agency so that operating procedures and staff skills will be upgraded on a continuing basis with resultant improvement in quality and reduction in cost.
- Produces special accounting plans, reports, and analyses involving complex accounting methods and principles as a basis for decision making by the chief fiscal officer and the department head.
- Constructs and maintains the department's accounting structure and cost accounting capabilities so the department can conform to legislative intent, meet state and federal regulatory requirements, and provide the department with reporting capabilities.
- Provides coordination and assistance in the revision of present systems and implementation of new systems and procedures that affect the fiscal division so that controls, services, and maximum utilization of available facilities may be maintained.
- Assists in the coordination and ongoing analysis and control of fiscal matters relevant to satellite institutions under departmental supervision.

Essential Requirements of Work

Knowledge, skills, and abilities necessary for functioning at full productivity. (Those asterisked are also essential at entry.)

* Extensive knowledge of accounting principles and practices.

Thorough knowledge of the department's accounting structure.

Thorough knowledge of the state's appropriation, budgetary, and accounting systems.

Thorough knowledge of federal government accounting, auditing, and reporting requirements.

Considerable knowledge of statutes pertaining to an individual's agency.

* Ability to plan, assign, and direct the work of a large number of professional and semiprofessional accounting employees.

* Ability to implement procedures to increase effectiveness and efficiency of employees.
* Ability to carry out departmental objectives with limited and infrequent supervisory conferences.
* Ability to prepare and interpret complex fiscal records and reports, recognize problems, and effect solutions.
* Ability to relate accounting to overall functions of the department.
* Ability to write and speak effectively.
* Ability to establish and maintain effective working relationships with managers, public, and other employees.

JOB D

Kind of Work

Difficult and responsible fiscal management and supervisory accounting work.

Difficulty and Responsibility of Work

Maintains a large and complex system of accounts. Serves as a section chief in the finance division of a very large department, maintains large state-federal or state-county accounts, and oversees a major statewide accounting function in the Department of Finance. Responsible for coordinating and supervising the various phases of the accounting function. Responsibility extends to the development of procedure and policies for the work involved. Supervises a staff of account clerks, accounting technicians, and accounting officers.

Principal Responsibilities

* Provides regular budget review so that program managers have adequate funds to be effective.
* Conducts financial analysis for economical and equitable distribution or redistribution of agency resource.
* Prepares long- and short-range program recommendations for fiscal action so that agency policies are consistent.
* Plans and directs the computerization of systems applied to fiscal services to ensure efficient operation.
* Develops and defines accounting office procedures to ensure the efficient delivery of fiscal services.
* Reviews and analyzes cost accounting computer output to ensure proper documentation of projected cost as required by federal policy and procedures.

- Prepares and supervises the preparation of federal budgets and grant requests, financial plans, and expenditure reports so that they accurately reflect needs and intent of the agency.
- Develops accounting and documentation procedures for county welfare departments so that state and federal auditing and reporting requirements are met.
- Establishes and maintains a financial reporting system for all federal and other nonstate funding sources so that all fiscal reporting requirements are adhered to on a timely and accurate basis.
- Assists grantee agencies in proper reporting procedures under federal grant programs so that requirements for reimbursement may be made on a timely basis.
- Determines the statewide indirect costs so that all state agencies are allocated their proportionate share of indirect costs.
- Supervises the review and processing of all encumbrance documents submitted to the Department of Finance so that necessary accounting information is recorded accurately and promptly in the accounting system.

Essential Requirements of Work

Knowledge, skills, and abilities necessary for functioning at full productivity. (Those asterisked are also essential at entry.)

Thorough knowledge of the department's accounting structure.
* Thorough knowledge of accounting principles and practices.
Considerable knowledge of the state's appropriation, budgetary, and accounting systems.
Working knowledge of statutes pertaining to an individual's agency.
* Ability to supervise clerical and accounting support staff.
* Ability to prepare and interpret complex fiscal records and reports, recognize problems, and effect solutions.
* Ability to relate accounting to overall functions of the department.
* Ability to write and speak effectively.
* Ability to establish and maintain effective working relationships with managers, public, and other employees.

JOB E

Kind of Work

Specialized bookkeeping and clerical work in the maintenance of financial records.

Difficulty and Responsibility of Work

Keeps financial records where the accounts are relatively simple, or assists accountants and accounting technicians in assigned work of greater difficulty where accounting operations are more complex and extensive. The work involves a combination of clerical and bookkeeping responsibilities requiring specialized training or experience. Receives direction from higher level accounting personnel in the form of detailed instructions and close review for accuracy and conformance with law, rules, or policy. Once oriented to the work, employee may exercise independent judgment in assigned duties.

Principal Responsibilities

- Maintains complete bookkeeping records independently where scope, volume, or complexity is limited or maintains a difficult part of an extensive bookkeeping operation.
- Codes and records all receipts and disbursement of funds.
- Prepares travel, account, invoice, and claim documents for payment.
- Reviews encumbrance or liquidation documents for accuracy and conformity with procedures and expedites financial transactions.
- Prepares financial information for reports and audits, invoices, and expenditure reports.
- Keeps general, control, or subsidiary books of accounts such as cash book appropriation and disbursement ledgers and encumbrance records.
- Accesses or inputs information to the statewide accounting system as directed.
- Performs related tasks as required.

Essential Requirements of Work

Knowledge, skills, and abilities necessary for functioning at full productivity. (Those asterisked are also essential at entry.)

- * Working knowledge of office procedures, methods, and equipment.
- * Working knowledge of modern bookkeeping practices.
- * Some knowledge of arithmetic and simple mathematics.
  Some knowledge of the state's appropriation, budgeting, and accounting system.
- * Ability to do detailed and repetitive work with speed and accuracy.
- * Ability to follow detailed instructions.
- * Ability to use a variety of office equipment.

JOB F

Kind of Work

Difficult semiprofessional accounting work.

Difficulty and Responsibility of Work

Performs varied and difficult semiprofessional accounting work within an established accounting system. Maintains a complex set of accounts and works with higher management outside of the accounting unit in planning and controlling expenditures. Works with higher level employees in providing technical fiscal advice and service to functional activities. This class is differentiated from the Accounting Technician level by the difficulty and complexity of work, considerably greater fiscal analysis, evaluation and planning responsibilities, and independence of action. Receives supervision from higher level management or accounting personnel. May provide lead work to lower level accounting, bookkeeping or clerical personnel.

Principal Responsibilities

- Assists the chief accounting officer in the preparation of all budgets to assure continuity in financial operations.
- Prepares and assembles the biennial budget and coordinates all accounting functions for a small department according to overall plan of department head and needs expressed by activity managers.
- Maintains cost coding and allocation system for a major department to serve as a basis for reimbursement.
- Provides accounting and budgetary controls for federal, state, and private grants including reconciling bank statements and the preparation of reports on the status of the budget and accounts.
- Evaluates the spending progress of budget activities, ensures that budgetary limits are not exceeded, and recommends or effects changes in spending plans.
- Provides technical services to divisions of an agency in the supervision of deposits, accounts payable, procurement, and other business management areas.
- Performs related work as required.

Essential Requirements of Work

Knowledge, skills, and abilities necessary for functioning at full productivity. (Those asterisked are also essential at entry.)

* Thorough knowledge of bookkeeping procedures and the ability to apply them to accounting transactions.
* Considerable knowledge of the state's appropriation, budgeting, and accounting system.
* Working knowledge of accounting and public financial administrations.
* Some knowledge of arithmetic and simple mathematics.

  Some knowledge of federal grant accounting and auditing and reporting requirements.
* Ability to use a variety of office equipment.
* Ability to write and speak effectively.
* Ability to establish and maintain effective working relationships with managers, the public and other employees.

JOB G

Kind of Work

Entry level professional accounting work.

Difficulty and Responsibility of Work

Performs professional accounting work as the fiscal officer of a small department, institution, or major division, or as an assistant to a higher level accountant in a large fiscal operation. Work involves providing a wide range of accounting services to professional and managerial employees. Assists in the development and maintenance of broad fiscal programs. Regularly performs complex fiscal analysis, prepares fiscal reports for management, and recommends alternative solutions to accounting problems. May supervise account clerks, accounting technicians, or clerical employees engaged in the fiscal operation. Receives supervision from a higher level accountant, business manager, or other administrative employee.

Principal Responsibilities

* Helps administrative employees develop budgets to ensure sufficient funds are available for operating needs.
* Monitors cash flow to ensure minimum adequate operating balance.
* Produces reports so that management has proper fiscal information.
* Submits reports to federal and state agencies to ensure financial reporting requirements are met.
* Analyzes and interprets fiscal reports so that information is available in useful form.
* Instructs technicians and clerks in proper procedures to ensure smooth operation of accounting functions.

- Investigates fiscal accounting problems so that adequate solutions may be developed.
- Recommends and implements new procedures to ensure the efficient operation of the accounting section.
- Interprets state laws and department policies to ensure the legality of fiscal transactions.

Essential Requirements of Work

Knowledge, skills, and abilities necessary for functioning at full productivity. (Those asterisked are also essential at entry.)

* Considerable knowledge of accounting principles and practices.

Considerable knowledge of the state's appropriation, budgetary, and accounting systems.

Working knowledge of fiscal analysis methods.

Working knowledge of federal government accounting, auditing, and reporting requirements.

* Ability to prepare and interpret complex fiscal records and reports, recognize problems, and effect solutions.

* Ability to write and speak effectively.

* Ability to establish and maintain effective working relationships with managers, public, and other employees.

JOB H

Kind of Work

Semiprofessional accounting work.

Difficulty and Responsibility of Work

Performs semiprofessional accounting work within an established accounting system. Responsible for maintaining accounting records on a major set of accounts, preauditing of transactions in a major activity, or handling cash receipts in a major facility, and for classifying transactions, substantiating source documents, balancing accounts, and preparing reports as prescribed. Responsible for recognizing errors or problems in the fiscal transactions of an agency and recommending alternative solutions for consideration by other staff. This level is differentiated from the account clerk, senior class, by the semiprofessional accounting work, less emphasis on transactional matters, and greater responsibility for the analysis and preparation of accounting records and reports. Must regularly exercise initiative and independent judgment and may provide lead-work direction to account clerks or clerical employees engaged in the fiscal operation. Receives supervision from an accounting technician, senior business manager, or professional accountant.

Principal Responsibilities

- Controls expenditures so they do not exceed budget totals and prepares allotment requests in the agency's budgetary accounts.
- Processes encumbrance changes of expenditures authorization and adjusts budget as necessary and desired.
- Reconciles department accounting records with the statewide accounting system records documents so that funds may be appropriated, allotted, encumbered, and transferred.
- Authorizes reimbursement for goods and services received by a major department.
- Develops and maintains a system of accounts receivable, including issuance of guidelines for participants and the preparation of state and federal reports.
- Provides daily accounting on loans receivable or financial aids for a major college.
- Audits cost vendor statements for conformity within departmental guidelines.
- Reconciles the payroll disbursements by payroll period for a major organization and prepares spending reports by AID.
- Supervises cash accounting unit and prepares reports on receipts and deposits.
- Performs related work as required.

Essential Requirements of Work

Knowledge, skills, and abilities necessary for functioning at full productivity. (Those asterisked are also essential at entry.)

- * Considerable knowledge of bookkeeping procedures and the ability to apply them to accounting transactions.
  Considerable knowledge of the state's appropriation, budget, and accounting system.
- * Some knowledge of accounting and public financial administration.
- * Some knowledge of arithmetic and simple mathematics.
- * Ability to use a variety of office equipment.
- * Ability to analyze financial records and reports, locate errors, and recommend solutions to procedural or other problems.
- * Ability to establish effective working relationships with the public and other employees.

Part 2

External Competitiveness: Determining the Pay Level

The objective of Part 2 is to discuss how employers position their pay relative to what competitors are paying. Exhibit II.1 shows how the policy regarding external competitiveness fits into the total pay model. It represents the second of the four major policy decisions in the model. The policy on external competitiveness is important because it expresses the organization's intentions regarding its pay relative to the pay of other employers competing in the same labor and product markets.

External competitiveness involves the determination of a pay level. Three "pure" alternatives exist—to lead competition, to match it, or to follow what competitors are paying. In practice, some employers use different policies for different units and/or job groups, and there are many different ways to put these policies into practice.

The determination of the policy on external competitiveness depends on three major factors: (1) labor conditions, stemming from competition in the labor market or labor union demands, (2) financial pressure stemming from product market conditions and the organization's financial vitality, and (3) the strategic and operating objectives that the organization has established.

External competitiveness is critical to the organization's success. Establishing a pay level translates external competitiveness into practice. The pay level has a twofold effect on pay objectives: (1) it directly affects the employer's operating costs (i.e., labor costs), and (2) it directly affects the employer's ability to attract and maintain a stable and qualified work force. Consequently, the policies and practices related to external competitiveness are among the most critical in compensation management.

In Chapter 6, the major factors affecting external competitiveness policies, consequences of these policies, and theories and research related to them are discussed. Chapter 7 discusses the decisions and techniques that translate an employer's external competitiveness policy into pay level.

EXHIBIT II.1
The Pay Model

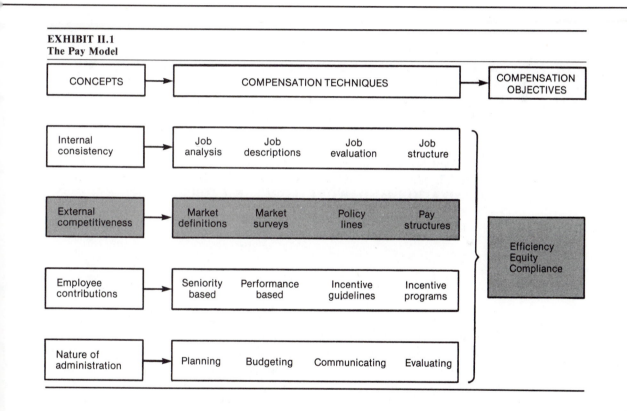

Chapter 6

External Competitiveness and the Pay Level

Every semester employers make job offers to graduating students. In 1986 students exchanged the data and discovered that the offers ranged from $18,000 to $37,000 per year. The most common was around $30,000. Early in the recruiting season students attributed this range to differences among themselves: grade point average, courses taken, interviewing skills, analytical and interpersonal abilities. But after some students rejected initial offers, they made an interesting discovery. Employers simply extended the same offer to other students. Why were the offers not changed when extended to different students? If an individual's qualifications do not explain differences in offers, what does? To be sure, some of the pay differences may be related to differences in students, but the better students seemed to get more offers rather than all the higher offers. Certainly, location has an effect: higher offers were made by firms located in San Francisco and New York City. The nature of the work also had some effect, with jobs in employment associated with somewhat lower offers than those in compensation and labor relations. A major difference in job offers was related to the industry in which the different firms compete. Offers from pharmaceuticals, brokerage houses, and high-technology firms tended to exceed those made by consumer products, insurance, banking, and heavy manufacturing firms.

The above experience is repeated year after year. Different employers offer different salaries for similarly trained students from the same school who will enter relatively similar human resource management jobs.[1] What determines these differences in pay levels, and what effects do these differences have on organization performance and employee work behavior? This chapter examines these questions.

EXTERNAL COMPETITIVENESS AND THE PAY MODEL

In practice, policies regarding external competitiveness translate into the employer's pay levels. It is important to understand the two concepts.

> **External competitiveness refers to the pay relationships *among* organizations and the *competitive positions* reflected in these relationships.**

> **Pay level refers to an *average* of the array of rates paid by an employer. It focuses attention on two aspects of pay: (1) the costs of human resources to the employer and (2) the use of pay to encourage workers to seek a job and remain with an employer.**

The link between pay level decisions and operating expenses is easy to understand. Labor costs constitute a significant portion of most organizations' total expenses. Other things being equal, the higher the pay level, the higher the labor costs. Furthermore, the higher the pay level relative to what competition pays, the greater the relative costs to produce similar products. So it would seem that the obvious conclusion is to set the minimum pay level possible.

However, other things are rarely equal. For example, a decision to establish a relatively high pay level may make it easier for the employer to attract and retain a highly qualified work force. One study concluded that high wages and high recruiting costs are substitutes for each other. High-wage employers are

---

[1]Albert Rees, "Information Networks in Labor Markets," *American Economic Review,* May 1966, pp. 559–66; and Albert Rees and George Schultz, *Workers and Wages in an Urban Labor Market* (Chicago: University of Chicago Press, 1970).

EXHIBIT 6.1
Salary Survey Results

Word Processing Operator, Lead

Duties
Assumes responsibility for directing work flow through the word processing center or cluster and provides administrative support to principals to improve overall productivity. Uses word processor to type high priority and confidential work.

High school graduate or equivalent, plus three years of work processing (mag card/tape/diskette) experience required.

Job title: Word Process Operator III	*Company Code*	*Minimum Rate*	*Mid Rate*	*Maximum Rate*	*Average Rate*	*Employee Population*
	D	$8.34	$9.71	$11.07	$9.40	1
	Y	7.35	8.65	9.95	9.40	1
	E	7.62	8.99	10.36	9.08	3
	YY	7.78	9.05	10.32	8.94	1
	B	6.84	8.56	10.26	8.37	2
	N	6.87	8.59	10.31	8.37	14
	W	5.96	8.99	10.28	8.08	1
	XX	6.89	8.10	9.72	8.05	12
	OO	5.53	7.19	8.84	7.65	2
	Q	6.45	8.60	10.23	7.58	3
	MM	5.70	7.13	8.56	7.40	2
	G	5.48	6.78	8.08	7.36	1
	R	6.20	7.63	9.05	7.36	3
Straight averages		6.69	8.31	9.77	8.26	46
Averages weighted by population		6.75	8.31	9.89	8.17	

Source: Dallas Area Electronics Survey. Survey sponsors: Recognition Equipment, Rockwell International, Collins Radio Group and Texas Instruments Inc.

---

able to attract and retain a work force better than low-wage competitors and thus do not have to recruit as extensively. However, other evidence suggests that high-wage employers also expend greater efforts on recruiting—that employers which offer relatively higher wages also exhibit greater recruiting expenses.[2] The logic behind this relationship between high pay level and recruiting behavior is that employers who search more for highly qualified people also pay more to hire them. So the result is that high-paying employers are more likely to attract larger applicant pools and higher quality applicants, which permits such employers to be more selective than would otherwise be the case.

So decisions regarding external competitiveness and pay level are important because they affect the quality of the work force as well as operating expenses and revenues.

No single "going rate." Considering its importance, it is surprising that so little is known about employers' pay policies regarding competitors and their pay level practices. We do know, as graduating students discover each year, that

---

[2]John M. Barron, John Bishop, and William C. Dunkelberg, "Employer Search: The Interviewing and Hiring of New Employees," *The Review of Economics and Statistics,* February 1985, pp. 43–52.

EXHIBIT 6.2
The Relationship of Company Pay Scales to Market Average

Company	*All Jobs (n = 21)* Percent	Company	Percent
A	+ 21.2	L	− .2
B	+ 17.5	M	− 1.4
C	+ 12.4	N	− 2.0
D	+ 8.7	O	− 4.5
E	+ 7.7	P	− 6.9
F	+ 7.4	Q	− 7.5
G	+ 5.1	R	− 8.1
H	+ 4.2	S	− 10.5
I	+ 2.8	T	− 11.5
J	+ 2.6	U	− 13.6
K	+ 2.5		

The highest 10 percent pay 16.5 percent above market: the highest 25 percent pay 7.5 percent above. The lowest 10 percent pay 11.3 percent below market: the lowest 25 percent pay 7.2 percent below.

Source: Reprinted by permission of the publisher from Kenneth E. Foster, "An Anatomy of Company Pay Practices," *Personnel,* September 1985, p. 68. © 1985 by the American Management Association.

the rates paid for similar jobs and skills vary widely among employers.[3] There is no single "going rate" for a job; rather, an array of rates exists. Notice in Exhibit 6.1 that the salary paid by firms participating in this survey for word processors varies from $5.48 per hour to $11.07 per hour. While some of this difference may be attributable to such factors as experience and seniority within the firm, much of it also reflects different pay levels among employers. The average rate paid by employers ranged from $7.36 per hour to $9.40 per hour.

A survey of aerospace firms reveals wide variation in competitive policies and pay levels.[4] Foster reports that in a survey of 21 firms, the top-paying firm paid more than 21 percent above the average pay in its market, and the bottom one paid more than 13 percent below market (i.e., below the overall average pay of all 21 firms). His figures are shown in Exhibit 6.2. Despite this apparently wide variation in pay levels, about 70 percent of the firms were within about 10 percent (plus or minus) of the market average.

Even more interesting is the fact that these firms exhibited different competitive positions for different job families. Exhibit 6.3 compares the relation-

---

[3]*College Placement Council Salary Survey* is published quarterly by the College Placement Council, Bethlehem, Pa. It reports starting salary offers to college graduates as collected by college placement offices. Data are reported by curriculum, by functional area, and by degree. It is one of several sources employers may use to establish the offers they extend to new graduates.

[4]Ken Foster, "An Anatomy of Company Pay Practices," *Personnel,* September 1985, pp. 67–71.

EXHIBIT 6.3
The Relationship of Company Pay Scales to Market Average

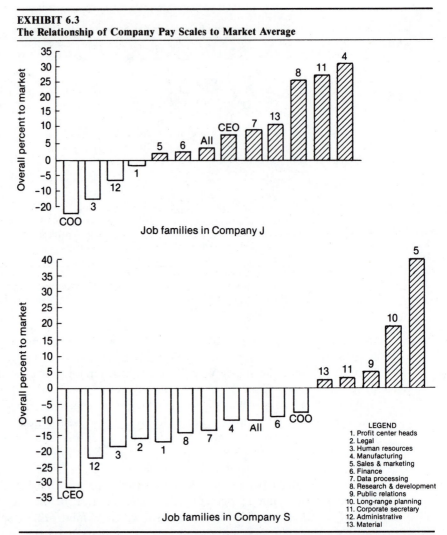

Source: Reprinted by permission of the publisher from Kenneth E. Foster, "An Anatomy of Company Pay Practices," *Personnel*, September 1985, pp. 69–70. © 1985 by the American Management Association.

ship of the pay levels of two firms (J and S) relative to the market for 13 job families. Note that in company J, average pay for 9 out of 13 job families is above the market. In firm S average pay is above the market in only five job families.

While it is risky to infer different competitive policies from these data, it is clear that different employers in the same industry exhibit different pay levels

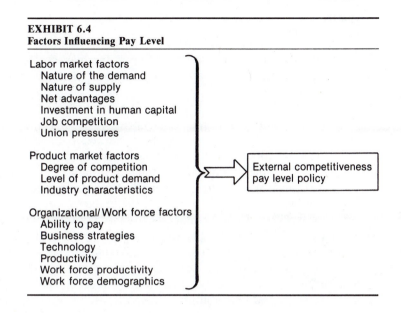

EXHIBIT 6.4
Factors Influencing Pay Level

Labor market factors
    Nature of the demand
    Nature of supply
    Net advantages
    Investment in human capital
    Job competition
    Union pressures

Product market factors
    Degree of competition
    Level of product demand
    Industry characteristics

Organizational/Work force factors
    Ability to pay
    Business strategies
    Technology
    Productivity
    Work force productivity
    Work force demographics

External competitiveness pay level policy

regarding their competitors.[5] Other evidence also suggests that different employers within the same industry adopt different policies and practices regarding external competition and pay levels.[6] The next section discusses the theories and research related to understanding the factors which determine these differences.

FACTORS INFLUENCING EXTERNAL COMPETITIVENESS AND PAY LEVEL

The factors which affect the determination of external competitiveness and pay level are grouped in Exhibit 6.4. They include the pressures exerted by (1) competition in labor markets for workers with sought-after skills and abilities; (2) competition in product and service markets, which affects the financial condition of the firm; and (3) characteristics unique to each organization and its work force, such as its ability to pay, business strategies, and the productivity and experience of its work force. These factors act in concert to influence pay levels set during the design and administration of pay systems.

---

[5] Erica Groshen, "Sources of Wage Dispersion: How Much Do Employers Matter?" Working paper, Department of Economics, Harvard University, December 1985; John Dunlop, "The Task of Contemporary Wage Theory," in *New Concepts in Wage Determination,* eds. George W. Taylor and Frank C. Pierson (New York: McGraw-Hill, 1975).

[6] Foster, "Anatomy"; George Milkovich, "Compensation Systems in High Technology Companies," Paper presented at the Conference on Human Resources in High Technology Firms,

LABOR MARKETS

The notion of a market is deceptively simple. Compensation managers often refer to it: "Our pay levels are based upon the market," "We pay competitively with the market," or "We are market leaders." For pay purposes, what precisely are markets?

Economists conceive of them as two basic types: the quoted price and the bourse.[7] Stores that label each item's price or ads that list a job opening's starting wage are examples of quoted price markets. Bourses involve haggling over the terms and conditions; buying a house or signing professional athlete's contracts are examples. Graduating students usually find themselves in a quoted market, though some haggling over the offer may occur. Both types involve an exchange between buyers and sellers; the "buyers" are employers and the "sellers" are workers. In labor markets the mechanisms developed to facilitate the exchange range from college recruiting to want ads and employment agencies.

Regardless of the mechanism, an exchange among employers and workers is necessary and does occur. The exchange involves sharing and evaluating information about the job opportunities and inducements offered by the employer and the skills and contributions offered by the worker. If the inducements and contributions offered are acceptable to both parties, some kind of a contract is executed. At times the contract is formal, such as those made with unions, professional athletes, and executive officers. At other times the agreement is informal, with an implied understanding or a brief letter. The result of the workings of the labor market is the allocation of employees to job opportunities at certain pay rates.

How Markets Work

Understanding markets requires analysis of the demand and supply of labor.[8] On the demand side, emphasis is on employers' hiring behavior and how much employers are able and willing to pay for labor. On the supply side, the focus is on the qualifications of workers and the pay that they are willing to accept in

---

UCLA Graduate School of Management, Los Angeles, June 1985; Frederic L. Pryor, "Incentives in Manufacturing: The Carrot and the Stick," *Monthly Labor Review,* July 1984, pp. 40–43; and David Balkin and Luis Gomez-Mejia, "The Relationship between Short-Term and Long-Term Pay Incentives in the High Technology Industry," Working paper, College of Business, Northeastern University, 1985.

[7]For more extended discussion of labor markets, see Arne L. Kalleberg and Aage B. Sorensen, "The Sociology of Labor Markets," *Annual Review of Sociology,* 1979, pp. 351–79; and Michael J. Piore, "Fragments of a 'Sociological' Theory of Wages," *American Economics Association,* May 1973, pp. 377–84.

[8]Ronald G. Ehrenberg and Robert S. Smith, *Modern Labor Economics* (Glenview, Ill.: Scott, Foresman, 1985).

EXHIBIT 6.5
Supply and Demand for M.B.A.s in the Short Run

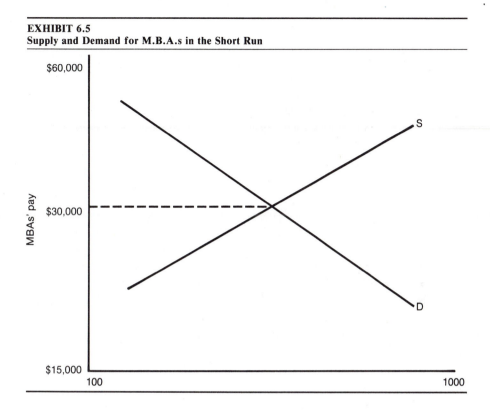

exchange for their services. Exhibit 6.5 shows a simple illustration of demand (line D) and supply (line S) for M.B.A.s. The vertical axis represents pay rates from $15,000 a year to $50,000 a year. The horizontal axis scale is the number of M.B.A.s demanded, ranging from 100 to 1,000. At the market level, demand is the sum of all employers' requirements for M.B.A.s at various pay levels. In a downward-sloping demand schedule, the higher the M.B.A. salaries, the fewer M.B.A.s employers will demand. Similarly, the entire market supply of M.B.A.s is the sum of all M.B.A.s who would be interested and available for jobs at different pay levels. In the illustration, the market-determined rate for M.B.A.s is $30,000. That is the rate at which the demand and supply of M.B.A.s are equal. We can think of the pay level as always affected by interaction of supply and demand in the market.

Labor Demand and the Marginal Revenue Product Model

Let us now switch our level of analysis from all employers to the single employer operating in the market. In analyzing a single employer's wage setting and employment behavior, economists simplify the environment with four basic assumptions.[9]

1. Employers seek to maximize profits (the difference between total revenues and total expenses).
2. Human resources are homogeneous and therefore interchangeable; an M.B.A. is an M.B.A. is an M.B.A.
3. The pay rates include *all* costs associated with employing human resources (holidays, benefits, and training, in addition to wages).
4. The markets faced by employers are competitive. This is an important assumption. It implies that there are so many buyers and sellers at any given time that the decisions made by any single employer or worker has negligible impact on the market.

In the near term, when an employer cannot change technology or capital and natural resources, its level of production can change only if the level of human resources employed is changed. Under such conditions:

> **The additional revenue generated when the firm employs one additional unit of human resources, with other factors held constant, is called the marginal revenue of labor.**

> **The additional output associated with the employment of one additional human resources unit, with other factors held constant, is the marginal product of labor.**

For example, if a compensation consulting firm can service 10 clients per month with two M.B.A.s and 16 with three, the marginal product (the change in output associated with adding additional units of labor) of employing the third M.B.A. is six. But the marginal product of a fourth M.B.A. may not be the same as the marginal product of the third M.B.A. In fact, when we add a fourth M.B.A. to the consulting firm, the marginal productivity falls to four. (Four additional clients can be serviced.) What happened?

The initial rise in productivity may have resulted from the three M.B.A.s working together to generate new ideas. Was the fourth M.B.A. of poorer quality than the third? The assumed homogeneity of factors of production (assumption two) rules this out. Diminishing marginal products result from the fact that

---

[9]For a more generalized discussion of marginal productivity, turn to a basic labor economics text such as Ehrenberg and Smith, *Modern Labor Economics*, or Lloyd G. Reynolds, *The Structure of Labor Markets* (New York: Harper & Row, 1951).

as human resources expand, each additional worker has a progressively smaller share of the other factors of production with which to work. Recall that in the short term other factors of production (e.g., office space, computer services) were fixed. As more M.B.A.s are brought into the firm, the marginal productivity must eventually decline.

In the short term, a single employer's demand for labor curve coincides with its marginal product of labor curve. The marginal product curve is downward sloping, indicating that each added unit of labor yields a progressively smaller increment in output.

In order to maximize profits (the first assumption), the employer will continue to employ additional labor until the marginal revenue generated by hiring the last employee is equal to the marginal expenses associated with employing that worker. Marginal revenue is simply the marginal product times the price consumers pay for that product. Since profits equal total revenues minus total expenses, if the labor's marginal revenue exceeds its marginal costs, profits are increased by hiring that additional unit of labor. Conversely, if marginal revenue is less than labor's marginal costs, the employer would lose money on the last hire and could increase profits by reducing labor. Hence, the level of employment that is consistent with profit maximization is that level at which the marginal revenue of the last hire is equal to its marginal costs.

Exhibit 6.6 shows the marginal revenue product model at both the level of the market and of a single employer. The pay level ($30,000) is determined at the market level stated earlier (left side of Exhibit 6.6). The interaction of the sum of *all* employers' demand for human resources and supply of human resources determines the level employers must pay. The employer is a pay level "taker," rather than pay level "maker." On the right side of Exhibit 6.6, supply and demand are analyzed at the level of the individual employer. The market has determined the pay rate ($30,000), and at that rate the individual employer can hire as many M.B.A.s as desired. The supply and demand lines intersect at 20; that is, this employer's marginal revenue will equal marginal cost upon hiring the twentieth M.B.A. So the task for a compensation manager is theoretically simple under the marginal product model: Determine the pay level set by market forces.

Objections to the marginal productivity model. A common objection is that employers have no idea what the marginal productivity of employees is. Compensation managers just do not ask, "What is the marginal revenue product of the last M.B.A. we want to hire?" Perhaps they do consider it, but simply express it differently. At Upjohn, before a new M.B.A. (or any degreed professional) is hired, the manager must justify it by comparing the expected compensation expenses to specific returns expected over a five-year period.[10]

---

[10]Henry L. Dahl, "Measuring the Human ROI," *Management Review,* January 1979, pp. 44–50.

EXHIBIT 6.6
Demand and Supply at the Market and Firm Level

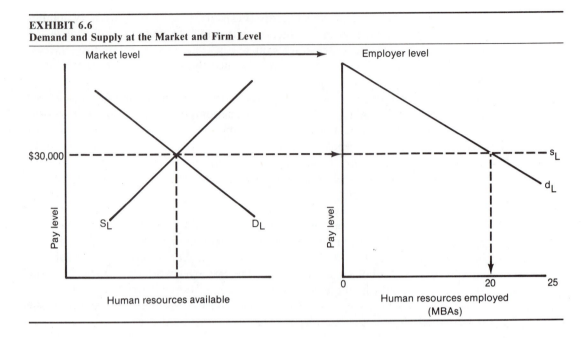

Other objections to the model question its ability to handle the complexities of determining pay in the real world. The model's assumptions oversimplify the real world. For example, the assumed degree of competition among buyers and sellers does not exist, nor are factors of production homogeneous, nor are all firms profit maximizers (some maximize market share, long-term profits, and so on). Despite these objections, the model still provides a valuable analytical framework for compensation managers.

Ideally, under the marginal productivity model we would pay individuals according to some function of their productivity times the market price of their product (marginal revenue product = marginal product × price). This is the perfect outcome measure in a conceptual sense. Unfortunately, there are some operational problems in measuring the outcome, specifically:

1. Placing a value on the goods or services an individual produces.
2. Determining individual values on products and services that are produced through joint efforts of different workers with a variety of talents. Labor is heterogeneous, not homogeneous.
3. Factoring the contributions of other resources (capital and raw materials) in the production process.

As a consequence of the difficulty of measuring marginal productivity and marginal revenue, compensation managers propose hypotheses about what types of things produce value in their organizations rather than trying to measure marginal revenue product directly. In the last two chapters we discussed job evaluation and compensable factors (skills required, financial accountability, external and internal contacts, etc.). In cases where the compensable factors are defined in terms of what management values in work, job evaluation can be thought of as assessing the job's contribution to organization goals (i.e., its marginal revenue product). Partial support for this notion is found in the policy-capturing (regression) approaches to establish the weights for compensable factors. Marginal productivity concepts are also applied in establishing the maximum and minimum rates jobs should be paid as well as linking the size of pay increases to performance or productivity improvements. So compensation decisions can be consistent with marginal productivity concepts, and these concepts can help us understand compensation decisions.

Labor Supply

In economic models, the supply of labor is a line or curve (lines *S* and *s* in Exhibit 6.6) representing the average pay required to attract different numbers of employees. Like demand curves, the exact shape of the supply of labor varies depending on the assumptions. In perfectly competitive markets, an employer faces a horizontal (elastic) supply curve: The market determines the price, and the individual employer can hire all the employees it wants, at that price. (See Exhibit 6.6, right side.) This model assumes that many workers are seeking jobs, they possess perfect data about job openings, and no barriers to mobility among jobs (no discrimination, licensing provisions, or union membership requirements) exist. Under the perfect competition model, the supply of labor is market driven, and the employer can hire all the employees it requires at the market-determined pay rate ($30,000 in the example in Exhibit 6.6).

As in the analysis of labor demand, these assumptions greatly simplify the real world. Perhaps some small employers, such as those in the service industry (e.g., fast foods and convenience stores), operate in such an environment, but most major employers do not.

As the assumptions of the model change to more accurately reflect reality, so do the supply curves. With an upward-sloping curve, from left to right, as shown in Exhibit 6.6, market level means that increased levels of human resources become available at higher pay levels. As pay increases, more people are willing to take a job. This relationship between the ability to attract human resources and the pay level is not meant to imply that pay is the sole determinant of human resource supply. It does imply that the pay level is an important factor influencing the supply of labor.

An upward-sloping supply of labor results from several factors. These include the "net advantage" offered to an individual, the training and investment in human capital required, the degree of competition for job openings, and union pressures.

Net advantage. More than 200 years ago Adam Smith argued that individuals consider the "whole of the advantages and disadvantages of different employments" and make decisions based on the alternative with the greatest "net advantage."[11] By this he meant that employers must offer higher pay rates to attract workers when

1. Greater time and expense is necessary to acquire skill and experience required to perform work.
2. Job security is tenuous.
3. Working conditions are disagreeable.
4. Chances of succeeding on the job are lower.

Individuals' net advantage calculations may include other elements, such as chances for promotion, opportunity for training, flexible work schedules, and coworker and supervisory relationships as well as the difficulties faced in simply commuting to and from the job. Cost of living is a major element in determining a job's net advantage. Pay levels may vary with living costs; high levels may be paid by firms located in areas with greater costs of living. However, for some jobs, particularly managerial and professional, many employers design a single nationwide pay structure which does not recognize geographic differentials. Reynolds argues that individual employees perceive different employers offering different combinations of pay and nonpay elements.[12] If employers wish to increase the level of human resources willing to accept employment, they may have to raise the pay level to offset the advantages found in other alternatives.

Training and investment in human capital. The expense of acquiring job-related skills also may create an upward-sloping supply curve. According to the human capital model, the value of an individual's skills and abilities is a function of the time, expenses, and other resources expended to acquire them.[13] Consequently, jobs that require long and expensive training (engineering, M.B.A.s, physicians) should receive higher pay levels than other jobs, such as clerical work and even elementary school teaching, which require less investment. According to this logic the time and expenses associated with acquiring the skills act as a barrier and restrict the ease of entry into occupations. Increasing the pay level for these occupations will induce people to develop their human capital and overcome the restrictions. So as pay level increases, the number of people willing to overcome barriers through training increases, creating an upward-sloping supply curve.

---

[11]Thomas A. Mahoney, *Compensation and Reward Perspectives* (Homewood, Ill.: Richard D. Irwin, 1979), p. 123.

[12]Reynolds, *Structure of Labor Markets.*

[13]Gary S. Becker, *Human Capital* (New York: National Bureau for Economic Research, 1964).

Job competition. Thurow, in the "job competition" model, asserts that workers do not compete for pay in labor markets.[14] Rather, pay for jobs is "quoted" or established, and workers compete through their qualifications for the job opportunities. A pool of applicants develops for every opportunity and individuals in the pool are ranked by prospective employers according to the skills, abilities, and experience required for the job. As the employer dips further and further into the applicant pool, individuals will require more training and will be less productive even though in a quoted market they will receive the same wage. Accordingly, the expenses (pay plus training) associated with each additional unit of labor in the pool increases, leading to an upward-sloping supply of labor curve.

Employer size and other factors. The size of an employer may also influence the shape of the supply curve. There is some evidence that larger organizations tend to pay more than smaller ones.[15] Under full-employment conditions, an employer who dominates the labor market has relatively few alternatives from which to attract new applicants. Any increase in employment requires that additional applicants must be induced to enter the labor supply, perhaps from schools, retirement, or more distant areas. Similarly, local applicants have very few alternatives and may have to commute to distant areas if they are rejected by the dominant employer. Corning Glass's influence in Corning, New York, might be an example. Such a dominant employer has relatively wide latitude in determining pay levels, since few alternative jobs exist. However, once the local labor supply is employed, small increases in the pay levels may not be effective in attracting more applicants. Then the supply curve, while upward sloping, may take on the shape of a "step" function, and require large pay increases to attract additional people. Rather than increasing the pay, the firm may opt to lower the job requirements (hire less skilled workers) but this pay savings would tend to be offset by increased training expenses. Small employers competing with a single dominant employer will experience considerable pressure to match the dominant employer's pay level or offer other advantages in order to obtain sufficient labor.

Finally, several other factors, such as geographic barriers, union requirements, lack of information about job openings, the degree of risk involved, and

---

[14]Lester C. Thurow, *Generating Inequality: Mechanisms for Distribution in the U.S. Economy* (New York: Basic Books, 1975).

[15]Richard Lester, "Pay Differentials by Size of Establishment," *Industrial Relations,* October 1967, pp. 57–67; Wesley Mellow, "Employer Size and Wages," *Review of Economics and Statistics,* 1982, pp. 495–501; Stanley H. Masters, "Wages and Plant Size: An Interindustry Analysis," *Review of Economics and Statistics,* August 1969, pp. 341–45; Thomas A. Pugel, "Profitability, Concentration, and the Interindustry Variation in Wages," *Review of Economics and Statistics,* May 1980, pp. 248–53; and Ephraim Klelman, "Wages and Plant Size: A Spillover Effect?" *Industrial and Labor Relations Review,* January 1971, pp. 243–48.

the degree of unemployment present in the market may all influence the supply of labor. For example, during high unemployment the supply curve would become relatively horizontal until the excess labor is absorbed.

In summary, the labor supply curve faced by firms in the short term depends on an individual's perceptions of net advantage, the extent of investment in human capital required, the degree of competition for job openings, the firm's size relative to the market, and other factors. The shape of the supply curve may vary from horizontal, with abundant supply at a given pay level, to upward sloping, requiring higher pay to increase the supply.

Union pressures. Employees organize unions to bargain collectively with management for outcomes they believe are unavailable to them as individuals. While these outcomes may seem self-evident, there have been a few studies of union member preferences. Wages and fringe benefits, along with job security and grievance handling, are among the most important outcomes.[16] When evaluating their unions, members ranked wage gains first, grievance handling second, fringes third, and job security fourth.[17] Unions' objectives are affected by economic conditions, political considerations within the union, and members' personal needs, among other factors.

Economic models suggest that unions' two basic goals are higher pay and increased membership. Increases in both are preferred, but usually trade-offs occur. If pay (marginal costs) increases more rapidly than productivity (marginal product) and the employer is unable to pass the increased costs on to the consumer, then employment (union membership) may be reduced. On occasion unions may succeed in negotiating both increased wages and membership.[18]

Labor economists have studied the effects of unions on wage levels for years.[19] The relative wage level of union versus nonunion employees seems to depend on the degree of concentration in the industry, the ability to pass wage increases on to consumers in the form of price increases, and the degree that the industry is unionized. Research suggests that unionized employees earn higher wages as compared to nonunion workers. Typical differences range from 5 to 15 percent.[20] More recent data show that wages of nonunionized employees

[16]Thomas A. Kochan, *Collective Bargaining and Industrial Relations* (Homewood, Ill.: Richard D. Irwin, 1980).

[17]John A. Fossum, *Labor Relations: Development, Structure, Process,* 3rd ed. (Plano, Tex.: Business Publications, 1985).

[18]Ibid.

[19]H. Gregg Lewis, "Union Relative Wage Effects: A Survey of Macro Estimates," *Journal of Labor Economics,* January 1983, pp. 1–27.

[20]Mark Killingsworth, "Union-Nonunion Wage Differentials," mimeo, Rutgers University, New Brunswick, N.J., 1981.

are rising faster than wages of unionized workers.[21] As this trend persists the union/nonunion differential narrows. The union impact on wages depends on the time period. The union/nonunion wage differential tends to be greatest during depressions or recessions and least during periods of expansion. For example, during 1932–33 (depression years), union presence may have meant more than 25 percent higher wages for unionized compared to nonunion workers.[22] The differential reached a low of about 2 percent in the late 1940s and it is below 10 percent in the mid-1980s. In a study of the effects of unions on pay levels of public sector employers, Lewin concludes that the average wage effect of public sector unions is +5 percent.[23] The greatest effects are reported for fire fighters (up to 18 percent differential attributed to presence of a union). At the other extreme, however, teachers' unions have not had as great an effect, with only 1 to 4 percent pay level differentials attributed to unions. In sum, it appears that the presence of unions does have a positive effect on pay levels, and this effect is greatest in the private sector during economic downturns and diminishes as the economy expands.

Of practical concern to the compensation manager is defining the specific objectives of each union that represents the organization's employees. Unfortunately, little research has been done that permits translating that objective into practice. In one study Olson measured union member preferences for bargaining outcomes.[24] Using pay increases as a base, he found the proportion of members preferring pension improvements, 42 percent; health insurance, 40 percent; job security, 21 percent; and grievance handling improvement, 15 percent.

Settlements with unions may also influence the compensation of nonunion employees.[25] For example, compensation managers frequently adjust management fringe benefits and services to at least match those negotiated with the

---

[21]D. J. B. Mitchell, "Union versus Nonunion Wage Norm Shifts," Working paper, UCLA, September 1985.

[22]Richard B. Freeman and James Medoff, *What Do Unions Do?* (New York: Basic Books, 1984).

[23]David Lewin, "Public Sector Labor Relations: A Review Essay," in *Public Sector Labor Relations: Analysis and Readings,* eds. D. Lewin, P. Feuille, and T. Kochan (Glen Ridge, N.Y.: Thomas Horton and Daughters, 1977).

[24]Craig A. Olson, "Scaling Union Member Preferences for Bargaining Outcomes," unpublished paper, Krannert Graduate School of Management, Purdue University, 1979.

[25]For studies of the spillover effect of unions on nonunion wages, see Daniel J. B. Mitchell, *Unions, Wages and Inflation* (Washington, D.C.: Brookings Institution, 1980); H. Gregg Lewis, *Unionism and Relative Wages in the United States* (Chicago: University of Chicago Press, 1963); Orley Ashenfelter and George E. Johnson, "Unionism, Relative Wages, and Labor Quality in U.S. Manufacturing Industries," *International Economic Review,* October 1972, pp. 488–507; and O. Eckstein and T. W. Wilson, "The Determination of Money Wages in American Industry," *Quarterly Journal of Economics,* 1962, pp. 379–414.

union. Pay levels for nonunion supervisors and clerical workers often are set to maintain a differential with union-negotiated wage levels. Finally, some employers adopt higher pay levels to help maintain a union-free status.

Relevant Markets and Multiple Pay Levels

As a practical matter, it has long been recognized that there is no such thing as a single, homogeneous labor market.[26] Rather, employers operate in many labor markets, each with unique demand and supply configurations. A major task for compensation managers is to define the labor markets that are relevant for pay purposes and to establish the appropriate pay levels. The three factors usually used to determine the relevant labor markets are the occupation (qualifications required), the geography (willingness to relocate and/or commute), and the other employers involved (particularly those who market similar goods or services).

Economists conceive of labor markets in terms of all three factors. They consider the skills and qualifications required in an occupation as important because they tend to limit mobility among occupations. This includes licensing and certification requirements as well as training and education. Accountants, for example, would have some difficulty in becoming dentists. Fogel stresses that labor markets are organized around occupations and states that "the forces of wage determination must necessarily be directed to occupations."[27]

Qualifications interact with geography to further define the scope of the relevant labor markets. Some skills, such as those possessed by degreed professionals (accountants, engineers, physicians), are recruited nationally. Others (technicians, crafts, and operatives) are recruited regionally and still others (office workers), locally. However, the geographic scope of a market is not fixed. It changes in response to workers' willingness to relocate or commute certain distances. This "propensity to be mobile" in turn may be affected by personal and economic circumstances as well as the pay level established by an employer. Configurations of local markets are even shaped by the availability of convenient public transportation. Furthermore, the geographic limits may not be the same for all in a broad skill group. All M.B.A.s (not a homogeneous group) do not operate in a national market; some firms recruit them regionally, others nationally.

[26]F. Ray Marshall, Allan G. King, and Vernon M. Briggs, Jr., *Labor Economics: Wages, Employment and Trade Unionism* (Homewood, Ill.: Richard D. Irwin, 1980).

[27]Walter Fogel, "Occupational Earnings: Market and Institutional Influences," *Industrial and Labor Relations Review,* October 1979, pp. 24–35. Also see Charles R. Greer, Jack Fiorito, and Robert C. Dauffenbach, "Uniformity and Variation in Compensability: A Potential Source of Incomparable Worth," unpublished paper, College of Business Administration, Oklahoma State University.

In addition to the occupation and its geography, the industry in which the employer competes also affects the relevant labor markets.[28] Industry effects occur by relating the qualifications to particular technologies and experience as well as by placing a limit on the employer's ability to pay, discussed in the next section. The importance of qualifications and experiences tailored to particular technologies is often overlooked in theoretical analysis of labor markets. But the plant manager of General Motors' diesel locomotive facilities in LaGrange knows that machinists and millwrights who help manufacture parts for locomotives have very different qualifications than those Seattle machinists and millwrights who help Boeing manufacture the 757.

Surprisingly little research has been done on determining the relevant labor markets for pay determination. Some work has been done with respect to the availability of various skills by minority and sex groups for employment and goal setting in affirmative action.[29] But compensation managers regularly define the relevant markets for various types of labor as part of the process of collecting external pay data. If the markets are incorrectly defined, the estimates of other employers' pay rates may be incorrect and the pay level inappropriately established. Most of the work on defining relevant markets has evolved through wage and salary survey practices. On this issue, academic research seems to offer little guidance to the compensation professional. For example, we have not even analyzed the applications for job vacancies to determine the nature of markets. Nor have we ever systematically collected data on the time it takes to fill a job vacancy.

PRODUCT MARKETS AND ABILITY TO PAY

Any organization must, over time, receive enough revenues to cover compensation and other expenses. In the private sector, revenues are generated through sales of products and services. It follows that an employer's ability to pay is constrained by its ability to compete. So the nature of the product market affects external competitiveness and the pay level the firm sets.[30]

The degree of competition among producers and the level of the demand for products are the two key product market factors. Both affect the ability of the organization to change the prices of its products and services. If prices can-

[28]Joseph W. Garbarino, "A Theory of Interindustry Wage Structure Variation," *Quarterly Journal of Economics,* May 1950, pp. 282–305.

[29]For example, see Frank Krzystofiak and Jerry Newman, "Evaluating Employment Outcomes: Availability Models and Measures," *Industrial Relations,* Fall 1982, pp. 277–92.

[30]Lewis, *Unionism and Relative Wages;* Mitchell, *Unions, Wages and Inflation;* Ross, "External Wage Structure;" and David G. Brown, "Expected Ability to Pay and Interindustry Wage Structure in Manufacturing," *Industrial and Labor Relations Review,* October 1962, pp. 45–62.

not be changed without suffering loss of revenues due to decreased sales, then the ability of the employer to pay higher rates is constrained.

In effect, the product market factors put a lid on the maximum pay level that an employer can set. If the employer pays more, then it has two options. It can try to pass on the higher pay level through price increases or hold prices fixed and allocate a greater share of total revenues to cover labor costs.

Consider the U.S. auto firms' recent experiences. For many years automakers were able to pass on increased pay levels to the consumer in the form of increased car prices. While competition among the the "Big Three" existed, they all passed on the pay increases. But then the product market revolutionized. The degree of competition from Japan and Korea increased, and due to a slowed economy, the total demand for cars actually declined. Both of these factors constrained the firms' ability to pay and their ability to change the pay level. In response, some autoworkers took pay cuts, accepted smaller wage increases, and agreed to work-rule changes intended to improve productivity.

So the nature of the product demand and the degree of competition in the industry influence the pay level and the ability to change it over time. An employer's ability to finance higher pay levels through price increases depends on the product market conditions.[31] Employers in highly competitive markets will be less able to raise prices without loss of revenues. At the other extreme, monopolists of a product (single sellers) with a very strong demand for the product will be able to raise prices.

Other factors besides the product market conditions affect the ability to pay. Some of these have already been discussed. The productivity of labor, the technology employed, the level of production relative to plant capacity available, and the extent of nonhuman resource expenses all affect ability to pay. These factors vary more across industries than within industries. The technologies employed and other conditions (consumer tastes) may differ among auto manufacturers but the differences are relatively small when compared to the technologies and product demand in other industries such as oil or banking. These across-industry differences permit firms to adopt different pay levels.

Pay contours. Variations in pay levels from industry to industry are well documented. Dunlop credited differences in wages paid to Boston truck drivers to the existence of wage contours, which he defines as

> a stable group of wage-determining units (bargaining units, plants, or firms) which are so linked together by (1) similarity of product markets, (2) resort to similar sources for a labor force, or (3) common market organization (custom) that they

---

[31]See Mahoney, *Compensation and Reward Perspectives,* pp. 115–23.

[32]Dunlop, "The Task of Contemporary Wage Theory." Also see David A. Pierson and Thomas A. Mahoney, "Labor Market and Employer Ability to Pay as Wage Contour Influences," *Southern Business Review,* Fall 1982, pp. 87–95.

have common wage-making characteristics. The wage rates for a particular occupation in a particular firm are not ordinarily independent of all other wage rates; they are more closely related to the wage rates of some firms than to others. A contour for particular occupations is to be defined in terms of both product market and the labor market. A contour, thus, has three dimensions: (1) particular occupations or job clusters, (2) a sector of industry, and (3) a geographical location.[32]

He noted that truck drivers in the coal industry for example were paid wage rates of about 75 percent of those paid to drivers in the oil industry. These observations, which apply to compensation managers, truck drivers, and most jobs, indicate that employers recruiting from the same labor supply may nonetheless pay significantly different wages. To these data we can add those from Foster's study shown in Exhibits 6.2 and 6.3. Not only do pay levels for the same job differ by industry, they also differ among employers within the same industry and the same geographic location.

ORGANIZATION AND WORK FORCE FACTORS

Conditions in the labor market and product market can be thought of as setting the limits within which the pay level can be established. Since the pay level directly affects operating costs, it must be set with an eye toward competitors' costs and ability to pay. Hence the conditions in the product market set the maximum beyond which the organization will be unable to competitively price its goods and services. The labor market pressures establish the minimum pay level that serves to attract and retain a pool of qualified workers. The floor to the minimum is set by minimum-wage legislation. If the compensation manager sets the pay level too low, managers will have trouble attracting and holding the types of employees required. Set the pay level too high and the employer's ability to sell products will be affected.

So the pressures in the product and labor markets create a range of possibilities within which the compensation manager can recommend the pay level be set. The situation facing compensation managers is described by Lester in the following terms: "Management in different organizations vary in their motivation patterns (willingness to pay) and in their compensation policies, and they can often set a pay level at various points within the range of possibilities." He goes on to stress "that it is naive . . . to talk of the 'competitive wage,' 'the equilibrium wage' or the 'wage that clears the market.' "[33]

Until now much of the discussion assumed employers operating in product markets and seeking profits. Public sector employers do not face product market pressures as private sector employers do. Their revenues are generated through lobbying for legislative budget allocations. These budgets are, in turn,

---

[33]Richard A. Lester, "A Range Theory of Wage Differentials," *Industrial and Labor Relations Review,* July 1952, pp. 483–500.

a function of the taxes levied in various jurisdictions. While perhaps not as finely tuned as some product markets, the voters' willingness to pay increased taxes for the services rendered acts as an upper boundary on the pay level analogous to product market forces.

Willingness to pay and pay strategies. Faced with a range of possibilities for setting the pay level, managers survey competitors in labor and product markets to estimate the salaries paid by others. Management motivations and strategies for setting the organization pay level relative to others may differ.[34] Some may opt to set the pay level relatively high in the range to "lead" competition. To the extent possible, they strive to buffer the organization from pressures in the labor and product markets. A lead position is designed to ensure few difficulties in recruiting and hiring as well as to induce the best qualified to apply and hold turnover to a desired level. However, a lead policy without offsetting productivity gains results in higher unit labor costs.

Others may decide to "pay with competition" (set the pay level at the average or median of going rates); others may choose to "follow" competition with pay but offer other advantages (job security or short commuting distances) that offset the higher pay offered by competitors. These policies and their consequences are discussed again in the next chapter. At this point it is important to know that employers have options regarding their pay policies toward competitors. Further, as we have already noted, that policy must be coordinated with the overall strategies for managing human resources.

Work force characteristics. The characteristics of the work force, such as its productivity, experience, and union affiliation, may affect the employer's pay level decision and consequently its competitive position. Employees with high productivity and more experience may be able to command higher salaries than less productive or less experienced workers. Union affiliation, as we have already noted, affects the pay level, and some evidence suggests that firms with higher proportions of male employees also seem to have pay levels that are higher than the average paid by competing firms.[35] While more research is required, it seems clear that unique characteristics of each organization and its work force affect the variations in pay levels and competitive policies that we observed earlier in this chapter.

---

[34]Sara L. Rynes, Donald P. Schwab, and Herbert G. Heneman III, "The Role of Pay and Market Pay Variability in Job Application Decisions," *Organizational Behavior and Human Performance* 31 (1983), pp. 353–64; and Kenneth G. Wheeler, "Perceptions of Labor Market Variables by College Students in Business, Education, and Psychology," *Journal of Vocational Behavior* 22 (1983), pp. 1–11.

[35]Groshen, "Wage Dispersion."

CONSEQUENCES OF PAY LEVEL DECISIONS

Earlier we noted the degree of competitiveness of the pay level has two major consequences: (1) its effect on operating expenses and (2) its effect on employee attitudes and work behaviors. These consequences, shown in Exhibit 6.7, have been discussed throughout this chapter. All we will do here is to note again a key premise of compensation management: that the competitive policy and the pay level are key decisions that affect the performance of the organization.

The pay level directly affects operating expenses and indirectly affects revenues. Wages paid represent an expense, so any decision that affects their level is important. Revenues are indirectly affected by the quality of the work force induced to join and the productivity and experience levels of those who stay. Reduction in turnover of high performers, increased experience levels, increased probability of remaining union free and reduction of pay-related grievances and work stoppages are examples of the work behaviors presumed to be affected by pay level decisions.

From a practical perspective, the manager of the pay system must consider all these factors when establishing the external competitiveness policy and determining how to put that policy into practice. The next chapter is devoted to how to set the policy and examines the alternative practices involved.

Before we proceed, let us reemphasize that the major reason we are interested in the external competitiveness policy and the pay level is that they have profound consequences on the organization objectives. As we have already noted, very little research exists to guide us in making pay level decisions. We have clearly established that differences among organizations' competitive policies and pay levels exist. What remains to be better demonstrated are the potential effects different policies will have.

EXHIBIT 6.7
Some Consequences of Pay Levels

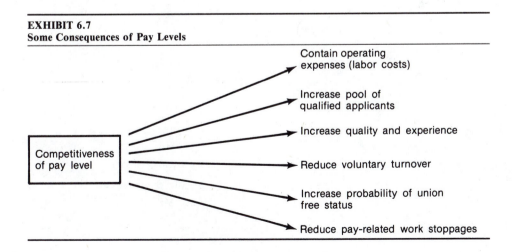

SUMMARY

The pay model used throughout this book emphasizes four basic policy issues—consistency, competitiveness, contributions, and administration. It also emphasizes that policies regarding these four issues need to be designed to achieve specific pay objectives. This section is concerned with external competitiveness, or pay comparisons among organizations. Does Apple Computer pay its bookkeepers the same wage that Virginia Electric and Power pays bookkeepers? Probably not. Different companies pay at different rates; the average of the overall array of rates in an organization constitutes the pay level. Each job family or functional specialty within the organization may have its own pay level. To achieve the objectives stipulated for the pay system, the pay level must be properly positioned relative to competitors. The next chapter discusses how the compensation professional determines this policy and considers the decisions involved and the variety of techniques available to implement decisions.

REVIEW QUESTIONS

1. Distinguish policies on external competitiveness from policies on internal consistency. Why is external competitiveness so important?
2. What factors influence an organization's external competitiveness?
3. Distinguish between marginal revenue and marginal product.
4. How do marginal revenue and marginal product affect an organization?
5. What does marginal revenue product have to do with pay?
6. What affects an organization's ability to pay?

Chapter 7

Designing the Pay Level and Structure

"The desired position in compensation is to be above the market—equal to or better than."

"Our pay philosophy is to be, on the average, better than the average."

"The policy for pay and benefits is to be in the top 10 percent."

"The company pays a slight premium in its nonunion plants over the wages paid in the general geographic area for similar work at union plants."

"The pay policy, an unwritten one, is to be competitive with the area. We use our own surveys. We check midpoints, and while the policy is to pay slightly above, in practice we pay at the midpoint. The salaried employees are below the midpoint and the hourly people are at the midpoint."

"Our goal is to be in the 65th percentile nationally."[1]

All the above statements are different organizations' policies regarding an employer's competitive position pay—the pay level. In the last chapter we discussed the factors that influence these pay policies. The rates competitors pay are critical; these include competitors in the product/service markets and labor markets. Other factors that influence the pay level include the nature of the labor markets, particularly the level of demand and supply available, and organizational factors such as the employer's financial condition, the technology, the work force demographics and productivity, the business strategies adopted, and the influence of unions.

In this chapter we examine how organizations use these factors to set externally competitive pay levels and structures. As part of this examination specific techniques and the major decisions in setting pay level are discussed.

MAJOR DECISIONS

The major techniques and decisions involved in setting an externally competitive pay level and designing the corresponding pay structures are shown in Exhibit 7.1. They include (1) clarify the employer's pay level policy; (2) determine the issues to be addressed in a survey; (3) design and conduct surveys; (4) interpret and apply survey results; and (5) design ranges, flat rates, and/or incentives. The approaches associated with each decision are discussed in the rest of the chapter. As you read through the chapter, you will become aware that each new decision may cause an employer to revise previous decisions. So the process may be better described as circular rather than linear. For example, the addition of incentives (decision 5) may cause the employer to revise its pay level

---

[1] Fred K. Foulkes, *Personnel Policies in Large Nonunion Companies* (Englewood Cliffs, N.J.: Prentice-Hall, 1980).

EXHIBIT 7.1
Determining Externally Competitive Pay Levels and Structures

External competitiveness: Pay relationships among organizations	→	Policy determination	→	Market definition	→	Conduct pay surveys	→	Draw policy lines	→	Competitive pay levels and structures

Some Major Decisions in Pay Level Determination
- Determine pay level policy
- Define purpose of survey
- Design and conduct survey
- Interpret and apply results
- Design ranges, flat rates, incentives

---

policy or decide that it needs a specialized survey to determine what types of incentives other employers are using. Or, in the face of market data, an employer may decide that it can no longer afford to maintain a lead position with pay. The point is that as data change, decisions may change.

DETERMINE PAY LEVEL POLICY

There are three classic pay level policies: to lead, to meet, or to follow competition. How does an employer choose a policy? Except for some dated studies, there is little research on what factors an employer actually uses to set a pay level policy. Some studies almost 40 years old report that "profit prospects" (anticipated ability to pay) and pay adjustments being made by other employers in the area (labor market conditions) are dominant factors. Unfortunately, more recent work has not been reported. In 1948, Lester had 63 firms rank seven factors they felt were most important.[2] His results, shown in Exhibit 7.2, reveal that rates paid by others and union pressures were most important, and the

---

EXHIBIT 7.2
Relative Importance of Pay Level Factors *(ranked by importance)*

1. Rates paid by other employers in the industry or area.
2. Union strength.
3. Cost of living changes.
4. Surplus/shortage of qualified workers.
5. Employee unrest.
6. Employers' overall financial position.
7. Firm's profits.

Adapted from Richard A. Lester, *Company Wage Policies* (Princeton, N.J.: Princeton University Press, 1948).

---

[2]Richard A. Lester, *Company Wage Policies* (Princeton, N.J.: Princeton University Press, 1948).

firm's financial position and company profits were least important. So what others pay appears to be a consistently important factor.

While the factors considered in setting pay may be stable, their relative importance may vary. For example, with inflation running over 12 percent in the late 1970s, the cost of living probably was a major factor in setting pay level. In fact, many employers reported granting special increases to offset effects of inflation for the first time in that period. In the 1981–83 economic recession some employers, particularly those in "smokestack industries," would probably have ranked ability to pay and profits as relatively important pay level factors. Other employers experiencing skill shortages, such as those in high technology and defense-related businesses, may have put greater weight on labor market factors and the ability to obtain critical skills. Unfortunately, this is all speculation; there is little research regarding which factors are most important, how these factors may shift over time, or what conditions may influence these shifts.

Given the choice to match, lead, or lag, evidence suggests that the most common policy is to *match* rates paid by competitors.[3] A 1951 study found that managers tended to justify this "matching" policy with three reasons: (1) failure to match competitors' rates would increase employee pay dissatisfaction; (2) over the long term, lower rates would limit the organization's ability to recruit; and (3) management was somehow obligated to pay prevailing rates. However, this study also found that employees were largely unaware of comparative pay levels among organizations. A more recent study of large, non-unionized companies found that most employers try to lead or at least match competition. This policy was seen as important for maintaining union-free status.[4] Little additional research on the choice of pay policies exists. Though as we shall see in this chapter, a firm's actual pay policy may be a function of which surveys are used, when they are used, and by whom, rather than its stated pay policy.

Policy effects. What difference does the pay policy make? The basic premise is that the competitive pay policy will affect compensation objectives and ultimately the organization's performance. The potential effects of alternative pay level policies on the compensation system objectives are shown in Exhibit 7.3.

Pay with competition. A pay with competition policy tries to ensure that an organization's labor costs are approximately equal to those of its competitors and that its wages be equally attractive to induce people to apply for employment. This policy avoids placing an employer at a disadvantage in pricing products or

---

[3]Kenneth E. Foster, "An Anatomy of Company Pay Practices," *Personnel,* September 1985, pp. 67–71.

[4]Lloyd G. Reynolds, *The Structure of Labor Markets* (Westport, Conn.: Greenwood Press, 1951); Foulkes, *Personnel Policies.*

EXHIBIT 7.3
Probable Relationships between Pay Level Policies and Objectives

	Compensation Objectives				
Policy	*Ability to Attract*	*Ability to Retain*	*Contain Labor Costs*	*Reduce Pay Dissatisfaction*	*Increase Productivity*
Pay above market (lead)	+	+	?	+	?
Pay with market (match)	=	=	=	=	?
Pay below market (lag)	−	?	+	−	?

in maintaining a qualified work force. But it does not provide an employer with a competitive advantage in its labor markets.

Lead policy. The rationale behind a lead policy is to maximize the ability to attract and retain quality employees and to minimize employee dissatisfaction with pay. Lead policies can serve as a signal to employees that the employer's entire human resource program is superior to that of its competitors. Some employers are able to pass higher pay rates on to consumers in the form of higher product prices. Sometimes an entire industry can pass high pay rates on to consumers if pay is a relatively low proportion of total operating expenses or if it is highly regulated. Petroleum and utilities are examples of such industries.

But what about adopting a leadership position within an industry? Does Exxon or Shell lead the other large petroleum/energy firms? If so, what are the advantages that accrue? If firms have similar technologies, other operating expenses are probably approximately equal. Does a lead policy within such an industry really permit the employer to select the best of the applicant pool? Assuming the employer is able to select the most qualified from this pool, does this higher quality talent translate into greater productivity, lower unit labor costs, improved product quality, and increased innovation? Do employees really view pay as a signal of the quality of an employer's entire personnel system? These are the premises that underlie a pay leadership policy. However, there is no research to support (or refute) it.

Lag Policy. Setting a lag pay policy to follow competitive rates may hinder a firm's ability to attract potential employees (Exhibit 7.3). A lag policy's effect on turnover is not at all clear. While lower pay levels probably contribute to turnover, the relationship between pay level policy and turnover is quite complex. Pay may be only one of many factors influencing turnover.[5] For example,

---

[5]Dan R. Dalton, W. D. Todor, and D. M. Krackhardt, "Turnover Overstated: The Functional Taxonomy," *Academy of Management Review* 7 (1982), pp. 117–23; Idalene F. Kesner and Dan R. Dalton, "Turnover Benefits: The Other Side of the 'Costs' Coin;" in *Employee Turnover: Causes, Consequences, and Control,* ed. W. H. Mobley (Reading, Mass.: Addison-Wesley Publishing, 1982), pp. 139–85; and B. M. Staw, "The Consequences of Turnover," *Journal of Occupational Behavior* 1 (1980), pp. 253–73.

alternative jobs available and length of service undoubtedly affect turnover, too. It is unclear how dissatisfied employees must be with pay before they will leave. Finally, some may see a pay policy as a signal of the quality of other personnel programs. It is possible for some employers to lag competition on pay but lead on other aspects of rewards (e.g., challenging work, desirable location, outstanding colleagues).

In summary, there is little evidence of the consequences of different pay level policies. It is not known whether the effects of pay level on the financial performance of a firm, its productivity, or its ability to attract and retain employees is sufficient to offset the effects on payroll costs. Nor is it known how much of a pay level variation makes a difference—will 5 percent or 10 percent or 15 percent be a noticeable difference? While lagging competitive pay could have a noticeable reduction in short-term labor costs, it is not known if this gain is accompanied by a reduction in the quality and performance of the work force.

So where does this leave the compensation professional? In the absence of convincing evidence, the least-risk approach is to set the pay level to match competition, though some employers vary their policy for different skills. They may adopt lead policies for certain critical skills, such as computer design engineers in the semiconductor industry, or financial analysts in brokerage houses. A competitive policy may be set for less critical skills, and a lag policy for jobs that are easily filled by the local labor market. A study of TRW, a large, highly decentralized firm, found that different business units established a variety of pay level policies.[6] Some of these differences reflected different industries in which the units operate (automotive versus defense related). Other differences reflected varying labor market conditions (high unemployment in Michigan and Ohio versus lower unemployment in Los Angeles) and business strategies (cost-plus defense contracts versus the highly competitive microchip market). Honeywell, another diversified firm, emphasizes in its communications to employees that the pay level policies are set independently by each of its business units. Under such decentralized approaches, an obvious concern is to achieve some degree of control and uniformity of policies, at least at the corporate level.

No matter what pay level policy is selected, it needs to be translated into practice. A first step is to identify the relevant external labor markets we are referring to when we set our pay level policy, and then survey that market to determine the competitor's existing pay rates.

WHY CONDUCT A SURVEY?

Most firms conduct or participate in several different pay surveys. Some writers claim that larger employers participate in up to 100 surveys in a single year,

---

[6]George T. Milkovich, "Pay Systems in a Highly Diversified Organization," Working paper, ILR School, Cornell University, Ithaca, N.Y., 1983.

though data from only a few select surveys are used to make compensation decisions.[7]

An employer will conduct/participate in a survey for a number of reasons: (1) to adjust the pay level in response to changing external pay rates, (2) to establish or price the pay structure, (3) to analyze personnel problems which may be pay related, (4) to attempt to estimate the labor costs of competitors in its product markets, or (5) to participate as "good citizens" in response to requests from other employers or public agencies.

Pay Level

Most organizations make adjustments to employees' pay on a regular basis. Perhaps as a result, employees have come to expect ever-increasing wages. Such adjustments can be based on performance, seniority, or simply the overall upward movement of pay rates in the economy. Market surveys provide information on pay rates among other employees. Periodic changes in overall rates guide employers to possible changes in their own overall rates in order to maintain or adjust their own wage level's relationship to the market. A major shift in employers' approach to regular (annual) adjustments in the pay level may be underway, particularly in industries facing competition from foreign producers with lower unit labor costs. Our experience suggests that more employers are delaying the adjustments of pay levels in an attempt to remain competitive with these foreign competitors.

Pay Structure

In addition to data on overall wage levels, many employers use market surveys as a check to validate their own job evaluation results. For example, internal job evaluation may place data processing jobs at the same level in the job structure as some secretarial jobs. But if the market shows vastly different pay rates for the two types of jobs, most employers will recheck their evaluation process to see if the jobs have been properly evaluated. Thus, the job structure that results from job evaluation may not match the pay structure found in the external market. Reconciling these two is a major issue confronting compensation professionals. As with so many procedures, it requires informed judgment based on the organization's specific circumstances and objectives.

---

[7]Kenneth E. Foster, "The Plus Side of Salary Surveys," *Personnel*, January/February 1963, pp. 35–43; S. Avery Raube, "Pay Surveys in Perspective," *Business Management Record*, May 1963, pp. 11–16; Barbara L. Fielder, "Conducting a Wage and Salary Survey," *Personnel Journal*, December 1982, pp. 879–80; and "New Techniques in Salary Surveys," *Business Management Record*, September 1963, pp. 28–31.

Belcher, Ferris, and O'Neill interviewed San Diego area organizations on their use of wage surveys. They found that adjustments to the pay structure were the most common uses of survey data.[8]

Survey results used to establish or adjust the pay level and price the job structure serve as crucial input for decisions which ultimately affect a firm's compensation objectives of efficiency and equity. An employer's labor costs and the competitiveness of its products and services are affected by the relationship between the organization's pay level and structure and the external market. Further, employers tend to rely on market data to justify pay differences among men and women in lawsuits brought under Title VII of the Civil Rights Act. Employers, for example, have successfully argued that the difference in pay between nurses and craftworkers is due to pay differences found in the external markets for these skills. This argument rests on the defensibility of the market data collected through wage surveys. Compensation professionals must ensure that their surveys will withstand illegal discrimination challenges.[9] Thus, surveys must be designed and managed carefully since their results are so significant to the organization.

Pay-Related Personnel Projects

Surveys used for special projects, often in response to problems that may be pay related, also provide important data. Examples include a survey of competitors' compensation practices for positions in which a company is experiencing abnormally high turnover among good performers. Or a special survey may determine starting salary offers that others are extending to college graduates. Many special studies are used to appraise the current pay practices for targeted groups, for example, patent attorneys or retail sales managers or chemical engineers. Using another example, General Mills may wish to exchange data with Nabisco, Keebler, and Frito Lay on a few jobs (e.g., district sales managers and merchandisers) where there is difficulty attracting and holding key people.

Estimate competitors' unit labor costs. Some firms, particularly in highly competitive businesses, such as producers of microcomputers, autos, and specialty steel products, are beginning to use salary survey data in their financial analysis of competitors' product pricing and manufacturing practices. The role of compensation professionals in this practice seems to be limited, but if this use of survey data becomes widespread, it may dampen employers' willingness to share detailed pay data with its product competitors.

---

[8]D. W. Belcher, N. B. Ferris, and J. O'Neill, "How Wage Surveys Are Being Used," *Compensation and Benefits Review,* September–October 1985, pp. 34–51.

[9]Sara L. Rynes and G. T. Milkovich, "Wage Surveys: Dispelling Some Myths about the 'Market Wage'," *Personnel Psychology,* Spring 1986, pp. 71–90.

The final purpose of surveys—to be a "good corporate citizen"—is least important. Some employers participate in many surveys simply as a courtesy to other employers. Due to the personnel expenses involved, some employers have become ve ry selective in agreeing to participate in surveys. So the first step is to identify the key issues the employer seeks to resolve in the survey. The area of salary surveys seems to be one where amount of data overruns its usefulness. Perhaps failure to specify the purpose of the analysis is why.

DESIGN AND CONDUCT SURVEYS

Surveys provide the data for setting the pay policy relative to competition and translating that policy into pay levels and structures. A survey is defined as:

> **The systematic process of collecting and making judgments about the compensation paid by other employers.**

The basic decisions in designing and conducting pay surveys are discussed in the following sections.

What Is the Relevant Market?

The answer to this question depends on the purpose of the survey. The goal is to either sample or obtain pay rates in the entire population of the relevant labor market. The relevant labor market includes those employers with whom an organization competes for employees.

Relevant labor markets are typically defined in terms of:

1. The occupation or skill required.
2. The geographic distance employees are willing to commute (or relocate).
3. Employers who compete for same skills.
4. Employers who compete with same products.

So the definition of relevant labor market will vary, depending on the particular job and skills we are looking at.

Exhibit 7.4 shows how qualifications interact with geography to define the scope of relevant labor markets. As the importance of the qualifications and complexity of qualifications increase, the geographic limits also increase. Compensation professionals tend to define competition on a national basis for certain managerial, professional, and technical (engineers and scientists) jobs, whereas clerical and production jobs tend to be priced in local and regional markets.

But these generalizations do not always hold true. For example, in areas with high concentrations of scientists, engineers, and managers (e.g., Boston,

EXHIBIT 7.4
Relevant Labor Markets by Geographic and Employee Groups

		Employee Groups/Occupations					
R E L E V A N T L A B O R M A R K E T	Geographic Scope	Production	Office and Clerical	Technicians	Scientists and Engineers	Managerial Professional	Executive
	Local: Within relatively small areas such as cities or MSAs (Metropolitan Statistical Areas) (e.g., Dallas metropolitan area)	Most likely	Most likely	Most likely			
	Regional: Within a particular area of the state or several states (e.g., oil producing region of southwestern U.S.)	Only if in short supply or critical	Only if in short supply or critical	Most likely	Likely	Most likely	
	National: Across the country				Most likely	Most likely	Most likely
	International: Across several countries				Only for critical skills or those in very short supply	Only for critical skills or those in very short supply	Some-times

Los Angeles, or Palo Alto), the primary market comparison may be regional, with national data used only secondarily.

In major metropolitan areas, the relevant market may be defined by commuting times and patterns. Some studies show that most people are willing to commute up to 45 minutes (one way) to work.[10] But obviously this varies by locale as well as by personal and economic circumstances. Further, managers can influence the willingness of people to commute through actions other than setting higher pay levels. For example, a firm may lobby the local transit authority for convenient bus routes and schedules or may sponsor company-owned vans and car pooling programs. One New York City department store buses 160 workers from Brooklyn to its suburban stores during busy holiday seasons so that stores will have an adequate supply of sales personnel. In this case, the local suburban supply of people willing to work for minimum wage is inadequate. Faced with a shortage of school teachers, New York City went to Spain to recruit qualified teachers who were willing to commit themselves to a job in New York for at least two years. The point is that most employers will take a variety of steps to increase the supply of labor before they will raise wages. But even raising wages may not always work.[11] For example, when Giant Foods

[10]David Peterson, "Defining Local Labor Markets," in *Perspectives on Availability,* ed. Kenneth McGuinness (Washington, D.C.: Equal Employment Advisory Council, 1977).

[11]Sylvia Nasar, "Jobs Go Begging at the Bottom," *Fortune,* March 17, 1986, pp. 33–35.

raised its hourly pay from $3.35 (the legal minimum) to $3.75 in the Chicago area, Wendy's and Burger King followed suit. The result was that Giant Food was paying more for the employees it already had, but was still shorthanded. So, from the perspective of attracting qualified people, both skills and geography (willingness to relocate or commute) are important factors in defining the relevant labor market.

From the perspective of cost control and ability to pay, the most important factor in defining the relevant market is competition in the product/service market. The pay rates of product/service competitors will affect both their cost of operations and their financial conditions (e.g., ability to pay). The attempt on the part of various airlines to seek wage reductions from employees to reduce operating expense and to enable lower, more competitive fares is an example. An employer must be competitive in the product/service markets in which it operates. So inclusion of product competitors in the wage survey is vital. However, this becomes more of a problem when the major competitors are setting prices for products based on wages paid in South Korea, Brazil, or China.

Some writers argue that if the skills are tied to a particular industry, as underwriters, actuaries, and claims representatives are to insurance, it makes sense to define the market on an industry basis.[12] If skills such as accounting, sales, or clerical are not limited to one particular industry, they argue that industry considerations are virtually meaningless. But that position ignores financial objectives of the employer. Pricing labor competitively with others who compete in the same industry with similar products and services is necessary to achieve the organization's financial objectives. Within these product/service market constraints, occupational and geographic factors come into play. Additionally, a firm's size (number of employees, total revenues, and assets) reflects its market dominance. If one firm is so dominant that it in effect makes the market, becoming a "wage maker" rather than a "wage taker," a survey that omitted that firm would not accurately capture the market.

A final consideration in determining the relevant market relates to EEO. As noted earlier, market data is increasingly being used in pay discrimination litigation to defend pay differentials.[13] If market data are to serve as criteria to explain and justify pay practices, the definition of the relevant markets and the survey methodology must be defensible. This means that it must be

1. Documented: An organization's policies regarding external wage comparisons should be specified, and actions taken in conducting surveys should be consistent with these policies.

---

[12]Allan N. Nash and Stephen J. Carroll, Jr., *The Management of Compensation* (Monterey, Calif.: Brooks/Cole Publishing, 1975).

[13]*Kouba and EEOC* v. *Allstate Insurance Company,* 1982, 691 F. 2d 873; and *Briggs* v. *City of Madison,* W. D. Wisc. 1982, 436 F. Supp. 435. Also see *In the Matter of Boston Survey Group,* Mass. Superior Court, Docket No. 56341, August 2, 1982; and Rynes and Milkovich, "Dispelling Myths."

2. Business related: Firms competing with similar products/services are included.

3. Work related: Employers of similar skills within similar geographic areas are included. Caution should be exercised here since some employers, by virtue of the nature of their product market or pressure from their unions may be able and/or willing to pay more (e.g., Arthur Anderson may be willing to pay its accountants in Chicago more than Marshall Field's department store pays, since accountants are more critical to revenues generated in Arthur Anderson than they are in Field's).

How Many Employers?

How many employers to include depends on the circumstances. Some larger firms with a lead policy may exchange data with only a few (6 to 10) top-paying competitors. A small organization in a metropolitan area dominated by two or three employers may decide to survey only smaller competitors, and try to lag the larger ones. National surveys conducted by consulting firms such as Organization Resource Counselor's SIRS, Hay's Middle Management, or Hewitt's 777 (see Exhibit 7.5) may include over 100 employers. Clients of these consultants often stipulate special analyses which report pay rates by selected industry groups, geographic region, and/or their pay levels (e.g., top 10%).

Who to Involve?

In most organizations the responsibility for managing the survey lies with the compensation professional. But since the pricing of human resources has a powerful effect on the bottom line, selected operating managers and employees are often involved, too. A recurrent theme in this text has been the need to get user acceptance of procedures and results through involvement in procedure design. This point is valid for job analysis, job evaluation, selecting compensable factors, and also for pricing. Recall that employees' perception of the equity of their pay will influence their work behaviors. Consequently, including managers and employees on task forces and/or surveying employees to discover what firms use for pay comparisons makes sense. Not only does broader involvement increase understanding and probably acceptance of results, but employees also are sources of suggestions about which employers to include and about the accuracy of the data other firms provide.

Third parties, outside consulting firms, are often used as protection from possible "price-fixing" lawsuits. The trade-off in hiring a third party versus managing the survey internally usually involves less control over the decisions that determine the quality and usefulness of the data when outsiders conduct the survey.

EXHIBIT 7.5
Consulting Firms Conducting National Surveys

Group	Survey Description	Method of Insuring Job Comparability	How Data Are Reported	Cost
Abbot, Langer and Associates 548 First Street Crete, IL 60417 (312) 672-4200	Conducts surveys of starting salaries of inexperienced college graduates and compensation in the accounting/ financial, data processing, engineering, field/bench service, industrial relations, legal, manufacturing, sales/marketing management, scientific/technical, security/loss prevention, and training/ development fields. Most of their surveys are sponsored by professional, technical, and business associations and periodicals.	Paragraph job descriptions, descriptions of duties and levels of responsibility, levels of supervisory responsibility, etc. are included, as appropriate. For example, for electrical/electronics engineers, eight levels of professional responsibility are described; in the data processing survey, 45 one-paragraph job descriptions are included.	Means, medians, first and third quartiles, and first and ninth deciles of base salary, salary range, and total compensation (salary plus commission, cash bonuses, and/or cash profit sharing), are reported by geographic area, type of employer, size of organization, experience, education, job function, supervisory responsibility, technical competence, etc., as appropriate.	$90–$295; discount to members of sponsoring societies and/or participants.
Administrative Management Society 2360 Maryland Road Willow Grove, PA 19090	Conducts and publishes three compensation surveys listing salary and corollary information for management, clerical, and data processing positions. In addition, an annual benefits survey is available.	Job titles and descriptions included.	Averages and quartiles reported by geographic area, industry and city.	$75 for members; $115 for nonmembers.
American Society for Personnel Administration (ASPA) c/o A. S. Hansen 606 N. Washington Street Alexandria, VA 22314	Survey of human resource positions in over 1,300 organizations of all sizes.	Over 37 human resource position job descriptions including title, written description, and typical reporting relationship.	For nationwide sample and individual cities by industry, including relationship of compensation to gross sales, assets, premiums, budget, and employment.	$125 for participants; $250 for nonparticipants in 1986. Costs may vary by year.
A. S. Hansen, Inc. 1080 Green Bay Road Lake Bluff, IL 60044 (312) 234-9550	National surveys by function (data processing, finance, accounting, legal, materials management). Canadian versions also available. Also, specialized industry surveys.	Job descriptions including title, written description, and reporting relationships. Level of job defined through Job Family Matrices.	See American Society for Personnel Administration for details.	Functional surveys: $125–$225 for participants; $350–$900 for industry surveys. Benefit survey, $500.
Executive Compensation Service Two Executive Drive Fort Lee, NJ 07024 (201) 585-9808	22 reports for United States and Canada; 21 reports for European nations. Company size range from under $10 million to over $10 billion in sales. Surveys include top and middle management as well as professional, scientific, technical, skilled trade, sales, hospital, health care, and supervisory personnel.	Over 1,100 positions described by function and reporting status. Data collection questionnaire sent to facility, followed by telephone contact if necessary.	Statistical tables, charts, and graphs. Supplement to top and middle management report allows use of regression analysis and shows interrelationships of jobs to sales volume.	$125–$275 for participants; $325–$575 for nonparticipants.

EXHIBIT 7.5 (*concluded*)

Group	Survey Description	Method of Insuring Job Comparability	How Data Are Reported	Cost
Growth Resources, Inc. 1 Newbury Street Peabody, MA 01960 (617) 535-5500	Officer Compensation Report specializes in smaller companies (sales $250,000 to $50 million). Salaries, bonuses, total compensation, benefits, perquisites, ownership. Related tax laws and all other aspects of officer pay reported. Manufacturing, technology, and service.	Full-page position specifications.	By industry group, company sales, profitability, and position.	$225 for participants; $400 for nonparticipants.
The Hay Group Compensation Information Center Philadelphia, PA 19103 (80 offices in 25 countries)	Produces more than 50 major surveys annually: 1. The Hay Compensation Comparisons summarizes cash compensation *practices* for management, professional, and exempt technical positions in all functions. Participants can request special analyses that focus on a particular industry, function, or location from the database of over 900 major organizations. Reports can be linked to similar surveys in 30 other countries. 2. Executive Compensation Comparisons reports information on salary, bonus, short-term incentives, long-term incentives, benefits, and perquisites for individual top corporate line and staff jobs. Participation in these two surveys is restricted to organizations that use the Hay Guide Chart Profile of job evaluation. Unrestricted participation surveys are also done by: industry sector (e.g., software, railroad companies); function (e.g., accounting, design, EDP, engineering, legal, manufacturing operations, personnel, sales); employee status (e.g., blue collar, nonexempt clerical); and for benefits, perquisites, and personnel practices.	Comparison base of over 2 million jobs is provided by use of units of job content (points), which describe relative size of job based on "certain measurable aspects" of job. Measurements can be derived from participant grades. Measurements can be generated with computer assistance by HAY VALUE. Data transmission can be by tape or diskette, through use of HAYSYNC telecommunications, or in hard copy.	Standard and custom reports include: tabular percentiles, linear representations of company policies, maturity curves, or multiple regression. Published annual report. Data can also be related to industry sector, company size, geographic or performance characteristics; or can be stated for selected peer groups. Analyses can connect foreign currency to U.S. dollar equivalents and after-tax dollars. Published annual report. Data can also be related to specific company characteristics for individual executive positions.	Generally $250 to $1,500, depending on company size. $350 per analysis. $900–$2,000, depending on company characteristics.
Hewitt Associates 100 Half Day Road Lincolnshire, IL 60015 (312) 295-5000	Total Compensation DataBase™ for top management includes base salaries, bonuses, basic and executive benefits, long-term incentives, and perquisites. Individual position data and detailed plan design features are covered. Three segments are currently available: general industrial/manufacturing, diversified financial, and media/broadcasting. User selects companies for comparison on any position(s) and/or design features desired.	Thorough written descriptions and organization definitions, including information on major areas of responsibility, board membership, and reporting relationships. Data edited manually and by computer and discussed with each participant.	A dollar value for *all* components of pay by position may be determined. Regression analysis on any of a number of variables may be used. Detailed design information, plan prevalence statistics, and average incentive plan award size information may also be reported.	Available to participants only. Manuals covering administrative practices and aggregate position information for the three segments cost $600, $200, and $900, respectively.

Organization	Description	Verification/Job Matching	Reports/Output	Cost
				Simple data retrievals on one or two items may start as low as $50–$75.
Management Compensation Services Suite 113 8687 East Via de Ventura Scottsdale, AZ 85258 (602) 994-1373	A Division of Hewitt Associates. About 20 surveys annually, including Project 777 (executive compensation in 400 manufacturers with sales over $100 million). Also have surveys of middle management, sales and sales management, and international executive compensation and perquisites in 48 countries. In addition, conduct industry surveys and act as third party for various association surveys (i.e., The American Hospital Association ASHPA Management Compensation Study).	Thorough written descriptions and organization definitions, primary and secondary scope measures, and reporting level. Data edited manually and by computer. Over 90 percent of participants contacted by phone to verify job matches and accuracy of data input.	Tabular and graphics displays, single and multiple regressions in hard copy and diskette. Scattergrams, customized comparison of participant's data to the survey and "Constant Group" trend reports. Participants may request custom reports selecting companies based on various characteristics such as size, short- and long-range corporate financial performance measures (ROE, ROA, ROC, ROS), location, reporting relationship, and type of business.	Except for association surveys, results are available only to participants. Participation fees vary from $240 to $1,700 depending on the survey.
Organization Resources Counselors, Inc. 1211 Avenue of the Americas New York, NY 10036 (212) 719-3400 11645 Wilshire Blvd. Los Angeles, CA 90025 (213) 820-3800	Salary Information Retrieval Systems (SIRS) includes data on more than 475 occupational groups in several industries from entry-level nonsupervisory through middle management. Also includes 250 nonexempt jobs for certain geographic clusters. Also does more specialized surveys (e.g., regional clerical, banking, computer programmers and systems analysts, electric utilities, and electronics manufacturing).	Paragraph descriptions of benchmark jobs. Jobs matched using leveling charts using factors of knowledge, accountability, and problem complexity, freedom to act, impact, supervision, and liaison; weights of these factors can be modified for each company. ORC visits each participant annually to verify job matches. SIRS database includes more than 1 million incumbents.	User may specify comparisons based on size, location, sales industry, and/or products. Averages, ranges, dollar and percentage differences, regression lines. All reports individually prepared to participant's specifications and include only those data participant requested.	Available only to participants.
Towers, Perrin Forster & Crosby 245 Park Avenue New York, NY 10167 (212) 309-3959	Compensation data bank unit does more than 100 domestic and international surveys. 1. CDB Cash Compensation Survey includes 30,000 executives at over 340 companies. Top executive and middle management positions are included. 2. CDB also has a Long-Term Incentive Plan Survey that measures the value and competitive standing of companies' long-term incentive grants. 3. International surveys in Belgium, Canada, Venezuela, Germany, Hong Kong, United Kingdom, France, Italy, Singapore, Korea, Switzerland, Taiwan, and Japan. 4. Other surveys typically by industry (finance, oil, chain restaurants, high tech, entertainment, consumer products).	Job scope (reporting level, employees supervised) and corporate finance information collected.	Multiple regression analysis provides a customized "going rate"; position summary table displays descriptive statistics, and incumbent comparison table displays "your data" alongside survey quartiles on job scope and incumbent data. Scatterplots indicate an organization's overall competitiveness. Data are reported on three PC programs which are compatible with the IBM PC and other personal computers.	$1,000–$1,300 for CDB membership; $900–$1,100 for Long-Term Incentive Plan Survey; $750–$3,500 for international surveys, depending on scope and location. $400–$800 for various PC diskettes.

The specter of charges of price-fixing is real.[14] Suits have been filed alleging that the exchange of survey data violates Section One of the Sherman Act, which outlaws conspiracies in restraint of trade, but thus far the suits have all been settled out of court. Typically, it has been the courts' interpretation of the Sherman Act that survey participants are guilty of price-fixing if the overall effect of the information exchange is to interfere with competitive prices. One case involved the Boston Survey Group, a 34-member association, which exchanged data on wages for a variety of clerical jobs. The survey reported the salaries of individuals in each job classification surveyed; each participating firm's information was clearly identified, and the results were reported by industry group. 9 to 5, a women's political action group, protested and forced the Massachusetts State Attorney General's office to investigate. A consent decree agreed to by the Boston Survey Group stipulates:

- The input of each participant will no longer be identified (i.e., results will be "blind").
- Only aggregated information will be reported for each participant; salaries of individual employees will not be published.
- No data will be published on a per-industry basis.
- Any classification surveyed which results in fewer than 10 reported incumbents will not be reported.
- Members may choose to allow their employees to see the aggregated survey results for their own jobs.

Prohibiting exchange of industry data eliminated the ability to make product market comparisons. This might not be important in clerical jobs, but industry groups are important when making comparisons in wages for other skills and jobs. For example, a Hewlett-Packard marketer's job is probably more similar to that of an AT&T Information Systems marketer than it is to one in Union Carbide. If the skills in question are generalized and thus transferable, the industry data can safely be ignored. However, industry data is crucial from a competitive product market perspective. Further, if the skills are highly specialized (e.g., semiconductor designer) then they may be industry specific and are not available across industries. The point is that if we are going to start regulating the collection of wage data, more caution than was apparently exercised by the Boston Survey Group is necessary.

Make or Buy?

The decision to retain outside expertise or design one's own survey includes a complex set of trade-offs. The availability of staff time and talent and the de-

---

[14]Gary D. Fisher, "Salary Surveys—an Antitrust Perspective," *Personnel Administrator,* April 1985, pp. 87–97, 154.

sire to control the quality of analysis and results are often given as reasons to tailor one's own survey. On the other hand, consulting firms offer a wide choice of ongoing surveys covering almost every job family and industry group imaginable. Additionally, most firms also undertake special study surveys. Exhibit 7.5 is only a partial description of some standard surveys offered by various consulting firms.

Criteria for selecting. Opinions about the value of alternative consultant surveys are rampant; research is not. Do Hay; Towers, Perrin, Foster & Crosby; or Hewitt's 777 surveys of managerial pay yield significantly different results? Many firms select one survey as their primary source and use others to cross-check or "validate" the results. Yet little systematic study of differences in market definition, participating firms, type of data collected, analysis performed, and/or results is available. Of increasing importance, can these various surveys successfully withstand pay discrimination litigation? Professional consultants who design employment tests for applicant selection report the test's performance against a set of measurements (reliability, validity, and so on). Analogous standards for pay surveys have not yet evolved. For example, little attention has been directed toward treating surveys as samples of a population of rates paid. Issues of sample design and statistical inferences are seldom considered.

Publicly available data. The Bureau of Labor Statistics (BLS) is a major source of publicly available pay data.[15] It publishes three basic surveys: area wage studies, industry wage studies, and a National Survey of Professional, Administrative, Technical, and Clerical Pay. In addition, most states and even some counties provide pay data to the public. Exhibit 7.6 illustrates the nature of BLS data. The data are inexpensive and readily available. Public sector employers seem to use BLS data more often than do private sector employers. Some private sector firms do track the rate of change in BLS data as a cross-check on other surveys, and for an organization with locations across the country, BLS data are useful for examining geographic differentials for various nonexempt jobs (e.g., file clerks in Chicago versus file clerks in Durham, North Carolina). While the BLS file clerk data may not be relevant to an organization's file clerk jobs, the variations among geographic areas or overtime may be of interest.

---

[15]U.S. Department of Labor, Bureau of Labor Statistics, *BLS Measures of Compensation* (Washington, D.C.: U.S. Government Printing Office, 1977), Bulletin 1941; David Lewin, "The Prevailing-Wage Principle and Public Wage Decisions," *Public Personnel Management,* November/December 1974, pp. 473–85; and L. Earl Lewis, "Federal Pay Comparability Procedures," *Monthly Labor Review,* February 1969, pp. 10–13.

EXHIBIT 7.6
Example of Bureau of Labor Statistics Area Wage Survey

Table A-12. Weekly earnings of office workers in establishments employing 500 workers or more in Chicago, Ill., March 1982

Occupation and industry division	Number of workers	Average weekly hours (standard)	Weekly earnings (in dollars) Mean	Median	Middle range	Under 140	140 and under 160	160-180	180-200	200-220	220-240	240-260	260-280	280-300	300-320	320-340	340-360	360-380	380-400	400-420	420-440	440-460	460-480	480-520	520-560	560 and over
File clerks	1,476	39.0	201.50	192.50	170.00-226.00	32	176	289	330	218	187	102	87	13	17	5	10	6	-	2	1	-	-	-	-	-
Manufacturing	204	39.5	219.50	215.50	195.00-238.00	-	3	20	34	54	47	19	15	4	4	3	-	-	1	1	1	-	-	-	-	-
Nonmanufacturing	1,272	39.0	198.50	189.00	167.00-222.00	32	173	269	296	164	140	83	72	9	13	2	10	6	-	2	1	-	-	-	-	-
Transportation and utilities	53	40.0	283.00	269.00	238.50-344.50	-	-	6	-	-	9	-	18	-	5	1	8	4	-	2	1	-	-	-	-	-
File clerks I	683	39.0	184.00	177.00	160.00-200.00	32	135	216	131	59	59	15	33	3	-	-	-	-	-	-	-	-	-	-	-	-
Nonmanufacturing	587	39.0	178.50	172.00	156.00-190.50	32	135	203	112	59	43	7	18	-	-	-	-	-	-	-	-	-	-	-	-	-
File clerks II	586	39.0	208.50	200.00	180.00-230.00	-	41	68	174	111	73	58	36	8	10	1	6	-	-	-	-	-	-	-	-	-
Manufacturing	96	39.5	215.00	211.00	194.00-230.00	-	3	7	15	32	26	8	-	-	4	1	-	-	-	-	-	-	-	-	-	-
Nonmanufacturing	490	38.5	207.50	198.50	180.00-230.00	-	38	61	159	79	47	50	36	8	6	-	6	-	-	-	-	-	-	-	-	-
File clerks III	207	38.5	238.50	227.00	208.00-254.00	-	-	5	25	48	55	29	18	2	7	4	4	1	1	3	1	-	-	-	-	-
Nonmanufacturing	195	38.5	236.50	226.00	206.00-250.00	-	-	5	25	48	50	26	18	1	7	4	6	1	1	2	-	-	-	-	-	-
Messengers	1,042	39.0	205.50	191.00	171.50-227.00	16	121	212	241	169	100	59	39	13	17	1	38	1	10	3	2	1	-	-	-	-
Manufacturing	215	39.0	212.00	203.00	188.00-227.00	16	4	9	60	64	29	23	8	3	7	1	1	1	4	3	1	-	-	-	-	-
Nonmanufacturing	827	39.0	204.00	189.00	168.00-225.50	-	117	203	181	105	71	52	31	10	10	-	38	-	6	-	2	1	-	-	-	-
Transportation and utilities	148	39.5	282.50	275.50	237.00-344.50	-	-	2	10	4	27	21	24	9	4	-	38	-	6	-	2	-	-	-	-	-
Switchboard operators	601	39.0	233.00	222.50	171.00-265.00	8	117	46	29	90	74	64	64	11	48	11	6	7	3	1	7	1	1	6	1	-
Manufacturing	119	39.5	275.50	254.50	231.00-309.00	-	-	2	7	8	23	16	16	1	17	6	5	7	1	1	7	1	1	1	1	-
Nonmanufacturing	482	39.0	222.00	212.50	158.00-258.00	8	117	44	22	82	51	41	48	10	31	5	1	3	3	-	6	-	-	5	1	-
Transportation and utilities	69	39.5	331.00	317.00	275.00-379.50	-	-	-	-	8	-	6	5	1	25	2	1	7	3	-	6	-	-	5	1	-
Switchboard operator-receptionists	297	39.5	252.00	246.00	217.50-270.50	-	-	6	10	59	52	72	50	25	2	-	10	5	-	-	-	-	2	4	-	-
Manufacturing	134	39.5	255.50	242.00	220.50-273.50	-	-	-	3	30	19	37	19	10	2	-	10	4	-	-	-	-	2	4	-	-
Nonmanufacturing	163	39.0	249.00	246.00	214.50-270.50	-	-	6	7	29	33	35	31	15	2	4	1	1	-	-	-	-	-	4	-	-
Order clerks	465	40.0	231.00	214.00	185.00-255.00	-	32	72	89	61	54	52	17	17	22	4	1	-	-	35	9	-	-	4	-	-
Manufacturing	255	40.0	267.50	251.00	217.00-287.50	-	-	16	23	36	33	52	17	17	12	4	1	-	-	35	9	-	-	4	-	-
Order clerks I	303	40.0	194.50	185.00	168.00-214.00	-	32	72	89	52	27	15	6	7	7	-	-	-	-	-	-	-	-	-	-	-
Manufacturing	121	40.0	220.50	217.50	188.00-251.00	-	-	16	23	27	35	12	6	7	3	-	-	-	-	-	-	-	-	-	-	-
Order clerks II	162	40.0	300.00	299.50	239.50-400.00	-	-	-	-	9	39	25	11	10	19	4	1	-	-	35	9	-	-	4	-	-
Accounting clerks	4,497	39.0	281.50	258.00	224.00-324.50	1	-	41	360	616	711	561	473	316	235	176	156	330	60	48	130	112	103	55	10	-
Manufacturing	1,291	39.5	292.50	272.00	230.00-333.00	1	-	18	58	144	233	117	121	117	103	73	52	45	38	18	33	22	55	42	10	-
Nonmanufacturing	3,206	39.0	277.00	254.00	220.00-319.50	-	-	23	302	472	478	444	352	201	132	103	104	285	22	30	97	90	48	16	6	-
Transportation and utilities	935	39.5	362.50	368.00	318.50-423.00	-	-	-	12	19	36	41	43	52	52	33	88	274	16	90	96	48	46	16	-	6
Accounting clerks I	614	39.5	254.50	235.50	204.50-276.00	1	-	18	120	77	116	87	48	18	25	15	35	4	8	12	5	15	10	-	-	-
Manufacturing	144	39.5	279.00	249.50	214.00-332.50	-	-	-	-	18	24	11	6	7	11	14	7	3	7	-	-	2	5	10	-	-
Nonmanufacturing	470	39.5	247.00	233.00	200.00-264.50	-	-	18	120	59	92	76	42	11	14	1	28	1	7	11	5	13	10	-	-	-
Transportation and utilities	142	39.5	307.00	308.00	239.50-344.50	-	-	-	12	10	15	17	11	5	14	1	27	-	1	11	5	13	13	-	-	-
Accounting clerks II	1,891	39.0	264.50	238.00	210.00-284.00	-	-	8	225	400	359	208	172	111	56	35	68	48	21	20	43	42	53	22	-	-
Manufacturing	578	39.5	265.50	240.00	222.00-284.00	-	-	3	26	99	160	99	74	38	14	37	14	9	11	6	9	9	55	6	-	-
Nonmanufacturing	1,313	39.0	265.50	237.00	207.00-287.50	-	-	5	199	301	199	145	98	73	40	33	54	11	10	14	34	33	48	16	-	-
Transportation and utilities	321	39.5	367.00	353.00	282.00-445.50	-	-	5	-	9	21	18	23	31	11	3	47	5	5	14	33	33	48	16	-	-
Accounting clerks III	1,327	39.0	298.00	274.50	239.00-368.00	-	-	-	5	126	203	217	155	103	47	27	61	265	14	3	49	-	12	33	-	-
Manufacturing	295	40.0	318.50	295.00	241.50-344.00	-	-	-	-	21	46	37	22	38	19	28	13	-	8	3	15	-	12	33	1	-
Nonmanufacturing	1,031	39.0	292.50	270.00	238.50-368.00	-	-	-	5	105	157	180	133	65	28	14	47	265	6	-	34	-	-	-	-	6

Which Jobs to Include?

A general guideline for all survey issues is to keep things simple. Select as few employers and jobs as necessary to accomplish the purpose. The more complex the survey, the less likely employers are inclined to participate unless the survey results are important to them also. On the other hand, some surveys, particularly from trade associations and public agencies, often are too general to be useful.

The decisions about which jobs to be included is a function of the purpose of the survey, the similarity of job content across employers, the range of jobs or skills to be studied, the diversity among firms surveyed, and the extent of the data requested.

Benchmark jobs approach. Typically, only key or benchmark jobs are included in surveys. Benchmark jobs are defined as reference points having the following characteristics:

- The contents are well known, relatively stable, and agreed upon by the employees involved.
- The supply and demand for these jobs are relatively stable and not subject to recent shifts.
- They represent the entire job structure under study.
- A sizable proportion of the work force is employed in these jobs.
- Some employers use the percentage of incumbents who are women and men to try to ensure that the benchmarks are free of possible employment discrimination.

Exhibit 7.7 shows a profile of an organization's functional areas (e.g., production, maintenance, services, laboratory, and office) and job grades. Benchmark

EXHIBIT 7.7
Representative Benchmark Jobs

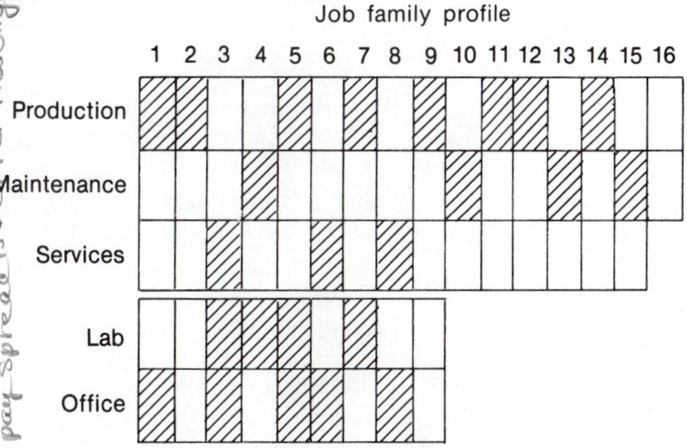

Job family profile

jobs should be chosen to represent all levels in the organization, and, if possible, all functions as well as minorities and women employees.

The point of using benchmark jobs is to be able to anchor the comparison of competitive pay rates with descriptions of similar types of work. Including the entire domain of work and jobs held by large numbers of employees helps ensure the accuracy and work relatedness of decisions based on survey results.[16] Descriptions of the benchmark jobs are included in the survey.

Skill-based/global approach. A skill-based or global approach does not emphasize comparisons of pay for specific jobs.[17] Instead, this approach recognizes that employers may tailor jobs to the organization or individual employee. Rarely do several organizations have identical jobs. This is particularly true in organizations that emphasize production work teams and task forces, or continuously adapt jobs to meet changing conditions. The skill-based approach may be better suited to survey pay levels in these situations.

With a skill-based approach, the rates paid to every individual employee in an entire skill group or function (e.g., all chemical engineers, or all computer scientists) become the reference point. Exhibits 7.8 and 7.9 show external market data on computer scientists with bachelor's degrees. These data permit determination of rates paid to B.S. computer scientists as well as that rate's relationship to years-since-degree (YSD). A skill-based approach simply substitutes a particular skill (represented by a B.S. in computer science in the example) and experience (YSD) for detailed descriptions of the work performed. In doing so, pressure is placed on managers to ensure that these computer scientists with specific experience are performing tasks whose value to the organization justifies the pay received.

Job value approach. A third approach to matching survey jobs is for an employer to use its job evaluation plan to evaluate the benchmark jobs provided in the survey.[18] For example, consider a survey which includes a job, senior personnel associate, and your employer's job, personnel specialist. The specialist seems to have similar but somewhat lighter responsibilities than does the

---

[16] Bruce Ellig, *Executive Compensation—A Total Pay Perspective* (New York: McGraw-Hill, 1982); Robert J. Greene, "How to Improve Job Pricing Techniques," *Compensation and Benefits Management,* Spring 1985, pp. 223–28.

[17] Harold B. Guerci, "Compensation Programs for Scientists and Professionals in Business," in *Handbook of Wage and Salary Administration,* ed. M. Rock (New York: McGraw-Hill, 1984), pp. 53/1–53/10.

[18] Kenneth E. Foster, "Acquiring Competitive Information from Surveys: An Empirical Approach," in *Handbook of Wage and Salary Administration,* 2nd ed., ed. Milton L. Rock (New York: McGraw-Hill, 1984), pp. 42/1–42/13; Edward Perlin, Irvin Bobby Kaplan, and John M. Curcia, "Clearing Up Fuzziness in Salary Survey Analysis," *Compensation Review,* Second Quarter 1979, pp. 12–25. Also see Bruce Ellig, "Salary Surveys: Design and Application," *Personnel Administrator,* October 1977, pp. 41–48.

EXHIBIT 7.8.
Scatterplot of Survey Data for Computer Programmers

YEARS OF PROGRAMMING EXPERIENCE

Scatterplot grid of MONTHLY SALARY (rows) versus YEARS OF PROGRAMMING EXPERIENCE (columns 1–37, +).

MONTHLY SALARY	TOTAL
2600 + OVER	42
2550 – 2599	16
2500 – 2549	14
2450 – 2499	25
2400 – 2449	13
2350 – 2399	32
2300 – 2349	37
2250 – 2299	38
2200 – 2249	33
2150 – 2199	55
2100 – 2149	63
2050 – 2099	88
2000 – 2049	101
1950 – 1999	96
1900 – 1949	123
1850 – 1899	147
1800 – 1849	144
1750 – 1799	155
1700 – 1749	146
1650 – 1699	169
1600 – 1649	167
1550 – 1599	139
1500 – 1549	159
1450 – 1499	146
1400 – 1449	170
1350 – 1399	144
1300 – 1349	171
1250 – 1299	124
1200 – 1249	147
1150 – 1199	110
1100 – 1145	104
1050 – 1099	110
1000 – 1049	52
950 – 999	38
900 – 949	22
850 – 899	9
800 – 849	6
750 – 799	4
700 – 749	1
UNDER 700	0

	1	2	3	4	5	6	7	8	9	10	11	12	13	14	15	16	17	18	19	20	21	22	23	24	25	26	27	28	29	30	31	32	33	34	35	36	37	+	TOTAL
TOTAL	111	430	209	205	232	265	295	263	249	197	136	137	139	94	86	69	64	56	31	34	18	11	3	3	3	3	0	0	0	1	1	0	1	0	0	0	0	0	3362
MEDIAN	1061	1162	1202	1389	1479	1559	1634	1677	1755	1851	1866	1902	1870	1916	1983	1987	2050	2033	1987	1850	1900	2175	1975	1975	2025	2025				1975	2225	2625							
MEAN	1174	1195	1220	1253	1399	1502	1636	1654	1762	1850	1899	1909	1875	1899	2037	2044	2025	2053	2038	1945	2031	2152	1969	2079	2079	2297				1991	2217	2954							
STD.DEV	218	187	142	211	240	235	244	265	263	240	320	324	272	337	320	376	328	368	340	386	310	267	40	418	425					0	0	0							

Source: Organization Resources Counselors, Inc.

EXHIBIT 7.9.
Maturity Curves Based on Scatterplot for Computer Programmers, Tenth through Ninetieth Percentile

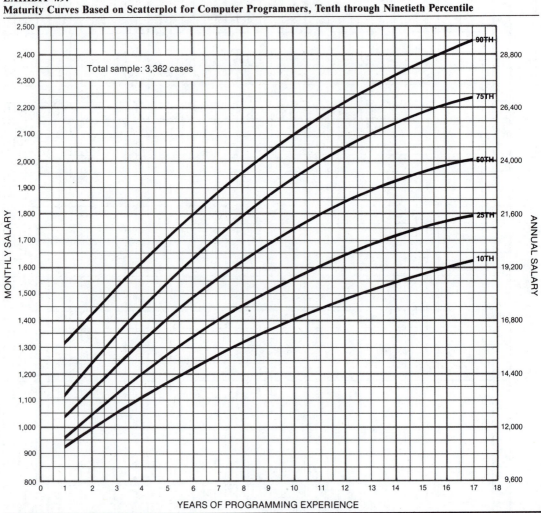

YEARS OF PROGRAMMING EXPERIENCE

Source: Organization Resources Counselors, Inc.

associate description in the survey. The job value approach involves evaluating the survey job, senior personnel associate, with your job evaluation system and comparing the results to your specialist job and taking account of any difference in points by making similar adjustments in the market data collected.

So the real issue is to ensure that the jobs or skill groups included in the survey provide data useful to design pay levels and structures. Depending on the purpose of the survey, either the key jobs approach, the skill-based approach, or the job value approach can do that.

What Information to Collect?

There are three basic types of data typically requested: (1) information about the nature of the organization, (2) information about the total compensation system, and (3) specific pay data on each incumbent in the jobs under study. Exhibilt 7.10 lists the basic types and the logic for including them.

No survey includes all the data that will be discussed. Rather, the data collected depends on the purpose of the survey and the jobs and skills included. Since no standards or guidelines on what to collect have been developed, compensation professionals must rely on their expertise and experience to make that decision.

EXHIBIT 7.10
Data Elements to Consider for Surveys and Their Rationale

Basic Elements	Examples	Rationale
Nature of organization		
Identification	Company name, address, contact person.	Further contacts.
Financial condition	Assets, sales, return on investment profits (after taxes).	Indicates nature of the product/ service markets, the ability to pay, size, and financial viability.
Employee	Total numbers.	
Size	Profit centers, product lines.	
Structure	Organizational charts.	Indicates how business is organized.
Nature of total compensation system		
Cash forms used	Basic pay, pay increase schedules, long- and short-term incentives, bonuses, cost of living adjustments, overtime and shift differentials.	Indicates the mix of compensation offered. Used to attempt to establish a comparable base.
Noncash forms used	Composition of benefits and services, particularly the degree of coverage and contributions to medical and health insurance and pensions.	
Incumbent and job		
Date	Date effective.	
Job	Match generic job descriptions, number of employees supervised, reporting levels.	Indicates degree of similarity with survey's key jobs.
Individual	Years since degree, education, date of hire.	Describes incumbents.
Pay	Actual rates paid to each individual, total earnings, last increase, bonuses, incentives.	

Nature of the organization. Information about the nature of the organization should permit the compensation professional to assess the similarities and differences among organizations in the survey. Financial information, size, and organization structure are usually included. Surveys of executives and upper level positions include more detailed financial and reporting relationships data. The logic for including this additional data is that compensation for these jobs is more directly related to the organization's financial performance. Surveys of lower level jobs typically collect only basic organization data.

The financial data seldom includes details on the firms' performance. Levels of revenues, sales, and profits are common, but other indicators such as return on investments or assets, changing market share, or changes in earnings are not. Such data could be used to analyze the pay range of strong versus weak performing firms or those with increasing market share versus those experiencing decline. More often than not, the financial data are simply used to group firms by size expressed in terms of sales or revenues.

Nature of the total pay system. All the basic forms of pay need to be covered in a survey in order to assess the similarities and differences in the pay packages offered and to accurately assess competitors' practices. For example, employers are increasingly offering various forms of team awards or individual incentives along with the base pay. Further, some employers roll these awards into the base pay, while others do not, and still others roll only a percentage of them into employees' base pay.

Yet it is particularly difficult to include *all* the pay forms in detail. For example, including details on benefits such as medical coverage deductibles, flexible benefit options, and even vacation policies quickly makes a survey too cumbersome. Methods to handle this problem range from a brief description of a benchmark benefit package to including only the most expensive and variable benefits or asking for an estimate of total benefit expenses as a percent of total labor costs. The point is that including some estimate of total compensation is important because we need to assess the entire compensation package offered by competitors.

Incumbent data. The most important data in the survey are the *actual* rates paid to each incumbent. Total earnings, hours worked, date and amount of last increase, bonus and incentive payments, and so on are included. However, the usefulness of each element needs to be balanced against the costs of trying to collect it. Again, keep things as simple as will provide the necessary information.

Enough data must be given to appraise the match between the key jobs in the survey and jobs within each company. Some personal data on each incumbent is also included to facilitate matching. The degree of match between the survey's key jobs and each company's jobs is assessed by various means. Hay Associates, for example, has installed the same job evaluation plan in many companies that participate in their surveys. Consequently, jobs in different organizations can be compared on their total job evaluation points and the distribution of points among the compensable factors. Other surveys simply ask participants to judge the degree of match.

Please check ( ) degree to which your job matches the benchmark job described in the survey:

My company's job is . . .
Of moderately less value   ( )
Of slightly less value   ( )
Of equal value   ( )
Of slightly more value   ( )
Of moderately more value   ( )

Still other survey designers periodically send teams of employees familiar with the key jobs to visit each participating organization to discuss the matches. Many public agency and trade association surveys often simply rely on each participant to match the key jobs as closely as possible.

EEO-related data. To date, no surveys collect data specifically for EEO purposes. Employers have been reluctant to collect such data, since it may be used against them in lawsuits. Some are now beginning to reexamine their surveys' role in measuring the relevant external labor market. For example, the fact that the city of Madison had difficulty attracting public health sanitarians to fill job vacancies was an important factor for the court that examined the pay differences between sanitarians (predominantly men) and nurses (predominantly women).[19] Since market data are increasingly important in explaining pay differences between men and women, it may become increasingly important to include data on the objectives of the pay system; for example, the ability to attract (length of vacancies), the ability to retain (turnover rates), and so on.

A compensation manager for Duke Power Company cautions that "most surveys are not of sufficient quality to justify their use as anything more than indicators of general salary levels and trends."[20] Despite the acceptance in the courts of "market data" as legal justification for salary differentials, the whole area of market data collection, analysis, and interpretation has not been subject to the same scrutiny as hiring practices and testing have. Whether they should is another question. Certainly, a survey analyst ought to have a sound, business-related rationale for every step in the process. But let us not forget what we are dealing with. Let us not make too fine a distinction based on data that are too general. Some surveys provide data that serve as a general guide to assess the adequacy of the whole pay structure, but not necessarily for the pay of specific jobs. Other surveys are designed to price specific jobs, and still others to assess only the rate of change in the rates paid. The purpose of the survey needs to be kept in mind when judging the data.

---

[19]*Briggs* v. *City of Madison.*

[20]T. Michael Fain, "Conducting Surveys," in *Handbook of Wage and Salary Administration,* 2nd ed. pp. 32/3–32/11.

EXHIBIT 7.11
Survey Questionnaire: An Illustration

Crafts — Assemblers and Operators

I. General Information

A. Company name: *Motor Research, Inc.*

B. Company representative providing information: *J. Rowe*

C. Title: *Compensation Analyst*

D. Company address: *Box 15, Moravia, N.Y.*

E. Telephone number: *607 263-9241*

F. Type of product or service: *Automotive test equipment*

II. Employment information

A. Number of shop foremen: *20*

B. Number of hourly employees: *593*

III. Personnel practices

A. Union status: Non-union *X*   Union_____

B. Overtime and shift differential — check one or both:

___*X*___Pay in excess of 40 hours/week
_____Pay in excess of 8 hours/day.

Shift differential:

Second shift: *92¢* /hour

Third shift: _____/hour

C. Number of paid holidays per year: _____*12*_____

D. Group medical insurance offered: Yes *X*   No_____

Approximate percentage of cost paid by company *10* %

E. Dental insurance offered: Yes_____ No *X*

Approximate percentage of cost paid by company __*—*__%.

Exhibit 7.11
(*concluded*)

		Wage Survey			
			Rate range		
Job classification	N/A*	Minimum	Maximum	# of employees	Weighted average
Welder – A		8.75	10.00	0	
Fitter – A		9.35	10.65	0	
Machinist – A		9.10	10.45	1	10.25
Painter – SENIOR		8.40	9.60	1	9.60
Blast Cleaner - GRIT – A		7.65	8.70	0	
Warehouseman – A		7.75	8.70	2	8.30
Shipping	✔				
Receiving	✔				
Assembly Mechanic – A		9.35	10.65	0	
Maintenance Mechanic – A		9.35	10.65	3	10.42
Machine Operator		7.65	8.70	0	
Burning Machine Operator		8.75	10.00	1	10.00
Press Brake Operator	✔				
Sheet Metal Mechanic	✔				
Forklift Operator/Materials Handler		6.25	7.10	0	

*Please check N/A if the job descriptions are not applicable or you do not have this particular job classification.

How to Collect the Data?

There are really only two basic methods used to collect pay data—interviews (in person or by phone) and mailed questionnaires. The purpose of the survey and the extensiveness of the data required usually determine the method. Special studies or double checking results is often done through phone interviews. Mailed questionnaires similar to the one in Exhibit 7.11 are probably most common. According to Nash and Carroll, field interviews with trained interviewers are the most effective.[21] The Bureau of Labor Statistics (BLS), the most experienced wage surveyor of all, uses field interviews. Obviously, this approach is costly and time-consuming. Rather than conduct field trips each year, some organizations use them every second or third year in order to hold down costs. Some employers rotate the responsibility for conducting and analyzing the survey among the participants; however, this practice risks maintaining confidentiality of the data provided by each participant.

---

[21]Nash and Carroll, *The Management of Compensation.*

Whichever data collection method is used, the participants are guaranteed confidentiality. Survey reports, usually shared only with participants and clients, summarize the data so that individual employees and organizations are masked. But in practice, seasoned compensation professionals often can recognize which data correspond to which firm.

Many aspects of pay surveys have been ignored by researchers. Little can be said about the effects of different formats in the accuracy of the data obtained. Little is known about ensuring comparability of key job matches or matching benefit packages. We don't even know how representative the survey participants are of some markets. The same lack of research plagues the analysis of survey results.

INTERPRET AND APPLY SURVEY RESULTS

To discover how survey data is actually analyzed, Belcher, based on taped interviews with 34 compensation professionals, reports:

> Every organization uses its own methods of distilling information from the survey; uses different surveys for different purposes; and uses different methods for company surveys. I could find no commonality in these methods of analysis by industry, by firm size or union presence. For example, some did nothing except read the entire survey, some emphasized industry data, others geographic competitors (commuting distances), some made comparisons with less than five competitors, some emphasized only large firms, others throw out the data from large firms.[22]

Their study identified 97 different methods of analysis used by these 34 professionals. Twenty-six of the 97 methods were used by four to six firms, 21 methods were used by only two or three firms, and 50 methods were used by only one firm.

Diversity rules in analyzing survey data. This may reflect the absence of a single correct approach, or more likely that compensation professionals have pragmatically adjusted their analysis to deal with a variety of circumstances. It may also reflect that many current approaches to analyzing survey data are not well grounded in business and work-related logic and therefore will not be able to withstand a legal challenge.

Certainly different approaches to analyzing data will produce a wide range of possible results. For example, what is the justification for excluding data from large (or small) employers? What is the rationale underlying disregarding all the pay rates that are "outlyers" or extreme values? There may be some good reasons for such decisions. But the logic needs to be stated and examined.

---

[22]Letter from D. W. Belcher to G. T. Milkovich, in reference to D. W. Belcher, N. Bruce Ferris, and John O'Neill, "How Wage Surveys Are Being Used," *Compensation and Benefits Review,* September-October 1985, pp. 34–51.

Check the Accuracy and Usefulness of the Data

If no standard approach exists, how should analysis proceed? Exhibit 7.12 defines a number of terms commonly used in analyzing survey data. These terms can be used to study an actual survey report. Exhibit 7.13 shows summary statistics reported by Organization Resource Counselors, Inc. for participants in their Salary Information Retrieval System. Exhibit 7.13 is from a report prepared on a buyer position for company E00l. For each of the 14 companies in the survey who reported this position, a variety of data are reported. Using our definitions in Exhibit 7.12, let us examine the data reported by company E040 for its senior buyer position. It reports five people in this position, paid a mean or average of $18,980 each. Let us assume that the individual salaries for these five people are $17,784; $18,236; $18,320; and $20,280 (two employees). The median wage is $18,320; the modal wage is $20,280. These figures are not reported in the survey; only the lowest actual rate ($17,784) and the highest ($20,280) are given. These actual salaries paid are well within the established, or permissible, range for this job at this company: the established range minimum is $15,912; and maximum is $24,596. Range spread (.55) is established minimum over established maximum. A lower number indicates a wider range. Ranges are discussed later in this chapter.

The bottom of Exhibit 7.13 shows data on all 14 companies combined into means and weighted means (each company's mean rate is weighted by the num-

---

EXHIBIT 7.12
Terms Used in Analyzing Data

Company A pays five employees wages of $12, $12, $13, $14, and $15.
Company B pays three employees wages of $9, $10, and $10.

Mean wage: Sum of wages paid to members of a group divided by number of people in the group.
   Company A mean wage = $13.33
   Company B mean wage = $ 9.67

Median wage: In a continuum, the wage in the middle.
   Company A median wage = $13.00
   Company B median wage = $10.00

Mode: The most frequently occurring wage.
   A modal wage = $12.00
   B modal wage = $10.00

Range spread: The distance from highest to lowest can be reported as actual dollars.
   Company A range = $3.00
   Company B range = $1.00
or, as ratio of minimum to maximum,
   Company A range = $ .80
   Company B range = $ .90

Weighted mean: Each company's mean wage is weighted by the number of people who occupy the group.
   Weighted mean of Company A and Company B wages = $11.88

EXHIBIT 7.13
Example of a Survey Report

REPORT PREPARED FOR ▶ C O M P A N Y   N O.   E001

Range spread, minimum to maximum (read .49 as 49%)

CO NO	BENCHMK JOB -------T I T L E S-------	NO OF EMP	AVER.	LOW	HIGH	MIN	MID	MAX	%SP	GR	FL SA
			--ACTUAL SALARIES--			----SALARY GRADE RANGE----					
E001	BUYER SENIOR	1*	17900	17900	17900	17000	21200	25400	.49	06	E
E040	BUYER SR	5	18980	17784	20280	15912	20254	24596	.55	05	E
E008	SENIOR BUYER	8	19240	17784	20592	15080	20488	25896	.72	04	E
E021	BUYER, SR	1	21480	21480	21480	16740	21462	26184	.56	25	E
E019	BUYER SENIOR	2	21450	19760	23140	16484	21424	26364	.60	58	E
E012	BUYER, SENIOR	5	21964	18356	24440	18356	22542	26728	.46	05	E
E019	BUYER SENIOR	4	22880	22100	24128	16848	21788	26728	.59	11	E
E029	SENIOR BUYER	11	22872	19476	25956	18456	22656	26856	.46	05	E
E020	BUYER SENIOR	6	20771	16598	22089	17804	22505	27206	.53	12	E
E018	BUYER SR	6	21672	20400	22944	17820	22590	27360	.54	21	E
E015	SENIOR BUYER	4	18772	17680	20488	15860	21710	27560	.74	05	E
E002	GROUP BUYER	1	23160	23160	23160	18960	23340	27720	.46	A4	E
E003	SR BUYER	2	24300	21600	27000	20460	25560	30660	.50	24	E
E026	BUYER	3	20643	20016	21828	20880	26106	31332	.50	08	E
E021	PURCHASING AGENT	2	20004	18996	21000	18192	23322	28452	.56	26	E
E009	BUYER/SUBCONTRACT ADMIN SR	20	25308	22200	28884	19524	24204	28984	.48	08	E
	TOTAL INCUMBENTS	81									
	TOTAL COMPANIES 14										
	WEIGHTED AVERAGE	80	22196	19846	24407	17983	22743	27503	.54		
	SIMPLE AVERAGE		21566	19826	23160	17825	22663	27501	.55		
	LOW		18772	16598	20280	15080	20254	24596	.46		
	HIGH		25308	23160	28884	20880	26106	31332	.74		
	COMPANY E001 AVERAGE	1	17900	17900	17900	17000	21200	25400	.49		

Annotations:
- Company's salary grade
- Identifies your company's data
- Average salary and paid range
- Established range (minimum, midpoint, maximum)
- FLSA status
- Number of incumbents reported to job
- Annual rates for exempt employees
- Number of companies reporting to this position
- Summary line weighted by number of incumbents — ♦WEIGHTED AVERAGE
- ♦Simple (unweighted) average line
- Lowest and highest data tabulated in each column above
- Your company's data repeated for ready comparison with summary lines — ▶ COMPANY E001 AVERAGE

♦NOTE: All summary lines exclude your company's data.

Source: Adapted from Organization Resources Counselors Inc., *Salary Information Retrieval System.*

ber of people that company employs in the job, for example, [(5 × $18,980) + (8 × $19,240) + (1 × $21,480) + (2 × $21,450) . . . /81]).

So what does one do with all these data? The first logical step is to make some judgment about how good a match these buyer positions are with your buyer position. Compare the job description used in the survey with your own company's job description. Even if the job descriptions are an exact match on job content, that does not mean that each company places the same value on that content. Therefore it is helpful to have further information on the value that each organization places on the job.[23] While Exhibit 7.13 gives us the salary grade where each company has slotted its buyer job, there is no information on where in the job structure this salary grade lies, so it appears to add little to our analysis.

If the job description of the buyer job in the survey does not match your own buyer's job, you may wish to weight the survey data according to the closeness of fit. This technique is called survey leveling. If the job in the survey has slightly greater responsibility than your buyer, survey data may be multiplied by .8, in order to bring it closer to a level of comparability to your position. This is an example of a rule of thumb used to modify survey data. The defensibility of this and other "adjustments to the data" is open to question. To date few outside of the compensation professions even realize these adjustments are made to survey results.

Several "quick" analyses provide further checks of the usefulness of survey data. One of these is to calculate the spread of rates between the highest and lowest salary paid to the survey job by all survey participants. For our buyer, the spread ($18,772/$25,308) is .74. A low ratio would reflect considerable dispersion in the data, in which case it might be advisable to reexamine the matching procedure used in the survey. It may also reflect employers' different pay level policies regarding the buyer function.[24]

Another way to check the usefulness of data is to look at the shape of the distributions of rates paid. In Exhibit 7.14, pay is on the horizontal axis; frequency of the rate is on the vertical axis. A bimodal (Figure B) or "rectangular" distribution (Figure C) may reflect problems with job matches, widely dispersed pay rates, or employers with widely divergent pay policies. Such a distribution may require further analysis to gain confidence in the data. For example, the distribution of rates for each buyer, when charted by the number of companies reporting a rate, approximates a normal distribution (Figure D). But if the frequency is weighted by the number of individuals in each company, the distribution loses its normal shape (Figure E). The 20 employees in company

---

[23]Ellig, *Executive Compensation;* Foster, "Acquiring Competitive Information."

[24]Erica Groshen, "Sources of Wage Dispersion: How Much Do Employers Matter?" working paper, Department of Economics, Harvard University, Boston, Mass., December 1985.

EXHIBIT 7.14
Illustrations of Distributions of Survey Pay Rates for Benchmark Jobs

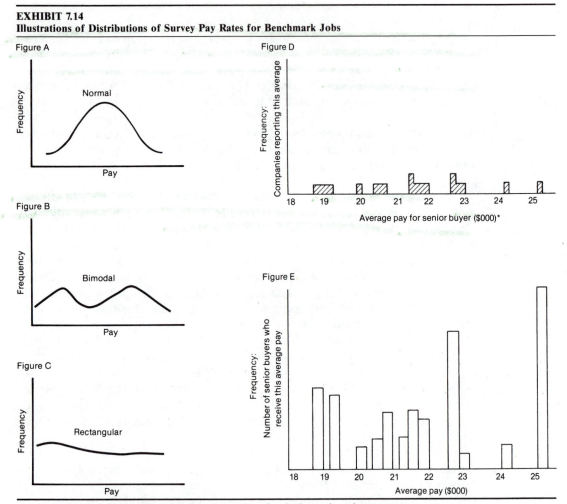

Note: Company averages are weighted by the number of senior buyers in each company.
*As reported in the SIRS Survey Report (Exhibit 7.13).

E009 distort the distribution. One correction may be to throw out data from that company. But that company's 20 incumbents constitute one fourth of the total incumbents in the survey. How to proceed depends on the purpose of the survey and other organization circumstances. If E009's rates are not high in other jobs, it would be nice to obtain a description of the buyer job in E009. The point is that what action to take depends on data available and the informed judgment of the analyst.

Before further examination of mechanics, it is useful to step back a moment and consider what surveys are trying to accomplish. The objective is to design pay levels and structures that employees feel are equitable and that will

EXHIBIT 7.15
Relationship between Internal Consistency and External Competitiveness

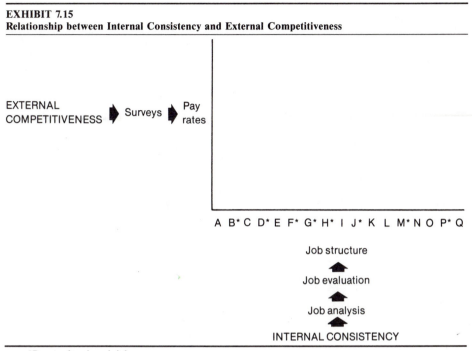

*Denotes benchmark jobs.

accomplish management's objectives. Two components of the pay model are emerging, and their relationship to each other is depicted in Exhibit 7.15.[25]

- An *internally equitable job structure* based on *job analysis* and *job evaluation* has been developed and is shown on the horizontal axis in Exhibit 7.15.
- Rates paid by *competitors in the external market* for benchmark jobs in that structure are based on the survey. The purpose of the survey is to help us position pay competitively in the external market (the vertical axis in Exhibit 7.15).

The next steps are to construct the market pay lines, to update the market data, and to set the employer's pay policy line and design the pay structure.

Construct Market Pay Lines

An essential part of constructing market lines involves abstracting and summarizing the detailed data collected in the surveys. A typical process includes start-

---

[25]Nancy Brown Johnson and Ronald A. Ash, "Incorporating the Labor Market into Job Evaluation: Clearing the Cobwebs," working paper, University of Kansas School of Business, Lawrence, Kans., 1985.

EXHIBIT 7.16
Scatterplot Depicting Relationship between Job Structure and Survey Data

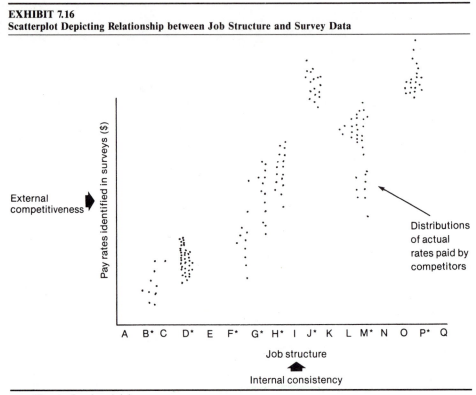

*Denotes benchmark jobs.

ing with a scatterplot of actual wages paid and ending with a series of lines that summarize these rates. Each key job has a distribution of rates, rather than a single rate in the market. Refer back to the distribution of rates for our buyer position, Exhibit 7.14. Let us assume the distribution approximates a normal distribution (Figure D), and that such a distribution exists for each of the other benchmark jobs in our survey. Exhibit 7.16 shows a scatterplot of these distributions for each benchmark job and their relationship to our job structure. In Exhibit 7.17, a bell curve is drawn which summarizes the scatterplots. Each of these distributions has means, medians, and so on, which also summarize the data. And all of these data are summarized further by constructing lines that reflect these distributions. Several methods to construct such lines can be used. A *single line* connecting the midpoints of each distribution (median or mean) is used by some. Exhibit 7.18 shows such a line (50th percentile). In addition to the midpoints, lines connect the 25th and 75th percentiles of each benchmark's pay distribution. Consider the 25th percentile line. It gives us a dollar amount for each key job. Twenty-five percent of our survey participants paid this rate or less for the job (e.g., 25 percent paid $17,784 or less to their buyers (Exhibit

EXHIBIT 7.17
Distribution of Rates

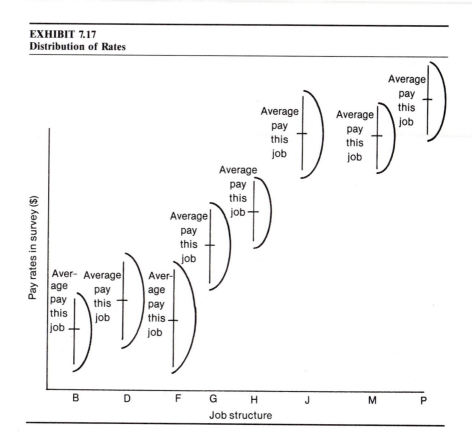

7.13). Often these lines are fitted to the data through a statistical procedure called regression analysis. Readers not familiar with regression analysis are urged to read the referenced materials.[26] So at this point the survey data have been analyzed for accuracy and summarized to be more manageable. The next step is to update the data.

Update the Survey Data

Often, three to six months (or more) may pass before all participating firms return their survey, data are coded and analyzed, and the report is available for use in decision making. By this time the survey data are outdated because market rates have probably already increased. Consequently, the data are usually

---

[26]George G. Judge, R. Carter Hill, and William E. Griffiths, *Introduction to the Theory and Practice of Econometrics* (New York: John Wiley & Sons, 1982); and N. H. Nie and C. H. Hull, *Statistical Package for Social Sciences* (New York: McGraw-Hill, 1970).

EXHIBIT 7.18
Constructing Pay Policy Lines

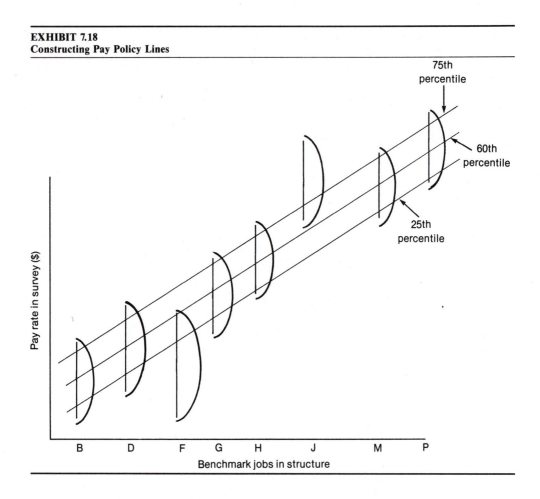

projected or updated to forecast the competitive rates for the future when the pay decisions are implemented.

. There are two issues involved in updating (often called "aging") the survey data. The first is *how much* (the amount) to update the data and the second is the *time horizon*. The amount chosen is based on several factors, including historical trends in the market data based on current and previous surveys, economic forecasts (prospects for the economy and the markets in which the employer operates, consumer price index, etc.), and the compensation manager's judgment.

The time horizon includes the current period and the plan period—the period (usually 12-month intervals) in which the compensation plan will be implemented and operate.

Exhibit 7.19 illustrates one of several approaches for updating. In the example, the pay rates collected in the survey were in effect as of January 1 of the

EXHIBIT 7.19
Updating Survey Data: An Illustration

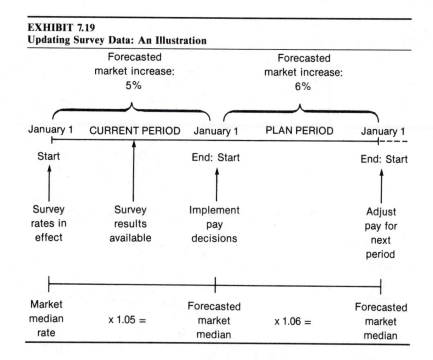

current year. The compensation manager will use these data for pay decisions that will go into effect January 1 of the next year, labeled *plan year* in the exhibit. According to historical trends reported in this and past surveys, the pay rates have been increasing by approximately 5 percent annually. If we assume the future will be like the past, then the market pay line is multiplied by 1.05 to account for the rise in pay that is expected to occur during the *current year.* If the compensation manager judges that the market is moving at a rate other than 5 percent, then a different rate can be used. To estimate what the market rates will be by the *end* of the plan year, a judgment is made about the rate of increase expected during the plan year and survey results are updated again on the basis of this judgment. In Exhibit 7.19 the assumed 6 percent increase during the plan year may be based on an expected increase in demand for the particular skills included in this survey. By the end of the plan year, the assumption is that the market will have increased by 1.05 × 1.06, or 1.13 percent, over January 1 of the current year.

Now that the survey data is updated, the employer's pay level can be set.

Set the Employer's Pay Level

The pay level policy for the organization can now be put into practice. Exhibit 7.20 shows the three classic policies and examples of how each is practiced. The objective is to set the pay level consistent with the organization's stated external

EXHIBIT 7.20
Putting Pay Level Policy into Practice

Policy	Mechanics	Illustration
I. Lead competition	Set our midpoint pay line (50th percentile or average) at the start of plan year to match competition by the *end* of the plan year or Set our midpoint pay (50th percentile) to match competition's 60 or 75th percentile or Set our midpoint pay to match only a few selected top paying competitors	
II. Pay with competition (lead/lag)	Set our midpoint pay line to match competition's at mid-year	
III. Follow competition	Set our midpoint pay line to be less than or match competition's at the *start* of the plan year	

competitiveness policy. In the case of lead policy, the illustration shows an organization setting its pay level (e.g., the median or mean rate) so it will be at least *equal* to the market's midpoints at the *end* of the plan year. A lead policy requires that they set it *above* the market rates at the start of the plan year. As the year progresses, the market rates are expected to increase so that the degree by which the organization leads will progressively decrease. At the end of the year the organization increases its pay level again for the following plan year.

As shown in Exhibit 7.20, there are alternative mechanisms that may be used to generate a policy line. To establish a competitive policy, the organization may use a lead/lag mechanism. The pay level is set so that it leads competition for half the year and lags for the other half. A "follow competition" policy involves setting the organization pay level so it lags the market level during the year.

EXHIBIT 7.21

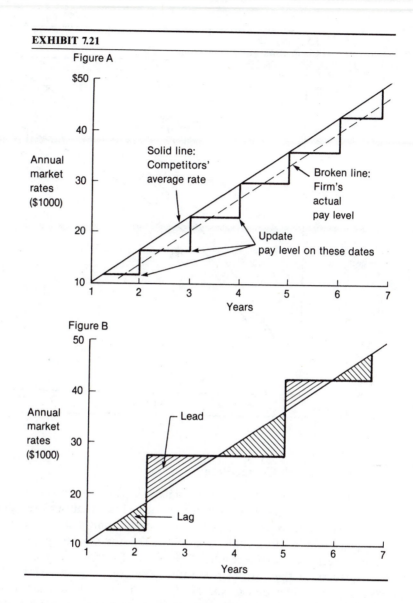

Figure A

Figure B

Recognize that practice does not always match policy. For example, the employer in Figure A of Exhibit 7.21 espouses a "meet competition" policy but because of the method used, it only "meets" competition on the first day of each year. The rest of the time its pay level is lagging or chasing its competitors. To achieve the "meets competition" policy the employer must "saw tooth" the market rate (Figure B), that is, set its pay level so it leads half the time and lags the other half.

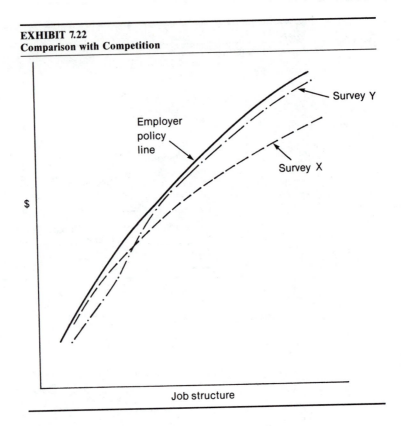

EXHIBIT 7.22
Comparison with Competition

Compare with Competition

Survey data are also used to analyze how an organization's current rates compare to the rates paid by competition. These analyses are relatively straightforward and there may be as many different approaches to them as there are compensation professionals. Exhibit 7.22 shows a company's pay level that lies between two survey results. The point of this analysis is to assess the competitiveness of the current pay rates. The company in Exhibit 7.22 feels that the employers included in survey Y make up its relevant labor markets. Survey X includes a wider variety of firms. Note that the company's current median rates lie on or above both market lines (based on median rates); thus the firm's pay practice is leading competition.

DESIGN PAY RANGES

The pay policy line has now been established based on the organization's policy regarding the external market and on the survey which provided actual rates paid by competitors. The next step is to design pay ranges for jobs inside the organization. Most discussions of pay ranges define what they are and explain how they are constructed. But why they are used and for what purpose are often unanswered questions. Ranges exist whenever two or more rates are paid to incumbents of a given job. Recall the "actual range" and "established range" data reported in Exhibit 7.13. Established ranges set upper and lower limits on the rates an employer will pay for a particular job.

Why Bother with Ranges?

Ranges provide a mechanism to deal with pressure from the external labor market and within the organization.[27] The wide variation of rates paid for similar jobs and skills reflects two *external* pressures:

1. The existence of quality variations (skills, abilities, experience) among individuals in the external market (e.g., company A has stricter hiring requirements for its buyer position than does company B, even though job descriptions are identical).
2. The recognition of differences in the productivity-related value to employers of these quality variations (e.g., buyers are more important to Neiman-Marcus than they are to Wal-Mart).

Both of these factors translate into a variety of rates in the external market rather than a single market rate for buyers.

Differences in rates paid to employees on the same job also should be consistent with an organization's pay policies and objectives. Hence ranges reflect the following internal pressures:

1. The intention to recognize individual quality and performance variations with pay (e.g., Carol, a buyer, makes better, more timely decisions for Neiman-Marcus than does Ed, but they both hold the same job and have the same responsibilities).
2. The intention to meet employee's expectations that pay increases will occur over time.

These two pressures translate into a range of rates for the buyer position in the organization. The advantage of using ranges is that they permit an employer to recognize individual differences, whether those differences are in performance or experience.

From an internal consistency perspective, the range established for any job should approximate the range of performance or experience differences that an employer wishes to recognize. From an external competitive perspective, the range acts as a control device. A range maximum sets the lid on what the employer is willing to pay for that work; the range minimum sets the floor.

---

[27]Jeff S. Emans and William W. Seithel, "Remedying Salary Inequities: Cleaning Up Your Act Systematically," *Compensation and Benefits Review,* July-August 1985, pp. 14–23.

But not all employers use ranges. For example, in cases where collective bargaining contracts establish wages, single *flat rates* rather than ranges are paid for each job. Hence, for example, all Senior Machinists II would receive $9.50 per hour regardless of performance or seniority. This flat rate is usually set to correspond to some midpoint on a survey of that job. Existence of a flat rate does not mean that performance variations do not exist. Flat rates reflect the parties' decision to ignore these variations when setting pay. Why would they wish to ignore performance differences? Unions (and many employees) may argue that performance measures are biased, or that work may be organized in a manner that permits little opportunity for individual differences in performance. If accurate measures of individual performance do not exist, then ranges need only accommodate seniority adjustments.[28] Some organizations pay a flat rate for a job and then attach a bonus or incentive to recognize performance variation.

Constructing Ranges

Designing ranges is relatively simple. There is no "best" approach, but three basic steps are typically involved.

1. Develop classes or grades. In Exhibit 7.23 the horizontal axis is the job structure generated through job evaluation. Recall that a grade or class is a grouping of different jobs; thus, each grade is made up of a number of jobs. The jobs in each grade are considered substantially equal for pay purposes. They may have approximately the same job evaluation points (e.g., within 20 or 30 points in a 500-point job evaluation plan). Each grade will have its own pay range, and all the jobs within the grade have that same range. Jobs in different grades (e.g., jobs D, E, and F in grade 2) should be dissimilar to those in other grades (grade 1, jobs A, B, and C) and will have a different range.

The use of job grades enhances an organization's flexibility and its ability to move people among jobs within a pay grade. No change in pay need be factored into the decision. Therefore, reassignment decisions can be made on the basis of organization or individual needs. Wolf makes the case that job grades also lend themselves nicely to job posting, and thus are congruent with promotion/allocation systems in the organization.[29] The salary grade is usually posted with the job description. Posting a grade rather than a fixed amount saves ex-

---

[28]James D. Finch, "Computerized Retrieval of Pay Survey Data, Linking Compensation Practices to Business Strategies," *Personnel Administrator,* July 1985, pp. 31–38.

[29]Martin Wolf, "Solving Technical Problems in Establishing the Pay Structure," in *Handbook of Wage & Salary Administration.* Job posting is a technique for filling job vacancies inside the organization. A description of the job is posted on bulletin boards or is published in employee newsletters. All employees are free to decide for themselves if they are interested in applying for the job.

EXHIBIT 7.23
Construct Grades or Classes

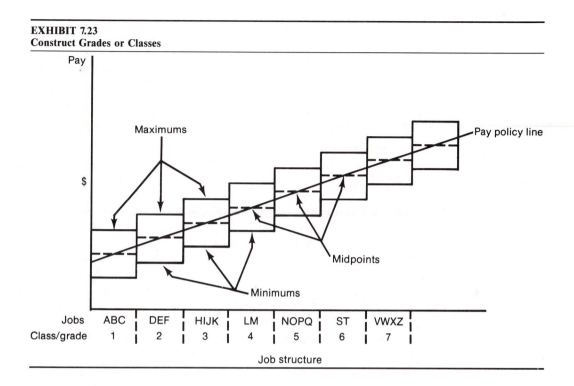

plaining to some employees why their similar jobs may have quite different actual salaries from the posted job.

But there are disadvantages to using salary grades, too. While grading recognizes the imprecision in job evaluation, it may be difficult to construct grades so that all jobs of identifiably similar content lie within the same grade. If jobs with relatively close job evaluation point totals fall on either side of grade boundaries (e.g., jobs E, F, and G have point totals within 30 points of each other, but E and F are in one grade, and G is in another), the magnitude of difference in salary treatment may be out of proportion to the magnitude of difference in job content. Resolving such dilemmas requires an understanding of the specific jobs, the needs of the organization, and the pressures it faces.

In Chapter 4 we stated that the number of grades or classes depended on the variety and diversity of the job involved, traditions in the workplace, and the career paths in the organization. To this list we now add the results of the survey data, particularly the slope of the pay curve and the pay differentials that are established between the grades. What is the correct number of job grades? Once more, our answer is, "it depends." Designing the grade structure that "fits" each organization involves trial and error until one seems to fit the best without too many problems.

Some consulting firms argue that grades are meaningless. They state that each job evaluation point has a dollar value, and therefore each job with its own point total should have its own range.[30] But many others fail to share their confidence in any job evaluation system's ability to generate the precise measurements necessary to support such a position.

2. Set midpoints, maximums, and minimums. The midpoint rates for each range are usually set to correspond to the pay policy line established earlier. The policy line represents the organization's pay level policy relative to what the competition pays for similar jobs. The maximums and minimums (the range width or spread) are usually based on what other employers are doing, the size of ranges identified in survey data, and some judgment about how the ranges fit the organization. Surveys usually provide data on both the actual maximum and minimum rates paid, as well as the established ranges (turn back to Exhibit 7.13 for an example). Some compensation professionals use the actual rates paid, particularly the 75th and 25th percentiles (if available) to establish the maximum and minimums; others use the mean of the established ranges reported in the survey as a starting point to design the ranges. The range spread, maximum over minimum, seems to vary from 10 to 100 percent. Some top level managerial positions commonly have range spreads of about 60 to 100 percent; entry to mid-level professional and managerial positions, between 35 to 50 percent; and for office production jobs, 10 to 25 percent is common. The wider ranges in the managerial jobs are designed to reflect the greater individual discretion in the work.

3. Degree of overlap. The differences in midpoints among ranges and the range spread determine the degree of overlap between adjoining grade ranges. What difference does overlap make? Consider the two extremes shown in Exhibit 7.24. A high degree of overlap and low midpoint differentials in Figure A indicate small differences in the value of jobs in the adjoining grades. Such a structure results in promotions (title changes) without much change in the rates paid. On the other hand, in Figure B, few grades and ranges result in wider range midpoint differentials and less overlap between adjacent ranges, and permit the manager to reinforce a promotion—a movement into a new range—with a greater amount of dollars. At some point the differential must be great enough to induce employees to seek and/or accept the promotion or to undertake the necessary training required. However, there is little research to indicate how much of a differential (just noticeable differences) is necessary to influence employees to take on additional responsibilities or invest in training.[31]

---

[30]Ibid.

[31]James Finch, "Computerized Retrieval"; P. Varadarajan and C. Futrell, "Factors Affecting Perceptions of Smallest Meaningful Pay Increases," *Industrial Relations,* Spring 1984, pp. 278–86; and Linda Krefting, Jerry Newman, and Frank Krzystofiak, "What is a Meaningful Pay Increase?" in *Perspectives on Compensation,* eds. L. Gomez-Mejia and D. Balkin (Englewood Cliffs, N.J.: Prentice-Hall, 1987).

EXHIBIT 7.24
Range Overlap

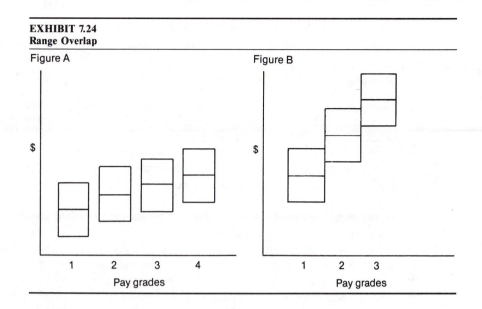

Figure A

Figure B

$ / Pay grades (1 2 3 4)

$ / Pay grades (1 2 3)

BALANCING INTERNAL AND EXTERNAL PRESSURES: ADJUSTING THE PAY STRUCTURE

Up until now we have made a distinction between the job structure and the pay structure. A job structure is generated through the process of job analysis and job evaluation. In it jobs are ordered on the basis of total points (point plan), classes and grades (classification plan), or ranks (ranking plan). The pay structure, on the other hand, is anchored by the organization's pay policy line, which is set using the market rates paid for key jobs.

Reconciling Differences

The problem with using two methods to create a structure is that you are likely to get two different structures. The order in which jobs are ranked on internal (job evaluation) and external (market surveys) factors may not completely agree. Certainly differences between the market rate and the job evaluation rank warrant a review of the basic decisions in evaluating and pricing that particular job. This may entail reviewing the job analysis, the job description sheets, and the evaluation of the job. It also means reexamining the market data as it pertains to the job in question. Often this reanalysis solves the problem. In cases where discrepancies persist, experienced judgment is required. Sometimes survey data is discarded; sometimes benchmark job matches are changed. Too frequently, decisions are made on the basis of expediency, and these decisions can undermine the integrity of the pay system. Reclassifying a market-sensitive job (supply and demand imbalance) into a higher salary grade, where it will tend to remain long after the imbalance has been corrected, will only create additional problems in the long run. Creating a special range which is clearly designated as market responsive may be a better approach.

Compression

Compression problems are classic examples of an imbalance between external competitive pressures and internal equity.[32] Compression results when wages for those jobs filled from outside the organization are increasing faster than the wages for jobs filled via promotion or from within the organization. The result is that as pay differentials among jobs become very small, the traditional pay structure becomes compressed. Examples are found in structures which include jobs paid at or near the minimum wage. Whenever Congress legislates changes in the minimum wage, the employer is faced with difficult choices. It can shift the entire pay structure higher to maintain the differentials with the new minimum wage and/or reduce the numbers employed to offset the higher costs and/or try to increase productivity through automation or other means.

Compression may also be found in engineering jobs where newly graduated engineers may command salaries almost equal to those paid to engineers with three to five years of service in a firm. And it often occurs in pay differences between the first-line supervisors and their subordinates. Gomez-Mejia and Balkin reported a study of compression in the salary differentials among professors in a business school.[33] Newly graduating assistant professor salaries, driven by extreme market forces, were increasing at a faster rate than more senior professor salaries, which were regulated by internal equity considerations. Faced with scarce resources, the dean channeled funds to attract new faculty and was unable to retain traditional wage differentials among the ranks. The dean abandoned internal equity in favor of external competitiveness for one segment of the job structure. Gomez-Mejia and Balkin point out that such action, while typical, may be dysfunctional. Senior faculty experiencing pay dissatisfaction from the compression searched for new jobs in other universities. Only the best performers were able to find new positions, so that the overall quality of the faculty declined.

Obviously these internal/external conflicts need to be resolved, and judgment is required in doing so. A manager may choose, as a matter of policy, to emphasize external over internal forces, or vice versa. Instead managers often choose a balancing act—responding to pressures, be they external or internal— to keep the best work force within some cost constraints.

---

[32]Thomas J. Bergmann, Frederick S. Hills, and Laurel Priefert, "Pay Compression: Causes, Results, and Possible Solutions," *Compensation Review* 15, no. 2 (1983), pp. 17–26.

[33]Luis R. Gomez-Mejia and David B. Balkin, "Causes and Consequences of Pay Compression: The Case of Business Schools," working paper, Management Department, University of Florida, Gainesville, Fla., November 1984.

In sum, the process of balancing internal and external pressures is a matter of judgment, made with an eye to the objectives established for the pay system. De-emphasizing internal pay relationships may lead to feelings of inequitable treatment among employees. These in turn may reduce employees' willingness to share new ideas on how to improve the work or improve the product's quality. Inequitable internal pay relationships may also lead employees to seek other jobs, file grievances, form unions, go out on strike, or refuse to take on greater job responsibilities. Neglecting external pay relationships, however, will affect both the ability to attract job applicants and the ability to hire those applicants who match the organization's needs. External pay relationships also influence the organization's labor costs and hence its ability to compete in the product/ services market.

Market pricing, reflecting an emphasis on external competitiveness, may be defined as pricing jobs so that the job worth and the pay structure are almost exclusively determined through reliance on external market data. Firms following such an approach typically have relatively informal job evaluation plans. They seek to match a large percentage of their jobs with market data and collect as much market data as possible. Usually the job evaluation process becomes a procedure to slot into the pay structure jobs that are truly unique to the company. This would be a very small percentage of the total jobs.

On the other side are organizations that emphasize internal equity: *pricing jobs in relationship to what other jobs within the organization are paid.* This policy emphasizes the importance of formal job evaluation plans and solid job matching for a few key benchmarks in the external market.

In Chapter 4, we stated that one prevailing view of job evaluation was that it "served to integrate the internal job structure with the rates paid in the external market." This is the fundamental logic underlying the factor comparison method where pay values are used to design the job comparison scale and the pay structure. The point plan also serves to integrate internal equity and the external market. It does this through policy capturing—using the pay rates for benchmark jobs to assign the weights to each compensable factor. Hence, the "agreed-upon rates of pay for benchmark jobs" serve as the criterion for deriving the weights for compensable factors.

SUMMARY

This chapter has detailed the basic decisions and techniques involved in setting pay levels and designing pay ranges. In most organizations surveys of other employers' pay rates are conducted and the results analyzed to determine competitive rates paid in the market. An employer using the survey results considers how it wishes to position its pay in the market: to lead, to match, or to follow competition. This policy decision may be different for different business units and even for different job groups within a single organization, depending on the circumstances. The pay policy is then translated into practice by setting pay policy lines. These lines reflect the employer's position in the market and serve as reference points around which pay ranges are established.

The use of ranges is a recognition of both external and internal pressures. No single going rate for a job exists in the market; rather an array of rates exists. This array results from variations in the quality of employees for that job and differences in employer policies and practices. It also reflects the fact that employers differ in the value attached to the jobs and qualifications. Internally, the use of ranges is consistent with variations in the discretion present in jobs. Some employees will perform better than others; some employees are more experienced than others. Pay ranges permit employers to value and recognize these differences with pay.

Let us step back for a moment to review what has been discussed and preview what is coming. We have examined two components of the pay model. Internal consistency issues and techniques including job analysis, job descriptions, and job evaluation, and the resulting job structure were discussed. External competitiveness issues and techniques, including policy determination, survey design and analysis, setting the pay policy line, and designing pay ranges have also been discussed. The next part of the book will examine issues involved in employee contributions—paying the individuals who perform the work. This is perhaps the most important part of the book. All that has gone before is a prelude, setting up the pay levels and pay structures within which individual employees are to be paid.

REVIEW QUESTIONS

1. Which pay level policy would you recommend to an employer? Why? Does it depend on circumstances faced by the employer? Which ones?
2. How would you go about designing a survey for setting pay for welders? How would you go about designing a survey for setting pay for financial managers? Do the issues differ? Will the techniques used and the data collected differ? Why or why not?
3. What factors determine the relevant market for a survey? Why is the definition of the relevant market so important?
4. In what situations would you recommend your employer use benchmark jobs in survey? When would you recommend a skill-based or job valuation approach?
5. What do surveys have to do with pay discrimination?
6. What factors would you consider in deciding the number of pay ranges to recommend?

Part 2
Compensation Applications

Case 1   Unimerge Corporation

Unimerge Corporation has recently developed a job evaluation plan using the Hay Guide Chart-Profile Method (see Appendix A to Chapter 4). The plan applies to all managerial and professional jobs at Unimerge. Hay consultants have worked with a committee from Unimerge to evaluate all jobs and to develop a job structure based on point assignments. Use of the plan has the solid backing of top management, which has been concerned with the haphazard and inconsistent methods previously used for evaluating and pricing jobs at Unimerge.

The compensation committee has now turned to the task of pricing jobs based on the point evaluations and the resulting structure. While the exact pricing methods are still under discussion, it has been agreed that Hay point ranges will be pegged to compensation ranges.

As methods for pricing the structure are being discussed in more detail, Unimerge's Vice President for Data Processing raises an issue that has just occurred to him. While he feels that the data processing jobs have been evaluated correctly, he notes that the market for these jobs has been very volatile. He has been forced over and over again to match outside pay offers in order to retain critical personnel. If the salaries are determined by Hay points, how will he be able to do this in the future? One of the other committee members suggests that when this occurs, the job in question could be assigned a higher point value.

1. You are the compensation manager responsible for maintaining the compensation program. How do you respond to the concerns of the data processing vice president?
2. How do you respond to the other committee member who proposes assigning a higher point value to jobs with volatile markets?
3. What policy and rationale do you propose for Unimerge for handling such situations in the future?

Case 2   *Hewlett-Packard Pay Policy*

The following is an excerpt from the pay policy of Hewlett-Packard. The policy is published and distributed for employee reference.

MEASURING THE COMPETITION

It is H-P's stated objective to have competitive salary curves that will give all employees the opportunity to be as well paid as employees of other leading companies with comparable jobs.

To ensure that this objective becomes a reality, H-P participates in salary surveys to determine the competitive market for the jobs performed at H-P.

Salary surveys are conducted at various times during the year to ensure that we keep in close contact with the ever-changing competitive job market.

From these surveys, the competitive average salary for each job is determined, and a decision is made about the position for our curve midpoints. (These midpoints are guidelines for the average pay for the jobs at H-P.)

Our philosophy of paying "among the leaders" ultimately guides this decision and establishes the relationship between our pay curve midpoint and the actual competitive average salary.

Depending on the companies surveyed, H-P establishes the relationship between present actual competitive salaries and our curve midpoints in one of the following ways:

- When compared with 5 to 10 truly leading companies, our midpoints will be approximately equal to the average of the competitive salary data for each benchmark job.

or

- Our midpoints will be 5 to 10 percent above the average of a group of 10 to 20 companies that have been selected from a broad survey because of their similarities to H-P.

or

- When using a broad survey of 30 or more companies selected by an outside consultant, our midpoints will be approximately 10 to 15 percent above the average paid by these companies.

As a final step in this process, H-P considers both the economic picture as forecasted by top economists and the expected change in the competitive job market over the next year.

Using this information, H-P projects the expected competitive salary movement one full year ahead in order to establish the pay curve midpoints for the next year.

Thus, in addition to our objective of paying among the leading companies, the curves are further adjusted upward to reflect anticipated competitive salary growth. When you hear that the "curves have gone up by 5, 7, or 10 percent," this means that the new curves are already at least 5, 7, or 10 percent ahead of the market when they are first used as tools for administering your salary.

This important point distinguishes H-P's pay program from most companies. What it means to you is that your pay curve is unlikely to ever be behind the competitive market.

Based on this policy and the discussion in Chapters 6 and 7:

1. Would you describe H-P's policy as one of leading, lagging, or matching the competition? Explain.
2. What factor influences the increasing competitiveness of H-P pay as the domain of comparison increases from 5 to 30 companies?
3. Why are midpoints used as comparison points for survey data?
4. If you were a local H-P manager involved in the selection of leading companies for survey purposes, what factors would you want to consider?

Case 3   *Industrial Relations Association of Tulsa*

Organizations have a wide range of methods for "distilling" salary survey information. The analysis and presentation of data in the form of salary recommendations involve common sense as well as technical sense. It also involves the ability to defend your analysis.

You are a compensation analyst for the Tulsa company participating in the survey reproduced in Exhibit 1 on page 264.

1. You are assigned to summarize the survey results for the clerical job series (jobs 001–009) and the accounting series (jobs 602–611) and to make salary structure adjustment recommendations for the two series.
2. Prepare your analysis in a combined graphic and narrative form, using either weighted average data, the salary range data (you will have to establish ranges based on "your reported weighted average" data), or a combination of both.
3. Assume in making your recommendations that your plan year commences three months from now and your company has a 5–10 percent lead policy with regard to the other companies in this survey.

EXHIBIT 1
Tulsa Survey Data

04616-2   AREA: TULSA   COMPANY:

JOB NUMBER	JOB CLASS TITLE	NUMBER OF PARTICIPATING COMPANIES	AVERAGE OF WEIGHTED AVERAGES	NUMBER OF EMPLOYEES	SALARY WEIGHTED AVERAGE	MINIMUM SALARY	MAXIMUM SALARY	YOUR REPORTED WEIGHTED AVERAGE
001	CLERK TYPIST B	10	912	40	903	776	1.101	848
003	CLERK TYPIST A	11	1.115	57	1.050	939	1.237	
004	SECRETARY C	14	1.009	110	1.108	863	1.235	988
005	SECRETARY B	19	1.176	136	1.223	974	1.402	1.226
006	SECRETARY A	20	1.342	74	1.344	1.047	1.538	1.686
007	GENERAL CLERK C	11	821	65	834	714	1.046	708
008	GENERAL CLERK B	15	916	131	927	800	1.154	922
009	GENERAL CLERK A	16	1.084	138	1.125	925	1.325	1.291
102	DETAIL DRAFTSMAN	11	1.119	46	1.100	965	1.370	1.191
103	PRODUCT DRAFTSMAN	15	1.250	61	1.288	1.074	1.531	1.454
104	DESIGN DRAFTSMAN	12	1.376	29	1.407	1.211	1.733	
105	PRODUCT DESIGNER	15	1.730	67	1.751	1.370	2.009	2.002
106	SENIOR PRODUCT DESIGNER	10	2.025	26	1.924	1.507	2.265	
111	ASSISTANT ENGINEER	11	1.602	27	1.728	1.321	2.038	1.825
112	DESIGN/DEVELOPMENT ENGINEER	9	1.391	38	2.039	1.448	2.263	2.242
113	SENIOR DESIGN/DEVELOPE ENG.	15	2.374	131	2.656	1.749	2.708	2.541
114	PROJECT ENGINEER	12	2.495	59	2.929	1.964	3.005	3.284
115	SENIOR PROJECT ENGINEER	11	2.664	28	2.693	2.072	3.140	3.379
116	SECTION CHIEF	11	3.098	39	3.388	2.357	3.788	4.330
201	INDUSTRIAL NURSE	10	1.464	21	1.361	1.231	1.836	1.453
301	KEYPUNCH OPERATOR B	8	1.025	38	931	909	1.229	801
302	KEYPUNCH OPERATOR A	13	897	40	914	792	1.132	873
306	COMPUTER OPERATOR B	13	1.118	47	1.097	989	1.380	1.071
307	COMPUTER OPERATOR A	15	1.347	59	1.408	1.129	1.584	1.649
308	PROGRAMMER/ANALYST	17	1.901	203	2.300	1.501	2.311	2.348
402	PRODUCTION CONTROL COOR.	13	1.628	81	1.804	1.300	1.962	1.511
403	FOREMAN MATERIAL HANDLING	18	1.869	77	2.118	1.523	2.234	2.198
404	SUPER. PLANT MATERIAL CONT.	14	2.094	23	2.140	1.638	2.551	2.404
506	FOREMAN-PLANT MAINTENANCE	16	2.098	55	2.298	1.727	2.582	2.126
507	MANAGER INDUSTRIAL ENG	10	2.951	10	2.951	2.331	3.655	2.805
508	PLANT ENGINEER	7	2.453	11	2.314	1.993	3.057	2.109
509	INDUSTRIAL ENG ANALYST	10	2.094	52	2.009	1.617	2.489	1.635
602	ACCOUNTANT B	17	1.411	50	1.481	1.238	1.840	1.525
603	ACCOUNTANT A	14	1.692	29	1.844	1.436	2.188	1.642
604	SUPERVISOR COST ACCOUNTING	13	2.202	18	2.147	1.721	2.695	1.915
606	CONTROLLER PLANT	11	3.436	11	3.436	2.690	4.110	
607	ACCOUNTING RECORDS CLERK	16	941	56	903	853	1.150	840
608	ACCOUNTING CLERK	16	1.103	62	976	954	1.316	1.113
609	CLERICAL ACCOUNTANT	10	1.254	31	1.251	1.055	1.506	1.670
611	SUPERVISOR GENL ACCTG	17	2.163	24	2.048	1.755	2.694	1.967
701	BUYER	19	1.482	40	1.559	1.257	1.895	1.339
702	SENIOR BUYER	16	1.964	70	1.961	1.506	2.337	1.823
704	PURCHASING AGENT	12	2.499	15	2.550	1.968	2.976	2.338
802	FOREMAN MANUFACTURING	20	1.970	383	2.189	1.628	2.403	2.074
803	GEN.-FOREMAN MANUFACTURING	13	2.361	73	2.318	1.852	2.801	2.237
805	PLANT SUPERINTENDENT	12	2.825	24	2.611	2.305	3.469	3.293
808	SUPERINTENDENT ASSEMBLY	6	2.814	19	2.908	2.341	3.638	2.707

Source: Industrial Relations Association of Tulsa.

Part 3

Employee Contributions: Determining Individual Pay

Thus far we have concentrated on two components of the pay model (Exhibit III.1). Internal consistency and the practices to ensure it—job analysis and job evaluation—provide guidance relating jobs to each other in terms of the content of the work and the relative contributions of the jobs to the organization's objectives. External competitiveness, or comparisons with the external labor market, raises issues of proper survey definitions, setting policy lines, and arriving at competitive pay levels and equitable pay structures. This part of the book deals with a third critical dimension of the pay system design and administration—paying individual employees performing the job.

How much should one employee be paid relative to another when they both hold the same jobs in the same organization? If this question is not answered satisfactorily, all prior efforts to evaluate and price jobs may have been in vain. For example, the compensation manager determines that all systems analysts should be paid between $18,000 and $26,000. But where in that range is each individual paid? Should a good performer be paid more than a poor performer? If the answer is yes, how should performance be measured and what should be the differential reward? Similarly, should the systems analyst with more years' experience (i.e., higher seniority) be paid more than a co-worker with less time on the job? Again, if the answer is yes, what is the trade off between seniority and performance in assigning pay raises. As Exhibit III.1 suggests, all of these questions involve the concept of employee contribution. For the next three chapters we will be discussing different facets of employee contribution.

Chapter 8 considers how pay affects performance. In particular, two questions are addressed: First, *should* pay systems be designed to affect performance? Second, *can* pay systems be designed to affect performance? Many of the answers to these questions come from theories of motivation and empirical research evaluating strategies to motivate employees in the workplace.

Chapter 9 looks at pay systems that assume performance can be objectively measured. In these times of productivity stagnation, such incentive systems are becoming increasingly attractive to organizations.

Finally, Chapter 10 focuses on more subjective performance measurement systems and their relationship to compensation in general and pay increases in particular.

EXHIBIT III.1
The Pay Model

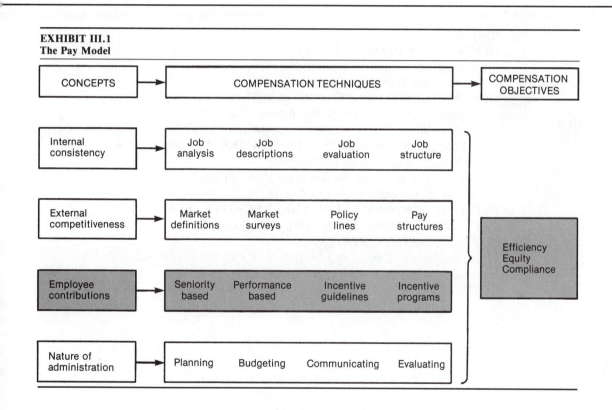

| CONCEPTS | COMPENSATION TECHNIQUES | COMPENSATION OBJECTIVES |

| Internal consistency | Job analysis | Job descriptions | Job evaluation | Job structure |

| External competitiveness | Market definitions | Market surveys | Policy lines | Pay structures |

| Employee contributions | Seniority based | Performance based | Incentive guidelines | Incentive programs |

| Nature of administration | Planning | Budgeting | Communicating | Evaluating |

Efficiency
Equity
Compliance

Chapter *8*

Employee Contributions: Pay and Performance

The Little Red Hen: A Productivity Fable

Once upon a time there was a little red hen who scratched about the barnyard until she uncovered some grains of wheat. She turned to other workers on the farm and said: "If we plant this wheat, we'll have bread to eat. Who will help me plant it?"

"We never did that before," said the horse, who was the supervisor.

"I'm too busy," said the duck.

"I'd need complete training," said the pig.

"It's not in my job description," said the goose.

"Well, I'll do it myself," said the little red hen. And she did. The wheat grew tall and ripened into grain. "Who will help me reap the wheat?" asked the little red hen.

"Let's check the regulations first," said the horse.

"I'd lose my seniority," said the duck.

"I'm on my lunch break," said the goose.

"Out of my classification," said the pig.

"Then I will," said the little red hen, and she did.

At last it came time to bake the bread.

"Who will help me bake the bread?" asked the little red hen.

"That would be overtime for me," said the horse.

"I've got to run some errands," said the duck.

"I've never learned how," said the pig.

"If I'm to be the only helper, that's unfair," said the goose.

"Then I will," said the little red hen.

She baked five loaves and was ready to turn them in to the farmer when the other workers stepped up. They wanted to be sure the farmer knew it was a group project.

"It needs to be cleared by someone else," said the horse.

"I'm calling the shop steward," said the duck.

"I demand equal rights," yelled the goose.

"We'd better file a copy," said the pig.

But the little red hen turned in the loaves by herself. When it came time for the farmer to reward the effort, he gave one loaf to each worker.

"But I earned all the bread myself!" said the little red hen.

"I know," said the farmer, "but it takes too much paperwork to justify giving you all the bread. It's much easier to distribute it equally, and that way the others won't complain."

So the little red hen shared the bread, but her co-workers and the farmer wondered why she never baked any more. [From *Federal News Clip Sheet,* June 1979].

Is the fable of the little red hen an accurate portrayal of American industry today? Do reward systems operate to discourage productive workers? Given the productivity lag discussed so frequently in the popular press, can we design compensation systems to spur productivity growth? If such a design is possible, is it desirable, or are other methods of approaching employee equity superior?

Answers to these questions are approached first in this chapter by defining the concept of employee equity as it relates to pay. With employee equity as a foundation, the remainder of the chapter explores the relationship between pay and performance. After all, if pay can motivate employees to perform better, the role of compensation and compensation managers in organizational success becomes crucial!

DEFINING EMPLOYEE EQUITY

On what basis should raises be granted? Make the initial assumption that organizations want to treat employees fairly (i.e., to ensure employee equity). Employee equity is defined here as:

> **Allocation of rewards (outcomes) to employees based on some standard of fairness consistently applied across individuals within the same job and organization.**

This definition immediately raises the question: "What standard of fairness should be used?" The strategy organizations adopt to answer this question provides the foundation for policies in employee equity.

Equivalent Treatment Standard

One route organizations can and do take is to adopt a standard of fairness based on equivalent treatment: all employees receive the same pay increase. One proponent of this standard of equity is unions. They argue, at times quite persuasively, that any effort to differentiate pay increases is destined to be unfair. Basing pay increases, for example, on the level of performance assumes that objective measures of performance exist. In the absence of objective performance measures, which unions argue is the rule rather than the exception, management has unlimited latitude in dispensing salary increases—a form of power that may result in inequitable treatment. (Chapter 17 will cover more extensively union roles in compensation administration.)

Differential Treatment Standard

The second strategy for organizations to adopt is one where the standard of fairness is based on differential treatment of employees: raises are distributed unequally according to some "fair" allocation rule. Prior to World War II the fair allocation rule was frequently individual need. The size of salary increases was based on an employee's need for the additional income. Under this system married men with large numbers of dependents received the largest increases. At the other extreme were women employees who were assumed to be working for pocket money and, hence, had a much lower need for raises. Vestiges of this philosophy still exist today, but discrimination laws and the women's movement have made it increasingly untenable.

An alternative allocation rule is based on individual performance differences. Recognizing individual differences in performance obviously assumes that workers are not interchangeable and equally efficient. Furthermore, the worth of jobs to an organization now becomes a function of both the job's value (i.e., pay structure determination as discussed in Chapters 6 and 7) and *the level*

EXHIBIT 8.1
A Comparison of U.S. and Canadian Standards of Fairness

	Location of Organization	
Basis of Salary Increase	*United States*	*Canada*
Merit only	57%	25%
Merit and general	28	53
General or cost of living	15	22

of individual performance in the job. Part of the reason pay ranges are established for jobs is to recognize these two distinct sources of value. Minimums and maximums of a pay range define the limits of a job's value. Within that range, though, value depends on some measure of individual performance.

Another way of looking at this is to extend further the concept of marginal revenue product (MRP) developed in Chapter 6. From an economic perspective wages should bear a close relationship to the value of products produced by a worker. If John Jones can produce 10 frisbees in an hour and those frisbees each sell for $4, John's pay should be some relatively constant proportion of that $40 market value. Granted the pay proportion might be smaller than the "slice" allocated to a marketing manager responsible for the overall frisbee marketing strategy. But John Jones's pay should be greater than the pay for anyone else who also produces frisbees but at a lower productivity level. When given a choice between these different standards of fairness, U.S. organizations in practice claim to use a differential treatment standard based on level of performance.[1]

If anything, the tendency to pay for performance (merit increases) in the United States is expected to increase: A recent survey indicates linking employees' pay to their performance is the foremost priority for 49 percent (426 organizations) of all senior human resource executives surveyed.[2] Why this interest in paying for performance? The pay model in Exhibit III.1 provides a clue. According to the model, employee equity is a function of seniority increases, performance evaluation, and pay increase guidelines. In fact, elaborating this model in Exhibit 8.2 yields:

Exhibit 8.2 indicates that employee work-related behavior is shaped by pay increase policies and guidelines. In fact, one of the goals of strategic planning is to reinforce this linkage.[3] The idea calls for design of reward and performance measurement systems which trigger employee behaviors necessary to

---

[1]Administrative Management Society, "1984 AMS Guide to Management Compensation," *Administrative Management Society* 84, no. 3 (1984), p. 3.

[2]CompFlash, "More Plaudits for Pay for Performance: Its Priority for Human Resource Executives," *AMA CompFlash* 84, no. 9 (1984), p. 7.

[3]Paul Stonich, "The Performance Measurement and Reward System: Critical to Strategic Management," *Organizational Dynamics* 12 (1984), pp. 45–57.

EXHIBIT 8.2
An Elaboration of the Employee Equity Concept

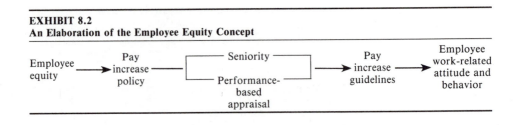

meet organizational goals. Recognize, though, that there are very real limits to the role of compensation in shaping behavior.[4] Other factors do influence performance! Consequently, compensation specialists must distinguish myth from reality and identify where compensation policies/practices can best be altered to maximize employee potential.

DETERMINANTS OF PERFORMANCE

What leads one employee to do a better job than another? In general there appear to be three factors that influence performance. First is the quality of the match between job requirements and individual ability. Everyone has heard stories of the supersalesperson who, when promoted to sales management, turned out to be worse than average. Skills that are exceptional for one line of work might be useless in another. Beyond the requirements/ability match though, there is the complex dimension of motivation. Why are some employees motivated to use their skills to best advantage while other employees "loaf" at every available opportunity? Finally, even highly skilled employees who are motivated to perform sometimes encounter conditions beyond their control (e.g., the bank loan officer with a goal to increase loans who is hampered by an unexpected sharp increase in interest rates).

All of these factors have been discussed in greater detail by Campbell and Pritchard.[5] Exhibit 8.3 illustrates these factors and suggests the role compensation may potentially play to influence them. Exhibit 8.3 suggests that compensation policies and practices may affect performance levels indirectly through the level of employee aptitude and skills (factors 1 and 2), and directly through employee motivation (choice to expend effort, degree of effort, and persistence of effort). Whether an organization should, in fact, attempt to tie pay to performance is dependent upon whether these linkages do exist. The next sections look first at some of the research findings on the role compensation plays in the ability → performance relationship, and then at the role compensation plays in the motivation → performance link.

---

[4]Ibid.

[5]John P. Campbell and Robert Pritchard, "Motivation Theory in Industrial and Organizational Psychology," in *Handbook of Industrial and Organizational Psychology,* ed. Marvin Dunnette (Chicago: Rand McNally, 1976).

EXHIBIT 8.3
Determinants of Employee Performance and the Role of Compensation

Determinant	Primary Source of Organizational Influence	Secondary Source of Organizational Influence
1. Aptitude level	Level of employee aptitude influenced by quality of selection policies and practices.	Quality of selection is affected by number of applicants, which is influenced by compensation and reward practices.
2. Skill level	Level of employee aptitude influenced by quality of selection policies and practices.	Quality of selection is affected by number of applicants, which is influenced by compensation and rewards, quality of training.
3. Choice to expend effort	Degree to which compensation practices are tied to employee performance.	
4. Choice of degree of effort to expend	Degree to which compensation practices are tied to employee performance.	
5. Choice to persist	Degree to which compensation practices are tied to employee performance.	
6. Understanding of work	Quality of job descriptions and supervisory explanations of performance requirements.	Quality of performance appraisal process.
7. Facilitating and inhibiting condition not under control of the individual	Unknown.	Unknown.

Ability → Performance Relationships

For years psychologists and others have recognized the existence of individual differences in ability.[6] The fact that ability is related to performance is also generally well accepted. The strength of this relationship is not, however, as high as might be expected. As an example, consider the strategy of an organization that hires individuals for assembly line jobs based on their scores on an intelligence test. The general rationale would run something like this: "IQ is a measure of general ability, and we want the highest-ability individuals available for all of our jobs." Needless to say, this strategy would be ineffective. Logic like this, used more frequently in the 1950s, resulted in lowered performance. Workers became overly bored with the routine nature of tasks. The lack of challenge actually resulted in subpar performance by these high-ability individuals.

Despite the less than perfect relationship between ability and performance, organizations have still adopted a number of policies and practices that are de-

---

[6]Leona Tyler, *The Psychology of Human Differences* (New York: Appleton-Century-Crofts, 1965).

signed to capitalize on the strength of this relationship; and incorporated into these procedures is a recognition of the role of money.

Selection and placement. Organizations have long realized the role of pay in the selection process. If an applicant pool is too small to ensure selection of sufficient numbers of qualified employees, one standard strategy is to raise the relative wage to attract more applicants.[7] In fact, the most recent economic thought, termed *efficiency wage theory,* suggests that organizations may be perfectly rational in offering wages greater than required by the market to attract workers. When firm A offers higher wages than its competitors, employees presumably face greater risks for performing at substandard levels: If caught, it is relatively more difficult (i.e., longer unemployment) to find a comparable alternative job. Presumably, then, workers in high-wage firms are less likely to shirk their task demands.[8]

Traditional selection theory also provides a rationale for paying wages above the market-clearing level. As noted in Chapter 6, paying above the market rate triggers several phenomena. First, the higher relative wage makes the opening more attractive. Recruitment is easier, and more individuals apply for the job. Second, the larger pool of applicants means more opportunity to select individuals whose abilities better match job requirements. The better a match between individual abilities and job requirements, the higher the expected job performance, other things equal.[9]

An essential ingredient in this scenario is the role of pay. This does not suggest that pay is the sole factor that attracts individuals to a firm. However, there is relatively strong evidence that job seekers do set a minimum pay level; and any wage offered that is lower than that minimum standard leads to refusal of an otherwise acceptable job offer.[10]

Training and development. Another way in which performance can be improved by acting upon the skill component of our equation is through training and development. The personnel process is highly subject to errors. For example, the selection process results, unfortunately, in a number of prediction er-

---

[7]Lloyd Reynolds, *Labor Economics and Labor Relations* (Englewood Cliffs, N.J.: Prentice-Hall, 1982).

[8]Robert E. Hall and David M. Lilien, "Efficient Wage Bargains under Uncertain Supply and Demand," *The American Economic Review* 69, no. 5 (1979), pp. 868–79; "Why Unemployment Sometimes Lingers on Stirs Renewed Interest," *The Wall Street Journal,* December 26, 1985, pp. 1, 26; Ian M. McDonald and Robert M. Solow, "Wage Bargaining and Employment," *The American Economic Review* 71, no. 5 (1981), pp. 896–908.

[9]L. H. Lofquist and R. V. Dawis, *Adjustment to Work* (New York: Appleton-Century-Crofts, 1969).

[10]H. R. Sheppard and A. H. Belitsky, *The Job Hunt* (Baltimore, Md.: Johns Hopkins University Press, 1966).

rors. Some job applicants do not end up performing as well in jobs as expected. To identify these errors the vast majority of organizations conduct formal performance evaluations. One outcome of this performance evaluation process is the identification of training and development needs intended to strengthen abilities necessary for improved job performance.

How does pay fit into this process? Are employees attracted to training programs because of anticipated future salary increases? One potential answer to these questions comes from human capital theory.[11] Becker, a major human capital theorist, argues that there are two different types of training: general and specific. General training is more frequently associated with formal educational institutions. It is argued that general training increases the value of an individual equally across all firms. For example, a bachelor's degree in English presumably increases a person's value to all organizations equally. Under these circumstances, Becker argues that the individual should bear the cost of training. This occurs, presumably, because the increased value of the employee is either recognized by the organization in the form of increased wages, or another organization will "pirate" the employee away.

In contrast, specific training is associated with an improvement in skills that are not of equal value across organizations. The primary beneficiary is the company employing the individual who receives training. For this type of training it is argued that the company should bear the costs of the training programs. Since the skills developed are of value only to one organization, the employee's value increases only for that organization. Salary increases need not be offered to induce the individual to stay with the firm because his or her value has not increased except in that firm. Since no pay increases result from this type of training, it is argued that the organization benefiting from the increased proficiency should bear the cost of training.

Most training provided by organizations falls between these two extremes of general and specific skills. Although there is no empirical support, conceptually this suggests that participation in training programs leads to increased compensation.

It is apparent that the ability-performance relationship is affected by pay levels. But this impact is indirect. Pay serves as an inducement that attracts high-ability individuals to the firm and which leads current employees to seek training designed to increase their abilities on the job. In fact, it appears that the direct impact of pay on performance really operates through the motivation component of the equation. When the pay model refers to pay inducing some type of behavior, it is actually referring to a dimension of motivation. The following section discusses some of the major theories and research dealing with the relationship between motivation and performance. Particular emphasis will be placed on the role pay assumes in this process.

---

[11]Gary Becker, *Human Capital* (New York: National Bureau of Economic Research, 1964).

Motivation → Pay → Performance Relationships

Many psychologists interested in the area of motivation agree that the key issue is the goal-directed nature of behavior.[12] If compensation managers could discover why behavior occurs and why it is directed toward one of countless possible goals, considerable progress could be made in improving employee job performance. Consider, for example, two operatives who work side by side on an assembly line in an automotive plant. One of the workers makes the appropriate welds in a timely fashion as cars pass on the line. The other expends considerable energy in finding ways to "beat the system": welds are missed; coat hangers are welded to parts of the body that are virtually undiscoverable until an owner takes the car in with complaints about an "irritating rattle." Each of these two employees works on the same line, with similar environment; each receives the same pay and works the same hours. Yet obviously their behavior is directed to entirely different goals.

Each of the theories discussed below sheds some light on this and countless other motivation problems experienced in the real world. The orientation taken will be to discuss these theories as they may bear on job performance. Again, particular emphasis will be placed on the role pay assumes in the motivation-performance link.

Content theories. Content theories can be distinguished by their emphasis on *what* motivates people rather than *how* people are motivated. The key variable in most of these theories is different types of needs. It has been speculated that psychologists have enumerated several hundred needs.[13]

The two most well-known content theories include the work by Maslow[14] and by Herzberg, Mausner, and Snyderman.[15] Maslow's theory is based on a hierarchy of five needs (Exhibit 8.4), each assumed to motivate behavior in varying degrees. Maslow argues that lower-level needs in the hierarchy are prepotent: Behavior is directed toward satisfying these needs until sufficient satiation occurs to make the next higher order need dominant. For example, illegal aliens entering the United States may well direct their behavior toward obtaining the necessary food to satisfy physiological needs of themselves and their families. If they obtain jobs that ensure consistent satisfaction of that need, the security need becomes dominant. Behavior is then directed toward obtaining

---

[12]Edwin Locke and J. Bryan, "Cognitive Aspects of Psychomotor Performance: The Effect of Performance Goals on Level of Performance," *Journal of Applied Psychology* 50 (1966), pp. 286–91; Edwin Locke, "The Motivational Effect of Knowledge of Results: Knowledge or Goal Setting?" *Journal of Applied Psychology* 51 (1967), pp. 324–29.

[13]Edward Lawler III, *Pay and Organizational Effectiveness: A Psychological View* (New York: McGraw-Hill, 1971).

[14]Abraham Maslow, *Motivation and Personality* (New York: Harper & Row, 1954).

[15]F. Herzberg, B. Mausner, and B. Snyderman, *The Motivation to Work* (New York: John Wiley & Sons, 1959).

EXHIBIT 8.4
Maslow's Hierarchy of Needs

1.	Physiological needs	The need for food, water, and air.
2.	Safety needs	The need for security, stability, and the absence from pain, threat, or illness.
3.	Social needs	Need for affection, belongingness, love.
4.	Esteem needs	Need for personal feelings of achievement or self-esteem and also a need for recognition or respect from others.
5.	Self-actualization needs	Need to become all one is capable of becoming, to realize one's own potential or achieve self-fulfillment.

---

physical and emotional security. Higher-order needs become progressively more important as lower-order needs are satisfied.

One of the major problems with this approach is that it is extremely difficult to identify which needs are prepotent at any given time. Without this information it is virtually impossible to determine how a work environment should be structured to improve performance. For example, research indicates that needs vary by age, geographic location (urban/rural), socioeconomic status, and sex, to name a few. There is even speculation that the needs of the general population have been shifting over time toward a greater concern for such higher-level needs as autonomy and self-actualization.[16]

What role does pay play in this process? One conclusion based on an extensive literature review is that pay can help satisfy esteem needs and physiological needs but is less useful for satisfying autonomy and security needs, and is least useful for satisfying social and self-actualization needs.[17]

In comparison, Herzberg's theory is very similar to Maslow's.[18] He argues that two types of factors are present across organizations: hygienes and motivators. Hygiene factors include such things as company policy/administration, supervision, salary, interpersonal relations, and working conditions. Motivators are represented by opportunities for advancement, achievement, responsibility, and recognition. In essence, it might be argued that Maslow's theory has gravitated in the same direction as Herzberg's. If in fact most lower-order needs are generally satisfied in our affluent society, then individual needs that are prepotent in Maslow's framework include esteem and self-actualization.[19] As conceived by Maslow, these needs are very similar to Herzberg's conception of advancement, achievement, and recognition. Since these factors are prepotent, they assume responsibility for a great deal of the goal direction of individuals. In Herzberg's terms they become the motivators, the factors that can lead to job satisfaction if met by the organization.

---

[16]Theodore Roszak, *The Making of a Counter Culture: Reflections on the Techno-Cractic Society and Its Youthful Opposition* (Garden City, N.Y.: Doubleday, 1969).

[17]Lawler, *Pay and Organizational Effectiveness.*

[18]Herzberg, Mausner, and Snyderman, *The Motivation to Work.*

[19]Roszak, *The Making of a Counter Culture.*

The one major difference that can be inferred from these two theories is the function assumed by pay. As already indicated, numerous studies have shown that pay can serve to satisfy, to some extent, Maslow's needs. In contrast, Herzberg's work is often interpreted as if he argued that pay is solely a hygiene factor. Pay is necessary at sufficient levels to thwart job dissatisfaction, but it is not appropriate for motivating behavior. In fact, this assessment is not correct. While Herzberg's theory can be attacked on a number of grounds, it is inappropriate to assume Herzberg relegated pay only to the status of a hygiene factor.[20] The original work by Herzberg also demonstrated that pay takes on significance as a source of satisfaction when it is perceived as a form of recognition or reward. In this context pay provides feedback to an employee in the form of recognition for achievement.

It is apparent from this summary of content theories that pay can serve to satisfy needs and impact on motivation. This discussion, however, has been silent on the mechanism by which this occurs. In fact, this is a general criticism of content theories. While it is apparent that pay can motivate behavior, one category of which is job performance, it is not at all clear *how* organizations can use pay to achieve this goal. In the following discussion of process theories of motivation more emphasis is placed on explaining the mechanisms that lead to motivation.

Process theories. Process theories of motivation focus on how people are motivated. They certainly recognize the role of content theories in examining the types of needs and reinforcers that are part of the motivational process, but they also attempt to explain how this process operates.

In explaining how motivation operates, some theories prominently mention the importance of rewards, including compensation. Others, while not denying a role for compensation, focus instead on other factors which affect individual motivation.

Reinforcement theories. Expectancy theory and operant conditioning theory both grant a prominent role to rewards (e.g., compensation). Pay motivates to the extent merit increases and other work-related rewards are allocated on the basis of performance.

Much of the operant conditioning literature focuses on the types of reinforcement strategies which best motivate high performance. Do workers respond better when rewards are based on their individual performance, or when their work units' success is the major determinant of rewards? Is a continuous reinforcement schedule (after each performance unit) motivationally superior to a variable reinforcement schedule? A summary of these findings is included in the section on pay for performance.

---

[20]R. J. House and L. A. Wigdor, "Herzberg's Dual-Factor Theory of Job Satisfaction and Motivation: A Review of the Evidence and a Criticism," *Personnel Psychology* 20 (1967), pp. 369–90.

EXHIBIT 8.5
A Composite Expectancy-Valence Model

Force to expend specific level of effort	Expectancy that specific level of effort will/will not accomplish task	Valence of task goal accomplishment/failure	Instrumentality of task accomplishment/failure for job outcomes	Valence of job outcomes	Instrumentality of job outcomes for need satisfaction	Valence of "basic" needs

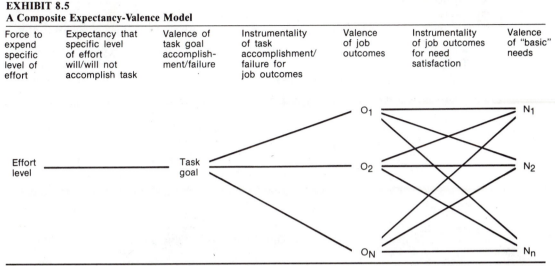

Note: For purposes of simplicity, this schematic portrays only one level of effort and one level of success on one task goal. A similar set of relationships exists for alternative levels of effort and alternative tasks or alternative levels of success.

Source: John P. Campbell and Robert Pritchard, "Motivation Theory in Industrial and Organizational Psychology," in *Handbook of Industrial and Organizational Psychology,* ed. Marvin Dunnette (Chicago: Rand McNally, 1976). Copyright © 1976, Marvin D. Dunnette. Reprinted by permission of John Wiley & Sons, Inc.

Of even greater interest to researchers over the past two decades has been the utility of expectancy, or VIE, theory. VIE is an acronym for valence (V), instrumentality (I), expectancy (E). Borrowing from earlier works,[21] Campbell and Pritchard present an excellent composite picture of the variables important in a VIE model.[22] Exhibit 8.5 summarizes this model.

The key variable to be explained in this model is effort level. According to Exhibit 8.5, effort level depends on three factors: (1) expectancy, (2) valence, and (3) instrumentality. Expectancy is viewed as a subjective probability estimate made by an individual as to whether a specific level of effort will result in task accomplishment. For example, if you were to have a test on the subject matter of this chapter tomorrow, what do you think the probability would be of getting an "A" if you studied hard for five hours tonight? In an organizational context employees would assess whether or not they could accomplish specific assignments made by their supervisor. These probabilities are assessed in numbers between .00 and 1.00. As the probability of a goal accomplishment rises

[21]V. H. Vroom, *Work in Motivation* (New York: John Wiley & Sons, 1964); G. Graen, "Instrumentality Theory of Work Motivation: Some Experimental Results and Suggested Modifications," *Journal of Applied Psychology* 53, no. 2 (1969), pp. 1–25; L. W. Porter and E. E. Lawler, *Managerial Attitudes and Performance* (Chicago, Ill.: Dorsey Press, 1968); Campbell and Pritchard, "Motivation Theory."

[22]Campbell and Pritchard, "Motivation Theory."

(approaches 1.00), the probability of expending a specific amount of effort rises.

The second factor in this model is goal valence. How much does an individual value (i.e., what is the anticipated satisfaction from) task accomplishment? To link Maslow's hierarchy of needs with this model, a task that satisfies a need which was prepotent would have a relatively high valence. Carrying the earlier illustration further, if you did not place a high value on earning an "A" in tomorrow's exam, even though it was within your capability (i.e., high expectancy), you would be less likely to expend the necessary effort. From an individual's perspective in an organization, consider a reward of a promotion, offered for successful accomplishment of a lengthy and difficult task. Most supervisors offering this promotion would assume subordinates would value highly this type of reward. Consider, however, the employees who are content with their existing job responsibilities and do not want to assume greater job responsibility. The low valence attached to this reward may lead to lower effort expenditure, a disappointment to supervisors who assume their employees hold consistent values.

Normally, completion of a task is not considered to have value in and of itself. In one sense this is correct. Most people associate work in organizations with the rewards that can be obtained from successful completion of that task. Actually, though, there is a reasonably large body of literature to indicate tasks can offer intrinsic rewards that occur simply because of performance and completion of task.[23] So a task goal can have a valence attached to it. More traditionally, though, people think about the rewards that result from task accomplishment, the so-called extrinsic rewards (e.g., pay, promotion) because they are outcomes resulting from performance of the task. It is in this linkage where the third component, instrumentality, becomes important. Assuming an employee accomplishes a task, what is the probability that a desired outcome or reward will result? If it is estimated that the subjective probability of obtaining a reward given task accomplishment is 1.00, then an employee is more likely to expend the necessary effort to start this sequence in motion. Instrumentality, as was true for expectancy, is expressed as a subjective probability varying between .00 and 1.00. Carrying the example with the test grade one step further, students might attempt to estimate the probability that obtaining an "A" on an exam tomorrow will result in an "A" for the entire course. Or, going even further, they might estimate the probability that obtaining an "A" in this course will lead to a good job offer. It is not a coincidence, for example, that finance majors probably expend more effort on obtaining "A's" in their finance courses. They view these courses as more relevant to their chosen career goals.

---

[23]See, for example, McNaly Csikszentmihalyi, "Play and Intrinsic Rewards," *Journal of Humanistic Psychology* 4 (1979), pp. 16–22; A Bandura, *Social Learning Theory* (Englewood Cliffs, N.J.: Prentice-Hall, 1977); E. Deci, "Notes on the Theory and Metatheory of Intrinsic Motivation," *Organizational Behavior and Human Performance* 15 (1975), pp. 130–45.

When students talk about course relevance in this context, they are expressing judgments that are considered instrumentalities in this model.

You will notice that the model in Exhibit 8.4 carries the idea of valences and instrumentalities out beyond the first level outcomes and their attached valences. In fact, this is a reasonable expression of reality that also portrays the role of pay in this model as it affects motivation. As Opsahl and Dunnette have noted, pay can serve as an *instrument* (this term is derived from the word *instrumentality* taken from the model).[24] Consider the manager who obtains a pay raise for an employee who performs well. By itself the pay raise may have no value. However, it can have a high instrumentality. Pay can be used to purchase goods that have a high valence. Given sufficient money the subjective probability that money can be used to buy a wide variety of desired goods is quite high (i.e., high instrumentality).

Note: this chain of events was triggered by a manager who established the pay-for-performance link. At least from an employee's perspective, *pay for performance* is partially an issue of instrumentality: "If I perform at the *desired* level considered excellent by my company, what is the probability I will be rewarded in turn with a corresponding pay increase?" Involved in this question is whether or not the company is viewed as paying for performance (i.e., allocating pay raises differentially to employees based on level of performance). This is just one of several questions that will be addressed after discussing the last theory relevant to the issues of pay for performance.

Equity theory. There has been some question about whether this theory is really a distinct theory or whether it can be subsumed under VIE theory.[25] Since equity theory plays such an important role in compensation, though, separate discussion is included here.

While there are a number of models[26] dealing with the equity concept, two have generated sufficient research or intriguing potential to warrant discussion. Adams argues that individuals compare their inputs and outcomes to those of some relevant other person in determining whether they are equitably (fairly) treated.[27] Stated another way, the comparison process can be expressed as a comparison of ratios:

---

[24]R. L. Opsahl and M. D. Dunnette, "The Role of Financial Compensation in Industrial Motivation," *Psychological Bulletin* 66 (1966), pp. 94–118.

[25]Lawler, *Pay and Organizational Effectiveness;* Campbell and Pritchard, "Motivation Theory."

[26]G. C. Homans, *Social Behavior: Its Elementary Forms* (New York: Harcourt Brace Jovanovich, 1961); E. Jaques, *Equitable Payment* (New York: John Wiley & Sons, 1961); M. Patche, *The Choice of Wage Comparisons* (Englewood Cliffs, N.J.: Prentice-Hall, 1961); J. S. Adams, "Wage Inequities, Productivity, and Work Quality," *Industrial Relations* 3, no. 1 (1963), pp. 9–16; J. S. Adams, "Injustices in Social Exchange," in *Advances in Experimental Social Psychology,* Vol. 2, ed. L. Berkowitz (New York: Academic Press, 1965), pp. 267–99.

[27]Ibid.

$$\frac{Op}{Ip} \text{ compared to } \frac{Oo}{Io}$$

where:

Op, Oo = Outcomes of person (p) or other (o)
Ip, Io = Inputs of person (p) or other (o)

This model suggests that people compare the rewards they receive, relative to the inputs they have to make to receive those rewards, to the same ratio for some relevant other. If the two ratios are not equal, the consequence is motivation to reduce the "perceived" inequity. A key in this explanation is the word *perceived*. The inequity could result because some individuals evaluate and classify as inputs and outcomes factors that other individuals might consider irrelevant. For example, a physically attractive salesperson might consider that a relevant input and expect to be compensated higher than a less attractive individual, other things equal. Yet the organization may consider this an irrelevant input, pay the two individuals equally, and never realize that the person views it as an inequitable exchange. Correspondingly, a person might evaluate an outcome as relevant that the organization is not even aware exists. As an example, consider a supervisor who keeps a particular employee abreast of information about company activities affecting the employee's job. Potentially, the supervisor could view this as a reward, treating the subordinate as a member of the "in" group, privy to information not disseminated to other subordinates.[28] If this is not perceived as a reward by the subordinate, yet the supervisor views it as a reward for above-average performance, feelings of inequity may result.

The impacts this perceived inequity may have on motivation and subsequent performance are pointed out by Adams.[29] Granted, inequity is viewed in this theory as a source of motivation. However, the consequences do not necessarily bode well for improved performance. As Adams notes, people can (1) cognitively distort their or other's inputs and/or outcomes, (2) attempt to change their or other's inputs and/or outcomes, (3) change the comparison person, or (4) reduce their involvement in the exchange relationship. Several of these consequences have negative implications for performance. For example, accusing employees of being rate busters and using social sanctions to get them to reduce outcomes could be viewed as an effort to get others to reduce inputs. An even better example would include certain unionization efforts. Consider a company that has a union representing all blue collar workers. If nonunionized clerical workers do not receive raises commensurate with those obtained by unionized workers, one possible outcome could be efforts by clerical workers to

---

[28]Fred Dansereau, G. Graen, and W. Haga, "A Vertical Dyad Linkage Approach to Leadership within Formal Organizations: A Longitudinal Investigation of the Role Making Process," *Organizational Behavior and Human Performance* 13 (1975), pp. 46–70.

[29]Adams, "Injustices in Social Exchange."

form their own union. This is particularly true if clerical workers use the unionized blue collar workers as relevant others and perceive that rewards for the two groups are out of balance, given inputs. In this case disgruntled clerical workers could view unionization as a way to improve outcomes and reestablish equity.[30]

The role money plays in equity theory is quite evident. Money is one of many outcomes that are evaluated in the exchange relationship. But since money is one of the most visible components and frequently one of the easiest to modify of the variables in the model, it becomes extremely important. As will be pointed out later, much of the research in equity theory involves varying pay levels or work level required and noting the inequity and subsequent behavior that occurs.

The second equity model of interest here was formulated by Elliot Jaques.[31] The major part of this model relevant to this discussion deals with Jaques's conception of how inequity arises. From Jaques's perspective, feelings of inequity are not dependent on the existence of a relevant other whose ratio of input to outcomes differs from the person's ratio. Rather, Jaques suggests that the relevant comparison in determination of equity is an internal standard. Presumably individuals have some internal standard of fairness based on accumulated past experiences against which current conditions are compared to determine fairness of, for example, current pay. From a compensation administrator's perspective, this can cause problems. A well-constructed and administered job evaluation system may reduce feelings of inequity in comparison with what other persons in the company may be receiving. If an internal standard is employed, however, any experiences in other organizations become relevant. This requires a compensation administrator to be equitable with respect to practices of other organizations. (Note: Adams's equity theory does not preclude a relevant other who is external to the organizations. Consequently the same implications could be inferred for this theory. However, it has been speculated that relevant other is more likely to be a co-worker than someone outside the firm.)

Most of the research relating equity theory to performance has stimulated inequity by either underpaying or overpaying individuals for tasks and then recording the impact on performance. At best the research has had mixed support.[32] Efforts during the 1980s have focused more on refining equity models to improve prediction and attempting to identify the behavioral and attitudinal consequences of inequity.[33]

---

[30]Chris Berger, Craig Olson, and John Boudreau, "The Effects of Unions on Work Values, Perceived Rewards, and Job Satisfaction," presented at the National Academy of Management meetings, August 1980.

[31]Jaques, *Equitable Payment*.

[32]Dyer and Schwab, "Personnel/Human Resource Management Research."

[33]D. M. Messick and K. S. Cook, eds., *Theories of Equity: Psychological and Sociological Perspectives* (New York: Praeger Publishers, 1983).

Social information processing theory. Recall that need theories focused on internally generated needs which induced behaviors designed to reduce these needs. Social information processing (SIP) theory counters need theory by focusing on external factors that motivate performance.[34] According to SIP theory, workers pay attention to environmental cues (e.g., performance levels of co-workers, goals imposed by supervisors) by cognitively processing this information in a way that may alter personal work goals, expectancies, and perceptions of equity.[35] In turn, this influences job attitudes, behavior, and performance. By far the strongest evidence that external factors influence motivation comes from the goal-setting research of Locke and associates.[36] A review of this literature indicates that the vast majority of studies on goal setting find a positive impact of goal setting on performance. Workers assigned "hard" goals consistently do better than workers told to "do your best."[37]

Notice, nothing in this discussion of SIP theory has suggested a role for compensation in the motivational process. The reason may be that researchers are unsure of the role. For example, goal-setting researchers are divided on whether compensation has an additive, interactive, or independent influence on goal setting. Locke and associates suggest that pay affects performance only by affecting the level of goals or individual commitment to achieving goals already established.[38]

A second perspective views goal setting and compensation as independent.[39] Still a third line of research counters the independence findings, maintaining that the joint presence of incentives and goal setting conditions has a negative effect on performance.[40] Perhaps the best summary, though, is to admit we still do not know enough about the motivational and cognitive processes which lead goal setting and compensation to trigger higher performance.[41] The next section explores this relationship between pay and performance.

---

[34]Terence R. Mitchell, Miriam Rothman, and Robert C. Liden, "Effects of Normative Information on Task Performance," *Journal of Applied Psychology* 70, no. 1 (1985), pp. 48–55.

[35]Ibid.

[36]Edwin A. Locke, Karyll N. Shaw, Lise M. Saari, and Gary P. Latham, "Goal Setting and Task Performance: 1969–1980," *Psychological Bulletin* 90 (1981), pp. 125–52.

[37]Ibid.

[38]Ibid.

[39]R. D. Pritchard and M. I. Curtis, "The Influence of Goal Setting and Financial Incentives on Task Performance," *Organizational Behavior and Human Performance* 10 (1973), pp. 175–83; J. R. Terborg and H. E. Miller, "Motivation, Behavior, and Performance: A Closer Examination of Goal Setting and Monetary Incentives," *Journal of Applied Psychology* 63 (1978), pp. 29–39.

[40]J. Mowen, R. Middlemist, and D. Luther, "Joint Effects of Assigned Goal Level and Incentive Structure on Task Performance: A Laboratory Study," *Journal of Applied Psychology* 61 (1981), pp. 598–603.

[41]Donald J. Campbell, "The Effects of Goal-Contingent Payment on the Performance of a Complex Task," *Personnel Psychology* 37 (1984), pp. 23–40.

PAY FOR PERFORMANCE: THE EMPIRICAL EVIDENCE

Laura Lasser

Early in this chapter discussion centered on the factors presumed to affect performance. Ideally, this would lead to identification of strategies that can be used by organizations to improve employee performance. This discussion has been leading up to the question: "Is pay the answer?" Can employee performance be affected by devising different pay strategies? The answer to this question depends on the answers to three subquestions: (1) Is money important to individuals? (2) *Should* pay increases be based on performance? (3) *Are* pay increases based on performance?

Is Money Important to Individuals?

From the motivational theories discussed earlier it is apparent there is no instinctive or basic need for money. Money becomes important insofar as it can satisfy recognized needs. For example, Lawler and Porter found that high-paid managers are more satisfied in the security need and the esteem need than low-paid managers.[42] Lawler infers from this and other research that money is capable of satisfying physiological, security, and esteem needs.[43] If these needs are satisfied by other means, or if they are not currently prepotent (in Maslow's terminology), then money is seen as having lower instrumental value and not particularly useful in motivating desired behavior.

If different needs are, in fact, prepotent across individuals, this information could be used to design a pay-for-performance system. Lawler argues for a two-step sequential process: (1) identify groups for which differential need strength is evident and (2) devise selection strategies that will identify those individuals who have needs that can be satisfied through a pay system tied to performance.[44] Such a strategy, if successful, would permit organizations that subscribe to a pay-for-performance philosophy to implement a wage and salary system designed to use pay for improved performance.

Until this occurs, however, there is evidence that organizations may be experiencing problems by assuming that employees place a high value on monetary rewards. One study suggests that managers overestimate the importance of pay to subordinates.[45] Given a belief that pay can motivate performance, supervisors become disillusioned when improved performance does not result from pay increases. This failure results in a general condemnation of pay as a moti-

potential weakness

---

[42]E. Lawler and L. Porter, "Perceptions Regarding Management Compensation," *Industrial Relations* 3 (1969), pp. 41–49.

[43]Lawler, *Pay and Organizational Effectiveness.*

[44]Ibid.

[45]F. A. Heller and L. W. Porter, "Perceptions of Managerial Needs and Skills in Two National Samples," *Occupational Psychology* 40 (1966), pp. 1–13.

Por. wext (handwritten marginalia)

vator. In reality, however, it may be more advantageous not to view money as the supreme motivator, but rather as one of the numerous factors in the work environment that affects employee motivation.

Should Pay Increases Be Based on Performance?

Given that money can satisfy at least a subset of basic needs, the question now becomes *should* salary increases be based on level of performance? Substantial evidence exists that management and workers alike believe pay *should* be tied to performance.

Dyer et al. asked 180 managers from 72 different companies to rate nine possible factors in terms of the importance they should receive in determining size of salary increases.[46] As Exhibit 8.6 indicates, workers believed the most important factor for salary increases should be job performance. Following close behind is a factor that presumably would be picked up in job evaluation (nature of job) and a motivational variable (amount of effort expended).

In a second study of managers similar results were obtained.[47] Quality of job performance and productivity were ranked first and third (of seven alternatives) respectively as criteria that should be used for determining salaries of managers in the private sector. For a similar group of managers in the public sector these two criteria ranked second and fourth.

The role that performance levels should assume in determining pay increases is less clear-cut for blue-collar workers.[48] As an illustration consider the frequent opposition to compensation plans that are based on performance (i.e., incentive piece-rate systems). Actually much of the discontent with performance-based plans is a reaction to the specific type of plan and the way it is administered. Lawler notes that "in many situations opposition to incentive pay comes about because the employees feel they cannot trust the company to administer incentive schemes properly.[49] From this data it appears there is some belief among employees that pay should be based on performance, particularly if the company can be trusted to administer the performance based plan effectively.

Should pay increases be based on performance? So far the evidence suggests employees believe pay should be tied to performance. A more important

---

[46]L. Dyer, D. P. Schwab, and R. D. Theriault, "Managerial Perceptions Regarding Salary Increase Criteria," *Personnel Psychology* 29 (1976), pp. 233–42.

[47]Edward Lawler, "Managers' Attitudes towards How Their Pay Is and Should Be Determined," *Journal of Applied Psychology* 50 (1966), pp. 273–79.

[48]Opinion Research Corporation, *Wage Incentives* (Princeton, N.J.: Opinion Research Corporation, 1946); Opinion Research Corporation, *Productivity from the Worker's Standpoint,* (Princeton, N.J.: Opinion Research Corporation, 1949); L. V. Jones and T. E. Jeffrey, "A Quantitative Analysis of Expressed Preferences for Compensation Plans," *Journal of Applied Psychology* 48 (1963), pp. 201–10.

[49]Lawler, *Pay and Organizational Effectiveness,* p. 61.

EXHIBIT 8.6
Mean Ratings of Criteria That *Should Be* Used to Determine Size of Salary Increases

Criteria	Mean Rating
1. Level of job performance	6.23
2. Nature of job	5.91
3. Amount of effort expenditure	5.56
4. Cost of living	5.21
5. Training and experience	5.15
6. Increases outside organization	4.64
7. Budgetary considerations	4.53
8. Increases inside organization	3.69
9. Length of service	3.31

Source: L. Dyer, D. P. Schwab, and R. D. Theriault, "Managerial Perceptions Regarding Salary Increase Criteria," *Personnel Psychology* 29 (1976), pp. 233–42. © 1976, Personnel Psychology, Inc.

question remains: Does tying pay to performance positively affect organizational profit? Do workers perform better when they receive pay contingent upon level of performance? Consider, for example, the Episcopal Diocese of Newark, New Jersey. Starting in 1986 priests were paid according to performance. Priests qualify for salary raises based on achievement of goals such as parish growth and quality of sermons. Apparently the church believes that tying pay to performance will enhance church goals. Are there any hard data to support this belief?[50]

Numerous studies indicate that tying pay to performance has a positive impact on employee performance.[51] A common type of study is to introduce an incentive system and observe whether workers, whose pay is now directly dependent on level of output, increase their levels of performance. Several studies indicate that introduction of an incentive system (e.g., piece rate) results in higher performance than occurs for workers receiving hourly pay.[52]

---

[50]"Pay for Priests," *The Wall Street Journal,* March 5, 1985, p. 1.

[51]George Green, "Instrumentality Theory of Work Motivation," *Journal of Applied Psychology* 53, no. 2 (1965), pp. 1–25; Lawler, "Manager's Attitudes"; D. P. Schwab and L. Dyer, "The Motivational Impact of a Compensation System on Employee Performance," *Organizational Behavior and Human Performance* 9 (1973), pp. 215–25; R. D. Pritchard, D. W. Leonard, C. W. Von Bergen, Jr., and R. J. Kirk, "The Effects of Varying Schedules of Reinforcement on Human Task Performance," *Organizational Behavior and Human Performance* 16 (1976), pp. 205–30; Donald Schwab, "Impact of Alternative Compensation Systems on Pay Valence and Instrumentality Perceptions," *Journal of Applied Psychology* 58 (1973), pp. 308–12.

[52]G. F. Latham and D. L. Dossett, "Designing Incentive Plans for Unionized Employees: A Comparison of Continuous and Variable Ratio Reinforcement Schedules," *Personnel Psychology* 31 (1978), pp. 47–61; G. A. Yukl and G. P. Latham, "Consequences of Reinforcement Schedules and Incentive Magnitudes for Employee Performance: Problems Encountered in an Industrial Setting," *Journal of Applied Psychology* 60 (1975), pp. 294–98; G. A. Yukl, G. P. Latham, and E. D. Pursell, "The Effectiveness of Performance Incentives under Continuous and Variable Ratio Schedules of Reinforcement," *Personnel Psychology* 29 (1976), pp. 221–31.

Another approach is to look at the top-performing organizations and see if they are also the top payers. Most commonly, these studies look at the compensation of chief executive officers (CEOs) in relation to organizational profits. While several studies have found negative relationships in this type of study, one recent piece of research found that the best performing companies pay 21 percent more in base salary to their CEOs, 67 percent more in the combined base salary and short-term incentives, and 140 percent more when the package also includes long-term incentives. The authors contend that previous studies were flawed because they failed to control for organizational size when studying the pay-performance relationship.[53]

Is Pay Based on Performance?

Whether due to blind faith, belief in expert testimony, or positive review of existing research, many companies claim that they base pay on performance.[54] One recent Conference Board study of 500 companies in a variety of industries indicates 95 percent of these companies base increases on individual performance.[55] And some 82 percent of these companies claim the pay for performance programs are successful. (Another 18 percent claim either the programs are a failure or are too new to evaluate.) So far, evidence suggests workers and managers think pay should be based on performance. There is also partial support for claiming that performance improves when pay is linked to levels of performance.

Despite these findings there is some evidence that organizations are moving in the opposite direction, away from compensation systems designed to tie pay to performance.[56] For example, Green and Podsakoff investigated the impact on performance of removing a performance-contingent pay plan.[57] Two paper mills employing 1,100 operative and managerial employees participated in a field experiment. One employer's incentive system was removed, and in the other, which served as a control, the pay incentive system remained intact. Performance ratings dropped significantly for the plant that removed the pay incentive system in comparison to the control plant.

---

[53]E. T. Redling, "Myth v. Reality: The Relationship between Top Executive Pay and Corporate Performance," *Compensation Review* 4 (1981), pp. 16–24.

[54]Bruce R. Ellig, *Executive Compensation: A Total Pay Perspective* (New York: McGraw-Hill, 1982); Edward E. Lawler, *Pay and Organizational Development* (Reading, Mass.: Addison-Wesley Publishing, 1981).

[55]CompFlash, "Companies Praise Pay-for-Performance Programs," *AMA CompFlash* 84, no.9 (1984), p. 6.

[56]C. Greene and P. Podsakoff, "Effects of Removal of a Pay Incentive: A Field Experiment," *Academy of Management Proceedings,* 1978, pp. 206–10.

[57]Ibid.

Does this suggest irrational behavior? Or is there some basis for arguing that the advantages of developing a pay-for-performance system are outweighed by the disadvantages.

PAY FOR PERFORMANCE: THE NEGATIVE EVIDENCE

Perhaps the biggest movement toward a pay-for-performance system was mandated by the Civil Service Reform Act of 1978. This act mandated that 50 percent of any pay increase was to be automatic, but the other 50 percent must be performance based. Here was an excellent opportunity to determine whether basing pay on performance (in part) would lead to improvements in performance. One study of managers in the Social Security Administration, an agency covered by the act, found merit pay had no impact on organizational performance.[58] Using a combination of objective (e.g., average number of days to pay certain claims) and subjective performance measures, there were no significant effects on performance from going to a merit pay system. In reporting these results, however, the authors also noted extremely low levels of trust in the merit system and how it operated within the agency. This highlights what some experts contend is a major problem with research on pay for performance: Most of the evidence arguing against a pay-for-performance system is based on problems in implementing the system.[59] If organizations provide the right climate and implement the system correctly, this argument is that pay-for-performance systems can successfully improve performance of employees. Perhaps the best summary of the kind of problems organizations encounter in implementing a pay-for-performance system is offered by Hamner.[60]

PAY FOR PERFORMANCE AND DESIGNING A COMPENSATION SYSTEM

Two issues become important in designing a pay-for-performance system. First, a system must be designed which fairly assesses and communicates the procedures to be followed; and second, a policy must be identified for determining the size of a pay increase associated with particular employee performance levels.

---

[58]Jane L. Pearce, William B. Stevenson, and James L. Perry, "Managerial Compensation Based on Organizational Performance: A Time Series Analysis of the Effects of Merit Pay," *Academy of Management Journal* 28, no. 2 (1985), pp. 261–78.

[59]Clay W. Hamner, "How to Ruin Motivation with Pay," *Compensation Review,* Third Quarter 1975, pp. 88–98; Herbert H. Meyer, "The Pay-for-Performance Dilemma," *Organizational Dynamics,* Winter 1975, pp. 71–78; CompFlash, "Companies Praise Pay-for-Performance Programs."

[60]Hamner, "How to Ruin Motivation with Pay."

Procedures to Design and Implement a Pay-for-Performance System

It seems apparent that a pay-for-performance policy could take on varying levels of importance in the design of a compensation system. At one extreme, pay for performance could be totally absent as a consideration in allocation of pay raises. Such a system could allocate raises on any number of bases other than performance: (1) across-the-board increases with the magnitude determined solely by the organization or in conjunction with a union(s), (2) cost-of-living increases tied to changes in the consumer price index (CPI), (3) increases based on seniority (assuming no relation to performance), or (4) some combination of the above.

A more moderate strategy would involve a role of lessened importance for pay for performance. This type of strategy has been advocated by Meyer.[61] Meyer suggests that pay systems be designed to specify, at the time of employment, initial salary and expected long-term salary adjustments, along with any factors (e.g., changing economic conditions) that could cause that schedule to fluctuate. This implicit contract would also include specification of necessary performance levels required to obtain the outlined progression of wage increases. During the course of employment any employee not meeting these minimum performance standards would be informed well in advance. Discussions with the supervisor at that point in turn would focus on the performance criteria that would have to be met for scheduled increases to be granted. Presumably a small percentage (Meyer recommends 5 to 10 percent) of employees would not meet performance expectations in this scenario and thus would not be granted the scheduled increase. Persistent failure to meet performance expectations might initially be met by scheduling formal or informal training sessions and ultimately might lead to dismissal.

In this type of system pay for performance becomes relevant only for the marginal employee. If performance does not meet some minimum standard, pay increases are withheld. With this type of strategy Meyer feels supervisors will be forced to identify intrinsic job rewards and make better use of extrinsic motivation, relegating pay to the role of attracting and retaining workers, with little impact on motivation.

How, then, are workers motivated under this system? Meyer views it as a two-component process. The first necessary ingredient is a well-designed human resources planning system. Jobs must be structured in logical promotion sequences. Accurate forecasts of job openings must be made. Thorough job analyses must be conducted to ensure that job requirements are well specified. Comprehensive records must be kept via some form of skills inventory system that indicates individual capabilities, training, interests, and job aspirations. Fi-

Only to People may strive ① standard. to meet the min.

---

[61]Meyer, "The Pay-for-Performance Dilemma."

nally, some method of job matching must be devised to ensure that the best-suited individuals are considered for particular jobs.[62]

The second step in Meyer's strategy, and the part designed to motivate high job performance, involves a strong promotion-from-within policy. High performers are rewarded with accelerated promotion opportunities. A well-developed human resources planning system is designed to complement a strong promotion-from-within policy. When employees acquire sufficient skills and experience for a promotion, such a system is designed to match them with appropriate job opportunities.

In summary, Meyer believes too much emphasis is placed on money as a prime motivator of performance. He believes more emphasis should be placed on the intrinsic rewards of jobs and the support of well-conceived human resources planning and promotion-from-within programs.

At the far end of the continuum is a strategy incorporating pay for performance that is based on two tenets: (1) there is substantial evidence that tying pay to performance results in higher levels of performance, and (2) most of the difficulties with this strategy arise in the implementation phase. Organizations do not pay sufficient attention to the full range of attitudinal and procedural changes that must accompany adoption of a pay-for-performance system. Given the importance this adoption might take for future productivity gains, the following issues consider strategies to facilitate a pay-for-performance system.

1. Pay is not perceived as contingent upon performance. Many organizations adopt a policy of secrecy in their wage and salary administration practices. In such cases a number of studies from Lawler indicate that managers regularly misperceive the levels of compensation of subordinates, peers, and superiors.[63] The nature of these errors tends to restrict the range of perceived salaries: Superiors are thought to receive less than their actual salaries and subordinates/peers are thought to receive more than is actually the case. This tends to compress the perceived wage scale and lowers motivation to perform: Subordinates with fewer job responsibilities are earning almost as much and any effort to obtain a promotion would result in a lower (perceived) increase than was felt justified.

---

[62]H. J. Bernardin, "The Effects of Rater Training on Halo Errors in Student Ratings of Instructors," *Journal of Applied Psychology* 63 (1978), pp. 301–8; W. C. Borman, "Effects of Instructions to Avoid Halo Error on Reliability and Validity of Performance Evaluation Ratings," *Journal of Applied Psychology* 60 (1975), pp. 556–60; G. P. Latham, K. N. Wexley, and E. D. Pursell, "Training Managers to Minimize Rating Errors in the Observation of Behavior," *Journal of Applied Psychology* 60 (1975), pp. 550–55.

[63]E. E. Lawler, "Managers' Perception of their Subordinates' Pay and of their Superiors' Pay," *Personnel Psychology* 18 (1965), pp. 413–22; Edward Lawler III, "Secrecy and the Need to Know," in *Managerial Motivation and Compensation,* ed. Henry Tosi, Robert House, and Marvin Dunnette (East Lansing, Mich.: Michigan State University Press, 1972), pp. 455–76.

Hamner argues that the secrecy surrounding pay increases may lead managers to believe that there is no direct relationship between pay and performance.[64] In fact it may lead to beliefs that salary administrators are trying to hide bad salary practices under a cloak of secrecy.

2. Performance ratings are viewed as biased. Given that the majority of performance evaluations are based on subjective judgments of supervisors, and not on objective criteria (e.g., units produced) many employees feel that ratings are biased. Substantial evidence exists to support this position. For example, several studies have shown that raters can agree reasonably well in their relative ratings of employees, but they do not discriminate particularly well across rating dimensions.[65] Dunnette and Borman have noted that "this means that different raters and/or methods tend to rank ratees similarly but that different facets or dimensions of job performance are poorly differentiated."[66] At least one study suggests that this problem can be overcome, however, if job dimensions are carefully defined so that raters understand fully the different performance dimensions being tapped.[67]

If performance ratings are viewed as biased, then the pay-performance link is particularly difficult to establish. If employees view the ratings they receive as arbitrary, little incentive exists to improve performance.

3. Rewards are not viewed as reward. The best example of this problem has been demonstrated by Meyer.[68] Assume, for the moment, that pay is supposed to be based on performance in company A. It would be expected that employees compare the pay increase they receive with that of other employees in the company. What happens if employees have an inflated view of their own performance relative to others in the company? They obviously conclude that pay is not tied to performance, otherwise their pay would be higher (given they see their performance as relatively high). This is exactly the problem that Meyer uncovered in a study of several occupational groups in a number of companies.[69] People were asked to rate themselves on job performance relative to other employees doing similar work.

Exhibit 8.7 shows some very startling results.

---

[64]Hamner, "How to Ruin Motivation with Pay."

[65]R. F. Burnaska and T. D. Hollmann, "An Empirical Comparison of the Relative Effects of Rater Response Biases on Three Rating Scale Formats," *Journal of Applied Psychology* 59 (1974), pp. 307–12; B. A. Freedman and E. F. Cornelius, "Effect of Rater Participation in Scale Construction on the Psychometric Characteristics of Two Rating Scale Formats," *Journal of Applied Psychology* 61 (1976), pp. 210–16.

[66]Marvin Dunnette and Martin Borman, "Personnel Selection and Classification Systems," *Annual Review of Psychology* 30 (1979), p. 488.

[67]T. L. Dickenson and T. E. Tice, "The Discriminant Validity of Scales Developed by Retranslation," *Personnel Psychology* 30 (1977), pp. 217–28.

[68]Meyer, "The Pay-for-Performance Dilemma."

[69]Ibid.

EXHIBIT 8.7
Self Ratings for Selected Employee Groups

Self Ratings	Employee Group			
	Blue-Collar Group, Plant A	Blue-Collar Group, Plant B	Engineers in Research Laboratory	Accountants in Several Companies
Top 10%	46%	40%	29%	37%
Top 25%	26	28	57	40
Top 50%	26	28	14	20
Bottom 50%	1	2	0	3
Bottom 25%	0	0	0	0
Bottom 10%	0	0	0	0
No response	1	2	0	0
	100%	100%	100%	100%

Across all occupational groups in several companies, in excess of 95 percent of the employees rated themselves above average. For each of the four groups at least 68 percent of the employees thought they were in the top 25 percent of all similarly situated employees in performance. Needless to say, this is statistically impossible. But the important point to note is that these employees expect a raise commensurate with their perceived performance. Imagine the confusion suffered by a manager who gives two subordinates a raise indicating they are in the top 25 percent of all employees (as opposed to, say, the top 50 percent), and it results in disappointment. The feedback conveyed by the raise deals a blow to the subordinates' self-esteem. They are rated lower than they believe (say top 10 percent) is justified. In this case a potential strategy for the "wronged" employees is to assume pay is not based on performance.

4. Managers of units using merit increases are more concerned with pay satisfaction than with job performance. One of the problems with a pay-for-performance system is that it is such a marked deviation from prior practices in most organizations. Employees become conditioned to receiving at least average performance ratings, no matter what their level of performance. This translates into a narrow band of merit increases with the poorest performer in a unit receiving only marginally less in a salary increase than outstanding performers. It comes as quite a shock when a pay-for-performance system is implemented and the pay increase differential broadens substantially. As might be expected, supervisors receive an upsurge of complaints. The problem that arises is that supervisors fail to trace complaint sources. The overwhelming majority of these complaints come from those employees who are hurt most: the relatively poor performers. The supervisor interprets this as general dissatisfaction with the new pay system and agitates for change.

With a change to a pay-for-performance system it is vital that supervisors receive extensive orientation on what to expect. If the system (i.e., pay based on merit) is poorly administered, any complaints that do arise should come from low producers. A falloff in pay satisfaction may well be an anticipated outcome.

5. Trust and openness about merit increases is low. Hamner argues that pay-for-performance systems cannot be introduced in a vacuum.[70] Other changes reflecting good human relations practices also must be introduced. For example, employees must be informed how the system will operate to ensure fair treatment. This requires a degree of openness in communications some organizations fear. Without appropriate explanations of the system, frequent feedback about performance, and openness about how the compensation system operates, the necessary climate of trust may not evolve.

6. Organizations fail to recognize sources of motivation other than money. One of the difficulties faced in compensation is the belief that money is a general panacea, capable of compensating for all other organizational problems. If one thing has been learned from the problems with poor productivity, absenteeism, and sabotage in the automobile industry, it is that money may attract workers to unsatisfying jobs; it may also help in retaining workers, at least in the short run. But the ability of money to motivate under conditions where numerous other factors work in opposition is limited at best. Money can be a motivator, but not to the exclusion of other factors, including the job itself.

Interestingly, there is even some evidence that money can detract from motivation. Numerous authors have argued that tasks have properties making them intrinsically rewarding (i.e., completing the task itself provides gratification).[71] They suggest that the intrinsic motivation that can result from a task may be impeded by extrinsic motivation and rewards. As has been explained elsewhere:

> The distinction between extrinsic and intrinsic motivation is the knowledge or feeling of personal causation. To the extent a person expects a reward for performing in a task he is unfree since he has not chosen the task for its own sake alone, the locus of causality is external and when rewards are important, dependence on the external source place the person in the position of Pawn.[72]

DeCharms argues that a task with intrinsic potential to motivate performance may actually yield lowered task motivation when an extrinsic reward (e.g., money) is offered for task performance.[73] In a series of works testing this hy-

[70]Hamner, "How to Ruin Motivation with Pay."

[71]R. DeCharms, *Personal Causation* (New York: Academic Press, 1968); E. L. Deci, "Effects of Externally Mediated Rewards on Intrinsic Motivation," *Journal of Personality and Social Psychology* 18 (1971), pp. 105–15.

[72]David W. Jones and Thomas C. Mawhinney, "The Interaction of Extrinsic Rewards and Intrinsic Motivations: A Review and Suggestions for Future Research," *Academy of Management Proceedings,* 1977, p. 62.

[73]DeCharms, *Personal Causation.*

pothesis, Deci has shown that pay for performance may actually reduce motivation on a task which has intrinsic motivational properties.[74]

Despite a reasonable amount of criticism of Deci's methods in this research, an important lesson should be learned: Pay systems, no matter how well designed, will not offset other strong negative aspects of work.[75] A pay system must complement a well-designed work environment rather than compensate for one that is poorly designed.

Current beliefs about design of pay-for-performance systems emphasize a total package that is consistent with strategic goals and management values.[76] One prescription for a successful pay-for-performance system includes 10 requisites:[77]

1. Trust and belief in management by employees.
2. Valid job evaluation system (so that "merit" money isn't used to correct distortions in a poor job evaluation system).
3. Performance criteria agreed upon by all levels of employees involved.
4. Job specific, results-oriented criteria which reduce subjective bias in interviewing.
5. Accurate performance appraisal. In the past 25 years, as a number of new performance evaluation formats have evolved (e.g., management by objectives, behaviorally anchored rating scales), each has been acclaimed as the solution to problems that have long plagued performance rating systems. Wide-scale adoption of these systems across organizations, and within organizations across different organization levels and job groups, has been somewhat disappointing. It would appear that no performance appraisal format is appropriate in all situations. As a consequence, different performance appraisal formats may be adopted for different situations.[78]
6. Appropriate administrative practices (e.g., minimize time between actual job performance and subsequent pay increase to maximize reinforcement value).
7. Provision of skilled feedback during appraisal sessions to ensure that employees are aware of correct work procedures.

---

[74]E. L. Deci, "Effects of Externally Mediated Rewards"; E. L. Deci, "Intrinsic Motivation, Extrinsic Reinforcement, and Inequity," *Journal of Personality and Social Psychology* 22 (1972), pp. 113–20; E. L. Deci, "Effects of Contingent and Noncontingent Rewards on Intrinsic Motivation," *Organizational Behavior and Human Performance* 8 (1972), pp. 217–29.

[75]B. J. Calder and B. M. Staw, "The Self Perception of Intrinsic and Extrinsic Motivation," *Journal of Personality and Social Psychology* 31 (1975), pp. 599–605.

[76]Nathan B. Winstanley, "Are Merit Increases Really Effective?" *Personnel Administrator* 4 (1982), pp. 23–31; Robert H. Rock, "Pay-for-Performance: Accent on Standards and Measures," *Compensation Review* 16, no.3 (1984), pp. 15–23.

[77]Winstanley, "Are Merit Increases Really Effective?"

[78]Michael Keeley, "A Contingency Framework for Performance Evaluation," *Academy of Management Review,* July 1978, pp. 428–38; Larry Cummings and Donald Schwab, *Performance in Organizations* (Glenview, Ill.: Scott, Foresman, 1973).

8. Trained managers. A program designed to illustrate common performance appraisal errors and train supervisors in providing employee feedback is useful to any organization seeking to implement a pay for performance system. An excellent summary of diverse training programs and their effectiveness is provided elsewhere.[79]

9. Program maintenance. Program updating where necessary and design of information systems that permit storage and retrieval of performance data help integrate these data into overall organizational decision-making processes.

10. Follow-up research must focus on the effectiveness of the performance appraisal and pay systems for motivating desirable employee behavior.

Policies for Pay Raise Levels

How large should pay increases be? There are three obvious actors with vested interests in the answer to this question, and each must be considered in arriving at an effective level of merit increase. First, the organization seeks to minimize payroll costs while maintaining some level of performance output. An individual occupying a job then should receive a raise (from the organization's perspective) of a magnitude dependent on individual performance, occupational marketability, centrality of the job and individual for achievement of organizational goals, and of course budget constraints.[80] Research indicates the size of a salary increase: diminishes when budgets are smaller, increases when performance is higher, and increases when the job is central to the organization's mission, other things equal.[81]

A second participant in the salary increase process is an employee's supervisor. Recent research on decision making related to salary increments indicates that supervisors in general tend to follow an adjustment approach to allocating salary raises. This type of system allocates larger raises to employees who are underpaid relative to peers at the same performance level.[82] Future research will need to determine what factors affect the type of allocation scheme supervisors select and to identify ways to ensure that procedures used by supervisors are consistent with organizational goals.

The final actor in the salary increase process is, of course, the employee receiving the pay increase. Considerable recent research indicates there are differ-

---

[79]Gary Latham and Kenneth Wexley, *Increasing Productivity through Performance Appraisal* (Reading, Mass.: Addison-Wesley Publishing, 1981).

[80]John Fossum and Mary Fitch, "Effects of Individual and Contextual Attributes on the Size of Recommended Salary Increases," *Personnel Psychology* 38 (1985), pp. 587–602.

[81]Ibid.

[82]M. H. Birnbaum, "Perceived Equity of Salary Policies," *Journal of Applied Psychology* 68 (1983), pp. 49–59.

ences across individuals in the size of a meaningful pay increase.[83] Presumably, if an organization offers a pay raise which is too small from an employee's perspective, the raise will not have the impact desired by the organization. Most current research focuses on factors which differentiate people in terms of how they attach value to money, and in particular, to pay increases. Pay increases seem to be valued either because of their positive impact on the purchasing power of the individual or because of their significance as a form of organizational recognition.[84] In the former case, salary increase magnitude would probably be compared against the size of the cost-of-living index. After all, a 6 percent increase during periods of 9 percent inflation is hardly grounds for celebration in the struggle to increase personal purchasing power. In contrast, if money is a form of organizational recognition, employees become concerned about the level of their raises in comparison to raises of others in the company. High relative raises act as feedback that performance is considered good by the powers that be.[85]

The total of this research indicates that appropriate pay size is not a fixed value. While we have made some progress in identifying the factors organizations consider important in establishing pay increase guidelines (Chapter 15), there are still huge gaps in our understanding of supervisory and subordinate reactions to these pay guidelines. To the extent either party is unhappy with the allocation scheme or level of pay raises chosen by the organization, unintended and potentially counterproductive consequences may be the result.

SUMMARY

On a superficial level the idea of pay for performance sounds like a viable policy to improve employee performance in organizations. After all, numerous studies have been summarized which show that employees who believe pay is dependent on performance actually perform at a higher relative level. Three key problems exist in translating this philosophy into a working practice. First, employees must value pay. While there is reasonable evidence to suggest that pay, at least indirectly, can satisfy individual needs, it should not be assumed that pay is the preeminent motivator capable of solving all organizational motivation problems. In essence, pay alone will not lead to achievement of high per-

---

[83]Linda A. Krefting, Jerry M. Newman, and Frank Krzystofiak, "What Is a Meaningful Pay Increase?" prepared for *Compensation: An Applied Approach,* eds. Luis R. Gomez-Mejia and David B. Balkin (Reston, Va.: Reston Publishing, forthcoming).

[84]Linda A. Krefting and T. A. Mahoney, "Determining the Size of a Meaningful Pay Increase," *Industrial Relations* 11 (1977), pp. 83–93.

[85]Krefting and Mahoney, "Determining the Size of a Meaningful Pay Increase"; Frank Krzystofiak, Jerry M. Newman, and Linda A. Krefting, "Determining the Size of a Meaningful Pay Increase," *Proceedings of the Midwest Academy of Management* (1982a), pp. 191–99; Frank Krzystofiak, Jerry Newman, and Linda Krefting, "Pay Meaning, Satisfaction, and Size of a Meaningful Pay Increase," *Psychological Reports* 51 (1982b), pp. 660–62.

formance expectations. This leads to the second point. If pay is to assume a role as motivator of performance, other detractors from this goal must be eliminated. This means an organization must develop sound human resources systems (e.g., selection, planning, performance evaluation, training) to complement the wage and salary system. Supervisors also must be trained to interact with subordinates about job expectations and provide feedback about job performance. Compensation does not, and never will be able to, exist in a vacuum. Even the best-designed compensation system will falter when other human resources systems are inadequately designed to meet organizational needs.

The third problem in developing a pay-for-performance system centers on the fact that employees must *believe* that pay is tied to performance. This implies more than a policy statement to this effect. Organization practices must convey that pay is actually tied to performance. This precipitates a number of thorny issues: (1) a reasonable amount of salary increases must be allocated to merit so that performance differences translate into meaningful differences in pay raises, (2) supervisors must be trained to discriminate among subordinates in performance; (3) supervisors must be willing and able (i.e., trained) to provide feedback to employees about performance; (4) this feedback must be accompanied by a supportive environment in which the supervisor views his or her role partially as a facilitator of employee performance (i.e., that performance is essentially a team effort); and (5) these practices must be adhered to consistently over time.

It is no small surprise that organizations fail to tie pay to performance effectively. When confronted with the choice between a commitment to all that pay for performance implies and adopting a far more tranquil strategy with fewer payoffs, the choice is frequently made to avoid the more costly long-term strategy. If this is the choice, then we would stop deluding ourselves that pay motivates and search for other strategies to motivate performance, such as that outlined by Meyer in this chapter.

REVIEW QUESTIONS

1. How does employee equity differ from internal equity? From external equity?
2. What are the possible standards of fairness in establishing employee equity?
3. How does the concept of marginal revenue product relate to employee equity?
4. How do selection, placement, and training decisions affect performance?
5. What is the difference between a content theory and a process theory of motivation? Give examples of each.
6. Explain how expectancy and instrumentality (VIE theory) can be used to improve compensation systems.
7. Identify and describe the major theories of equity. Give examples of how they relate to job compensation.
8. Is money important to individuals? Explain, referring to relevant research.
9. Is pay based on performance? Why or why not?
10. How should a pay system be developed to best link pay to performance?

Chapter 9

Objective Performance-Based Pay Systems: Incentive Systems and Gain-Sharing Plans

Bill Miller, a new assembler, whispers confidentially to Herb Parry, the worker at the next station: "What's that guy behind us doing with the stopwatch and clipboard?" "Geez!" replied Herb. "When were you born? The company is trying to mess with us again by putting in a new incentive system. The creep with the stopwatch probably just wrote a book on compensation and thinks he knows how to

299

make us work harder. Just do like I tell you, kid, and we'll beat this guy. No one's going to mess with us."

A long-time mechanic for a gas station quite unexpectedly finds himself at the Pearly Gates talking to St. Peter.
Mechanic: "But I can't be dead, I'm only 38 years old."
St. Peter: "I'm sorry, our records show you are 58."
Mechanic: "Please, St. Peter, check again. I know I'm only 38."
(St. Peter departs and after some time returns with a huge ledger book.)
St. Peter: "I'm sorry. We've checked and rechecked our records. I assure you they are quite accurate. You are 58 years old."
Mechanic: "But your records must be wrong. Here, look! I've got a birth certificate in my wallet. That will prove my age."
St. Peter (dismissing the birth certificate): "Tut, Tut, my boy. Our records are completely accurate. You are 58."
Mechanic: "How could your records be more accurate than a birth certificate?"
St. Peter: "If you insist, I will explain the process." (St. Peter pauses to add up some totals.) "According to our records you have tuned-up 6,000 cars; changed the oil and filters on another 11,800; completed transmission overhauls on 400 more cars; and relined the brakes on 1,200 others. According to the blue book used by all gas stations to estimate time for such tasks to bill customers, you must be at *least* 58 years old!"

The stories introducing this chapter share three common elements characteristic of performance-based pay systems. First, employees have needs. Admittedly this is a simple observation. But if an organization's compensation package does not recognize and satisfy these needs, the potential for motivating desired employee performance is lost. Compensation represents just a cost on a balance sheet rather than a productive tool to shape employee behavior.

The second characteristic of performance-based pay systems is that organizations have objectives and any shaping of employee behavior should be oriented to these objectives.[1] Again, this is a simple observation. Far simpler, indeed, than the task of designing pay systems supportive of diverse and complex organizational objectives. For example, should pay systems be identical in two firms, one with an objective of maximizing return on investment and the other interested in maintaining a stable and secure operation? And would the compensation system in these firms be similar to one in an organization seeking sales growth and a high market share? The answer to both these questions is probably *no!* And compensation managers must recognize these differences in designing compensation systems.

---

[1]Gary Latham and Kenneth Wexley, *Increasing Productivity through Performance Appraisal* (Reading, Mass.: Addison-Wesley Publishing, 1981).

Third, a performance-based pay system must be able to link achievement of organizational objectives with satisfaction of individual needs. In this case the linking pins are performance evaluation and pay plan design.

> **Performance evaluation (or performance appraisal): A process to determine the correspondence between worker behavior/task outcomes and job expectations (performance standards).**

> **Pay plan design: A process to identify pay levels, components, and timing which best match individual needs and organizational requirements.**

In other words, the performance evaluation process is designed to ensure that workers perform tasks that help organizations achieve their objectives. In turn, pay systems are designed to satisfy individual objectives or needs.[2]

Exhibit 9.1 puts these two processes into the total framework of a performance-based pay system. Notice, worker outcomes in the form of individual performance data are compared against performance standards generated from organizational objectives and a thorough analysis of the job. The complexity of the performance evaluation process hinges on the performance standards and individual performance data. The more objective these two are, the simpler is the evaluation process. Consider, for example, IBM employees selling personal computers. Both performance standards and individual performance can be gauged in dollar figures. Compare this with trying to evaluate a personnel assistant's performance against such vague performance standards as reliability (how dependable the person is) and initiative.

A fascinating phenomenon occurs here. As performance standards and performance data become more objective, less time is spent on evaluation and more on constructing pay systems to meet individual needs and organizational objectives.

Notice cells A and B in Exhibit 9.2. The focus here is on relatively objective performance evaluation systems. Output is concrete and measurable. Evaluation is straightforward: Are quantity standards being met? The major debate, as noted later, is over the difficulty of the performance standards. Combined with this are relatively sophisticated efforts to design pay systems: the incentive and gain-sharing plans to be discussed shortly.

In contrast, when evaluation standards and performance data are more subjective (C and D), effort is channeled to the development of evaluation sys-

---

[2]R. V. Dawis and L. H. Lofquist, *Adjustment to Work* (New York: Appleton-Century-Crofts, 1969).

EXHIBIT 9.1
Performance Evaluation and Pay Linkages

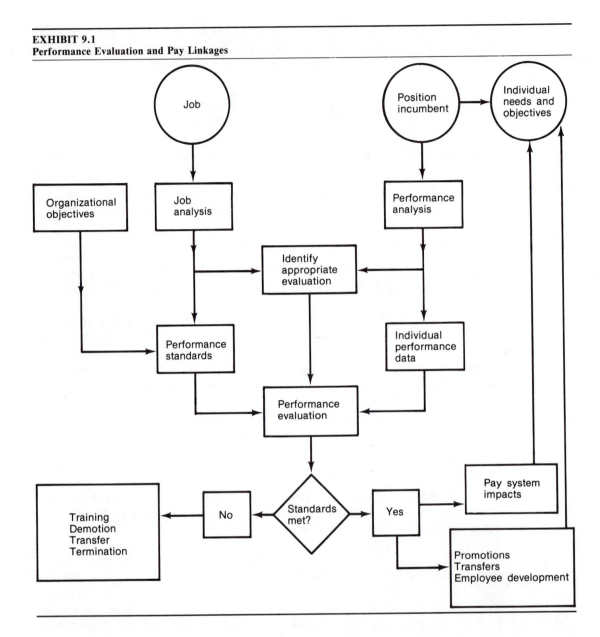

tems that are accurate and fair, as illustrated in the next chapter. The evaluation process is considerably more elaborate and complex. Perhaps because these systems are more subjective, and employee acceptance more tenuous, pay systems tied to them are less complex and less rigidly dependent on evaluation results.

EXHIBIT 9.2
Categorization of Pay-for-Performance Systems

		Tie between Pay and Performance	
		Direct *(A)*	*Indirect* *(B)*
Objectivity of Performance Measurement	*Objective*	Performance evaluation involves counting output. Pay system may be individual incentive plan.	Performance evaluation involves counting output. Pay system may be group gain-sharing plan.
	Subjective	*(C)* Performance evaluation may be management by objectives. Base pay depends on time worked, not output. Pay increments based on achievement of objectives.	*(D)* Performance evaluation more subjective and less evidently tied to performance. Base pay depends on time worked, not output. Pay increments based on subjective performance evaluation.

The remainder of this chapter covers performance-based pay systems with objective performance standards, or incentive and gain-sharing plans.

ISSUES IN ADOPTION AND DEVELOPMENT OF INCENTIVE AND GAIN-SHARING PLANS

Adoption Issues

About 20 years ago, a series of factors was discovered that related to incentive system adoption. Interestingly, incentive plans tend to be more prevalent in industries sharing four characteristics:[3]

1. High labor costs.
2. High cost competition in product markets.
3. Slow or nonexistent advancements in technology.
4. High potential for production bottlenecks.

In large part, these observations still tend to be borne out. Consider the clothing industry. Labor is a large proportion of total costs for production of clothing. The market is extremely cost competitive, particularly when the inter-

---

[3]Robert B. McKersie, Carroll F. Miller, and William E. Quarterman, "Some Indicators of Incentive Plan Prevalence," *Monthly Labor Review,* May 1964, pp. 271–76.

national production of clothing and inroads made into U.S. markets are considered. The technology for making clothing has not advanced very quickly, and there is a reasonably high potential for bottlenecks in the production of the final good. Similar kinds of problems face the steel industry, which in recent years has been accused of being negligent in its adoption of new technologies. This, combined with severe competition from overseas steel markets, makes the advantages of incentive systems appear more attractive.

In contrast, the automobile industry is characterized by relatively restrained use of incentive systems. While it faces problems similar to the steel industry in terms of foreign competition, technological advances tended in the past to keep labor costs down to a level where price competition with foreign producers was at least feasible. This, combined with the United Auto Workers stand against incentive systems, had resulted in relatively infrequent adoption of them (we will discuss union attitudes toward incentive systems in general in Chapter 17).

Since this early study was done, a number of other factors have been identified which affect incentive system adoption: (1) organizational strategy, (2) managerial value system, (3) organizational design and work relationships, (4) unit and individual performance standards, and (5) unit and individual performance.

Organizational strategy. As organizations grow and change to meet environmental demands, the design of compensation systems to support both change and stabilization is vital. Research on this change process and the accommodation of compensation systems to change has focused thus far on linking compensation design to diversification strategy.[4]

As organizations prosper and grow they must decide, as part of their overall organizational strategy, what the nature of the growth (if any) will be. For example, organizations can choose to diversify into new product or service lines. Should this diversification be through acquisition of existing firms or through internal expansion? Further, if the decision is to expand, will expansion be along similar or different product lines? Research indicates that the decision to diversify and the mode (acquisition or expansion) have an impact on compensation system design.[5]

Some organizations pride themselves on stability and growth through "tried and true" methods (i.e., growth through internally generated diversification or

---

[4]Jeffrey Kerr, "Diversification Strategies and Managerial Rewards: An Empirical Study," *Academy of Management Journal* 28, no. 1 (1985), pp. 155–79; R. A. Pitts, "Incentive Compensation and Organization Design," *Personnel Journal* 53 (1974), pp. 338–44.

[5]R. A. Pitts, "Incentive Compensation and Organization Design"; Kerr, "Diversification Strategies and Managerial Rewards: An Empirical Study"; R. P. Reumelt, "Diversity and Profitability," paper presented at the Academy of Management meetings, Western Region, Sun Valley, Idaho, 1977.

through further penetration of existing markets).[6] It is just these organizations which are also likely to have compensation systems that promote stable employment relationships. Rewards are based on seniority. Any incentive systems used in this type of organization are likely to take a long-run perspective on profits and are apt to foster interdependence among divisions through goals emphasizing *both* divisional and organizational performance.[7]

In contrast, some firms adopt a more risk-taking approach to growth, actively prospecting for acquisitions and generally pursuing external diversification programs.[8] These organizations promote more entrepreneurial behavior for employees.[9] Entrepreneurial behavior is reinforced by designing bonus and incentive systems that encourage autonomy and competitive drive. Bonuses may assume a much larger role in these organizations than they assume in those characterized by more conservative values.[10] Incentives are likely to stress short-term performance on relatively objective measures of divisional performance. Concern for shaping cooperative behavior among units is conspicuously absent. Autonomy and competition are valued, and the compensation system reflects these concerns.[11]

Management values. A related factor influencing compensation design is the existing management value system. Incentive systems are more readily accepted when management values promote stable work relationships. Trust between workers and management is strong.[12] This trust evolves, in part, as workers experience a work environment where cyclical employment patterns are avoided and fears of job loss diminish. In turn, this stability lessens the fears that introduction of an incentive system is a "management plot" to increase production and to lay off workers.

Continued viability of an incentive system, though, depends on management's ability to face the more difficult behavioral consequences of incentive compensation. Remember, incentives create a spread between the pay levels of individuals and groups. As the spread increases, so may the dissatisfaction of

---

[6]M. Leontiades, *Strategies for Diversification and Change* (Boston: Little, Brown, 1980).

[7]Arch Patton, "Why Incentive Plans Fail," *Harvard Business Review,* May–June 1972, pp. 58–66; Kerr, "Diversification Strategies and Managerial Rewards: An Empirical Study"; Jerry M. Newman, "Selecting Incentive Plans to Complement Organizational Strategy," in *Current Trends in Compensation Research and Practice,* ed. L. Gomez-Mejia and D. Balkin, forthcoming.

[8]Leontiades, *Strategies for Diversification and Change.*

[9]Pitts, "Incentive Compensation and Organization Design"; M. S. Salter, "Tailor Incentive Compensation to Strategy,"*Harvard Business Review* 51, no. 3 (1973), pp. 94–102.

[10]Kerr, "Diversification Strategies and Managerial Rewards."

[11]Newman, "Selecting Incentive Plans to Complement Organizational Strategy."

[12]Patton, "Why Incentive Plans Fail"; Kerr, "Diversification Strategies and Managerial Reward: An Empirical Study"; Pitts, "Incentive Compensation and Organization Design."

lower-paid individuals. Organizations and managers unable to bear the heat of this disapproval should avoid incentive systems.

Organizational design and work relationships. A compensation system also complements the way organizational units are designed to interact. Autonomous units with sole responsibility for particular goods or services are ideal for objective, results-oriented performance measures. Independent units can be held accountable for successfully meeting targets; and incentive systems can tie rewards to those performance targets.[13]

As autonomy decreases, though, divisional performance measures become less viable. Rather, the interdependence among groups, divisions, and the organization in decision making is reflected in performance measures and incentive standards that reflect combined performance of all three entities.

Unit and individual performance standards. The last section may leave the impression that performance standards are easily manipulated and can trigger all sorts of desired performance. Be careful! Research indicates that inappropriate choice of performance standards is the single biggest cause of certain incentive system failures. If performance can't be measured validly and objectively, the potential advantage of incentive systems is greatly reduced.[14]

Unit and individual performance. Compensation, as noted earlier, is intended to attract, retain, and motivate workers. Incentive systems are useful on the last of these objectives: When performance is sub par, incentives may motivate higher performance. However, it is not clear that incentives are nearly so effective in helping to attract or retain employees. Take, as an example, firms dependent on high technology and highly skilled employees with technical skills in scarce supply. Compensation design here might focus more on base salary and less on incentives, seeking to maximize retention rather than level of production.

Similarly, adoption of an incentive system probably has implications for the types of workers such a system might attract. What does an economically motivated person look like? Is there any such animal? Can selection strategies be developed to fill jobs with these people? Or can current employees be trained in this need? While little empirical work addresses the issue, motivation theories from Chapter 8 suggest the process people may follow in determining whether

---

[13]Pitts, "Incentive Compensation and Organization Design"; Newman, "Selecting Incentive Plans to Complement Organizational Strategy"; and Organizational Analysis and Practice, *Strategic Issues in Reward Systems: An Analysis of Incentive Systems* (Ithaca, N.Y.: Organizational Analysis and Practice, 1982).

[14]Organizational Analysis and Practice, *Strategic Issues in Reward Systems;* Jude T. Rich and John A. Larson, "Why Some Long-Term Incentives Fail," *Compensation Review* 16, no. 1 (1984) pp. 26–37.

EXHIBIT 9.3
Pros and Cons, Incentive (payment by results) Plans

Advantages

1. Payment by results systems can make a substantial contribution to a rise in productivity, to lower production costs, and to increased earnings or workers.
2. In general, less direct supervision is required to maintain reasonable levels of output than under payment by time.
3. Workers are encouraged to pay more attention to reducing lost time and to make more effective use of their equipment.
4. In most cases, systems of payment by results, if accompanied by improved organizational and work measurement, enable labor costs to be estimated more accurately than under payment by time and so facilitate the application of modern systems of standard costing and budgetary control.

Disadvantages

1. Generally, introduction of a payment-by-results system leads to a deterioration in the quality of the product. Additional expense is involved in the application of an adequate system of quality control.
2. If the task is set too high or there is a low guaranteed minimum wage, the health, efficiency, and morale of the workers may be adversely affected.
3. The risk of accidents may be increased.
4. Inaccurate rate setting under an incentive scheme or wide differences in the ability or capacity of workers working in close proximity may lead to large differences in earnings and ill-feelings between the workers.
5. Additional expense involved in employing the personnel required to install and administer a system of payment of results; in some cases this expense may be out of proportion to the potential savings in costs.
6. Workers may tend to oppose the introduction of new machinery or methods, or other changes in conditions of production, which would necessitate a restudy of the job.

Source: Pinhas Schwinger, *Wage Incentive Systems* (New York: Halsted, 1975). © 1975, Keter Publishing Company.

an incentive system is favorable. Specifically, equity theory suggests that the reward value relative to effort must be greater than 1.00 (reward exceeds effort) and that the ratio should favorably compare to other relevant employees. Furthermore, expectancy theory indicates the monetary reward must be valued, the performance-pay link must be visible, and employees must believe that effort leads to high performance.[15]

For a different perspective on factors to consider in selecting an incentive/ gain-sharing plan, Exhibit 9.3 notes a more general set of issues in incentive system adoption.

Development Issues

Should rewards be paid to individual employees for individual performance? Or should larger groups be the unit of focus? What should be the standard that triggers incentives? And what should be the form (frequency of incentives)? All of these issues are discussed in this section.

_____

[15]Organizational Analysis and Practice, *Strategic Issues in Reward Systems*.

Group or individual plans? Level of aggregation. Level of aggregation refers to the size of the work unit for which performance is measured (e.g., individual, work group, department, plant, organization) and to which rewards are distributed. The issue is important for three reasons. First, contrasting motivational forces are unleashed by an organization's decision to aggregate. What type of employee behavior best fits organizational needs? Individual incentive systems are generally associated with more competition, increased pressure on individuals to perform and to accept responsibility for their own actions, increased risk-taking behavior, and lower acceptance of management values/job demands which don't directly affect incentive output.[16] Alternatively, group incentive plans reinforce behaviors which promote collective rather than individual success. The perceived connection between pay and performance may be lessened, but this may be offset by an increase in cooperation and joint effort among employees working for a shared reward based on aggregate performance. In deciding on an appropriate plan, organizations ought to consider the four factors noted in Exhibit 9.4.[17] Also note, though, that the trend in recent years has been away from individual incentive plans and toward group plans.[18] The concern seems to be that individual incentive plans are extremely costly and difficult to administer. Further, unions fear that individualized pay will be based on "biased" management standards. Couple these constraints with a growing interest in increased teamwork/cooperation and the movement to group plans becomes more understandable.

Of course, combinations of these plans are also possible. One of the most popular is to measure performance at the plant or total organization level but to distribute rewards at the individual level, based on some supervisory evaluation of individual performance. One variation currently used by a prominent organization is illustrated in Appendix A at the end of this chapter.

A second reason why the issue of aggregation is important centers on technical constraints. The nature of an organization's technology, both in production and in information processing, constrains choice. In general, individual incentive systems are less appropriate where:[19]

1. Individual contributions of workers are difficult to measure, either because of interdependent work flows or because of machine-controlled work pace.
2. Work stoppages are regular and uncontrollable.

---

[16]Organizational Analysis and Practice, *Strategic Issues in Reward Systems;* Pinhas Schwinger *Wage Incentive Systems* (New York: Halsted, 1975); Kerr, "Diversification Strategies and Managerial Rewards: An Empirical Study"; Salter, "Tailor Incentive Compensation to Strategy."

[17]Edward Lawler III, *Pay and Organization Development* (Reading, Mass.: Addison-Wesley Publishing, 1981).

[18]Hewitt Associates, *An Overview of Productivity-Based Incentive Systems,* May 1985, Document P3022/2625.

[19]Organizational Analysis and Practice, *Strategic Issues in Reward Systems;* Schwinger, *Wage Incentive Systems.*

EXHIBIT 9.4
Factors Influencing Aggregation Level

Characteristic	*Individual Level of Incentives Appropriate*	*Group Level of Incentives—Unit, Department, Organization— Appropriate*
Performance measurement	Good measures of individual performance exist. Task accomplishment not dependent on performance of others.	Output is group collaborative effort. Individual contributions to output cannot be assessed.
Organizational adaptability	Individual performance standards are stable. Production methods and labor mix relatively constant.	Performance standards for individuals change to meet environmental pressures on relatively constant organizational objectives. Production methods and labor mix must adapt to meet changing pressures.
Organizational commitment	Commitment strongest to individual's profession or superior. Supervisor viewed as unbiased and performance standards readily apparent.	High commitment to organization built upon sound communication of organizational objectives and performance standards.
Union status	Nonunion. Unions promote equal treatment. Competition between individuals inhibits "fraternal" spirit.	Union or nonunion. Unions less opposed to plans that foster cohesiveness of bargaining unit and which distribute rewards evenly across group.

3. The management information and cost accounting systems are relatively primitive.

The key to these constraints is that performance must be measurable, and the agent (who completed the work) must be identifiable. Usually these limitations become more severe the lower the level of analysis (e.g., individuals).[20] After all, most organizations can provide performance data (e.g., profits) for the entire organization. When the unit of analysis is smaller, though, it becomes more and more difficult to decide on objective measures of performance and to attribute that performance to specific individuals or groups.

Finally, level of aggregation is also important because the choice frequently influences the objectivity of the performance standards and, consequently, the type of pay system that evolves. If the existing information system can provide only very subjective supervisory ratings at the individual level of performance, it may be appropriate to focus on a higher level measure. Moving to higher levels of aggregation yields performance measures with a more objective base (profit, cost effectiveness). And, as noted earlier, these objective performance measures allow implementation of compensation systems directly tied to (group) output.

---

[20]Newman, "Selecting Incentive Plans to Complement Organizational Strategy."

EXHIBIT 9.5
Illustration of a Bonus Payment System in a Large Retail Store

Time Frame for Goal Attainment	Performance Standard	Bonus
June 1986–June 1987	Increase sales volume by 6 percent and reduce customer complaints by 10 percent.	20 percent of base pay as of June 1987.

Form of incentive. Incentive and gain-sharing plans can involve three forms of payment: base pay, commission, and bonus. Base pay, if used at all in an incentive scheme, is a guaranteed level of payment irrespective of output. Typically this base pay compensates for such activities as handling customer returns, fielding complaints, and waiting for machines to be repaired. All these examples restrict employee production, which is typically tied to incentive payments. Consequently this alternative compensation may be considered appropriate.

A commission is any form of payment tied directly to achievement of performance standards.[21] Any salesperson is typically on a commission base, for example. Commissions are especially desirable because wage payments are directly tied to some form of profits index (sales, production level). Employee costs, then, rise and fall in line with revenues. When firms can least afford high labor costs (recession) employees have the lowest sales level and the smallest commissions.

Perhaps the form of incentive increasing in popularity most rapidly is the bonus. A bonus is a lump sum payment to an employee in recognition of goal achievement. Typically the goal is not expressed in standard output but represents a major step toward achievement of organizational goals. Herein lies a distinct advantage. Performance goals can be changed yearly to reflect the changing nature of organizational objectives.[22] Upon completion, a previously agreed-upon bonus is owed the employee (frequently a percentage of base pay; see Exhibit 9.5).

One industry where bonuses are particularly popular is the highly competitive, high technology industry. A Hay survey of 33 large high tech companies showed that the top 7 percent of managerial, professional, and technical employees were eligible for bonuses. In smaller high tech organizations (less than $100 million sales versus $1 billion sales for the larger companies) 47 percent of

---

[21]Gerry Phillips, "Matching the Compensation Plan to the Sales Role," *Canadian Business Review,* Spring 1977, pp. 62–66; Ernest C. Miller, "How Companies Set the Base Salary and Incentive Bonus Opportunity for Chief Executive and Chief Operating Officers . . . A Compensation Review Symposium," *Compensation Review* 7 (Fourth Quarter, 1976), pp. 66–72; John P. Steinbrink, "How to Pay Your Sales Force," *Harvard Business Review* 56, no. 4 (1978), pp. 111–22.

[22]J. Moynahan, *Designing an Effective Sales Compensation Program* (New York: Amacom, 1980).

all managerial, professional, and technical employees get bonuses. These percentages are generally higher than are found in other manufacturing industries (e.g., large manufacturing firms average approximately 3 percent participation rates).[23]

Another form of payment attaining some popularity over the past several years is lump sum payments. Lump sum payments are generally granted in lieu of wage increases and are preferred because base pay and pay-related benefits don't change. Approximately 7 percent of all 1984 contracts had provisions for lump sum payments.[24]

Frequency of incentives. Instrumental conditioning experiments indicate that rewards work best when administered immediately after task completion. This conjures up images of monkeys pressing bars and immediately receiving bananas from a chute. Obviously, this kind of compensation system would not be very popular or practical with humans. The most frequent concession is to pay incentives on standard time schedules: weekly, monthly, quarterly, and yearly. Unfortunately, though, task cycles are not conveniently equivalent to calendar cycles.[25] Employees end up receiving incentives at times far removed from the accomplishments triggering the rewards. A more viable strategy would adopt a performance contract mechanism. Upon completion of agreed-upon work at an agreed-upon date, an incentive will be paid. If the time frame is too short to make payment practical, regular feedback about incentive accumulations should be provided until payment can be made.

Another subset of the frequency question is the issue of long-term and short-term incentive plans. Much of the popular press has criticized American business for taking too short a perspective on organizational goals. Emphasizing short-run profits to the detriment of longer-run objectives, so this argument goes, frequently hurts us in international competition with countries such as Japan which take a more long-range perspective on business prospects. There is research to support this criticism. Short-term incentive plans are more prevalent in American companies than are long-term plans. For example, one study found 75 percent of firms ($n = 110$) had short-term plans, while only 55 percent had long-term incentive plans.[26] This emphasis on the short run may be changing, though. Organizations are showing increased interest in designing incentive plans that both meet organizational objectives *and* are consistent with time frames of differing durations.[27] This focus shifts discussions away from

[23]CompFlash, "Survey Shows Bonuses Are the Way to Go," *AMA CompFlash* 85-07 (1985), p. 4.

[24]Compflash, "Gaining Popularity: Lump Sum Payments in Lieu of Wage Increases," *AMA CompFlash* 85-05 (1985), p. 4.

[25]P. Clark, *Organizational Design* (London: Travistock, 1972).

[26]Compflash, "Short-Term Plans Outnumber Long-Term Plans," *AMA CompFlash* 85-06 (1985), p. 1.

[27]Bruce R. Ellig, "Incentive Plans: Short Term Design Issues," *Compensation Review* 16, no. 3 (1984), pp. 26–36.

EXHIBIT 9.6
Common Performance Measures Used in Incentive Plans

Measure	*Definition*	*Organization*
1. Operating margin (percent)	*Total sales and revenues less total costs and expenses* divided by total sales and revenues.	American Motors, American Airlines.
2. Operating return on assets	*Operating income* divided by average total assets.	General Motors, Borg-Warner, Federated Department Stores, Texas Instruments.
3. Earnings per share	*Income available to common stockholder* divided by average number of common shares outstanding.	Jewel Company, Winn Dixie Stores.
4. Return to equity	*Income available to common stockholder* divided by common equity (market value of common stock).	Polaroid, Deere & Company, Burlington Industries.

---

the less productive question, "Should we use short-term or long-term incentive plans?" toward the more relevant question, "What should be the nature of the mix and objectives of each type of plan?" Organizational success then becomes a function of identifying consistent short- and long-run goals and ensuring both are met. Several authors suggest a key element in forging this interdependence is selecting appropriate measures of organizational performance.[28] Both the financial research literature and the human resources management literature currently are debating the relative merits of such organizational effectiveness measures as earnings per share, return on equity, return on investments, and growth.[29] (Exhibit 9.6 illustrates measures used by different organizations.)

INDIVIDUAL INCENTIVE PLANS

All incentive plans have one common feature: an established standard against which worker performance is compared to determine wages. For individual incentive systems this standard is compared against individual worker performance. From this basic foundation, a number of seemingly complex and divergent plans have evolved. Before discussing the more prevalent of these plans, however, it is important to note that each varies along two dimensions and can be classified into one of four cells illustrated in Exhibit 9.7.

The first dimension on which incentive systems vary is in the method of rate determination. Plans either set up a rate standard based on units of pro-

---

[28]Ellig, "Incentive Plans: Short Term Design Issues"; Rich and Larson, "Why Some Long Term Incentives Fail."

[29]Bruce R. Ellig, "Incentive Plans: Over the Long Term," *Compensation Review* 16, no. 2 (1984), pp. 39–54; Ellig, "Short Term Design Issues."

EXHIBIT 9.7
Individual Incentive Plans

		Method of Rate Determination	
		Units of Production per Time Period *(1)*	*Time Period per Unit of Production* *(2)*
Relationship Between Production Level and Pay	*Pay Constant Function of Production Level*	Straight piecework plan.	Standard hour plan.
	Pay Varies as Function of Production Level	*(3)* Taylor differential piece-rate system. Merrick multiple piece-rate system.	*(4)* Halsey 50–50 method. Rowan plan. Gantt plan.

duction per time period or on time period per unit of production. On the surface, this distinction may appear trivial but, in fact, the deviations arise because tasks have different cycles of operation.[30] Short-cycle tasks, those that are completed in a relatively short period of time, typically have as a standard a designated number of units to be produced in a given time period. For long-cycle tasks, this would not be appropriate. It is entirely possible that only one task or some portion may be completed in a day. Consequently, for longer-cycle tasks, the standard is typically set in terms of time required to complete one unit of production. Individual incentives are based on whether or not workers complete the task in the designated time period.

The second dimension on which individual incentive systems vary is the specified relationship between production level and wages. The first alternative is to tie wages directly to output, so that wages are some constant function of production. In contrast, some plans vary wages as a function of production level. For example, one common variation is to provide higher dollar rates for production above the standard than for production below the standard.

Specific Plans

Each of the plans discussed in this section has as a foundation a standard level of performance determined by some form of time study or job analysis completed by an industrial engineer or trained personnel administrator. (Exhibit 9.8 provides an illustration of a time study.) The variations in these plans occur in either the way the standard is set or the way wages are tied to output. Following Exhibit 9.7 there are four general categories of plans.

---

[30]Thomas Patten, *Pay: Employee Compensation and Incentive Plans* (New York: Macmillan, 1977); Schwinger, *Wage Incentive Systems*.

EXHIBIT 9.8
Example of a Time Study

Task: Drilling operation.

Elements:
1. Move part from box to jig.
2. Position part in jig.
3. Drill hole in part.
4. Remove jig and drop part in chute.

Notes and Remarks	Observation Number	Elements			
		(1)	*(2)*	*(3)*	*(4)*
	1	.17	.22	.26	.29
	2	.17	.22	.27	.34
	3	.16	.21	.28	.39
	4	.18	.21	.29	.29
	5	.19	.20	.30	.36
	6	.25	.21	.31	.31
	7	.17	.23	.29	.33
Observed time		.17 (mode)	.21 (mode)	.29 (median)	.33 (mean)
Effort rating	(130%)	1.30	1.30	1.30	1.30
Corrected time		.2210	.2730	.3370	.4290
Total corrected time					1.2600

Allowances:
Fatigue	5%	
Personal Needs	5%	
Contingencies	10%	
Total	20% (of total corrected time of 1.2600)	.2520
Total allotted time for task		1.5120

Source: From *Performance Appraisal and Review Systems* by Stephen J. Carroll and Craig E. Schneier. Copyright © 1982 by Scott, Foresman and Company. Reprinted by permission.

1. Cell 1. The most frequently implemented incentive system is a straight piecework system. Rate determination is based on units of production per time period, and wages vary directly as a function of production level. A standard is developed reflecting the units of output a worker is expected to complete in, say, an hour. Workers are paid for each unit of output. Consequently workers who consistently exceed the established standard receive higher than average wages.

The major advantages of this type of system is that it is easily understood by workers and, perhaps consequently, more readily accepted than some of the other incentive systems. The major disadvantages center on the difficulty in setting a standard. For example, the industrial engineer charged with establishing a standard for the drilling operation in Exhibit 9.8 may be expected to observe numerous drillers performing the task. The time study expert would then derive a standard indicating the number of holes it should be possible to drill in a given time period by workers performing at a normal rate. The accuracy of the industrial engineer's measurements, the workers chosen to observe, and the definition of a normal rate of speed all influence the final standard.[31] An inappropriate standard can result in labor dissension (too high a standard) or excessive labor costs (too low a standard). Either outcome is likely to result in deteriorating labor-management relations. Consequently great care must be taken to ensure that both management and the workers have a role in establishing standards. Very frequently in unionized firms this is formally ensured through inclusion of standards as a negotiable issue in the contract language.

2. Cell 2. There are two relatively common plans that set standards based on time per unit and tie incentives directly to level of output: (1) standard hour plans and (2) Bedeaux plans. A standard hour plan is a generic term for plans setting incentive rate based on completion of a task in some expected time period. A common example can be found in any neighborhood gasoline station or automobile repair shop. Let us assume you need a new transmission. The estimate you receive for labor costs is based on the mechanic's hourly rate of pay, multipled by a time estimate for job completion derived from a book listing average time estimates for a wide variety of jobs. If the mechanic receives $30 per hour and a transmission is listed as requiring four hours to remove and replace, the labor costs would be $120. All this is determined in advance of any actual work. Of course, if the mechanic is highly experienced and fast, the job may be completed in considerably less time than indicated in the book. However, the job is still charged as if it took the quoted time to complete. This is the basic mechanism of a standard hour incentive plan. If a task can be completed in less than the designated time, a worker is still paid at a rate based on the standard time allotted for that job times an hourly rate. Standard hour plans are more practical than a straight piecework plan for long-cycle operations and jobs that are nonrepetitive and require numerous skills for completion.[32]

A Bedeaux plan provides a variation on straight piecework and standard hour plans. Instead of timing an entire task, a Bedeaux plan requires division of a task into simple actions and determination of the time required by an average skilled worker to complete each action. After the more fine time analysis of tasks, the Bedeaux system functions similarly to a standard hour plan. Workers receive a wage incentive for completing a task in less than standard time. This incentive is a direct function of the time saved in completing the task.

3. Cell 3. The two plans included in cell 3 provide for variable incentives as a function of units of production per time period. Both the Taylor plan and the Merrick plan provide different piece rates, depending on the level of production relative to the standard. To illustrate this, consider the contrasts of these plans

---

[31]Stephen Carroll and Craig Schneier, *Performance Appraisal and Review Systems* (Glenview, Ill.: Scott, Foresman, 1982).

[32]Patten, *Pay: Employee Compensation and Incentive Plans;* Schwinger, *Wage Incentive Systems.*

with a straight piece-rate plan. A straight piece-rate plan varies wages directly with output. If workers reach standard production, they receive the standard wage. Eighty percent of standard production results in 80 percent of standard wage. Plotting a graph with percentage of standard production on one axis and percentage gain in base hourly rate on the other, the slope for a straight piece-rate system would be 1.00. Both the Taylor and Merrick plans would have variable slopes depending on production levels of workers. For example, the Taylor plan establishes two piecework rates. One rate goes into effect when a worker exceeds the established standard for a given time period. This rate is set higher than the regular wage incentive level. A second rate is established for production below standard, and this rate is lower than the regular wage.

The Merrick system operates in the same way, except three piecework rates are set: (1) high—for production exceeding 100 percent of standard; (2) medium—for production between 83 percent and 100 percent of standard; and (3) low—for production less than 83 percent of standard.[33]

Both these systems are designed to reward highly the efficient worker and penalize the inefficient worker. Quite obviously there are infinite variations on the number and type of piecework rates that could be established. While these two plans are designed to encourage the highly efficient, they are not as penalty-laden for less efficient workers as their now defunct predecessors.

4. Cell 4. The three plans included in cell 4 provide for variable incentives as a function of a standard expressed as time period per unit of production. The three plans include the Halsey 50–50 method, the Rowan plan, and the Gantt plan.

The Halsey 50–50 method derives its name from the shared split between worker and employer of any savings in direct cost. An allowed time for a task is determined via time study. The savings resulting from completion of a task in less than the standard time are allocated 50–50 (most frequent division) between the worker and the company.

The Rowan plan is similar to the Halsey plan in that an employer and employee both share in savings resulting from work completed in less than standard time. The major distinction in this plan, however, is that a worker's bonus increases as time required to complete the task decreases. For example, if the standard time to complete a task is 10 hours and it is completed in 7 hours, the worker receives a 30 percent bonus. Completion of the same task in six hours would result in a 40 percent bonus above the hourly wage for each of the six hours.

The Gantt plan differs from both the Halsey and Rowan plans in that standard time for a task is purposely set at a level requiring high effort to complete. Any worker who fails to complete the task in standard time is guaranteed a preestablished wage. However, for any task completed in standard time or less,

---

[33]Schwinger, *Wage Incentive Systems.*

earnings are pegged at 120 percent of the time saved. Consequently worker's earnings increase faster than production whenever standard time is met or exceeded.

GROUP INCENTIVE PLANS (GAIN–SHARING PLANS)

In one sense, group incentive plans are similar to individual incentive plans. An attempt is made to tie pay to performance by giving workers an additional payment when there has been an increase in profits or a decrease in costs to the firm. All plans begin by comparing inputs to outcomes. In this case labor inputs are compared to some measure of production outputs. In a basic sense incentives are awarded when some base period calculation of labor inputs and production outputs are exceeded, either by reducing labor inputs, increasing production outcomes, or both. It should be stressed, though, that these improvements don't necessarily result because employees individually or collectively decide to work harder. Indeed, it is probably more common that improvements arise because employees work smarter, identifying means to perform tasks more efficiently without working harder.

Deviation from individual incentive plans obviously arises because incentives are based on some measure of group performance rather than individual performance. Incentives are based on a comparison of present profits or costs against historical cost accounting data on the same figures. When the organization achieves greater profits or lower costs relative to a base year, groups participating in the incentive plan receive a portion of the accrued funds.

Complexity is introduced into these formulas, though, because different organizations have different goals. Different strategies and management value systems yield different solutions to some of the common questions organizations must answer in selecting one of the several different types of gain sharing plans:[34]

1. Strength of reinforcement. What role should base pay assume relative to incentive pay? Incentive pay tends to encourage only those behaviors which are rewarded. For example, try returning an unwanted birthday present to a store which pays its sales force solely for new sales! Tasks which carry no rewards are only reluctantly performed (if at all!).

2. Scope of the formula. Formulas can vary in the scope of inclusions for both the labor inputs in the numerator and productivity outcomes in the denominator.[35] For example, the standard could be as narrowly defined as reducing labor costs or it could incorporate a wide range of alternative organizational goals. Efforts to improve quality could be reinforced by focusing on reductions in

---

[34]Max Bazerman and Brian Graham-Moore, "PG Formulas: Developing a Reward Structure to Achieve Organizational Goals," in *Productivity Gainsharing,* ed. Brian Graham-Moore and Timothy Ross (Englewood Cliffs, N.J.: Prentice-Hall, 1983).

[35]Newman, "Selecting Incentive Plans to Complement Organizational Strategy."

customer complaints, increases in market share, or some other measure selected to reflect management concerns. Great care must be exercised, though, to ensure that the behaviors reinforced actually affect the desired bottom line goal. Getting workers to expend more effort, for example, might not always be the desired behavior. Increased effort may bring unacceptable levels of accidents. Or it may even be preferable to encourage cooperative planning behaviors that result in smarter, rather than harder, work.

3. Perceived fairness of the formula. Not all incentive systems cover all employees in a firm. In fact it is common to limit eligibility to individuals in key positions whose income exceeds certain minimum standards.[36] When multiple plans are implemented which cover different groups of employees and which have different goals, coordination to ensure equity becomes increasingly important.

4. Ease of administration. Sophisticated plans with involved calculations of profits or costs can become too complex for existing company information systems. Increased complexities also require more effective communications and higher levels of trust among participants.

5. Production variability. One of the major sources of problems in gain-sharing plans is failure to set targets properly.[37] For example, consider the company that sets a target of 6 percent return on investment. When this level is reached, it triggers an incentive for eligible employees. Yet, in a product market where the average for that year is 15 percent return on investment, it is apparent that no incentive is appropriate for our underachiever.[38] Such problems are particularly insidious during economic swings and for organizations which face volatile economic climates. Care must be taken to ensure that the link between performance and rewards is sustained. This means that environmental influences on performance, not controllable by plan participants, should be factored out when identifying incentive levels.

Exhibit 9.9 illustrates three different formulas which can be used as the basis for gain-sharing plans. The numerator, or input factor, is always some labor cost variable, expressed in either dollars or actual hours worked. Similarly, the denominator is some output measure such as net sales or value added. Each of the plans determines employees' incentive based on the difference between the current value of the ratio and the ratio in some agreed-upon base year. The more favorable the current ratio relative to historical standards, the larger the incentive award.[39] The three primary types of gain-sharing plans, differentiated by their focus on either cost saving (the numerator of the equation) or some measure of profits (the denominator of the equation), are noted below.

---

[36]Ellig, "Incentive Plans: Short Term Design Issues."

[37]Rich and Larson, "Why Some Long Term Incentives Fail."

[38]Patton, "Why Incentive Plans Fail."

[39]Newman, "Selecting Incentive Plans to Complement Organizational Strategy."

EXHIBIT 9.9
Three Gain-Sharing Formulas

	Scanlon Plan (single ratio variant)	*Rucker Plan*	*Improshare*
Numerator of ratio (input factor)	Payroll costs	Labor cost	Actual hours worked
Denominator of ratio (outcome factor)	Net sales (plus or minus inventories)	Value added	Total standard value hours

Adapted from M. Bazerman and B. Graham-Moore, "P.G. Formulas: Developing a Reward Structure to Achieve Organizational Goals," in *Productivity Gainsharing,* ed. B. Graham-Moore and T. Ross (Englewood Cliffs, N.J.: Prentice-Hall, 1983).

Cost Savings Plans

⇒ *Scanlon Plan.* Scanlon plans are designed to lower labor costs without lowering the level of a firm's activity. Incentives are derived as a function of the ratio between labor costs and sales value of production (SVOP).[40] The SVOP includes sales revenue and the value of goods in inventory. To illustrate how these two figures are used to derive incentives under a Scanlon plan, consider Exhibit 9.10.

In practice, this $50,000 bonus in Exhibit 9.10 is not all distributed to the work force. Rather, 25 percent is distributed to the company and 25 percent of the remainder is withheld and placed in an emergency fund to reimburse the company for any future months when a "negative bonus" is earned (i.e., when the actual wage bill is greater than the allowable wage bill). The excess remaining in the emergency pool is distributed to workers at the end of the year.

EXHIBIT 9.10
Examples of a Scanlon Plan

1985 Data (Base Year) for Alcon, Ltd.		
SVOP	=	$10,000,000
Total wage bill	=	4,000,000
$\dfrac{\text{Total Wage Bill}}{\text{SVOP}}$	=	$4,000,000 \div 10,000,000 = .40 = 40\%$

Operating Month, August 1987			
SVOP	=	$950,000	
Allowable wage bill	=	.40 ($950,000)	= $380,000
Actual wage bill (August)	=	330,000	
Savings	=	50,000	

$50,000 available for distribution as a bonus.

[40]A. J. Geare, "Productivity from Scanlon Type Plans," *Academy of Management Review* 1, no. 3 (1976), pp. 99–108.

Rucker plan. The Rucker plan involves a somewhat more complex formula than a Scanlon plan for determining worker incentive bonuses. Essentially, a ratio is calculated that expresses the value of production required for each dollar of total wage bill. Consider the following illustration.[41]

1. Assume accounting records show the company put $.60 worth of electricity, materials, supplies, and so on into production, to produce $1.00 worth of product. The value added is $.40 for each $1.00 of sales value. Assume also that records show that 45 percent of the value added was attributable to labor; a productivity ratio (PR) can be allocated from the formula:

2. PR × 45% = 1.00. Solving yields PR = 2.22.

3. If the wage bill equals $100,000, the *expected* production value is the wage bill ($100,000) × PR (2.22) = $222,222.22.

4. If *actual* production value equals $280,000.00, then the savings (actual production value minus expected production value) equals $57,777.78.

5. Since the labor contribution to value added is 45 percent, the bonus to the work force should be .45 × $57,777.78 = $26,000.00 (rounded).

6. The savings are distributed as an incentive bonus according to a formula identical to the Scanlon formula—75 percent of the bonus is distributed to workers immediately and 25 percent is kept as an emergency fund to cover poor months. Any excess in the emergency fund at the end of the year is then distributed to workers.

Implementation of the Scanlon/Rucker Plans

There are two major components vital to the implementation and success of a Rucker- or Scanlon-type plan: (1) a productivity norm and (2) development of effective worker committees. Development of a productivity norm requires both effective measurement of base year data and acceptance by workers and management of this standard for calculating bonus incentives. Effective measurement requires that an organization keep extensive records of historical cost relationships and make them available to workers or union representatives to verify cost accounting figures. Acceptance of these figures, assuming they are accurate, requires that the organization choose a base year that is neither a "boom" nor a "bust" year. The logic is apparent. A boom year would reduce opportunities for workers to collect bonus incentives, and a bust year would lead to excessive bonus costs for the firm. The base year chosen also should be fairly recent, allaying worker fears that changes in technology or other factors would make the base year unrepresentative of a given operational year.

The second ingredient of Scanlon/Rucker plans is a series of worker committees (also known as productivity committees or bonus committees). The pri-

---

[41]Geare, "Productivity from Scanlon Type Plans."

mary function of these committees is to evaluate employee and management suggestions for ways to improve productivity and/or cut costs. Operating on a plantwide basis in smaller firms, or a departmental basis in larger firms, these committees have been highly successful in eliciting suggestions from employees. It is not uncommon for the suggestion rate to be above that found in companies with standard suggestion incentive plans.[42]

It is this climate the Scanlon/Rucker plans foster that is perhaps the most vital element of success. Numerous authors have pointed out that these plans have the best chance for success in companies with competent supervision, cooperative union-management attitudes, strong top management interest and participation in the development of the program, and management open to criticism and willing to discuss different operating strategies. It is beyond the scope of this discussion to outline specific strategies adopted by companies to achieve this climate, but the key element is a belief that workers should play a vital role in the decision-making process.

Similarities and Contrasts between Scanlon and Rucker Plans

Scanlon and Rucker plans differ from individual incentive plans in their primary focus. Individual incentive plans focus primarily on using wage incentives to motivate higher performance through increased effort. While this is certainly a goal of the Scanlon/Rucker plans, it is not the major focus of attention. Rather, given that increased output is a function of group effort, more attention is focused on organizational behavior variables. The key is to promote faster, more intelligent and acceptable decisions through participation. This participation is won by developing a group unity in achieving cost savings, a goal that is not stressed, and often stymied, in individual incentive plans.

Even though Scanlon and Rucker plans share this common attention to groups and committees through participation as a linking pin, there are two important differences between the two plans. First, Rucker plans tie incentives to a wide variety of savings, not just the labor savings focused on in Scanlon plans.[43] Second, this greater flexibility may help explain why Rucker plans are more amenable to linkages with individual incentive plans.

Improshare

Improshare (IMproved PROductivity through SHARing) is a relatively new gain-sharing plan which has proven easy to administer and to communicate.[44]

---

[42]Ibid.

[43]Patten, "Pay: Employee Compensation and Incentive Plans"; Schwinger, *Wage Incentive Plans.*

[44]Graham-Moore and Ross, *Productivity Gainsharing.*

EXHIBIT 9.11
A Comparison among Gain-Sharing Plans

	Behavioral and Organizational Issues in Choosing a Plan				
	Strength of Reinforcement	*Scope of Formula*	*Perceived Fairness of Formulation*	*Ease of Administration*	*Production Variability*
Scanlon	Reinforcement hindered because incentives tied to group performance.	Narrowly concerned with labor costs and sales.	Simplicity of formula and broad base of cooperation yield perception of fairness.	Simplicity makes administration easy.	Rapid peaking of production cycles not easy to deal with.
Rucker	Reinforcement only hindered because incentives tied to group performance.	Even more narrow than Scanlon in that sales value of production is corrected for inflation.	Complexity slightly reduces perceived fairness. Requires somewhat less cooperative effort than Scanlon.	Value added concept and formula exclusions difficult to administer.	Formula for calculating value added specifically deals with changing economic conditions.
Improshare	Reinforcement only hindered because incentives tied to group performance.	Narrow measures of labor hours saved.	Lack of employee involvement in development of plan may reduce perceived fairness.	Simplicity makes administration easy.	Management must closely monitor inventory to ensure variability in economic conditions is reflected in production changes.

First, a standard is developed which identifies the expected hours required to produce an acceptable level of output. This standard comes either from time and motion studies conducted by industrial engineers or from a base period measurement of the performance factor. Any savings arising from production of agreed-upon output in fewer than expected hours are shared by the firm and by the worker.[45]

Exhibit 9.11 compares these three types of gain-sharing programs on the five dimensions discussed earlier.[46]

Profit-Sharing Plans

The second general category of group incentive plans includes all profit-sharing plans, whether the profit shared is distributed currently or deferred until later (typically at retirement, disability, severance, or death).[47] While provisions of

---

[45]Newman, "Selecting Incentive Plans to Complement Organizational Strategy."

[46]Ibid.

[47]Robert McCaffery, *Managing the Employee Benefits Process* (New York: AMACOM, 1983).

the Employee Retirement Income Security Act (ERISA) have taken some of the incentive out of implementing incentive plans, recent estimates still suggest that about 20 percent of the private nonfarm work force receives some kind of profit sharing.[48] In the past three or four years, though, there has been a shift to thrift savings plans (Chapter 12) and away from profit-sharing plans, largely because of the instability of corporate profits. This comes despite some evidence that profit sharing may result in significant performance improvements.[49]

Profit-sharing plans, as is evident from the name, focus on profitability as the standard for group incentives. These plans typically can be found in one of three combinations. First, cash or current distribution plans provide full payment to participants soon after profits have been determined, usually quarterly or annually. As might be expected, the incentive value of profit distribution declines as the time between performance and payoff increases and as the size of the payoff declines relative to previous years. Second, deferred plans have a portion of current profits credited to employee accounts, with cash payment made at time of retirement, disability, severance, or death.[50] Because of certain tax advantages, this is the fastest-growing type of profit-sharing system, with approximately 80 percent of the companies with some form of profit-sharing plans using the deferred option.[51] The median range of profits distributed runs from 14 percent to about 33 percent.[52] Third, combination plans incorporate aspects of both current and deferred options. A portion of profits is immediately distributed to employees with the remaining amount set aside in designated accounts. About 20 percent of all companies with profit-sharing plans have this option.

There are certain similarities between profit-sharing plans and the other group incentive plans discussed. Both types of plans foster a climate where cost-cutting suggestions are more acceptable to employees. Furthermore, both types of plans are designed to pay out incentives when the organization is most able to afford them. However, the similarities end here. While a cash or current distribution plan carries some motivational incentive, thus resembling Scanlon/Rucker plans, deferred-payment plans more closely resemble a pension fund. The incentive value of working to increase current profits when rewards are distributed much later is, at best, minimal. To balance this disadvantage, profit-sharing plans have two distinct advantages. First, they do not require elaborate cost accounting systems to calculate incentives to be allocated to employees.

---

[48]Bureau of National Affairs, "Incentive Pay Schemes Seen as a Result of Economic Employee Relation Change," *BNA Daily Report,* October 9, 1984, p. cc-1.

[49]General Accounting Office, "Productivity Sharing Programs: Can They Contribute to Productivity Improvement?" March 31, 1981 (Washington, D.C.: government document).

[50]Schwinger, *Wage Incentive Systems.*

[51]McCaffery, *Managing the Employee Benefits Process.*

[52]Patten, "Pay: Employee Compensation and Incentive Plans"; Schwinger, *Wage Incentive Systems.*

Second, and perhaps more important, profit-sharing plans have been implemented in organizations that cover the entire spectrum in size. Admittedly there are definite tendencies for smaller organizations to opt for a current distribution plan and for larger organizations to choose the deferred option, but until there is more evidence that Scanlon/Rucker plans can be adapted successfully to larger organizations, profit-sharing plans seem to represent the major alternative for organizations of any size.

Effectiveness of Gain-Sharing Plans

Although there are many case studies of gain-sharing programs in the literature, very few of them report hard data collected in a well-controlled study. Many of the better studies, however, do report positive results from such plans. The General Accounting Office, for example, interviewed 36 companies with gain-sharing programs. Estimates indicated an average of 17 percent savings from these programs.[53] Perhaps the best study, though, reports an extensive literature search on gain-sharing studies.[54] Of the 33 programs with sufficient detail for comparison, virtually all reported only post hoc analyses; hence it is virtually impossible to make any but the most preliminary conclusions. The data are encouraging, though: (1) some level of productivity increase, rise in quality, or cost reduction was reported by 75 percent of the companies; (2) 75 percent of the companies indicated an increase in ideas, suggestions and innovations by employees; (3) among participants the programs were generally popular, with 64 percent reporting improved morale or quality of work life; and (4) about 50 percent of the participants reported improved communications, either between superiors and subordinates, labor and management, or both.

Why do gain-sharing programs work? Unfortunately there is almost no information available to answer this question.[55] The most plausible speculation, though, suggests that gain-sharing programs succeed because they change the culture of the firm. Employees at all levels develop a broader perspective about the organization's objectives and greater commitment to achieving them.[56]

INDIRECT COMPARISONS OF INDIVIDUAL AND GROUP INCENTIVE PLANS

Much time has been spent discussing the various types of plans and their viability in different organizational environments. It is appropriate now to report

---

[53]General Accounting Office, "Productivity Sharing Programs: Can They Contribute to Productivity Improvement?"

[54]R. J. Bullock and E. E. Lawler, "Gainsharing: A Few Questions and Fewer Answers," *Human Resource Management* 23, no. 1 (1984), pp. 23–40.

[55]Ibid.

[56]Ibid.

some of the results in companies that have used incentive plans. The strategy will be to discuss first individual then group incentive plans and then report on the relatively limited research that has compared the two types of plans simultaneously.

Perhaps the most thorough summary of individual incentive plan results comes from Edward Lawler.[57] In a review of numerous incentive plans it is concluded that even the most conservative estimates suggest that productivity can be increased by 10 to 20 percent.

DIRECT COMPARISONS OF GROUP AND INDIVIDUAL INCENTIVE SYSTEMS

There have been a number of studies directly comparing group versus individual incentive plans. The most thorough of these studies was conducted by London and Oldham.[58] As they note, prior studies fail to include one important factor: In comparisons of group versus individual incentive plans it is typical to contrast one group plan against multiple individual plans. For example, both Marriott and Schwab suggest that individual incentive plans may be superior to group plans in increasing employee productivity.[59] However, both studies used a single group incentive strategy: one in which bonuses are based on the average performance of the entire group. London and Oldham expanded this comparison to also include comparisons where bonuses are based on performance of the highest performer in the group and another program with bonuses based on the lowest performer in the group. Productivity under these three group plans in a laboratory setting were compared against results using an individual piece-rate system and a fixed-rate (i.e., straight hourly wages) system. Performance was approximately equal under the high-performance group incentive system and the individual piece-rate system. Both of these plans resulted in significantly better performance than for any of the other programs.

While these results need to be replicated in a field setting (i.e., an organization), they suggest that group incentive plans can be structured to approximate the productivity results obtained under individual incentive plans. Whether the other advantages of group incentive plans outlined earlier are still retained remains to be seen in future research studies.

In comparison, most of the studies reporting results from group incentive plans (primarily Scanlon/Rucker plans) have indicated productivity or profit

[57]Edward E. Lawler III, *Pay and Organizational Effectiveness: A Psychological View* (New York: McGraw-Hill, 1971).

[58]M. London and B. Oldham, "A Comparison of Group and Individual Incentive Plans," *Academy of Management Journal* 20, no. 1 (1977), pp. 34–41.

[59]R. Marriott, "Size of Working Group and Output," *Occupational Psychology* 23 (1949), pp. 47–57; D. P. Schwab, "Impact of Alternative Compensation Systems on Pay Valence and Instrumentality Perceptions," *Journal of Applied Psychology* 58 (1973), pp. 308–12.

increases in a range of 4.5 percent to 23.7 percent for periods of time between 1 and 17 years.[60] Firms at the high successful end of this continuum tend to be smaller and more stable, and experience less industrial conflict than those that benefit less.[61] It is tempting to conclude from the similar size of these productivity gains that individual and group incentive plans are equally effective. Data from more direct comparisons of the two types of plans partially supports this conclusion.

SUMMARY

The decision to establish a performance-based pay system requires that organizations measure performance accurately and fairly. This chapter has discussed pay systems based on objective performance measures (incentive systems). The diversity of individual and group incentive plans potentially available to an organization may appear overwhelming at first. But, as we have noted, organizational characteristics and compensation policy objectives serve well to narrow down the list of suitable alternatives. The major caution to recognize is that incentive systems are not a panacea for all productivity problems. Granted, tying pay to performance can have a positive motivational impact, hence improving productivity. But this system must be fostered by a climate of trust in which both management and workers participate in establishing fair standards and mutually agreeable administrative rules.

REVIEW QUESTIONS

1. How do pay systems differ when performance standards are objective versus subjective?
2. What types of issues should firms consider before adopting an incentive/gain-sharing plan?
3. What does level of aggregation mean in compensation? How does it relate to development of incentive plans?
4. How do individual incentive systems differ? Compare and contrast two existing systems to illustrate your points.
5. When is a group incentive or gain-sharing plan preferred over an individual incentive plan?
6. Describe how a Scanlon plan operates. Why are such plans frequently effective?
7. How do profit-sharing plans differ from Scanlon/Rucker type plans?

---

[60]E. S. Puckett,"Productivity Achievements—A Measure of Success," in *The Scanlon Plan,* ed. F. C. Lesieur (Cambridge, Mass.: MIT Press, 1978), pp. 109–18; F. Lesieur and E. Puckett, "The Scanlon Plan Has Proved Itself," *Harvard Business Review* 47 (1969), pp. 109–18.

[61]Bullock and Lawler, "Gainsharing: A Few Questions and Fewer Answers."

Appendix A

Example of an Integrated Incentive Plan (Selected Sections)

J. C. Penney Company
Management Incentive Plan Guide
General Office, Zone, and District Personnel

This material sets forth the principles, policies, and procedures that will guide the administration of the Penney incentive plan for general office, zone, and district management personnel. It is presented in the following sections:

1. Purpose and Philosophy of the Plan.
2. Eligibility for Participation.
3. The Incentive Fund.
4. Distribution of the Incentive Fund.
    a. Allocating Department and Zone Funds.
    b. Determining Individual Awards.
5. Timing and Method of Payment.
6. Summary of Responsibilities for Plan Administration.

PURPOSE AND PHILOSOPHY OF THE PLAN

The purpose of the management incentive plan is to motivate Penney management personnel to increase company profits. In order to achieve this objective, incentive payments will be related directly to company profit performance, department performance, zone performance (where applicable), and individual performance.

The philosophy underlying the plan recognizes that both salary and incentive payments play a part in providing recognition and rewards that help motivate individual performance. However, incentive payments differ from salaries in two respects. One is that incentive payments are one-time, rather than continuing payments. A second is that incentive payments are related directly to

327

profits, whereas salaries are related to the long-term value of the job as performed by the incumbent. Because of these differences in the characteristics of these two forms of compensation, there will be differences in the way they are administered.

Some of the more important differences resulting from the one-time character of incentive payments are the following:

1. Incentive payments will tend to reflect company and individual performance in the year just ended; while salary payments, since they are the cumulative result of successive salary reviews, will reflect performance over a longer period of time.
2. Incentive payments can be used with more flexibility than salary adjustments to reward outstanding performance. This is primarily because the company can grant an unusually large incentive award in one year without committing itself to higher compensation costs in future years.
3. Incentive payments can be used to penalize as well as to reward. While salaries customarily move upward only, incentive awards may be reduced from one year to the next either because of lower company profits or because of poorer individual performance.

The second major distinction between incentive payments and salary adjustments lies in the relationship to company profits. Salaries are related to company profits only remotely. With incentive payments there is a direct, immediate relationship. This relationship has been established to motivate all Penney associates who influence company profits significantly to make a maximum contribution toward this key objective.

The greater an individual's opportunity to influence company profits, the more logical it is that he should have an important stake in those profits. Hence the proportion of total compensation paid in the form of incentive award, rather than salary, will be greatest for those associates with greatest degree of responsibility for company profits. Consequently, changes in company profits will have a more pronounced effect on the total compensation of higher level executives than on the compensation of those at lower levels.

It has been traditional in the Penney Company to place heavy emphasis on relating individual compensation to profits—store profits in the case of store management, and company profits in the case of general management. The salary portion of total compensation traditionally has been relatively modest. Despite the rise in salary levels under the new salary plan, the spirit of this tradition will be continued in order to maintain management incentive to build profits. Consequently, salaries, particularly for higher level positions, will be lower than salaries paid by other companies for comparable positions, and incentive award (at least in reasonably good profit years) will be larger than those paid by other companies.

ELIGIBILITY FOR PARTICIPATION

Eligibility for the management incentive plan is limited to those associates whose responsibilities are such that they make a significant impact on company profits, either long term or short term or both. Eligibility shall be determined by analysis of each Penney associate's opportunity to contribute to profits. Since position grades in the salary structure reflect the relative worth of positions, they serve as a useful point of departure for determining eligibility. However, they shall not be applied automatically but shall be used as a general guide.

Eligibility shall begin at a lower level in the salary structure for zone and district positions than for general office positions. The reason is that transfers between zone and district positions and store positions can be made more easily if the compensation patterns for these two groups are compatible. Incentive payments for store personnel begin at a relatively low total compensation level (and rightly so, because these incentive payments are based on profits or sales at the store level); whereas incentive payments for general office personnel are applied only to those at higher compensation levels with an opportunity to influence company profits (because these incentive payments are related to company profits). Thus, if zone and district eligibility did not begin well below the compensation level required among the general office group, transfers between store positions and zone and district positions would require unusually large salary adjustments.

To determine eligibility, the following ground rules shall be applied in each area of operations.

For the general office, the plan shall include all associates who are classified in grade 10 and above, plus selected associates whose positions are in grade 9. Corporate department heads shall review the performance of associates in grade 9 annually and nominate for eligibility in the coming year those whose performance is considered superior. These nominations shall be subject to review and approval by the Pay Administration Committee.

For zone and district positions, the plan shall include all associates who are classified in grade 7 and above, plus selected associates from grade 6. Zone managers shall review performance of associates in grade 6 annually and nominate for eligibility in the coming year those whose performance is considered superior. These nominations shall be subject to review and approval by the director of store operations and the Pay Administration Committee.

From time to time, the board of directors may wish to grant special awards for outstanding accomplishments to associates who are not eligible for regular incentive payments. Such special awards shall not be taken from the management incentive fund.

THE INCENTIVE FUND

In order to relate incentive awards to company profits, all awards shall be paid from a fund generated by company profits. The amount of this incentive fund for any year shall be determined by the following formula: 5 percent of net profits before deducting federal taxes and before deducting the incentive fund itself, but after deducting 10 percent of invested capital (total shareholders' equity plus any long-term debt).

For example, using the appropriate figures for 1960, the incentive fund calculation would be:

Net profits before deducting federal taxes and incentive fund.	$97,425,000
10 percent of invested capital (shareholders' equity only, since there was no long-term debt).	− 30,825,000
	$66,600,000
	× 5%
Incentive fund.	$ 3,330,000

If we assume that net profits before deducting federal taxes and the incentive fund increase to $110,000,000 and that invested capital increases to $400,000,000, the calculations would be:

Net profits before deducting federal taxes and incentive fund.	$110,000,000
10 percent of invested capital.	− 40,000,000
	$ 70,000,000
	× 5%
Incentive fund.	$ 3,500,000

Thus, when company profits increase by more than 10 percent of any additional invested capital, the fund will increase; when company profits do not increase as much as 10 percent of added invested capital, the fund will decrease.

The provison for a deduction or "set-aside" of 10 percent of invested capital accomplishes two purposes:

1. It ensures that the fund will increase only if the company earns at least a reasonably good return on any increased capital investment. (A 10 percent before-tax return can be considered "reasonably good" in today's investment market.) It thus helps focus attention on protection of the shareholders' interests.
2. It maximizes the impact of profit on the fund, hence emphasizes the need for building profits.

In order to ensure that individual incentive payments are directly related to company profit performance, substantially all of the fund generated in one year shall be distributed at the close of that year. No reserve shall be established to even out the effect of good and poor profit years, nor shall any ceiling be established on the size of the fund. (However, company directors have the authority to reduce an unreasonably large fund.)

Although care has been taken to develop an incentive fund formula that minimizes the need for future change, it is possible that unforeseen changes in conditions will necessitate such a change. It shall be the responsibility of the

Board Management Compensation Committee to review the fund formula annually, with the assistance of the comptroller and manager of pay administration, and to decide on any changes that are needed.

DISTRIBUTION OF THE INCENTIVE FUND

The intent in distributing the incentive fund is to provide appropriate recognition for both individual and group performance. Group performance at the over-all company level is recognized by the fact that the size of the fund itself depends on company profit performance. Group performance at the general office and zone levels is recognized by allocating the fund among general office departments and the zones (including districts) on a basis that takes the performance of each group into account. Individual performance is recognized by determining the portion of the department or zone allocation to be awarded to plan participants on the basis of their individual performance.

Chapter 10

Subjective Performance Evaluation and Merit Pay

The Harper

According to one version of Aesop's fables, a man who used to play upon the harp, and sing to it, in little alehouses, and made a shift in those narrow confined walls to please the dull sots who heard him, from hence entertained an ambition of shewing his parts on the public theatre, where he fancied he could not fail of raising a great reputation and fortune in a very short time. He was accordingly admitted upon trial; but the spaciousness of the place, and the throng of the people, so deadened and weakened both his voice and instrument, that scarcely either of them could be heard, and where they could, his performance sounded so poor, so low, and wretched, in the ears of his refined audience, that he was universally hissed off the stage.

Moral: As beauty is in the eyes of the beholder, so too is a performance evaluation in the eyes of the rater.

Although the last chapter dealt with performance-based pay systems, relatively little mention was made of the performance measurement techniques involved. Objective performance data lends itself readily to objective counting and verification procedures. A punch press operator who works all day to produce 3,000 widgets can readily verify this number if desired. This objective evaluation system, in turn, is the foundation for pay systems heavily dependent on output. The sophisticated linkages between pay and output (e.g., variable levels, timing, and even forms of pay) are possible only because output measurement is so free from distortion.

This chapter deals with an entirely different set of circumstances. In the majority of jobs, objective performance standards are not feasible. Either job output is not readily quantifiable or the components that are quantifiable do not reflect important job dimensions. A secretarial job could be reduced to words per minute and errors per page of typing. But many secretaries, and their supervisors, would argue this captures only a small portion of the job. Courtesy in greeting clients and in answering phones, initiative in solving problems without running to the boss, dependability under deadlines—all of these intangible qualities can make the difference between a good and a poor secretary.

How, then, should performance be measured when the data are so elusive? What does a unit of courtesy or initiative look like? Such subjective concepts require subjective judgments for performance evaluation. This chapter deals with the continuing efforts to find evaluation formats and strategies to reduce this subjectivity. The ultimate goal, as yet not achieved, is to find ways to evaluate performance that are perceived as fair and accurately reflecting work output. Until this is accomplished, though, employees quite naturally will be reluctant to have pay systems finely tuned to "measured" variations in performance. As a consequence, pay systems related to subjective performance evaluation ought to reflect only gross changes in output.

EXHIBIT 10.1
Standards of Comparison Used in Different Rating Formats

	Relative Comparison against:	*Absolute Comparison against:*		
	Performance of Other Employees	*Adjective Descriptors*	*Expected Job Behaviors*	*Expected Job Outcomes*
Type of Format	1. Ranking	2. Adjective checklist 3. Standard rating scale	4. Behaviorally anchored rating scale (BARS)	5. Management by objectives (MBO)
	--- 6. Essay ---			

Unfortunately, organizations operate as if their appraisal systems are more accurate than they actually are.[1] Quite naturally, then, employees feel inequitably treated. One poll, in fact, found 30 percent of employees believed their performance appraisals were ineffective. This credibility gap and the growing general concern about errors in appraisal have spurred research to improve accuracy in appraisal. Early research along these lines centered on identifying appraisal formats that would improve the accuracy of rater efforts. More recent attention has focused on the raters themselves, attempting to identify how raters process information used to derive appraisal ratings. Knowing how raters process information, including how irrelevant information plays a role in the evaluation of employees, may permit more effective training programs designed to show raters appropriate procedures. The first two sections of this book deal with these two research directions and the useful information they have uncovered.

PERFORMANCE EVALUATION FORMATS

Exhibit 10.1 illustrates six types of evaluation formats falling into two general categories.[2] By themselves in one category are all evaluation methods involving some ranking procedure to compare employees with each other. All other procedures compare performance data against one of three absolute standards: adjectives, behaviors, and outcomes. Finally, an essay format, because of the wide discretion allowed a rater in completing an evaluation, could involve any of the above formats.

---

[1] N. B. Winstanley, "How Accurate Are Performance Appraisals?" *Personnel Administrator* 25 (August 1980), pp. 41–44.

[2] Larry L. Cummings and Donald P. Schwab, *Performance in Organizations* (Glenview, Ill.: Scott, Foresman, 1973).

Ranking Procedures

Employees are compared against each other in terms of the overall value of their performance to the organization. There are a number of ways these rankings can be obtained.

First is a straight ranking procedure. The highest performer is identified and successive individuals are ordered by level of overall performance. A second strategy involves alternate ranking. The top and bottom performances in the unit are identified and removed from the list. From the remaining list, then, the next best and worst performers are selected. This process continues until all employees have been ranked. Third, on a paired comparison procedure each employee is compared (paired) with every other employee. One's ranking depends on the number of total times an employee is ranked higher in performance than the other employee in each pair.

Finally, forced distribution ranking literally forces evaluators to distribute rankings according to some predetermined distribution. A typical procedure would be to approximate a normal distribution:

Number of Employees	Lowest 10%	Next 20%	Middle 40%	Next 20%	Highest 10%
40	4	8	16	8	4

Adjective Checklists

For an adjective checklist, raters must check the descriptors that most reflect an employee's performance. Each descriptor previously has been evaluated to determine how favorable or unfavorable it is for successful job performance (e.g., aloof, demanding, temperamental).[3] A variant on this format also attempts to equate checklist items for social desirability (perceived positive or negative connotations generally attached to a word). For whichever format is used, though, the overall performance score is the sum of scores on each of the items checked.

Standard Rating Scales

All of the variants on rating scales share two underlying commonalities. First, one or more performance standards are developed and each is defined for the appraiser. Second, each performance standard has a measurement scale attached to it, indicating varying levels of performance on that dimension. Appraisers rate appraisees by checking the point on the scale that best represents the appraisee's performance level. Variations on the rating scale format occur in the extent to which points or anchors along the scale are defined. For example, Exhibit 10.2 compares two different anchoring methods.

---

[3]Frank Barron, "Complexity-Simplicity as a Personality Variable," in *Problems in Human Assessment,* eds. Douglas Jackson and Samuel Messick (New York: McGraw-Hill, 1967).

EXHIBIT 10.2
Methods of Anchoring Rating Scales

Single Word Anchor Scale

Performance dimension	(1)	(2)	(3)	(4)	(5)
Leadership ability	Well above average.	Above average.	Average.	Below average.	Well below average.

Short Phrase Anchor Scale

Performance dimension	(1)	(2)	(3)	(4)	(5)
Job knowledge	Is extremely well informed about all facets of job.	Is well informed on important dimensions of job.	Has sufficient knowledge of job dimensions to perform job adequately.	Lacks necessary information about job dimensions.	Is misinformed or lacks knowledge on important job dimensions.

Employees are assigned a scale level reflecting their performance on each dimension. Overall performance is some weighted average (weighted by the importance the organization attaches to each dimension) of the ratings on all dimensions. Appendix A at the end of this chapter gives examples of standard rating scales and the total appraisal form for some well-known organizations.

Behaviorally Anchored Rating Scales

Behaviorally anchored rating scales (BARS) are a variant on standard rating scales in which the various scale levels are anchored with behavioral descriptions directly applicable to jobs being evaluated (Exhibit 10.3). By anchoring scales with concrete behaviors, firms adopting a BARS format hope to make evaluations less subjective. The six steps in developing a behaviorally anchored rating scale are listed in Exhibit 10.4.

Management by Objectives (MBO)

There is a major obstacle to defining MBO. As has been noted elsewhere: "MBO, like ice cream, comes in 29 flavors."[4] Since this comment was written, both the number of ice cream flavors and the number of different approaches to MBO have increased. Despite this confusion, a working definition can be de-

---

[4]J. S. Hodgson, "Management by Objectives: The Experiences of a Federal Government Department," *Canadian Public Administration* 16, no. 4 (1973), pp. 422–31.

EXHIBIT 10.3
Behaviorally Anchored Rating Scale: Resident Adviser, University Housing

Performance Dimension
> Concern for individual dorm residents: Attempts to get to know individual dorm residents and responds to their individual needs with genuine interest. This resident adviser could be expected to:

Rating Scale

(1)	(2)	(3)	(4)	(5)
Recognize when a floor member appears depressed and ask if person has problem he/she wants to discuss.	Offer floor members "tips" on how to study for a course he/she has already taken.	See person and recognize him/her as a floor member and say "hi."	Be friendly with a floor member; get into discussion on problems, but fail to follow up on the problem later on with student.	Criticize a floor member for not being able to solve his/her own problems.

EXHIBIT 10.4
Procedures in Developing a Behaviorally Anchored Rating Scale

1. Supervisors of a group of employees, performing similar jobs, are asked to identify those broad sets of job activities that comprise the job. For programmer analysts, examples of such "performance dimensions" might be coding and documentation.
2. The same supervisors generate a set of critical incidents (behaviors they have seen performed by subordinates) that represent actual examples of very good and very poor subordinate performance on each of the dimensions.
3. Each member of a second, independent group of supervisors then is instructed to categorize each incident into the performance dimension most appropriate. If there is not high agreement among the supervisors (e.g., 70 percent) about which category an incident belongs in, the incident is deleted as being too ambiguous.
4. For each remaining incident the same group of supervisors rates the incident on a "good-bad" continuum, typically using a 1 to 5 scale. Items with high disagreement between supervisors (e.g., standard deviations greater than 1.0) are also discarded as being to ambiguous.
5. The remaining incidents may be used to anchor the various scale points on a numerical scale for each performance dimension. For example, an incident with a mean rating (from the second supervisory group) of 2.5 would be used as an anchor one half of the way between the scale values of 2 and 3. Presumably these anchors allow supervisors to compare their employees against a common set of standards, thereby reducing error.
6. The resultant set of performance dimensions, each with a set of ordered and scaled incidents, is referred to as BARS.

---

veloped. (Components of successful MBO programs are illustrated in Exhibit 10.5). MBO is both a planning and appraisal process. Organization goals or plans are identified and each successive organizational hierarchy is charged with identifying work objectives that will support attainment of organizational goals. This identification of work objectives is a participatory process requiring discussion between both supervisor and subordinate in identifying appropriate

EXHIBIT 10.5
Components of a Successful MBO Program

	Total Number of Responses*	Percentage of Authorities in Agreement
1. Goals and objectives should be specific.	37	97
2. Goals and objectives should be defined in terms of measurable results.	37	97
3. Individual goals should be linked to overall organization goals.	37	97
4. Objectives should be reviewed "periodically."	31	82
5. The time period for goal accomplishment should be specified.	27	71
6. Wherever possible, the indicator of the results should be quantifiable; otherwise, it should be at least verifiable.	26	68
7. Objectives should be flexible; changed as conditions warrant.	26	68
8. Objectives should include a plan of action for accomplishing the results.	21	55
9. Objectives should be assigned priorities of weights.	19	50

*In this table the total number of responses actually represents the total number of authorities responding; thus, the percentages also represent the percent of authorities in agreement with the statements made.

Source: Mark L. McConkie, "A Clarification of the Goal Setting and Appraisal Process in MBO," *Academy of Management Review* 4, no. 1 (1979), pp. 29–40. © 1979, Academy of Management Review.

goals.[5] Once goals have been mutually determined, they become the standards against which employee performance is evaluated. Level of performance evaluation is directly equated with degree of goal accomplishment. The final evaluation (overall rating) is expressed numerically and represents a subjective estimate of both goal difficulty and degree of attainment (e.g., hard goals which are completely achieved should result in an overall rating of five on a scale with five as the maximum).

Essays

Using an open-ended format, the appraiser is asked to write an essay descriptive of employee performance. Since the descriptors used could range from comparisons with other employees through adjectives, behaviors, and goal accomplishments, the essay format can take on characteristics of all the formats discussed previously.

---

[5]Mark L. McConkie, "A Clarification of the Goal Setting and Appraisal Processes in MBO," *Academy of Management Review* 4, no. 1 (1979), pp. 29–40.

EVALUATING PERFORMANCE APPRAISAL FORMATS

A review of the literature indicates five dimensions against which different appraisal formats can be compared: (1) employee development potential, (2) administrative ease, (3) personnel research potential, (4) cost, and (5) validity. Admittedly, different organizations will attach different weights to these dimensions. For example, a small organization in its formative years is likely to be very cost conscious. A larger organization with more pressing affirmative action commitments might place relatively high weight on validity and nondiscrimination criteria and show less concern about cost issues. A progressive firm concerned with employee development will demand a format allowing rich employee feedback. Less enlightened organizations may be concerned solely with costs. The dimensions for evaluating appraisal include the following five.[6]

Employee Development Criteria

Does the method communicate the goals and objectives of the organization? Is feedback to employees a natural outgrowth of the evaluation format, such that employee developmental needs are identified and can be attended to readily?

Administrative Criteria

How easily can evaluation results be used for administrative decisions concerning wage increases, promotions, demotions, terminations, and transfers? Comparisons among individuals for personnel action require some common denominator for comparison. Typically this is a numerical rating of performance. Evaluation forms that do not produce numerical ratings cause administrative headaches.

Personnel Research

Does the instrument lend itself well for validating employment tests? Applicants predicted to perform well can be monitored through performance evaluation. Similarly, the success of various employee and organizational development programs can be traced to impacts on employee performance. As with the administrative criteria, though, evaluations typically need to be quantitative to permit the statistical tests so common in personnel research.

---

[6]Bruce McAfee and Blake Green, "Selecting a Performance Appraisal Method," *Personnel Administrator* 22, no. 5 (1977), pp. 61–65.

EXHIBIT 10.6
True Rating Errors: An Illustration and Definition

	(1)	(2)	(3)	(4)

```
        High
        P │ Al          P │ Al        P │          P │
        e │             e │ Sue       e │          e │
        r │             r │ Bill      r │          r │
    T   f │         R   f │        R   f │      R   f │
    r   o │         a   o │        a   o │      a   o │ Al
    u   r │ Sue     t   r │        t   r │      t   r │ Sue
    e   m │         e   m │        e   m │      e   m │ Bill
        a │         d   a │        d   a │      d   a │
        n │             n │            n │ Al       n │
        c │             c │            c │ Sue      c │
        e Low│ Bill     e │            e │ Bill     e │

                     Leniency       Severity      Central
                     error          error         tendency
                                                  error
```

Error

Leniency—Rated performance consistently exceeds true score performance of ratees.
Severity—Rated performance consistently lower than true score performance of ratees.
Central tendency—Rated performance falls in middle of rating scale, irrespective of true score performance of ratees.
Halo—Rating on one performance dimension strongly influences (i.e., highly correlated with) rating on other performance dimensions, irrespective of true score relationship across dimensions.

Economic Criteria

Does the evaluation form require a long time to develop initially? Is it time-consuming for supervisors to use in rating their employees? Is it expensive to use? All of these factors increase the format cost.

Validity

By far the most research on formats in recent years has focused on reducing error and improving accuracy. Success in this pursuit would mean decisions based on performance ratings (e.g., promotions and merit increases could be made with greater confidence). In general, the search for the "perfect format" to eliminate rating errors (see Exhibit 10.6 for definitions and examples of true rating errors) and improve accuracy has been unsuccessful. The high acclaim, for example, accompanying introduction of BARS has not been supported by research.[7] Exhibit 10.7 provides a relative comparison among the six rating for-

---

[7]H. John Bernardin, "Behavioral Expectation Scales v. Summated Ratings: A Fairer Comparison," *Journal of Applied Psychology* 62 (1977), pp. 422–27; H. John Bernardin, Kim Alvares, and C. J. Cranny, "A Re-comparison of Behavioral Expectation Scales to Summated Scales," *Journal*-

EXHIBIT 10.7
An Evaluation of Performance Appraisal Formats

	Employee Development Criteria	Administrative Criteria	Personnel Research	Economic Criteria	Validity
Ranking	Poor—ranks typically based on overall performance, with little thought given to feedback on specific performance dimensions.	Poor—comparisons of ranks across work units to determine merit raises are meaningless. Other administrative actions similarly hindered.	Average—validation studies can be completed with rankings of performance.	Good—inexpensive source of performance data. Easy to develop and use in small organizations and in small units.	Average—good reliability but poor on rating errors, especially halo.
Adjective checklist	Average—general problem areas identified for employee, but little information on extent of problem or behaviors/outcomes necessary to change evaluation.	Average—adjective rankings can be tallied for merit decisions.	Good—checklists equated for social desirability may yield relatively uncontaminated performance data.	Average—expensive to develop.	Good—usually good content validity and equating items for social desirability will reduce rating errors.
Standard rating scales	Average—general problem areas identified. Some information on extent of developmental need is available, but no feedback on necessary behaviors/outcomes.	Average—ratings valuable for merit increase decisions and others. Not easily defended if contested.	Average—validation studies can be completed, but level of measurement contamination unknown.	Good—inexpensive to develop and easy to use.	Average—content validity is suspect. Rating errors and reliability are average.
Behaviorally anchored rating scales	Good—extent of problem and behavioral needs are identified.	Good—BARS good for making administrative decisions. Useful for defense if contested because job-relevant.	Good—validation studies can be completed and measurement problems on BARS less than many other criterion measures.	Average—expensive to develop but easy to use.	Good—high content validity. Some evidence of inter-rater reliability and reduced rating errors.
Management by objectives	Excellent—extent of problem and outcome deficiencies are identified.	Poor—MBO not suited to merit income decisions. Level of completion and difficulty of objectives hard to compare across employees.	Poor—nonstandard objectives across employees and no overall measures of performance make validity studies difficult.	Poor—expensive to develop and time consuming to use.	Excellent—high content validity. Low rating errors.
Essay	Unknown—depends on guidelines for inclusions in essay as developed by organization or supervisors.	Poor—essays not comparable across different employees considered for merit or other administrative actions.	Poor—no quantitative indices to compare performance against employment test scores in validation studies.	Average—easy to develop but time consuming to use.	Unknown—unstructured format makes studies of essay method difficult.

mats in terms of their performance on the five dimensions for evaluating appraisal formats.

HOW RATERS PROCESS INFORMATION

This decade has witnessed an explosion of research on how people process information to arrive at, among other things, final performance ratings. Many experts believe this is a potentially more fruitful research direction to help improve performance rating than are previous efforts to improve rating formats.[8] Already this research has yielded models of how people review information and make judgments. Combine this with systematic research testing parts of these models and there is quickly developing a body of information on how to improve the rating process.

Models of the Appraisal Process

Cognitive models tend to outline the performance appraisal process in similar ways. Raters go through stages, some of them quite unconscious, when they attempt to rate the performance of other employees. First, the rater observes the behavior of a ratee. Second, this behavior is encoded as part of a total picture of the ratee (e.g., one way of saying this is that we form stereotypes about people). Third, we store this information in memory, which is subject to both short- and long-term decay. Simply put, we forget things! Fourth, when it comes time to evaluate a ratee, the rater reviews the performance dimensions and retrieves stored observations/impressions to determine their relevance to the performance dimensions. Finally, the information is reconsidered and integrated with other available information as the rater makes the final ratings.[9]

Quite unintentionally, when people process this information, errors occur: behavior is observed incorrectly; impressions are formed which are incorrect stereotypes of employees; when information is stored some of it is forgotten; recall is influenced by extraneous factors. At virtually every stage raters can make errors that result in evaluations which are not an accurate reflection of employee performance. Fortunately, some high-quality research has allowed us

---

of Applied Psychology 61 (1976), pp. 284–91; C. A. Schriesheim and U. E. Gattiker, "A Study of the Abstract Desirability of Behavior-Based v. Trait-Oriented Performance Rating," *Proceedings of the Academy of Management* 43 (1982), pp. 307–11; F. S. Landy and J. L. Farr, "Performance Rating," *Psychological Bulletin* 87 (1980), pp. 72–107.

[8]Landy and Farr, "Performance Rating."

[9]Landy and Farr, "Performance Rating"; A. S. Denisi, T. P. Cafferty, and B. M. Meglino, "A Cognitive View of the Performance Appraisal Process: A Model and Research Propositions,"*Organizational Behavior and Human Performance* 33 (1984), pp. 360–96; Jack M. Feldman, "Beyond Attribution Theory: Cognitive Processes in Performance Appraisal," *Journal of Applied Psychology* 66, no. 2 (1981), pp. 127–48; W. H. Cooper, "Ubiquitous Halo," *Psychological Bulletin* 90 (1981), pp. 218–44.

to identify, and thus try to correct, some of the errors made in rating other employees.

Errors in the Rating Process

Ideally, raters should attend exclusively to performance-rated factors when they observe employee behavior. In fact all of the processing stages should be guided by *performance relevancy*. Unless a behavior (or personality trait) affects performance it should not influence performance ratings! Fortunately, performance actually does play an important role, perhaps the major role, in determining what rating an employee receives.[10] On the negative side, though, are many other factors which should not be considered in the rating process but which appear to influence ratings (i.e., they cause errors in the evaluation process).[11]

Errors in observation (attention). Generally, researchers have varied three types of input information to see how raters observe and what they attend to. The first set of data manipulated are characteristics of the ratees themselves. Reasonably consistent information indicates that males are rated higher than females (other things equal) and that the rating of blacks and whites depends on the race of the rater (same race, higher ratings).[12]

Researchers also vary characteristics of the input data to see if this influences performance ratings. Both the pattern of performance (performance gets

[10]Leo Leventhal, Raymon Perry, and Philip Abrami, "Effects of Lecturer Quality and Student Perception of Lecturer Experience on Teacher Ratings and Student Achievement," *Journal of Educational Psychology* 69, no. 4 (1977), pp. 360–74; Angelo Denisi and George Stevens, "Profiles of Performance, Performance Evaluations, and Personnel Decisions," *Academy of Management* 24, no. 3 (1981), pp. 592–602; Wayne Cascio and Enzo Valenzi, "Relations among Criteria of Police Performance," *Journal of Applied Psychology* 63, no. 1 (1978), pp. 22–28; William Bigoness, "Effects of Applicant's Sex, Race, and Performance on Employer Performance Ratings: Some Additional Findings," *Journal of Applied Psychology* 6l, no. 1 (1976), pp. 80–84; Dorothy P. Moare, "Evaluating In-Role and Out-of-Role Performers," *Academy of Management Journal* 27, no. 3 (1984), pp. 603–18.

[11]H. J. Bernardin and Richard Beatty, *Performance Appraisal: Assessing Human Behavior at Work* (Boston: Kent Publishing, 1984).

[12]Edward Shaw, "Differential Impact of Negative Stereotyping in Employee Selection," *Personnel Psychology* 25 (1972), pp. 333–38; Benson Rosen and Thomas Jerdee, "Effects of Applicant's Sex and Difficulty of Job on Evaluations of Candidates for Managerial Positions," *Journal of Applied Psychology* 59 (1975), pp. 511–12; Gail Pheterson, Sara Kiesler, and Philip Goldberg, "Evaluation of the Performance of Women as a Function of their Sex, Achievement, and Personal History," *Journal of Personality and Social Psychology* 19 (1971), pp. 114–18; W. Clay Hamner, Jay Kim, Lloyd Baird, and William Bigoness, "Race and Sex as Determinants of Ratings by Potential Employers in a Simulated Work Sampling Task," *Journal of Applied Psychology* 59, no. 6 (1974), pp. 705–11; and Neal Schmitt and Martha Lappin, "Race and Sex as Determinants of the Mean and Variance of Performance Ratings," *Journal of Applied Psychology* 65, no. 4 (1980), pp. 428–35.

better or worse over time) and the variability of performance (consistent versus erratic) influence performance ratings, even when the level of performance is controlled.[13] Not surprisingly, workers with an ascending pattern of performance are seen as more motivated, while those who are more variable in their performance are tagged as lower in motivation. All of us have seen examples of workers (and students) who intuitively recognize this type of error and try to use it to their advantage. The big surge of work at the end of an appraisal period is often designed to "color" a rater's perceptions.

Errors in storage and recall. Research suggests that raters store information in the form of trait-based schemata.[14] More importantly, perhaps, people tend to recall information in the form of schemata or trait categories also. For example, a rater observes a specific behavior (i.e., an employee resting during what are obviously work hours). The rater stores this information not as the specific behavior, but rather in the form of a trait, such as "that worker is lazy." Specific instructions to recall information about the ratee, as for a performance review, elicit the trait—lazy. Evidence indicates that in the process of forming impressions or making predictions about others, people organize behavioral information into trait categories.[15] Further, in the process of recalling information, rater recall may be colored by, or consistent with, the schema (or trait categorization or implicit personality theory) but inconsistent with actual events.[16] The entire rating process, then, may be heavily influenced by these cognitive schema which we adopt; and the schema may or may not be accurate! One of the most obvious examples of this processing error is evident in sex ste-

[13]Denisi and Stevens, "Profiles of Performance, Performance Evaluations, and Personnel Decisions"; William Scott and Clay Hamner, "The Influence of Variations in Performance Profiles on the Performance Evaluation Process: An Examination of the Validity of the Criterion," *Organizational Behavior and Human Performance* 14 (1975), pp. 360–70; Edward Jones, Leslie Rock, Kelly Shaver, George Goethals, and Laurence Ward, "Pattern of Performance and Ability Attributions: An Unexpected Primacy Effect," *Journal of Personality and Social Psychology* 10, no. 4 (1968), pp. 317–40.

[14]Landy and Farr, "Performance Rating"; Bernardin and Beatty, *Performance Appraisal: Assessing Human Behavior at Work.*

[15]K. M. Jeffrey and W. Mischel, "Effects of Purpose on the Organization and Recall of Information in Person Perception," *Journal of Personality* 47 (1979), pp. 297–419; C. Hoffman, W. Mischel, and K. Masse, "The Role of Purpose in the Organization of Information about Behavior: Trait-Based v. Goal-Based Categories in Person Cognition," *Journal of Personality and Social Psychology* 4 (1981), pp. 211–25.

[16]N. Cantor and W. Mischel, "Traits v. Prototypes: The Effects on Recognition and Memory," *Journal of Personality and Social Psychology* 35 (1977), pp. 38–48; R. J. Spiro, "Remembering Information from Text: the 'State of Schema' Approach," in *Schooling and the Acquisition of Knowledge,* ed. R. C. Anderson, R. J. Spiro, and W. E. Montague (Hillsdale, Calif.: Erlbaum Assoc., 1977); T. K. Srull and R. S. Wyer, "Category Accessibility and Social Perception: Some Implications for the Study of Person Memory and Interpersonal Judgments," *Journal of Personality and Social Psychology* 38 (1980), pp. 841–56.

reotyping. A female ratee is observed, not as a ratee, but as a female ratee. A rater may form impressions based on stereotypic beliefs about women rather than the reality of the work situation. Performance ratings are then influenced by the gender of the ratee, quite apart from any performance information.

Errors in storage and recall also appear to arise from memory decay. At least one study indicates that rating accuracy is a function of the delay between performance and subsequent rating. The longer the delay, the less accurate the ratings.[17]

Errors in evaluation. The context of the actual evaluation process also can influence evaluations.[18] Several researchers indicate that the purpose of evaluation affects the rating process. Supervisors who know ratings will be used to determine merit increases are less likely to discriminate among subordinates than when the ratings will be used for other purposes.[19] Being required to provide feedback to subordinates about their ratings also yields less accuracy than does a secrecy policy.[20] Presumably anticipation of an unpleasant confrontation with the angry ratee "persuades" the rater to avoid confrontation. How? By giving ratings which are higher than justified.

IMPROVING EVALUATIONS

Raters are capable of making errors in all the stages of information processing which characterize the rating process. Thus far this chapter has been quite pessimistic about the potential to correct this situation. This section identifies what is known about improving evaluation—the so-called tips to a better appraisal.

Format Selection

Historically, the selection of a performance appraisal has been guided primarily by fads and fashions. Organizations have been disposed to jump on the proverbial "bandwagon" by adopting the latest "in" format. Little consideration is given to the organization's needs, employee needs, or the types of jobs being evaluated. These factors are vital in the strategic selection of a performance appraisal format. And, because these factors vary across organizations and within

[17]Robert Heneman and Kenneth Wexley, "The Effects of Time Delay in Rating and Amount of Information Observed on Performance Rating Accuracy," *Academy of Management Journal* 26, no. 4 (1983), pp. 677–86.

[18]Robert Liden and Terence Mitchell, "The Effects of Group Interdependence on Supervisor Performance Evaluations," *Personnel Psychology* 36, no. 2 (1983), pp. 289–99.

[19]Winstanley, "How Accurate Are Performance Appraisals?"; Landy and Farr, "Performance Rating"; Heneman and Wexley, "The Effects of Time Delay in Rating and Amount of Information Observed on Performance Rating Accuracy."

[20]Cummings and Schwab, *Performance in Organizations*.

organizations, across jobs and individuals, a contingency approach to format selection may be the most appropriate strategy. The argument is made that no single evaluation format may be entirely appropriate across all jobs and individuals in an organization. It may be appropriate to adopt different appraisal formats for different situations. Advocates of this contingency approach argue that the nature of the task and/or past performance of the individual may warrant an array of formats rather than a single format.

Keeley suggests that the choice of an appraisal format is dependent on the type of tasks being performed.[21] He argues that tasks can be ordered along a continuum from those that are very routine in nature to those for which the appropriate behavior for goal accomplishment is very uncertain. In Keeley's view, different appraisal formats require assumptions about the extent to which correct behavior for task accomplishment can be specified. The choice of an appraisal format requires a matching of formats with tasks that meet the assumptions for that format. At one extreme of the continuum are behavior-based evaluation procedures that define specific performance expectations against which employee performance is evaluated. Keeley argues behaviorally anchored rating scales fall into this category. The behavioral anchors define specific performance expectations representing different levels of performance possible by an employee. Only for highly routine, mechanistic tasks is it appropriate to specify behavioral expectations. For these routine tasks it is possible to identify the single sequence of appropriate behaviors to accomplish a goal. Consequently it is possible to identify behavioral anchors for a performance scale that illustrate varying levels of attainment of the proper sequence of activities.

However, when tasks become less routine, it becomes more difficult to specify a single sequence of procedures that must be followed to accomplish a goal. Rather, multiple strategies are both feasible and appropriate to reach a final goal. Under these circumstances, Keeley argues the appraisal format should focus on evaluating the extent to which the final goal is accomplished.[22] Thus, for less certain tasks a management by objective (MBO) strategy would be appropriate. As long as the final goal can be specified, performance can be evaluated in relation to that goal without specifying or evaluating the behavior used to reach that goal. The focus is exclusively on the degree of goal accomplishment.

At the other extreme of the continuum are tasks that are highly uncertain in nature. A relatively low consensus exists about the characteristics of successful performance. Moreover, the nature of the task is so uncertain it may be difficult to specify expected goals. For this type of task, Keeley argues that judgment-based evaluation procedures are most appropriate. Subjective estimates are made by raters about the levels of employee performance on tasks for

---

[21]Michael Keeley, "A Contingency Framework for Performance Evaluation," *Academy of Management Review* 3 (July 1978), pp. 428–38.

[22]Ibid.

which neither the appropriate behavior nor the final goal are well specified. The extent of this uncertainty makes this type of appraisal very subjective, and may well explain why trait-rating scales are openly criticized for the number of errors that result in performance evaluation.

A second contingency approach advocated by Cummings and Schwab combines both a task dimension and an evaluation of past employee performance in determining the appropriate appraisal format.[23] Unlike Keeley's approach, however, the appropriate format is determined by past employee performance and not task specificity. Cummings and Schwab argue that the type of tasks assigned to an individual should be a function of past performance. High performers are given tasks that have relatively uncertain behavioral requirements and perhaps even uncertain goal specification. Presumably this is both a reward to the employee and an affirmation by the supervisor that performance need not be monitored as closely. In contrast, average and below average performers are assigned to tasks that are increasingly more specified in terms of behavioral requirements. In turn, the level of task specificity defines the appropriate evaluation format. Exhibit 10.8 outlines the various approaches recommended by Cummings and Schwab and the evaluation formats they feel are appropriate for each.

Training Raters

Although there is some evidence that training is not effective[24] or is less important in reducing errors than other factors,[25] the majority of findings are quite supportive of training raters as an effective method to reduce appraisal errors.[26] Rater training programs can be divided into three distinct categories:[27]

1. Rater error training, in which the goal is to reduce psychometric errors (i.e., leniency, severity, central tendency, halo) by familiarizing raters with their existence.

---

[23]Cummings and Schwab, *Performance in Organizations.*

[24]H. J. Bernardin and E. C. Pence, "Effects of Rater Training: Creating New Response Sets and Decreasing Accuracy," *Journal of Applied Psychology* 6 (1980), pp. 60–66.

[25]Sheldon Zedeck and Wayne Cascio, "Performance Appraisal Decision as a Function of Rater Training and Purpose of the Appraisal," *Journal of Applied Psychology* 67, no. 6 (1982), pp. 752–58.

[26]H. J. Bernardin and M. R. Buckley, "Strategies in Rater Training," *Academy of Management Review* 6, no. 2 (1981), pp. 205–12; D. Smith, "Training Programs for Performance Appraisal: A Review," *Academy of Management Review* 11, no. 1 (1986), pp. 22–40; B. Davis and M. Mount, "Effectiveness of Performance Appraisal Training Using Computer Assisted Instruction and Behavioral Modeling," *Personnel Psychology* 3 (1984), pp. 439–52; H. J. Bernardin, "Effects of Rater Training on Leniency and Halo Errors in Student Ratings of Instructors," *Journal of Applied Psychology* 63, no. 3 (1978), pp. 301–8; J. M. Ivancevich, "Longitudinal Study of the Effects of Rater Training on Psychometric Error in Ratings," *Journal of Applied Psychology* 64, no. 5 (1979), pp. 502–8.

[27]Bernardin and Buckley, "Strategies in Rater Training."

EXHIBIT 10.8
A Contingency Evaluation Approach Based on Past Employee Performance

Program	Past Employee Performance	Type of Tasks Assigned to Employee	Appropriate Evaluation Format
Developmental Action Program (DAP)	Consistently high performance in past with demonstrated potential for growth.	Tasks for which there is considerable discretion in way goals are accomplished.	1. MBO. 2. BARS.
Maintenance Action Program (MAP)	1. Average acceptable performance with low potential for growth, or 2. Above average performance working on job with low discretion.	Tasks for which: 1. Clearly defined and communicated goals are established, and 2. The method for carrying out tasks is frequently improved by the technology or the supervisor, and 3. Close direction and frequent evaluation is possible.	1. Conventional trait rating. 2. BARS. 3. Weighted checklist. 4. Forced choice.
Remedial Action Program (RAP)	Employees who are clearly below acceptable performance standards.	Highly structured tasks for which it is possible to: 1. Provide feedback about why performance is inadequate, 2. Provide behavioral critical incidents to point out examples of poor and acceptable performance, 3. Develop a structured program for correction with performance measures and time perspectives clearly explained and frequently reviewed.	1. BARS.

Source: L. L. Cummings and D. P. Schwab, *Performance in Organization* (Glenview, Ill.: Scott, Foresman, 1973). Reprinted with permission.

2. Performance dimension training, with supervisors exposed extensively to the performance dimensions to be used in rating.
3. Performance standard training designed to provide raters with a standard of comparison or frame of reference for making ratee appraisals.

Several generalizations about ways to improve rater training can be summarized from this research. First, lecturing to ratees about ways to improve ratings generally is ineffective. Second, individualized or small group discussion sections are more effective in conveying proper rating procedures. Third, when these sessions are combined with extensive practice and feedback sessions, the rating accuracy is significantly improved. Fourth, longer training programs (more than two hours) generally are more successful than are shorter programs. Fifth, performance dimension training and performance standard training (as explained above) generally work better than rater error training, particularly when the two superior methods are combined. Finally, the greatest success has come from efforts to reduce halo errors and improve accuracy. Leniency errors have proved the most difficult form of error to eliminate. This shouldn't be surprising. Think about the consequences to a supervisor of giving inflated ratings versus accurate or even deflated ratings. The latter two courses are certain to result in more complaints and, possibly, reduced morale. The easy way out is to artificially inflate ratings. Unfortunately, this positive outcome for supervisors may come back to haunt them; with everyone receiving relatively high ratings there is less distinction between truly good and poor performance, and less emphasis on pay for performance.

Eliminating errors in the actual appraisal. Several researchers have indicated that errors can also be prevented in the planning and actual conduct of appraisal interviews.[28] While Exhibit 10.9 provides a detailed discussion of the elements of a good appraisal, the essence can be distilled down to eight requirements:[29]

1. Maintain records of employee performance, both as documentation and to jog the memory.
2. Conduct a performance diagnosis to determine in advance if the problem arises because of motivation, skill deficiency, or external environmental constraints.[30] In turn this tells the supervisor whether the problem requires "motivation-building," training, or efforts to remove external constraints.
3. Participate in appraisal between superior and subordinate—not unilateral "discussion."
4. Promote goal achievement through team effort between supervisor and subordinate.
5. Set goals to focus work efforts and provide a basis for comparison of results versus goals.

---

[28]Bernardin and Buckley, "Strategies in Rater Training"; Winstanley, "How Accurate Are Performance Appraisals?"; Bernardin and Pence, "Effects of Rater Training: Creating New Response Sets and Decreasing Accuracy"; J. M. Ivancevich, "Subordinates' Reactions to Performance Appraisal Interviews: A Test of Feedback and Goal Setting Techniques," *Journal of Applied Psychology* 67 (1982), pp. 581–87; D. Cederblom, "The Performance Appraisal Interview: A Review, Implications and Suggestions," *Academy of Management Review* 7 (1982), pp. 219–27; S. Snell and K. Wexley, "Performance Diagnosis: Identifying the Causes of Poor Performance," *Personnel Administrator,* April 1985, pp. 117–27; J. M. Ivancevich and J. T. McMahon, "The Effects of Goal Setting, External Feedback, and Self-Generated Feedback on Outcome Variables: A Field Experiment," *Academy of Management Journal* 25 (1982), pp. 359–72; A. S. Denisi and W. A. Blencoe, "Level and Source of Feedback and Determinates of Feedback Effectiveness," *Proceedings of Academy of Management* 42 (1982), pp. 175–79.

[29]Winstanley, "How Accurate Are Performance Appraisals?"; Bernardin and Buckley, "Strategies in Rater Training"; Ivancevich, "Subordinates' Reactions to Performance Appraisal Interviews: A Test of Feedback and Goal Setting Techniques"; Cederblom, "The Performance Appraisal Interview: A Review, Implications and Suggestions."

[30]Snell and Wexley, "Performance Diagnosis: Identifying the Causes of Poor Performance."

EXHIBIT 10.9
Tips on Appraising Employee Performance

Preparation for the Performance Interview
1. Keep a weekly log of individual's performance. Why?
    A. It makes the task of writing up the evaluation simpler. The rater does not have to strain to remember six months or a year ago.
    B. It reduces the chances of some rating errors (e.g., recency, halo).
    C. It gives support/backup to the rating.
2. Preparation for the interview should *not* begin a week or two before it takes place. There should be continual feedback to the employee on his/her performance so that (*a*) problems can be corrected before they get out of hand, (*b*) improvements can be made sooner, and (*c*) encouragement and support are ongoing.
3. Allow sufficient time to write up the evaluation. A well-thought-out evaluation will be more objective and equitable. Sufficient time includes (*a*) the actual time necessary to think out and write up the evaluation, (*b*) time away from the evaluation, and (*c*) time to review and possibly revise.
4. Have employees fill out an appraisal form prior to the interview. This prepares employees for what will take place in the interview and allows them to come prepared with future goal suggestions, areas they wish to pursue, and suggestions concerning their jobs or the company.
5. Set up an agreed-upon, convenient time to hold the interview (at least one week in advance). Be sure to pick a nonthreatening day.
6. Be prepared!
    A. Know what you are going to say. Prepare an outline (which includes the evaluation and future goal suggestions).
    B. Decide on developmental opportunities *before* the interview. Be sure you know of possible resources and contacts.
    C. Review performance interview steps.
7. Arrange the room in such a way as to encourage discussion.
    A. Do not have barriers between yourself and the employee (such as a large desk).
    B. Arrange with secretary that there be no phone calls or interruptions.

Performance Appraisal Interview (Steps)
1. Set the subordinate at ease. Begin by stating the purpose of the discussion. Let the individual know that it will be a two-way process. Neither superior nor subordinate should dominate the discussion.
2. Give a general, overall impression of the evaluation.
3. Discuss each dimension separately. Ask the employee to give his/her impression on own performance first. Then explain your position. If there is a problem on some, try *together* to determine the cause. When exploring causes, urge the subordinate to identify three or four causes. Then, jointly determine the most important ones. Identifying causes is important because it points out action plans which might be taken.
4. Together, develop action plans to correct problem areas. These plans will flow naturally from the consideration of the causes. Be specific about the who, what, and when. Be sure to provide for some kind of follow-up or report back.
5. Close the interview on an optimistic note.

Communication Technique Suggesions
1. Do not control the interview—make it two-way. Do this by asking open-ended questions rather than submitting your own solutions. For example, rather than saying, "Jim, I'd like you to do these reports over again," it would be better to say, "Jim, what sort of things might we do here?" Avoid questions that lead to one-word responses.
2. Stress behaviors and results rather than personal traits. Say, "I've noticed that your weekly report has been one to two days late in the last six weeks," rather than, "You tend to be a tardy, lazy person."
3. Show interest and concern. Instead of saying, "Too bad, but we all go through that," say, "I think I know what you're feeling. I remember a similar experience."
4. Allow the subordinate to finish a sentence or thought. This includes being receptive to the subordinate's own ideas and suggestions. For example, rather than saying, "You may have something there, but let's go back to the real problem," say, "I'm not certain I understand how that relates to this problem. Why don't you fill me in on it a bit more?"

These last four suggestions emphasize problem analysis rather than appraisal. Of course, appraisal of past performance is a part of problem analysis, but these suggestions should lead to a more participative and less defensive subordinate role. These suggestions will also help improve creativity in problem solving. The subordinate will have a clearer understanding of why and how he/she needs to change work behavior. There should be a growth of climate of cooperation, which increases motivation to achieve performance goals.

6. Focus discussions, with performance and ways to improve it as the target.
7. Provide minimal criticism with focus on the future and strategies to achieve future goals.
8. Eliminate multipurpose appraisal systems. Developmental objectives to provide individuals needed skills cannot be achieved in an interview where the ratee knows the results will also bear on the size of any merit raise. Interviews with different purposes should be separated in time.

EQUAL EMPLOYMENT OPPORTUNITY (EEO) AND PERFORMANCE EVALUATION

Equal employment opportunity and affirmative action have influenced human resource decision making for more than 20 years now. While there are certainly critics of these programs, there has been at least one important trend traceable to the civil rights vigil in the workplace. Specifically, EEO has forced organizations to document decisions and to ensure they are firmly tied to performance or expected performance. Nowhere is this more apparent than in the performance appraisal area. Performance appraisals are subject to the same scrutiny as employment tests. Consider the use of performance ratings in making decisions about promotions. In this context, a performance appraisal takes on all the characteristics of a test used to make an initial employment decision. If employees pass the test (i.e., are rated highly in the performance evaluation process), they are predicted to do well (i.e., have promotion potential) at higher level jobs. This interpretation of performance evaluation as a test, subject to validation requirements, was made in *Brito* v. *Zia Company*.[31] In this case, Zia Company used performance ratings based on a rating format to lay off employees. The layoffs resulted in a disproportionate number of minorities being discharged. The court held that:

> Zia, a government contractor, had failed to comply with the testing guidelines issued by the Secretary of Labor, and that Zia had not developed job-related criteria for evaluating employees' work performance to be used in determining employment promotion and discharges which is required to protect minority group applicants and employees from the discriminatory effects of such failure.[32]

Since the *Brito* case there has been growing evidence that the courts have very specific standards and requirements for performance appraisal.[33] One study,

---

[31]*Brito* v. *Zia Company,* 478 F. 2d. 1200 (1973).

[32]Barbara Schlei and Paul Grossman, *Employee Discrimination Law* (Washington, D.C.: Bureau of National Affairs, 1976), p. 173.

[33]G. L. Lubben, D. E. Thompson, and C. R. Klasson, "Performance Appraisal: The Legal Implications of Title VII," *Personnel* 57, no. 3 (1980), pp. 11–21; H. Feild and W. Halley, "The Relationship of Performance Appraisal System Characteristics to Verdicts in Selected Employment Discrimination Cases," *Academy of Management Journal* 25, no. 2 (1982), pp. 392–406; *Albermarle Paper Company* v. *Moody,* U.S. Supreme Court, nos. 74–389 and 74–428, 10 FEP Cases 1181 (1975); also *Moody* v. *Albermarle Paper Company,* 474 F. 3d. 134.

summarizing the factors influencing court evaluations of performance appraisal systems, identified four factors which appear to make a difference.[34] First, courts are favorably disposed to appraisal systems which give specific written instructions on how to complete the appraisal. Presumably, more extensive training in other facets of evaluation would also be viewed favorably by the courts. Second, organizations tend to be able to support their cases better when the appraisal system is behaviorally based rather than trait oriented. In part this probably arises because behaviorally oriented appraisals have more potential to provide workers feedback about developmental needs. Third, as pointed out by every basic personnel book ever printed, and reinforced by this text, the presence of adequately developed job descriptions provides a rational foundation for personnel decision making of every form. The courts reinforce this by ruling more consistently for the defendant (company) when their appraisal systems are based on sound job descriptions. Fourth, courts also approve of appraisal systems which require that supervisors feed back to employees results of the appraisal. Absence of secrecy permits employees to identify weaknesses and to challenge undeserved appraisals.

What will be the probable thrust of future EEO cases dealing with performance appraisal? If performance evaluations continue to be treated as tests, a number of trends can be predicted. First, the courts will continue to require that performance standards are content valid (i.e., they must be related to the job being evaluated). This means that dimensions on which performance is to be rated must be derived from job analysis, reflecting content of the job in question. Second, it is also likely the courts will insist that performance evaluations be as free as possible from errors based on subjective judgments (e.g., halo, leniency, severity, central tendency). Partial support for these predictions comes from a Supreme Court case, *Albermarle Paper Co.* v. *Moody*.[35] In this case, Albermarle used a rating system based on overall job performance to evaluate employee performance. The Court found this inappropriate:

> Albermarle's supervisors were asked to rank employees by a "standard" that was extremely vague and fatally open to divergent interpretations. Each job grouping contained a number of different jobs, and the supervisors were asked, in each grouping to "determine which ones (employees) they felt, irrespective of the job that they were actually doing, but in their respective jobs, did a better job than the person they were rating against. . . ." There is no way of knowing precisely what criteria of job performance the supervisor was considering, the same criteria or whether, indeed, any of the supervisors actually applied a focused and stable body of criteria of any kind.[36]

---

[34]Feild and Hally, "The Relationship of Performance Appraisal System Characteristics to Verdicts in Selected Employment Discrimination Cases."

[35]*Albermarle Paper Company* v. *Moody;* also *Moody* v. *Albermarle Paper Company.*

[36]Schlei and Grossman, *Employee Discrimination Law,* p. 173.

A third possible requirement for performance evaluation could be that the process be empirically validated (i.e., some demonstration that the performance ratings for employees predict, in the case of promotions, performance on the job after promotion). If this requirement is mandated, current organizational practices will have to be dramatically altered. In a survey of company performance appraisal practices, not one of 217 companies using performance appraisal results to make promotion decisions had completed an empirical study to determine if the ratings were a good predictor of later job performance after promotion.[37]

If EEO infiltrates the performance evaluation area to any serious extent, two formats appear most likely to survive the encounter: behaviorally anchored rating scales and management by objectives. Each requires close attention to job content in establishing performance dimensions or objectives. Each focuses on assessment of concrete observable performance dimensions. And each has the latitude to provide employees with specific feedback about performance, lessening the chances of charges based on subjective biases.

In effect, EEO may force a renaissance in performance evaluation. An incentive will exist for organizations to consider carefully the issues discussed in this chapter and elsewhere in constructing a nonbiased performance evaluation system.

TYING PAY TO SUBJECTIVELY APPRAISED PERFORMANCE

Most people have come to expect at least annual pay increases. The difficulty arises in trying to shape these expectations so that employees view raises as a reward for performance. Chapter 8 illustrated this difficulty in theoretical terms. Now it is addressed from a pragmatic perspective. Very simply, organizations frequently grant increases that are not designed or communicated to be related to performance. The three pay increase guidelines that fit this mold will be discussed briefly before outlining a standard based on merit.[38]

Two types of pay increase guidelines provide equal increases to all employees. The first, a general increase, typically is found in unionized firms. A contract is negotiated that specifies an across-the-board (equal) increase for each year of the contract. Similar increases would occur because of cost-of-living adjustments (COLA), but these would be triggered by changes in the consumer price index (CPI) (Chapter 17).

The third form of guideline comes somewhat closer to tying pay to performance. Longevity (seniority) increases tie pay increases to a preset progression pattern based on seniority. For example, a pay grade might be divided into 10

---

[37]Robert I. Lazer, "The Discrimination Danger in Performance Appraisal," in *Contemporary Problems in Personnel*, eds. W. Hammer and F. Schmidt (Chicago: St. Clair Press, 1977), pp. 239–45.

[38]*Compensating Salaried Employees during Inflation: General vs. Merit Increases* (New York: Conference Board, Report no. 796, 1981).

EXHIBIT 10.10
Performance Rating/Salary Increase Matrix

Position in Range \ Performance Rating	Unsatisfactory	Improvement Needed	Competent	Commendable	Superior
Fourth quartile	0%	0%	4%	5%	6%
Third quartile	0%	0%	5%	6%	7%
Second quartile	0%	0%	6%	7%	8%
First quartile	0%	2%	7%	8%	9%
Below minimum of range	0%	3%	8%	9%	10%

equal steps, and employees move to higher steps based on seniority. To the extent performance improves with time on the job, this method has the rudiments of paying for performance.

By far the most popular form of pay guideline for exempt employees is one based on merit or performance.[39] Invariably these guidelines take one of two forms. The simpler version specifies pay increases permissible for different levels of performance.

	(1)	(2)	(3)	(4)	(5)
Performance level	Outstanding	Very Satisfactory	Satisfactory	Marginally Satisfactory	Unsatisfactory
Merit increase	10–12 percent	7–10 percent	5–7 percent	3–5 percent	0 percent

Increase ranges may be included in each performance category to give supervisors some discretion in the amount of increases.

More complex guidelines tie pay not only to performance but also to position in the pay range. Exhibit 10.10 illustrates such a system for a food market firm.

The percentages in the cells of Exhibit 10.10 are changed yearly to reflect changing economic conditions, but they usually maintain two relationships across all organizations. First, as would be expected in a pay-for-performance system, lower performances are tied to lower pay increases. In fact, in many organizations the poorest performers receive no merit increases. The second relationship is that pay increases decrease (percentage) as employees move through a pay range. For the same level of performance, employees low in the range receive higher percentage increases than employees who have progressed farther through the range. In part this is designed to forestall the time when employees reach the salary maximum and have salaries frozen. In part, though, it is also a

---

[39]Ibid.

cost-control mechanism tied to budgeting procedures, as discussed in Chapter 15.

Designing Merit Guidelines

Designing merit guidelines involves answering three questions. First, what should the poorest performer be paid as an increase? Notice, this figure is seldom negative! Wage increases are, unfortunately, considered an entitlement. Wage cuts tied to poor performance are very rare. Most organizations, though, are willing to give no increases to very poor performers.

The second question involves average performers. How much should they be paid as an increase? Most organizations try to ensure that average performers are kept whole relative to cost of living. This dictates that the midpoint of the merit guidelines equal the percentage change in the local or national cost-of-living index (usually the CPI).

Finally, how much should the top performers be paid? In part, budgetary considerations (Chapter 15) answer this question. But there is also growing evidence that employees vary in the size of increases that they consider meaningful (Chapter 8). Continuation of this research may help determine the approximate size of increases not only for top performers but for all employees.

SUMMARY

The process of appraising employee performance can be both time-consuming and stressful. These costs are compounded if the appraisal system is poorly developed or if a supervisor lacks appropriate training to collect and evaluate performance data. Development of a sound appraisal system(s) requires an understanding of organizational objectives balanced against the relative merits of each type of appraisal system. For example, despite its inherent weaknesses an appraisal system based on global ranking of employee performance may be appropriate in smaller organizations which, for a variety of reasons, choose not to tie pay to performance. In contrast, a sophisticated management-by-objective appraisal system may not be appropriate for such a company.

Similarly, training supervisors effectively to appraise performance requires an understanding of organizational objectives. We know relatively little about the ways in which raters process information and evaluate employee performance. However, a thorough understanding of organizational objectives combined with a knowledge of common errors in evaluation can make a significant difference in the quality of appraisals.

REVIEW QUESTIONS

1. Compare the six evaluation formats in terms of their utility for making administrative decisions.

2. Which types of appraisal formats are most likely to be useful for employees seeking to improve their performance? Why?

3. Compare and contrast the strengths and weaknesses of behaviorally anchored rating scales versus management by objectives.

4. What steps might be taken to ensure a firm's appraisal system was nondiscriminatory?

5. How do organizations design merit pay guidelines? What decisions must be made in this process?

Appendix A

Examples of Appraisal Forms: 3M, Xerox
(next 10 pages)

Note: The form for Xerox Corporation allows managers to identify different performance factors for each job. Once factors are listed, though, a standard rating format is used.

3M'S POSITION-TAILORED
PERFORMANCE REVIEW

MAIL TO:	Manager's Name J. J. Mc Habe	Manager's Address	Date Prepared

Employee Name John T. Doe		Personnel Action Code	Employee Number 1234567
Position Title Sales		Country Canada	Date PDQ Completed 01/04/83
Functional Area Engineering		Date Entered Present Position / /	Appraisal Period From / / To / /

Section I–Overall Performance

Check the box below that best summarizes this employee's overall job performance in terms of the job requirements. Your rating should take into account

1. The degree to which the job requirements have been satisfied.
2. The difficulty of the job requirements.
3. The employee's methods for satisfying job requirements.

☐	Excellent	Achievements consistently far exceed the position's key objectives.
☐	Better than satisfactory	Achievements consistently meet and frequently exceed the position's key objectives or requirements.
☐	Satisfactory	Achievements consistently meet the position's key objectives or requirements. Accomplishments may exceed work requirements in some areas.
☐	Needs further improvement	Achievements partially meet the position's key objectives or requirements. With improvement, performance should become satisfactory.
☐	Unsatisfactory	Achievements do not meet the position's key objectives or requirements.

Major job responsibilities during appraisal period: List, in order of importance, what this employee was supposed to do during this appraisal period.

Time spent in major functions

80%	Representing
70%	Coordinating
60%	Administration
50%	Consulting
40%	Monitoring business indicators
30%	Controlling
20%	Supervising
12%	Other
10%	Planning and organizing

Accomplishments for this appraisal period: List significant accomplishments or results achieved during this appraisal period related to the major job responsibilities listed above. Explain any lack of results.

3M'S POSITION-TAILORED PERFORMANCE REVIEW	John T. Doe PDQ Completed 01/04/83

Section II–Performance Factors

This section contains nine job performance factors, definitions of these factors, and examples of each factor. Rate this employee's job performance by:

1. Reading the definitions and examples of each factor.
2. Rating the employee on each factor by placing an X in the appropriate box of the shaded column. If a factor is not applicable, write "NA" in the Comments section for that factor.

The Comments section for each factor can be used to expand upon the ratings made.

1. **Economics management:** Uses information, finances, equipment, and supplies to maximize long-term profit; achieves forecasts and objectives.

   - Determining plans and performance objectives of an organization the size of 3M, worldwide.
   - Determining plans and performance objectives of an organization the size of a sector.
   - Determining plans and performance objectives of an organization the size of a group or international geographic area.
   - Forecasts manpower requirements.
   - Reviews and, if necessary, revises budget allocations.

Rating
Far exceeds requirements
Exceeds requirements
Meets all requirements
Partially meets requirements
Does not meet requirements
Comments:

2. **Emphasizing goals and productivity:** Setting and attainment of high performance standards for self and group in line with company goals.

   - Developing implementation strategy for long-range plans.
   - Planning and coordinating the introduction of new products or services.
   - Determining plans to phase out unprofitable products/services.
   - Setting selling prices.
   - Making additions to headcount that are within the approved budget.

Rating
Far exceeds requirements
Exceeds requirements
Meets all requirements
Partially meets requirements
Does not meet requirements
Comments:

3. **Organizing and facilitating work:** Plans, organizes, and ensures effective job performance through oral and written communication and delegation of tasks to subordinates.

   - Hiring an individual for an approved position.
   - Determining reductions in employee headcount, should this become necessary.
   - Revising the structure of an organization having 400 or more employees.
   - Evaluating an organization of 200–400 employees to determine the best allocation and utilization of resources.
   - Scheduling work of subordinates so that it flows evenly and steadily.

Rating
Far exceeds requirements
Exceeds requirements
Meets all requirements
Partially meets requirements
Does not meet requirements
Comments:

4. **Managing subordinates:** Emphasizes cooperation and teamwork among subordinates; motivates subordinates.

   - Allocating and scheduling resources to ensure that they will be available when needed.
   - Developing operational policies and procedures under which managers are expected to perform.
   - Establishing parameters to guide the planning of organizations in excess of 800 employees.
   - Giving guidance to other organizations for planning beyond one year.
   - Recommending changes in policy and procedures.

Rating
Far exceeds requirements
Exceeds requirements
Meets all requirements
Partially meets requirements
Does not meet requirements
Comments:

3M'S POSITION-TAILORED PERFORMANCE REVIEW	John T. Doe PDQ Completed 01/04/83

5. Knowledge of job: Has and regularly updates knowledge of job-related concepts and/or skills.

- Determining implementation methods for meeting operational objectives established by others.
- Makes use of assigned administrative or technical staff.
- Defines areas of responsibility for managerial personnel.
- Interacts face-to-face with subordinates on an almost daily basis.
- Assigns priorities for others on no less than a quarterly basis.

Far exceeds requirements
Exceeds requirements
Meets all requirements
Partially meets requirements
Does not meet requirements
Comments:

6. Problem solving and decision making: Monitors and analyzes situations, identifies problems, and makes appropriate decisions to resolve problems.

- Develops executive level management talent.
- Reviews subordinates' work almost continually.
- Reviews subordinates' work methods for possible increases in productivity.
- Motivates subordinates to change or improve performance.
- Analyzes subordinates' weaknesses and training needs.

Far exceeds requirements
Exceeds requirements
Meets all requirements
Partially meets requirements
Does not meet requirements
Comments:

7. Appraisal and development of subordinates: Evaluates subordinates objectively on a regular basis and is active in the setting and attainment of objectives for subordinates.

- Guides subordinates on technical aspects of the job.
- Monitors subordinates' progress toward objec. of unit and adjusts activ. as necessary to reach them.
- Provides complete instructions to subordinates when giving assignments.
- Delegates work, assigns responsibility to subordinates, and establishes appropriate controls.
- Maintains a smooth working relationship among various individuals who need to work cooperatively.

Far exceeds requirements
Exceeds requirements
Meets all requirements
Partially meets requirements
Does not meet requirements
Comments:

8. Equal opportunities: Utilizes skills and talents of subordinates and ensures equal opportunities for all subordinates.

Far exceeds requirements
Exceeds requirements
Meets all requirements
Partially meets requirements
Does not meet requirements
Comments:

9. Other:

Far exceeds requirements
Exceeds requirements
Meets all requirements
Partially meets requirements
Does not meet requirements
Comments:

3M'S POSITION-TAILORED PERFORMANCE REVIEW	John T. Doe PDQ Completed 01/04/83

Section III–Development Plan

This section helps develop the jobholder's skills as they pertain to this position.

Relative strengths	Specific recommendations for better utilizing strengths	Target date
	Manager:	
	Employee:	
	Human resources:	

Relative weaknesses	Specific recommendations for improving current job performance	Target date
	Manager:	
	Employee:	
	Human resources:	

3M'S POSITION-TAILORED **PERFORMANCE REVIEW**	John T. Doe PDQ Completed 01/04/83

Section IV–Overall Comments

Comments of J. J. Mc Habe

Comments of reviewer

Comments of John T. Doe

Section V–Signatures

This performance review has been reviewed and discussed with the employee:

Employee Signature: John T. Doe	Manager Signature: J. J. Mc Habe	Reviewer Signature
Date	Date	Date

XEROX EXEMPT SALARY
PROGRAM PERFORMANCE APPRAISAL

Name	
Title	
Division/Department	
Period reviewed from	To
Reviewed by	
Title	

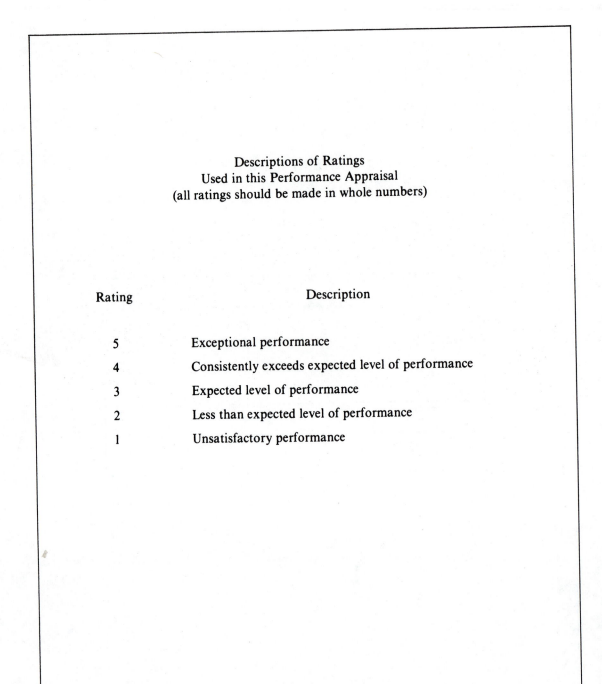

Descriptions of Ratings
Used in this Performance Appraisal
(all ratings should be made in whole numbers)

Rating	Description
5	Exceptional performance
4	Consistently exceeds expected level of performance
3	Expected level of performance
2	Less than expected level of performance
1	Unsatisfactory performance

Part I

Employee lists activities in order of importance.

Manager appraises performance against standards of performance considered attainable most of the time by a majority of employees qualified to perform the assignment.

Activity (to be completed by the employee):

Appraisal (to be completed by the manager):

Activity:

Appraisal:

Activity:

Appraisal:

Activity:

Appraisal:

Part IV

Summary appraisal and/or additional comments:

Overall summary appraisal:
(check the overall rating)

In reaching the summary rating the manager is expected to consider each of the activities. Since the weightings assigned to various activities are intended merely to show their relative importance, no precise formula should be applied. Managers are to exercise sound judgment and discretion in reaching the summary rating.

Unsatisfactory performance	Less than expected level of performance	Expected level of performance	Consistently exceeds expected level of performance	Exceptional performance

Written by	Title	Date

Additional approvals

Employee review of the performance appraisal:
    I have reviewed this appraisal and discussed the contents with my manager. My signature means that I have been advised of my performance and does not necessarily imply that I agree with the appraisal or the ratings.

Employee signature:	Date

Employee's comments (optional): If the employee wishes to do so, any comments concerning the appraisal, for example, agreement or disagreement, may be indicated here.

Salary range:	Minimum $	Midpoint $	Maximum $	Date as of

Part 3
Compensation Applications

Case 1   *Great Lakes Ornamental Supplies*

Great Lakes Ornamental Supplies (GLOS) designs and manufactures metal stair railings for commercial and residential customers. The company was founded in 1946 by Jake Weatherbee, a man fiercely dedicated to building the highest quality railings possible. This emphasis on high quality quickly established a reputation for Jake and ensured him continuing business from customers interested in top quality products. Between 1946 and 1975 Jake's share of the market gradually rose to 9 percent. Since then the market has stabilized and Jake has been quite content to maintain his market share and reputation for quality.

Jake's senior vice president in this enterprise is Amos Taylor. Amos began his career with GLOS in 1952 as Jake's first full-time salesperson. Repeated success as the top salesperson led to Amos's promotion to vice president of sales in 1964 and senior vice president in 1972. Amos, too, is proud of the quality railings GLOS designs and manufactures. He has frequently been heard to tell customers: "I don't have to be a salesman with these railings, they sell themselves."

Amos's nephew, Larry Hart, is vice president for manufacturing. He has a reputation as a demanding but fair boss. Workers are expected to come to work on time and complete assignments as directed. If they perform up to expectations, Larry will back them up 100 percent in fighting for wage increases and other forms of reward.

Larry has a meeting today with Jake. He's certain Jake wants to talk about the annual wage increases. He hopes Jake has recommended a large increase for the welding department. Despite high turnover rates those guys have really pulled together and done a job. Despite a 25 percent reduction in departmental employment over the past year, the gang has turned out as many units as they did last year.

Role for Jake Weatherbee

You have a meeting today with Larry Hart, your vice president for manufacturing. Larry is a good man but you're a bit concerned he doesn't share your love of GLOS. Certainly he doesn't seem to care as much as you about quality. Over the past four months there have been four complaints about structural weaknesses in newly installed railings. This is more complaints than the company normally gets in a year! To convey your displeasure you have decided to increase the budget of the welding department only 3 percent. You hope when word gets around that all the other departments received a 10 percent increase, the welding department will improve its performance. If this doesn't work, maybe it's time to reprimand Larry Hart.

Role for Larry Hart

You are very concerned about the way wage increases are allocated at GLOS. When you first started with the company in 1968 there were only 75 employees. Since Jake knew everyone and could keep track of their performance, it seemed appropriate that he determine both departmental budgets and individual wage increases. Since 1965, though, the company has grown to 217 employees. It is apparent that Jake simply can't know all the employees well enough to recommend individual raises. Moreover, there is also some evidence that Jake isn't aware of departmental records either. You have had three people leave the welding department in the past year. These were the first turnovers in that department in four years. Rumor has it among the welders that the company doesn't appreciate them. They turn out more units than anyone else in the industry, yet no one seems to care. You care; and you have tried to show it. But you'd better back up your words with cold, hard cash. You've prepared records showing improved productivity in the group. You're particularly proud of this since the unit switched over to a new welding process. It took some getting used to, but the group worked extra hard and got the job done, even short three welders. You think they deserve large raises and replacements for the lost workers.

It's time to meet with Jake Weatherbee.

1. What is the strategic plan of the company? How well does it fit in with compensation practices?
2. What compensation problems exist in GLOS? How does the issue of equity play a role?
3. What other elements of the reward system (i.e., other elements of the system that reinforce behavior) aren't operating well? What changes in behavior will be necessary for Jake and Larry to correct those problems?

Case 2   *Quayle Pharmaceutical*

Quayle Pharmaceutical is a medium-sized pharmaceutical company located in Sherwood, New Jersey. Most of Quayle's profits over the past 20 years have

EXHIBIT 1
Quayle Pharmaceutical Productivity Trends, 1982–1986*

1982	1983	1984	1985	1986
127,000	123,000	122,786	104,281	100,222

*Dollars gross revenue generated per employee in 1967 dollars.

EXHIBIT 2
Turnover Percentages, All Occupations, 1982–1986

1982	1983	1984	1985	1986
14%	12.5%	19.0%	15.3%	11.1%

EXHIBIT 3
Absenteeism, Average Days per Employee, 1982–1986

1982	1983	1984	1985	1986
*	*	9.6	9.7	10.2

*Records not available.

been generated by high volume production of drugs used by veterinarians in the care of domesticated animals. Since there is only a small markup in this market, Quayle must make its profit from high volume. With somewhat loose quality control laws for drugs distributed to veterinarians, Quayle historically has been able to achieve unit production levels which are high for the pharmaceutical industry.

Unfortunately, in the past two years productivity has significantly deteriorated at Quayle. Records for the past five years are provided in Exhibit 1. In addition, turnover and absenteeism are up (Exhibits 2 and 3).

John Lancer, president of Quayle Pharmaceutical, is deeply concerned. The key to Quayle's success has always been its high productivity and resulting low unit production costs. For some reason profits have been down 18 percent during the past two years (1985 = −13 percent; 1986 = −23 percent). Mr. Lancer has an annual stockholders' meeting in two weeks and he's determined he'll go in with some answers. Maybe they can't correct the drop-off in time for the meeting, but heads will roll if he doesn't get some answers. All department heads subsequently are sent detailed letters outlining the profit picture and requesting explanations.

Ralph Simpson is the top human resources person at Quayle Pharmaceutical. As Director of Human Resources Management he was informed by John Lancer three weeks ago that a marked drop in profits had occurred over the past year. Mr. Simpson offers the data in Exhibit 4 as a possible explanation for the profit decline.

EXHIBIT 4
Attitude Survey toward Compensation: Level and Administration

N = 1,427 (87 percent response rate)
Questions 1–15

Column A Scaling	Column B Scaling	Column C Scaling
1 = Very important to me	1 = Very satisfied	1 = Very dependent
2 = Important to me	2 = Satisfied	2 = Dependent
3 = Neither important nor unimportant	3 = Neutral	3 = Unsure
4 = Unimportant to me	4 = Dissatisfied	4 = Rarely dependent
5 = Very unimportant to me	5 = Very dissatisfied	5 = Never dependent

Indicate how important the following rewards available to Quayle employees are to you in column A. Indicate how satisfied you are with the level Quayle delivers in column B. How dependent are these rewards on your performance? (Column C)

		A	B	C
1.	A good salary	2	2	4
2.	An annual raise equal to or greater than the cost of living	1	2	5
3.	A profit sharing plan	5	3	3
4.	Paid sick days	5	3	5
5.	Vacation	3	1	5
6.	Life insurance	4	1	5
7.	Pension	4	1	5
8.	Medical plan	3	1	5
9.	Opportunity for advancement	2	5	5
10.	Job security	1	2	2
11.	Good supervisors	2	2	5
12.	Opportunity to develop new skills	2	5	5
13.	Good co-workers	3	3	5
14.	Steady hours	3	2	2
15.	Feedback about performance	1	5	3

1. Do Exhibits 1, 2, and 3 suggest any problems which might explain or be related to the profit declines?
2. Given the discussion of motivation theory in your text, do the data in Exhibit 4 suggest that productivity declines may be due to motivation problems? What other human resource management explanations are plausible?

Case 3   *Tinker Food Markets*

Tinker Food Markets were founded by Jonathon Tinker in Philadelphia shortly after the Depression. Since 1938 the chain has grown from 1 store to 86 supermarkets in Pennsylvania and southern New York. Until 1948 the stores were operated by one of Mr. Tinker's descendants. In 1948 the firm went public and the Tinker family gradually moved out of leadership roles. By all accounts, Tinker's problems number from this period of Tinker family withdrawal. The company is now heavily unionized, with virtually all nonexempt employees and approximately 15 percent of the exempt employees unionized. Pay raises for union employees are across-the-board and negotiated between the union and management. Nonunion employees generally receive an across-the-board increase also, generally pegged to the union's negotiated rate. Performance appraisals are conducted by supervising employees. The appraisal form consists of one performance-related question: "Overall, how well do you think this employee performed during the past year?" Employees are not told the results of this appraisal and it is generally believed that the question is only used to determine promotability.

Employees have no opportunity to respond to poor ratings and, in fact, don't even know when ratings are poor. The end result is suspicion and mistrust. There have been numerous complaints that the system must be unfair. In general the complaints tend to come from the poorer performers. Supervisors respond very rapidly to these complaints, though, and usually ensure that the person receives a larger than average raise to lessen the dissatisfaction.

1. The new Tinker management would like to establish a pay-for-performance system. What does this mean for them?
2. What changes will have to be made in the way the system operates now?
3. How might these changes be implemented?
4. Which of the nonmonetary changes do you think will help motivate better performance? Defend your position.

Case 4   *Assessing the Environment for Developing an Incentive Plan*

Tasks

1. Identify an organization for which you can get reasonably thorough information about products, methods of production, nature and extent of competition, morale of workers, and attitude of company toward workers. Your information source might be: (*a*) yourself in past or current jobs, (*b*) a friend or relative, (*c*) classmates.
2. Develop a structured interview questionnaire outlining the questions which you think need to be asked to assess whether your company could benefit from an incentive system. Be sure that your questions cover all the areas of concern noted in Chapter 10 of your text.
3. Which type of incentive or gain-sharing plan do you think would be most effective in your organization? Extensively document your position. If no incentive system would be appropriate, also defend your position.

Case 5   *"The Ratebusters"*

Carlisle Controls manufactures small servocontrol valves used in aircraft of all kinds, including space shuttles regularly sent into orbit. About 75 percent of Carlisle's business comes from government contracts. To win these contracts Carlisle must bid lower (among other requirements) than other competitors. Up until five years ago this wasn't difficult. Carlisle had no competitors! At that time, though, a patent on the valve ran out and a number of other organizations began machining these parts. To reduce labor costs, Carlisle implemented an incentive system based on the following rate schedule:

Number Valves Machined per Hour*	Payment Schedule
10	$ .60 per valve
11–20	.80 per valve
21 +	1.00 per valve

*Counted only if 0 defects.

Of the 10 machinists operating on this schedule, 9 produce an average of 12 valves per hour. Rarely does this group turn out less than 10 valves or more than 15 in an hour. The 10th machinist is an exception. He regularly machines between 23 and 25 valves per hour.

According to an industrial engineering consultant that Carlisle hired last year, the separate motions involved in machining a valve require 2.5 minutes. With allowances for fatigue and personal needs each valve could be machined in three minutes by a trained machinist working under normal conditions.

Role for Alan Young

You are 29 years old, married, and have two children. Six months ago your mother-in-law moved in with your family. Since you believe very strongly in the family unit, you are happy to have her; but the extra financial burden has been difficult to bear. To meet the extra costs you have been working especially hard to turn out more valves and earn a higher incentive. In the past you have always tried to produce around 18–20 valves an hour. The guys have kidded you about being a ratebuster, but it just seemed like good-natured jibes. Now you are turning out 25 valves during a good hour. You've always been good with machines, plus you know a few tricks to cut down the number of movements needed to machine a valve. Sure you have to press to turn out the last three in an hour, but it's worth it to know your family has a comfortable income.

Lately you have noticed the other machinists don't seem to be as friendly. There have even been occasional flashes of anger when one or two guys have noticed how many valves you were finishing. It's now to the point where George King wants to talk to you. George is one of the machinists you like; but if he tries to pressure you to reduce your output . . . well he can go stuff it.

Role for George King

You have been with Carlisle for 15 years now, second highest seniority in the department. You think Carlisle is a good place to work. They try to look after their people. The only time Carlisle hasn't done right by you was during the last big slump in the aerospace industry. All but three machinists in your department were laid off that time. You're determined you won't go through another stretch of unemployment like that again. Eighteen months without a job almost made you an alcoholic and destroyed your marriage. You've got everything back together again and nothing is going to mess things up.

The guys you work with are all pretty straight; all except Al Young, that is. He's always been a bit of a maverick. Most of the guys have agreed to hold production to 15 or less pieces. Who cares what that industrial engineer said was possible. It's too tough to turn out 20 pieces every hour. Besides, if everyone increases their output, what's to stop Carlisle from getting rid of some of the guys. It just isn't worth it. Now all of a sudden Al Young is turning out as many as 25 pieces an hour. The guys tolerated it when he did 20 pieces an hour, but now he's rubbing your nose in it. It's time to set that guy straight. In fact, maybe you'll just go see him now.

Students will play the roles of George King and Alan Young. Each will rationalize his position. Their meeting should address the following issues.

1. Given your understanding of corporate America, are George King's concerns legitimate?
2. What might Carlisle do to reduce the existing tension between Alan and the rest of the group?
3. How do you think an industrial engineer establishes productivity standards? How might these standards be flawed?

Case 6   *Minnesota Electric*

Minnesota Electric makes lamps for residential customers and high intensity bulbs for commercial use. The industry is quite competitive, with foreign manufacturers claiming 40 percent of the market. Profits and sales have risen in all but six of the years since the company was founded in 1958. All six years shared one common attribute: new housing sales were at record lows. Eighty percent of Minnesota Electric's market is in furnishing fixtures for new homes.

Minnesota Electric is viewed as a good company to work for. They believe strongly in employee participation and in the basic dignity of workers. This attitude is reflected in the successful operation of quality circles, the continuing presence of highly effective suggestion plans, and the general high morale of employees. Further evidence of this commitment to its employees is Minnesota Electric's reluctance to reduce its work force when demand drops. In fact, there have been no general work force reductions in 22 years. Reductions in overtime have generally been sufficient reaction to decreased demand.

You have the following information about Minnesota Electric.

	1983	1984	1985	1986	1987
Sales value of production (SVOP)	$15,000,000	$17,500,000	$19,000,000	$16,000,000	*
Total wage bill	5,000,000	6,000,000	9,000,000	8,000,000	*

	Current Operating Month, January 1988
Sales value of production	$1,500,000
Wage bill	666,666

*Data available in four weeks. Changeover to new computer system delayed output.

Minnesota Electric has decided to implement a Scanlon Plan for the 610 workers in its New Brighton, Minnesota, plant. Given the above information and your knowledge of Scanlon Plans (and incentive systems in general) from the text, design a Scanlon Plan and determine the bonus to be distributed as of the coming January. At a minimum your plan should include:

1. An implementation strategy, including specific communication tools.
2. Development of a target standard against which current wages and SVOP can be compared. This should include justification for which historical data is used and why.

Case 7 *Keysoft Enterprises Appraisal Interview*

Keysoft writes and markets software packages for microcomputers. Founded in 1973 by two former employees of IBM, Keysoft gradually has moved to a place of prominence and respect in this highly competitive and volatile industry. Last year the company employed 150 people. At that time James Burton III, president of Keysoft, decided to introduce a formal Human Resources program. Part of this program is a new appraisal system for exempt employees illustrated in Exhibit 1. Mr. Burton borrowed this appraisal format from a friend who

EXHIBIT 1
Appraisal Form—Exempt Employees

☐ Annual   ☐ Interim   ☐ Probationary   Original to local file, duplicate to employee.

Employee's Name (Last, First, Middle initial)	File Number	Job Title	Company Seniority Date	Organization Code No.

Evaluation Period	Instructions: Rate the employee on the major performance areas listed below by placing an "X" on the scale. Be sure to consider the entire year's performance, not just a major or recent occurrence. You should be able to substantiate your rating with measurable and/or observable information. Include appropriate written comments of a summary nature for each performance category shown below.
From To / / / /	

PRODUCTIVITY/VOLUME OF WORK: Examples—Contribution to unit objectives, revenue generation, calls, data input, passengers processed, does his/her share.

Comments:

```
├──────────┼──────────┼──────────┼──────────┤
```
Far below what   About the same   Far above what
others in the   as others   others
group contribute   contribute   contribute

QUALITY OF WORK: Examples—Errors, customer contact skills, complaint letters, completeness of assignment, files in order, appearance (if related to job).

Comments:

```
├──────────┼──────────┼──────────┼──────────┤
```
Far below   About the same   Far above
others in the   as others in the   others in the
group   group   group

TEAMWORK: Examples—Works well with other employees, helps others when time is available, supportive of decisions, works well in group situations.

Comments:

```
├──────────┼──────────┼──────────┼──────────┤
```
Not concerned   Usually puts the   Outstanding
about the needs   needs of the   team player,
of the team   team ahead of   always puts
                       own needs   team needs first

INTERPERSONAL RELATIONS: Examples—Communication skills, ability to get along with customers, peers, and management.

Comments:

```
├──────────┼──────────┼──────────┼──────────┤
```
Lacks   Demonstrates   Has
interpersonal   good interpersonal   outstanding
skills, very   relations and is   interpersonal
often has   effective in   relations with
conflicts with   dealing with   customers and/
customers and/   customers and/   or members of
or members of   or members of   the group
the group   the group

DEPENDABILITY/ATTENDANCE: Comments:	Days Absent	No. of Occurrences	Days Late

Summary Comments:

Evaluator's signature	Date / /	Reviewed by: Evaluator's Supervisor's signature	Date / /
Signature of employee (Optional)	Date / /	Conference with employee held on:	Date / /

owns a string of convenience food stores. This will be the first time the appraisal forms have been tried out on Keysoft employees.

Students will play each of the two roles, Sarah Brown and Jeff Morrow. Each participant should read the company history and the assigned role. Sarah Brown also should read about conducting an appraisal interview (see Exhibit 10.9). Both employees should fill out the appraisal form in Exhibit 1, rating Jeff on the dimensions indicated. This will provide a starting point for discussions during the interview.

Role for Sarah Brown, Supervisor

Today you will be conducting your first appraisal interview with the new format Jim Burton has been pushing. Frankly you wish you could try it out on someone besides Jeff Morrow. While he's been a very good employee in the past, you notice that in the last six months his performance has dropped. He doesn't seem to get along very well anymore with the other creative programmers. One incident, in particular, sticks out. Jeff was working on a new spreadsheet program when Sam Daniels asked for help on one of the games he was creating. Not only did Jeff refuse, but he started screaming at Daniels to do his own work. You can't tolerate this kind of behavior. Employees are expected to cooperate with each other.

You're also concerned that Jeff hasn't been creating as many software programs lately. Normally he can write about two programs a year. But he has been working on this program for almost a year with no tangible output. Jeff just doesn't seem to be as productive as he used to be.

Role for Jeff Morrow, Programmer

Keysoft just isn't the company it used to be. All your problems started about two years ago. About that time they hired a bunch of new programmers who just don't have that creative flair. You helped them for the first year. But they keep coming back for more and more. It got to the point about six months ago where you had to tell them to do their own work. Sam Daniels is the worst of the lot. He's in over his head and expects you to bail him out. You're tired of covering for him. In fact, you lost your temper with him about five months ago. You regret screaming at him but he just won't let you do your job.

You are excited about the upcoming appraisal interview with Sarah Brown, your supervisor. She didn't give you as big a raise last year as you deserved, but you're sure she'll make up for it this year. After all, didn't you carry three programmers for almost a year with some of your more creative ideas? Besides that, you are almost done with that spreadsheet program that has taken a year to write. It's by far the most sophisticated program you've ever written. If it doesn't outperform the market leaders and make the company $2 million in the first year, you'll be very surprised. You can smell success, and you're sure Sarah will be just as enthusiastic.

Following Jeff and Sarah's interview, students should discuss the following questions.

1. Were any of the difficulties in the appraisal interview magnified because of the poor quality of the appraisal format? Explain your answer.
2. Was Sarah Brown able to recognize where differences of opinion existed with Jeff Morrow? Was she able to resolve these differences? What is (are) the key(s) to successfully resolving these differences?
3. Do you think Jeff Morrow's performance will improve as a result of this interview? Why or why not?

Case 8   *Developing a Merit Pay Guide for Keysoft Enterprises*

As noted in the history of Keysoft Enterprises in the previous case, James Burton III (president of Keysoft) wants to upgrade the existing human resources

EXHIBIT 1
Merit Pay Guide for Last Year

Position in Salary Range / Performance	Well below Average	Below Average	Average	Above Average	Well above Average
Above grade maximum (red circle)	0 — 0	2 — 0	3 — 5	4 — 5	5 — 15
Q4	0 — 0	3 — 0	4 — 10	5 — 10	6 — 15
Q3	0 — 0	4 — 0	5 — 5	6 — 25	7 — 10
Q2	2 — 0	5 — 2	6 — 9	7 — 9	8 — 10
Q1	2 — 0	6 — 3	7 — 6	8 — 5	9 — 6

Notes: 1. Cost of living rose 6 percent last year.
2. Numbers at lower right corner of each cell represent the number of employees falling into that cell during the previous year. These figures should be used to calculate budgetary implications of any proposed merit guide.

system. One part of the system which will follow the same format, though, is the merit pay guide. Please read about merit pay guides in Chapter 10 of your text. Exhibit 1 shows the merit pay guide used by Keysoft last year. Next year's guide should follow the same general format. Specifically: (1) higher performers should receive larger increases, (2) employees with salaries in lower quartiles of a pay grade should receive larger increases than employees in higher quartiles, and (3) average performers with salaries in the middle of a pay grade should receive increases equal to the cost of living. In addition, Mr. Burton would like the new merit guide to reflect the following policy decisions:

1. Performance differences between employees should be rewarded with even larger salary-increase differences between employees than in past years.
2. No red circle employee should receive a pay increase.
3. Total increases should not exceed 8 percent on average for all employees.

Develop a merit pay guide to reflect these policies. Remember, there is no one right answer, but you should document how your merit pay guide conforms to Keysoft policies.

Case 9 *Evaluating Keysoft's Performance Appraisal System*

Keysoft Enterprises (see History of Keysoft in Case 7, the Keysoft Appraisal Interview case) uses a performance evaluation form (Exhibit 1) to appraise incumbents of the seven nonexempt jobs described below. Identify the strengths and weaknesses of this evaluation form relative to the criteria outlined in Chapter 10 of your text (i.e., employee development criteria, administrative criteria, personnel research, economic criteria, and validity). Be specific in your discussion.

JOB DESCRIPTIONS FOR KEYSOFT NONEXEMPT JOBS

Messenger

1. *Duties:* Performs under direct supervision, collection, sorting, and distribution of mail and incoming and outgoing interoffice correspondence as required. Performs errands and other related duties. Distributes or collects miscellaneous materials. Posts bulletin board notices. Operates simple mechanical reproduction machines, such as ditto duplicator and addressograph, and collates reports.

EXHIBIT 1
Keysoft Nonexempt Performance Appraisal

Name _____   Date of Hire _____

Position _____   Department _____

Absentee Record: _____ Miscellaneous illness   _____ Total
                           _____ Single illness   _____ Days late
                           _____ Other

PLEASE COMPLETE AND RETURN TO THE HUMAN RESOURCES DEPARTMENT NO LATER
THAN: _____

Rating Scale:

| 1 = Unacceptable performance | 2 = Minimally acceptable performance | 3 = Average performance | 4 = Good performance | 5 = Outstanding performance |

Number		Rating	Comments
1	Theoretical knowledge		
2	Business maturity and productivity		
3	Willingess to act and make decisions		
4	Analytical capacity		
5	Quality of work and judgment		
6a	Personality in internal relations		
6b	Tact and persuasiveness in customer and public relations		
7a	Leadership		
7b	Organizational ability and control		
8	Physical capacity		
	Overall evaluation =		

2. *Requirements for entering:* High school graduate or equivalent. Must be physically fit, must give evidence of intelligence, ability, and responsibility to indicate possible eventual ability to advance to higher rated work.

Typist

1. *Duties:* Performs under general supervision typing of technical and business correspondence, reports, and statements, including long carriage statement work and setting up of tables taken from copy or from machine. Performs other types of miscellaneous clerical work and acts as receptionist when required.

2. *Requirements for entering:* High school graduate or equivalent. Must demonstrate ability to pass satisfactorily company typist test by performing accurately at the rate of at least 50 words per minute.

Secretary

1. *Duties:* Schedules appointments, gives information to callers, takes dictation, and otherwise relieves officials of clerical work and minor administrative and business details.
   a. Reads and routes incoming mail.
   b. Locates and attaches appropriate file to correspondence to be answered by employer.
   c. Takes dictation by hand or by machine and transcribes notes on typewriter.
   d. Composes and types routine correspondence.
   e. Files correspondence and other records.
   f. Answers telephone and gives information to callers or routes calls to appropriate official.
   g. Schedules appointments for employer.
   h. May oversee clerical workers.

2. *Requirements for entering:* High school graduate or equivalent. Must be neat in appearance and have a pleasing personality. Must have broad experience in stenographic work and have demonstrated the capacity to handle secretarial duties as well as the qualities of integrity and intelligence.

Intermediate Clerk I (General)

1. *Duties:* Under general supervision or under the direction of a higher rated clerk performs a wide range of specialized clerical and/or payroll duties of an analytical nature, some of which may be in the scope of or be a part of the duties of other clerical jobs. May also direct the work of one or more lower rated clerks; and in so doing, may plan and lay out tasks for such in-

dividuals. May use usual office machines and equipment, calculating machines, etc. May have numerous contacts with vendors, common carriers, or government agencies.

2. *Requirements for entering:* High school graduate or equivalent. Must have four years of experience in clerical duties. Must have demonstrated ability to analyze the problems arising in previous assignments, to handle a variety of detail pertaining to established procedures, as well as the ability to exercise discretion concerning operating routine and detail. Must have experience necessary to originate investigations of various phases of work assignments or to assemble data for the purpose of such investigations.

Programming Clerk I

1. *Duties:* Under general supervision, carries out a variety of duties to assist technical personnel by relieving them of the routine tasks involved in project work, computer programming, and preparation of work for the computer. May be called upon to write computer programs of a moderate complexity, or parts of such programs. May act as contact with remote users of the computer to receive data, prepare it for submission to the computer, and return answers to the remote user. May direct the work of lower rated programming clerks and staff assistants.

2. *Requirements for entering:* Education requirements are the same as for Programming Clerk II. Must have received for at least one year the top progression rate of Programming Clerk II and have demonstrated a higher caliber of aptitude, skill, and job performance.

Programming Clerk II

1. *Duties:* Under general supervision, carries out a variety of duties to assist technical personnel by relieving them of the routing tasks involved in project work, computer programming, and preparation of work for the computer. May be called upon to write simple computer programs or parts of programs. May act as contact with remote users of the computer to receive data, prepare it for submission to the computer, and return answers to the remote users. May assist higher and lower rated clerical personnel in the performance of their work as required.

2. *Requirements for entering:* High school graduate from college preparatory course or equivalent, with two years of algebra, plane geometry, and at least one physical science. Two years of experience as math clerk, or the equivalent in outside training or experience. Demonstration of ability by successful passing of the appropriate written test of achievement, or by successful completion of a two-year course in computer programming in a recognized

technical school. Must exhibit a higher caliber of aptitude, skills, and job performance.

Senior Programming Clerk

1. *Duties:* Under limited supervision, performs a variety of advanced clerical duties to assist technical personnel by relieving them of selected tasks involved in project work, computer programming, and preparation of work for the computer. May be called upon to code or write programs of greater complexity than are undertaken by Programming Clerk I, or parts of such programs. May act as contact with remote users of the computer to receive data, prepare it for submission to the computer, and return answers to remote users. May direct the work of lower rated programming clerks and staff assistants.

2. *Requirements for entering:* Educational requirements are the same as for Programming Clerk II. Must have received for at least one year the top progression rate of Programming Clerk I and have demonstrated a higher caliber of aptitude, skill and job performance. Must have complete knowledge of functional and operating procedures of clerical programming group (if applicable; or must be able to work alone in the conduct of the required duties if the work assignments are so constituted) and must have demonstrated capacity to assume responsibility and to exercise soundly independent judgment and initiative.

Part *4*

Employee Benefits

The area of employee benefits represents more of a mystery than any other covered thus far in this book. The reason is simple. Benefit practices today are based on faith rather than facts. Consider, for example, the compensation objectives noted in the pay model, Exhibit IV.1.

Does effective employee benefits administration facilitate organization performance? Or do employee benefits impact upon an organization's ability to attract, retain, and motivate employees? Conventional wisdom says employee benefits can affect retention, but there is little research to support this conclusion. A similar lack of research surrounds each of the other potential payoffs to a sound benefits program.

Is it any wonder, then, why firms are becoming increasingly concerned about the steadily rising costs of benefits? They represent a labor cost with no apparent returns.

Balanced against this is the perception of employee benefits as an entitlement. Employees believe they are entitled to continued benefits as a term of employment. Efforts to reduce benefit levels or eliminate parts of the package altogether would meet with employee resistance and dissatisfaction.

Somewhere between these two perspectives is the probable truth about employee benefits. Operating on this assumption, this part of the book takes the perspective that organizations must control costs of benefits wherever possible and increasingly seek ways to maximize the returns from benefit expenditures. As a first step in this direction, Chapter 11 identifies issues organizations should face in developing and maintaining a benefits program. A model of the benefits determination process also is presented to provide a structure for thinking about employee benefits.

Chapter 12 provides a summary of the state of employee benefits today. Hopefully this will provide the groundwork for innovative and effective benefit packages of tomorrow.

EXHIBIT IV.1
The Pay Model

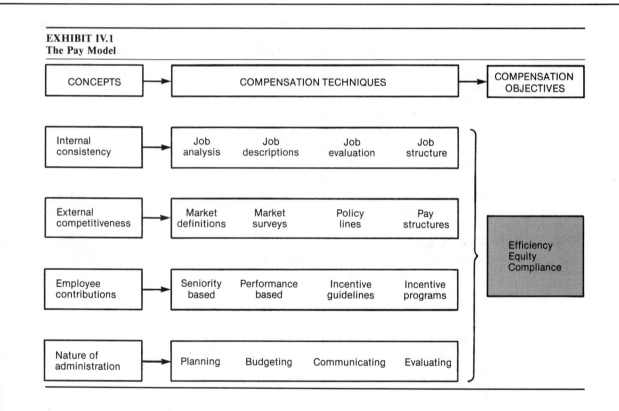

Chapter *11*

The Benefits Determination Process

Item 1: Oneida silversmith employees can rent, at reduced rates, cottages and camp-sites on company-owned property on New York's Lake Oneida.[1]

Item 2: Ingersoll Rand Company, Woodcliffe Lake, N. J., lets staffers plant gardens on its grounds and even plows, fertilizes, and waters the plots.[2]

Item 3: Other benefits from assorted companies: Hypnosis cure for smoking; tear gas classes; weekly barbecue; high school graduation gift; on-site barber shop; on-site department store; company pro shop.[3]

Item 4: Half of payroll costs may go for employee benefits by decade's end, up from 37 percent currently, some consultants predict.[4]

Are items 1 through 3 isolated cases of liberal employee benefits, or do they foreshadow a reality predicted by the doomsayers in item 4? How can employee benefits expand this rapidly, especially when we compare with the following brief chronicle of "benefits" of the past:[5]

- A carriage shop published a set of rules for employees in 1880 that stated, in part: "Working hours shall be from 7 A.M. to 9 P.M. every day except the Sabbath. . . . After an employee has been with this firm for five years he shall receive an added payment of five cents per day, provided the firm has prospered in a manner to make it possible. . . . It is the bounden duty of each employee to put away at least 10 percent of his monthly wages for his declining years so he will not become a burden upon his betters."

- In 1915, employees in the iron and steel industry worked a standard 60 to 64 hours per week. By 1930 that schedule had been reduced to 54 hours.

- It was not until 1929 that the Blue Cross concept of prepaid medical costs was introduced.

- Prior to 1935 only one state (Wisconsin) had a program of unemployment compensation benefits for workers who lost their jobs through no fault of their own.

- Before World War II very few companies paid hourly employees for holidays. In most companies employees were told not to report for work on holidays and to enjoy the time off, but their paychecks were smaller the following week.

---

[1] Andrea Stone, "Innovative Benefit Programs Perk Up," *USA Today* (January 31, 1986), p. 30.

[2] *The Wall Street Journal,* June 10, 1980, p. 1.

[3] Hewitt Associates, "Innovative Benefits" (Lincolnshire, Ill.: Hewitt Associates, 1982).

[4] *The Wall Street Journal,* June 10, 1980, p. 1.

[5] Robert W. McCaffery, *Managing the Employee Benefits Program* (New York: American Management Association, 1972).

- Aid for permanently and totally disabled workers under the Social Security Act did not begin until 1954, and several more years had elapsed before employees under age 50 were covered.
- Not until July 1966 did hospitalization and medical care benefits (Medicare) for persons over age 65 become operative under Social Security.

In reality, employee benefits have expanded rapidly. Although esoteric benefits are the rarity, organizations still expend over $7,000 per employee per year on benefits costs.[6]

Employee benefits—that part of the total compensation package, other than pay for time worked, provided to employees in whole or in part by employer payments (e.g., life insurance, pension, workers' compensation, vacation).

Employee benefits can no longer realistically be called "fringe" benefits. Benefits represent an ever-escalating percentage of total payroll. And neither the percentage of payroll nor the types of benefits provided can be considered a *fringe*. In most cases both the organization and its employees consider these benefits *major* cost/benefit features of the world of work. For example, it has been estimated that General Motors Corporation pays more for employee medical benefits alone than it does for all the steel necessary to produce its yearly output of automobiles.[7] This rather startling fact underscores a major escalation of benefits costs in comparison to other costs of production. Consider the following example comparing cost changes for the period 1955–1975 (Exhibit 11.1).[8]

EXHIBIT 11.1
Cost Changes for Selected Factors, 1955–1975

Factors	Rise in Cost (percentage) 1955–1975
Average worker base annual income	+92
Consumer price index	+98.6
Corporate taxes	+100
Benefits	+397

Source: John P. Hanna, "Can the Challenge of Escalating Benefits Costs Be Met?" Reprinted from the November 1977 issue of *Personnel Administrator.* Copyright 1977, The American Society for Personnel Administration, 606 North Washington Street, Alexandria, VA 22314. ($40 per year.)

---

[6]U.S. Chamber of Commerce, *Employee Benefits, 1983* (Washington, D.C.: U. S. Chamber of Commerce, 1984).

[7]John Hanna, "Can the Challenge of Escalating Benefits Costs Be Met?" *Personnel Administration* 27, no. 9 (1977), pp. 50–57.

[8]Ibid.

Employee benefits rose over a 20-year period at a rate almost four times greater than employee wages or the consumer price index. The result was a $550 billion price tag in 1983 for employee benefits. This is more than five times the amount spent on benefits in 1967 ($100 billion).[9]

Another way of portraying the dramatic increase in benefit costs is to trace changes reported by the U.S. Chamber of Commerce in its annual benefits survey. Exhibit 11.2 shows the change in benefit costs for selected organizations during the decades of the 1960s and 1970s.[10]

For all companies in the Chamber of Commerce survey during 1983, benefits payments totaled 36.6 percent of payroll. This represents an expenditure of $7,582 per employee per year.[11]

Around these average figures, considerable variation exists in the benefits provided and their costs. Benefits, for example, range from a high of 47 percent of payroll in the primary metal industries to a low in wholesale/retail trade of 29 percent.[12]

EXHIBIT 11.2
Change in Benefits Costs: 1959, 1969, 1980 (N = 140 Organizations)

	1959	*1969*	*1980*
Percentage of payroll (total)	24.7	31.1	41.4
Legally required benefits	3.5	5.3	8.1
Pension, insurance, and other agreed-upon payments	8.5	10.4	15.2
Rest periods, lunch breaks	2.2	3.1	3.8
Payments for time not worked (holidays, vacations, etc.)	8.4	10.1	11.9
Profit sharing, bonuses	2.1	2.2	2.4

Source: *Employee Benefits, 1980* (Washington, D.C.: Chamber of Commerce of the United States, 1980), p. 27.

WHY THE GROWTH IN EMPLOYEE BENEFITS?

Wage and Price Controls

During both World War II and the Korean War the federal government instituted strict wage and price controls. The compliance agency charged with enforcing these controls was relatively lenient in permitting reasonable increases in benefits. With strict limitations on the size of wage increases, both unions and employers sought new and improved benefits to satisfy worker demands.

---

[9]U.S. Chamber of Commerce, *Employee Benefits, 1980* (Washington, D. C.: U. S. Chamber of Commerce, 1981).

[10]Ibid.

[11]U.S. Chamber of Commerce, *Employee Benefits, 1983*.

[12]Ibid.

Unions

The climate fostered by wage and price controls created a perfect opportunity for unions to flex their muscles, newly acquired under the Wagner Act of 1935. Several National Labor Relations Board rulings during the 1940s conferred legitimacy upon negotiations over employee benefits. Absent the leverage to raise wages very much, unions fought for the introduction of new benefits and the improvement of existing benefits. Success on this front during the war years lead to further postwar demands. Largely through the efforts of unions, most notably the auto and steelworkers, several benefits common today were given their initial impetus: pattern pension plans, supplementary unemployment compensation, extended vacation plans, and guaranteed annual wage plans.[13]

Employer Impetus

It would be a mistake to assume that the war years provided the only incentive fostering a receptive benefits climate. In fact, many of the benefits in existence today were provided at employer initiative. Much of this employer receptivity can be traced to pragmatic concerns about employee satisfaction and productivity. Rest breaks often were implemented in the belief that fatigue increased accidents and lowered productivity. Savings and profit-sharing plans (e.g., Procter & Gamble's profit-sharing plan was initiated in 1885) were implemented to improve performance and provide increased security for worker retirement years. Indeed, many employer-initiated benefits were designed to create a climate in which employees perceived that management was genuinely concerned for their welfare.

Cost Effectiveness of Benefits

One final, and important, impetus for the growth of employee benefits is their cost effectiveness in three situations. The first advantage is that most employee benefits are not taxable. Provision of a benefit rather than an equivalent increase in wages avoids payment of federal and state personal income tax. Remember, though, recurrent tax reform proposals may eliminate much of the tax advantage of employee benefits. Recent proposals, if adopted, could lead to several benefits being counted as taxable income:

1. Portions of employer health contributions.
2. Group life insurance premiums.
3. Dependent life insurance.
4. Educational assistance.
5. Legal services.
6. Cafeteria pay plans.[14]

---

[13]McCaffery, *Managing the Employee Benefits Program.*

[14]Carson E. Beadle, "Taxing Employee Benefits: The Impact on Employers and Employees," *Compensation Review* 17, no. 2 (1985), pp. 12–19.

Already there has been one minor casualty, with the Deficit Reduction Act (Defra) of 1984 limiting the types of benefits which can be included in cafeteria plans (e.g., no parking fees paid, limits on vacation homes). Obviously, taxation of any or all of these benefits would reduce or eliminate their advantage over allocating the corresponding amount to direct wages.

A second cost effectiveness component of benefits arises because many group-based benefits (e.g., life, health, and legal insurance) can be obtained at a lower rate than could be obtained by employees acting on their own. Group insurance also has relatively easy qualification standards, permitting a set of employees who might not otherwise qualify (e.g., an employee with a heart condition who becomes eligible for group life insurance at a nonprohibitive rate after being denied individual insurance). Third, a well-designed benefits plan that meets employee needs may yield advantages far beyond the dollar cost. In an economic sense, if the utility of the cash value of a benefit is less than the utility of the benefit itself, the organization has made a wise investment decision.

THE VALUE OF EMPLOYEE BENEFITS

Given the rapid growth in benefits and the staggering cost implications, it seems only logical that employers must derive commensurate return on this investment. In fact, there is at best only anecdotal evidence that employee benefits are cost justified. This evidence falls into three categories.[15] First, employee benefits are widely claimed to help in the retention of workers. Benefit schedules are specifically designed to favor longer-term employees. For example, retirement benefits increase with years of service, and most plans do not provide for full employee eligibility until a specified number of years of service has been reached. Equally, amount of vacation time increases with years of service; and finally, employees' savings plans, profit-sharing plans, and stock purchase plans frequently provide for increased participation or benefits as company tenure increases.

There is some research to indicate that benefits may increase retention. Two studies uncovered a negative relationship between fringe benefit coverage and job change patterns.[16] A more detailed follow-up study, though, found only two types of benefits curtailed employee turnover: pensions and medical coverage.[17] Virtually no other employee benefit had a significant impact on turnover behavior.

---

[15]Donald P. Crane, *The Management of Human Resources,* 2nd ed. (Belmont, Calif.: Wadsworth, 1979); Foegen, "Are Escalating Employee Benefits Self-Defeating?" *Pension World* 14, no. 9 (September 1978), pp. 83–84, 86.

[16]Olivia Mitchell, "Fringe Benefits and Labor Mobility," *Journal of Human Resources* 17, no. 2 (1982), pp. 286–98; Bradley Schiller and Randal Weiss, "The Impact of Private Pensions on Firm Attachment," *Review of Economics and Statistics* 61, no. 3 (1979), pp. 369–80.

[17]Olivia Mitchell, "Fringe Benefits and the Cost of Changing Jobs," *Industrial and Labor Relations Review* 37, no. 1 (1983), pp. 70–78.

Employee benefits also are lauded for their presumed impact on employee satisfaction. A recent survey by the Opinion Research Corporation casts doubt on this claim, though.[18] There has been a sharp drop in satisfaction with employee benefits over the past decade, with the lowest satisfaction marks going to disability, life, and health insurance. This decline in satisfaction is attributed to a failure of benefits programs to adjust to the changing characteristics of the work force. Ever-increasing numbers of women in the labor force, coupled with increasing numbers of dual career families and higher educational attainments, suggest changing values of employees.[19] Changing values, in turn, necessitate a reevaluation of benefits packages.

Finally, employee benefits also are valued because improved retention and increased satisfaction will, some organizations hope, have bottom-line effects on profitability. This is consistent with the old adage: "A happy worker is a productive worker."

Unfortunately, the research supporting these declarations is relatively scant, particularly in relation to the huge costs incurred in the name of employee benefits. Further cause for pessimism comes from several studies indicating that employees are not aware of, or undervalue, the benefits provided by their organization.[20] In one study, employees were asked to recall the benefits they received.[21] The typical employee could recall less than 15 percent of them. In another study with a somewhat different approach, M.B.A. students were asked to rank-order the importance attached to various factors influencing job selection.[22] Presumably the large percentage of labor costs allocated to payment of employee benefits would be justified if benefits turned out to be an important factor in attracting good M.B.A. candidates. Of the six factors ranked, employee benefits received the lowest ranking. Opportunity for advancement (1), salary (2), and geographic location (3) all ranked considerably higher than benefits as factors influencing job selection. Compounding this problem, these students also were asked to estimate the percentage of payroll spent on employee benefits. Slightly less than one half (46 percent) of the students thought that benefits comprised 15 percent or less of payroll. Nine out of 10 students (89 percent) thought benefits accounted for less than 30 percent of payroll. Only 1 in 10 students had a reasonably accurate or inflated perception of the magnitude of employee benefits.[23]

---

[18] *The Wall Street Journal,* April 30, 1985, p. 1.

[19] Ibid.

[20] Marie Wilson, Gregory R. Northcraft, and Margaret A. Neale, "The Perceived Value of Fringe Benefits," *Personnel Psychology* 38 (1985), pp. 309–20.

[21] William Halley, Jr., and Jack Ingram III, "Communicating Fringe Benefits," *Personnel Administration,* no. 2 (1973), pp. 20–26.

[22] Richard Huseman, John Hatfield, and Richard Robinson, "The MBA and Fringe Benefits," *Personnel Administration* 23, no. 7 (1978), pp. 57–60.

[23] Ibid.

The ignorance about the value of employee benefits inferred from these studies can be traced to both attitudinal and design problems. Looming largest is the attitude problem. Benefits are taken for granted. Employees view them as a right with little comprehension of, or concern for, employer costs.[24]

As an interesting illustration demonstrating that this trend can be reversed, the 1982 agreement between General Motors and the United Auto Workers included a provision tying employee benefits to level of absenteeism. Employees who were chronically absent over a six-month period faced reductions in vacations, holidays, and sickness/accident pay proportionate to their percentage of absenteeism (e.g., 20 percent absenteeism resulted in an identical reduction in holiday pay). Recent data indicate that the absenteeism rate has dropped from 11 percent to 9 percent.[25] Even this small success should encourage benefits managers to try other innovative programs. Otherwise, benefits are viewed as an entitlement and don't receive the close scrutiny in planning and administrative phases that is warranted.

KEY ISSUES IN BENEFITS PLANNING AND ADMINISTRATION

Benefits Planning Issues

First, and foremost, the components of a benefits plan should complement the remainder of the compensation program.[26] For example, if a major compensation objective is to attract good employees, the benefits program would be designed with this in mind. Benefits would be designed with rapid, or instant, eligibility provisions and attractive vesting requirements. Conversely, an organization with a turnover problem might choose to design a benefits package that improves progressively with seniority, thus providing a reward for continuing service.

Second, the benefits plan should be competitive, adequate, and cost effective. To be competitive, an employer might establish an objective that the overall value of a benefits package would be comparable to that of designated firms in a benefits survey. To be adequate, however, more subjective evaluations come into play. Most organizations considering the question of adequacy evaluate the financial liability of employees with and without a particular benefit (e.g., employee medical expenses with and without medical expenses benefits). There is no magic formula for defining benefits adequacy.[27] In part, the answer may lie in the relationship between benefits adequacy and the third plan objec-

---

[24]Foegen, "Are Escalating Employee Benefits Self-Defeating?"

[25]*The Wall Street Journal,* March 19, 1985, p. 1.

[26]Jerry Rosenbloom and G. Victor Hallman, *Employee Benefit Planning* (Englewood Cliffs, N.J.: Prentice-Hall, 1981).

[27]M. Meyer, *Profile of Employee Benefits* (New York: The Conference Board, Report no. 813, 1981), p. 2.

tive: cost effectiveness. More organizations need to consider whether employee benefits are cost justified. Consider, for example, the health care area. There was a 93 percent increase in health care prices between 1973 and 1980. Some organizations have begun to redefine the adequacy criterion to overcome strong perceptions of cost ineffectiveness. The end result is higher deductibles and greater sharing of premium payments with employees. At the extreme, some experts have even suggested limiting health coverage solely to catastrophic illness. Any cost savings would then be shared with employees. Such cost-benefit analyses must become a stronger feature in both planning and administration of benefits.

Benefits Administration Issues

Three major administration issues arise in setting up a benefits package: (1) Who should be protected or benefitted? (2) How much choice should employees have among an array of benefits? (3) How should benefits be financed?[28]

Every organization has a variety of employees with different employment statuses. Should these individuals be treated equally with respect to benefits coverage? Should, for example, a retired automobile executive be permitted to continue purchasing cars at a discount price, a benefit that could be reserved solely for current employees? In fact, a series of questions must be answered:

1. What probationary periods (for eligibility of benefits) should be used for various types of benefits? Does the employer want to cover employees and their dependents more or less immediately upon employment or provide such coverage for employees who have established more or less "permanent" employment with the employer? Is there a rationale for different probationary periods with different benefits?
2. Which dependents of active employees should be covered?
3. Should retirees (as well as their spouses and perhaps other dependents) be covered, and for which benefits?
4. Should survivors of deceased active employees (and/or retirees) be covered? And if so, for which benefits? Are benefits for surviving spouses appropriate?
5. What coverage, if any, should be extended to employees who are suffering from disabilities?
6. What coverage, if any, should be extended to employees during layoff, leaves of absence, strikes, and so forth?
7. Should coverage be limited to full-time employees?[29]

The answers to these questions depend on the policy decisions regarding adequacy, competition, and cost effectiveness discussed in the last section.

---

[28]Rosenbloom and Hallman, *Employee Benefit Planning,* pp. 427–31.
[29]Ibid.

The second administrative issue concerns choice (flexibility) in plan coverage. In the standard benefits package employees typically have not been offered a choice among employee benefits. Rather, a package is designed with the "average" employee in mind and any deviations in needs simply go unsatisfied. The other extreme (discussed in greater detail later) is represented by "cafeteria-style" plans. Under this concept employees are permitted great flexibility in choosing benefits options of greatest value to them. Picture an individual allotted x dollars walking down a cafeteria line and choosing menu items (benefits) according to their attractiveness and cost. The flexibility in this type of plan permits the structuring of packages with maximum impact on employee needs.[30] (See Exhibit 11.3.)

In between these two extremes is an increasingly popular range of options permitting companies to provide some flexibility in benefits choice without going to the extreme of a cafeteria-style plan. Such a plan might provide, for example, (1) optional levels of group term life insurance; (2) the availability of death or disability benefits under pension or profit-sharing plans; (3) choices of covering dependents under group medical expense coverages; (4) a variety of participation, cash distribution, and investment options under profit-sharing, thrift, and capital accumulation plans.[31]

The level at which an organization finally chooses to operate on this choice/flexibility dimension really depends on its evaluation of the relative advantages/disadvantages of employee choice noted in Exhibit 11.3.[32]

EXHIBIT 11.3
Advantages and Disadvantages of Flexible Benefit Programs

Advantages
1. Employees choose packages that best satisfy their unique needs.
2. Flexible benefits help firms meet the *changing* needs of *changing* work force.
3. Increased involvement of employees and families improves understanding of benefits.
4. Flexible plans make introduction of new benefits less costly. The new option is added merely as one among a wide variety of elements from which to choose.
5. Cost containment: Organization sets dollar maximum. Employee chooses within that constraint.

Disadvantages
1. Employees make bad choices and find themselves not covered for predictable emergencies.
2. Administrative burdens and expenses increase.
3. Adverse selection. Employees pick only benefits they will use. The subsequent high benefit utilization increases its cost.

---

[30]TPF & C Survey Report, *Flexible Benefit Programs: A Comprehensive Look at Flexible Spending Accounts and Broad-Based Plans* (New York: Towers, Perrin, Forster & Crosby, 1985).

[31]Kenneth Shapiro, "Flexibility in Benefit Plans," in *1983 Hay Compensation Conference Proceedings* (Philadelphia: Hay Management Consultants, 1983).

[32]Commerce Clearing House, *Flexible Benefits* (Chicago: Commerce Clearing House, 1983); American Can Company, *Do It Your Way* (Greenwich, Conn.: American Can Co., 1978); L. M. Baytos, "The Employee Benefit Smorgasbord: Its Potential and Limitations," *Compensation Review,* First Quarter 1970, pp. 86–90.

The final administrative issue involves the question of financing benefits plans. Alternatives include:

1. Noncontributory (employer pays total costs).
2. Contributory (costs shared between employer and employee).
3. Employee financed (employee pays total costs for some benefits—by law the organization must bear the cost for some benefits).

Exhibit 11.4 shows the arguments for each of these three methods of financing. In general, organizations prefer to make benefits options contributory, reasoning that a "free good," no matter how valuable, is of less value to an

---

EXHIBIT 11.4
Advantages of Different Types of Benefit Financing Plans

Arguments for noncontributory financing:

1. All eligible employees are covered: Under a noncontributory plan, all eligible employees who have completed the probationary period, if any, are covered by the plan. This feature can avoid employee and public relations problems that might arise under a contributory plan. For example, otherwise eligible employees may not elect coverage under a contributory plan and hence, they and/or their dependents may not be covered when a loss or retirement occurs.
2. Tax efficiency: In most cases, employer contributions to an employee benefit plan do not result in current gross income to the covered employees for federal income tax purposes, even though these contributions are normally deductible by the employer as a reasonable and necessary business expense.
3. Group purchasing advantages: To the extent that all eligible employees are covered, as opposed to less than all under a contributory plan, the employer may be able to secure more favorable group rates or other conditions of coverage then would otherwise be the case.
4. Union or collective bargaining pressures: Labor unions generally favor noncontributory plans.
5. Ease and economy of administration: Since payroll deduction is not necessary under a noncontributory plan, benefit and accounting records are easier to maintain.

Arguments for contributory financing:

1. More coverage and/or higher benefits possible: Given a certain level of employer contribution toward the cost of an employee benefit plan, employee contributions may make possible a more adequate plan, or they may enable a plan to be installed in the first place.
2. Possible greater employee appreciation of the plan: When employees contribute to a plan, they will have greater appreciation for the benefits that they are helping to finance. They will not take such benefits for granted.
3. Possible lessening of abuses of benefits: In a vein similar to the previous argument, employees will be less likely to abuse an employee benefit plan if they know that such abuses may increase their own contribution rates.

Arguments for employee-pay-all financing:

1. Separate optional plans may be offered: Some employers offer employees the opportunity of purchasing additional, supplementary coverages at group rates, without individual underwriting, which are separate from the benefits of the regular employee benefit plan. These coverages might include, for example, additional accident insurance, life insurance, hospital indemnity coverage to supplement Medicare. These additional coverages are normally on an employee-pay-all-basis.
2. Benefits not otherwise available: Employee-pay-all financing may be the only basis on which an employer feels it can offer the coverage. In the future, such a plan might be shifted to a contributory or even to a noncontributory basis.

Source: Jerry S. Rosenbloom and G. Victor Hallman, *Employee Benefit Planning*, © 1981, pp. 427, 429–34. Reprinted by permission of Prentice-Hall, Englewood Cliffs, NJ.

employee. Furthermore, employees have no personal interest in controlling the cost of a free good.

COMPONENTS OF A BENEFITS PLAN

Exhibit 11.5 outlines a model of the benefits determination process over time. The remainder of this chapter briefly explains the model and then reviews each of its important components.

The central dynamic of a benefits program involves a negotiating process. While the term *negotiating* typically is associated with a union environment, the process is viewed much more broadly here. Negotiation in this context involves a maximum bilateral effort to satisfy the preferences of both the employer and employee. The crucial element of this process is that it involves a *joint* determination of a benefits package. Joint determination implies that maximal effectiveness of a benefits program requires a reorientation in benefits planning, design, and implementation. Given the costs of benefits, it is no longer

EXHIBIT 11.5
A Model of the Benefits Determination Process

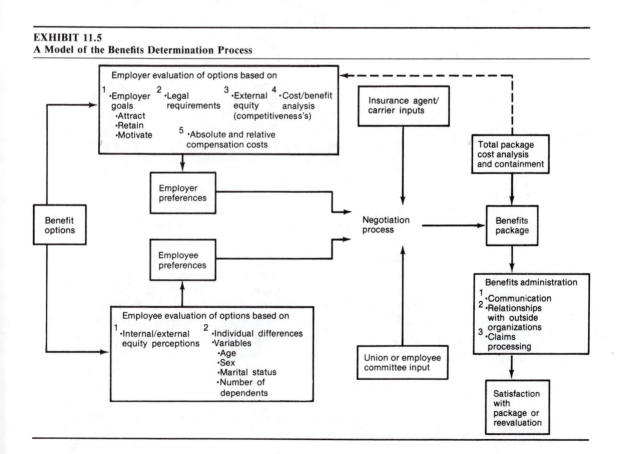

appropriate for top executives or benefits managers to make assumptions about employee needs and design programs based on these all-too-frequently faulty assumptions. Nor is it realistic for employees to expect employers readily to provide every benefit that may "catch their fancy." Rather, employers must develop mechanisms to identify employee needs and to determine the potential costs of these benefits. Correspondingly, employees must expect that the negotiation process involving benefits will be placed in a much broader cost framework that mandates employer consideration of total package costs—a consideration which, in all likelihood, will yield more employer opposition to new benefits options in the decades ahead.

Participating in this negotiation process are a number of interested parties with varying levels of input into the final benefits package. Two of the minor participants are insurance agents and union negotiators. Insurance agents may become involved by providing cost information on different alternatives. Unions, if present, play a somewhat larger role by negotiating for benefits that best represent the collective needs of employees.

Far larger roles in the choice of a final benefits package are played by both employee and employer and their preferences. The next sections review the factors which affect these sets of preferences.

Employer Preferences

As Exhibit 11.5 indicates, a number of factors affect employer preference in determining desirable components of a benefits package. One of the most important, but least effectively considered, is the structure of the package existing from prior years. Many benefits managers fail to recognize the difficulty of eliminating an option once it has been established and accepted by employees. Historically, benefits managers negotiated or provided benefits on a "package" basis rather than a cost basis. The current cost of a benefit would be identified and, if the cost seemed reasonable, the benefit would be provided for (or negotiated with) employees. The crucial error in this process was a failure to recognize that rising costs of this benefit were expected to be borne by the employer. The classic example of this phenomenon is health care coverage. An employer considering a community based medical plan like Blue Cross-Blue Shield (BC-BS) during the early 1960s no doubt agreed to pay all or most of the costs of one of the BC-BS options. As costs of this plan skyrocketed during the 60s and 70s, the employer was expected to continue coverage at the historical level. In effect, the employer became locked into a level of coverage rather than negotiating a level of cost. In subsequent years, then, the spiraling costs were essentially out of the control of the benefits manager.

Admittedly, in subsequent years coverage may be reduced or employee contributions on an option may be required, but the blow to employee perceptions of equity may be severe. A more prudent strategy to determine employer preferences would be a complete cost-benefit analysis and forecasts of future costs *prior to* adopting a particular option.

Cost-benefit analysis. A major reason for the proliferating costs of benefits programs is the narrow focus of benefits administrators. Too frequently the costs/benefits of a particular benefit inclusion are viewed in isolation, without reference to total package costs or forecasts of rising costs in future years. To control spiraling benefits costs, administrators should adopt a broader, cost-centered approach. As a first step, this approach would require policy decisions on the level of benefits expenditures acceptable both in the short and long run. The ability of benefits administrators to control costs within these parameters would be an important dimension in their performance evaluations. As a second step, this approach would require benefits administrators, in cooperation with insurance carriers and armed with published forecasts of anticipated costs for particular benefits, to determine the cost commitments for the existing benefits package. Budget dollars not already earmarked may then be allocated to new benefits that best satisfy organizational goals. Factors affecting this decision include an evaluation of benefits offered by other firms and the competitiveness of the existing package. Also important is compliance with various legal requirements as they change over time (Chapter 12). Finally, the actual benefit of a new option must be explored in relation to employee preferences. Those benefits which top the list of employee preferences should be evaluated in relation to current and future costs. Because future costs estimates may be difficult to project, it is imperative that benefits administrators reduce uncertainty. If a benefit forecast suggests future cost containment may be difficult, the benefit should be offered to employees only on a cost-sharing basis. Management determines what percentage of cost it can afford to bear within budget projections, and the option is offered to employees on a cost-sharing basis, with projected increases in both employer and employee costs communicated openly. In the negotiation process, then, employees or union representatives can evaluate their preference for the option against the forecasted cost burden. In effect, this approach defines the contribution an employer is willing to make, in advance. And it avoids the constraints of a defined benefit strategy that burdens the employer with continued provision of that defined benefit level despite rapidly spiralling costs.

External equity. Two important considerations establish external equity in a benefits program. One of the issues that must be confronted is the absolute level of benefits payments relative to important product and labor market competitors. A policy decision must be made about the position (market lead, market lag, or competitive) the organization wants to maintain in its absolute level of benefits relative to the competition. Many employers adopt a benefit a competitor has initiated only to find some time later that it is inappropriate given the makeup of the organization. A classic example is the employer who installs an education reimbursement plan in an organization with an aging work force. Data suggest this composition of employees is less likely to use this benefit, and consequently place relatively low value on it.

One of the best strategies to determine *external equity* is to conduct a benefits survey. Alternatively, many consulting organizations, professional associations, and interest groups collect benefits data that can be purchased. Perhaps the most widely used of these surveys is the annual benefits survey conducted by the U.S. Chamber of Commerce. To illustrate typical inclusions in a survey, the survey used by the U.S. Chamber of Commerce is reproduced in Exhibit 11.6.[33]

Legal requirements. Since the turn of the century both the state and federal governments have shown considerable interest in the benefits area. In particular, governmental policy consistently has been to legally require employers to provide a cushion of economic and social security. Employers are legally required to finance all or part of the costs of workers' compensation, unemployment insurance, social security, and pension plans.[34]

Absolute and relative compensation costs. Any evaluation of employee benefits must be placed in the context of total compensation costs. Cost competitiveness means the total package must be competitive—not just specific segments. Consequently, decisions on whether to adopt certain options must be considered in light of the impact on total costs and in relationship to expenditures of competitors (as determined in benefits surveys such as the Chamber of Commerce survey discussed later in this chapter.)

Employee Preferences

Employee preferences for various benefit options are determined by individual needs. Those benefits perceived to best satisfy individual needs are most highly desired. In part these needs arise out of feelings of perceived equity or inequity. For example, consider government employees living in the same neighborhood as autoworkers. Imagine the dissatisfaction with government holidays created when they discover the autoworkers are home the whole week between Christmas and New Year's Day. The perceived unfairness of this difference need not be rational. But it is, nevertheless, a factor that must be considered in determining employee needs. Occasionally this comparison process leads to a "bandwagon" effect, where new benefits offered by a competitor are adopted without careful consideration simply because the employer wants to avoid hard feelings. This phenomenon is particularly apparent for employers with strong commitments to maintaining a totally or partially nonunion work force. Benefits obtained by a unionized competitor or a unionized segment of the firm's work

---

[33]U.S. Chamber of Commerce, *Employee Benefits, 1984.*

[34]James Ledvinka, *Federal Regulation of Personnel and Human Resource Management* (Belmont, Calif.: Kent Publishing, 1982).

EXHIBIT 11.6
Copy of Questionnaire Used in Chamber of Commerce Employee Benefits Survey—1984

This survey is confidential. Data of individual firms will not be disclosed. Data furnished will be published only in the form of totals for groups of companies. Only persons handling the research will see your report.

1. **Coverage.** If you have several divisions or plants, data covering any typical group of employees will be satisfactory.
2. **Employees Covered in Survey.** Except for banks, financial institutions, etc., limit data included in this report to hourly-rated employees and to salaried employees who are paid on a similar basis. That is, include data for salaried employees if their pay varies depending on whether they work overtime or less than full time, but do not include them if they receive their regular daily or weekly pay regardless of hours worked. Since this definition would exclude many employees of banks, financial institutions, etc., for these firms, please include all nonsupervisory employees and all working supervisors, regardless of their method of payment. Please exclude all officers of company. Hospitals having difficulty making this employee separation can also include data for all employees.
3. **Approximate or Incomplete Data.** If you are unable to give exact data for the various items in the questionnaire, please give estimates—we would prefer a good estimate to a blank space. If you are unable to break down the data on payments exactly as we have outlined it, please give the data that is available. Please indicate the items for which payments were made but for which you cannot give separate figures.
4. **Question A. Gross Payroll Data.** For this item report actual wages (not take-home pay after deductions have been made). Report on line A-1 the straight-time wages for all hours, including pay for time not worked, plus payments in lieu of vacations and holidays. Report premium and bonus payments on other lines. Thus, if an employee receives $10 an hour for straight time and $5 additional for overtime after 40 hours, for each hour of overtime worked after 40 hours, $10 would be entered on line A-1, and $5 on line A-2.
5. **Items C-1, C-4, and C-6. Pension and Insurance Premiums.** For pension and insurance premiums, report net payments after deducting any dividends or credits returned to employer by insurer. In pension programs the company's long-term commitment is fixed, not tied to profits. Profit-sharing payments are reported as Item F-1.
6. **Item C-4. Life Insurance.** Exclude premiums for life insurance purchased under a pension plan. Such premiums should be reported under Item C-1.
7. **Item C-6. Medical Care Insurance.** Include premiums which supplement medicare coverage of retired employees.
8. **Item F-1. Profit-Sharing Payments.** Company contributions are based on current profits of the business, fluctuating with current profit levels.
9. **Item F-2. Contributions to Employee Thrift Plans.** Company contributions are not tied to current profit levels but are a fixed proportion of amount contributed by employees.
10. **Question G. Employee Payroll Deductions.** For this question report deductions from employee pay. Employer contributions are reported in questions B and C.
11. **Question H. Employee Hours.** This is the number of hours worked or paid for, corresponding to earnings given on line A-1. Employee hours for full-time employee. Report the total number of hours for a typical full-time employee in 1984. It would be the number of hours representing the wages shown on line A-1, including paid vacation period, paid holidays, and paid sick leave. If hours would not be the same for all employees, show hours for the majority of employees.

EXHIBIT 11.6 (*continued*)

CONFIDENTIAL

EMPLOYEE BENEFITS SURVEY—1985

Show actual data or best estimate for employees covered in survey.

A. GROSS PAYROLL FOR EMPLOYEES IN SURVEY:

- For this item, report **actual** wages (**not** take-home pay after deductions have been made). Report on line A-1 the straight-time wages for all hours, including pay for time not worked, plus payments in lieu of vacations and holidays.
- Report premium and bonus payments on lines other than line A-1. Thus, if the rate is $10.00 an hour for straight time and $5.00 additional for overtime after 40 hours, for each hour of overtime worked after 40 hours, $10.00 would be entered on line A-1, and $5.00 on line A-2.

Total amount for 1985

1. Straight time for employees in survey	$_____	33
2. Overtime premium pay	$_____	45
3. Holiday premium pay	$_____	57
4. Shift differential	$_____	69
5. Earned incentive or production bonus	$_____	81
6. Other (Specify: _____)	$_____	93
7. TOTAL GROSS PAYROLL	$_____	105

Include BONUS AND PREMIUM PAY ONLY on lines 2-6. Report straight-time pay on line 1.

B. LEGALLY REQUIRED PAYMENTS (employer's share only):

1. Old-Age, Survivors, Disability, and Health Insurance (employer FICA taxes)	$_____	120
2. Unemployment Compensation (federal and state taxes)	$_____	132
3. Workers' Compensation (estimate cost if self-insured)	$_____	144
4. Railroad Retirement Tax	$_____	156
5. Railroad Unemployment and Cash Sickness Insurance	$_____	168
6. State sickness benefits insurance	$_____	180
7. Other (Specify: _____)	$_____	192
8. TOTAL	$_____	204

C. VOLUNTARY OR AGREED-UPON PAYMENTS (employer's share only):

ITEMS C-1, C-4 AND C-6—PENSION AND INSURANCE PREMIUMS. For pension and insurance premiums, report net payments after deducting any dividends or credits returned to employer by insurer. In **pension programs**, the company's long-term commitment is fixed, not tied to profits. Profit-sharing payments are reported as item F-1.

ITEM C-4—LIFE INSURANCE. Exclude premiums for life insurance purchased under a pension plan. Such premiums should be reported under item C-1.

ITEM C-6—MEDICAL CARE INSURANCE. Include premiums which supplement Medicare coverage of retired employees.

1. Pension plan premiums under insurance and annuity contracts (net)	$_____	219
2. Payments to uninsured trusteed pension plans	$_____	231
3. Pension payments under unfunded pension programs	$_____	243
4. Life insurance premiums (net)	$_____	255
5. Death benefits not covered by insurance	$_____	267
6. Hospital, surgical, medical, and major medical insurance premiums (net)	$_____	279
7. Hospital, surgical, medical, and major medical payments self-insured	$_____	291
8. Life and health insurance combined	$_____	303
9. Short-term disability, sickness or accident insurance (company plan or insured plan)	$_____	315
10. Salary or wage continuation or long-term disability (insured, self-administered, or trust)	$_____	327
11. Dental insurance premiums	$_____	339
12. Discounts on goods and services purchased from company by employees	$_____	351
13. Employee meals furnished by company	$_____	363
14. Child care	$_____	375
15. Parking	$_____	387
16. Physical and mental fitness programs	$_____	399
17. Other (vision care, prescription drugs, etc. Specify: _____)	$_____	411
18. TOTAL	$_____	423

EXHIBIT 11.6 (*concluded*)

D. PAID REST PERIODS, COFFEE BREAKS, LUNCH PERIODS, WASH-UP TIME, TRAVEL TIME, CLOTHES-CHANGE TIME, GET-READY TIME, ETC.

Total amount for 1985

- This should be reported *if* time is paid for, whether or not there is a formal work rule providing for such time off. A simple rule of thumb is that if employees typically take two 10-minute rest periods per day, this would amount to approximately 4% of gross payroll; if two 15-minute breaks are taken, the figure would come to 6% of gross payroll (Item A-7). $ _____ 438

E. OTHER PAYMENTS FOR TIME NOT WORKED:
- If you lack exact data for these items, please give your best estimate.

1. Payments for or in lieu of vacations..	$ _____ 450
2. Payments for or in lieu of holidays not worked...........................	$ _____ 462
3. Sick leave pay...	$ _____ 474
4. Payments required under guaranteed workweek or work year	$ _____ 486
5. Jury, witness, and voting pay allowances..................................	$ _____ 498
6. National Defense, State or National Guard duty	$ _____ 510
7. Payment for time lost due to death in family or other personal reasons	$ _____ 522
8. Maternity leave pay	$ _____ 534
9. Other (Specify: _____)	$ _____ 546
10. TOTAL	$ _____ 558

F. OTHER ITEMS:

1. Profit-sharing payments (Company contributions are based on current profits of the business, fluctuating with current profit levels).	
(a) Current cash payments...	$ _____ 573
(b) Payments to deferred profit-sharing trusts	$ _____ 585
2. Contributions to employee thrift or stock purchase plans (Company contributions are *not* tied to current profit levels, but are a fixed proportion of amount contributed by employees).	$ _____ 597
3. Christmas or other special bonuses (not tied to profits), service awards, suggestion awards, etc.	$ _____ 609
4. Employee education expenditures (tuition refunds, seminar attendance, etc.)	$ _____ 621
5. Payments to union stewards or officials for time spent in settling grievances or in negotiating agreements	$ _____ 633
6. Special wage payments ordered by courts, wage adjustment boards, etc...........................	$ _____ 645
7. Other (Specify: _____)	$ _____ 657
8. TOTAL	$ _____ 669

G. EMPLOYEE PAYROLL DEDUCTIONS: (employees' share only):
- For this question, report deductions from *employee* pay. Employer contributions are reported in questions B and C.

1. Old-Age, Survivors, Disability, and Health Insurance (employee FICA taxes)	$ _____ 684
2. Railroad Retirement Tax	$ _____ 696
3. State sickness benefits insurance tax.......................................	$ _____ 708
4. Pension plan premiums or contributions	$ _____ 720
5. Life insurance premiums	$ _____ 732
6. Hospital, surgical, medical, and major medical insurance premiums or contributions	$ _____ 744
7. Other (Specify: _____). Do not include deductions for income tax........	$ _____ 756
8. TOTAL	$ _____ 768

H. EMPLOYEE HOURS
- These figures include hours worked or paid for, including time actually worked, *plus* holidays, vacation, sick leave, and other time paid for but not worked.

1. **Employee hours for full-time employee.** Report the total number of hours for a typical full-time employee in 1985, including paid vacation period, paid holidays, paid sick leave, etc. If hours would not be the same for all employees, show hours for the majority of employees, calculated as follows.

Total hours of a **typical full-time employee** during 1985:

$$\underline{\qquad\qquad} \times \quad 52 \quad = \quad \underline{\qquad\qquad} \; 783$$

average number of hours per week per employee   total hours during 1985 per employee

2. The total number of hours of all employees worked or paid for, covering all employees in the survey, corresponding to earnings given on line A-1, is calculated as follows.

Total hours of **all employees** in survey during 1985:

$$\underline{\qquad\qquad} \times \quad \underline{\qquad\qquad} \quad = \quad \underline{\qquad\qquad} \; 795$$

total hours per employee in 1985   number of employees included in your survey data   total hours of all employees in 1985

PRIMARY STANDARD INDUSTRIAL CLASSIFICATION CODE (SIC Code)   =   _____

- If you do not know your SIC Code, please give a description of the type of business and/or the principal lines or products manufactured or handled.

_____

_____

force are frequently passed along to nonunion employees. While the effectiveness of this strategy in thwarting unionization efforts has not been demonstrated, many nonunion firms would prefer to provide the benefit as a safety measure.

A major assumption in empirical efforts to determine employee preferences is that preferences are somehow systematically related to what are termed demographic differences. The demographic approach assumes that demographic groups (e.g., young versus old, married versus unmarried) can be identified for which benefits preferences are fairly consistent across members of the group. Furthermore, it assumes that meaningful differences exist between groups in terms of benefit preferences.

There is some evidence that these assumptions are only partially correct. In an extensive review of employee preference literature, Glueck traced patterns of group preferences for particular benefits.[35] As one might expect, older workers showed stronger preferences than younger workers for pension plans.[36] Also, families with dependents had stronger preferences for health/medical coverage than families with no dependents.[37] The big surprise in all these studies, though, is that many of the other demographic group breakdowns fail to result in differential benefit preferences. Traditionally, it has been assumed that benefit preferences ought to differ among males versus females, blue collar versus white collar, married versus single, young versus old, and families with dependents versus those with none. Few of these expectations have been borne out by these studies. Rather, the studies have tended to be more valuable in showing preference trends that are characteristics of all employees. Among the benefits available, health/medical and stock plans are highly preferred benefits, while such options as early retirement, profit sharing, shorter hours, and counseling services rank among the least-preferred options. Beyond these conclusions, most preference studies have shown wide variation in individuals with respect to benefit preferences.

The weakness of this demographic approach has led some organizations to undertake a second and more expensive empirical method of determining employee preference: surveying individuals about needs. One way of accomplishing this requires development of a questionnaire on which employees evaluate various benefits. For example, Exhibit 11.7 illustrates two types of questionnaire formats.

While other strategies for scaling are available (e.g., paired comparison),

---

[35]William F. Glueck, *Personnel: A Diagnostic Approach* (Plano, Tex.: Business Publications, 1978).

[36]Ludwig Wagner and Theodore Bakerman, "Wage Earners' Opinions of Insurance Fringe Benefits," *Journal of Insurance,* June 1960, pp. 17–28; Brad Chapman and Robert Otterman, "Employee Preference for Various Compensation and Benefits Options," *Personnel Administrator* 25 (November 1975), pp. 31–36.

[37]Stanley Nealy, "Pay and Benefit Preferences," *Industrial Relations* (October 1963), pp. 17–28.

EXHIBIT 11.7
Questionnaire Formats for Benefits Surveys

A. Ranking method
Rank order the following benefits from 1 (high) to 4 (low) in terms of their value to you.
_____Health/medical coverage.
_____Extended holiday schedule.
_____Pension plan.
_____Life insurance.

B. Likert-type scale
How important are each of the following benefits to you (check one for each benefit).

	(1) Very Important	*(2)* Important	*(3)* Neutral	*(4)* Unimportant	*(5)* Very Unimportant
Health/medical coverage	_____	_____	_____	_____	_____
Extended holiday schedule	_____	_____	_____	_____	_____
Pension plan	_____	_____	_____	_____	_____
Life insurance	_____	_____	_____	_____	_____

---

the most important factor to remember is that a consistent method must be used in assessing preferences on a questionnaire. Switching between a ranking method and a Likert-type scale may, by itself, affect the results.[38]

A third empirical method of identifying individual employee preferences is commonly known as a cafeteria-style plan (also called, at various times, a supermarket plan or smorgasbord plan). Picture a cafeteria that offers different benefit options at varying prices. Employees are allotted a fixed amount of money and permitted to spend that amount in the purchase of benefit options. A cafeteria-style plan operates very much in this manner. From a theoretical perspective, this approach to benefits packaging is ideal. Employees directly identify the benefits of greatest value to them, and by constraining the dollars employees have to spend, benefits managers are able to control benefits costs.

The simplicity and apparent validity of this approach for identifying employee preferences has generated considerable interest in American industry.[39] Beyond the pioneering efforts of American Can Company, TRW, and Education Testing Service, current estimates indicate 90 percent of all companies (1,100 surveyed) are considering, or have in place, elements of a flexible benefits plan.[40] This suggests that flexible benefits really exist in far more than the

---

[38]George T. Milkovich and Michael J. Delaney, "A Note on Cafeteria Pay Plans," *Industrial Relations* (February 1975), pp. 112–16.

[39]Concern exists that tax laws may change to lessen attractiveness of these plans.

[40]CompFlash, "Flexible Compensation," *AMA CompFlash* 84–7 (1984), p. 4.

40 companies typically cited as adoptees.[41] For example, virtually all organizations with pensions have electives to cover spouses or others. Another 50 percent of all companies have an option allowing employees to supplement their group life insurance plans.[42] Even the proliferation of articles on how to set up successful flexible benefits plans attests to their increasing popularity.[43]

The Negotiation Process

It would be nice to believe that determination of benefits is a bilateral process. Unfortunately, there are numerous cases where this appears not to be true. In some cases organizations provide benefits without consulting employees about their preferences. In other cases a union representing employees will push hard for a benefit that is granted by management's negotiator without conferring with the benefits managers about long-term cost implications. Neither strategy is optimal. Rather, multiple groups should be involved in a negotiating process, and this holds true whether the firm is unionized or not. On management's side, the labor relations expert (if any) must be in constant touch with the benefits manager to identify options and their cost implications. In turn, the benefits manager must decide whether the organization should directly finance the benefit or obtain indirect coverage through an agent or carrier. If this latter option is chosen, the agent can provide valuable costing information and suggestions on plan design.

From the employee's side, unions must be sensitive to which benefit options are most important to union members. Formal or informal polling provides the input for initial demands. As cost implications are determined and as the relative priority of specific benefits becomes clearer for both parties, the negotiations can proceed more rationally.

Administering the Benefits Program

The job description for an employee-benefits executive found in Exhibit 11.8 indicates that administrative time is spent on two functions that require further discussion: (1) communicating about the benefits program, and (2) claims processing.[44]

---

[41]Shapiro, "Flexibility in Benefit Plans."

[42]Ibid.

[43]Peter W. Stonebraker, "A Three-Tier Plan for Cafeteria Benefits," *Personnel Journal* 44 (December 1984), pp. 51–57; Lance D. Tane, "Guidelines to Successful Flex Plans: Four Companies' Experiences," *Compensation and Benefits Review*, 1984, pp. 38–45; Peter W. Stonebraker, "Flexible and Incentive Benefits: A Guide to Program Development," *Compensation Review* 17, no. 2 (1985), pp. 40–53; Robert C. Wender and Ronald L. Sladky, "Flexible Benefit Opportunities for the Small Employer," *Personnel Administrator* 34 (December 1984), pp. 113–19.

[44]McCaffery, *Managing the Employee Benefits Program.*

[Handwritten marginal notes:]

why the growing trend toward Flexible benefit plans:

1. Demographic shift in the workforce (= People are different)
   → used to be design around married, male breadwinner w/ 2.3 kids etc, now also employ young unmarried mothers etc.
   Shift in attitudes (= People want more input)

2. (= People want more input)

3. Co. specific reason is that most organizations can't afford all benefit plans for all people

EXHIBIT 11.8
Job Description for Employee-Benefits Executive

Position
    The primary responsibility of this position is the administration of established company benefits programs. Develops and recommends new and improved policies and plans with regard to employee benefits. Assures compliance with ERISA requirements and regulations.

Specific Functions
1. Administers group life insurance, health and accident insurance, retirement programs, and savings plans.
2. Processes documents necessary for the implementation of various benefits programs and maintains such records as are necessary.
3. Recommends and approves procedures for maintenance of benefits programs and issues operating instructions.
4. Participates in the establishment of long-range objectives of company benefits programs.
5. Conducts surveys and analyzes and maintains an organized body of information on benefits programs of other companies.
6. Informs management of trends and developments in the field of company benefits.
7. Gives advice and counsel regarding current developments in benefits programs.
8. Acts as liaison between company and banks, insurance companies, and other agencies.
9. Conducts special studies as requested by management.
    In addition, the employee-benefits executive may be responsible for various employee services, such as recreation programs, advisory services, credit unions, and savings bond purchase programs.

Source: Robert McCaffery, *Managing the Employee Benefits Program* (New York: American Management Association, 1983), p. 25.

Employee Benefits Communication

The most frequent method for communicating employee benefits is the employee-benefits booklet.[45] A typical booklet would contain a description of all benefits, including levels of coverage and eligibility requirements. For new employees this benefits manual might be accompanied by either a verbal presentation or, more frequently these days, an audiovisual presentation. While some organizations may have periodic sessions with employees (e.g., once per year), a more typical approach would be one-on-one discussions between the benefits administrator and an employee seeking information on a particular benefit.

A current popular communication tool for employee benefits invokes the flexibility of computers to provide individualized benefits statements for each employee. These tailor-made reports indicate package components and provide selected cost data about the options. Despite this and other innovative plans to communicate employee benefit packages, failure to understand benefits components and their value is still one of the root causes of employee dissatisfaction with a benefits package.[46] Recommendations to overcome this problem include the following four suggestions:[47]

---

[45]Maria McNally, "Employee Benefits Communications," in *Employee Benefits Management*, ed. H. Wayne Snider (New York: Risk and Insurance Management Society, 1980), pp. 153–64.

[46]Reported in "Yider-Heneman Creativity Award Supplement," *Personnel Administration* 26, no. 11 (1981), pp. 49–67.

[47]McCaffery, *Managing the Employee Benefits Program*.

1. Development of a benefits manual for employees that outlines their entitlements and restrictions on benefits coverage.
2. Periodic explanation (particularly for new employees) of more widely used and/or misunderstood benefits.
3. A willingness to provide "spot" counseling to employees who have questions about particular benefits. Not only a formal mechanism is required, but also an attitude that it is appropriate for employees to seek counseling.
4. Cost data—perhaps most important, employees should be aware of the costs incurred in providing benefits to them. A number of different strategies are available for conveying cost information.
   a. Total annual cost—frequently employees are amazed at the total costs borne by an employer for a benefits program. This can be a particularly useful tool if comparisons are made with past years to show escalating costs.
   b. Percentage of payroll—a particularly valuable comparison to demonstrate competitiveness with other firms.
   c. Average cost per employee per year—this means of communicating costs is most useful for employees who view their salaries in annualized terms (e.g., exempt employees, particularly managerial, professional, and executive levels).
   d. Average cents per hour—this approach is most appropriate for employees who view wages on an hourly basis (i.e., hourly staff).
   e. Employer/employee cost ratios—these figures are essential both as a summary statistic and to demonstrate to employees the proportions (and dollars) paid on each benefit by the employer and employee.

Relationship with Outside Organizations

Virtually all employee benefits come under the scrutiny of some government agency. Some employee benefits, such as the legally required unemployment compensation, workers' compensation, and social security, require extensive liaison with government agencies. For example, workers' compensation and unemployment compensation claims by employees require employer contacts with the appropriate agencies. Companies that establish a reputation of being communicative and cooperative can expect objective reviews of all claims and challenges to claims.[48]

Claims Processing

As noted by one expert, claims processing arises when an employee asserts that a specific event (e.g., disablement, hospitalization, unemployment) has occurred

---

[48]Robert McCaffery, *Managing the Employee Benefits Program,* rev. ed. (New York: American Management Association, 1983).

and demands that the employer fulfill a promise of payment.[49] As such, a claims processor must first determine whether the act has, in fact, occurred. If the answer is yes, the second step involves determining if the employee is eligible for the benefit. If payment is not denied at this stage, the claims processor calculates payment level. It is particularly important at this stage to ensure coordination of benefits. If multiple insurance companies are liable for payment (e.g., working spouses covered by different insurers) a good claims processor can save from 10 to 15 percent of claims cost by ensuring that the liability is jointly paid.[50]

While these steps are time-consuming, most of the work is quite routine in nature. The major job challenges come in those approximately 10 percent of all claims where payment is denied. A benefits administrator must then become an adroit counselor, explaining the situation to the employee in a manner that conveys the equitable and consistent procedures used.

Cost Analysis and Containment

Cost containment is easily the biggest issue in benefits planning and administration today.[51] Escalating costs of the 1960s and 1970s, combined with disappointing evidence that benefits have little impact on shaping positive employee behaviors, have molded the cost-cutting drives of the 1980s. Increasingly, employers are auditing their benefits options for cost containment opportunities. The terminology of cost containment is becoming a part of every employee's vocabulary; Exhibit 11.9 provides definitions of some common cost containment terms. Additional discussion of cost containment strategies for specific benefits is included in Chapter 12.

Monitoring the Benefits Environment

The model of the benefits process (Exhibit 11.5) presented earlier has a final variable—satisfaction with pay package. In effect, this variable is included because a benefits package must have a monitoring process. The key to this monitoring function is that both employers and employees must periodically (at *least* once yearly) assess whether specific components and the total benefits package are meeting desired goals. From the employer's perspective, it is important to ensure: compliance with changing legal requirements, competitiveness with relevant organizations, and cost effectiveness of existing options. In turn, employees must evaluate how well benefits satisfy their changing needs. To the extent either party is dissatisfied with the outcomes of this monitoring process, it may signal a need for change in some of the benefits components discussed in the next chapter.

---

[49]Bennet Shaver, "The Claims Process," in *Employee Benefit Management,* ed. H. Wayne Snider, pp. 141–52.

[50]Thomas Fannin and Theresa Fannin, "Coordination of Benefits: Uncovering Buried Treasure," *Personnel Journal,* May 1983, pp. 386–91.

[51]McCaffery, *Managing the Employee Benefits Program.*

EXHIBIT 11.9
A Basic Primer of Cost Containment Terminology

Deductibles: An employee claim for insurance coverage is preceded by the requirement that the first x dollars be paid by the claimant.

Coinsurance: A proportion of insurance premiums are paid by the employee.

Benefit cutbacks: Corresponding to wage concessions some employers are negotiating with employees to eliminate or reduce employer contributions to selected options.

Defined contribution plans: Employers establish the limits of their responsibility for employee benefits in terms of dollar contribution maximum.

Defined benefits plans: Employers establish the limits of their responsibility for employee benefits in terms of a specific benefit and the options included. As the cost of these options rises in future years the employer is obligated to provide the benefit as negotiated, despite its increased cost.

Dual coverage: In families where both spouses work there is frequently coverage of specific claims from each employer's benefit package. Employers cut costs by specifying payment limitations under such conditions.

Benefit ceiling: Establishing a maximum payout for specific claims (e.g., limiting liability for extended hospital stays to $150,000).

SUMMARY

Given the rapid escalation in the cost of employee benefits over the past 15 years, organizations would do well to evaluate the effectiveness of their benefits adoption, retention, and termination procedures. Specifically, how does an organization go about selecting appropriate employee benefits? Are the decisions based on sound evaluation of employee preferences balanced against organizational goals of legal compliance and competitiveness? Do the benefits chosen serve to attract, retain and/or motivate employees? Or are organizations paying billions of dollars of indirect compensation without any tangible benefit? This chapter has outlined a benefits determination process that identifies major issues in selecting and evaluating particular benefit choices. The next chapter catalogues the various benefits available and discusses some of the decisions confronting a benefits administrator.

REVIEW QUESTIONS

1. Why have employee benefits as a proportion of total labor costs expanded so dramatically since World War II?
2. What does the term *cost effective* mean? Are employee benefits cost effective?
3. What are the advantages of flexible (cafeteria-style) benefits over standard benefit packages? The disadvantages?
4. How is the concept of external equity similar or different in discussing pay versus benefits?
5. How might a benefits administrator effectively measure employee preferences for different types of benefits?
6. Design a program to communicate effectively an employee benefits program. What are the key elements of this communication?

Chapter *12*

Benefits Options

Human resources professionals share three widely held views about benefits administration. First, the number of employee benefits and the laws affecting them have been escalating rapidly. Second, a good benefits administrator can save an organization substantial sums of money through proper benefits plan design and effective administration of benefits. Third, proficiency in benefits plan administration requires years of experience. The first two of these statements were endorsed in Chapter 11. The third statement, however, requires qualification. Admittedly, the number of benefit options and choices can, at times, be quite overwhelming. Even trained human resource professionals can err in their evaluation of the package. For example, one study asked both college graduates and human resource professionals to rank order 11 different benefits equated for costs to a company.[1] The HR professionals' role was to estimate the graduates' responses. Surprisingly, at least to the recruiters, the college graduates placed high value on medical/life insurance, company stocks, and pensions. Lesser importance was placed on holidays and scheduling conveniences (e.g., flextime, four-day work week). The recruiters systematically underestimated the value of most of the top benefits and overestimated the value of the time and schedule benefits. Despite the surprises, though, and despite the obvious magnitude of benefits information, there are still some basic issues which can be identified as equally relevant across different organizations. These commonalities serve as a foundation for aspiring benefits plan administrators. After categorizing benefits, these issues will be discussed as they relate to each benefit category. Exhibit 12.1 provides the most widely accepted categorization of employee benefits. In their annual report based on a nationwide survey of employee benefits, the U.S. Chamber of Commerce identifies five categories of benefits.[2] Since this breakdown is familiar to benefits plan administrators, it will be used to organize this chapter and illustrate important principles affecting administration of each benefit type. Exhibit 12.2 provides Department of Labor data on employee participation in selected benefits programs.[3] Notice the high rate of participation for such common benefits as life/health insurance and pension plans. These participation rates are only exceeded by those of legally required benefits.

LEGALLY REQUIRED BENEFITS

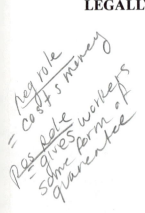

Virtually every employee benefit is *affected* by statutory or common law (many of the limitations are imposed by tax laws). In this section the primary focus will be on benefits that are *required* by statutory law: workers' compensation, social security, and unemployment compensation. The one exception to this coverage will be the inclusion of equal employment opportunity laws as they affect employee benefits—a legal minefield for benefits managers, lawyers, and executives.

---

[1]Kermit Davis, William Giles, and Hubert Feild, "Compensation and Fringe Benefits: How Recruiters View New College Graduates' Preferences," *Personnel Administrator,* January 1985, pp. 43–50.

[2]U.S. Chamber of Commerce, *Employee Benefits, 1985* (Washington, D.C.: Chamber of Commerce, 1984).

[3]U.S. Department of Labor, *Employee Benefits in Medium and Large Firms, 1983,* Bulletin 2213, August 1984.

EXHIBIT 12.1
Categorization of Employee Benefits

Type of Benefit (total employee benefits as percent of payroll):
1. Legally required payments (employer's share only):
    a. Old-age, survivors, disability, and health insurance (employer FICA taxes)
    b. Unemployment compensation (federal and state taxes)
    c. Workers' compensation (estimate cost if self-insured)
    d. Railroad retirement tax
    e. Railroad unemployment and cash sickness insurance
    f. State sickness benefits insurance
2. Pension and insurance premiums; voluntary or agreed-upon payments (employer's share only):
    a. Pension plan premiums under insurance and annuity contracts (net)
    b. Payments to uninsured trusteed pension plans
    c. Pension payments under unfunded pension programs
    d. Life insurance premiums (net)
    e. Death benefits not covered by insurance
    f. Hospital, surgical, medical, and major medical insurance premiums (net)
    g. Hospital, surgical, medical, and major medical payments (self-insured)
    h. Life and health insurance combined
    i. Short-term disability, sickness, or accident insurance (company plan or insured plan)
    j. Salary or wage continuation or long-term disability (insured, self-administered, or trust)
    k. Dental insurance premiums
    l. Discounts on goods and services purchased from company by employees
    m. Employee meals furnished by company
    n. Miscellaneous payments (child care, parking, physical and mental fitness programs, vision care, prescription drugs, etc.)
3. Paid rest periods, coffee breaks, lunch periods, wash-up time, travel time, clothes-change time, get-ready time, etc.
4. Other payments for time not worked:
    a. Payments for or in lieu of vacations
    b. Payments for or in lieu of holidays not worked
    c. Sick leave pay
    d. Payments required under guaranteed workweek or work year
    e. Jury, witness, and voting pay allowances
    f. National Defense, State or National Guard duty
    g. Payment for time lost due to death in family or other personal reasons
    h. Maternity leave pay
5. Other items:
    a. Profit-sharing payments (company contributions are based on current profits of the business, fluctuating with current profit levels)
        (1) Current cash payments
        (2) Payments to deferred profit-sharing trusts
    b. Contributions to employee thrift or stock purchase plans (company contributions are *not* tied to current profit levels, but are a fixed proportion of amount contributed by employees)
    c. Christmas or other special bonuses (not tied to profits), service awards, suggestion awards, etc.
    d. Employee education expenditures (tuition refunds, seminar attendance, etc.)
    e. Payments to union stewards or officials for time spent in settling grievances or in negotiating agreements
    f. Special wage payments ordered by courts, wage adjustment boards, etc.

Source: Chamber of Commerce of the United States, *Employee Benefits Survey, 1985.*

EXHIBIT 12.2
Summary: Percent of Full-Time Employees by Participation in Employee Benefit Programs, Medium and Large Firms, 1983

Employee Benefit Program	All Employees	Professional and Administrative Employees	Technical and Clerical Employees	Production Employees
Paid:				
Holidays	99	99	100	98
Vacations	100	100	100	99
Personal leave	25	31	35	17
Lunch period	11	4	5	17
Rest time	74	58	76	80
Sick leave	67	92	91	42
Sickness and accident insurance	49	29	34	67
Noncontributory*	41	22	26	57
Long-term disability insurance	45	66	58	28
Noncontributory*	34	47	42	23
Health insurance for employee	96	98	95	96
Noncontributory*	65	62	54	71
Health insurance for dependents	93	95	91	92
Noncontributory*	43	42	35	47
Life insurance	96	97	95	95
Noncontributory*	80	79	78	81
Retirement pension	82	86	84	79
Noncontributory*	75	79	79	72

Note: Participation is defined as coverage by a time off, insurance, or pension plan. Employees subject to a minimum service requirement before they are eligible for a benefit are counted as participants even if they have not met the requirement at the time of the survey. If employees are required to pay part of the cost of a benefit, only those who elect the coverage and pay their share are counted as participants. Benefits for which the employee must pay the full premium are outside the scope of the survey. Only current employees are counted as participants; retirees are excluded even if participating in a benefit program.

*All coverage in the benefit program is provided at no cost to employee. Supplemental life insurance and pension plans, not tabulated in this bulletin, may be contributory.

Workers' Compensation

Workers' compensation is an insurance program, paid for by the employer, designed to protect employees from expenses incurred for a work-related injury or disease. An injury or disease qualifies for workers' compensation if it results from an accident that arose out of, and while in, the course of employment. An employee may receive workers' compensation benefits for:

1. Permanent total disability and temporary total disability.
2. Scheduled injuries—loss of use of a body member.
3. Survivor benefits for fatal injuries.
4. Medical expenses.
5. Rehabilitation.
6. Disfigurement.

Of these six benefit payments, the medical expenses category is the most expensive, accounting for more than 30 percent of workers' compensation pay-

EXHIBIT 12.3
Commonalities in State Workers' Compensation Laws

Issue	Most Common State Provision
Type of law	• Compulsory ($N = 47$ states). • Elective ($N = 3$ states).
Self insurance	• Self-insurance permitted ($N = 47$ states).
Coverage	• All industrial employment. • Farm labor, domestic servants and casual employees usually exempted. • Compulsory for all or most public sector employees ($N = 47$ states).
Occupational diseases	• Coverage for all diseases arising out of and in the course of employment. No compensation for "ordinary diseases of life."

ments. Exhibit 12.3 summarizes the most common features of the various state laws.[4]

Workers' compensation can consist of either monetary reimbursement or payment of medical expenses. The amount of compensation is based on fixed schedules of minimum and maximum payments. Disability payments are often tied to the employee's earnings, modified by such economic factors as the number of dependents.

The employee receives workers' compensation, regardless of fault in an accident. Detailed record keeping of work accidents, illnesses, and deaths are required by state statute.

States require that employers obtain workers' compensation insurance through a private carrier or, in some states, through participation in a state fund. The employer is liable for premium payments; the employee does not pay for this insurance.

Some states provide "second injury funds" to relieve an employer's liability when a preemployment injury combines with a work-related injury to produce a disability greater than that caused by the latter alone. For example, if a person with a known heart condition breaks an arm in a fall triggered by a heart attack, medical treatments for the heart condition would not be paid from workers' compensation insurance; treatment for the broken arm would be compensated.

The cost of workers' compensation, as well as level of protection, varies widely from state to state. In some states employers pay more for workers' compensation than they do for state income tax. Given these high costs, it seems appropriate to spend a moment evaluating the effectiveness of the workers' compensation system. First, a brief historical review of workers' compensation will help place this discussion in perspective.

---

[4] U.S. Chamber of Commerce, *Analysis of Workers' Compensation Laws, 1985* (Washington, D.C.: Chamber of Commerce, 1985), Publication no. 6803.

The first workers' compensation state laws to survive the constitutionality question were passed in 1911. By 1920, all but six states had passed some form of workers' compensation law. All 50 states currently have one. The passage of these first laws is attributable to two related events. First, prior to passage of the first state laws (1907–1908), the accident rate in industry attained an unacceptable level: "approximately 30,000 workers died from occupational-related accidents."[5]

In addition to this high accident rate, workers had no protection for work-related accidents. The only source of remedy for workers injured on the job required legal resolution.

Under common law prevailing at that time, injured employees rarely received favorable treatment in the court. An employer could use any one of three defenses with reasonable assurance of success: (1) "contributory negligence"—recovery denied to the worker if it could be shown the worker contributed in any way to the injury, (2) "fellow servant" doctrine—recovery denied if a co-worker contributed in some way to the accident, (3) "assumption of risk"—as a last resort an employer could claim that the employees knew of the job hazards and willingly assumed them upon acceptance of employment.

Needless to say, many accident cases were successfully defended by employers using one of these three lines of defense. As accident rates mounted, however, public support grew for some form of worker compensation.

The result of this rising sentiment, tempered by more than 60 years of experience and modification, is the modern workers' compensation system. According to the National Commission on State Workmen's Compensation Laws, the existing workers' compensation system should achieve five major objectives.[6] The following paragraphs outline these objectives and assess the degree to which they have been achieved.

First, workers' compensation is designed to pay certain, prompt, and reasonable compensation to victims of work accidents. Little can be said about the promptness of payments, since few jurisdictions collect or report such data. The reasonableness of compensation, however, is more easily assessed. Most states attempt to provide an injured worker with 50 to 67 percent of lost income. According to Paul, though, this compensation level frequently is not achieved in practice.[7] Numerous states set maximum weekly benefits that fall below the target policy. Of even more concern, many jurisdictions provide for benefits that are below the poverty threshold. While some progress has been made in the years since these data were collected (1971–1972), considerable room for improvement still exists.

---

[5] Robert J. Paul, "Workers' Compensation: An Adequate Employee Benefit?" *Academy of Management Review,* October 1976, p. 113.

[6] Ibid.

[7] Ibid.

Second, workers' compensation attempts to eliminate delays, costs, and wastes of personal injury litigation. The existing system is based on the no-fault concept, presumably eliminating the need to undertake costly battles to establish guilt or innocence. This goal has been largely achieved, despite some administrative problems in minimizing delays and costs.

Third, the law seeks to study and attempt to reduce the number of accident cases rather than to conceal them. While data on accident reduction records are not widely available, workers' compensation has two components that could provide incentive for development of a safe work environment. First, since most employers are experience rated (insurance premiums vary directly with the number of accidents experienced), they have a monetary incentive to reduce accidents.[8] Second, most laws require accurate records on accident data which, if assembled, could provide added insight into safety modification procedures appropriate for various industries. Unfortunately, many employers do not respond to this component of the law. Consequently the resulting accident data are often sketchy and of little value in accident prevention.

Perhaps the most convincing evidence that workers' compensation laws have not met public expectations about accident prevention can be inferred from passage of the Occupational Safety and Health Act (OSHA) of 1970.[9] The provisions of OSHA are designed to improve working conditions in industry, thereby reducing worker accidents and job-related illnesses. Passage of the act suggests that the reactive approach (i.e., react to injuries after the fact through compensation) is insufficient incentive to stem job-related accidents.

Fourth, workers' compensation requires firms to provide prompt and adequate medical treatment. This provision has been a major contribution of workers' compensation laws. Most jurisdictions provide full medical treatment for injured workers without legal limitation on the time or cost of treatment.

Fifth, the law provides for rehabilitation of workers unable to return to their former jobs. Prior to the early 1970s this provision was the least effective aspect of existing workers' compensation programs. However, massive reforms of the law during the 1970s have resulted in additional rehabilitative benefits while a disabled employee enrolls in a retraining program.

Social Security

Today most working Americans and their families are protected by social security. Whether a worker retires, becomes disabled, or dies, social security benefits are paid to replace part of the lost family earnings. Indeed, ever since its passage in 1935, the Social Security Act has been designed and amended to provide a foundation of basic security for American workers and their families.

---

[8]Ibid.

[9]James Ledvinka, *Federal Regulation of Personnel and Human Resource Management* (Belmont, Calif.: Wadsworth Publishing, 1982).

EXHIBIT 12.4
Social Security through the Years

1935:   Original provisions of the law
Federal old-age benefits program.
  Public assistance for the aged, blind, and dependent children who would not otherwise qualify for social security.
Unemployment compensation.
  Federal state program for maternity care, crippled children's services, child-welfare services.
Public health services.
Vocational rehabilitation services.

Changes in the law since 1935
1939:   Survivor's insurance added to provide monthly life insurance payments to the widow and dependent children of a deceased worker.
1950–
1954:   Old-age and survivor's insurance was broadened.
1956:   Disability insurance benefits provided to workers and dependents of such employees.
1965:   Medical insurance protection to the aged and later (1973) the disabled under age 65 (medicare).
1972:   Cost-of-living escalator tied to the consumer price index—guaranteed higher future benefits for all beneficiaries.
1974:   Existing state programs of financial assistance to the aged, blind, and disabled were replaced by SSI (supplemental security income) administered by the Social Security Administration.

Exhibit 12.4 identifies initial coverage of the law and subsequent broadening of this coverage over the years.[10]

The money to pay these benefits comes from the social security contributions made by employees, their employers, and self-employed people during working years. As contributions are paid in each year, they are immmediately used to pay for the benefits to current beneficiaries. Herein lies a major problem with social security. While the number of retired workers continues to rise (because of earlier retirement and longer life spans), no corresponding increase in the number of contributors to social security has offset these costs. Combine these increases with other cost stimulants (e.g., liberal cost-of-living adjustments) and the outcome is not surprising. To maintain solvency, there has been a dramatic increase in both the maximum earnings base and the rate at which that base is taxed. Exhibit 12.5 illustrates the trends in tax rate, maximum earnings base, and maximum tax for social security.

The combined impact of these schedules for employers is twofold. Consider, for example, employees who earned $45,000 in 1986. They will have deducted from their wages $3,003 to reflect payments in maximum counted earnings of $42,000 (7.15 percent of $42,000). The first obvious impact on an employer is that he must also pay $3,003. Less obviously, though, an employer should con-

---

[10]William J. Cohen, "The Evolution and Growth of Social Security," in *Federal Policies and Worker Status Since the Thirties,* ed. J. P. Goldberg, E. Ahern, W. Haber, and R. A. Oswald (Madison, Wis.: Industrial Relations Research Association, 1976), p. 62.

EXHIBIT 12.5
Tax Rates, Maximum Earnings Base, and Maximum Social Security Tax

Year	Taxation Rate on Covered Earnings		Total × Maximum Earnings Base		Maximum Social Security Tax (dollars)
	For Retirement Survivors and Disability Insurance (percent)	For Hospital Insurance (percent)	Total (percent)	Maximum Earnings Base (dollars)	
1978	5.05%	1.00%	6.05% ×	$17,700	$1,070.85
1979	5.08	1.05	6.13 ×	22,900	1,403.77
1980	5.08	1.05	6.13 ×	25,900	1,587.67
1981	5.35	1.30	6.65 ×	29,700	1,975.05
1982	5.40	1.30	6.70 ×	32,400	2,170.80
1983	5.40	1.30	6.70 ×	35,700	2,391.90
1984	5.40	1.30	7.0 ×	37,800	2,646.00
1985	5.70	1.35	7.05 ×	39,600	2,791.80
1986	5.70	1.45	7.15 ×	42,000	3,003.00
1987	5.70	1.45	7.15 ×	*	—
1990	6.2	1.45	7.65 ×	*	—
2000	6.2	1.45	7.65 ×	*	—

*Automatic adjustments based on average earnings level.
Source: Social Security Administration (SSA) Bulletin No. 79-10044, 1979, and Annual Statistical Supplement, 1984–85.

sider this social security contribution when determining appropriate pension benefits. A targeted level of pension benefits that neglects social security contributions results in retirement income subsidized by the employer in excess of forecasted objectives.

For social security to maintain its status as a major form of income protection, significant changes must be made in the current system. Estimates for the period 1982–2056 predict an average annual expenditure of 14.09 percent of taxable payroll (i.e., payout to social security recipients). Given that the average annual income to fund these payouts is only expected to be 12.27 percent of taxable payroll, the social security fund faces a substantial deficit.[11] Although improving economic conditions have somewhat lessened the social security crisis, some hard decisions still must be made. Exhibit 12.6 lists some proposed changes in social security as well as the savings estimated from each change.

In the past several years a dissenting view has been voiced about the future of social security. This opposition claims that doomsayers' warnings of social security failure are making far too pessimistic assumptions about future economic conditions. As support, unpublished data from the Social Security Administration has been released showing that the fund is running an annual operating surplus of $6.8 billion in 1986. This is forecasted to increase to $55.1 billion per year in 1990 and $192 billion in the year 2000.[12] Thus, it is still un-

---

[11]Haeworth Robertson, "The Social Security Fix," *Compensation Review* 3 (1983), pp. 63–70.
[12]"Social Security Taxes Too High, Kemp Says," *Buffalo News,* February 26, 1986, p. 1.

EXHIBIT 12.6
Savings from Proposed Changes in Social Security *(billions of dollars)*

Proposal	Savings, 1982–1986*
Tax the first six months of sick-pay benefits.	$ 2.6
Lengthen basic averaging period for computing retirement benefits.	1.3
Change inflation indexing of "bend points"—income levels used to calculate benefits.	4.2
Reduce benefits for early retirees.	17.6
Eliminate benefits for children of early retirees.	1.9
Apply the maximum disability payment for a family to retirement and survivor cases.	2.9
Eliminate "windfall" benefits to public pensioners.	0.6
Eliminate all nonmedical disability benefits.	7.7
Increase the waiting period before receiving disability to six months from five months.	1.4
Require the estimated length of a disability to be 24 months instead of 12 months.	2.8
Require a worker to have had disability insurance for 30 out of the 40 previous quarters to qualify for disability payments.	10.0
Move date for yearly cost of living increase to October from July.	6.3
Raise levels of extra income after retirement that are permitted before social security benefits are cut.	(6.5)†
Total savings to social security.	$46.4

*Calendar years.
†Added costs to system.
Source: Social Security Administration.

clear how much trouble the social security fund really has, and the consequent impact this will have on payroll taxes.

Unemployment Insurance

The earliest union efforts to cushion the effects of unemployment for their members (*c.* 1830s) were part of benevolent programs of self-help. These efforts took the form of crises contributions by working members for their unemployed brethren.[13] With passage of the unemployment insurance law (as part of the Social Security Act of 1935), this floor of security for unemployed workers became less dependent upon the philanthropy of fellow workers. Since unemployment insurance laws vary state by state, this review will cover some of the major characteristics of different state programs.

Financing. Unemployment compensation paid out to eligible workers is financed exclusively by employers who pay federal and state unemployment insurance tax. The tax amounts to 6.2 percent of the first $7,000 earned by each worker. The state unemployment commission (or its equivalent) receives 5.4

---

[13]Raymond Munts, "Policy Development in Unemployment Insurance," in *Federal Policies and Worker Status Since the Thirties,* ed. Goldberg, Ahern, Haber, and Oswald.

percent of this 6.2 percent, and the remainder goes to the federal government for administrative costs and to repay federal government loans to the extended unemployment compensation account. All states allow for experience rating, charging lower percentages to employers who have terminated fewer employees. (The tax rate may fall to 0 percent in some states for employers who have had no recent experience with former employees collecting chargeable unemployment insurance.)

During the late 1970s and early 1980s many state funds were severely drained by the prolonged recession. To keep their unemployment funds solvent, states borrowed from the federal government. Since that time 12 states and the District of Columbia have been past due on loan repayment. To repay the federal government an additional 1.9 percent tax surcharge (above the current .8 percent of the 6.2 percent total payroll tax returned to the federal level) was levied on the first $7,000 of employee income for each employer in the troubled states.[14] The pressure to increase payroll taxes and reduce benefit outlays has led to increased numbers of unemployed who are uninsured. Much of this increase can be traced to increased disqualification periods for voluntary job leavers and higher earnings requirements to become eligible for unemployment insurance.[15]

Eligibility. To be eligible for benefits, an unemployed worker must: (1) be able, available, and actively seeking work; (2) not have refused suitable employment; (3) not be unemployed because of a labor dispute (except Rhode Island and New York); (4) not have left a job voluntarily; (5) not have been terminated for gross misconduct; and (6) have been previously employed in a covered industry or occupation, earning a designated minimum amount for a designated period of time.

These eligibility criteria eliminate many individuals who might otherwise qualify for UI.[16] Of the 5,076,000 people unemployed in 1974, "672,000 had never been in the labor force and therefore failed to meet the minimum employment earnings criterion. Another 431,000 were teenagers who had left the labor force and subsequently reentered; they also were unlikely to have met the minimum employment earnings criterion. Additionally, 585,000 people were prime-age adults who voluntarily left their last jobs and so were ineligible. These 1,688,000 persons, one third of the unemployed, were very likely ineligible for UI benefits."[17]

---

[14]"U.S. Penalizes Firms in States Past Due on Jobless Payments," *The Wall Street Journal,* December 4, 1984, p. 1.

[15]Gary Burtless and Wayne Vroman, "The Performance of Unemployment Insurance Since 1979," *IRRA Proceedings,* December 2, 1984, pp. 138–46.

[16]Gary S. Fields, "Direct Labor Market Effects of Unemployment Insurance," *Industrial Relations* 16, no. 1 (February 1977), pp. 33–44.

[17]Ibid.

Coverage. All workers except a few agricultural and domestic workers are currently covered by unemployment insurance (UI) laws. These covered workers (97 percent of the work force), though, must still meet eligibility requirements to receive benefits.

Duration. Until 1958 the maximum number of weeks any claimant could collect UI was 26 weeks. However, the 1958 and 1960–61 recessions yielded large numbers of claimants who exhausted their benefits, leading many states temporarily to revise upward the maximum benefits duration. The most recent modification of this benefits duration (1982) involves a complex formula that ensures extended benefits in times of high unemployment. Extended benefits will be paid when either of two conditions prevails: (1) when the number of insured unemployed in a state reaches 6 percent, or (2) when the rate experienced is greater than 5 percent and at least 20 percent higher than in the same period of the two preceding calendar years over a 13-week time frame.[18]

Weekly benefits amount. Those unemployed workers who do meet eligibility requirements are entitled to a weekly benefit amount designed to equal 50 percent of the claimants' lost wages. In reality, though, the weekly benefit amount compensates for about 66.6 percent of the net income loss of UI recipients.[19] The disparity arises because UI benefits are not taxed. Consequently, a dollar amount targeted at 50 percent of the average income while working results in a larger net income percentage because of no deductions for federal/state income tax and social security payments.

This level of payment has frequently raised the question of whether UI participants have sufficient incentive actually to seek a job, rather than postponing job search behavior until benefits are near expiration. This controversy requires further examination.

UI and the incentive to work. It has been suggested that "the low rate of income loss for many covered workers tends to remove the financial inducement to avoid unemployment or to return to work."[20] To determine if this argument is valid, numerous studies have looked at the incidence of unemployment (number of times) and duration of unemployment (weeks per spell of unemployment) comparing employees covered and not covered by UI. One review of these studies indicates that, for the most part, there is a small but significant positive relationship between UI and duration of unemployment.[21]

[18]C. Arthur Williams, John S. Turnbull, and Earl F. Cheit, *Economic and Social Security,* 5th ed. (New York: John Wiley & Sons, 1982).

[19]Martin Feldstein, "Economics of the New Unemployment," *The Public Interest* 33 (1973), pp. 3–42.

[20]Fields, "Direct Labor Market Effects of Unemployment Insurance."

[21]Clair Vickery, "Unemployment Insurance: A Positive Reappraisal," *Industrial Relations* 18, no. 1 (Winter 1979), p. 18.

While covered workers may have somewhat longer periods of unemployment than ineligible workers, some evidence indicates that covered workers have a lower frequency of unemployment. Moreover, some evidence suggests that UI may have more impact on the composition of the unemployed than on the level of unemployment.

> This occurs because as UI recipients want to be recalled or search longer for their next job, the job seekers not eligible for UI have improved access to the available vacancies. Since the unemployed who are not eligible for UI are primarily new or recent entrants to the labor market, the jobs for which they are qualified require less experience. The UI system was specifically designed to discourage the experienced unemployed from taking such jobs on a temporary basis while they waited to return to jobs that utilized their experience.[22]

The accumulation of evidence suggests that UI does create some disincentive to work. However, the impact is not large in comparison to the value of the social welfare role played by unemployment compensation.

Controlling unemployment taxes. Every unemployed worker's unemployment benefits are "charged" against one or more companies. The more money paid out on behalf of a firm, the higher is the unemployment insurance rate for that firm. Couple the increased insurance premiums with the costs of replacing a terminated worker (Exhibit 12.7), and it is apparent that the costs of terminations are high. Efforts to control these costs quite logically should begin with a well-designed human resources planning system. Realistic estimates of human resources needs will reduce the need for hasty hiring and morale-breaking terminations. Additionally, though, a benefits administrator should attempt to audit prelayoff behavior (e.g., lateness, gross misconduct, absenteeism, illness, leaves of absence) and compliance with UI requirements after termination (e.g., job refusals, insufficient duration of covered work). Exhibit 12.8 outlines the types of areas to monitor if unemployment costs are to be cut.

EQUAL EMPLOYMENT OPPORTUNITY AND BENEFITS

Two Equal Employment Opportunity laws have substantial impacts on benefits policy and procedures: Title VII of the Civil Rights Act of 1964 and the Age Discrimination in Employment Act (1967). Both laws have provisions outlawing differential contributions to or coverage from benefit plans when such differential treatment is based on protected group status (in these cases, sex and age).

Civil Rights Act

Title VII of the Civil Rights Act prohibits discrimination in terms and conditions of employment (including benefits) that is based on race, color, religion,

---

[22]Ibid.

EXHIBIT 12.7
Cost Elements in Replacing a Terminated Worker

	Direct	*Indirect*	*Total*
Added overhead costs			
Employment agency fee	$___	$___	$___
Advertising	___	___	___
Recruitment	___	___	___
Public relations activities	___	___	___
Processing applications	___	___	___
Interviewing, reference check	___	___	___
Psychological testing	___	___	___
Orientation materials (films, brochures)	___	___	___
Medical exam	___	___	___
Accounting and payroll entries	___	___	___
Pension plan, health insurance	___	___	___
Workers' compensation premiums	___	___	___
Increased social security payments	___	___	___
Increased unemployment insurance premiums	___	___	___
Added operating costs			
On-the-job training	___	___	___
Supervisor's time with new employee	___	___	___
Formal training program participation	___	___	___
Material spoilage	___	___	___
Increased inspection	___	___	___
Temporary employees hired to make up for low output of new hires	___	___	___
Overtime paid to maintain productivity	___	___	___
Loss of productivity between separation of former employee and hire of new employee	___	___	___
Loss of productivity between time of decision to quit (discharge) and actual quit (discharge)	___	___	___
Severance pay	___	___	___
Estimated cost per replacement	$___	$___	$___

Source: Allan Janoff, "You Can Reduce Your Unemployment Taxes." Reprinted the January 1976 issue of *Personnel Administrator,* copyright 1976, The American Society for Personnel Administration, 606 North Washington Street, Alexandria, VA 22314, $40 per year.

sex, or national origin. One interpretive issue related to benefits that has arisen since passage of the act involves sex discrimination. In particular, should pregnant women be permitted health, disability, and/or sick leave benefits because of pregnancy? In the 1976 case of *Gilbert* v. *General Electric Corporation* the Supreme Court held that the disability insurance program was not sex discriminatory under Title VII.[23] Reasoning that men and women were covered under the GE plan equally except for one condition, pregnancy, the Court ruled no insurance plan must be all inclusive. This decision met with sufficient opposition from women's organizations, unions, civil rights groups, and sympathetic legislators to be overturned by law in 1978. The pregnancy disability amendment, as it is called, "prohibits the denial of health, disability, or sick leave benefits to

---

[23]429 US 125.

EXHIBIT 12.8
Areas to Monitor in Cutting UI Costs

Cost Control Survey

Cause—Do you: Yes   No   Sometimes

Lateness
1. Tell employee whom to call when late?
2. Keep documented history of lateness and warning notices?
3. Suspend chronically late employees before discharging them?

Absenteeism
1. Tell employees whom to call when absent?
2. Rule that three days absent without calling in is reason for automatic discharge?
3. Keep documented history of absence and warning notices?
4. Request doctor's note on return to work?

Illness
1. Keep job open, if possible?
2. Offer leave of absence?
3. Request doctor's note on return to work?

Pregnancy
1. Follow EEOC ruling "no discharge"?
2. Request doctor's note indicating how long employee may work?
3. Change jobs within company when practical?
4. Offer maternity leave?
5. Recall to work four weeks following birth?

Leave of absence
1. Make written approval mandatory?
2. Stipulate date for return to work?
3. Offer position at end of leave?

Leave job voluntarily
1. Conduct exit interview?
2. Obtain a signed resignation statement?
3. Mail job abandonment letter?
4. Mail job review questionnaire three to six months after separation?

Cause—Do you: Yes   No   Sometimes

Layoff
1. Hire employees with established "benefit year" if you anticipate layoffs?
2. Keep employees on when the cost to replace them would more than offset paying their salary?
3. Transfer employees to different departments?
4. Have a flexible work week that reflects high and low periods of productivity?
5. Temporarily lay off employees for one week during slack periods?
6. Attempt to find temporary or part-time jobs for laid-off employees?

Job refusal
1. Issue a formal notice to employees collecting benefits to return to work?
2. Require new employees to stipulate, in writing, their availability to work overtime, night shifts, etc.?

Not qualified
1. Set probationary periods to evaluate new employees?
2. Conduct followup interviews one to five months after hire?

Deliberate unsatisfactory performance
1. Document all instances, recording when and how employee did not meet job requirements?
2. Require supervisors to document the steps taken to remedy the situation?
3. Require supervisors to document employee's refusal of advice and direction?

Violation of Company Rules
1. Make sure all policies and rules of conduct are understood by all employees?

EXHIBIT 12.8
(concluded)

Cost Control Survey

Cause—Do you:

	Yes	No	Sometimes
2. Require all employees to sign a statement acknowledging acceptance of these rules?			
3. Meet with employee and fill out documented warning notice?			
4. Discharge at the time violation occurs, or suspend?			

Wrong benefit charges

	Yes	No	Sometimes
1. Check state charge statement for:			
a. Correct employee?			
b. Correct benefit amount?			
c. Correct period of liability?			

Claim handling

	Yes	No	Sometimes
1. Assign a claims supervisor or central office to process all separation information?			
2. Respond to state claim forms on time?			
3. Use proper terminology on claim form and attach documented evidence regarding separation?			
4. Attend hearings and appeal unwarranted claims?			
5. Conduct availability checks and rehire employees collecting benefits?			

Administration

	Yes	No	Sometimes
1. Have a staff member who knows unemployment insurance laws and who:			
a. Works with the personnel department to establish proper use of policies and procedures?			
b. Anticipates and reports costly turnover trends?			
c. Successfully protests unwarranted claims and charges for unemployment benfits?			
d. Recommends appropriate tax remedies to:			

Cause—Do you:

	Yes	No	Sometimes
(1) Verify the contribution rate assigned by the state?			
(2) Test for rate modification?			
(3) Test for voluntary contribution and advisability of a joint account?			
(4) Determine advantage of transfer of experience resulting from mergers, acquisitions, or other corporate changes?			

Communication

	Yes	No	Sometimes
1. Hold periodic workshops with key personnel to review procedures and support effort to reduce turnover costs?			
2. Immediately investigate who, or what, is responsible for costly errors and why?			

Management reports

	Yes	No	Sometimes
1. Point to turnover problems as they occur by:			
a. Location?			
b. Department?			
c. Classification of employee?			
d. Job position?			
2. Evaluate the effectiveness of current policies and procedures used to:			
a. Recruit?			
b. Select?			
c. Train?			
d. Supervise?			
e. Separate?			
3. Help create policies, procedures for:			
a. Less costly layoffs?			
b. Increased survival rate?			
c. Retention of employee?			

Source: Allan Janoff, "You Can Control Your Unemployment Taxes." Reprinted from the January 1976 issue of *Personnel Administrator*, copyright, 1976, The American Society for Personnel Administration, 606 North Washington Street, Alexandria, VA 22314, $40 per year.

pregnant women temporarily disabled by childbirth itself or by a medical condition incurred before or after childbirth."[24] Such coverage applies only if a valid benefits plan is already in effect and if the pregnant employee is medically able to work.

A second area where sex discrimination may exist is in pension plans. Two types of plans have been alleged to be discriminatory:

1. A plan requiring women to contribute a higher premium than men in order to receive the same benefits as a man, other things equal.
2. A plan requiring women to contribute the same amount but receive less benefits than a man, other things equal.[25]

The Supreme Court in the *Manhart* case (reaffirmed and extended in the *Nerris* case) rejected the defense that the higher payment rate was justified on actuarial grounds because women as a class live about five years longer than men;[26] therefore, the cost of a pension plan for the average retired woman was greater than the cost for the average retired man.[27] In rejecting this claim, the Supreme Court agreed that actuarial tables show the average woman living longer than the average man. However, for many individual cases, women live shorter lives than men. Title VII clearly applies to the individual and, thus, the Court ruled against decisions based on class characteristics. This decision means not only that women receive the same pension but also contribute the same amount, other things equal. The added costs of this coverage, therefore, are borne by the company.

Age Discrimination in Employment Act

The Age Discrimination in Employment Act prohibits job-related discrimination against individuals between the ages of 40 and 70 (excluding highly paid executives). Since 1978, when amendments to ADEA raised the age limit for protected group status from 65 to 70, the impact on benefits plans has been threefold:

1. In the area of pensions, should workers who have reached the "normal" retirement age (65) be permitted to accrue service credits (and hence greater benefits) for their pension plan? According to Congress, the answer is no.[28]

---

[24]Geraldine Leshin, *EEO Law: Impact on Fringe Benefits* (Los Angeles: University of California, Institute of Industrial Relations, 1979), p. 22.

[25]Ibid.

[26]*City of Los Angeles Department of Water and Power* v. *Manhart et al.,* 98 US 1370; Paul Schultz and Cheryl Fells, "Current Developments in Employee Benefits," *Employee Relations Law Journal* 9 (1981), pp. 62–73.

[27]Leshin, *EEO Law: Impact on Fringe Benefits,* p. 45.

[28]Ibid.

Employers need not grant service credits for employment after age 65, without fear of violating either ADEA or the Employee Retirement Income Security Act (ERISA, 1974).

2. What happens to employee life insurance coverage for years worked after age 65? Employers may not eliminate life insurance coverage after age 65. However, reduction of benefits is permitted if an employer can demonstrate the higher costs that would be entailed in continuing benefit coverage at the pre-65 age level.[29]

3. An employer may not reduce *total* health benefits for employees between the ages of 65 and 70. This issue is relevant because employees become eligible for medicare at age 65. The employer may reduce company health insurance only by the amount of medicare coverage.

The remainder of this chapter examines employee benefits that are not legally required. However, if the employer chooses to provide these benefits, many of them are subject to certain regulatory and taxation laws (e.g., pensions, profit sharing, life insurance, educational benefits). The review follows the categorization listed earlier in this chapter.

PENSIONS, INSURANCE, AND OTHER AGREED UPON PAYMENTS

This category includes the following types of benefits:

1. Pension plans.
2. Life insurance coverage.
3. Hospital, surgical, medical, and major medical insurance coverage.
4. Salary continuation or long-term disability protection.
5. Short-term disability protection.
6. Dental insurance coverage.
7. Discounts on goods and services purchased from company by employees.
8. Employee meals furnished by company.
9. Miscellaneous payments (e.g., legal insurance, termination pay, moving expenses).

Two of these categories are self-explanatory (7, 8). The remainder require some comment, since several are some of the more volatile areas in employee benefits plans today.

Deferred Compensation/Pension Plans

The last chapter noted that a high relationship exists between employee age and preference for a pension plan. While this need for old age security may become more pronounced as workers age, it is evident among younger workers also.

---

[29]Ibid.

This security motive and certain tax advantages have fostered the rise of deferred compensation programs. Deferred compensation programs provide income to an employee at some future time as compensation for work performed now. Two types of deferred compensation plans will be discussed to varying degrees here: (1) stock option plans and (2) pension plans.

Not surprisingly, both of these deferred compensation plans are subject to stringent tax laws. For deferred compensation to be exempt from current taxation specific requirements must be met. To qualify (hence labeled a "qualified" deferred compensation plan), an employer cannot freely choose who will participate in the plan. This requirement eliminated the common practice of discriminating in favor of executives and other highly compensated employees.[30] The major advantage of a qualified plan is that the employer receives an income tax deduction for contributions made to the plan even though employees may not yet have received any benefits. The disadvantage arises in recruitment of high-talent executives. A plan will not qualify for tax exemptions if an employer pays high levels of deferred compensation to entice executives to the firm, unless proportionate contributions also are made to lower level employees.

Stock option plans. The Economic Recovery Tax Act of 1981 restored popularity to stock options as a form of deferred compensation. Exhibit 12.9 outlines the various types of stock options and the features that make them attractive.

Pension plans. The second form of deferred compensation is the well-known pension plan. All pension plans have at least four common characteristics. First, they involve deferred payment to a former employee (or surviving spouse) for past services rendered. Second, they all specify a normal retirement age at which benefits begin to accrue to the employee. While 65 is the "normal" retirement age, a number of events have led this age to be used as a guideline rather than an inflexible standard. At one extreme is the Age Discrimination in Employment Act, which permits most employees to work until age 70. At the other extreme is the social trend for earlier retirement. To deal with the uncertainty generated by these divergent trends, many companies operate as if 65 is the normal retirement age and adjust pensions according to actuarial cost deviations from this norm.

A third characteristic of pension plans is the benefits formula employed. These formulas can vary on at least two dimensions: (1) whether employees are required to contribute to the pension fund and (2) whether the program is a defined benefit plan (plan specifies pension level and payments by company geared to maintaining this level) or a defined contribution plan (company pay-

---

[30]Ernst and Whinney, *Tax Aspects of Compensation Planning* (New York: Ernst & Whinney, 1979).

EXHIBIT 12.9
Stock Option Packages

Type	Features	Selected Advantages and Disadvantages
Incentive stock option (ISO)	Select executives are given option to purchase stock at some later point for the fair market price as determined at the time option is granted. To meet IRS rules, must not exceed $100,000 per year and options must be exercised in order they are granted.	Employee purchases stock when price exceeds option price (i.e., no risk gains from stock market). No tax at time option is exercised. Potential of only capital gains tax rate if held specified time.
Stock appreciation rights (SAR)	Executives are given right to receive amount equal to future appreciation on stock, often in lieu of exercising stock option.	Executives are not required to finance purchase of stock, yet still receive benefit of any price increase. No tax liability to executive until SAR exercised.
Nonqualified stock option	Executives are given option to buy stock for specific number of years, with no limit on amount of stock optioned and no limit on allowed exercise period.	Company receives tax deduction and no charge to earnings. Less attractive to executives because tax is at individual rather than capital gains tax rate.
Performance share/ performance unit plans	Executives are given hypothetical stock units at beginning of review period. Number of units cashed is function of long-term goal achievement.	No tax or accounting advantages to company. Quite expensive. Executives receive benefits of increasing stock price and rewards based on achievement of long-run corporate goals.

ments are specified and the investment success with these funds determines pension levels). A typical pension plan design varies pension level by years of service. Exhibit 12.10 illustrates three common pension plans.

Pension levels may adjust for losses of purchasing power due to inflation. The prevalent pension plan design in public sector plans (Federal Civil Service Retirement System, some state and municipal retirement systems, social security

EXHIBIT 12.10
Examples of Pension Plan Language

Company	Current Annual Normal Retirement Benefit
Allied	Greater of *a* or *b*: (*a*) 1.1 percent of final average pay plus .4 percent of final average pay in excess of average social security age base, all times credited service, or (*b*) 2.0 percent of final average pay times credited service up to 25 years, minus 64 percent of social security.
Amerada Hess	1.6 percent of final average pay less 1.5 percent of social security, all times credited service (maximum 50 percent social security offset)
Beatrice Foods	Greater of *a* or *b*: (*a*) 1.4 percent of final average pay less 1.5 percent of social security, all times credited service (maximum 50 percent social security offset) or (*b*) 1.0 percent of final average pay times credited service.

system, Uniformed Services Retirement System) is automatically to adjust pension benefits to reflect changing living costs.[31] The preferred mechanism is to tie pension change to the consumer price index (CPI).

With the large changes in the CPI during the late 1970s and early 1980s many private sector firms are reluctant to become contractually (or even non-contractually) bound to the CPI index for pension changes. Rather, private employers have generally preferred to adjust pension payments upward on an ad hoc basis.

Payments are also affected by the Retirement Equity Act of 1984. This act is designed to eliminate discrimination in pensions against women. Essentially the law recognizes that women have more gaps in their employment history and reduces the allowed penalty imposed under the Employee Retirement Income Security Act.[32]

The final element of pension plans that should be universal, but is not, is integration with social security benefits. About one third of the plans monitored by the Department of Labor have a provision for integration with social security benefits.[33] One integration approach reduces normal benefits by a percentage (usually 50 percent) of social security benefits.[34] Another feature employs a more liberal benefits formula on earnings that exceed the maximum income taxed by social security. Regardless of the formula used, about two thirds of U.S. companies do not employ the cost-cutting strategy. Once a company has targeted the level of income it wants to provide employees in retirement, it makes sense to design a system that integrates private pension and social security to achieve that goal. Any other strategy is not cost effective.

ERISA

Private pension plans ran into serious criticism in the recession of the early 1970s for a number of reasons. Many people who thought they were covered were not because of complicated rules, insufficient funding, irresponsible financial management, and employer bankruptcies. Some pension funds, including both employer-managed and union-managed funds, were accused of mismanagement; other pension plans required long vesting periods. The Employee Retirement Income Security Act was passed in 1974 in response to these criticisms.

---

[31]Robert Frumkin and Donald Schmitt, "Pension Improvements Since 1974 Reflect Inflation, New U.S. Law," *Monthly Labor Review* 102, no. 4 (1979), pp. 18–22.

[32]Anna Rappaport, "Employee Benefits, Financial Security, and Family Structure in the Post Retirement Equity Act Environment,"*Employee Benefits Journal,* June 1985, pp. 9–16.

[33]Frumkin and Schmitt, "Pension Improvements Since 1974 Reflect Inflation, New U.S. Law."

[34]Jerry S. Rosenbloom and G. Victor Hallman, *Employee Benefit Planning* (Englewood Cliffs, N.J.: Prentice-Hall, 1981).

ERISA does not require that employers offer a pension plan, but pension plans in effect are rigidly controlled by ERISA provisions. These provisions were designed to achieve two goals: (1) "to protect the interest of 35 million workers who are covered today by private retirement plans, and (2) to stimulate the growth of such plans."[35]

The actual success of ERISA in achieving these goals has been mixed at best. In the first two full years of operation (1975–1976) more than 13,000 pension plans were terminated. A major factor in these terminations, along with the recession, was ERISA. Employers complained about the excessive costs and paperwork of living under ERISA. Some disgruntled employers even claimed ERISA was an acronym for "Every Ridiculous Idea Since Adam." To examine the merits of these claims, let us take a closer look at the major requirements of ERISA.

Eligibility. Employees must become eligible for a pension plan after one year of service or at age 25, whichever comes later. However, if an employee younger than 25 has continuous service with the firm, he or she becomes eligible for years' credit equal to seniority at age 25 (providing seniority is at least one year).

Funding. Funded pension plans finance future payments by setting money aside in special funds. Nonfunded, or pay-as-you-go, plans deduct pension payments from current funds. ERISA requires an employer to pay annually the full cost of current benefit accruals, as well as amortize payments on past liabilities. Present IRS regulations disallow tax-deductible funding of past amounts in fewer than 10 years. Thus, companies have no incentive to bring their plans to 100 percent funding sooner. Another funding issue occurs when benefit increases are granted retroactively, but the company does not immediately fund these benefit increases. ERISA funding requirements and the potential size of unfunded liabilities have woven a tangled web that has collapsed merger talks and spawned amendments, none of which has proven satisfactory. The difficulty requires understanding the distinction between a defined contribution plan and a defined benefit plan.

As noted earlier, a defined contribution plan states what level of assets will be put into a plan, for example, "10 percent of salaries paid." A defined benefit plan specifies the level of benefits that will be paid, for example, "$450 per month beginning at age 65 and continuing for the life of the recipient." A defined benefit plan carries greater uncertainty as to what level of funding is required to meet obligations; consequently the size of the employer's liability is also uncertain. To avoid this uncertainty, many employers switched from de-

---

[35]Robert D. Paul, "The Impact of Pension Reform on American Business," *Sloan Management Review* 18 (1976), p. 59.

fined benefit to defined contribution plans. Further funding uncertainty arises when more than one employer contributes to a pension plan. Such multi-employer pension plans cover one fourth of all American workers in private industry who have defined benefit pension plans. In such cases, not only the potential liability is unknown, but also the financial condition of other employers may be unknown. The fate of the remaining participants is uncertain if one employer pulls out of the agreement.

The Multi-Employer Pension Plan Amendment Act of 1980 addressed some of these issues. The act broadened the definition of defined benefit plans so that the vast majority of plans (including some previously considered defined contribution plans, thus extending potential liability) were covered. Under the Multi-Employer Pension Plan Amendment, employers who now participate in multi-employer pension plans face liabilities if they withdraw from such plans, with the amount of liability determined by the amount of unfunded vested liability of the plan (nonforfeitable benefits obligations) and the withdrawing employer's level of participation. No distinction is made between voluntary and involuntary withdrawal; bankruptcies and buyouts are treated alike. Reaction to this amendment has been hostile; many employers claim that it imposes unrealistic financial burdens and discourages them from joining such multi-employer plans.

Pensions also are having some interesting impacts on strategic planning of organizations. In 1983, 400 of the biggest companies had $42 billion in pension overfunding. This is an attractive stimulant to other organizations looking for acquisitions. The acquiring company can terminate the pension, retrieve the excess funding, and start a new pension plan. This possibility resulted in wide-scale reduction of pension expenses in 1983 (60 percent of the major industrial firms cut pension expenses by an average of 3.5 percent).[36] While this reduces the probability of a takeover, it also lessens the chance that current contribution levels will meet future payment requirements.

Vesting and portability. These two concepts are sometimes confused but have very different meanings in practice. Vesting refers to the length of time an employee must work for an employer before he or she is entitled to benefits accruing in the pension plan. The vesting concept has two components. First, any contributions made by the employee to a pension fund are immediately and irrevocably vested. The vesting right becomes questionable only with respect to the employer's contributions. As mandated by ERISA, employer contributions must vest at least as quickly as one of the following three definitions: (1) Ten-year service schedule—credits accrue to an employee's account but are not vested until completion of 10 years of service. (2) Graded 5/15 schedule—after 5 years

---

[36]"Business Reduces Pension Funding to Cut Costs, Fend Off Takeovers," *The Wall Street Journal,* October 11, 1984, p. 35.

of service an employee is guaranteed 25 percent of accrued benefits. Each year until 10 years adds an additional 5 percent. The following 5 years up to 15 years' service result in an additional 10 percent accrual/year (at which time the benefits are 100 percent vested). (3) The rule of 45—vesting begins when an employee's age and service equal 45 (providing a minimum of five years' service have been achieved). At this point benefits are vested at the 50 percent level. Each additional year of service increases vesting by 10 percent up to the maximum of 100 percent.

The vesting schedule an employer uses is often a function of the demographic makeup of the work force. An employer who experiences high turnover may wish to use the 10-year service schedule. By so doing, any employee with fewer than 10 years' service at time of termination receives no vested benefits. Or the employer may use the 5/15 graded schedule in the hopes that earlier benefits accrual will reduce undesired turnover. The strategy adopted is, therefore, dependent on organizational goals and work force characteristics. Recent data suggest vesting after 10 years is the most popular formula, with 80 percent of one sample opting for this alternative.[37]

Portability of pension benefits becomes an issue for employees moving to new organizations. Should pension assets accompany the transferring employee in some fashion?[38] ERISA does not require mandatory portability of private pensions. On a voluntary basis, though, the employer may agree to let an employee's pension benefits transfer either to an individual retirement account (IRA) or in a reciprocating arrangement, to the new employer. For an employer to permit portability, of course, the pension rights must be vested.

Fiduciary responsibility. Today over $400 billion exist in private pension accounts in the United States. Unrestrained investment of these funds by a company representative could lead to substantial abuse.[39] Consequently ERISA stipulates that the fiduciary entrusted with investment decisions is legally obligated to follow a "prudent man" rule. Included in the operational definition of a prudent man are certain prohibitions against investments made in self-interest.

Pension Benefit Guaranty Corporation. Despite the wealth of constraints imposed by ERISA, the potential still exists for an organization to go bankrupt, or in some way fail to meet its vested pension obligations. To protect individuals confronted by this problem, employers are required to pay insurance

---

[37]Wyatt Company, *Top 50: A Survey of Retirement, Thrift and Profit-Sharing Plans* (New York: Wyatt Company, 1984).

[38]Susan M. Phillips and Linda P. Fletcher, "The Future of the Portable Pension Concept," *Industrial and Labor Relations Review* 30 (1977), p. 197.

[39]Mark Gertner, "ERISA and the Investment Decision Making Process: The Past, the Present, and the Future," *Employee Benefits Journal,* June 1985, pp. 28–35.

premiums to the Pension Benefit Guaranty Corporation (PBGC) established by ERISA. In turn, the PBGC guarantees payment of vested benefits to employees formerly covered by terminated pension plans.

Updating Pensions

The future of pensions depends on two related issues. First, will ERISA evolve sufficiently to reduce the flood of criticism? And second, will other retirement income arrangements evolve to lessen the importance of traditional pension plans?

A number of changes should be made in ERISA to reverse the trend toward pension plan terminations. First, the fiduciary responsibilities must be altered so that the prudent man rule permits reasonable investment of pension funds. As it stands now, many firms are forced to obtain external consultants to make the expert decisions the prudent man rule mandates. Fear of making a poor pension investment in an uncertain environment has led many companies to obtain insurance against personal liability for poor "crystal ball gazing."

A second area of major concern is the administrative burden of ERISA.[40] One 1975 estimate by Standard Oil of California placed the costs of total compliance with administrative requirements at $2.5 million.[41] Admittedly, when start-up costs are factored out, the cost burden for most companies will be considerably less than this. Whatever the final cost to companies, however, many consider them too high. This results in widespread plan termination rather than plan adoption, thus thwarting the original goal of ERISA.

Despite these criticisms the impact of ERISA has not been wholly negative. The reporting provisions of the act that contribute to the administrative burden also aid in the communication of pension plan benefits to employees. A second benefit of ERISA is the focus placed on unfunded pension liabilities of companies. Absent ERISA's requirement of scheduled payments to meet past pension liabilities, many organizations could have continued for years assuming they could pay benefits out of current assets. The potential for disaster in such a strategy is obvious. ERISA forces pension managers to determine the extent of these liabilities and gradually diminish them over time.

One possible final benefit of ERISA is the obvious potential for financial gain by employees. Ehrenberg and Smith, however, make the case that workers pay for their own benefits in trade-offs made between current wages and benefits in the total compensation package. Focusing on ERISA's vesting provisions, they indicate that in a competitive market the added pension costs incurred by vesting drive down wages, and thus penalize workers who prefer a

---

[40]Paul, "The Impact of Pension Reform on American Business." See also Judy Olian, Stephen Carroll, and Craig Schneier, "Pensions and Personnel/Human Resource Management," Working paper prepared for the President's Commission, 1980.

[41]Paul, "The Impact of Pension Reform on American Business."

relatively high current wage. According to their analysis, ERISA is of benefit only to two groups of workers: those who believed they were likely to receive a pension when in fact they would not have without the legislation, and those workers who either through ignorance or lack of choice cannot find a job with another employer who offers a better compensation package.[42] Without question, however, the greatest beneficiaries of ERISA are the retired workers who presently receive pension benefits courtesy of the Pension Benefit Guaranty Corporation.

The future of pensions also is linked to the evolution of other retirement income arrangements. One of the more interesting is called a simplified employee pension (SEP) and is intended to markedly reduce the paperwork for regular pension plans. By using a form of an individual retirement account (IRA) contract, employers contribute directly into it rather than operating their own pension plan.[43] While an IRA account does not qualify as an employee benefit (and is not being discussed here) because no employer contributions are involved, SEPs are gradually becoming a popular benefit alternative to the more burdensome regular pension plans.[44]

But should companies go through the trouble of changing their existing pension system? And if the answer is yes, how should the change be implemented? In answer to the first question, it appears there are several rewards to restructuring a retirement program: (1) potentially reduce plan cost (pension plus thrift saving costs currently total about 10 percent of pay); (2) gain employee assistance by restructuring the package from a defined benefit to defined contribution system; (3) improve plan design by eliminating redundant benefits (e.g., overlap between social security and pension); (4) tie level of retirement benefits to the fortunes of the company to allow payments into the pension fund to vary with the organization's ability to pay.[45]

How should this restructuring occur? First and foremost, the process must be well planned. A replacement income study should be completed. This involves looking at a range of hypothetical employees and comparing their pre- and postretirement net incomes. Is the postretirement income adequate? Does it meet company targets? Are there any redundancies contributing to the not uncommon problem of having employees who retire and receive more than when they were working?[46] If restructuring is deemed necessary (because target pen-

---

[42]Ronald Ehrenberg and Robert Smith, *Labor Economics* (Glenview, Ill.: Scott, Foresman, 1982).

[43]Rosenbloom and Hallman, *Employee Benefit Planning.*

[44]"Simplified Employee Pensions," *The Wall Street Journal,* February 12, 1985, p. 31.

[45]Laurence Brennan, "Updating the Traditional Corporate Retirement Program, Part I," *Compensation Review* (First Quarter 1984), pp. 11–25; Judy Olian, Stephen Carroll, Jr., and Craig Eric Schneier, "It's Time to Start Using Your Pension System to Improve the Bottom Line," *Personnel Administrator,* April 1985, pp. 77–83, 152.

[46]Brennan, "Updating the Traditional Corporate Retirement Program, Part I."

sion income exceeds desired levels), there are a number of ways to alter the pension formula or change method of calculating career earnings which yield less expensive pension alternatives.[47]

Insurance Plans

Four types of insurance plans are included as employee benefits: (1) health-related insurance plans, (2) legal insurance plans, (3) dental plans, and (4) life insurance. By far the most costly and well-entrenched of these in American industry are health-related insurance plans. The American health system today costs in excess of $200 billion annually.[48] Health care costs represented 5.9 percent of gross national product in 1965 and 10.5 percent in 1983. There was a 400 percent increase in health care costs between 1970 and 1981.[49] Most costly technology, increased numbers of elderly, and a system which does not encourage cost savings have all contributed to the rapidly rising costs of medical insurance. In the past 10 years, though, employers have begun to take steps designed to curb these costs. After a discussion of the types of health care systems, these cost-cutting strategies will be discussed.

An employer's share of health care costs is contributed into one of five health care systems: (1) a community-based system, such as Blue Cross (hospitalization)-Blue Shield (doctors' fees); (2) a commercial insurance plan; (3) self-insurance; (4) a health maintenance organization (HMO); or (5) a preferred provider organization (PPO).

Of these five, plans 1 to 3 operate in a similar fashion. Two major distinctions exist, however. The first distinction is in the manner payments are made. With Blue Cross-Blue Shield the employer-paid premiums guarantee employees a direct service, including room, board, and any necessary health services covered by the plan. Coverage under a commercial insurance plan guarantees fixed payment for hospital service to the insured, who in turn reimburses the hospital. And finally, a self-insurance plan implies that the company provides coverage out of its own assets, assuming the risks itself within state legal guidelines.

The second distinction is in the way costs of medical benefits are determined. Blue Cross-Blue Shield operates via the concept of community rating. In effect, insurance rates are based on the medical experience of the entire community. Higher use of medical facilities results in higher premiums. In contrast, insurance companies operate off a narrower experience rating base, preferring to charge each company separately according to its medical facility usage. Finally, of course, the cost of medical coverage under a self-insurance program is

[47]Ibid.

[48]Herbert Notkin and Leland V. Meader, "The American Health Care System," *Personnel Administrator* 23, no. 5 (1978), pp. 33–39.

[49]Daniel Stone and E. G. Sue Reitz, "Health Care Cost Containment and Its Impact on Employee Relations," *Personnel Administrator* 29 (1984), pp. 27–33.

directly related to usage level, with employer payments going directly to medical care providers rather than to secondary sources in the form of premiums.

As a fourth delivery system health maintenance organizations offer comprehensive benefits for a fixed fee. Health maintenance organizations offer routine medical services at a specific site. Employees make prepayments in exchange for guaranteed health care services on demand. By emphasizing preventive treatment and early diagnosis, HMOs reduce the need for hospitalization to about one half the national average.[50] By law employers of more than 25 employees are required to provide employees the option of joining a federally qualified HMO. If the employee opts for HMO coverage the employer is required to pay the HMO premium or an amount equal to the premium for previous health coverage, whichever is less.

Finally, preferred provider organizations represent a new form of health care delivery in which there is a direct contractual relationship between and among employers, health care providers, and third-party payers.[51] An employer is able to select providers (e.g., selected doctors) who agree to price discounts and strict utilization controls. In turn, the employer influences employees to use the preferred providers through financial incentives. Doctors benefit by increasing patient flow. Employers benefit through increased cost savings. And employees benefit through wider choice of doctors than might be available under an HMO. Whether other benefits or disadvantages of PPOs surface depends on broader exposure and experimentation with this newest cost-cutting alternative.

Health care: Cost control strategies. There are basically three general strategies available to benefit managers for controlling the rapidly escalating costs of health care.[52] First, organizations can motivate employees to change their demand for health care, through changes in either the design or the administration of health insurance policies. Included in this category of control strategies are: (1) deductibles (the first x dollars of health care cost are paid by the employee); (2) coinsurance rates (premium payments are shared by company and employee); (3) maximum benefits (defining a maximum payout schedule for specific health problems); (4) coordination of benefits (ensure no double payment when coverage exists under the employee's plan and a spouse's plan); (5) auditing of hospital charges for accuracy; (6) requiring preauthorization for selected visits to health care facilities; (7) mandatory second opinion whenever surgery is recommended.[53]

---

[50]Janice Ross, "Attacking Soaring Health Benefit Costs," *Pension World* 14, no. 1 (1978), p. 51.

[51]Thomas Billet, "An Employer's Guide to Preferred Provider Organizations," *Compensation Review* 16, no. 4 (1984), pp. 58–62.

[52]Regina Herzlinger and Jeffrey Schwartz, "How Companies Tackle Health Care Costs: Part I," *Harvard Business Review* 63 (July–August 1985), pp. 69–81.

[53]Herzlinger and Schwartz, "How Companies Tackle Health Care Costs: Part I"; Regina Herzlinger, "How Companies Tackle Health Care Costs: Part II," *Harvard Business Review* 63

EXHIBIT 12.11
Selected Cost Control Strategies and Their Effectiveness

	Number of Companies Using Strategy	*Percentage Considering Strategy*	
Cost Control Strategy		*Most Effective*	*Least Effective*
Claims and use review	137	46	7
Auditing insurers	189	42	18
Business coalitions	182	30	18
Offer alternative delivery systems	138	28	15
Identify high-cost providers	109	11	7
Cost control task forces	114	10	3
Company negotiated provider contracts	38	7	1
Company negotiated hospital contracts	17	6	1

Source: Regina Herzlinger, "How Companies Tackle Health Care Costs: Part II," *Harvard Business Review* 63, September–October 1985, p. 109.

The second general cost control strategy involves changing the structure of health care delivery systems and participating in business coalitions (for data collection and dissemination). Under this category falls the trend toward HMOs and PPOs. Even under more traditional delivery systems, though, there is more negotiation of rates with hospitals and other health care–delivery agents.[54]

The final cost strategy involves promotion of preventive health programs. No-smoking policies and incentives for quitting smoking are popular inclusions here. But there is also increased interest in healthier food in cafeterias/vending machines, on-site physical fitness facilities, and early detection screening to identify possible health problems before they become more serious.

Exhibit 12.11 shows typical cost control strategies and an assessment of how effective each has been. Exhibit 12.12 provides a more specific example of cost-cutting, outlining the procedures ITT has adopted to cut costs.

Salary continuation as a long-term disability plan. A number of benefit options provide some form of protection for disability. For example, workers'

(September–October 1985), pp. 108–20; Gary McIlroy, "Health Care Cost Containment in the 1980s," Compensation Review ?? (Fourth Quarter 1983), pp. 15–31; CompFlash, "New Health-Cost Containment Steps Taken by IH," *AMA CompFlash* 84-2 (1984), p. 4; Billet, "An Employer's Guide to Preferred Provider Organizations"; Stone and Reitz, "Health Care Cost Containment and Its Impact on Employee Relations"; Compensation Currents, "Benefits," *Compensation Review* 15, no. 3 (1983), p. 11; Robert Cooper, *Health Care Cost Containment Procedures and Practices* (Brookfield, Wis.: International Foundation of Employee Benefit Plans, 1983); Health Research Institute, *Health Care Cost Containment* (Walnut Creek, Calif.: Health Research Institute, 1983); Judy Waldo Bracken, "Getting through the Maze: Knowing the Fundamentals of Employee Health Benefit Planning," *Personnel Administrator* 29, no. 5 (1984), pp. 64–74; Kenneth Clarke and Lisa Groves, "Medical Plan Changes: Are You Doing Enough to Contain Costs?" *Personnel Administrator* 30 (September 1985), pp. 115–19.

[54]Cooper, "Health Care Cost Containment Procedures and Practices."

EXHIBIT 12.12
International Telephone and Telegraph Health Care Cost Control Strategies, 1984

1. Raise deductible from $100 per person ($200 per family) to $150 per person ($300 per family).
2. Eliminate three-month deductible carryover provision.
3. Introduce employee contribution of $5 per month.
4. Introduce retiree/dependent/spouse contribution of $5 per month.
5. Require second opinion on surgery.
6. Outpatient surgery covered 100 percent—selective types.
7. 100 percent coverage home health care upon approval.
8. Require certification of medical necessity for weekend admission to hospital.
9. 100 percent coverage for birthing centers.

compensation covers disabilities that are work related. Even social security has provisions for disability income to those who qualify. Beyond these two legally required sources, though, there are two similar sources of disability income: employee salary continuation plans and long-term disability plans.

Many companies have some form of salary continuation plan that pays out varying levels of income depending on duration of illness. At one extreme is short-term illness covered by sick leave policy and typically reimbursed at a level equal to 100 percent of salary.[55] After such leave benefits run out, disability benefits become operative. The benefit level is typically less than 100 percent of salary, and may be multitiered. An example of a multitiered plan follows the quite liberal formula noted in Exhibit 12.13.

Most private disability income benefits are provided through plans under-written by insurance companies. Typically these plans become effective when an employee salary continuation plan expires. So, for example, an injured worker covered by the payment schedule in Exhibit 12.13 would start collecting long-term disability (LTD) after 52 weeks.[56] Most company LTD plans then provide

EXHIBIT 12.13
An Example of a Multitiered Salary Continuation Plan

Duration of Illness	*Percentage of Salary to Individual*
Less than 26 weeks	100
26–52 weeks	75
More than 52 weeks	See long-term disability plan

Organizations may only pay that portion not covered by social security and up to a maximum dollar amount, e.g., $100,000.

---

[55]Employee Benefit Plan Review, "Disability Plan Survey Identifies Common Elements," *Employee Benefit Plan Review* 10 (April 1981), p. 9.

[56]William Wiatrowski, "Employee Income Protection against Short Term Disability," *Monthly Labor Review,* February 1985, pp. 33–38.

between 50 and 66 percent of an employee's wages for a period varying between two years and life.[57]

Legal insurance and dental plans. Prior to the 1970s, prepaid legal insurance was practically nonexistent. In recent years, however, prepaid legal insurance has become an increasingly popular benefit. Tremendous variety exists in the structure, options, delivery systems, and attorney compensation mechanisms.[58] Across these plans, there are still some commonalities.[59] A majority of plans provide routine legal services (e.g., divorce, real estate matters, wills, traffic violations) but exclude provisions covering felony crimes, largely because of the expense and potential for bad publicity.[60] Employees with legal problems either select legal counsel from a panel of lawyers selected by the firm (closed-panel mechanism) or freely choose their own lawyers with claims reimbursed by an insurance carrier.[61]

A benefits manager considering inclusion of this benefit in the total package should be aware of some important cost implications. First, fees frequently range in the neighborhood of $30 to $60 per hour. Second, combine this cost with an employee utilization rate that rises from approximately 10 percent of all employees in the first year to a ceiling of approximately 30 percent, and costs may be a serious constraint to be evaluated in advance of offering the legal benefit.[62]

As Exhibit 12.14 indicates, dental insurance is also becoming a popular new benefit option. As a subset of this option, *prepaid* dental insurance is also gen-

---

EXHIBIT 12.14
Dental Plan Popularity

Covered Mouths: Dental insurance spreads—as do worries over costs.

Dental plans enroll 70 million persons, twice as many as in 1975, and the number may hit 99 million by 1985, says the American Dental Association. But recent jumps in dental costs force concerns like General Electric Company, which launches a plan July 1, to pay fixed amounts for procedures, rather than a proportion of dentists' fees.

Under Cities Service Co.'s dental plan, begun June 1, workers must share premium costs—which is unusual but which may become more common, experts predict. Mathematica Inc., Princeton, N.J., rejects offering the benefit when employees refuse to share premiums. Other small companies, such as Ragaire Corp., Cleburne, Tex., say they can't afford dental insurance when employees want it to pay "for everything."

Among existing plans, inflation prompts some employers to postpone braces coverage and other improvements, Prudential Insurance says.

Source: *The Wall Street Journal,* June 10, 1980, p. 1. Reprinted by permission of *The Wall Street Journal,* © Dow Jones & Company, Inc., June 10, 1980. All rights reserved.

---

[57]Rosenbloom and Hallman, *Employee Benefit Planning.*

[58] Sandy DeMent, "Prepaid Legal Service Plans: Past Developments, Present Status, and Future Prospects," *Pension World* 14, no. 7 (1978), pp. 11–20, 22–24.

[59]Ibid.

[60]Ibid.

[61]Ibid.

[62]Ibid.

erating interest. Of the 99 million Americans with dental insurance, approximately 7-10 percent have prepaid insurance. Bearing similarity to an HMO, this type of plan enlists a group of dentists who agree to treat company employees in return for a fixed monthly fee per employee.[63] This arrangement is designed to lower administrative costs and reduce the incentive for overtreatment.

Life insurance. One of the most common employee benefits offered by organizations is some form of life insurance. Typical coverage would be a group term insurance policy with a face value of one to two times the employee's salary. Most plan premiums are paid completely by the employer, and slightly over 80 percent include retiree coverage.[64] The policy provides protection against loss of life for a specified period, but provides no cash surrender value or investment value.[65] About two thirds of all policies include accidental death and dismemberment clauses.[66] To discourage turnover, almost all companies make this benefit forfeitable at termination.

Miscellaneous Benefits

Paid rest periods, lunch periods, wash-up time, travel time, clothes-change time, and get-ready time benefits are self-explanatory. Most work-time-off arrangements evolved historically on an informal basis or were negotiated in labor contracts.

PAYMENT FOR TIME NOT WORKED

Included within this category are several self-explanatory benefits:

1. Paid vacations and payments in lieu of vacation.
2. Payments for holidays not worked.
3. Paid sick leave.
4. Payments for National Guard or army or other reserve duty; jury duty and voting pay allowances; payments for time lost due to death in family or other personal reasons.

Judging from employee preferences discussed in the last chapter and from observation of negotiated union contracts, pay for time not worked continues to be a high-demand benefit. Twenty years ago it was relatively rare, for exam-

---

[63]"Dental Insurance Program Gains Favor Among Firms," *The Wall Street Journal,* September 21, 1984, p. 31.

[64]Allan Blostin, "Is Employer Sponsored Life Insurance Declining Relative to Other Benefits?" *Monthly Labor Review,* September 1981, pp. 31–33.

[65]Ernst and Whinney, *Tax Aspects of Compensation Planning.*

[66]Blostin, "Is Employer Sponsored Life Insurance Declining Relative to Other Benefits?"

ple, to grant time for anything but vacations, holidays, and sick leave. Now, many organizations have a policy of ensuring payments for civic responsibilities and obligations. Any pay for such duties (e.g., National Guard, jury duty) are usually nominal, so companies often supplement this pay, frequently to the level of 100 percent of wages lost.

OTHER EMPLOYEE BENEFITS

Under this heading the U.S. Chamber of Commerce typically includes various forms of profit-sharing plans. As defined by the Internal Revenue Service, various plans may be regarded as profit-sharing plans:

1. Thrift savings plans.
2. Deferred compensation plans.
3. Stock bonus plans.
4. ESOPs (employee stock ownership plans).

Categories 2 and 3 have been discussed elsewhere, so the focus here is on thrift savings plans and ESOP plans.

Employee thrift plans were initially introduced after World War II as a supplement to retirement plans. The typical thrift plan today is designed to assist American workers in meeting savings goals.[67] As an illustration, one survey of 246 companies with savings plans showed that most employers (83 percent) encouraged savings by matching employee contributions.[68] The most common contribution was 50 cents for every dollar, up to a maximum dollar amount (usually 5–10 percent of pay). A popular alternative has been to tie employer contribution levels to some measure of annual profitability.

Current interest in savings plans centers on what are popularly called 401(k) plans, so named after the section of the Internal Revenue Code describing them.[69] One survey of 401(k) plans placed participation at about 43 percent of companies.[70] Conversion of an existing savings plan to a 401(k) plan is actually quite easy. Most existing savings plans allow employees to contribute through payroll deduction. To encourage participation the company matches employee contributions, typically at the 50 percent level. Conversion to a 401(k) plan requires an administrative change from after-tax payroll deduction to pre-tax salary deferral. Hence, the participating employee does not pay current income or Social Security tax and the employer contribution is still deductible to the company.

---

[67]Robert D. Ready and Albert S. Schlactmeyer, "Trends within a Trend . . . Employee Savings Plans (Past, Present, and Future)," *Pension World* 14, no. 10 (1978), pp. 23–24, 26–28.

[68]CompFlash, "Tax Benefits Encourage Participation in Savings Plans," *AMA CompFlash* 84-5 (1984), pp. 4–5.

[69]Jerald Levy, "401(k) Plans—A Primer," *Employment Benefits Journal,* September 1985, p. 13; Howard Sontag, "Codas: Better than IRAs?" *Compensation* 3 (1982), pp. 14–22.

[70]CompFlash, "Popularity of 401(k) Plans Grows," *AMA CompFlash* 84-12 (1984), p. 6.

EXHIBIT 12.15
Illustration of a PAYSOP Plan

Company Participants	Salary	Percentage Compensation	Dollar Value of Securities Available for Allocation	Actual Allocation
Mr. W	$ 20,000	20K/140K = 14	$1,000	$ 140
Mr. X	30,000	30K/140K = 21	1,000	210
Ms. Y	40,000	40K/140K = 29	1,000	290
Ms. Z	50,000	50K/140K = 36	1,000	360
Total	$140,000			Total $1,000

Source: Adapted from Howard V. Sontag and Gary G. Quintiere, "PAYSOPs: ERTA's Revised TRASOPs," *Compensation Review* 14 (1982), pp. 14–27.

Finally, employee stock ownership plans (ESOPs) involve employer contributions in the form of stock ownership. Two variants on ESOPs have emerged in recent years.

A TRASOP (Tax Reduction Act stock ownership plan) is a form of ESOP that meets specific requirements of the Tax Reduction Act of 1975, as amended. Its attractiveness rests on two major factors. First, employers are essentially making payments to a trust that invests in the employer's stock. If the TRASOP meets Internal Revenue Service standards, this payment may be tax deductible: "In its original form, a TRASOP provided an extra 1 percent investment credit to any corporation willing to place that amount in trust for employee investment in employer stock."[71] While employees build up equity in the organization, the employer accumulates necessary capital from the sale of stock—a sale financed by an employer investment that is tax deductible. Some experts have argued that this stock accumulation will eventually lead to employee ownership of the organization. While some organizations dread this possible outcome, others view it as a low-probability occurrence and believe stock ownership will spur a healthy drive by employees for increased productivity and profitability.

Beginning in 1983 TRASOPs underwent a change based on provisions of the Economic Recovery Tax Act of 1981. In place of the 1 percent investment-based tax credit (1.5 percent if we add the .5 percent credit allotted to plan sponsors who permitted and matched voluntary employee contributions) is a payroll-based tax credit of .5 percent in 1983–84, and rising to .75 percent for 1985–87. Thus, for a participating organization with total payroll of $50 million, the additional credit for the plan sponsor would be $250,000 in 1983–84 and $375,000 in 1985–87. This switch to a payroll-based tax credit presumably reflects Congress' intention to provide greater benefits to labor-intensive firms at the expense of capital-intensive firms favored under the old TRASOP stan-

---

[71]Jeffrey R. Gates, Peter S. Egan, and Gail V. Kellogg, "TRASOPs—More Attractive after the Revenue Act of 1978," *Financial Executive,* January 1979, p. 44.

dards.[72] Exhibit 12.15 illustrates how these new PAYSOPs, so named for the credit tied to company payroll, operate.

SUMMARY

Since the 1940s employee benefits have been the most volatile area in the compensation field. From 1940 to 1980 these dramatic changes came in the form of more and better forms of employee benefits. The result should not have been unexpected. Employee benefits are now a major, and many believe prohibitive, component of doing business. Look for the decade of the 1980s to be dominated by cost-saving efforts to improve the competitive position of American industry. A part of these cost savings will come from tighter administrative controls on existing benefit packages. But another part, as already seen in the auto industry, may come from a reduction in existing benefits packages. If this does evolve as a trend, benefits administrators will need to develop a mechanism for identifying employee preferences (in this case "least preferences") and use those as a guideline to meet agreed upon savings targets.

REVIEW QUESTIONS

1. Are workers' compensation laws effective? Defend your answer.
2. Why is the social security system in trouble?
3. Explain the role of "experience rating" in employee benefits.
4. Discuss the relationship between UI and the incentive to work.
5. Explain the conflict between actuarial tables and equal employment opportunity laws.
6. What is the difference between vesting and portability?
7. What features would you include in a medical coverage plan to minimize costs?

---

[72]Howard V. Sontag and Gary G. Quintiere, "PAYSOPs: ERTA's Revised TRASOPs," *Compensation Review* 14 (1982), pp. 14–27.

Part 4
Compensation Application

Mondaille Hydraulics

Mondaille Hydraulics manufactures pumps for construction equipment and residential homes. In six months contract negotiations are scheduled with the bargaining representative for all blue collar workers, Local 1099 of the United Auto Workers. The president of your company, Forrest Sutton, is convinced that he must get concessions from the workers if Mondaille is to compete effectively with increasing foreign competition. In particular, Mr. Sutton is displeased with the cost of employee benefits. He doesn't mind conceding a small wage increase (maximum 3 percent), but he wants the total compensation package to cost 3 percent less for union employees during the first year of the new contract. Your current costs are shown in Exhibit 1.

Your labor relations assistant has surveyed other companies obtaining concessions from UAW locals. You also have data from a consulting firm which indicates employee preferences for different forms of benefits (Exhibit 2). Based on all this information you have two possible concession packages which the union just might accept, labeled Option 1 and Option 2 (Exhibit 3).

1. Cost out these packages given the data in Exhibits 1 and 2 and the information contained from various insurance carriers and other information sources (Exhibit 4).
2. Which package should you recommend to the president? Why?
3. Which of the strategies do you think need not be negotiated with the union before implementation?

446

EXHIBIT 1
Current Compensation Costs

Average yearly wage	$16,224.00
Average hourly wage	$ 9.86
Dollar value of yearly benefits, per employee	$ 6,084.00
Total compensation (wages plus benefits)	$21,638.76
Daily average number of hours paid	7.5

Benefits (by category)	Dollar Cost/ Employee/Year
1. Legally required payments (employer's share only)	$1,459
a. Old-age, survivors, disability, and health insurance (FICA taxes)	951
b. Unemployment compensation	229
c. Workers' compensation (including estimated cost of self-insured)	262
d. Railroad Retirement Tax, Railroad unemployment and cash sickness insurance, state sickness benefits insurance, etc.	16
2. Pension, insurance, and other agreed-upon payments (employer's share only)	2,069
a. Pension plan premiums and pension payments not covered by insurance-type plan (net)	885
b. Life insurance premiums; death benefits; hospital, surgical, medical, and major medical insurance premiums, etc. (net)	954
c. Short-term disability	65
d. Salary continuation or long-term disability	49
e. Dental insurance premiums	49
f. Discounts on goods and services purchased from company by employees	16
g. Employee meals furnished by company	32
h. Miscellaneous payments (compensation payments in excess of legal requirements, separation or termination pay allowances, moving expenses, etc.).	16
3. Paid rest periods, lunch periods, wash-up time, travel time, clothes-change time, get-ready time, etc. (90 minutes)	573
4. Payments for time not worked	1,623
a. Paid vacations and payments in lieu of vacation (16 days average)	803
b. Payments for holidays not worked (9 days)	557
c. Paid sick leave (10 days maximum)	213
d. Payments for State or National Guard duty; jury, witness, and voting pay allowances; payments for time lost due to death in family or other personal reasons, etc.	49
5. Other items	360
a. Profit-sharing payments	196
b. Contributions to employee thrift plans	49
c. Christmas or other special bonuses, service awards, suggestion awards, etc.	65
d. Employee education expenditures (tuition refunds, etc.)	32
e. Special wage payments ordered by courts, payments to union stewards, etc.	16
Total	$6,084.00

EXHIBIT 2
Benefit Preferences

Benefit Type or Method of Administering	Importance to Workers
Pensions	87
Hospitalization	86
Life insurance	79
Paid vacation	82
Holidays	82
Long-term disability	72
Short-term disability	69
Paid sick leave	70
Paid rest periods, lunch periods, etc.	55
Dental insurance	51
Christmas bonus	31
Profit sharing	21
Education expenditures	15
Contributions to thrift plans	15
Discount on goods	5
Fair treatment in administration	100

Note: 0 = Unimportant; 100 = Extremely important.

EXHIBIT 3
Two Possible Concession Packages

Option 1

Implement COPAY for Benefit	Amount of COPAY
Pension	$200.00
Hospital, surgical, medical and major medical premiums	250.00
Dental insurance premiums	15.00

Reduction of Benefit

Eliminate 10-minute paid break (workers leave work 10 minutes earlier)

Eliminate one paid holiday per year

Coordination with legally required benefit; Social Security coordinated with Mondaille pension

Option 2

Improved claims processing
  Unemployment compensation
  Workers' compensation
  Long-term disability

Require probationary period (one year) before eligible for:
  Discounts on goods
  Employee meal paid by company
  Contributions to employee thrift plans

Deductible ($100 per incident)
  Life insurance; death benefits; hospital, etc.
  Dental insurance

COPAY	Amount of COPAY
Hospital, surgical, medical and major medical premiums	$200.00

EXHIBIT 4
Analysis of Cost Implications for Different Cost-Cutting Strategies: Mondaille Hydraulics

Cost-Saving Strategy	*Savings as Percent of Benefit-Type Cost*
COPAY	Dollar for dollar savings equal to amount of COPAY
Deductible ($100 per incident)	
Life insurance premiums, death benefits, hospital, etc.	6%
Dental insurance	30
Require probationary period before eligible (one year)	
Discount on goods and services	10
Employee meals furnished by company	15
Contributions to employee thrift plans	10
Improved claims processing	
Unemployment compensation	8
Workers' compensation	3
Long-term disability	1
Coordination with legally required benefits	
Coordinate Social Security with Mondaille Pension Plan	15

Part 5

Government's Role and Compliance

We have now completed the discussion of three basic policies in the pay model used in this book. The first, which focused on determining the structure of pay, dealt with internal consistency. Determining the pay level based on external competitiveness was the second basic policy decision we examined. The third dealt with determining the pay for individual employees according to their contributions. These policy decisions, regarding consistency, competitiveness, and contributions, are directed at achieving the objectives of the pay system.

Before taking up the fourth basic policy decision, the nature of administration, we need to consider the significant role government and legislation play in the management of compensation. Laws and regulations are the most obvious intervention by government into compensation management. Laws serve to regulate pay decisions, much as employer policies do. Examples are readily apparent: minimum wage legislation is the most obvious. Others include the Equal Pay Act and Title VII of the Civil Rights Act, which prohibit pay discrimination.

But government is more than a source of laws and regulations. It is a major player in the marketplace, and consequently affects both the supply and demand for labor. Government affects the demand for labor in several ways: as a major employer, as a consumer of goods and services, and through its fiscal and monetary policies. Similarly, it affects the supply of labor—as a competitor looking to employ labor but also by setting licensing standards (e.g., teachers, physicians, barbers) and through appropriating funds for education and training programs that affect the nature of skills possessed by potential employees.

This part of the book has two chapters devoted to examining government as a major force which needs to be considered in the design and management of pay systems (see Exhibit V.1). Chapter 13 examines government's role in general and also several laws. Pay discrimination, a critical concern in contemporary compensation management, is considered in Chapter 14.

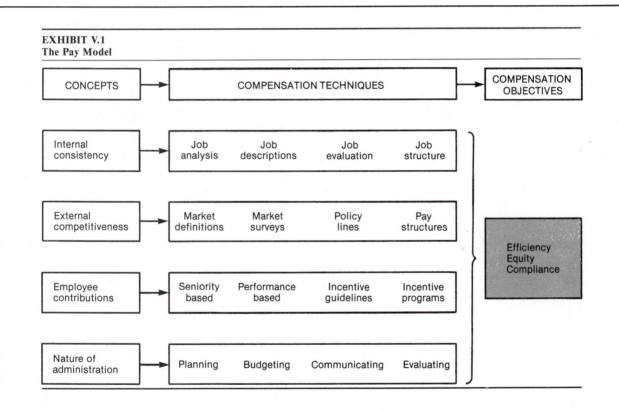

EXHIBIT V.1
The Pay Model

| CONCEPTS | COMPENSATION TECHNIQUES | COMPENSATION OBJECTIVES |

| Internal consistency | → | Job analysis | Job descriptions | Job evaluation | Job structure |

| External competitiveness | → | Market definitions | Market surveys | Policy lines | Pay structures |

| Employee contributions | → | Seniority based | Performance based | Incentive guidelines | Incentive programs |

| Nature of administration | → | Planning | Budgeting | Communicating | Evaluating |

Efficiency
Equity
Compliance

451

Chapter 13

The Government's Role in Compensation

A majority of the workers in the cotton mills are under 16, and the ages of them run down to 6 and 7. . . . The hours that these children work is well nigh incredible. Either they toil from six in the morning until six at night, or from six at night until six in the morning. The average daily wage of the men is 57 cents, of the women 39 cents, of the children 22 cents.[1] Said one . . . superintendent of a . . . glass plant: "I shall oppose every attempt at improved child-labor laws. Some people are born to work with their brains and some with their hands. Look at these," pointing to a line of "glass" boys, "they are not fitted to do anything else."[2]

---

[1] Edwin Markham, Benjamin B. Lindsey, and George Creel, *Children in Bondage* (New York: Hearst's International Library Company, 1914), pp. 25, 46.

[2] Ibid., p. 67.

The above excerpts describe conditions during a period when employment relations were without government regulation. Today we hear of the economic effect of regulations, but less often about the price paid for unregulated conditions. Like so many aspects of human resource management, balance is required between massive governmental intervention on the one hand and a lack of regulation on the other.

While the degree of enforcement may fluctuate with the political climate, the overall tendency has been toward ever-increasing regulation. Consequently the regulatory climate—the laws and the regulations issued by governmental agencies created to enforce the laws—represents a significant influence on compensation decisions.

GOVERNMENT INFLUENCES ON PAY

The government influences compensation practices and wages both directly and indirectly. Its direct effect on wages is through legislation such as the minimum wage law, which sets a floor on what an employer must pay, or the Equal Pay Act, which requires that pay differences among employees doing the same job cannot be based on the sex of the employee. Through such laws, the government involves itself directly in the wage-setting process. But it also has indirect effects, as shown in Exhibit 13.1. Governmental actions often affect both the demand and supply of labor; consequently, wages also are affected. Protective legislation often restricts the supply of labor in an occupation. For example, requiring plumbers to be licensed restricts the number of people who can legally offer plumbing services. While these licensing requirements are initiated in the

EXHIBIT 13.1
Government Effects on Wages and Practices

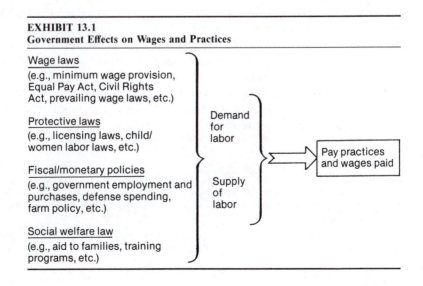

name of consumer protection, they also constrain the labor supply and put upward pressure on wages.

Legislation aimed at protecting specific groups also tends to restrict that group's full participation in the labor supply. Compulsory schooling laws, for example, restrict the supply of 15-year-olds available to sell hamburgers. Laws intended to protect women from certain types of working conditions also limit the hours women could work and the amount of physical labor they performed. Such laws also may have restricted access to many well-paying occupations. Other indirect effects of government on labor supply and hence wages include government-sponsored training and social welfare programs (e.g., aid to families with dependent children).

Government actions also affect the demand for labor. First, employment at all levels of government has grown from around 6 million employees in 1946 to 16.4 million in 1984.[3] While the federal government grew rapidly in the 1930s and 1940s, current growth is more rapid at state and local levels. Yearly growth rates at the state and local level of 5 percent were common in the 1960s and the 1970s.[4] In many regions (e.g., state capitals, county seats, etc.) the government is the dominant employer; consequently, it is a major force in determining the wages paid. In addition to being a major employer, government is a major consumer. Federal expenditures as a percent of the GNP have risen from 7.3 percent in 1902 to 24 percent in 1985.[5] A decision by the government to purchase 10 B-757 aircraft from Boeing has a dramatic effect on the demand for labor in Seattle, where Boeing is located.

Government fiscal and monetary policies that affect the economy indirectly affect market forces which, in turn, influence wages. Examples abound. Foreign trade policies, money supply decisions, farm policy—all these governmental actions have indirect effects on wages paid. Restricted farm exports mean farmers will have less money, which means manufacturers of farm equipment and fertilizer will hire fewer people. Lowered interest rates mean more people can afford to purchase houses, which means jobs not only for builders but also for employees of appliance, furniture, and carpet manufacturers. Lower tax rates mean more cash for all taxpayers, which, at least according to some economic theorists, translates into a boost for all employers and an increased demand for labor. Tax subsidies for hiring certain disadvantaged youth have the intent of stimulating a weak demand for such employees. So government's effect on wages is wide-ranging and pervasive.

---

[3] U.S. Department of Commerce, Bureau of Census, *Statistical Abstract of the United States, 1986,* 106th ed. (Washington, D.C.: U.S. Government Printing Office, December 1985).

[4] Ibid.

[5] *Economic Report of the President,* transmitted to Congress February 1986 (Washington, D.C.: U.S. Government Printing Office, 1986).

GOVERNMENT AND THE PAY MODEL

Regulatory compliance is one of the objectives of the pay model used in this book. The compensation techniques (job analysis and evaluation, surveys, ranges, performance appraisal, increase guidelines, and so on) and the results of those techniques (pay levels, pay structures, individual pay, and pay forms) must all be designed to be in compliance with the laws.

Some might argue that laws and regulations serve as constraints rather than objectives in the pay model. Whether or not they constrain depends on the philosophy of compensation management in a particular organization. Laws and regulations can serve as both constraints and objectives.

Regulations as Constraints

Once legislation is passed and interpretive regulations are published, the compensation manager must design systems to comply with them. Whether or not this leads to the results that are intended by legislation, managers must ensure that their practices are in compliance or be willing to go to court to seek clearer interpretation of the laws. For example, throughout the 1950s and early 1960s, Sears Roebuck & Company was lauded in textbooks and the popular press as a fair-minded employer willing to go to considerable expense to recruit and train minority group members and locate retail stores in neighborhoods where minority groups were concentrated. In 1963, equal employment opportunity legislation was passed. Prior to legislation, Sears had evolved policies and programs designed to increase minority employment. These programs relied in part on starting people in part-time positions and moving them into full-time positions as their skills developed and openings became available. But the Equal Employment Opportunity Commission (EEOC), the federal agency charged with enforcing equal opportunity legislation, required different and additional approaches. Sears managers had already accepted the goal of affirmative action and argued that they were not discriminating. EEOC disagreed and filed suit, alleging that Sears violated Title VII of the Civil Rights Act. Eventually, Sears filed a countersuit against the Commission. While some issues between Sears and the EEOC have been settled, mostly in Sears's favor, litigation continues. Whether these suits and countersuits will lead to practices that were more equitable than previous behavior is unknown. Certainly the EEOC members that required Sears to change its practices must have believed so. In contrast to employers who routinely refused applications for certain jobs from blacks or women, Sears's practices were ahead of their time. The point is that once legislation has been passed, all employers must comply with it. Some behaviors intended to discriminate may be made illegal; so may be some behaviors intended to enhance the employment status of minorities. If the legislation's exact intent is unclear, it may require interpretation through the courts.

Writing about the legislative and regulatory process, Ledvinka states, "It is more important to understand why the regulations are the way they are than to understand what the regulations say management can or cannot do."[6] By understanding the regulatory process, managers can better comply with the intent of legislation. According to Ledvinka, problems in society instigate a pressure for legislative action. If enough support develops, often as a result of compromises and trade-offs, laws are passed. Once passed, agencies must enforce the laws through rulings, regulations, inspections, and investigations. Management responds to enforcement by auditing and/or altering personnel practices, defending lawsuits, and lobbying for policy change.

Regulations as Objectives

But if the regulatory process constrains employers' behavior, it also provides opportunities to influence what legislation is passed and how legislation is interpreted. The nature of legislation can also be influenced. Employers lobby through their governmental relations units or through a consortium of employers, such as Business Roundtable or American Compensation Association. Testimony is often given before committees drafting legislation. To influence legislation requires the compensation professional to establish links with the firm's law department as well as with professional societies.

Employers also influence court interpretation of legislation through defending their practices during litigation, although this is a costly procedure and not one many employers seek. An example of employer influence on legislation is the Equal Pay Act, in which Congress chose skill, effort, responsibility, and working conditions as factors to define equal work.[7] These factors were chosen largely because Congress became aware of them through lobbying efforts as the criteria commonly used by employers and unions to evaluate jobs. So laws and regulations serve as both constraints within which to operate and objectives. Compensation professionals need to put greater emphasis on proactive activities intended to shape the legislation and regulations or to defend sound pay practices in the courts.

Let us now look at some specific compensation legislation.

MINIMUM WAGES AND COMPENSABLE TIME

The main legislation in this category is the Fair Labor Standards Act and the Portal-to-Portal Act. The Fair Labor Standards Act is the oldest and has the broadest coverage.

---

[6] James Ledvinka, *Federal Regulation of Personnel and Human Resource Management* (Boston: Kent Publishing Company, 1982).

[7] Equal Employment Opportunity Commission, *Legislative History of Titles VII and XI of Civil Rights Act of 1964* (Washington, D.C.: U.S. Government Printing Office, 1968).

Fair Labor Standards Act of 1938 (FLSA)

FLSA has four major provisions:

1. Minimum wage.
2. Hours of work.
3. Child labor.
4. Equal pay.

Minimum wage. When first enacted in 1938, the minimum wage was $.25 per hour. As of January 1981 it was changed to $3.35 per hour.[8] Forty-seven states also have minimum wage laws (shown in Exhibit 13.2), which cover employees exempt from FLSA. Coverage of the minimum wage provision does not extend to all employees. For example, current regulations allow the Department of Labor to authorize pay for full-time students at 83 percent of the federal minimum wage, but the certification period cannot exceed one year. Exemp-

EXHIBIT 13.2
Basic Hourly Minimum Wage Rates under State Laws

1. Alabama	None	27. Montana	$3.05
2. Alaska	$3.85	28. Nebraska	$1.60
3. Arizona	None	29. Nevada	$2.75
4. Arkansas	$3.15	30. New Hampshire	$3.35
5. California	$3.35	31. New Jersey	$3.35
6. Colorado	$3.00	32. New Mexico	$3.35
7. Connecticut	$3.37	33. New York	$3.35
8. Delaware	$3.00	34. North Carolina	$3.35
9. D.C.	$3.35–$3.95	35. North Dakota	$2.80–$3.10
10. Florida	None	36. Ohio	$2.30
11. Georgia	$3.25	37. Oklahoma	$3.35
12. Hawaii	$3.35	38. Oregon	$3.35
13. Idaho	$2.30	39. Pennsylvania	$3.35
14. Illinois	$3.35	40. Puerto Rico	55¢–$3.35
15. Indiana	$2.00	41. Rhode Island	$3.35
16. Iowa	None	42. South Carolina	None
17. Kansas	$1.60	43. South Dakota	$2.80
18. Kentucky	$2.60	44. Tennessee	None
19. Louisiana	None	45. Texas	$1.40
20. Maine	$3.55	46. Utah	$2.50–$2.75
21. Maryland	$3.35	47. Vermont	$3.35
22. Massachusetts	$3.35	48. Virginia	$2.65
23. Michigan	$3.35	49. Washington	$2.30
24. Minnesota	$3.35	50. West Virginia	$3.05
25. Mississippi	None	51. Wisconsin	$3.25
26. Missouri	None	52. Wyoming	$1.60

Note: Rates currently in effect at time of publication.
Source: *BNA Policy and Practice Series* Wages and Hours (Washington, D.C.: Bureau of National Affairs, 1986).

[8] Peyton K. Elder and Heidi D. Miller, "The Fair Labor Standards Act: Changes of Four Decades," *Monthly Labor Review* 93 (1970), pp. 10–16.

tions may also be granted for handicapped workers, apprentices, and learners. The bulk of such exemptions are utilized in the restaurant industry.[9] Proposals for a two-tier minimum wage, which would specify a lower minimum for teenagers, appear from time to time, but thus far have not generated sufficient political support. While the minimum has been unchanged since 1981, the purchasing power of $3.35, adjusted for inflation, has declined by 18 percent. A minimum wage study commission has proposed indexing the minimum to reflect changes in average hourly earnings.[10] Thus, as overall wages rose, so would the minimum. But again, no action has been taken on this recommendation.

Effects of minimum wage provisions. Minimum wage legislation was intended to provide an income floor for workers in society's lowest paid and least productive jobs.[11] Much of the research on minimum wage provisions has focused on its effects on income and employment levels.

Income effects. Who benefits by changes in the minimum wage rates? Some evidence suggests that adult women have been the primary beneficiaries, because higher rates have attracted them into full-time from part-time employment.[12] Other evidence suggests that all workers have benefited; as the pay rate at the lowest end of the scale has moved up, so have pay rates above it, in order to maintain pay differentials among jobs.[13] The shift in the pay structure resulting from an increased minimum wage is greater in some industries than others. For example, the lowest rates paid in the steel, chemical, oil, and pharmaceutical industries are well above minimum wage; any legislative change would have little direct impact on the labor bill of employers in these industries. Changes in the minimum wage will greatly affect labor costs of retailing and service firms, however. These businesses employ many clerks and sales personnel at or near the minimum wage. As the minimum increases, the increase ripples upward through the entire pay structure. Hence, pay of all personnel is increased to maintain pay differentials. The resulting higher labor bill increases the possibility of substituting capital for jobs (e.g., introducing automated inventory control systems, or prepacked frozen french fries) or holding down employment levels (e.g., fewer sales personnel) to control labor costs.

---

[9]July 16, 1982, Federal Register (47 FR 31010).

[10]Sar Levitan and Isaac Shapiro, "The Working Poor Deserve a Raise"; and Marvin H. Kosters, "An Increase Would Hurt Teen-Agers," both in *The New York Times,* March 30, 1986, p. F2.

[11]Edward M. Gramlich, "Impact of Minimum Wages on Other Wages, Employment, and Family Incomes," *Brookings Papers on Economic Activity* no. 2 (1976), pp. 409–51; Finis Welch, *Minimum Wages: Issues and Evidence* (Washington, D.C.: American Enterprise Institute, 1978).

[12]Donald O. Parsons, *Poverty and the Minimum Wage* (Washington, D.C.: American Enterprise Institute, 1980).

[13]Sar A. Levitan and Richard S. Belous, "The Minimum Wage Today: How Well Does It Work?" *Monthly Labor Review,* July 1979, pp. 17–21; Gramlich, "Impact of Minimum Wages."

So people working at or near the minimum wage who continue to work definitely do benefit from mandated minimum wage increases, and other workers in higher level jobs in those same companies may also benefit. Yet as labor costs increase, fewer workers will be hired if the increased costs can not be passed on to consumers or offset by increased productivity.

Employment effects. Many economists believe that employment opportunities for inexperienced and unskilled youth have been hurt by the minimum wage.[14] Employers may reason that the skills this group possesses are not commensurate with their costs. If a higher wage is to be paid, the employer will try to find more experienced or skilled workers. The stubbornly high rate of unemployment among teenagers is consistent with this argument. Is the problem of youth unemployment exacerbated by minimum wage legislation? Focusing on unemployment rates of various population segments draws attention away from the wide variety of possible causes of unemployment. Instead, the law's effect on *employment opportunities* for teenagers has been suggested as an alternative measure which is independent of population size and less subject to misinterpretation.[15] A 25 percent increase in the minimum wage will be associated with a 3.5 to 5.5 percent reduction in teenage employment. Presumably, similar results would hold for other unskilled and inexperienced workers, too. Some demographers predicted that the decreased birthrates in the 1960s and 1970s would eventually reduce youth employment without further governmental intervention.[16] And recent experience is beginning to corroborate this. For example, a 1985 Bureau of National Affairs survey found that 30 percent of the fast food stores had job vacancies that had gone unfilled for a month or more.[17]

Minimum wage legislation causes income for some workers to increase and employment opportunities for some workers to decrease. But what are the societywide effects of minimum wage legislation? How well does it work as an antipoverty program? A study of the impact of changes in minimum wages on low-wage adult females concludes:

> The modest increases in earnings among adult females from poverty families estimated here (as a result of increases in minimum wage) are unlikely to be sufficiently valuable from a social perspective to offset the labor market difficulties imposed on . . . young persons, male and female.[18]

---

[14]Brigitte H. Selle Kaerts and Stephen W. Welch, "An Economic Analysis of Minimum Wage Noncompliance," *Industrial Relations,* Spring 1984, pp. 244–59.

[15]Robert S. Goldfarb, "The Policy Content of Qualitative Minimum Wage Research," *Proceedings of the 27th Annual Meeting 1974,* Industrial Relations Research Association, pp. 261–68. A classic piece on minimum wage is George J. Stigler, "The Economics of Minimum Wage Legislation," *American Economic Review* 36 (June 1946), pp. 358–65.

[16]Clark Kerr and Jerome Rosow, eds., *Work in America: The Decade Ahead* (New York: Van Nostrand Reinhold, 1979).

[17]S. Naser, "Jobs Go Begging at the Bottom," *Fortune,* March 17, 1986, pp. 33–35.

[18]Parsons, *Poverty and the Minimum Wage,* p. 62.

Proposed amendments. In the face of mixed evidence, should the proactive compensation manager urge relaxation of the minimum wage? Or increases? The answer probably depends on the legislation's effects on the employer's labor costs. Compensation professionals in retail and service firms will probably oppose increases whereas those in high wage firms will be indifferent. The Minimum Wage Study Commission, established by Congress in 1977, made the following recommendations in late 1981.

*[handwritten margin note: Compensation manager's view *]*

A proposed youth differential allowing a lower rate for jobs held by unskilled, inexperienced youth should be rejected.

Index the minimum wage to reflect changes in average hourly earnings in private business.

Eliminate the bulk of the exemptions.

Reduce noncompliance by permitting class action lawsuits, increasing penalties, and targeting enforcement efforts.

Retain the executive, administrator, and professional exemptions.

Limit student certification exemptions to high school students.

To date no action has been taken on these recommendations. The Reagan administration, however, continues to advocate a differential minimum wage as a way to reduce youth unemployment.

Hours of work. The overtime provisions of the FLSA require payment at one and a half times the standard for work over 40 hours per week.[19] There is a "union contract exemption" covering employees working under guaranteed annual employment agreements. Many union contracts provide for overtime after a shorter work week, some as short as 25 hours.[20]

The overtime provision is aimed at sharing available work. It seeks to make hiring more workers a less costly option than scheduling overtime for current employees. But overtime pay for current employees is often the least costly option. This is due to (1) an increasingly skilled work force, with higher training costs per employee and (2) higher fringe benefits, the bulk of which are fixed per employee. These factors have lowered the point at which it pays employers to schedule longer hours and pay the overtime premium, rather than hire, train, and pay fringes for more employees. Models to examine the break-even points between working overtime and hiring additional workers have been designed.[21] These models compare added expense of time and a half wages to the added fringe benefits and training costs required for new hires.

---

[19]29 Code of Federal Regulations, Chap. V, Secs. A.3-A.5

[20]T. A. Kochan, H. C. Katz, and N. R. Mower, "Worker Participation and American Unions," in *Challenges and Choices Facing American Labor,* ed. T. Kochan (Cambridge, Mass.: MIT Press, 1985), pp. 271–306.

[21]M. L. Spruill, M. J. Wallace, and A. Glasberg, "Staffing Analysis Cost Technique," *Managerial Planning* 26 (1978), pp. 32–38.

Several amendments to increase the overtime penalty have been offered. These typically seek to increase the penalty, reduce the standard workweek to less than 40 hours, or repeal some of the exemptions. Only about 58 percent of all employees are covered by the overtime provision at present.[22]

Effects of the overtime provision. Unions typically support efforts to raise the overtime wage because they believe such a change will result in higher employment levels and more union members. Employers typically oppose efforts because changes will result in greater costs for them. Recent research concludes that the maximum employment gain from changing overtime provisions would be .5 to 1.5 percent in manufacturing and .8 to 2.1 percent in nonmanufacturing, and there is pessimism as to whether even these gains could be achieved.[23]

In addition to increased costs, some researchers have investigated overtime's effect on worker satisfaction. Generally, as hours of work increase, both pay satisfaction and job satisfaction decrease. But any negative effects of overtime vary with the reasons for using overtime.[24] For example, is overtime scheduled because of growing workload, or because of inefficient work scheduling? If overtime is required because of what employees consider to be inadequate management, they are probably going to resent the requirement. But, working overtime is not always viewed negatively. Most union contracts specify that overtime hours be offered to members on the basis of seniority, which implies that the chance for extra work is desirable.[25] An auto worker reminisced, "We used to get together on Thursday and say, 'Let's all work Saturday and get some overtime.' So we would purposely scrap 500 axles that would have to be rebuilt on the weekend. You do that now, and you work yourself out of a job, pal. That axle's going to cost twice as much and the Japanese will move in."[26]

So what difference does overtime make to the compensation professional who does not schedule axle production? The hours of work provision of FLSA requires that records be kept of actual time worked by employees in covered jobs. This brings up two issues of interest: (1) What is and is not included in "actual time worked"? and (2) Which jobs are covered?

Exempt and nonexempt. Whether jobs are classified as exempt or nonexempt from the FLSA is of major importance. Nonexempt jobs must comply

---

[22]Ronald G. Ehrenberg and Paul L. Schumann, *Longer Hours or More Jobs?* (Ithaca: New York State School of Industrial and Labor Relations, Cornell University, 1982).

[23]Ibid.

[24]Lloyd S. Baird and Philip J. Beccia, "The Potential Misuse of Overtime," *Personnel Psychology* 33, no. 3 (Autumn 1980), pp. 557–66.

[25]John A. Fossum, *Labor Relations* (Plano, Tex.: Business Publications, 1982), p. 194.

[26]Richard Danjin, quoted in John Simmons and William Mares, *Working Together* (New York: Alfred A. Knopf, 1983).

EXHIBIT 13.3
Some Exemptions to the Minimum Wage and Overtime Provisions of the Fair Labor Standards Act

Section 13(a)(1)	Outside salesmen, professional executive, and administrative personnel ("including any employee employed in the capacity of academic administrative personnel or teacher in elementary or secondary schools").
Section 13(a)(3)	Employees of certain seasonal amusements or recreational establishments.
Section 13(a)(5)	Fishing and first processing at sea employees.
Section 13(a)(6)	Agricultural employees employed by farms utilizing fewer than 500 man-days of agricultural labor, employed by a member of their immediate family, certain local seasonal harvest laborers and seasonal hand harvest laborers 16 years of age or under, and employees principally engaged in the range production of livestock.
Section 13(a)(7)	Employees exempt under Section 14 of the Act (certain learners, apprentices, students and handicapped workers).
Section 13(a)(12)	Seamen on foreign vessels.
Section 13(a)(15)	Babysitters employed on a casual basis and persons employed to provide companion services.
Section 7(b)	Certain employees under collectively bargained guaranteed annual wage plans and wholesale or bulk petroleum distribution employees.
Section 7(i)	Certain commission salesmen in retail or service establishments.
Section 13(b)(1)	Motor carrier employees.
Section 13(b)(2)	Railroad employees.
Section 13(b)(3)	Airline employees.
Section 13(b)(6)	Seamen.
Section 13(b)(12)	Agricultural employees.
Section 13(b)(15)	Maple sap employees.
Section 13(b)(29)	Employees of amusements or recreational establishments located in a national park or national forest or on land in the National Wildlife Refuge System.

with the FLSA, which means they must be paid time and a half for hours worked overtime and extensive records must be kept and filed with the Department of Labor. Overtime pay is not required for exempt jobs, nor is record-keeping of hours worked. Today the FLSA, amended several times since it was first passed in 1938, covers many jobs. However, there are exemptions, and they are the most complex part of the act. Some of the exemptions are shown in Exhibit 13.3. For example, professional, executive, and administrative jobs are exempt. So are many jobs in the transportation industry.

Some exemptions suspend only certain provisions of the act, while others suspend all provisions. Some apply to all employees of certain businesses, others to only certain employees. To compound the confusion, exemptions may overlap. Repeated amendments to the act have made the distinction between exempt and nonexempt difficult to determine. Ledvinka observed, "As soon as the distinction between exempt and nonexempt begins to emerge clearly from court cases, the act is amended, setting off a new round of court cases."[27]

---

[27]Ledvinka, *Federal Regulation*, p. 250.

The Wage-Hour Division of the Department of Labor, which is charged with enforcement of the FLSA, provides strict criteria that must be met in order for jobs to be considered professional and exempt from minimum wage and overtime provisions. Professionals must:

Do work requiring knowledge generally acquired by prolonged, specialized study, or engage in original and creative activity in a recognized artistic field.

Consistently exercise discretion or judgment.

Do work that is primarily intellectual and nonroutine.

Devote at least eighty percent of their work hours to such activities.[28]

There are also criteria for exempt status for executives. Executives must:

Primarily undertake management duties.

Supervise two or more employees.

Have control (or at least great influence) over hiring, firing, and promotion.

Exercise discretionary powers.

Devote at least 80 percent of their work hours to such activities.[29]

There are similar criteria for administrative and sales workers and employees in transportation and other industries as well.[30]

Child labor. The child labor provision of FLSA states that minors must be over 18 to work in hazardous occupations and above 16 or 14 in other occupations. The age varies, depending on the type of work and whether or not the employer is the child's parent. This provision generates little controversy today. As the excerpts at the beginning of the chapter indicate, this is a change from the attitudes prevailing in society in the early 1900s.

The fourth major provision of FLSA, equal employment, will be discussed in the next chapter. Equal employment was not covered in the original 1938 FLSA. It was added as an amendment in 1963, called the Equal Pay Act, and is today of major importance. The whole topic of wage discrimination merits a separate chapter. (See Chapter 14.)

Portal-to-Portal Act of 1947

Recall that FLSA requires records of time actually worked by covered employees. But when does the workday begin? Is it when the employee arrives at the actual job site? Or on the employer's premises? Think of working in an underground coal mine. Underground travel time to get to the actual work site is under the control of the employer and may be substantial. According to current interpretation of FLSA and the courts, this travel time should be part of the

---

[28]29 Code of Federal Regulations, Chap. V, Sec. 541.3.

[29]Ibid., Sec. 541.1

[30]Ibid., Secs. 541.2 and 541.500.

hours worked and included in calculating pay and overtime rates. But in *Anderson* v. *Mt. Clemens Pottery* the courts extended this "travel time" concept to manufacturing, ruling that time spent walking between the plant gate and the work bench as well as time spent on certain "make-ready" activities was all "compensable working time."[31] A flood of lawsuits for wages owed followed, prompting Congress to pass the Portal-to-Portal Act. The act provides that time spent on activities before beginning or after completion of the "principal activity" is compensable only if payment is required under a contract or has customarily been counted as work time prior to the *Mt. Clemens* case. In other words, if time spent on makeready activities was not counted as work hours before, the employer need not begin counting that time now. This addition of "custom" is the most important feature of the act.

The next group of laws set pay for work done to produce goods and services contracted by the federal government. These are called "prevailing wage" laws.

PREVAILING WAGE LAWS

A government-defined prevailing wage is the minimum wage that must be paid for work done on covered government projects or purchases. In practice these prevailing rates have been union rates paid in various geographic areas,[32] and have become a higher minimum wage on covered projects. The original purpose was to prevent the government from undercutting local workers. For example, if a government project of the magnitude of Hoover Dam were to pay low wages to construction workers, their sheer force of size may drive down the entire wage structure in the area. So the government has required that surveys identify the prevailing wage in an area, and that wage becomes the mandated minimum wage on the government-financed project.

Contractors object to this requirement because it frequently means they have to match a wage rate that only a minority of area workers, 30 percent or more, are receiving. Business and taxpayer groups argue that prevailing rates result in higher costs than necessary on government projects. Unions, on the other hand, argue that fringe benefits are not included in the calculation of prevailing wages, and therefore it understates actual rates.[33]

In 1982 new regulations were proposed that would define prevailing wage in any area as (1) the wage paid to a majority of area employees in the job classification (that provision remained unchanged from the previous regulations) *or* (2) a wage calculated under a new weighted average formula, if a majority of area employees do not happen to work at a single rate.[34] However, the Building

---

[31]*Anderson* v. *Mt. Clemens Pottery Co.*, 6 WH Cases 595, USDC E. Michigan.

[32]F. Ray Marshall, Allan M. Cartter, and Allan G. King, *Labor Economics* (Homewood, Ill.: Richard D. Irwin, 1976), p. 240.

[33]Ibid.

[34]May 28, 1982, Federal Register (47 FR 23644).

and Construction Trades Department of the AFL–CIO protested, arguing that the purpose of prevailing wage legislation is to protect the wages of workers, while the purpose of the new regulations is to reduce costs.[35] The appeals court has upheld the Labor Department's revisions.[36]

The main prevailing wage laws are (1) Davis-Bacon (1931), which covers mechanics and laborers on public construction projects with expenditures over $2,000; (2) Walsh-Healey Public Contracts Act (1936), which extends the provisions of Davis-Bacon to manufacturers or suppliers of goods for government contracts over $10,000; (3) Service Contract Act (1965), which extends coverage to suppliers of services in excess of $2,500 (e.g., cleaning, catering) to the federal government; and (4) National Foundation Arts and Humanities Act (1965), which covers professionals, laborers and mechanics working on projects that receive funding from the Foundation. Only those employees directly engaged in producing or furnishing for the federal contract are covered; other employees of the manufacturer/supplier are not.

In addition to a prevailing wage, Walsh-Healey also requires:

1. One and a half times the regular pay rate for hours over 8 per day or 40 per week must be paid.
2. Sanitary and nonhazardous working conditions must be maintained.
3. Payroll records must be kept.
4. Employees must be above 16 years.

Walsh-Healey predates the FLSA. The FLSA duplicates some Walsh-Healey requirements and extends them to additional employees.

Up to this point we have discussed the FLSA, the Portal-to-Portal Act, and prevailing wage legislation, much of which was originally passed in the 1930s and 1940s in response to social issues of that time. In the 1960s, the equal rights movement pushed different social problems to the forefront. The Equal Pay Act and the Civil Rights Act were passed. Because of their substantial impact on human resource management and compensation, they are discussed at length in the next chapter. Additional rights legislation includes the Pregnancy Discrimination Act and the Age Discrimination in Employment Act (Exhibit 13.4).

EQUAL RIGHTS LEGISLATION

Age Discrimination in Employment Act of 1967

The Age Discrimination in Employment Act, passed in 1967 and amended in 1978, protects workers between the ages of 40 and 70 from employment dis-

---

[35] *Building and Construction Trades Department, AFL-CIO* v. *Donovan*, Docket No. 82-1631.
[36] July 26, 1982, Federal Register (47 FR 32070).

EXHIBIT 13.4
Federal Laws: Equal Employment Opportunity

Regulation	Major Provisions
Equal Pay Act	A 1963 amendment to FLSA; equal pay required for male and female workers doing "substantially similar work" in terms of skill, effort, responsibility, and working conditions. Exemptions allowed for seniority, merit pay, and piece work systems.
Title VII of Civil Rights Act	(1) Prohibits discrimination in all employment practices on basis of race, sex, color, religion, national origin, or pregnancy.
	(2) Bennett Amendment links Title VII with the Equal Pay Act by providing that it is not unlawful to differentiate on the basis of sex in determining pay if such differentiation is authorized by the Equal Pay Act.
Age Discrimination Act	Protects employees aged 40–70 against age discrimination.
Pregnancy Discrimination Act	Disability and medical benefits plans cannot single out pregnancy for differential treatment. Pregnancy must be covered to same extent that other medical conditions are covered.

crimination due to age.[37] To date this act has been applied principally to retirement, promotion, and layoff policies, but it applies to all personnel decisions. The purpose of the act is to "promote employment of older persons on their ability rather than age; to prohibit arbitrary age discrimination in employment; to help employers and workers find ways of meeting problems arising from the impact of age on employment."[38] The law forbids mandatory retirement prior to age 70 (with some exceptions); limiting or classifying employees in any way that would adversely affect their status because of age; reducing any employee's wage rate to comply with the act; or discriminating in compensation or terms of employment because of age. Individual states frequently have laws protecting employees not covered by federal law.

Age discrimination focuses attention on the compensation issue of paying for performance and the relationship between performance and age. For example, the career stage literature often assumes a "decline" stage in later years, though the age of decline varies.[39] However, the literature on aging does not support such an assumption.[40] Variations in performance exist at all ages, in-

---

[37]29 U.S.C. Sec. 621-634 (1970 and Supp. V. 1975) as amended by Public Law 95-256 (1978).

[38]Ibid.

[39]Douglas Hall, *Careers in Organizations* (Santa Monica, Calif.: Goodyear Publishing, 1976); J. Rush, A. Peacock, and G. Milkovich, "Career Stages: A Partial Test of Levinson's Model of Life/Career Stages," *Journal of Vocational Behavior* 16 (1980), pp. 347–59; D. J. Levinson, C. Darrow, E. Klein, M. Levinson, and B. McKee, *The Seasons of a Man's Life* (New York: Alfred A. Knopf, 1978); and E. G. Schein, *Career Dynamics* (Reading, Mass.: Addison-Wesley Publishing, 1978).

[40]Mildred Doering, Susan Rhodes, and Michael Schuster, *Managing the Aging Workforce,* Report to the General Electric Foundation (Syracuse, N.Y.: Syracuse University, June 1980).

EXHIBIT 13.5
Sandia's Age-Related "Stretchout" Program

	Age			
Interval	*29 and Under*	*30–35*	*36–45*	*46 and Over*
12 months	5.0%	7.5%	10.0%	12.5%
15 months	5.0%	5.0%	7.5%	10.0
18 months	5.0%	5.0%	5.0%	7.5%
21 and over	5.0%	5.0%	5.0%	5.0%

cluding among older workers. A pay system that purports to pay for performance must be sure that performance appraisal systems are not biased by age, or that appraisers do not assume a lower performance level simply because a worker is older.

The most important Supreme Court ruling on age discrimination thus far is *Mistretta* v. *Sandia Corporation.*[41] Sandia had a policy of granting no raise smaller than 5 percent, on the philosophy that a raise of less than 5 percent decreased motivation. If performance did not merit at least a 5 percent increase, Sandia felt it was better to give that employee no increase. Sandia also had a "stretchout" program that varied with the performance level. However, the stretchout also varied with age, as Exhibit 13.5 indicates.

For example, if a worker's performance was judged to merit only the minimum 5 percent increase, a worker aged 29 or less could receive that raise 12 months after a previous raise; a worker aged 30 to 35 would need to wait 15 months for such a raise; a worker aged 36 to 45 would receive the 5 percent raise after 18 months, and a worker over 45 years of age would need to wait 21 months for such a raise. Workers over age 45 could receive raises 12 months after previous raises only if their performance was so outstanding that it merited a 12.5 percent increase. This stretchout policy was judged to be age-related and therefore discriminatory against workers in the protected age group.

The Sandia system of age banding clearly differentiated employees on the basis of age. But in most cases it is difficult to document age discrimination because age is so closely correlated to seniority, and it is not illegal to vary treatment of employees on the basis of seniority. Another difficulty in pinpointing age discrimination is the frequently higher base position of an older worker. For example, older workers have lower promotion rates than younger workers, but this difference reflects the lower number of possible positions available into which older workers could be promoted. Additionally, lower salary increases for older workers may reflect their higher position in the pay ranges for particular jobs. To lessen the impact of any performance declines on costs, some experts recommend a base price for adequate performance in a job, and a bo-

---

[41]*Mistressa* v. *Sandia Corp.* U.S. District Court 21, FEP Cases 1671, 1978.

nus for quantifiable results above satisfactory.[42] The chapters on employee contributions discuss various ways of linking pay and performance. But the best advice in regard to the regulatory compliance objective is to avoid assuming performance differences on the basis of age, sex, race, or other illegal criteria. The focus should be on accurate performance appraisal.

Pregnancy Discrimination Act of 1978

This act is actually an amendment to Title VII of the Civil Rights Act. It requires employers to extend to pregnant women the same disability and medical benefits provided other employees.[43] The Pregnancy Discrimination Act forbids exclusion of pregnancy from the list of disabilities for which the employer compensates absent employees. It does not require an employer to offer a disability plan, nor does it prevent a dollar limit being placed on reimbursement of medical costs. The law merely places disability benefits for pregnant employees on an equal footing with those of nonpregnant employees.

In *McNulty* v. *Newport News Shipbuilding* (1983), the Supreme Court applied the Pregnancy Discrimination Act to pregnancy benefits received by spouses of male employees.[44] The employer had set a limit on maternity benefits for employee spouses, but did not limit payments for any other medical conditions. The Court ruled that whatever benefits package is offered to female employees, including medical care for spouses and dependents, must be offered equally to male employees. In other words, no limitation can be put on pregnancy expenses that is not applied to other medical conditions. The decision does not bar employers from limiting all medical costs for dependents, say to 50 percent of expenses, if they impose the same limit on all dependents, regardless of sex. All employee spouses must be treated the same, and while this treatment need not be identical to treatment for employees, maternity benefits cannot be treated differently from other medical conditions.

Equal Benefits Payouts versus Equal Benefit Costs

The issue of equal benefit treatment for all employees is complicated by the insurance industry practice of charging differential rates based on sex (Exhibit 13.6).[45] For example, because women as a group live longer than men, they

---

[42]Samuel T. Beachman, "Managing Compensation and Performance Appraisal Under the Age Act," *Management Review,* January 1979, pp. 51–54.

[43]Patricia M. Lines, "Update: New Rights for Pregnant Employees," *Personnel Journal* 58, no. 1 (January 1979), pp. 33–37.

[44]"Court Rules Health Plans Must Be Equal," *Ithaca Journal,* June 21, 1983, p. 22.

[45]"Sex and the Insurance Policy," *Business Week,* February 7, 1983, pp. 83–87.

EXHIBIT 13.6
How Much More Women Pay for Insurance than Men

Coverage	Lifetime Cost Differential for Women
Medical	
Typical hospital-surgical policy from State Farm Mutual for years 25 to 64. $100 daily room and board; $2,000 surgical. Includes pregnancy complications. Excludes normal pregnancy, childbirth	+ $ 6,862
Disability	
Typical disability policy for years 25 to 64 from Allstate Life. $700/ month base benefit. Excludes pregnancy, childbirth, miscarriage, abortion. Includes complications and nonelective caesarean section	+ 4,854
Life insurance and pension	
Typical policy for age 65 retirement from Minnesota Mutual. Life insurance before age 65, $100,000. Monthly pension starting at age 65, $1,000. Pay premiums for years 35 to 54. Dividends estimated by company deducted	+ 5,856
Automobile	
Typical liability and physical damage policy, using factors rated by Insurance Services Office. Primary classifications: youthful operator; good student; unmarried; owner or principal operator; drive to work or business use, medium-size town. For years 17 to 24	− 1,840
Total difference	$15,732

Source: National Organization for Women.

theoretically collect pensions for a greater number of years and therefore are more costly for the pension provider unless the monthly pension payment is made smaller. If a pension is taken as a lump-sum payment, or paid out over a limited number of years, then the sex of the pensioner makes no difference. But if the pensioner wishes to purchase an annuity that will continue payments until death, a woman will receive a lower monthly annuity payment than a man will, assuming both retire at the same age and both pay the same lump sum for their annuity. For years many employers required greater pension contributions from women employees than from men, or alternatively, paid lower annuities to women than to men when they retired. But in 1978 the Supreme Court ruled that an employer violates Title VII of the Civil Rights Act if it requires unequal pension plan *contributions* based on sex.[46] The fact that women as a group live longer than men does not justify unequal treatment of a specific woman employee, who may or may not live longer than any specific male employee. Lower courts have applied this reasoning to pension *benefits* or payouts in addition to pension contributions, and this issue is currently working its way through the courts.

---

[46]*Los Angeles Dept. of Water and Power v. Manhart et al.,* 435 U.S. 702, 1978.

WAGE AND PRICE CONTROLS

Wage control programs typically aim at maintaining low inflation at low levels of unemployment. They frequently focus on limiting the size of the pay raises as well as the rate of increases in the prices charged for goods and services.

Control programs can vary in their stringency. In 1942, for example, wages were frozen at a level that prevailed on September 15 of that year.[47] The government established "going rates" for key occupations and then permitted pay increases up to the minimum of a going rate bracket. Benefits could be instituted only if employers could show that they were customary in an area. Despite these restrictions, because of the demand and supply imbalances created by World War II, the basic wage increased 24 percent between January 1941 and July 1945.

Another freeze was ordered in 1951, but by now many union members had labor contracts that provided automatic wage increases tied to the cost of living as well as annual "productivity" raises.[48] Once stabilization officials decided to permit the continued operation of these contracts, they were forced to sanction similar raises for other groups of employees.

Rather than an across-the-board wage freeze, the Council of Economic Advisers (CEA) in the early 1960s tried a more moderate approach. It tied wage rate and benefit increases to overall productivity increases, reasoning that acceptance of this guide would maintain stability of labor cost per unit of output for the overall economy. But many economists question the usefulness of guidelines tied to productivity on the grounds that inflation typically is caused by unmet demand, whereas productivity guidelines focus on supply rather than demand.[49] Additionally, there are serious difficulties in measuring the productivity factor to which wages are tied.[50] Productivity is only one of many factors related to pay, and any national productivity rate is meaningless when applied to a specific employer's productivity.

In 1971 the Nixon administration, facing a 6 percent inflation rate and an unemployment level just over 5 percent, imposed freeze and control measures that rivaled those of World War II. These policies were able to slow inflation to just over 3 percent through most of 1971 and 1972.[51] But once the controls were relaxed, prices rose rapidly: over 6 percent in 1973 and 11 percent in 1974. Galbraith interprets the rapid growth of postcontrol inflation as proof that the controls were effective and should have remained in place. Friedman interprets

---

[47] *Wage and Salary Controls Handbook* (Washington, D.C.: Bureau of National Affairs, May 3, 1972).

[48] Ibid.

[49] Marshall, Cartter, and King, *Labor Economics.*

[50] Solomon Fabricant, "Which Productivity? Perspectives on a Current Question," *Monthly Labor Review,* June 1962, pp. 18–24.

[51] Marshall, Cartter, and King, *Labor Economics.*

the same data to indicate that wage-price controls merely redistributed inflation over time but did not eliminate it.[52]

Mitchell and Weber argue that controls can be useful in the short run, and the point of their research is to find ways to minimize the dislocations related to controls in future applications.[53]

The Council on Wage and Price Stability during the Carter administration tried to minimize problems by opting for less encompassing voluntary wage guidelines.[54] Employers were provided formulas to determine their own compliance with pay standards. Those that did not comply were subject to government scrutiny and possible government manipulation of import restrictions and government purchases to favor employers who complied and penalize noncompliance. However, even though flexibility had been a goal of the program, an absolute standard soon developed, along with a bureaucracy to consider exceptions to the standard.

So wage controls or guidelines can vary in the broadness of application and in the stringency of the standard. The standard for allowable pay increases can range from absolute denial during a freeze to increases equal to some productivity or price change measure.

How successful are wage controls in achieving their goal of reducing inflation? Economists disagree. Cartter, Marshall, and King conclude:

1. No western country has had successful guidelines for long periods of time, though there have been short-run successes during periods of crisis.
2. The most successful experiences have come where centralized labor and management organizations agreed to wage-price policies and governments used these policies as supplements to, rather than substitute for . . . other economic policies to overcome inflationary pressures.[55]

Eventually any freeze or outside control exerted at an arbitrary point in time cannot help but be inequitable to some employers and employees, since the wage-setting process is ongoing. Both unions and managers are united in their concern for employee equity under wage controls.[56] They are also united in

---

[52]Ibid.

[53]George P. Schultz and Kenneth W. Dam, "Reflections on Wage and Price Control," *Industrial and Labor Relations Review,* January 1977, pp. 139–51; Arnold R. Weber and Daniel J. B. Mitchell, "Further Reflections on Wage Controls: Comment," *Industrial and Labor Relations Review,* January 1978, pp. 149–58. See also George P. Schultz and Kenneth W. Dam, "Reply," *Industrial and Labor Relations Review,* January 1978, pp. 159–60; and Daniel J. B. Mitchell and Ross E. Azevedo, *Wage-Price Controls and Labor Market Distortions* (Los Angeles: Institute of Industrial Relations, University of California, 1976).

[54]Lucretia Dewey Tanner and Mary Converse, "The 1978–80 Pay Guidelines: Meeting the Need for Flexibility," *Monthly Labor Review,* July 1981, pp. 16–21.

[55]Cartter, Marshall, and King, *Labor Economics,* p. 326.

[56]*A Position Statement on the Revised Voluntary Wage Guidelines,* (Scottsdale, Ariz.: American Compensation Association, August 28, 1979).

their interest in the administration of a government control program. Programs usually start out simple, but as requests for exceptions mount, so does the bureaucracy. The administrators of the 1978–80 Carter pay guidelines prided themselves on an average response time to requests for exceptions of 40 days.[57] But in periods in which responses are required to meet rapidly changing conditions, affected employees are not willing to wait 40 days, and compensation professionals are forced to figure ways around the regulations.

In the face of possible bureaucratic and employee equity problems, how can compensation managers best protect their employees and managers facing government intervention in the wage-setting process? Those companies that seem to suffer the least disruptions are the ones that have sound and flexible compensation systems in place, with well-thought-out policies that demonstrably have been followed in the past. Such companies can document what they have done and why they did it, and are far more able to handle government intervention than employers that have no formal pay systems and cannot justify their behavior. The same is true with any other area of government interest, be it meeting FLSA pay and recordkeeping requirements, or complying with equal rights legislation. A system based on work- and business-related logic is an employee's and employer's best protection.

REGULATION OF BENEFITS

We have already mentioned the requirements that benefits packages must be nondiscriminatory on the basis of sex, race, religion, and national origin. Additional governmental effects on benefit options are discussed in Chapter 12. Government has its impact in two ways. The first is by legally requiring that some specific benefits be provided, either at employer expense or as an expense shared between employer and employee. Workers' compensation, social security, and unemployment insurance are all legally required. Workers' compensation and unemployment insurance are completely employer-financed, whereas employees and employers jointly contribute to social security.

The second way the government influences benefits is through its tax policy. Benefits are, in general, tax-free to employees and a tax-deductible expense to employers, providing certain conditions are met. These conditions change frequently, almost with every legislative session, but their general aim is to ensure that a benefit package is structured to be available to all employees rather than to a select few, and to be sure that tax-free cash is not funneled to employees under the guise of benefits, thus escaping the long arm of the IRS. These issues are discussed in the benefits chapters.

---

[57]Tanner and Converse, "The 1978–80 Pay Guidelines."

SUMMARY

Compliance with laws and regulations is treated as an objective in the pay model. It can be a constraint and/or an opportunity.

The regulatory environment faced by a compensation professional certainly constrains the decisions that can be made. Once laws are passed and regulations published, employers must comply. But a proactive compensation manager can influence the nature of regulations and their interpretation. Astute professionals must be aware of legislative and judicial currents, to protect both employers' and employees' interests, and to ensure that compensation practices conform to judicial interpretation.

How can a compensation professional best undertake these efforts? First, join professional associations to stay informed on emerging issues and to act in concert to inform and influence public and legislative opinion. Second, constantly review compensation practices and the results of their application. The equitable treatment of all employees is the goal of a good pay system, and that is the same goal of the legislation. Where interpretations of equitable treatment differ, informed public discussion is required. Such discussion cannot occur without the input of informed compensation professionals.

REVIEW QUESTIONS

1. What is the nature of government's role in compensation?
2. Explain why changes in the minimum wage can have differential effects on employees.
3. How could a compensation professional model the effect of minimum wage on a specific employer's labor bill?
4. Your employer's production manager has recommended adding a third shift of workers. What advice can you give?
5. What kinds of proactive activities can an employer undertake to enhance the regulatory environment?
6. Could the pay objective of regulatory compliance ever conflict with other objectives? Could it conflict with the employer's notion of consistency or competitiveness? An employee's notion of equity? If so, how would you deal with such situations?

Chapter *14*

Pay Discrimination

Chapter Outline

The . . . wage curve . . . is not the same for women as for men because of the more transient character of the service of the former, the relative shortness of their activity in industry, the differences in environment required, the extra services that must be provided, overtime limitations, extra help needed for the occasional heavy work, and the general sociological factors not requiring discussion herein. Basically then we have another wage curve . . . for women below and not parallel with the men's curve.[1]

It has been suggested that the concept of discrimination is vague. In fact it is clear and simple and has no hidden meanings. To discriminate is to make a distinction, . . . and these differences in treatment which are prohibited . . . are those based on the five forbidden criteria: race, color, religion, sex, and national origin. [Floor debate preceding passage of Title VII, Interpretive Memorandum, Senators Clark and Case, floor managers, Title VII, 110 Congressional Record 7218 (1964)][2]

The pay practice described above, taken from a 1939 job evaluation manual, is now prohibited by law. Discriminatory practices, such as paying women and minorities less than white men for equal work, contributed to the need for legislation. Legislation, in turn, requires interpretation by regulatory agencies and courts. And despite the assurances offered during the heat of congressional debates, definitions of pay discrimination and the interpretation of the laws enacted to prohibit it have been neither clear nor simple. The laws pertaining to pay discrimination, their interpretation, and implications for pay systems are the subject of this chapter.

PAY DISCRIMINATION: WHAT IS IT?

Over 20 years have passed since the laws intended to prohibit pay discrimination were enacted; a number of issues remain unresolved. The most basic of these is defining pay discrimination. To better understand pay discrimination, it is useful to begin by distinguishing between *access* and *valuation* discrimination.[3]

Access Discrimination

Access discrimination focuses on the staffing and allocation decisions made by employers (e.g., recruiting, hiring, promoting, training, and layoffs). Access

---

[1]The job evaluation manual was introduced as evidence in *Electrical Workers (IUE)* v. *Westinghouse Electric Corp.,* 632 F.2d 1094, 23 FEP Cases 588 (3rd Cir. 1980), cert. denied, 452 U.S. 967, 25 FEP Cases 1835 (1981).

[2]Interpretive memorandum, Title VII, 110 Cong. Rec. 7213 (1964).

[3]Kenni Judd and Luis Gomez-Mejia, "Comparable Worth: A Sensible Way to End Pay Discrimination, or the Looniest Idea Since Looney Tunes?" in *Perspectives on Compensation,* eds. L. Gomez-Mejia and David Balkin (Englewood Cliffs, N.J.: Prentice-Hall, 1987).

discrimination denies particular jobs, promotions, or training opportunities to qualified women or minorities. Signs of such discrimination, outlawed by Title VII of the Civil Rights Act of 1964, still persist. For example, in 1982, nearly 20 years after the passage of Title VII, more than half of all women workers were employed in only 20 out of a total of 427 occupations.[4] Analyzing how employers share employment and training opportunities with minority and women is beyond the intent of this book, but the interested reader will find the references useful for further study.

Valuation Discrimination

Valuation discrimination focuses on the pay women and minorities receive for the jobs they perform. Discrimination occurs when minorities or women employees are paid less than white males are paid for performing equal work (i.e., paying women less than men who are working side by side, in the same plant, doing the same work, producing the same results). This definition of pay discrimination hinges on the standard of *equal pay for equal work*.

But many believe this definition does not go far enough. They believe that valuation discrimination can also occur when men and women hold entirely different jobs (i.e., when job segregation or access discrimination exists). Consider jobs in different progressions or career paths (e.g., office/clerical, crafts, operatives). The jobs within each of these progressions may be primarily staffed by one gender. For example, office and clerical jobs may be staffed predominantly by women, and craft jobs staffed predominantly by men. Is it illegal to pay employees in one career path less than employees in the other are paid, if the two groups are performing work that is not equal in content or results, but is "in some sense of comparable worth" to the employer?[5]

Here the proposed definition of pay discrimination hinges on the standard of *equal pay for work of comparable worth*. Existing federal laws do not support the equal pay for work of comparable worth standard. But some argue that the issue has not yet been adequately tested.[6] Several states have enacted

---

[4]Andrea H. Beller, "Occupational Segregation and the Earnings Gap," in *Comparable Worth: Issue for the 80's,* Vol. 1 (Washington, D.C.: U.S. Civil Rights Commission, 1985); Andrea Beller, "Trends in Occupational Segregation by Sex and Race: 1960–1981," in *Sex Segregation in the Workplace: Trends, Explanations, and Remedies,* ed. Barbara F. Reskin (Washington, D.C.: National Academy Press, 1985); B. F. Reskin and H. I. Hartmann, eds., *Women's Work, Men's Work: Sex Segregation on the Job* (Washington, D.C.: National Academy Press, 1985); Women's Bureau, Office of the Secretary, U.S. Dept. of Labor, Bulletin 298, *Time of Change: 1983 Handbook on Women Workers,* 1983; B. Turner and C. Wilson, Testimony for the National Committee on Pay Equity before the Joint Economic Committee, April 10, 1984.

[5]Donald J. Treiman and H. J. Hartmann, eds., *Women, Work and Wages* (Washington, D.C.: National Academy Press, 1981).

[6]Mary Heen, "A Review of Federal Court Decisions under Title VII of the Civil Rights Act of 1964," in *Comparable Worth and Wage Discrimination,* ed. Helen Remick (Philadelphia: Temple University Press, 1984).

laws which require a comparable worth standard for state and local government employees, and some predict that such legislation will be extended to other states and eventually to the private sector.

So two standards for defining pay discrimination need to be considered— equal pay for equal work, and equal pay for work of comparable worth. For an understanding of the legal foundations of each, let us turn to the legislation and key court cases.

THE EQUAL PAY ACT

The two major laws prohibiting pay discrimination are the Equal Pay Act (EPA) of 1963 and Title VII of the Civil Rights Act of 1964.[7] The EPA forbids wage discrimination

> between employees on the basis of sex when employees perform equal work on jobs in the same establishment requiring equal skill, effort, and responsibility and performed under similar working conditions. . . . Pay differences between equal jobs can be justified when that differential is based on (1) a seniority system; (2) a merit system; (3) a system measuring earnings by quality or quantity of production; or (4) any factor other than sex.[8]

Thus the EPA embodies for women the "equal work" definition of pay discrimination. It spells out with relative clarity that only comparisons among equal jobs are to be considered in measuring pay discrimination, and includes some worker-related characteristics which are legitimate reasons for pay differences.

The act defines equal work by four factors: (1) skill, (2) effort, (3) responsibility, and (4) working conditions. As noted during our discussion of job evaluation (Chapters 4 and 5), these factors or some variation of them are commonly used in most job evaluation plans. The drafters of the EPA simply incorporated job evaluation concepts into the act's language.

Differences in pay between men and women employed in equal work are permitted under the EPA by the four exceptions or *affirmative defenses*. Differences in pay for equal work are legal if they are based on (1) differences in seniority, (2) differences in quality of performance, (3) differences in quality or quantity of production, or (4) some factor other than sex.

Although the EPA is relatively specific, numerous cases were brought before the courts to further clarify its provisions. Some important cases are sum-

---

[7]The 14th Amendment also provides equal treatment under the law and some cases involving pay discrimination have been heard under it, especially since *Mescall* v. *Burrus,* 603 F.2d 1266, 1271 (7th Cir. 1979); most, however, have been brought jointly with a Title VII claim.

[8]29 U.S.C. § 206(d) (1979). Since the EPA is an amendment to the Fair Labor Standards Act, it originally exempted the same occupational groups as did the FLSA. However, with the passage of the Education Amendments of 1972, EPA exemptions for bona fide executives, administrators, professionals, and outside salesmen were eliminated [29 U.S.C. § 213(a) (1970)].

marized in Exhibit 14.1. Three major implications of these cases for compensation decisions are:

- Definition of equal work: How equal is equal?
- Four factor definitions: What is meant by equal skill, effort, responsibility, and working conditions?
- Factor other than sex: What are these "other factors?"

Definition of Equal

After years of judicial indecision, the court in 1970 established guidelines to define equal work in the *Schultz* v. *Wheaton Glass Company* case. Wheaton Glass Company maintained two job classifications for selector packers in its production department, male and female. The female job class carried a pay rate 10 percent below that of the male job class. The company claimed that the male job class included additional tasks that justified the pay differential, such as shoveling broken glass, opening warehouse doors, doing heavy lifting, and the like. The plaintiff claimed that the extra tasks were infrequently performed,

EXHIBIT 14.1
Selected Wage Discrimination Cases

Major Cases	Issues	Findings	Implications for Compensation Practices
Schultz v. *Wheaton Glass*, 1970 421 F. 2d 259	Two jobs had been historically segregated by sex with the men's jobs carrying the higher pay rate. This pay differential was based on the fact that men sometimes performed tasks the women did not. Performance of these extra tasks was considered of economic benefit to the company.	Pay differential was based on sex since the jobs performed by men and women were nearly identical with respect to skill, effort, responsibility and working conditions; additional tasks performed by men did not justify wage difference since the tasks were not performed by all men in the job.	Under EPA, equal pay for equal work means equal pay for "substantially similar" work. Evaluation of jobs must reflect real differences in skill, effort, responsibility and working conditions if wage differentials are to be justified. "Economic benefit" of the additional tasks is not a legitimate "other than sex" factor unless the job pricing system supports it.
Corning Glass Works v. *Brennan*, 1974 417 U.S. 188	Some night shift jobs had originally been open only to men and carried a higher rate than the same day shift jobs open to women. Although the employer later opened the night shift jobs to all and established a uniform shift differential the original wage difference for men was preserved. Was this difference justified on basis of "dissimilar" working conditions?	A shift differential could be a factor other than sex, but in this case the shift differential was explained by a desire of the employer to compensate men, who worked at night, more than women, who worked during the day.	Traditional considerations involved in development of universal job factors will be considered by the court, but are not necessarily legal.

EXHIBIT 14.1
(*continued*)

Major Cases	Issues	Findings	Implications for Compensation Practices
Brennan v. *Prince William Hospital Corporation,* 1974 417 U.S. 188	Wage differentials were maintained between the jobs held by men and those held by women because the frequency of tasks performed in each job was different, the location in which tasks were carried out was not the same, and the men's jobs carried some additional tasks. Hiring criteria for the two jobs, however, were the same.	Wage differentials were sex based because jobs were similar in skill, effort, responsibility, and working conditions despite the differences in frequency with which tasks were performed or differences in location. The extra tasks performed by men were carried out by only some of the men, on occasion, required no special skill or training, and were never open to women.	Differences in frequency with which tasks are performed is not evidence of difference in effort or responsibility and location differences in themselves do not constitute dissimilar work conditions. Legitimate differences in skill must reflect differences in hiring criteria or in job training.
Lemons v. *City and County of Denver,* 1980 620 F. 2d 228	Plaintiffs argued that nurses were underpaid by the city, which paid the prevailing wage for their occupation in the community, because the community had historically discriminated against women's jobs.	There is no authorization under Title VII to adjust market disparities. As long as there is equal access to all jobs, there is no need to disregard community wage rates in assessing job worth.	The market factor is legitimate in job pricing so long as all jobs involved are equally open to both sexes.
Gunther v. *County of Washington,* 1981 U.S. Supreme Court 451 U.S. 161	Plaintiffs used employer's deviation from job evaluation plan as evidence of intentional discrimination.	The court found that this case did not involve the notion of comparable worth but that "to hold sex-based wage discrimination violates Title VII only if it also violates the EPA would be denying relief to victims of discrimination who did not hold the same job as a high paid man."	Supports the overriding nature of findings of intentional sex discrimination. How to measure intentional discrimination as well as the nature of jobs to be compared becomes an issue. Cases examined would imply that job segregation or misuse of employer's job evaluation system which undervalues wages for women may be considered as evidence of intentional discrimination.
Briggs v. *City of Madison,* 1982 W.D. Wisc. 436 F. Supp. 435	Plaintiffs claimed that their jobs were similar to those of more highly paid males in terms of skill, effort, responsibility and working conditions. They rejected the employer's justification of market necessity noting that (1) the market reflected historic sex discrimination; (2) an appeal to the market is not legitimate; and (3) positions in "female" jobs sometimes remained open but wages weren't increased as a result.	The court found that the disputed jobs were substantially similar in effort, skill, responsibility, and working conditions and thus should be similarly compensated. However the wage differential was still justified by the higher market rate required to attract and retain those in the "male" jobs. It noted that there was nothing in Title VII holding an employer responsible for the historic discrimination reflected in the marketplace. Without convincing evidence of intent to discriminate, an appeal to the market is legitimate.	Again, evidence of intent to discriminate is required to override an appeal to market value. However, the fact that the court was convinced of the internal comparability of jobs as presented in this case may mean increased scrutiny of the market defense. Wage survey techniques and the use of their results should be sound, timely, and consistently applied without bias.

EXHIBIT 14.1
(concluded)

Major Cases	Issues	Findings	Implications for Compensation Practices
Kouba and EEOC v. Allstate Insurance Company, 1982 691 F. 2d 873	Plaintiff claimed that past salary used to set minimum salary during training and after discriminated on basis of sex because past salary reflected widespread historical discrimination, and resulted in female sales agents receiving lower salaries than male agents. Defendant claimed business reasons dictated use of past salary information.	Appeals court ordered the lower court to examine the business reasons cited by employer as basis for salary. Noting that a salary determination factor that causes male/female wage differentials cannot be used without an acceptable business reason, "a factor used to effectuate some business policy is not prohibited simply because a wage differential results." The EPA "entrusts employers, not judges, with making the often uncertain decision of how to accomplish business objectives."	The use of past salary, or any other factor in setting pay, is legal if done for acceptable business reasons, even though a wage differential may result. Focus must be on the reason for the use of the factor, and whether business reasons reasonably explain the use of that factor.
Taylor v. Charley Brothers Company, 25 FEP Cases 602 (W.D. Pa. 1981)	Warehouse jobs paid on basis of warehouse products handled, rather than work done. Women all in one lower paying department; men in another. Can pay discrimination exist among dissimilar jobs?	Employer's pattern and practices of treating women employees unequally in other employment decisions (e.g., hiring, placement, promotion) can provide inference of intent to discriminate on pay for dissimilar jobs, too.	Pay must be based on work performed. Failure to make any effort to examine job content may, combined with other behaviors, indicate intent to discriminate in pay for dissimilar jobs.
Spaulding v. University of Washington, 35 FEP Cases 217 (9th Cir. 1984)	Faculty of a predominantly female department claimed that they were underpaid on the basis of sex in comparison with faculty of other, comparable departments. Defendant claimed reliance on external market rates in setting wages, an employment practice that plaintiffs stated was discriminatory in impact although facially neutral.	Existence of wage differences between similar jobs is not sufficient to establish intent to discriminate. Employer's nonpay behavior did not show discriminatory intent. A compensation system based on market forces is not the type of specific employment practice necessary to support a disparate impact claim.	Use of wage survey data that incorporates past sex discrimination in the relevant market does not subject the employer to disparate impact claims. "(E)mployers deal with the market as a given and do not meaningfully have a 'policy' about it."
American Federation of State, County, and Municipal Employees (AFSCME) v. State of Washington, 578 F. Supp. 846, 33 FEP Cases 808 (W.D. Wash. 1983)	Employee union claimed that the state discriminated when it failed to implement a comparable-worth study which it had commissioned. Study had been commissioned in response to widespread allegations of discrimination. The study showed that employees in female-dominated jobs were compensated less than employees in male-dominated jobs, although *the dissimilar jobs were of comparable worth.*	Commissioning the study does not require the state to implement its recommendations. Although the state may choose to enact a comparable worth plan, it is not obligated to eliminate economic inequalities that it did not create in the market. "Economic reality is that the value of a particular job to an employer is but one factor influencing the rate of compensation for that job."	Setting wages according to prevailing market rates is not evidence of intent to discriminate. Employer is not bound by a study it commissions, but may use it as a diagnostic tool. Labor market conditions, bargaining demands and the possibility that another study could give different results may also be considered.

and not all men did them.[9] Further, these extra tasks performed by some of the men were regularly performed by employees in another classification ("snap-up boys"), and these employees were paid only 2 cents an hour more than the women. Did the additional tasks performed by some members of one job class render the jobs unequal? The court decided not. It ruled that the equal work standard required only that jobs be *substantially* equal, not identical. The extra duties performed by the men did not justify paying the men 10 percent more than the women were paid. "Substantially equal work" based on the *Wheaton Glass Company* case has become the standard for assessing whether or not jobs are equal.

Additionally, the courts have generally held that the *actual work performed* is the appropriate data to use when deciding if jobs are substantially equal. This was established in several cases, including *Hodgeson* v. *Brookhaven General Hospital* (Exhibit 14.1), where it was found that the duties employees actually performed were different from those in the written descriptions of the job. These cases reinforce the point made in the chapter on job analysis: Compensation decisions must be based on the actual work employees perform, and any summary of that work, such as written job descriptions, must accurately capture that work.

Definitions of the Four Factors

The Department of Labor provides these definitions of the four factors.[10]

- Skill: Experience, training, education, and ability as measured by the performance requirements of a particular job.
- Effort: Mental or physical. The amount or degree of effort (not type of effort) actually expended in the performance of a job.
- Responsibility: The degree of accountability required in the performance of a job.
- Working conditions: The physical surroundings and hazards of a job including dimensions such as inside versus outside work, heat, cold, and poor ventilation.

Guidelines to clarify these definitions have evolved through court decisions.

---

[9]Plaintiffs are those who bring suit to obtain a remedy for injury to their rights. Defendants are those (usually the employer) who explain current practices to answer the suit.

[10]U.S. Department of Labor, *Women Workers Today* (Washington, D.C.: 1976); U.S. Department of Labor, *The Earnings Gap between Women and Men* (Washington, D.C.: 1976); U.S. Department of Labor, *Equal Pay for Equal Work under the Fair Labor Standards Act* (Washington, D.C.: Interpretative Bulletin, August 31, 1971); U.S. Department of Labor, *Brief Highlights of Major Federal Laws and Order on Sex Discrimination in Employment* (Washington, D.C.: February 1977).

Differences in efforts and skill requirements for hospital aides (females) and orderlies (males) were examined in *Hodgeson* v. *Brookhaven General Hospital*. The primary tasks of both jobs involved general patient care. However, the hospital claimed that additional tasks assigned male orderlies required greater effort (e.g., restraining violent patients, dealing with disoriented patients) or greater skill (e.g., catheterization) than did any of the additional tasks assigned female aides. In another case (Exhibit 14.1, *Brennan* v. *Prince William Hospital)*, the employer also claimed that additional tasks assigned male orderlies required more skill than did any tasks assigned female aides despite the fact that the hiring and organizational training requirements for the two jobs were identical.

Prince William Hospital had formerly grouped orderlies and aides into one job classification and paid one wage rate. The hospital preferred to have orderlies assigned to assist with male patients, and aides assigned to women's wards. But when the hospital ran into difficulty in attracting a sufficient number of orderlies (males), it divided the two jobs into two classifications, assigned a few additional job duties to the orderlies, and raised the wage attached to that job. The court found that at this particular hospital, those additional duties (catheterization) were performed infrequently, and that newly hired orderlies were paid the higher wage even before they had been taught the additional task. Therefore the wage discrepancy was not justified.

Based on these and other discussions, it appears that for an employer to support a claim of *unequal* work, the following conditions must be met:

1. The effort/skill/responsibility must be substantially greater in one of the jobs compared.
2. The tasks involving the extra effort/skill/responsibility must consume a *significant amount* of time for *all* employees whose additional wages are in question.
3. The extra effort/skill/responsibility must have *a value commensurate* with the questioned pay differential (as determined by the employer's own evaluation).

Cooper and Barrett compared a number of cases that provide information on what constitutes equal.[11] While they agree with the general pattern identified above, they point out that questions remain. For example, according to various court rulings, where 36 percent or more of time is spent in additional duties, jobs are dissimilar. Where 10 percent or less of the time is spent in additional duties, jobs are similar. (Except in one orderlies versus aides case, the 2 percent of the time that orderlies drove ambulances convinced the First Circuit Court that the jobs were unequal.) But that still leaves the range between 10 and 36 percent.

---

[11]Elizabeth A. Cooper and Gerald V. Barrett, "Equal Pay and Gender: Implications of Court Cases for Personnel Practices," *Academy of Management Review* 9, no. 1 (1984), pp. 84–94.

The courts have also dealt with equal working conditions. In *Brennan* v. *Corning Glass Works,* Corning claimed that night and day shift inspector jobs were unequal because the time of day worked constituted "dissimilar working conditions." Corning did have historical reasons for assuming the jobs were dissimilar: the State of New York's "protective legislation" previously prohibited women from working nights. Corning's shift differential arose during this time. The 1974 court ruled that the time of day did not constitute dissimilar working conditions because the definition of working conditions in Corning's job evaluation plan did not include shift differentials. That is not to say that shift differentials are illegal, but if they are paid, the employer must clearly state that its purpose is to compensate workers for unusual conditions, and it must be separate from the base wage for the job.

Similarly, pay differences between men and women on substantially equal work cannot be justified by a union contract or by the fact that women accepted a lower starting wage for the job.[12]

Factors Other than Sex

Under the Equal Pay Act *unequal* pay for equal work may be justified through the four affirmative defenses: seniority, merit, performance-based incentive system, or a factor other than sex. Factors other than sex include shift differentials, temporary assignments, bona fide training programs, differences based on ability, training, or experience, and others.[13]

Recently factors other than sex were interpreted as a broad general exception that may include business reasons advanced by the employer. In *Kouba* v. *Allstate* (Exhibit 14.1), Allstate Insurance Company paid its new sales representatives a minimum salary during their training period. After completing the training, the sales reps received a minimum salary or their earned sales commissions, whichever was greater. The minimum salary paid during training needed to be high enough to attract prospective agents to enter the training program, yet not so high as to lessen the incentive to earn sales commissions after training. Allstate argued that the minimum salary needed to be calculated individually for each trainee, and the trainee's past salary was a necessary factor used in the calculation. But Allstate's approach resulted in women trainees generally being paid less than male trainees, since women had held lower paying jobs before entering the program. Allstate maintained the pay difference resulted from acceptable business reasons: a factor other than sex.

---

[12]U.S. Department of Labor, *Equal Pay;* Thomas J. Bergmann and Frederick S. Hills, "Internal Labor Markets and Indirect Pay Discrimination," *Compensation Review,* Fourth Quarter 1982, pp. 41–50.

[13]Bona fide is interpreted here as (1) established, either formally or informally; (2) systematically applied in a nondiscriminatory fashion; and (3) communicated to all covered employees. H.R. Rep. No. 309, 88th Cong. 1st Sess. 3 (1963).

Lola Kouba didn't buy Allstate's arguments. She argued that acceptable business reasons were limited to "those that measure the value of an employee's job performance to his or her employer." But the court rejected Kouba's argument. It said that Allstate's business reasons for a practice must be evaluated for reasonableness. A practice will not automatically be prohibited simply because wage differences between men and women result.

The court did not say that Allstate's "business" reasons were justified. It did say that Allstate's argument could not be rejected *solely because the practice perpetuated historical differences in pay*. Rather, Allstate needed to justify the business relatedness of the practice. In other words, the factor "other than sex" must be demonstrably business related.

The case was settled out of court, so no legal clarification of Allstate's rationale was ever provided. Thus, the definition of "factor other than sex" remains somewhat murky. It does seem that pay differences for equal work can be justified for demonstrably business-related reasons. But what is and is not demonstrably business related has not yet been catalogued.

Reverse Discrimination

Several cases deal with the important issue of reverse discrimination against men, when pay for women is adjusted. In these cases, men have claimed that they were paid less than women doing similar work, simply because they were men. In one case, the University of Nebraska created a model to calculate salaries based on values estimated for a faculty member's education, field of specialization, years of direct experience, years of related experience, and merit.[14] Based on these qualifications, the university granted raises to 33 women whose salaries were less than the amount computed by the model. However, the university made no such increases to 92 males whose salaries were also below the amount the model set for them based on their qualifications. The court found this system a violation of the Equal Pay Act. It held that, in effect, the university was using a new system to determine a salary schedule, based on specific criteria. To refuse to pay employees of one sex the minimum required by these criteria was illegal.

In another case, the male faculty at Northern Illinois University sued to have a model the university developed to adjust women faculty salaries applied to them, also.[15] But there was an important difference. The regional Office of

---

[14]*Board of Regents of University of Nebraska* v. *Dawes,* 522 F.2d 380, 11 FEP Cases 283 (8th Cir. 1976); 424 U.S. 914, 12 FEP Cases 343 (1976). The *Dawes* and *Ende* cases are contrasted in K. M. Weeks, "Equal Pay: The Emerging Terrain," *College and University Law,* Summer 1985, pp. 41–60.

[15]*Ende* v. *Board of Regents of Northern Illinois University,* 37 FEP Cases 575 (7th Cir. 1985). Peter Saucier wonders whether affirmative action plans are "a factor other than sex" in "Affirmative Action and the Equal Pay Act," *Employee Relations Law Journal* 11, no. 2 (Winter 1985/86), pp. 453–66.

Civil Rights had found reasonable cause to believe that Northern Illinois University was discriminating against women faculty. The university did not dispute this finding. Instead, it sought to correct salary differences based on a model similar to the one used at Nebraska.

The NIU model was used to allocate *a one-time salary adjustment* to overcome the results of past discrimination against women, and was not a permanent change in the compensation system. Therefore the court ruled that it did not need to be applied to men. Nebraska, on the other hand, used a salary model that was *not* tailored to correct past discrimination. Rather, Nebraska developed a new way to calculate salaries and therefore must apply it to all faculty members equally.

So what does this have to do with compensation management? Viewed collectively, the courts have provided reasonably clear directions. The design of pay systems must incorporate a policy of equal pay for substantially equal work. The determination of substantially equal work must be based on the actual work performed (the job content) and must reflect the skill, effort, and responsibility required, and the working conditions. It is legal to pay men and women who perform substantially equal work differently if the pay system is designed to recognize differences in performance, seniority, quality and quantity of results, or certain factors other than sex, in a nondiscriminatory manner. Further, to minimize vulnerability to reverse discrimination suits, if a new pay system is designed, it must be equally applied to all employees. If, on the other hand, a one-time adjustment is made to correct past problems, it need only apply to the affected group.

But what does this tell us about discrimination on jobs that are *not substantially equal*—dissimilar jobs? For example, suppose that almost all women employees worked in one job classification: office/clerical. Further suppose that the employer granted cost of living increases semiannually to all job classes *except* the one, office/ clerical. The office/clerical jobs are not "substantially equal" to the other jobs, so the Equal Pay Act does not apply. Can the office/ clerical employees still charge their employer with pay discrimination? Yes, under Title VII of the Civil Rights Act.

TITLE VII OF THE CIVIL RIGHTS ACT

Title VII prohibits discrimination on the basis of sex, race, color, religion, or national origin in any employment condition, including hiring, firing, promotion, transfer, compensation, and admission to training programs.[16] Title VII was amended in 1972 and 1978. The 1972 amendments strengthened enforcement and expanded coverage to include employees of government and educa-

---

[16]29 U.S.C. § 206 (d) (1) (1970). Its coverage is broader, also. Employers, employment agencies, labor organizations, and training programs involving 15 or more employees and some 120,000 educational institutions fall under its jurisdiction.

tional institutions, as well as private employers of more than 15 persons. The pregnancy amendment of 1978 made it illegal to discriminate based on pregnancy, childbirth, or related conditions.

Defining Discrimination

Since 1964 the courts have evolved two theories of discrimination behavior under Title VII: (1) disparate treatment and (2) disparate impact. Exhibit 14.2 contrasts the two theories.

EXHIBIT 14.2
Discriminatory Behavior

Disparate Treatment	*Disparate Impact*
1. Different standards for different individuals or groups.	1. Same standards have differing consequences.
2. Intent to discriminate may be inferred by behaviors.	2. Discrimination shown by general statistical impact; discriminatory intent need not be present.
3. Employer can justify actions by absence of discriminatory intent and exercise of reasonable business judgment.	3. Employer can justify pay differences through business necessity.

Disparate treatment. Disparate or unequal treatment includes those practices in which an organization treats minorities or women less favorably than others are treated, either openly or covertly. Under this definition, a practice is unlawful if it applies different standards to different employees, for example, rejecting women but not men applicants if they have school-aged children (different standards). The mere fact of unequal treatment may be taken as evidence of the employer's intention to discriminate.

Disparate impact. Personnel practices that have a differential effect on members of protected groups are illegal under the disparate or unequal impact theory of Title VII, unless the differences can be justified as necessary to the safe and efficient operation of the business or are work related. The major case which established this interpretation of Title VII is *Griggs* v. *Duke Power Co.,*[17] in which the Court struck down employment tests and educational requirements that screened out a greater proportion of blacks than whites. Even though the practices were applied equally—both blacks and whites had to pass the tests—they were prohibited because (1) they had the consequence of excluding a protected group (blacks) disproportionately and (2) they were not related to the jobs in question.

---

[17]*Griggs* v. *Duke Power Co.,* 401 U.S. 414 (1971).

Under the disparate impact theory of discrimination, whether or not the employer intended to discriminate is irrelevant. Thus a personnel decision can, on its face, seem neutral, but if the results of it are unequal, the employer must demonstrate that the decision is either work related or a business necessity.

These two theories of discrimination have been well established in employment or access discrimination issues.[18] They have been more difficult to apply to pay issues. The difficulty stems from the fact that different pay may be legal for dissimilar work. To understand the evolving status of pay discrimination under Title VII, we examine two basic questions.

1. Can pay discrimination exist in different pay rates for dissimilar jobs?
2. What constitutes pay discrimination in dissimilar jobs?

Pay Discrimination and Dissimilar Jobs

The Supreme Court, in *Gunther* v. *County of Washington* (Exhibit 14.1), determined that pay discrimination may occur in establishing pay differences for dissimilar jobs. In this case, four jail matrons in Washington County, Oregon, claimed that their work was comparable to that performed by male guards. Both the county's own wage survey and its assessment of job worth had indicated that the matrons should be paid about 95 percent as much as guards. Instead, their pay was only about 70 percent that of the guards. Lower courts refused to consider the matrons' case on the grounds that their evidence did not *meet the equal work requirement of the Equal Pay Act.* The Supreme Court overturned the lower courts and stated that a Title VII pay case was not bound by the definitions of equal work or the affirmative defenses of the Equal Pay Act.

Prior to *Gunther,* the relationship between EPA and Title VII was unclear. Many felt that the existence of the Equal Pay Act meant that all pay discrimination charges had to be brought under that law and meet that law's definitions of equal work and the four defenses.[19] But in *Gunther,* the Supreme Court ruled that "to hold that sex-based wage discrimination violates Title VII only if it also violates the EPA would be denying relief to victims of discrimination who did not hold the same jobs as a higher paid man." The Court also went out of its way to state what it was *not* ruling on:

---

[18]For a review of EEO laws and litigation, see Ruth G. Shaefer, *Nondiscrimination in Employment—And Beyond,* Report No. 782 (New York: The Conference Board, 1980); *Fair Employment Practices* (Washington, D.C.: Bureau of National Affairs, 1984); *Pay Equity and Comparable Worth* (Washington, D.C.: Bureau of National Affairs, 1984); John B. Golper, "The Current Legal Status of Comparable Worth," *Labor Law Journal* 34 (September 1983), pp. 563–80; Karen S. Koziara, D. Pierson and R. E. Johannesson, "The Comparable Worth Issue: Current Status and New Directions," *Labor Law Journal* 34 (August 1983), pp. 504–9.

[19]Lawrence Z. Lorber, J. Robert Kirk, Stephen L. Samuels, and David J. Spellman III, *Sex and Salary* (Alexandria, Va.: The ASPA Foundation, 1985).

We emphasize at the outset the narrowness of the question before us in this case. Respondents' claim is not based on the controversial concept of "comparable worth," under which the plaintiff might claim increased compensation on the basis of a comparison of the intrinsic worth or difficulty of their job with that of other jobs in the same organization or community. Rather, respondents seek to prove, by direct evidence, that their wages were depressed because of intentional sex discrimination, consisting of setting the wage scale level lower than its own survey of outside markets and the worth of the jobs warranted.

(The case was returned to a lower court for additional evidence of discrimination, and was eventually settled out of court.)

So the *Gunther* case established that charges of pay discrimination on dissimilar (not equal) jobs could be brought under Title VII. But it did not consider what might constitute pay discrimination in dissimilar jobs under Title VII. To examine this question we discuss three possible approaches: (1) where the employer exhibited a pattern of discrimination in many of its personnel practices beyond wage setting, (2) where the employer used market data to justify pay differences, and (3) where the employer conducted a pay equity study using job evaluation to determine jobs of "comparable worth."

Proof of Discrimination: Pattern of Personnel Practices

Under this approach, employees seek to prove the discrimination pervades the entire employment relationship, including the pay system. In *Taylor* v. *Charley Brothers Company* (Exhibit 14.1), a wholesale distributor maintained two separate departments based on what products were handled, not on what work was done. For example, warehouse workers who handled frozen food were in department 1; those who handled health and beauty aids were in department 2. Charley Brothers hired only men for the first department; women applicants were not even considered for positions in that department. If female applicants specifically requested department 1, they were told that the work there required greater physical strength, but they were not told that jobs in department 1 also paid more. Additional evidence indicated that no males were considered for jobs in department 2, and that both company officials and union officials discouraged female employees from bidding for jobs in department 1. Clearly, the company's hiring and job assignment policies violated Title VII in that women were denied equal access to jobs, but did its pay policies discriminate, too? The Court held that both the EPA and Title VII were violated. In those jobs that were substantially equal in both departments 1 and 2—receivers, order selectors, and pack-up persons—the differential pay meant that the EPA was violated. But the Court went beyond this and said that Charley Brothers intentionally discriminated in its entire pay system. Women were paid substantially less than men in the all-male department simply because they worked in a department populated only by women and not because the jobs they performed were inherently worth less than jobs performed by men. The Court took as evidence of the company's intent to discriminate the fact that it had never undertaken any type of evaluation of any of the jobs, its practice of segregating women within the one department, and various discriminatory remarks made by officials of the company.[20] Sufficient proof of Charley Brothers' intention to discriminate was shown through the pattern of its personnel practices, including pay, regardless of the dissimilarity of the jobs involved.

Cases of such blatant discrimination are probably rarer today. It is relatively easy to obtain agreement as to the existence of discrimination in situations where evidence exists in almost every personnel decision. Most situations are less clear.

Consider, for example, the case in which the pay rates for two obviously dissimilar jobs are determined. Examples include the pay rates for nurses versus tree trimmers or nurses versus sanitarians or even professors of nursing versus professors of business administration. If these jobs are dissimilar and if no pattern of discrimination in hiring, promotion, or other personnel decisions exists, then what constitutes pay discrimination?

Proof of Discrimination: Use of Market Data

In the case of *Lemons* v. *The City and County of Denver* (Exhibit 14.1), nurse Mary Lemons claimed that her job, held predominantly by women, was illegally paid less than the jobs held predominantly by men (tree trimmers, sign painters, tire servicemen, etc.). Lemons claimed that the nurse's job required greater education and skill. Therefore, to pay the male jobs more than the nurses' jobs simply because the male jobs commanded higher rates in the local labor market was discriminatory. She argued that the market reflected historical underpayment of "women's work." Lemons claimed the existence of pay differences for women's versus men's work was a sign of job discrimination. The court disagreed, adding that "market disparities are not among those Title VII seeks to adjust."[21] Thus, the situation identified by *Lemons*—pay differences in dissimilar jobs—did not by itself constitute proof of intent to discriminate.

In another case, *Briggs* v. *City of Madison* (Exhibit 14.1), pay differences between *substantially similar* jobs were considered. Here the court determined that, if jobs are substantially similar, then the existence and size of any pay differences are relevant in establishing discrimination. The court ruled that though the jobs of nurse and public health sanitarian were not equal, they were "substantially similar." But the pay differences between the two jobs were great.

---

[20]The union was also accused of discrimination against female employees. The courts accepted as evidence discriminatory statements made by union leaders, but did not hold them liable for their behaviors, since they had not made the hiring and allocation decisions.

[21]George T. Milkovich and Renae Broderick, "Pay Discrimination: Legal Issues and Implications for Research," *Industrial Relations* 21, no. 3 (Fall 1982), pp. 309-17.

The court felt that if the jobs were similar, the pay should be, too. The fact that it wasn't constituted initial evidence of discrimination because

> it rests upon the logical premise that jobs which are *similar* in their requirements of skill, effort, and responsibility and in their working conditions are of comparable value to an employer. . . . Jobs of comparable value would be compensated comparably but for the employer's discriminatory treatment of the lower paid employees.[22]

However, the city of Madison successfully rebutted the initial case of discrimination with evidence from the external labor market. According to labor market data, sanitarians throughout the state were paid salaries comparable with those in Madison. The salary the city was offering for sanitarians was raised because the city had experienced difficulty (long periods to fill job vacancies) in attracting qualified sanitarians. So the city was able to justify the pay differences using market data.[23]

The courts have continually upheld employers' use of market data to justify pay differences for different jobs. *Spaulding* v. *University of Washington* (Exhibit 14.1) developed the argument in greatest detail. In this case, the predominantly female faculty of the Department of Nursing claimed that it was illegally paid less than faculty in other departments.

Spaulding alleged disparate treatment in setting nursing professors' pay in comparison to pay in "comparable" departments. The statisticians for Spaulding presented a model which controlled for the effects of level of education, job tenure, and other factors. They asserted that any pay difference not accounted for in their model was discrimination. But the courts have been dubious of statistics. One judge, in *Wilkins* v. *University of Houston,* even quoted Mark Twain: "There are three kinds of lies: lies, damned lies, and statistics."[24] The *Spaulding* judge observed that the model "unrealistically assumed the equality of all master's degrees, ignored job experience prior to university employment and ignored detailed analysis of day-to-day responsibilities." Without such

---

[22]George T. Milkovich, "Wage Discrimination and Comparable Worth," *ILR Report* 19, no. 2 (Spring 1982), pp. 7–12; Ronald L. Oaxaca, "Sex Discrimination in Wages," *Discrimination in Labor Markets,* eds. O. Ashenfelter and A. Rees (Princeton, N.J.: Princeton Press, 1973); A. S. Blinder, "Wage Discrimination: Reduced Form and Structural Estimates," *Journal of Human Resources* 8, no. 4 (1973), pp. 436–55; Ronald Oaxaca, "Male-Female Wage Differentials in Urban Labor Markets," *International Economic Review* 27, no. 3 (1973), pp. 332–50; E. Robert Livernash, ed., *Comparable Worth: Issues and Alternatives* (Washington, D.C.: Equal Employment Advisory Council, 1980).

[23]In 1983, Madison, Wisconsin's city government enacted guidelines requiring that the wage structures of private businesses that contract with the city be reviewed "to determine whether comparable pay exists for comparable positions." To comply, vendors must set percentage goals for hiring women and minorities and maintain the same percentage goals for distribution of salaries. For example, if a contractor's work force is 30 percent female, 30 percent of its wages must be paid to females. (Information from Lorber et al., *Sex and Salary.*)

[24]*Wilkins* v. *University of Houston,* 695 F.2d 134, FEP Cases 318 (5th Cir. 1983).

data, "we have no meaningful way of determining just how much of the proposed wage differential was due to sex and how much was due to academic discipline."

But the court went beyond criticizing the model. It ruled on the use of competitive market data as a policy. The court held that every employer who is constrained by market forces must consider market values in setting labor costs. "Naturally, market prices are inherently job-related." Employers who rely on the market deal with it as a given and do not meaningfully have a "policy" about it in the relevant Title VII sense, according to the court. Allowing reliance on the market to constitute a facially neutral policy for disparate impact purposes "would subject employers to liability for pay disparities with respect to which they have not, in any meaningful sense, made an independent business judgment."

Is there a "market policy"? Recall from the market survey discussion (Chapter 7) all the decisions that go into designing and conducting a survey. What employers constitute the "relevant market"? Does the relevant market vary by occupation? Do different market definitions yield different wage patterns? Clearly, judgment is involved in answering these questions. Yet the courts have thus far neglected to examine those judgments for possible bias. Perhaps the pattern of judgment does indeed constitute a "policy" in a Title VII sense.

Spaulding and other court cases have tended to view the market as a "given" that allows little room for discretion. If that is so, then according to Rynes and Milkovich, the employer's role is to "find out precisely what that rate is. If, on the other hand, a *range* of possible wages exists for any given job, then . . . the observed, or measured, market wage will depend on where the wage data is collected, . . . (and) *sampling* becomes critical."[25]

Should market survey procedures be subject to the same issues that surround other statistical procedures (e.g., availability analysis for fairness in hiring and promotion, or validity and job-relatedness of tests)? While Rynes and Milkovich do not take a position on this question, they point out that "judgment enters into virtually every step of the wage survey process, and each successive judgment may modify the eventual results."[26] Clearly not all employers are the "price takers" that the courts have assumed.

Proof of Discrimination: Jobs of "Comparable Worth"

A third approach to attempting to determine pay discrimination on jobs of dissimilar content hinges on finding a standard by which to compare the value of jobs. The standard must do two things. First, it must permit jobs with dissimi-

---

[25]Sara L. Rynes and George T. Milkovich, "Wage Surveys: Dispelling Some Myths about the 'Market Wage'," *Personnel Psychology,* Spring 1986, pp. 71–90.

[26]Ibid.

lar content to be declared equal or "in some sense comparable."[27] Second, it must permit pay differences for dissimilar jobs that are not comparable. Job evaluation has been proposed as that standard.[28] If an employer's own job evaluation study shows jobs of dissimilar content to be of equal value to the employer, then isn't failure to pay them equally proof of intent to discriminate? The issue has been considered in *AFSCME* v. *State of Washington* (Exhibit 14.1).

In 1973, the state of Washington commissioned a study of the concept of comparable worth (discussed later in this chapter) and its projected effect on the state's pay system. The study concluded that by basing wages on the external market, the state was paying women approximately 20 percent less than it was paying men in jobs deemed of comparable value to the state. The state took no action on this finding, so AFSCME, the employees' union, sued to force implementation of a compensation system based on comparable worth as outlined in the study. The union alleged that since the state was aware of the adverse effect of its present policy, failure to change it constituted discrimination. But the court ruled that an employer merely being aware of adverse consequences for a protected group did not constitute discrimination. "The plaintiff must show the employer chose the particular policy because of its effect on members of a protected class. We also reject AFSCME's contention that, having commissioned the study, the state of Washington was committed to implement a new system—we reject a rule which would penalize rather than commend employers for their effort and innovation in undertaking such a study."[29]

AFSCME v. *State of Washington* differs from previous cases that used market data in that this is the first case where the evidence that the jobs were in any sense "equal" was developed by the employer. But even though the state had commissioned the study, it had not agreed to implement the study's results. Therefore the employer had not, in the court's view, admitted the jobs were equal or established a pay system which purported to pay on the basis of "comparable worth" rather than markets.

If the state had adopted a policy of paying on a basis of "comparable value," then the noted pay discrepancies might have been illegal. That issue remains to be tested in the courts.

---

[27]Treiman and Hartmann, *Women, Work and Wages.*

[28]Livernash, *Comparable Worth;* Helen Remick, "Strategies for Creating Sound, Bias Free Job Evaluation Plans," *Job Evaluation and EEO: The Emerging Issues* (New York: Industrial Relations Counselors, 1978); David J. Thomsen, "Eliminating Pay Discrimination Caused by Job Evaluation," *Personnel* 55, no. 5 (September–October 1978), pp. 23–36; Marc J. Wallace, Jr., Charles H. Fay, and Richard W. Beatty, "Pay Equity and Equal Employment Opportunity: An Analysis of the Legal, Research, and Professional Debate," unpublished paper, University of Kentucky, Lexington.

[29]The AFSCME case is discussed in length in Lorber, *Sex and Salary,* and *Pay Equity and Comparable Worth.*

So where does this leave us? Clearly Title VII prohibits intentional discrimination in compensation if it is based on sex or other prescribed factors, whether or not the employees in question hold the same or different jobs. Discrimination may be proved by direct evidence of an employer's intent (e.g., an overall pattern of behavior that demonstrates disparate treatment). However, "Job evaluation studies and comparable worth statistics alone are insufficient to establish the requisite inference of discriminatory motive."[30] On the other hand, the disparate impact standard, where no proof of discriminatory intent is required, at least, so far appears to be inappropriate for broad challenges to general compensation policies.

To date, Title VII rulings have several implications for compensation management. First, it is clear that pay discrimination is not limited only to equal jobs; it may also occur in setting different rates for different jobs.[31] Next, it is also clear from these cases that the courts are not about to rule use of external market rates illegal.[32] Competitive market pricing, by itself, does not appear to constitute a policy that has disparate impact, though that issue may still be open to question. Further, to prevail in a disparate treatment allegation, plaintiffs need to demonstrate a pattern of discrimination practices that is specific and deliberate—"regularly and purposefully treat(ing) women differently and generally less favorably than men."[33] Simply demonstrating pay differences on jobs that are not equal is insufficient to prove discrimination.

What additional implications for the design and administration of pay systems can be drawn? These court decisions imply that pay differentials between dissimilar jobs will not be prohibited under Title VII if the differences can be shown to be based on the content of the work, its value to the organization's objectives, and the employer's ability to attract and retain employees in competitive external labor markets. The courts appear to recognize that "the value of a particular job to an employer is but one factor influencing the rate of compensation for a job."[34]

THE EARNINGS GAP

According to the Bureau of Labor Statistics, women working full-time in the first quarter of 1985 had median wage and salary earnings of $268 a week, 66

---

[30]David A. Cathcart and Pamela L. Hemminger, *Developments in the Law of Salary Discrimination* (Los Angeles: Gibson, Dunn and Crutcher, 1985).

[31]*AFSCME* v. *State of Washington.*

[32]*Briggs* v. *City of Madison; Spaulding* v. *University of Washington.*

[33]*Taylor* v. *Charles Brothers Company.*

[34]*AFSCME* v. *Washington.*

EXHIBIT 14.3
Female-Male Ratios of Median Usual Weekly Earnings of Full-Time Wage and Salary Workers, by Age, 1971–1983
(adjusted for male-female differences in full-time hours)*

	Year										
								Second Quarter 1979	Annual Average		
Age	May 1971	May 1973	May 1974	May 1975	May 1976	May 1977	May 1978		1979	1982	1983
Total, 16 years and over	.68	.68	.67	.68	.68	.67	.67	.68	.68	.71	.72
16–19	.94	.86	.87	.90	.90	.92	.91	.90	.92	.91	.96
20–24	.85	.83	.82	.82	.86	.84	.80	.81	.82	.88	.89
25–34	.73	.72	.72	.73	.74	.72	.73	.74	.73	.79	.80
35–44	.66	.61	.61	.63	.61	.62	.59	.64	.64	.66	.66
45–54	.62	.62	.62	.63	.62	.61	.59	.63	.61	.64	.63
55–64	.67	.69	.65	.67	.67	.65	.65	.66	.64	.65	.67

*Female-male earnings ratios were adjusted for differences in hours worked by multiplying by age-specific male-female ratios of average hours worked per week (for nonagricultural workers on full-time schedules).

Source: Earnings by age and sex are from unpublished tabulations from the Current Population Survey provided by the Bureau of Labor Statistics, U.S. Department of Labor. Hours data are from U.S. Bureau of Labor Statistics, Employment and Earnings series, January issues, annual averages.

percent of the $404 earned by men.[35] While this difference has fluctuated over time, as shown in Exhibit 14.3, it has been extremely persistent. In fact, some suggest the earnings gap goes back to Leviticus:

> And the Lord spoke unto Moses . . . thy valuation for the male from twenty years old even unto sixty years old, even thy valuation shall be fifty shekels of silver, after the shekel of the sanctuary. And if it be a female, then thy valuation shall be thirty shekels.[36]

While some biblical scholars dispute this interpretation of Leviticus, the Lord's ratio of 30 to 50 shekels is close to current earnings ratios.

Close examination of the data in Exhibit 14.3 reveals that the earnings gap varies by age of workers; it is the greatest (63–67 percent) in older workers and the narrowest (96 percent) among younger workers. In fact the age variable is probably highly correlated with other factors that affect the earnings gap.

Research on the Earnings Gap: A Mixed Bag

Why does the earnings gap persist? Pay determination is a complex process, with many factors involved; Exhibit 14.4 lists some of these factors. While a complete discussion of earnings differentials among social groups and occupations is beyond the purpose of this book, an understanding of the factors in-

---

[35]*Monthly Labor Review,* January 1986.

[36]Leviticus 17:1–4. While this citation appears frequently in comparable worth literature, many biblical scholars disagree with an interpretation that attaches differential wages to men and women. Instead, the topic in Leviticus is redeeming vows. In this light, the 50-shekel ransom would appear to be a penalty that falls heavier on men than women.

EXHIBIT 14.4
Possible Determinants of Pay Differences

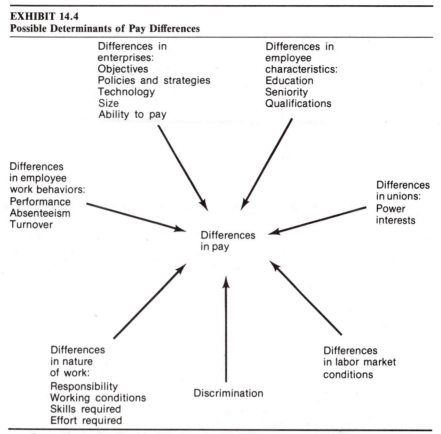

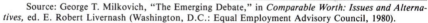

Source: George T. Milkovich, "The Emerging Debate," in *Comparable Worth: Issues and Alternatives,* ed. E. Robert Livernash (Washington, D.C.: Equal Employment Advisory Council, 1980).

volved is important, particularly as they are relevant to the management of compensation.

One factor, perhaps the most important one, is the differences in the nature of jobs held by men and women. Exhibit 14.5 shows that the distributions of women and minorities among occupations differ from that for white men. Further, the BLS reports that half of all working women are employed in only 20 of the 427 occupations.[37] While recent data confirm that these patterns are changing, with women gaining access to a wider array of occupations, significant differences in the occupational distribution by race and sex remain.

Another factor affecting the earnings gap is that women and minorities tend to hold the lower paying jobs in each occupation. The labor force participation rate of women (the percent of all women 16 years of age and over who

---

[37]Turner and Wilson, Testimony.

EXHIBIT 14.5
Gender and Race Differences in Occupational Distribution, 1984

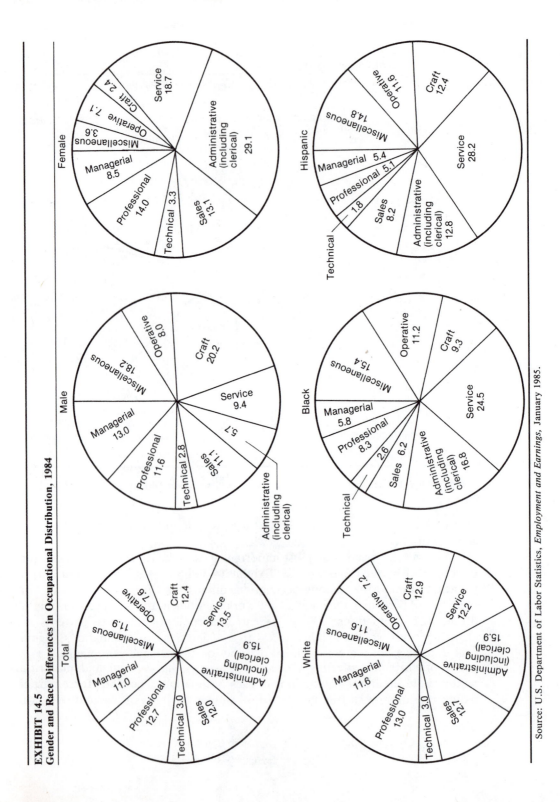

Source: U.S. Department of Labor Statistics, *Employment and Earnings*, January 1985.

are in the labor force) has increased dramatically; in 1983, the rate was 53 percent, and women made up 44 percent of the civilian labor force.[38] However, new entrants to the labor force are more often employed in relatively low-paying positions, which tend to hold down women's median earnings. While differences in employment behavior of women (e.g., greater turnover and absenteeism) do explain some of the earnings gap, that pattern is changing. Not only are women joining the labor force at greater rates, but women are staying in the labor force at rates increasingly similar to those for men.[39]

The empirical evidence does support the proposition that a large part of the earnings gap may be attributed to the high proportions of women in lower paying occupations and lower paying jobs within occupations, rather than to women and men being paid unequally in similar jobs.[40] When men's and women's earnings are analyzed within occupations, the wage differentials are less than those in the labor force at large. One study showed that in narrowly defined occupations, the average pay of men exceeds that of women, but these differences nearly disappear when each occupation is further classified by skill and experience.[41] Men and women are paid about the same wages on the same job (equal pay for equal work), but a much smaller proportion of women hold senior level posts in any occupation. Some evidence suggests that within the same occupation, firms employing predominantly women tend to pay a lower average wage than those employing predominantly men.[42] As the chapter on market surveys indicated, employers of the same skills in different industries may have different wage policies and consequently different rates (e.g., secretaries and accountants are paid less by banks than are secretaries and accountants employed by petroleum firms). Groshen, for example, reports that employees can get as much as a 20 percent increase in pay simply by switching industries (while performing the same job).[43] Freeman and Leonard report that their research shows

---

[38]James P. Smith and Michael P. Ward, *Women's Wages and Work in the Twentieth Century* (Santa Monica, Calif.: Rand Corporation, 1984).

[39]Paula England, "Do Men's Jobs Require More Skill than Women's?" *ILR Report* 19, no. 2 (Spring 1983), pp. 20–23; and Paula England and Steven P. McLaughlin, "Sex Segregation of Jobs and Male-Female Income Differentials," in *Discrimination in Organizations,* ed. Rodolfo Alvarez (San Francisco: Jossey-Bass, 1979).

[40]G. Johnson and G. Solon, *Pay Differences between Women's and Men's Jobs* (Cambridge, Mass.: National Bureau of Economic Research, Inc., 1984).

[41]Beller, "Occupational Segregation"; Solomon W. Polachek, "Women in the Economy: Perspectives on Gender Inequality," *Comparable Worth: Issue for the 80's,* Vol. 1 (Washington, D.C.: U.S. Commission on Civil Rights, 1985); Claudia Goldin, *Occupational Segregation by Sex: The Roles of Supervisory Costs and Human Capital, 1890–1940,* (Cambridge, Mass.: National Bureau of Economic Research, 1984); Mary Corcoran and Gregory J. Duncan, "Work History, Labor Force Attachment, and Earnings Differences between the Races and Sexes," *Journal of Human Resources* 14 (Winter 1979), pp. 3–20.

[42]Johnson and Solon, *Pay Differences.*

[43]Erica L. Groshen, "Sources of Wage Dispersion: How Much Do Employers Matter?" Working paper, Harvard University Department of Economics, December 1985.

that differences in unions affect differences in earnings.[44] Belonging to a union in the public sector seems to raise female wages more than it raises male wages. They found no such gender effects for union membership in the private sector. The point is that using the earnings gap to infer discriminatory behavior on the part of those involved in the pay determination process is difficult, since so many factors are involved.

Inferring from aggregated data. Some studies of the earnings gap have little relevance to understanding discrimination in pay-setting practices.[45] While actual pay decisions occur at the level of the individual employer, union, and/ or employee, with few exceptions most analysis of the earnings gap is conducted at aggregated levels. Such aggregated data studies often do not adequately include factors used in wage-setting practices, such as differences in employee work behavior; in the education, skills, and abilities to perform specific jobs; in the specific content of the work; in the interaction or match between employee qualifications and the work requirements; in the employer's pay policies; or in union objectives and power relative to employers. *Research on the pay-setting process and the role discrimination plays must be performed at the level at which wages are set: at the level of the employer, union, and job.* Inferring and evaluating from aggregated data is misleading. For example, factors explaining pay differences between Mrs. Jones and Mr. Jones must be examined by looking at their jobs, their personal skills, and their employers. Let us assume Mr. and Mrs. Jones both have college degrees (his is in psychology, hers is in computer science); both are in sales (he in shoes and she in mainframe computers) and both work for private employers (he for J. C. Penney and she for IBM). They probably have very different salaries, but most aggregated data would show them to have similar skills and similar jobs.

The problems with proxies. While many studies of male/female wage differences include some of the pay-setting factors, none of the published studies includes all of them. This is not always because researchers are not aware of these factors; the omissions are due in large part to two problems. First, there is a lack of adequate publicly available data; and second, proxies used are often too abstract.[46] Consider a study which treats all employee experience as equal (measured as age minus years of education minus five years) and all fields of

---

[44]Richard B. Freeman and Jonathan S. Leonard, *Union Maids: Unions and the Female Workforce* (Cambridge, Mass.: National Bureau of Economic Research, 1985).

[45]Treiman and Hartmann, *Women, Work and Wages,* chap. 2.

[46]Barbara R. Bergmann, "Occupational Segregation, Wages, and Profits When Employers Discriminate by Race or Sex," *Eastern Economic Journal* 1 (1974), pp. 103–16; Oaxaca, "Sex Discrimination in Wages," *Discrimination in Labor Markets;* Rosabeth Kantor and Barry Stein, eds., *Life in Organizations* (New York: Basic Books, 1979). For additional references, see C. Selden, E. Mutari, M. Rubin, and K. Sacks, *Equal Pay for Work of Comparable Worth* (Chicago: American Library Association, 1982).

education as equal (measured as years of education completed). Differences in types of experiences and the nature of education affect pay; such studies cannot measure these effects. Most studies use proxies for all factors that cannot be measured directly. Thus, years of education may serve as a proxy for all the differences in a person's skills and abilities; performance may be measured inversely by absenteeism; or differences among employers may be inferred from major industrial classifications. One study even uses number of children as a proxy for time spent away from the job.[47]

Another problem with using proxies is that possession of a qualification or skill does not mean it is work related. Examples of cab drivers, secretaries, locomotive engineers, or house painters with college degrees are numerous. Many studies of the earnings gap are done at a level that cannot discern many of the detailed employee/job/employer characteristics that are actually used in setting pay. As one reviewer has written, "It is not the quantity of the studies that is lacking; it is the quality."[48] So aggregated data tell us there is an earnings gap. This gap is the result of a number of factors, including discrimination. But we cannot say if discrimination is occurring, or to what extent, without looking at specific cases.

Wages for "women's work." The evidence is clear that as women enter the labor force in increasing numbers, the jobs they hold tend to be lower paying and in only a narrow range of occupations. This continued concentration, for whatever reason, raises a basic question: Why are jobs held predominantly by women, almost without exception, paid less than jobs held predominantly by men? Are women's jobs fairly valued, by the same standards that are used to value other jobs, or have they been systematically undervalued and/or underpaid?[49] Do job evaluation systems give adequate recognition to job-related contributions in those jobs held primarily by women? An example: the state of Washington conducted a study which concluded that the job of a licensed practical nurse required skill, effort, and responsibility equal to that of a campus police officer. In 1978 the state paid the licensed practical nurse, on average, $739 a month. The campus police officer was paid, on average, $1,070 a month. These salary differences were not related to productivity-related job content characteristics included in the study.[50]

---

[47]Barbara Norris, "Comparable Worth, Disparate Impact, and the Market Rate Salary Problem: A Legal Analysis and Statistical Application," *California Law Review* 71, no. 2 (March 1983), pp. 730–40.

[48]Donald P. Schwab, "Using Job Evaluation to Obtain Pay Equity," in *Comparable Worth: Issue for the 80's,* Vol. 1.

[49]Sharon Toffey Shepela and Ann T. Viviano, "Some Psychological Factors Affecting Job Segregation and Wages," in *Comparable Worth and Wage Discrimination,* ed. H. Remick (Philadelphia: Temple University Press, 1984).

[50]Helen Remick, "Beyond Equal Pay for Equal Work: Comparable Worth in the State of Washington," in *Equal Employment Policy for Women,* ed. Ronnie Steinberg-Ratner (Philadelphia:

It is this type of wage difference (e.g., nurses' versus police officers' wages) that is controversial. Some argue that pay differences are the result of consistent undervaluing of work done by women, and it ought to be illegal.[51] If jobs require comparable skill, effort, and responsibility, the pay must be comparable, no matter how dissimilar the job content may be. Others respond that pay differences between men and women are the result of many factors, not the least of which are market factors, for which no acceptable substitute is available.[52] And they question who or what, if not market-based factors, will determine wages for such dissimilar jobs as nurses and police officers. But critics respond that current pay differentials based on market forces are discriminatory. The market is faulty, they argue, because it reflects historic *access discrimination,* when employers simply refused to hire women for most jobs.[53] Women were restricted to only a few job categories, resulting in an oversupply of people to fill these jobs and artificially holding down wages for women's jobs relative to the rates paid for other jobs. Pay systems that value jobs today based on their market rates, these critics assert, incorporate and perpetuate this past discrimination against women and minorities. This is so, they argue, because market influences historically tend to undervalue jobs dominated by women (e.g., clerks, nurses, librarians, teachers). Therefore, they argue, jobs held predominantly by women ought to be paid at the market rate for "comparable" jobs held predominantly by men.[54]

But proponents of continuing reliance on market forces in the pay determination process argue that market forces are the best available measure of the value of work and employee qualifications. Whatever its flaws, there exists no adequate substitute. Indeed, market advocates argue that no mechanism that excludes market factors for determining job worth is feasible.[55]

Differing Public Policy Options

All the rhetoric boils down to two basic policy options directed at the reduction of the earnings gap. The first focuses on the access discrimination: ensuring that the distribution of employment and educational opportunities is not dis-

---

Temple University Press, 1980), pp. 405–48; Ronnie J. Steinberg, "'A Want of Harmony': Perspectives on Wage Discrimination and Comparable Worth," in *Comparable Worth and Wage Discrimination,* ed. H. Remick.

[51]Paula England, "Socioeconomic Explanations of Job Segregation," in *Comparable Worth and Wage Discrimination,* ed. Remick.

[52]George H. Hildebrand, "The Market System," in *Comparable Worth: Issues and Alternatives,* ed. E. R. Livernash (Washington, D.C.: Equal Employment Advisory Council, 1980).

[53]Bergmann, "Occupational Segregation, Wages, and Profits When Employers Discriminate by Race or Sex."

[54]Helen Remick, "Dilemmas of Implementation: The Case of Nursing," in *Comparable Worth and Wage Discrimination.*

[55]Hildebrand, "The Market System."

criminatory. The second aims at the realignment of wage structure: valuation discrimination. While both have the same intended consequence—to reduce the earnings gap between men and women—their approaches differ.

During the 1970s, interpretation and enforcement of pay discrimination legislation was consistent with the first strategy: eliminate access discrimination through the fair distribution of employment and education opportunities. Regulatory agencies urged that vacancies in jobs, training, and education programs in which women and minorities were underrepresented (or in some cases excluded) be filled by women and minorities at rates greater than their representation in the available labor supply until the underrepresentation was corrected. Thus, reduction in the earnings differentials was sought through desegregating jobs, hiring affirmatively, and offering equal pay for equal work.

Many women currently in the labor force have invested in years of experience and training for their jobs, and simply may not want access to other, higher paying jobs.[56] Proponents of realigning the work structure maintained that focusing solely on job opportunities and equal pay for equal work overlooks a major source of potential discrimination. It is that jobs held predominantly by women may be less valued precisely because they are "women's work," rather than for any productivity or work-related attributes of the work performed. The argument is that these wages may have been artificially depressed relative to what those wages would be if the jobs were performed by white males.

The second policy option, realignment of the wage structure, relies on the comparable worth standard of pay discrimination—equal pay for jobs that are dissimilar in content but of comparable worth. Let us turn next to examine comparable worth. First we examine the concept and related legislative developments.

COMPARABLE WORTH

Comparable worth as the standard for pay discrimination has been debated off and on since World War II.[57] During the debate leading to passage of the Equal Pay Act in the 1960s, a proposed bill read "to prohibit employers from maintaining wage differentials for work of *comparable* character on jobs the performance of which required *comparable* skills."[58] Representative St. George pro-

---

[56]Brigette Berger, "Comparable Worth at Odds with American Realities," in *Comparable Worth: Issue for the 80's*, Vol. 1; Michael Evan Gold, *A Dialogue on Comparable Worth* (Ithaca, N.Y.: ILR Press, 1983). Gold provides a thoughtful discussion of the issue of comparable worth and proposed approaches to operationalize the concept.

[57]Martha May, "The Historical Problem of the Family Wage," *Feminist Studies* 8 (Summer 1982), pp. 399–424; Ronnie Steinberg-Ratner, "Research: Wage Discrimination and Pay Equity," in *Preliminary Memorandum on Pay Equity*, eds. N. Perlman and B. Ennis (Albany: Center for Women in Government, State University of New York, 1980).

[58]Hearings . . . on H. R. 8898, 10266, Part I, 87th Cong., 2d Sess. (1962).

posed, and the House of Representatives agreed to, the word *equal* for comparable, arguing that

> the term "comparable" lacked meaning and would provide too much latitude to the Department of Labor, who would enforce the bill.[59]

Representative Goodell stated,

> when the House changed the word "comparable" to "equal" the clear intention was to narrow the whole concept. We went from "comparable" to "equal" meaning that the jobs involved should be virtually identical, that they would be very much alike or closely related to each other. We do not expect the Labor Department people to go into an establishment and attempt to rate jobs that are not equal.[60]

The National Academy of Science (NAS) report on the topic recognizes the difficulty of determining comparable worth and suggests that within an employer jobs "in some sense comparable" in their value to the organization ought to be equally compensated whether or not their work content is substantially equal.[61] The NAS authors suggest that rather than being some immutable standard universal to all employers and all jobs across the entire U.S. economy, a comparable worth standard would require only that whatever characteristics of jobs are considered worthy of compensation by a single employer (excluding market considerations) should be equally regarded, irrespective of the sex of the job incumbent.[62]

Legislative Developments

Comparable worth is, first and foremost, a political issue. People who share a set of beliefs about how pay should be determined in society wish to convince a sufficient number of others that their approach is "fairer" or more "equitable." The courts, as we have discussed, do not seem inclined to interpret present laws in a manner that encompasses comparable worth. Consequently, comparable worth proponents continue to lobby for either new legislation or voluntary action on the part of employers which would include the comparable worth standard.

Much of this political activity is occurring in state and local governments. Fourteen state legislatures have adopted the equal pay for comparable work standard as amendments to their equal pay acts.[63] Massachusetts and Oklahoma

---

[59]108 Cong. Rec. 14767–14769.

[60]109 Cong. Rec. 9197.

[61]Nancy Perlman and Bruce Ennis, "Achieving Comparable Compensation for Work of Comparable Value," (Albany: Center for Women in Government, State University of New York, 1980).

[62]Treiman and Hartmann, *Women, Work and Wages,* p. 9.

[63]Alice Cook, "Comparable Worth: Recent Developments in Selected States," *Proceedings of the 1983 Spring Meeting of the Industrial Relations Research Association,* Honolulu, March 1983, pp. 494–504; and *Pay Equity and Comparable Worth,* BNA Special Report (Washington, D.C.: Bureau of National Affairs, 1984).

specify that wages must be equal for those performing "comparable work," while Oregon, Alaska, and West Virginia require pay equity for performing work of a "comparable character."[64] Coverage of these statutes varies from state to state. In some, such as Hawaii, they apply to state and county employees.[65] In others, such as Minnesota, they apply to all public employers (e.g., every municipality, school, and mosquito control district).[66] The Minnesota law is included as Appendix A to this chapter.

Action at the federal level focuses on rhetoric and commissioning studies.[67] A proposal for a "pay equity study" of federal government employees has aroused opposition from business groups, which feel the study will be structured to conclude that pay adjustments are necessary. Extending this conclusion to the private sector is seen as the next logical step, one that concerns them.

Comparable worth and job evaluation. In 1980, Schwab stated, "At present, there is no mechanism for defensibly establishing comparable worth. Certainly job evaluation does not do it."[68] Since then over 20 states have conducted "pay equity" studies in which job evaluation was used to establish jobs of comparable worth. Indeed, the Minnesota comparable worth statute mandates the use of job evaluation, and most of the bills pending in other states use the Minnesota statute as a model. A policy of equal pay for jobs of comparable worth is established through the following four basic steps:

1. Adopt a single job evaluation plan applied to all jobs within a facility.
2. Calculate the gender representation (percentage male and female employees) of each job group. Any job group in which 70 percent or more of the incumbents are one gender is considered sex segregated.
3. Jobs with equal job evaluation points and sex segregation should be paid equally (i.e., single policy line).
4. The wage-to-job evaluation point ratio should be based on the wages paid to male-dominated jobs.[69]

---

[64]*Pay Equity,* p. 55.

[65]Ibid., p. 56.

[66]Ibid., p. 58.

[67]"Federal Agency Actions," "Federal Legislative Actions," and "Interest Groups" in *Pay Equity and Comparable Worth;* Geraldine Ferraro, "Bridging the Gap, Pay Equity and Job Evaluation," *American Psychologist* 39, no. 10 (1984), pp. 1166–70; and The Equal Employment Advisory Council, "Twenty Questions on Comparable Worth," in *Current Issues in Human Resource Management,* ed. S. Rynes and G. Milkovich (Plano, Tex.: Business Publications, 1986).

[68]Donald P. Schwab, "Job Evaluation and Pay Setting: Concepts and Practices," in *Comparable Worth: Issues and Alternatives,* ed. E. Robert Livernash (Washington, D.C.: Equal Employment Advisory Council, 1980).

[69]Also see "EEO Policy and Research Developments in the 1970s" (edited symposium) *Industrial Relations* 21, no. 3 (1983); and "Pay Discrimination: Legal Issues and Implications for Research," *Industrial Relations* 21, no. 3 (1983), pp. 309–18.

EXHIBIT 14.6
Job Evaluation Points and Salary

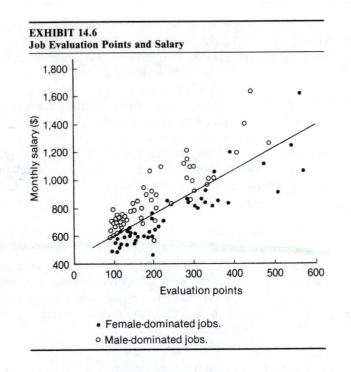

Consider Exhibit 14.6. The solid dots are jobs held predominantly by women (i.e., female representation greater than or equal to 70 percent). The circles are jobs held predominantly by men (i.e., greater than or equal to 70 percent men). The policy line (solid) for the women's jobs is below and less than the policy line for male jobs (dotted line). A comparable worth policy would use the results of the single job evaluation plan (x axis) and price all jobs as if they were male-dominated jobs. Thus all jobs with 100 job points would receive $600, all those with 200 points would receive $800, and so on. So comparable worth is technically feasible. Whether or not it is defensible is another matter.

Proponents of comparable worth are of two minds when it comes to job evaluation. Some see it as the primary technique for establishing jobs of comparable worth, as illustrated above.[70] Others admit it is too subjective to rely on.[71] While there is disagreement, Remick is perhaps the most specific. She de-

---

[70]Helen Remick, ed. *Comparable Worth and Wage Discrimination* (Philadelphia: Temple University Press, 1984).

[71]Ruth G. Blumrosen, "Wage Discrimination, Job Segregation and Title VII of the Civil Rights Act of 1964," *University of Michigan Journal of Law Reform* 12, no. 397 (1979), pp. 17–23; Richard W. Beatty and James R. Beatty, "Some Problems with Contemporary Job Evaluation Systems," in *Comparable Worth and Wage Discrimination;* Robert Madigan, "Comparable Worth Judgments," *Journal of Applied Psychology* 70, no. 1 (1985), pp. 137–47; Robert Grams and Donald Schwab, "An Investigation of Systematic Gender-Related Error in Job Evaluation," *Academy of Management Journal* 28, no. 2 (June 1985), pp. 279–90.

EXHIBIT 14.7
Inequalities in Point-to-Dollar Relationships

A. Inequality of Pay in Relation to Job Evaluation Points

City or State	Job Title	Monthly Salary	Difference	Number of Points
Minnesota	Registered nurse (F)	$1,723	$537	275
	Vocational education teacher (M)	2,260		275
San Jose, California	Senior legal secretary (F)	665	$375	226
	Senior carpenter (M)	1,040		226
	Senior librarian (F)	898	$221	493
	Senior chemist (M)	1,119		493
Washington State	Administrative services manager A (F)	1,211	$500	506
	Systems analyst III (M)	1,711		426
	Dental assistant I (F)	608	$208	120
	Stockroom attendant II (M)	816		120
	Food service worker (F)	637	$332	93
	Truck driver (M)	969		94

B. Inequality of Job Evaluation Points in Relation to Pay

City or State	Job Title	Monthly Salary	Point Difference	Number of Points
Minnesota	Health program representative (F)	$1,590	82	238
	Steam boiler attendant (M)	1,611		156
	Data processing coordinator (F)	1,423	65	199
	General repair work (M)	1,564		134
San Jose, California	Librarian I (F)	750	164	228
	Street sweeper operator (M)	758		124

Note: F = Female; M = Male.
Source: Ronnie J. Steinberg, "Identifying Wage Discrimination and Implementing Pay Equity Adjustments," in *Comparable Worth: Issue for the 80's,* Vol. 1 (Washington, D.C.: U.S. Commission on Civil Rights, 1985).

fines comparable worth as "the application of a single, biased free point factor job evaluation system within a given establishment, across job families, both to rank order jobs and to set salaries."[72] This definition seeks to minimize the influence of external markets for female-dominated jobs (e.g., markets for clerical or nursing skills). How dollars are actually attached to job evaluation points under such a plan is not well developed. Based on recent applications of this approach, it seems that the market rates for male-dominated jobs are used to convert the job evaluation point-to-salaries. The point-to-salaries ratio of male-dominated jobs would then be applied to female-dominated jobs. Steinberg, in Exhibit 14.7, points out the wide range of point-to-dollar relationships that presently exist in Minnesota, San Jose, and Washington, all of which work to the detriment of women. For example, in Minnesota both registered nurses (fe-

[72]Helen Remick, "Major Issues in *a priori* Applications," in *Comparable Worth and Wage Discrimination,* p. 99.

males) and vocational education teacher positions (male) receive 275 job evaluation points, but a $537 difference exists in their monthly pay.

Since past pay legislation has outlawed lowering any wage to make pay equal, a comparable worth policy may require employers to pay all employees at the highest market line or point-to-dollar ratio that exists for any segment of its employees. This translates into the rate paid for jobs held predominantly by men. Bellak raises a host of issues under such an arrangement:

- Would the unions give up their right to negotiate contracts independent of the pay arrangements in the other segments of the organization (i.e., would unions B, C, D, E, etc., have to agree to the same point/dollar relationship as union A, which signed the first agreement)?
- If the individual unions negotiated jointly for the same point/pay relationship, would there be any need for more than one union?
- How would an organization entice people into jobs where there were shortages because of distasteful work, if there were not premium pay for the same points, or more pay for fewer points (as in the sanitarians/nurses case previously discussed)?
- If one unit in a firm pays only base salary, will it have to increase its compensation level if another unit in the same firm introduces an incentive plan suitable for the business sector in which it competes?
- Must a state pay the same dollars for the same points to employees who work and live in a low-cost rural area as they do to employees in the high-cost large cities?
- Must a high-tech company raise the pay of its accountants (male-dominated) to equal the pay of its engineers (also male-dominated) for the same points?[73]

Underlying Bellak's points is a more basic one, which is whether legally mandating a job evaluation approach is defensible. Many employers do not use job evaluation at all. A myriad of approaches are used to determine pay ranging from market pricing to knowledge-based pay to gain sharing to maturity curves. A mandated job evaluation approach simply does not fit all circumstances.

Single versus multiple plans. A key issue in Remick's definition of comparable worth is a single plan applied across job families. This issue of single versus multiple plans has not yet been tested in the courts. An employer may be able to justify the use of multiple plans by demonstrating the full range of the work performed and the inadequacy of a single set of factors to adequately describe and evaluate that range of work. In practice, the overwhelming majority

---

[73]Alvin O. Bellak, "Comparable Worth: A Practitioner's View," in *Comparable Worth: Issue for the 80s,* Vol. 1.

of employers that use job evaluation use more than one plan to cover all jobs. A partner at Hay Associates observed,

> We, ourselves, do not know of a single case, in all the years before and after the legislation of 1963 and 1964, where a large and diverse organization in the private sector concluded that a single job evaluation method, with the same compensable factors and weightings, was appropriate for its factory, office, professional, management, technical, and executive personnel in all profit center divisions and all staff departments.[74]

Rosen, Rynes, and Mahoney add,

> The problem of making global assessments of a position's overall contribution to organizational goals and objectives cannot be underestimated. As work increases in complexity and interdependence, it becomes progressively more difficult to define common criteria of worth and to assess the unique contribution of any given position to the organization.[75]

Yet the use of a single plan seems crucial to comparable worth: As the NAS study concludes, "Whatever characteristics of jobs are considered worthy of compensation by a single employer should be equally regarded, irrespective of the sex of the job incumbent."[76]

How to conduct such an evaluation in a bias-free manner is difficult to imagine. There is no way to discern with certainty what the absolute point value of any particular job is, despite the ratios found by Steinberg; such a value does not exist. People who advocate such approaches credit job evaluation with more explanatory power than it possesses. By relying solely on job evaluation they are putting all their eggs in a loosely woven basket.

Union Developments

Unions support "pay equity" as a concept. Some interpret pay equity to mean comparable worth; others use pay equity as a more all encompassing, less well-defined term. Some unions, such as the American Federation of State, County, and Municipal Employees (AFSCME) and the Communication Workers of America (CWA) actively support comparable worth and have negotiated comparable worth–based pay increases, lobbied for legislation, filed legal suits, and attempted to educate their members and the public about comparable worth.[77]

---

[74]Ibid.

[75]Benson Rosen, Sara Rynes, and Thomas A. Mahoney, "Compensation, Jobs, and Gender," *Harvard Business Review,* July/August 1983, pp. 170–90.

[76]Treiman and Hartmann, *Women, Work and Wages.*

[77]Sara Rynes, T. Mahoney, and B. Rosen, "Union Attitudes toward Comparable Worth," in *Pay Equity in Comparable Worth;* Karen Shallcross Koziara, "Comparable Worth: Organizational Dilemmas," *Monthly Labor Review,* December 1985, pp. 13–16; Barbara N. McLennan, "Sex Dis-

But trade-offs between higher wages and fewer jobs make some unions reluctant to aggressively support comparable worth. Examples include unions in industries facing stiff foreign competition (e.g., International Ladies' Garment Workers' Union and the United Steel Workers). Trade-offs between higher wages and fewer jobs are more likely in some industries than in the public sector, which faces less competition for its services and is better able to absorb a wage increase.[78]

So the amount of union support for comparable worth is directly related to its effects on the membership. As labor leader George Meany observed when some economists sought his support for an alternative method for calculating cost-of-living wage adjustments: "Show me what difference it will make in my pay, and I'll tell you whether I support it."

Nationally the AFL–CIO adopted a resolution calling for its affiliated unions to:

1. Treat sex-based pay inequities in contract negotiations like all other inequities that must be corrected.
2. Initiate joint union-employer pay equity studies, as AFSCME has already done with a number of public employers.
3. Take all other appropriate action to bring about true equality in pay for work of comparable value and to remove all barriers to equal opportunity for women.[79]

Some argue that the earnings gap can be handled within the existing collective bargaining process. In 1983, AFSCME struck the city of San Jose, California, over a demand for "equity adjustments" for clerical jobs compared to carpenters and technicians.[80] The city and union eventually agreed to a two-year

---

crimination in Employment and Possible Liabilities of Labor Unions," *Labor Law Journal,* January 1982, pp. 26–35; *Breaking the Pattern of Injustice* (Washington, D.C.: American Federation of State, County, and Municipal Employees, 1983); *Pay Equity: A Union Issue for the 1980s,* American Federation of State, County, and Municipal Employees, 1625 L Street N.W., Washington, D.C. 20036, 1980; *Ourself: Women and Unions,* Food and Beverage Trades Department, AFL–CIO, Washington, D.C., March 1981; Lisa Portman, Joy Ann Grune, and Eve Johnson, "The Role of Labor," in *Comparable Worth and Wage Discrimination.*

[78]Barbara R. Bergmann, "The Economic Case for Comparable Worth," and Mark R. Killingsworth, "The Economics of Comparable Worth: Analytical, Empirical, and Policy Questions," both in *Comparable Worth: New Directions for Research,* ed. H. Hartmann (Washington, D.C.: National Academy Press, 1985).

[79]Winn Newman, "Pay Equity Emerges as a Top Labor Issue in the 1980s," *Monthly Labor Review,* April 1982, pp. 49–51; Susan L. Josephs, "Equal Pay and Comparable Worth: Collective Bargaining Approaches," unpublished paper, Ohio State University, Columbus. See also *Highlights of Recent Labor Union Activity* (Washington, D.C.: National Committee on Pay Equity, 1983).

[80]Robert L. Farnquist, David R. Armstrong, and Russell P. Strausbaugh, "Pandora's Worth: The San Jose Experience," *Public Personnel Management,* Winter 1983, p. 358–78; "Background Material on the San Jose Situation," Comparable Worth Project Clearinghouse, 488 41st St., No. 5, Oakland, CA 94609, Fall 1982. Comparable Worth Project also publishes a quarterly newsletter on activities of unions, employers, and others, available by subscription.

contract which included $1.4 million for "equity adjustments" in salaries for jobs held predominantly by women. The AFSCME president stated that the agreement shows "pay discrimination can be dealt with at the collective bargaining table."[81] Other settlements have also included special equity adjustments.

Costs

Opposition to comparable worth legislation is almost a reflex action for many employers. Legislation constrains their ability to act, to redesign pay systems, and to meet changing conditions. In addition, legislation usually translates into increased costs. Nevertheless, some employers that oppose a mandated approach to comparable worth are investigating how it could be implemented and its expected costs.

Some cost data are publicly available. A study in Pennsylvania reports "the average difference between existing wages for female jobs and predicted wages for female jobs based on wages for male jobs was $1.10 per hour," or $2,228 annually per affected employee.[82] Minnesota's Department of Employment Relations estimated the administrative cost of installing that state's comparable worth system at $85,000. Minnesota's actual wage adjustment allocation was $21.8 million to provide increases to 8,225 workers in female-dominated occupations over a two-year period. They estimate costs eventually at 4 percent of payroll.[83] Other states have spent varying amounts on studies of their pay systems. North Carolina's study cost $650,000, New York's $500,000. Note that these are only study costs. Implementing the concept is much more expensive. The state of Washington is implementing a comparable worth plan expected to cost $482 million even though the courts held it was not legally required to do so.[84]

How generalizable are these figures? Cook estimated costs at .7 percent to 5 percent of payroll, but she did not report the underlying models used to arrive at those estimates.[85] A simple model shown in Exhibit 14.8 allows us to

---

[81]*Pay Equity: A Union Issue for the 1980s.*

[82]David A. Pierson and Karen S. Koziara, *Study of Equal Wages for Jobs of Comparable Worth* (Philadelphia: Center for Labor and Human Resource Studies, 1981).

[83]Nina Rothchild, "Overview of Pay Initiatives, 1974–1984," in *Comparable Worth: Issue for the 80's,* Vol. 1.

[84]*Options for Conducting A Pay Equity Study of Federal Pay and Classification Systems* (Washington, D.C.: U.S. General Accounting Office, 1985); and "Washington State Settles Bias Case," *The New York Times,* January 2, 1986, p. 1.

[85]Cook, "Developments in Selected States." Some economists are beginning to model the costs and effects of comparable worth at an aggregated level, including Mark R. Killingsworth, "The Economics of Comparable Worth: Analytical, Empirical and Policy Questions," in *Comparable Worth,* ed. Heidi I. Hartmann (Washington, D.C.: National Academy Press, 1985), pp. 86–115; and Ronald Ehrenberg and Robert Smith, *Comparable Worth in the Public Sector* (Cambridge, Mass.: National Bureau of Economic Research, 1984), NBER Working Paper, 1471. See also San-

---

EXHIBIT 14.8
Preliminary Calculations of Comparable Worth's Addition to Wage Bill

---

$$\text{Percent increase} = DF$$

where

D = Percent differential between wage for female-dominated occupations and comparable male-dominated occupations

F = Percent of total wages presently paid to members of female-dominated occupations

If D = 20% F = 30%, comparable worth adds 6 percent to total wage bill.

If D = 15% F = 20%, comparable worth adds 3 percent to total wage bill.

---

make an initial estimate of the cost of comparable worth adjustments. Perlman and Grune estimate a 5 to 20 percent pay difference in male-female jobs that have the same job evaluation points in most firms.[86] We can use their 20 percent figure as the size of the wage adjustment required and further assume that 25 percent of the firm's entire payroll is earned by people whose wages need to be increased. Based on the formula in Exhibit 14.8, the adjustment is a 5 percent increase in the employer's total wage bill. In organizations where wage differences are less than 20 percent, or where a smaller percent of the total wage bill is paid to female-dominated jobs, the percentage would be smaller.

A 5 percent increase in total wage costs may not be too high a price for some employers—those that can pass the costs on in the form of higher prices or increased taxes, or those whose overall labor costs are a very small portion of total costs (e.g., petroleum firms). Conversely, those employers facing greater competition and with a higher percentage of employees receiving adjustments will find a 5 percent increase in their wage costs intolerable.

Obviously, the model in Exhibit 14.8 oversimplifies the real costs involved. It calculates the cost for only a single period; it does not include increased cost resulting from benefits tied to pay level (e.g., pensions, overtime pay, social security) and other factors.

Alternatives

While advocates try to gain support for comparable worth by using the term *pay equity*—no one wants to be against equity—many believe the whole notion is wrongheaded for interfering in a system that manages to get people to do unpopular jobs and immoral for holding out false hope. O'Neill calls this "chang-

---

dra E. Gleason and Collette Mosher, "Comparable Worth in the Public Sector: Why This Issue Won't Fade Away," mimeo, 1985; Sandra E. Gleason and Collette Mosher, "Some Neglected Policy Implications of Comparable Worth," *Policy Studies Review,* May 1985, pp. 595–600.

[86]Nancy Perlman and Joy Ann Grune, "Comparable Worth Testimony of the National Committee on Pay Equity," Presented before the U.S. House of Representatives, Subcommittees on Civil Service, Human Resources and Compensation and Employee Benefits, 1982.

ing the rules in the middle of the game, for no good reason."[87] Rather than encouraging women to move into higher paying job categories, the notion in effect penalizes those who have made the effort to do so. For example, if a woman takes the training necessary to become a computer programmer only to find the pay differential between clerk and programmer narrowed through comparable worth, her efforts to become a programmer have less monetary worth than she anticipated.

But the pay determination process has always had a political aspect. Minimum wage legislation is an example. Unionized workers have frequently been able to obtain higher wages than comparable unorganized workers. So if women can convince employers to adopt comparable worth, why shouldn't they? The issue then becomes, should it be mandated? Or should it be part of the ongoing collective bargaining process?

The bottom line is that there simply is no intrinsic economic worth to any one job or group of jobs or job structure.[88] Why should a nurse be paid more than a ditch digger? Why should a ditch digger be paid more than a nurse? Within limits, workers are paid what is required—to get people to take jobs and perform them satisfactorily. What it takes to get people to do work is determined through the confluence of many forces: the markets, unions, individual preferences, and so on. Who is to say another system is "fairer"? Fairer to whom? Put in this manner, comparable worth is clearly a political issue.

Finally, little attention has been paid to how effectively comparable worth will close the earnings gap.[89] Since differential earnings between men and women are the key rationale given for its adoption, the policy ought to be evaluated in terms of its ability to reduce the gap. As Minnesota and other states proceed, that data will begin to be available. Minnesota is already experiencing a few problems with fire fighters who were less enamored with the concept when their job was judged comparable to that of a librarian. The press reports the fire fighters suggesting to the public, "Next time you have a fire, call a librarian."[90] Perhaps the librarian's response should be, "Next time you want to know what's in a book, ask a fire fighter." Nevertheless, the results in the states may influence the willingness of private sector employers as well as Congress to adopt the comparable worth standard as a national policy.

---

[87]June O'Neill, "An Argument Against Comparable Worth," in *Comparable Worth: Issue for the 80's,* Vol. 1.

[88]Frederick S. Hills and Thomas J. Bergmann, "Conducting an Equal Pay for Equal Work Audit," in *Perspectives on Compensation,* eds. L. Gomez-Mejia and D. Balkin (Englewood Cliffs, N.J.: Prentice-Hall, 1987); and Jerald Greenberg and Ronald L. Cohen, eds. *Equity and Justice in Social Behavior* (New York: Academic Press, 1982).

[89]Heidi Hartmann, ed., *Comparable Worth: New Directions for Research* (Washington, D.C.: National Academy Press, 1985); Robert Buchele and Mark Aldrich, "How Much Difference Would Comparable Worth Make," *Industrial Relations,* Spring 1985, pp. 222–33.

[90]Cathy Trost, "In Minnesota, 'Pay Equity' Passes Test, but Foes See Trouble Ahead," *The Wall Street Journal,* May 13, 1985, p. 35.

Beyond considering what an employer's policy regarding comparable worth ought to be, there are several actions compensation professionals need to consider to help ensure that the pay system achieves compliance. Many of these, such as selecting a job evaluation plan and factors, and weighing those factors, have been discussed throughout the book.

SUMMARY

Pay discrimination laws require special attention for several reasons. First, these laws regulate the design and administration of pay systems. Second, the definition of pay discrimination, and thus the approaches used to defend pay practices, are in a state of flux. Many of the provisions of these laws simply require sound pay practices which should have been employed in the first place. And sound practices are those with three basic features:

1. They are work related.
2. They are related to the mission of the enterprise.
3. They include an appeals process for employees who disagree with the results.

Achieving compliance with these laws rests in large measure on the shoulders of compensation professionals. It is their responsibility to ensure that the pay system is properly designed and managed.

Should comparable worth be legally mandated? Comparable worth is at its core a political issue and, not surprisingly, opinions vary. But how much, if any, comparable worth policy will diminish the earnings differential remains an unanswered question. The earnings differential is attributable to many factors. Discrimination, whether it be access or valuation, is but one factor. Others include market forces, industry and employer differences, union bargaining priorities, and more. Compensation professionals need to critically examine traditional pay practices to ensure they are complying with regulations. Certainly the focus needs to be on pay discrimination.

Is all this detail on interpretation of pay discrimination really necessary? Yes. Without understanding the interpretations of pay discrimination legislation, compensation managers risk violating the law, exposing their employer to considerable liability and expense, and losing the confidence and respect of all employees when a few are forced to turn to the courts to gain nondiscriminatory treatment.

REVIEW QUESTIONS

1. What is the difference between access and valuation discrimination?
2. Differentiate between disparate impact and disparate treatment, using pay practices as your examples. (Your illustrative practices may be legal or illegal.)

3. What is the relationship between the Equal Pay Act and Title VII of the Civil Rights Act?
4. What are the reasons given to indicate a need for a comparable worth standard? Why hasn't a comparable worth standard been embraced by employers?
5. What are the pros and cons of labor market data in setting wages? Can you defend their use?
6. How would you design a pay system that was based on comparable worth?

Appendix A

Minnesota Law on Equitable Compensation (excerpts)

An Act

H.F. No. 2005

Chapter No.

relating to employment; providing for equitable compensation relationships among certain government employees; amending Minnesota Statutes 1981 Supplement, Sections 43A.01, by adding a subdivision; 43A.02, by adding subdivisions; 43A.05, by adding a subdivision; and 43A.18, Subdivision 8.

BE IT ENACTED BY THE LEGISLATURE OF THE STATE OF MINNESOTA:

Section 1. Minnesota Statutes 1981 Supplement, Section 43A.01, is amended by adding a subdivision to read:

Subd. 3. [EQUITABLE COMPENSATION RELATIONSHIPS.] It is the policy of this state to attempt to establish equitable compensation relationships between female-dominated, male-dominated, and balanced classes of employees in the executive branch. Compensation relationships are equitable within the meaning of this subdivision when the primary consideration in negotiating, establishing, recommending, and approving total compensation is comparability of the value of the work in relationship to other positions in the executive branch.

Sec. 2. Minnesota Statutes 1981 Supplement, Section 43A.02, is amended by adding a subdivision to read:

Subd. 6a. [BALANCED CLASS.] "Balanced class" means any class in which no more than 80 percent of the incumbents are male and no more than 70 percent of the incumbents are female.

Sec. 3. Minnesota Statutes 1981 Supplement, Section 43A.02, is amended by adding a subdivision to read:

Subd. 14a. [COMPARABILITY OF THE VALUE OF THE WORK.] "Comparability of the value of the work" means the value of the work measured by the composite of the skill, effort, responsibility, and working conditions normally required in the performance of the work.

Sec. 4. Minnesota Statutes 1981 Supplement, Section 43A.02, is amended by adding a subdivision to read:

Subd. 22a. [FEMALE–DOMINATED CLASS.] "Female-dominated class" means any class in which more than 70 percent of the incumbents are female.

Sec. 5. Minnesota Statutes 1981 Supplement, Section 43A.02, is amended by adding a subdivision to read:

Subd. 27a. [MALE–DOMINATED CLASS.] "Male-dominated class" means any class in which more than 80 percent of the incumbents are male.

Sec. 6. Minnesota Statutes 1981 Supplement, Section 43A.05, is amended by adding a subdivision to read:

Subd. 5. [COMPARABILITY ADJUSTMENTS.] The commissioner shall compile, subject to availability of funds and personnel, and submit to the legislative commission on employee relations by January 1 of each odd-numbered year a list showing, by bargaining unit, and by plan for executive branch employees covered by a plan established pursuant to section 43A.18, those female-dominated classes and those male-dominated classes in state civil service for which a compensation inequity exists based on comparability of the value of the work. The commissioner shall also submit to the legislative commission on employee relations, along with the list, an estimate of the appropriation necessary for providing comparability adjustments for classes on the list. The commission shall review and approve, disapprove, or modify, the list and proposed appropriation. The commission's action shall be submitted to the full legislature in the same manner as provided in section 3.855 and section 43A.18 or section 179.14, subdivision 5, provided that the full legislature may approve, reject, or modify the commission's action. The commission shall show the distribution of the proposed appropriation among the bargaining units and among the plans established under 43A.18. Each bargaining unit and each plan shall be allocated that proportion of the total proposed appropriation which equals the number of positions in the unit or plan approved by the commission for comparability adjustments divided by the total number of positions on the list approved by the commission for comparability adjustments. Distribution of any appropriated funds within each bargaining unit or plan shall be determined by collective bargaining agreements or by plans.

Sec. 7. Minnesota Statutes 1981 Supplement, Section 42A.18, Subdivision 8, is amended to read:

Subd. 8. [COMPENSATION RELATIONSHIPS OF POSITIONS.] In preparing management negotiating positions for compensation which is established pursuant to subdivision 1, and in establishing, recommending, and approving total compensation for any position within the plans covered in subdivisions 2, 3 and 4, the commissioner shall assure that:

(a) Compensation for positions in the classified and the unclassified service compare reasonably to one another;

(b) Compensation for state positions bears reasonable relationship to compensation for similar positions outside state service;

(c) Compensation for management positions bears reasonable relationship to compensation of represented employees managed;

(d) Compensation for positions within the classified service bears reasonable relationships among related job classes and among various levels within the same occupation; and

(e) Compensations bear reasonable relationships to one another within the meaning of this subdivision if compensation for positions which require comparable skill, effort, responsibility, and working conditions is comparable and if compensation for positions which require differing skill, effort, responsibility, and working conditions is proportioned to the skill, effort, responsibility, and working conditions required.

Sec. 8. [ALLOCATION.]

The amount recommended by the legislative commission on employee relations pursuant to section 6 to make comparability adjustments shall be submitted to the full legislature by March 1 of each odd-numbered year. The legislature may accept, reject, or modify the amount recommended. The commissioner of finance, in consultation with the commissioner of employee relations, shall allocate the amount appropriated by the legislature, on a pro-rata basis, if necessary, to the proper accounts for distribution to incumbents of classes which have been approved for comparability adjustments.

Funds appropriated for purposes of comparability adjustments for state employees shall be drawn exclusively from and shall not be in addition to the funds appropriated for salary supplements or other employee compensation. Funds not used for purposes of comparability adjustments shall revert to the appropriate fund.

Sec. 9. [EXCEPTION.]

The provisions of this act do not apply to the positions in Minnesota Statutes 1981 Supplement, Section 43A.08, Subdivision 1, Clause (g).

Part 5
Compensation Applications

Case 1   EEO at Sun State—A

You are a new personnel generalist at Sun State. You worked there last summer as an intern, and your boss, Georgia Santos, was very pleased with the job analysis and job descriptions you did during the summer. In fact, those job descriptions provided the basis for a complete job evaluation done this past year. As your first assignment, Georgia has asked you to assess Sun State's vulnerability to charges of pay discrimination. She says they do not discriminate against women, yet she has heard rumors that someone intends to file charges against them. Lisa Johnson was in complaining about her most recent raise. Lisa has a good performance record and received a generous raise based on her performance. However, Lisa said her pay was still below that of the males in her group, and that Sun State is notorious for its poor treatment of women.

Georgia has provided you the data in Exhibit 1. She has asked you for a report on the state's pay practices from an EEO perspective. She wants you to identify differences in treatment between males and females and decide if these differences are a result of discrimination or if they can be explained by some other factors. You have decided to begin your analysis by calculating separate means for males and females for the variables given in Exhibit 1.

1. Do whatever further analysis you believe will be useful and write the report for Georgia Santos.
2. Based on your analysis, what conclusions can be made about the state's pay system?
3. If you identify any problems, make specific recommendations for remedying them.
4. You may also recommend further data collection. If you do, specify the data to be collected and why you feel it is needed.

EXHIBIT 1
Sun State Personnel Inventory Sheet

Employee	Job Evaluation Points	Age	Sex	Years at Sun	Years on Present Job	Performance Rating*	Monthly Salary
1. Jim	350	24	M	2	2	5	$1,000
2. Henry	350	30	M	5	5	5	1,400
3. Patsy	350	34	F	4	4	4	1,200
4. Don	350	50	M	20	20	1	1,800
5. Jane	425	32	F	10	2	3	2,800
6. Bruce	425	45	M	15	10	3	4,000
7. Joan	425	24	F	1	1	4	2,500
8. Bill	425	34	M	5	5	4	3,000
9. Phil	600	35	M	10	5	2	3,500
10. Katie	600	36	F	8	8	3	2,800
11. Patricia	600	25	F	4	3	4	2,900
12. Jason	600	45	M	20	10	2	3,800
13. Patrick	600	30	M	7	7	5	4,200
14. John	700	38	M	8	8	1	4,600
15. Vera	700	52	F	25	15	5	5,000
16. Dennis	700	45	M	19	16	4	4,600
17. Susan	700	49	F	20	14	5	4,700
18. Laura	400	28	F	6	4	3	1,800
19. Tom	400	50	M	20	8	3	3,400
20. Carol	400	30	F	5	3	5	2,000
21. Richard	500	52	M	22	12	3	3,200
22. Mark	500	66	M	25	10	3	3,200
23. Ann	500	38	F	8	3	4	2,800
24. Janet	500	25	F	2	1	5	2,400
25. Sam	800	47	M	10	10	3	5,200
26. Charles	475	32	M	10	4	3	2,400
27. Lisa	475	35	F	3	3	4	2,400
28. Matthew	475	40	M	8	8	2	3,000
29. Michael	475	35	M	6	6	4	2,800
30. Sharon	475	42	F	12	4	3	2,500
31. Mary	475	29	F	4	2	5	2,100

*1 = Unsatisfactory performance; 5 = Outstanding performance.

EEO at Sun State—B

You finished your report to Georgia Santos last week. Thus far, you have not met with her to get her reaction to it. You are in the employee cafeteria when Lisa Johnson approaches.

Lisa asks how you like working for the state. She's heard you've done some EEO analysis and asks you point blank, "Do you think Sun State's pay system is nondiscriminatory?"

1. You remember that your boss mentioned Lisa's complaints about possible sex discrimination. What will you tell Lisa?

2. Following this incident, you decide to write a memo to your boss regarding communication about the pay system. What pay communication policy do you recommend for the state?

Case 2 *Unions and Social Issues: Comparable Worth*

ADVANCE PREPARATION

At least one week prior to the exercise, participants should read pages in the text and identify the pros and cons of comparable worth. One student will be assigned to play the role of Marc Russell and one student to play the role of Ann Baycroft. All other students should read both roles to familiarize themselves with *both* positions.

BACKGROUND

The International Union of Clerical Employees was formed in 1951 to provide a collective voice for the growing number of clerical workers in the private sector. Under the continuing direction of Marc Russell, International President, the IUCE now focuses on all nonexempt office employees. By 1975 the union had 225,000 members. However, as other unions have experienced declining enrollment and sought new unionization targets, it has been increasingly difficult for the IUCE to increase its membership. In fact, since 1980 there has been a small decline to the current level of 212,000 members.

Membership in the IUCE is about 85 percent female and 12 percent black or other minority. Union leadership at the international level is about 30 percent male and 70 percent female. At the local union level leadership is about 74 percent male and 25 percent female.

Role for Marc Russell, IUCE International President

Over the past three years you have become increasingly concerned about the stagnant membership drive efforts. Increasing militancy of management and competition for membership from other unions has made the union growth curve take a downward dip.

One way to reverse the trend, according to your executive vice president (Sally Feldman), is to champion the cause of equal pay for women. With women having 85 percent of the votes in the union, it certainly is politically viable for you to endorse equal pay for comparable work. The women, after all, believe they should get the same pay as men when they do a job of comparable worth to the company. Why should a male custodian get paid twice as much as a female secretary?

You're not opposed to women in the workplace, but this idea concerns you for two reasons. First, if the competitive market pays custodians twice as much as secretaries, you're not sure how some law is going to negate that difference. After all, how can you suspend supply and demand in a free society? Second, you're not sure how the worth of jobs is going to be measured to determine which jobs are of comparable worth. You're familiar with job evaluation, but it seems to support the idea that men's jobs frequently are worth more to the company. The whole issue seems highly political, and you're not sure you should get involved right now.

Role for Ann Baycroft, Assistant Director, Center for Women in Industry

The Center for Women in Industry (CWI) is a nonprofit research organization located in Syracuse, New York. Its central purpose is to conduct research designed to facilitate the transition to and progress in industry for women of all races, colors, and creeds. Current efforts by the CWI are aimed at achieving equal pay for jobs of comparable worth. You have been assigned to talk with Marc Russell, president of the International Union of Clerical Employees. If possible you would like his support for this cause. In fact, he seems like an almost ideal supporter. On pragmatic grounds, almost all of his votes come from women. Support for comparable worth should get enthusiastic support from his membership.

On moral grounds you also feel the cause is just. Women have been conditioned to believe they shouldn't work. And if they do work, there are certain jobs which are women's jobs. Your research shows that the crowding of women into these jobs forces wages lower. Still worse, it appears that existing job evaluation systems systematically overvalue the unique aspects of male jobs and undervalue the important differences in women's jobs. You intend to ask Marc Russell for support in lawsuits and legislation designed to completely overhaul existing compensation systems. One half the population should no longer be forced to work for an unfair wage.

Part 6

Managing the System

Let us return to the pay model, shown in Exhibit VI.1. We have covered three basic policy decisions—consistency, competitiveness, and contribution—along with the specific techniques and decisions required to achieve objectives such as unit efficiency, equity toward employees, and compliance with regulations. We have also examined in the preceding two chapters the role of government in design of pay systems and pay discrimination. Now we take up the fourth, and last, basic policy decision shown in the pay model, the nature of the administration of the system. Many facets of pay administration have already been examined. Yet several important issues remain. These are covered in this final part of the book.

The most important remaining issue concerns controlling costs. In fact, one of the key reasons for being systematic about pay decisions is to control costs. Some basic questions that need to be answered include: What are the labor costs associated with recommended pay decisions? How can the labor costs be contained? How are these costs to be budgeted and managed?

In addition to these questions, there are other administration issues that also need to be considered. The best-designed system in the world will founder if it is ineffectively implemented and managed. Should line managers participate in administering the system? To what extent? What should line managers and employees be told about the pay system? Why? Can the pay system be evaluated? How are compensation departments structured and staffed in different organizations?

The objective of Part 6 is to answer these questions and discuss the techniques involved in administering the pay system. Techniques for budgeting and implementing are discussed in Chapter 15. Chapter 16 examines compensation systems designed for employee groups working in special circumstances. These include executives, international employees, sales personnel, scientists and engineers, and first-level supervisors. As noted throughout the book, unions often play a significant role in the pay determination process. The book therefore concludes with a separate chapter, 17, devoted to the role of unions in compensation management.

EXHIBIT VI.1
The Pay Model

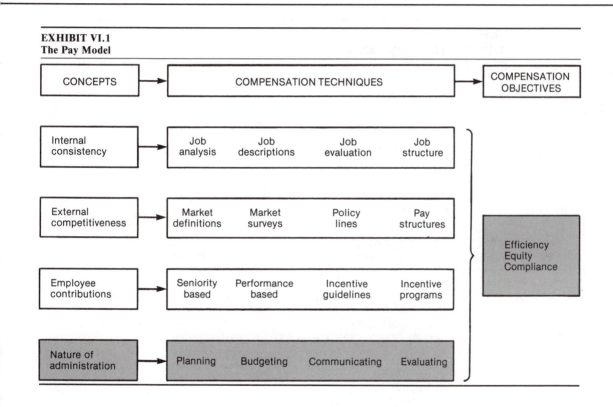

| CONCEPTS | → | COMPENSATION TECHNIQUES | → | COMPENSATION OBJECTIVES |

Internal consistency → Job analysis / Job descriptions / Job evaluation / Job structure

External competitiveness → Market definitions / Market surveys / Policy lines / Pay structures

Employee contributions → Seniority based / Performance based / Incentive guidelines / Incentive programs

Nature of administration → Planning / Budgeting / Communicating / Evaluating

Efficiency
Equity
Compliance

523

Chapter *15*

Budgeting and Administering

John Russell, former American Compensation Association Board member, recently retired. He was then approached by his Missouri community to develop a salary plan for the city. John worked on it diligently and submitted the plan.

Subsequently, he decided to run for the position of alderman on the city council, and was elected. His salary program was then brought before the council for a vote. Russell's vote was against his own program. His vote was among the majority and the plan was rejected. John explained his behavior by commenting, "I never realized how tight the budget was!"[1]

John's dilemma is shared by all compensation professionals and line managers. Budgets are an important part of the administration of compensation; they serve to allocate financial resources. While budgeting occurs as part of compensation administration, it also is part of managing human resources and the total organization. Creating a compensation budget involves trade-offs among the basic pay policies—how much to spend emphasizing internal consistency compared to external competitiveness or compared to employee's contributions. Trade-offs also occur over short- versus long-term incentives, over pay increases contingent on performance versus seniority, and over direct pay (cash) compared to benefits. Budgeting also involves trade-offs between how much to emphasize compensation compared to other aspects of human resource management. In such cases managers must decide the financial resources to deploy toward compensation compared to staffing (e.g., work force size and job security) compared to training (e.g., work force skills) and so on. The human resource budget implicitly reflects the organization's human resource strategies; it becomes an important part of the human resource plan. Finally, budgeting in the total organization involves allocating financial resources to human resources and/or technology, capital improvements, and the like. So from the perspective of a member of the city council, John Russell ended up making different resource allocation decisions than he might have made from the perspective of the compensation manager.

The four basic pay policies dealing with consistency, competitiveness, contribution, and administration serve to guide and regulate pay decisions. In turn, the compensation systems (techniques) are designed to be consistent with these policies and to achieve specific pay objectives. Pay systems are intended to serve as mechanisms that assist managers to make better decisions about pay. How the pay systems are used by managers involves the administration of pay.

ADMINISTRATION AND THE PAY MODEL

Consider making pay decisions without a formal system. Under such an arrangement each manager would have total flexibility to pay whatever seemed to

---

[1] "Russell Reverses Roles," *ACA News,* June/July 1978, p, 2.

work at the moment. Total decentralization of compensation decision making, carried to a ridiculous extreme, would result in a chaotic array of rates. Employees would be treated inconsistently and unfairly. The objectives of individual managers and some employees may be served, but the overall fair treatment of employees and the organization's objectives may be ignored.

Ideally, any management system, including the compensation system, implies goal-directed behavior. Compensation is managed to achieve the three pay model objectives: equity, efficiency, and compliance. Properly designed pay techniques, such as job evaluation, surveys, gain sharing, performance evaluation, and the like, help managers achieve these objectives.

Rather than goal-directed tools, however, pay systems often degenerate into bureaucratic burdens. Pay techniques become ends in themselves rather than focusing on objectives.[2] Operating managers may complain that pay techniques are more a hindrance than a help, and these managers are frequently correct. So any discussion of the nature of pay administration must again raise the question: What does this technique do for us? How does it help managers better achieve their objectives?

This chapter discusses the nature of compensation administration, which is the fourth major and final building block in the pay model used in this book. The basic premise is that while it is possible to design a system that includes internal consistency, external competitiveness, and employee contributions, the system will not achieve its objectives without competent administration.

While many pay administration issues have been discussed throughout the book, a few remain to be called out explicitly. Therefore, this chapter covers a variety of compensation administration issues, including (1) inherent controls, (2) forecasting and budgeting, (3) procedural equity, (4) structuring the compensation function, and (5) auditing and evaluating the pay system.

CONTROLLING COMPENSATION SYSTEMS: INHERENT CONTROLS

Pay systems have two basic processes which serve to control pay decision making: (1) those inherent in the design of the techniques and (2) the formal budgeting process.

Think back to the several techniques already discussed: job analysis and evaluation, policy lines, range minimums and maximums, performance evaluation, gain sharing, salary increase guidelines. In addition to their primary purposes, they also regulate managers' pay decisions by limiting what managers may do. Controls are imbedded in the design of these techniques to ensure that decisions are directed toward the pay system's objectives. A few of these controls are examined below.

---

[2]See, for example, R. Henderson, *Compensation Management* (Reston, Va.: Reston Publishing, 1985).

Range Maximums and Minimums

These ranges set the maximum and minimum dollars to be paid for specific work. The maximum is an important cost control: It represents the highest value the organization places on the output of the work. The individual skills and abilities possessed by employees may be more valuable in another job, but the range maximum represents what all the work produced in a particular job is worth to the organization. For example, the job of account clerk is in a pay range with a maximum that is the highest an organization will pay an account clerk, no matter how well the clerk performs the job. Pressures to pay over the range maximum occur for a number of reasons—for example, when employees with high seniority reach the maximum or when promotion opportunities are scarce. If employees are paid over the range maximum, these rates are called *red circle rates.* Most employers "freeze" red circle rates until the ranges are shifted upward by market update adjustments so that the rate is back within the range again. If red circle rates become common throughout an organization, then the design of the ranges and the evaluation of the jobs need to be reexamined.

Range minimums are just that: the minimum value placed on the work. Often rates below the minimum are used for trainees, but paying below the minimum seems to be an uncommon practice. Sometimes overzealously cost-conscious managers pay the absolute minimum needed to fill a job. However, this should be a very short-term action. Employees quickly perceive internal inequities, which leads to turnover, pay-related grievances, and increased interest in union membership. Below minimum payment may also occur for those employees who receive rapid promotions. Outstanding performers or women and minorities under an affirmative action plan may be examples. Some managers may find it difficult to grant the sizable pay increases required under such circumstances. Such behavior leaves the employer vulnerable to pay discrimination charges.

Finally, two-tier arrangements as a device to control labor costs should be mentioned. Two-tier structures differentiate pay for the same jobs based on employees' dates of hire. So employees hired after a specified date will receive lower wages than their more senior peers working on the same jobs. Two-tier wage structures are especially common in airlines, shipbuilding, and meatpacking. In 1985 the United Postal Service employees agreed that new employees would receive 10–30 percent less than incumbents for up to three years. USAir implemented a "B pay scale" for newly hired workers which is as much as forty percent lower than the "A scale" for existing employees.[3]

---

[3]Edwin Colodny, "Airline Deregulation Revisited," *USAir,* August 1986, p. 11; Miriam Goldberg, "Two-Tier Wage Settlements and Collective Bargaining Prospects," *Wharton Quarterly Model Outlook,* April 1985; Peter Capelli and Timothy Harris, "Airline Union Concessions in the Wake of Deregulation," *Monthly Labor Review* 108, no. 5 (1985), pp. 37–39; Daniel J. B. Mitchell, "Concession Bargaining and Wage Determination," *Business Economics,* July 1985, pp. 45–50; and Lee Balliet, "Labor Solidarity and the Two-Tier Collective Bargaining Agreement," paper presented at Industrial Relations Research Association meetings, Dallas, Tex., December 30, 1984.

Compa-Ratios

Range midpoints reflect the pay policy line of the employer in relationship to external competition. To assess how managers actually pay employees in relation to the midpoint, an index called a *compa-ratio* is often calculated.

$$\text{Compa-Ratio} = \frac{\text{Average rates actually paid}}{\text{Range midpoint}}$$

A compa-ratio of less than 1.00 means that, on average, employees in that range are paid below the midpoint. Translated, this means that managers are paying less than the intended policy. There may be several valid reasons for such a situation. The majority of employees may be new or recent hires; they may be poor performers; or promotion may be so rapid that few employees stay in the job long enough to get into the high end of the range.

A compa-ratio greater than 1.00 means that, on average, the rates exceed the intended policy. The reasons for this are the reverse of those mentioned above: A majority of workers with high seniority; high performance; low turnover; few new hires; or low promotion rates. A compa-ratio of 1.00 means that the average pay rate equals the intended policy. Compa-ratios may be calculated for individual employees, for each range, for organization units, or for functions.

So the relationship of actual salaries paid to the midpoint of the pay structure is an inherent control to assess how well actual practice corresponds to intended policy. Any significant and persistent deviations (high or low compa-ratios) should be investigated. While valid reasons for such deviations exist, other reasons may be that managers are overly generous or stingy compared to the policy designed into the pay system.

Range maximums, minimums, and midpoints help control pay for employees by job group. Other inherent controls affect individual pay.

There are basically two decisions involved in the control of individual employees' pay. One is the hiring rates offered to prospective employees (controlled in part by the range minimum), and the other is the amount and timing of pay increases.

Increase Guidelines

Increase guidelines that specify amount and timing of pay increases on an organization-wide basis are another example of an inherent control designed into the pay technique. These guidelines, illustrated in Chapter 10, Exhibit 10.10, are designed to ensure consistent treatment of employees by different managers throughout the organization.

Other examples of controls designed into the pay techniques include the mutual sign offs on job analysis and job descriptions required of supervisors and subordinates. Another is slotting new jobs into the pay structure via job evaluation, which helps ensure that jobs are compared on the same factors.

Formal appeals processes are another control, which helps ensure that employees' feelings of inequitable treatment are voiced and understood. All these controls are intended to help achieve the pay objectives. In addition to these inherent controls, there is the formal budgeting process.

FORECASTING AND BUDGETING

Compensation is a significant part of operating expenses in any organization. Controlling these expenses is one of the principal reasons for installing a formal pay system in the first place. As noted earlier, the principal mechanism used to control all operating expenses, including those associated with compensation, is the budgeting process.

Budgeting helps to ensure that future financial expenditures are coordinated and controlled. The budget becomes a plan within which managers operate and a standard against which managers' actual expenditures are evaluated. Pay budgeting involves forecasting the compensation costs associated with employing human resources for the next plan year. Both the total financial expenditures required by the compensation system during the next period and the amount of the pay increases required are estimated.

There are two basic approaches to generating compensation budgets: (1) "bottom up," in which individual employees' pay rates for the next plan year are forecasted and summed to create an organization's total budget and (2) "top down," in which a total pay budget for the unit is determined and allocated "down" to individual employees during the plan year.

Bottom Up: Forecasting Individuals' Pay

Bottom up budgeting requires managers to estimate the pay increase they will recommend for each of their subordinates during the upcoming plan year. Exhibit 15.1 shows an example of the process involved. Each of the steps within this compensation forecasting cycle is described below.

1. *Instruct managers in compensation policies and techniques.* Train managers in the concepts of a sound pay-for-performance policy and in standard company compensation techniques such as the use of pay increase guidelines and budgeting techniques. Also communicate the salary ranges and market data.
2. *Study pay increase guidelines.* Review with the managers the purpose of increase guidelines and how to use them.
3. *Distribute forecasting instructions and worksheets.* Furnish managers with the forms and instructions necessary to preplan increases.

Exhibits 15.2 and 15.3 are examples of the forecasting worksheets that might be provided. In Exhibit 15.2, we see the pay history for an individual employee, Sarah Ross. Her performance rating history, past raises, and timing of these raises are included. Some compensation professionals argue that provid-

EXHIBIT 15.1
Compensation Forecasting and Budgeting Cycle

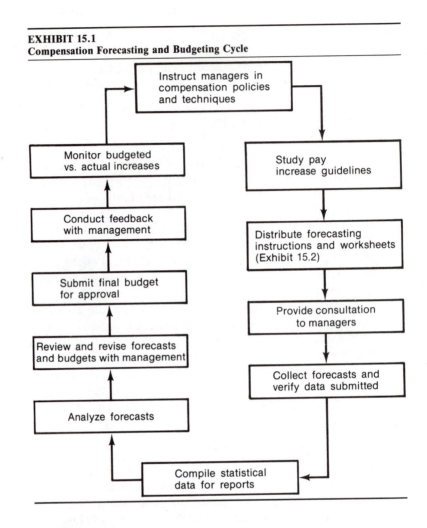

ing such detailed data and recommendations to operating managers makes the system too mechanical. The result, they argue, is to remove the manager from planning and making judgments about individual employee pay. On the other hand, such histories ensure that managers are at least aware of this information and that pay increases for any one period should be part of a continuing message to individual employees, not some ad hoc response to short-term changes. On the bottom line of Exhibit 15.2, Ms. Ross's supervisor has recommended a raise of $2,496, to be given in September 1987, 10 months after her last raise. This increase amounts to 10 percent of her base salary ($24,960) and converts to 12 percent on an annualized (12-month) basis. The range maximums, minimums, and midpoints for Ms. Ross's job are shown on the right of the bottom line. If she is given this recommended raise, her compa-ratio will be .98, meaning she will be paid just slightly below the range midpoint of $28,016 for her job.

EXHIBIT 15.2
Pay History

COMPANY		YEAR END	LOCATION						DATE PREPARED	

NAME	Sarah Ross	YEAR END EXPERIENCE	EMPLOYMENT DATE	YEAR AND SERVICE	YEAR FIRST DEGREE	HIGHEST DEGREE	HIGHEST DISCIPLINE	SOC SEC NO
		4	08-22-82	21/04	82	BS	Acctg.	458-56-5332

POSITION	Accountant	CLASSIF LEVEL	EMPL MO LEVEL	DATE ASSIGNED TO POSITION	DATE ASSIGNED TO CLASS LEVEL OF POSITION
		26		08-22-82	08-22-82

EMPLOYEE APPRAISALS

FOR BUDGET YEAR	PERFORMANCE RATING	POTENTIAL	RANK	TOTAL RANK
1985	2.0	28	2	7
1986	2.0	28	4	27
1987	3.0	28	3	49

SOC SEC NO 458-56-5332

PREVIOUS SALARY CHANGES

DATE	AMOUNT	#	MONTHS INTERVAL	ANNUAL VALUE	FIC	SALARY	SALARY RANGE UPPER BAND OR RANGE MAX	BAND MIDPOINT	LOWER BAND OR RANGE MIN	#	REMARKS	SUPERVISORS INITIALS
02 01 86	1920	8.3	10	10		23040						
12 01 **						24960					**Projected-Current year	

POLICY FORECAST

CAC- B	DATE	AMOUNT	#	MONTHS INTERVAL	ANNUAL VALUE	FIC	SALARY	UPPER BAND OR RANGE MAX	BAND MIDPOINT	LOWER BAND OR RANGE MIN	#	REMARKS	SUPERVISORS INITIALS
	09 01 87	2496	10.0	10	12		27456	30018	28016	25214	98		(A)

EXHIBIT 15.3
Pay Forecasting and Planning Worksheet

SALARY WAGE SCHEDULE _____

DEPARTMENT _Shipping_

MANAGER _Kramden_

EMPLOYEE NAME (ALTERNATE RANKED)	PAY RATE AS OF DATE	JOB'S NEW PAY RANGE			PROBATION OR PROMOTION INCREASE	PROJECTED 1st PERIOD INCREASE					PROJECTED 2nd PERIOD INCREASE					PROJECTED PAY RATE AS OF DATE
		MINIMUM	MIDPOINT	MAXIMUM		MERITS $	%	SPECIALS $	%	TOTAL ($)	MERITS $	%	SPECIALS $	%	TOTAL ($)	
Sarah Ross	9-87					1971	8%	525		2496						
Paul Formtest	8-87					2808	13½%			2808						
Al Smith	10-87					1601	7%			1601						
	A									B					C	

NUMBER OF EMPLOYEES _____

$$\frac{B + C}{A} = \underline{\quad} \%$$

APPROVALS _____

AND _____

DATE _____

In Exhibit 15.3, Ms. Ross's supervisor will enter salary recommendations for her and her colleagues for the upcoming time period.

4. *Provide consultation to managers.* Offer advice and salary information services to managers upon request.
5. *Collect forecasts and verify data submitted.* Audit the increases forecasted to ensure they do not exceed the pay guidelines and are consistent with appropriate ranges.
6. *Compile statistical data for reports.* Prepare statistical data in order to feed back the outcomes of pay forecasts and budgets.
7. *Analyze forecasts.* Examine each manager's forecast and recommend changes based on noted inequities among different managers.

In Exhibit 15.4, the compensation department has returned to the supervisor (Ralph Kramden) a printout of his recommendations for Sarah Ross and other employees (both non-exempt and exempt) he supervises and a month-by-month breakdown of salary expenses for the next two years, assuming his salary recommendations are approved. So by the end of 1988, Kramden's compensation budget is $122,366.40 for the six employees under his supervision.

8. *Review and revise forecasts and budgets with management.* Consult with managers regarding the analysis and recommended changes.
9. *Submit final budget for approval.* Obtain top management approval of forecasts.
10. *Conduct feedback with management.* Present statistical summaries of the forecasting data by department and establish unit goals.
11. *Monitor budgeted versus actual increases.* Control the forecasted increases versus the actual increases by tracking and reporting periodic status to management.

The result of the forecasting cycle is a budget for the upcoming plan year for each organization's unit as well as estimated pay treatment for each employee. The budget does not lock in the manager to the exact pay change recommended for each employee. Rather, it represents a plan, and deviations due to unforeseen changes such as performance improvements, unanticipated promotions, and the like are common.

This approach to pay budgeting requires managers to plan the pay treatment for each of their employees. It places the responsibility for pay management on the managers. In effect, a pay system has been designed to achieve equity, efficiency, and compliance, and the managers use it to forecast next year's pay actions. The compensation professional takes on the role of adviser to operating management use of the system.

Top Down: Planned Level Rise

Top down, unit level budgeting involves estimating the pay increase budget for an entire organization unit. Once the total budget is determined, it is then allo-

EXHIBIT 15.4
Analysis of Pay Forecasts and Budgets

DATE:19JAN87

CC:XYZ   SUPERVISOR   NAME:RALPH KRAMDEN

JOB CODE	EMPLOYEE NAME	STS	HOURLY RATE	NEW SALARY	EFF DATE	MONTHS SINCE LAST INCR	PLANNED RTG	-PLAN INCREASE AMOUNT- MERIT	SPECIAL	TOTAL	COMPA-RATIO	NEW JOB
NONEXEMPT												
T56	OX MEYER	FT	7.46	15,516.80	FEB87	6	2	.36		.36	90.4	
			7.83	16,286.64	NOV87	9	2	.37		.37	94.9	
X92	OS JONES	FT	8.22	17,097.60	MAR88	4	2		.39	.39	99.6	T51
			7.19	14,955.20	AUG87	13	1		.94	.94	95.8	X90
Z15	WD PLANTER	FT	7.10	14,768.00	SEP87	20	3	.38	.22	.60	86.0	
EXEMPT												
M22	JP FORMSTEST	FT	11.35	23,608.00	AUG87	19	2	2808		2808	99.0	
M55	S ROSS	FT	13.20	27,456.00	SEP87	10	3	1971	524	2496	98.0	
P17	AP SMITH	FT	11.77	24,481.60	OCT87	14	3	1601		1601	102.8	

(PLANNED ENDING SALARY)   TOTAL NONEXEMPT   46,820.80
(PLANNED ENDING SALARY)   TOTAL EXEMPT   75,545.60

TOTAL KRAMDEN   122,366.40

PLANNED EXPENSE BY MONTH-CY87   (ROUNDED TO NEAREST HUNDRED DOLLARS)

	JAN	FEB	MAR	APR	MAY	JUN	JUL	AUG	SEP	OCT	NOV	DEC	TOTAL
TOTAL NONEXEMPT	3.4	3.5	3.5	3.5	3.5	3.5	3.5	3.7	3.8	3.8	3.8	3.8	43.3
TOTAL EXEMPT	5.7	5.7	5.7	5.7	5.7	5.7	5.7	6.0	6.2	6.3	6.3	6.3	71.0
TOTAL KRAMDEN	9.1	9.2	9.2	9.2	9.2	9.2	9.2	9.7	10.0	10.1	10.1	10.1	114.3

PLANNED EXPENSE BY MONTH-CY88   (ROUNDED TO NEAREST HUNDRED DOLLARS)

	JAN	FEB	MAR	APR	MAY	JUN	JUL	AUG	SEP	OCT	NOV	DEC	TOTAL
TOTAL NONEXEMPT	3.8	3.8	3.9	3.9	3.9	3.9	3.9	3.9	3.9	3.9	3.9	3.9	46.8
TOTAL EXEMPT	6.3	6.3	6.3	6.3	6.3	6.3	6.3	6.3	6.3	6.3	6.3	6.3	75.5
TOTAL KRAMDEN	10.1	10.1	10.2	10.2	10.2	10.2	10.2	10.2	10.2	10.2	10.2	10.2	122.3

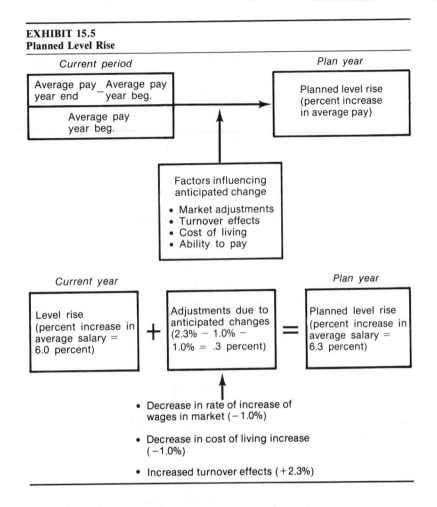

EXHIBIT 15.5
Planned Level Rise

Current period

$$\frac{\text{Average pay year end} - \text{Average pay year beg.}}{\text{Average pay year beg.}}$$

Plan year

Planned level rise (percent increase in average pay)

Factors influencing anticipated change
- Market adjustments
- Turnover effects
- Cost of living
- Ability to pay

Current year

Level rise (percent increase in average salary = 6.0 percent)

$+$

Adjustments due to anticipated changes (2.3% − 1.0% − 1.0% = .3 percent)

$=$

Plan year

Planned level rise (percent increase in average salary = 6.3 percent)

- Decrease in rate of increase of wages in market (−1.0%)
- Decrease in cost of living increase (−1.0%)
- Increased turnover effects (+2.3%)

cated to each manager, who plans how to distribute it among subordinates. There are many approaches to unit level budgeting in use. Two typical ones will be considered.[4] They differ in the choice of financial index used as a control measure. One approach is controlling to a planned level rise; the other is controlling to a planned compa-ratio.

Planned level rise. A planned level rise is the percentage increase in average pay for the unit which is planned to occur. Top management will set this figure

[4]For alternative approaches to pay forecasting and budgeting, see Bashker Biswas and Thomas M. Hestwood, "Projecting Base Payroll Costs," *Compensation Review,* Third Quarter 1975, pp. 47–53; Warren C. Axelrod, "Evaluating Salary Increases," *Personnel Journal,* December 1978, pp. 676–79; Thomas Plumberg, "A Model for Estimating Payroll Expenses," *Compensation Review,* First Quarter 1981, pp. 23–29.

in consultation with the compensation professional and others (e.g., finance) after considering such factors as anticipated rates of change in market data, changes in cost of living, the employer's ability to pay, and the effects of turnover and promotions. The variables, as shown in Exhibit 15.5, used in establishing the planned level rise are:

1. Current level rise: This figure is calculated as the average of all salaries at the end of the current period, minus the average of all salaries at the beginning of the period, divided by the average salary at the beginning. It is the percentage increase in the average rate paid that has occurred during the present time period. In the example shown in Exhibit 15.5, the current level rise is 6.0 percent.

2. Adjustments due to anticipated changes: This adjustment is partly quantitative and partly judgmental. It assesses the effects of such factors as changes in market rates, changes in the financial health of the organization (ability to pay), and turnover effects. Turnover effects account for the downward pressure on average salaries as highly paid employees leave or retire and are replaced by employees whose pay is usually lower in the pay range for that job. These lower paid employees may be less experienced and perhaps less productive. Only the decreased costs, not the possible lower productivity, are reflected in the turnover effects.

If the new employees are paid less than those they replace, why is the turnover effect shown in Exhibit 15.5 as a plus 2.3 percent? The answer is that the lower rates paid to these new employees create a downward pressure on the *average* rate paid. If employers wish to maintain a competitive position in the external market, they must offset this downward pressure by *increasing* the rate of change (+2.3 percent) in the average rate paid. The logical next question is, why bother? Why not simply permit the percentage increase on the average rate to decline? Most employers do. A few argue that if they did this, then the average salary paid would deteriorate in the marketplace, increasing the likelihood of losing qualified employees and decreasing the chances of recruiting equally qualified replacements.

In our exhibit, top management has decided that market changes this year have been smaller than in the previous year (−1 percent), which is fine, since the organization's financial position has deteriorated (−1 percent). Combining these adjustments to our +2.3 percent turnover effect gives an adjustment factor of +0.3 percent and a planned level rise of 6.3 percent. This means that the organization has set a target of 6.3 percent as the present increase in average salary that will occur in the next budget period. It does not mean that everyone's increase will be 6.3 percent. It means that at the end of next year's budget, the average salary calculated to include all employees will be 6.3 percent higher than it is now.

This figure at the unit or corporate level is then pushed down to individual managers, who will use it as a guideline to determine individual employee increases. Several more calculations are involved. These are discussed next.

Participation rate. This is the total number of employees anticipated to receive pay increases in the plan year, divided by the total number of employees eligible to receive increases. The participation rate may be less than 100 percent, meaning that some employees will not get pay increases in this upcoming plan year. They may be marginal performers, or they may have just received an increase and are not eligible for another until some time beyond the next year. The participation rate may also be greater than 100 percent in cases with new hires who may get pay increases every six months for the first year or two, or in some assembly and office and clerical jobs where increases are smaller but more frequent.

Exhibit 15.6 uses the 6.3 percent from Exhibit 15.5 as the targeted planned level rise. The first row shows that the total payroll ($2,205,200) will increase by $138,928. The 190 employees will receive a typical raise of $.20, or 3.5 percent. But because the participation rate is 180 percent, most employees will receive two increases in the budget period. The current average hourly rate of $5.60 will increase by $.36 by year-end. The next eight rows show the numbers of employees and their current average pay, by pay grade. Then it works backward to calculate an estimated typical increase, given estimated participation rates for each pay grade. (This example assumes that no turnover occurs.) While the overall payroll impact is 6.3 percent, adjustments are made differentially among pay grades. For example, in pay grade 3, a typical raise this year will be 20 cents an hour, or 3.8 percent. Note that the 190 percent participation rate means that most employees in grade 3 will receive two increases during the year. Thirty-four increases (190 percent participation rate $\times$ 18 employees) will be given to those 18 employees in pay grade 3; 16 will get two raises, and two will get one raise. So the typical increase is 20 cents—and the overwhelming majority of employees will get two such raises in the time period. The point of planned level rise budgeting is that the amount to increase the average pay level is set by top management and allocated down to lower level managers.

EXHIBIT 15.6
Budgeting to Planned Level Rise Target: 6.3 Percent, or $138,928, Increase from This Year

(1)	(2)	(3)		(4)	(5)	(6)		(7)
	Present	Payroll Increase				Typical Increase		Current
Pay	Payroll			Employee	Participation			Average/Hourly
Grade	this Grade	Percent	Amount	Population	Rate	Amount	Percent	Rate*
Targets	$2,205,200	6.3%	$138,928	190	180%	$.20	3.5%	$5.60 + .36
1	98,000	3.6	3,528	12	100	.15	3.6	4.25
2	56,300	6.3	3,547	6	180	.17	3.5	4.89
3	182,300	7.2	13,126	18	190	.20	3.8	5.27
4	348,000	6.3	21,924	32	180	.20	3.5	5.66
5	733,700	6.6	48,600	61	180	.23	3.7	6.26
6	124,000	4.3	5,332	10	140	.20	3.1	6.46
7	598,600	6.7	40,106	46	190	.24	3.5	6.70
8	64,300	4.3	2,765	5	170	.17	2.5	6.70

*Based on 48 weeks per year, 40 hours per week.

Top Down: Compa-Ratio

Under this approach to budgeting, a "planned compa-ratio" is established as the target rather than a rise in the average pay level. Recall that

$$\text{Compa-Ratio} = \frac{\text{Average rate paid}}{\text{Range midpoint}}$$

The only real difference between this approach and the planned level rise approach is that a planned compa-ratio plays a more formal role; many of the same factors are used in both approaches. Exhibit 15.7 shows an approach used by one employer. The planned compa-ratio (box 3) is set by adjusting the unit's current compa-ratio in light of the unit's current ability to attract and retain employees and its pay level policy. By combining the planned compa-ratio with market adjustments (box 4) and turnover effects, the required percentage increase in average pay, or the level rise (box 5), is calculated. The exhibit does not show us how the employer arrives at the various figures (e.g., planned compa-ratio, ability to pay). It merely shows generally how these various figures interact.

EXHIBIT 15.7
Unit Budget Process: Control to Planned Compa-Ratio

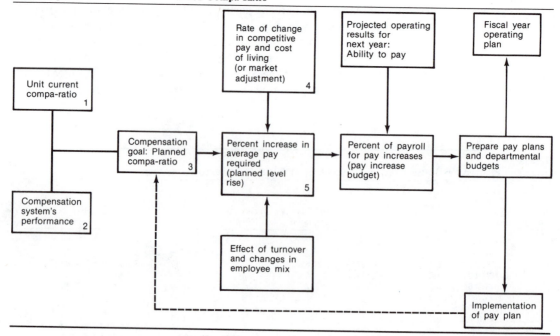

Exhibit 15.8 illustrates the calculations in a planned compa-ratio approach. The unit in the example has the same 80 employees during the entire period, and its compa-ratio is .97 at the end of the current year. The planned compa-ratio is 1.06, based on current experience and judgment. A planned compa-ratio of 1.06 means that at the end of the next budget period, the average rate paid is to be 6 percent above the average range midpoint. Reasons for setting it above 1.00 may include paying higher wages as part of a nonunion strategy, or it may be a recognition that the stable work force is gaining in seniority and experience and deserves pay that is on average above the midpoint of the ranges.

In addition to moving individuals relatively higher in their pay ranges, the ranges and midpoints are also being adjusted (step 3) on the basis of anticipated changes in the rates paid by competitors in the external market. In the example, the 10 percent update in structure adjustment results in new totals and average range midpoints for the plan year ($2,177,659 and $27,221). So this unit is making two pay adjustments at once. First, it is moving its entire pay structure up by 10 percent (to adjust for market increases) by adjusting range midpoints. Second, it is moving its employees to a higher position in that new range (to account for more experienced work force) by adjusting its compa-ratio.

EXHIBIT 15.8
Estimated Budget *(Method: controlling to planned compa-ratio)*

Period	Employees in Unit	Total Pay	Average Pay	Total Midpoints	Average Midpoints	Compa-Ratio
End of						
current year	80	$1,920,300				.97[1]
Plan year			$24,004	$1,979,690	$24,746	
Begin	80	1,920,300	24,004	2,177,659[3]	27,221[3]	.88[2]
End	80	2,308,319[4]	28,853[4]	2,177,659	27,221	1.06[2]
Change	—	388,019	4,849	—	—	
Percentage change	—	20.2	20.2	—	—	

Calculations steps:

(1) Current compa-ratio: $.97 = \dfrac{\text{Total pay}}{\text{Total midpoints}} \left(\dfrac{1,920,300}{1,979,690}\right) \text{or} \dfrac{\text{Average pay}}{\text{Average midpoints}} \left(\dfrac{24,004}{24,746}\right)$

(2) Plan year compa-ratio:

   Beginning: $.88 = \left(\dfrac{1,920,300}{2,177,659}\right)$

   End planned: 1.06 set by management policy

(3) Range midpoint adjustments: ($1,979,690 × 1.10 = $2,177,659; $24,746 × 1.10 = $27,221) assume estimated market increase: 10 percent

(4) Estimated total payroll: $\text{Planned compa-ratio} = \dfrac{\text{Total pay}}{\text{Total midpoints}} \text{ or } \dfrac{\text{Average pay}}{\text{Average midpoints}}$
   End plan year

   $1.06 = \dfrac{\$2,308,319}{\$2,177,659} \text{ or } \dfrac{\$28,853}{\$27,221}$

Source: Adapted from *Cert III Manual,* American Compensation Association.

The estimated total payroll and change in payroll that results from these two adjustments can now be calculated (step 4). This is done by using the planned compa-ratio (1.06) and the adjusted total range midpoints ($2,177,659) and solving for the total pay expected at plan year end.

Step 4:

$$\text{Planned Compa-Ratio} = \frac{\text{Total pay}}{\$2,177,659}$$

$$\text{Plan year end total pay} = 1.06 \times \$2,177,659$$

$$\text{Budgeted total pay} = \$2,308,319$$

This amounts to a $388,019 increase ($2,308,319 − $1,920,300) from the total pay at the beginning of the plan year (see the table in Exhibit 15.8) and represents 20.2 percent change in total pay, assuming a 100 percent participation rate.

Distributing the budget to subunits. Recall that our focus here is on top-down budgeting. Whichever method is used to generate the unit budget, once estimated it is distributed down to the subunit managers. Once again, a wide variety of methods to determine what percent of the salary budget each manager should receive exists.[5] Some use a uniform percentage, in which each manager gets an equal percentage of the budget based on the salaries of each subunit's employees. Others vary the percentage allocated to each manager based on each subunit's compa-ratios, and/or any pay-related problems, such as turnover or performance, which have been identified in that subunit. In effect, a planned compa-ratio may be established for each subunit.

Once salary budgets are allocated to each subunit manager, they become a constraint: a limited fund of money that each manager has to allocate to subordinates. Typically, pay increase guidelines (such as those discussed in Chapter 10) are used to help managers make these allocation decisions.

Top down versus bottom up. Rather than treating individual forecasting (bottom up) versus unit budgeting (top down) as alternatives, many organizations employ both approaches. Usually, this means generating the unit's budget first and then forecasting individual pay increases to ensure that the budget is appropriate. Whichever method is used, the formal budgeting process is a vital part of the pay system. It is through budgeting that compensation cost objectives are achieved.

Analyzing Costs

Exhibit 15.9 shows how to cost out a wage proposal. The exhibit is self-explanatory, so spend some time and work through the calculations. Such cost-

---

[5]Ralph W. Ells, *Salary Budgeting* (Madison: University of Wisconsin Bureau of Business Research, Wisconsin Commerce Reports, October 1958).

EXHIBIT 15.9
Costing a Wage Proposal

Wages

1. *Average Hourly Rate* (see example 1)
   a. Multiply the number of employees times the hourly rate in each wage category.
   b. Add the results obtained for each wage category.
   c. Divide the total hourly rate by the total number of employees. This will give a "weighted" average which will properly take into consideration the population variances in each wage category.

Example 1:

Labor Grade	Number of Employees		Hourly Rate		Total Hourly Rate
1	5	×	$4.00	=	$ 20.00
2	10	×	3.80	=	38.00
3	15	×	3.60	=	54.00
4	20	×	3.40	=	68.00
Totals	50				$180.00

$180.00 ÷ 50 = $3.60 (weighted average hourly rate)

2. *Cents per Hour Increase per Employee* (see example 2)
   a. Multiply the cents per hour increase times the number of employees in each wage category.
   b. Add the number of employees in each wage category.
   c. Add the total cents per hour increase obtained for each wage category.
   d. Divide *b* into *c*. This will give a "weighted" average which will properly take into consideration the population variances in each wage category.

Example 2:

Labor Grade	Number of Employees		Cents per Hour Increase		Total Cents per Hour Increase
1	5	×	$.05	=	$ .25
2	10	×	.05	=	.50
3	15	×	.05	=	.75
4	20	×	.10	=	2.00
Totals	50				$3.50

$3.50 ÷ 50 = $.07 (weighted average cents per hour increase)

3. *Percent Increase per Employee* (see example 3)
   To obtain this, use the same calculation as 2 above, except substitute the percent amount of increase figure for cents per hour in 2*a*.

Example 3:

Labor Grade	Number of Employees		Percent Increase		Total Percent Increase
1	5	×	6%	=	30%
2	10	×	3	=	30
3	15	×	3	=	45
4	20	×	2	=	40
Totals	50				145%

145 ÷ 50 = 2.9% (weighted average percent increase)

4. *Annual Cost of a Cents per Hour Increase* (see example 4)
   To obtain this you should multiply the cents per hour increase times number of employees times 2,080 (52 weeks × 40 hours). The annual increased cost for each category can be figured, but normally only the total increased cost is calculated; to do this use the (weighted) *average* cents per hour increase

EXHIBIT 15.9
(concluded)

Wages

amount. Also, remember each annual cost increase is added to each succeeding cost increase; thus, if your costs are increased $7,280 in each of two years, your cost increase in the second year is $14,560.

Example 4:

Labor Grade	Number of Employees		Total Hours Worked		Cents per Hour Increase	Annual Cost
1	5	× 2,080 =	10,400	×	$.07	$ 728.00
2	10	× 2,080 =	20,800	×	.07	1,456.00
3	15	× 2,080 =	31,200	×	.07	2,184.00
4	20	× 2,080 =	41,600	×	.07	2,912.00
Totals	50	× 2,080 =	104,000	×	.07	$7,280.00

Benefits

5. *Vacation* (see example 5)
   a. Calculate the number of employees who will be eligible.
   b. Multiply that number times the average hourly rate (after any wage increase) times increased hours of vacation.
   c. Divide *b* by the total number of work hours of all employees (total population × 2080). This will give you the cents per hour increase per employee in the first year it is granted. To obtain the cost in each succeeding year, add the number of employees eligible in the first year to the number eligible in each succeeding year. Then calculate the new average hourly rate and complete the calculation.

Example 5:
If vacation is increased from three weeks after 18 years of service to three weeks after 15 years of service and is as follows:

Number of Employees	Years of Service
5	17
5	16
10	14

(*a*) First year:

Number of Employees Eligible		Average Rate		Increased Vacation		Total Annual Cost
10	×	$3.67	×	40 hrs.	=	$1,468.00

		Total Hours Worked		Cents per Hour
$1,468.00	÷	104,000	=	$.0141

(*b*) Second year:

20 × $3.74 × 40 = $2,992.00
$2,992.00 ÷ 100,000 = $.030 cents per hour

6. *Insurance* (see example 6)
   Calculate the total increased annual premium cost to be paid by the company (this can usually be obtained from the insurance carrier). Divide this amount by the total number of work hours for all employees. This will give you the cents per hour cost per employee.

Example 6:

Total Annual Cost		Total Hours Worked		Cents per Hour
$5,000	÷	104,000	=	$.0408

ing is commonly done prior to recommending a pay increase. It is also used in preparation for collective bargaining. For example, it is useful to have in mind the dollar impact of a 1 cent per hour wage change, and a 1 percent change in payroll as one goes into bargaining.[6] Knowing these figures, negotiators can quickly compute the impact of a request for a 9 percent wage increase. The calculations are straightforward and serve as useful standards for analysis.

Total compensation costs. Thus far the costs of benefits and other forms of pay (deferred plans, savings plans, bonuses) have not been incorporated into the budgeting process. At some point, the costs of benefits and cash compensation must be combined. This usually occurs after separate budgets for cash compensation and benefits are calculated. Not only must the costs associated with all compensation be generated, but the allocation of the organization's financial resources among the different forms of pay needs to be managed. Back in the first chapter, the need to better manage the allocation of financial resources among different pay forms was discussed. Particularly important is the proportion of labor costs allocated to performance and incentive-based pay compared to the proportion spent on entitlements, such as many services and benefits. The management of total compensation represents an important development in the field. The budgeting process, with its emphasis on cost controls and analysis of allocation of financial resources to different forms of pay, should play an increasingly important role in compensation management.[7]

Budgeting enables managers to foresee the financial impact of pay expenditures on the organization's performance. This encourages them to better manage the expenditures and distribution of compensation dollars.

Use of Computers

If you've been thinking to yourself during these various budgetary calculations, "there's got to be an easier way," you're right. Computer software is commercially available to analyze almost any aspect of compensation information you can think of.

Computers can provide analysis and data that will improve the administration of the pay system. For example, computers can easily check the accuracy of past estimates in comparison to what actually occurred (e.g., the percent of employees that actually did receive a merit increase, and the amount). Alternate

---

[6]Stephen Holoviak, *Costing Labor Contracts* (New York: Praeger Publishing, 1984); and Myron Gable and Stephen Holoviak, "Determining the Cost of Supplemental Benefits," *Compensation and Benefits Review,* September–October 1985, pp. 22–33.

[7]Robert E. Allen and Timothy J. Keaveny, "Costing Out a Wage and Benefit Package," *Compensation Review,* Second Quarter 1983, pp. 27–39; and Gable and Holoviak, "Determining the Cost of Supplemental Benefits."

wage proposals can be quickly simulated and their potential effects compared, using spreadsheet programs.

But computers have wider applications to compensation administration besides costing.[8] In fact, every aspect of compensation may benefit from computer applications. For example, we discussed computerized job analysis and job evaluation and its advantages over conventional methods. Software is also available to evaluate salary survey data and incentive and gain-sharing results.

So computers have become a tool and can aid the compensation professional in designing and managing the pay system to accomplish its objectives. This technology is changing the basic nature of compensation administration. More than ever, the compensation professional can focus on careful examination and analysis of the data—to ensure that the administration of the pay system is directed to the organization's goals and strategies.

The Role of Cost of Living

What role do changes in the cost of living play in determining the compensation budget or in making adjustments in pay? Note that both methods of top down budgeting consider changes in the cost of living when setting the planned level rise in average rates paid. While there is little research to support it, employees undoubtedly compare their pay increases to changes in their cost of living, and unions consistently argue that increasing living costs justify adjustments in pay.[9] So let's examine what the cost of living is, how it is measured, and its possible uses.

A distinction. First, it is important to distinguish among three related concepts: the cost of living, changes in prices in product and service markets, and changes in wages in labor markets. As Exhibit 15.10 shows, changes in wages in labor markets are measured through wage surveys. These changes are incorporated into the system through market adjustments in the budget and updating the policy line and range structure. The second concept, price changes of goods and services in product and service markets, is measured by several government indexes, one of which is the consumer price index. The third concept, the cost of living, is more difficult to measure. Employees' expenditures on goods and services depend on many things: marital status, number of dependents, ages of children, personal preferences, and so on. Different employees probably experience different costs of living, and the only accurate way to measure them is to examine the personal financial expenditures of each employee.

---

[8]James D. Finch, "Computerized Retrieval of Pay Survey Data," *Personnel Administrator,* July 1985, pp. 31–38.

[9]Daniel J. B. Mitchell, "Should the Consumer Price Index Determine Wages?" *California Management Review,* Fall 1982, pp. 5–19.

EXHIBIT 15.10
Three Distinct but Related Concepts and Their Measures

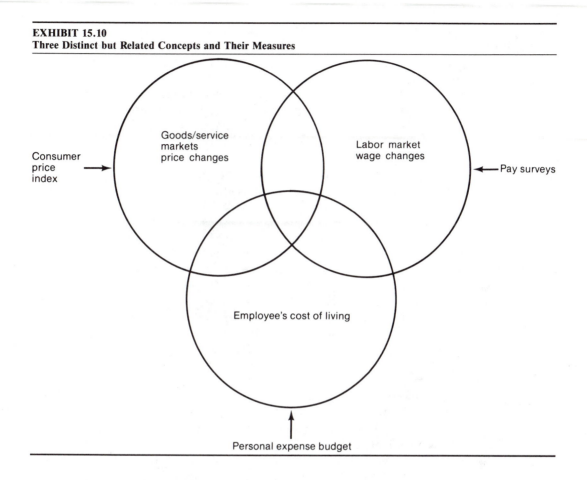

The three concepts are interrelated. Wages from the labor market are costs of producing goods and services, and changes in wages create pressures on prices. Similarly, changes in the prices of goods and services create needs for increased wages in order to maintain the same lifestyle. Most people refer to the consumer price index (CPI) as a "cost of living" index. Strictly speaking, it is not. Many employers choose, as a matter of pay policy or in response to union pressures, to tie wages to some measure of change in prices of goods and services. A measure commonly chosen is the CPI. But in doing so, employers are confounding the concepts of living costs and labor market costs. The CPI does not necessarily reflect an individual employee's cost of living.

What is the CPI? The consumer price index (CPI) measures changes over time in prices of a hypothetical market basket of goods and services. The present index is based on a 1972–73 study of the actual buying habits of 38,000 individuals. From this study, 265 categories of major expenditures were derived, and weights were assigned based on each category's percentage of total expenditures. For example, the index gives a weighting of 5.02 percent to auto purchases. This means that of the total money spent by all 38,000 people in the 1972–73 study, 5.02 percent of it was spent to buy new cars. This weighting plan measures both the price of cars and the frequency of new car purchases. To determine the new car component for today's CPI, today's price of a new car identically equipped to the one purchased in 1972–73 is multiplied by the factor weight of 5.02 percent. The result is called today's *market basket price* of a new car.

CPI figures are adjusted so that a base period of 1967 equals 100. For example, a CPI of 330 in 1987 indicates that it costs $330 in 1987 to buy the same goods and services that cost $100 in 1967.

Uses of the CPI. The CPI is the subject of public interest because changes in it trigger changes in employers' pay budgets, labor contracts, social security payments, federal and military pensions, and food stamp eligibility. One source estimates that over half the U.S. population is affected by payout changes tied to the CPI.[10] Tying budgets or payouts to the CPI is called indexing. Up until the mid-1960s, very little was indexed. By 1981 a 1 percent increase in the CPI triggered transfer payments and wage increases estimated at $2 billion.[11] In the mid-1980s, less rapid changes in prices, and even price decreases in some commodities, have lessened interest in the CPI. Still, its effects are substantial.

Geographical differences in the CPI. In addition to the national CPI, separate indexes are calculated monthly for five metropolitan areas and bimonthly for 23 other metropolitan areas and various regions.[12] These local CPIs typically are more variable than the national indexes. They do not, as some mistakenly believe, indicate whether prices are absolutely higher in a particular area. Changes in the CPI only indicate whether prices have increased more or less rapidly in an area since the base period. For example, a CPI of 210 in Chicago and 240 in Atlanta does not necessarily mean that it costs more to live in Atlanta. It does mean that prices have risen faster in Atlanta since the base year 1967 than they have in Chicago, since both cities had bases of 100 in 1967.

Thus far in this chapter we have examined the control process in pay systems. First we discussed some of the controls built into the various pay techniques during their design. Next, the formal budgetary process was examined.

---

[10] Jerry Newman, "The Consumer Price Index: Issues and Understanding," Paper presented at the American Compensation Association, National Conference, Scottsdale, Ariz., October 22, 1981.

[11] Alan S. Blinder, "The Consumer Price Index and the Measurement of Recent Inflation," in *Brookings Papers on Economic Activity* 2, eds. William C. Brainard and George L. Perry (Washington, D.C.: Brookings Institution, 1980).

[12] Mitchell, "Should the CPI Determine Wages?"

In the rest of the chapter, we will discuss other pay administration issues, beginning with reconsidering the notion of procedural equity and the need to evaluate the effectiveness of any pay system.

PROCEDURAL EQUITY

Earlier in this book, we stressed the importance of procedural equity—that employees must feel that the pay system is fair. Ensuring procedural equity is an integral part of the pay administration. Employees' perceptions about the pay system are shaped through the treatment they receive by managers, through the formal communication programs about pay, and through employee participation in various aspects of the design of the system. Additionally, there should be some way for employees to appeal the results of their treatment by the system. Communication and appeals procedures or "speak ups" are our next topics.

Communication

Salaries of the executives in publicly held corporations are published in annual financial reports. Similarly, collective bargaining agreements spell out in detail pay rates for covered employees. And if you know which budget books to examine, you can even find the salaries of most public officials. But these groups constitute only a fraction of all employees. Most employees are not told what their co-workers are being paid. The literature on compensation management usually exhorts employers to communicate pay information; however, there is no standard approach on what to communicate to individuals about their own pay or that of their colleagues.

Two reasons are usually given for communicating pay information. The first is that considerable resources have been devoted to design a fair and equitable system. For managers and employees to gain an accurate view of the pay system and perhaps influence their attitudes about it, they need to be informed.

The second reason is that according to some research, employees seem to misperceive the pay system.[13] For example, they tend to overestimate the pay of those with lower level jobs and to underestimate the pay of those in higher level jobs. In other words, they tend to think that the pay structure is more compressed than it actually is. What difference does this make? Consider the reason for pay differentials in the first place. They were designed to help motivate em-

---

[13]Thomas A. Mahoney and William Weitzel, "Secrecy and Managerial Compensation," *Industrial Relations* 17, no. 2 (1978), pp. 245–51; "Administering Pay Programs . . . An Interview with Edward E. Lawler III," *Compensation Review*, First Quarter 1977, pp. 8–16; and Julio D. Burroughs, "Pay Secrecy and Performance: The Psychological Research," *Compensation Review*, Third Quarter 1982, pp. 44–54.

ployees to seek promotions—to undertake the training, to gain the experience required, and to accept greater responsibilities. If differentials are underestimated, their motivational value is diminished.

Further, there is some evidence to suggest that the goodwill engendered by the act of being open about pay may also affect perceptions of pay equity.[14] Interestingly, the research also shows that employees in companies with open pay communication policies are as inaccurate in estimating pay differentials as those in companies where pay secrecy prevails. However, employees under open pay policies tend to express greater satisfaction with their pay and with the pay system. So there may be some goodwill engendered by the presence of a communication system, even if employees do not accurately translate communicated policy into actual salary results.

What to communicate. The first point to be made about pay communication is that if the pay system is not based on work-related or business-related logic, then the wisest course is probably to avoid formal communication until the system is put in order. In other words, pay secrecy may allow poor practices to go undetected, or at least unchallenged. However, avoiding *formal* communication is not synonymous with avoiding communication. Employees are constantly getting intended and unintended messages through the pay treatment they receive.

The second point is that achieving a fair and equitable pay system requires active involvement and feedback from managers and employees. An open policy helps ensure that employees understand how their pay is determined. The third point is that providing accurate pay information may cause some initial short-term concerns among employees. Over the years, employees probably have rationalized a set of relationships between their pay and the perceived pay and efforts of others. Receiving accurate data may require those perceptions to be adjusted.

Exhibit 15.11 is one major employer's communications policy. Many employers communicate the range for an incumbent's present job and for all the jobs in a typical career path or progression that employees can logically aspire to. This provides employees some means to judge their own pay. As job posting becomes more common, pay rates for a wider variety of jobs become more public. Often one practice is at odds with another, however. For example, some companies do not communicate ranges to job incumbents, but do list the ranges for vacant jobs in their job posting system. Incumbents in the posted job or related jobs simply go to the posting board to figure out their own ranges and how their pay corresponds to the posted range.

In addition to ranges, some employers communicate the typical pay increases that can be expected for poor, satisfactory, and top performance. The

---

[14]Ed Lawler III, "The New Pay," in *Current Issues in Human Resource Management,* eds. Sara L. Rynes and George T. Milkovich (Plano, Tex.: Business Publications, 1986), pp. 404–12.

EXHIBIT 15.11
Typical Communications Policy

Program Communications

A. To supervisors. New ranges and guides should be published to affected supervisors upon approval together with a memo explaining the change and outlining the program review, the changes made, the effective date, the new ranges and guides, and any instructions for communication to employees.

B. Supervisors should communicate to affected employees. Employees should understand that our salary ranges are reviewed periodically and that they are competitive with the market. They should be told the dollar value for their salary range and the A–B–C performance definitions. They should know the supervisor's evaluation of their performance—the reasons for his position in the range. Guides are not discussed.

---

rationale given is that employees exchange data (not always factual) and/or guess at normal treatment, and the rumor mills are probably incorrect. Providing accurate data may have a positive effect on employee work attitudes and behaviors. One potential danger in divulging increase schedule data is the inability to maintain that schedule in the future, for reasons outside the control of the compensation department (e.g., economic or product market conditions). The employee needs to be aware of this caveat. Nevertheless, pay increase data, coupled with performance expectations, should enhance employee motivation, which is a prime objective of the pay system.

Perhaps the most important information to be communicated is the work-related and business-related rationale on which the system is based. Some employees may not agree with these rationales or the results, but at least it will be clear that pay is determined by something other than the whims or biases of their supervisors.

Finally, it is doubtful that anyone will recall the detailed information provided. But at least they will know the data are available and the compensation department is one place to get it.

Proactive versus reactive. More often than not pay communication seems to be initiated in response to some challenge. Operating managers may question the results; employees may question their pay increase compared to the latest CPI figures; or minorities and women may take issue with their pay in comparison to the pay of white men.

Some pay professionals take a more proactive approach. They reason that a pay system, properly designed, is intended to influence employee work attitudes and behaviors. To help accomplish these objectives, managers' and employees' perceptions of the pay system need to be influenced; hence actively communicating about the system, its rationale, and its results is in order. And this communication should occur before challenges and misperceptions arise.

The benefits section of this book called out the legal requirements to communicate certain benefits provisions in the Employee Retirement and Income Security Act. The failure to understand benefit provisions is cited as one of the root causes of employee dissatisfaction with benefit packages.[15] Thus, information on the total pay system needs to be communicated to help achieve the pay system's objectives.

Communication and pay satisfaction. Managers who prefer to limit pay communication with employees implicitly assume that employees will become dissatisfied with their own pay if they obtain more information. But this assumption raises two issues. First, it indicates that managers believe their pay system treats employees inequitably or that the present system is not based on work-related logic. Second, research is not clear on how employees make pay comparisons. Most theories indicate that employees compare their pay with that of others around them. Their perceptions about what other employees are actually paid may or may not be accurate, but it is a factor in how employees feel about their own pay.

Most of the research on pay satisfaction and secrecy has concentrated on the accuracy of employees' judgments about the pay of their subordinates and superiors, and the correlation between this accuracy and pay satisfaction. The argument is that reduced secrecy will contribute to improved satisfaction. Not all researchers have found a consistent relationship between communication, accuracy of compensation perceptions, and pay satisfaction.[16] So communication by itself may not measurably contribute to pay satisfaction. Clearly, communicating cannot overcome indefensible pay practices. Pay satisfaction, as noted in various places in this book, is very complex. But if managers believe their pay system to be equitable and can demonstrate its work-related logic to employees, there is a strong likelihood of gaining employee acceptance and confidence by being open about it.

Appeals

Despite an organization's best attempts to help employees understand how their pay is set, employees sometimes feel they have been unjustly treated, either in assessing their own performance, in evaluating their job, or even in considering external competition. Disagreements over pay, or any part of the pay delivery system, can and do occur. Many organizations have designed procedures for handling these disagreements. These procedures provide a mechanism for em-

[15]Robert McCaffery, *Managing the Employee Benefits Program* (New York: AMACOM, 1983); and Chris Berger, "The Effects of Pay Level, Pay Values and Fringe Benefits on Pay Satisfaction," Working paper, Krannert School of Management, Purdue University, Lafayette, Indiana, 1983.

[16]E. E. Lawler and J. G. Rhode, *Information and Control in Organizations* (Santa Monica, Calif.: Goodyear Publishing, 1976); E. E. Lawler and G. D. Jenkins, *Employee Participation in Pay Planning,* Unpublished technical report to Department of Labor, Ann Arbor, Michigan, 1976; E. E. Lawler, *Pay and Organization Development* (Reading, Mass.: Addison-Wesley Publishing, 1981); and G. Douglas Jenkins, Jr., and Edward E. Lawler, "Impact of Employee Participation in Pay Plan Development," *Organizational Behavior and Human Performance* 28 (1981), pp. 111–28.

ployees and managers to voice their disagreements and receive a hearing. They help ensure that pay communication is a two-way process.

Employees who belong to a union collectively bargain some of their disagreements and take others through a formal grievance procedure.[17] "Voice" procedures designed for managerial, professional, and other nonunionized employees, especially for compensation questions, are typically less formal.

Types of appeals systems. The type of system an organization uses may depend on the types of problems it deals with and its compatibility with other organizational structures.

Procedures can vary on two dimensions:

1. **Degree of formality.** High formality means explicit statements concerning appealable issues, steps to follow, and roles and responsibilities of parties.
2. **Degree of independence from management.** Are workers forced to complain to their immediate superiors, or does the system use people further removed?[18]

Some organizations have several conflict resolution systems. In IBM's "Speak Up" program, employees may take their questions to their immediate managers or a manager one level beyond. Emphasis is on handling conflicts informally at first, but if the employee does not feel satisfied, more formal written complaints occur. Under IBM's "Open Door" program, employees are encouraged to write to any manager, including the chief executive. All letters are answered and responses are followed up with visits from employee relations professionals. IBM reports that both systems get amazingly heavy use by employees.

Participation of Managers and Employees

As far back as Chapter 1, this text emphasized manager and employee participation in designing pay systems as a means of gaining their acceptance and understanding of results. Most employers make use of compensation committees to review the results and recommendations of the compensation professionals. Membership on these committees varies, but they usually include key financial and operating managers. An example of a charter for one of these committees is in Appendix B to this chapter.

In addition to managers, employee participation may be beneficial. For example, employees may be asked to sign off on the analysis of their jobs, they

---

[17]Robert T. Boisseau and Harvey Caras, "A Radical Experiment Cuts Deep into the Attractiveness of Unions," *Personnel Administrator,* October 1983, pp. 76–79.

[18]John D. Aram and Paul F. Salipante, Jr., "An Evaluation of Organizational Due Process in the Resolution of Employee/Employer Conflict," *Academy of Management Review* 6, no. 2 (1981), pp. 197–204.

may serve on compensation task forces that select compensable factors, and they may indicate which employers they feel should be included in pay surveys. A growing number of employers offer employees some participation in the choice of benefits.

Lawler argues persuasively that employee participation can make a difference in the success of a pay system.[19] Focusing on performance-based pay systems, he cites two work groups doing the same kinds of jobs and operating under similar pay incentive plans. One group had high productivity that continued to increase; the other had low and stable productivity. The first group had a long history of participating in decision making and had voted on the incentive plan when it was first installed. The second group had no such participative history; their plan was imposed by management.

According to Lawler, a design process that includes employees can be quite successful in overcoming resistance to change. Accordingly, employees have more information about a plan and are more likely to believe a pay-performance relationship exists. Employees become committed to the plan; they have control over what happens; and they trust the system. Encouraging a cooperative rather than adversarial relationship is the goal of employee participation. The underlying premise is that such an atmosphere will better allow employees to perform their jobs and contribute a creative spark to the organization.

Another approach that some organizations have adopted to minimize divisions among employee groups and to engender a source of participation is the all-salaried work force.

All-Salaried Work Force

The all-salaried work force, an old concept, is being reexamined in light of the need to increase employee participation and commitment. The all-salaried concept includes removing all time clocks, equalizing benefits for all employees, and converting hourly pay rates to biweekly rates. The objective is to improve the employee's commitment to the work by adopting a more egalitarian approach to pay practices. The effects of an all-salaried approach have not been researched. Some claim labor costs will be reduced; however, equalizing fringes for all employees will probably raise benefit costs. Others claim the all-salaried concept is part of a broader effort to improve the climate of the organization. To overcome the potentially adversarial relationship that often arises between employee and employer, this improved climate, they claim, will in turn lead to increased worker participation, acceptance, and commitment.

In a recent study, TRW emphasized that the all-salaried program is part of a participative employee relations philosophy.[20] Such a philosophy goes beyond

---

[19]Jenkins and Lawler, "Impact of Employee Participation in Pay Plan Development."

[20]Ian Ziskin, "The All-Salaried Work Force," Report to Corporate Compensation Department, TRW, Cleveland, Ohio, 1982.

the pay system and requires adjustment in all human resource management systems. Foulkes observed, "The fact that all employees are paid by the same method is not the critical variable—rather, what is important is the climate of respect, trust, and confidence."[21]

STRUCTURING THE COMPENSATION FUNCTION

Compensation professionals seem to be constantly reevaluating where within the organization the responsibility for the design and administration of pay systems should be located. The organizational arrangements of the compensation function vary widely.[22]

An important issue related to structuring the function revolves around the degree of decentralization (or centralization) in the overall organization structure. *Decentralized* refers to a management strategy of giving separate organization units the responsibility to design and administer their own systems. This contrasts with a centralized strategy, which locates the design and administration responsibility in a single corporate unit. Some firms, such as Citibank and Pacific Gas and Electric, have relatively large corporate staffs whose responsibility it is to formulate pay policies and design the systems. Administration of these policies and systems falls to those working in various units, often personnel generalists. Such an arrangement runs the risk of formulating policies and practices that are well tuned to overall corporate needs but less well tuned to each unit's particular needs and circumstances. The use of task forces, with members drawn from the generalists in the affected units, to design new policies and techniques helps diminish this potential problem.

Other highly decentralized organizations, such as TRW and Honeywell, have relatively small corporate compensation staffs (two or three professionals). Their primary responsibility is to manage the systems by which executives and the corporate staff are paid. These professionals operate in a purely advisory capacity to other organization subunits. The subunits, in turn, may employ compensation specialists. Or the subunits may choose to employ only personnel generalists rather than compensation specialists, and may turn to outside compensation consultants to purchase the expertise required on specific compensation issues.

Another structural variation, found at Control Data Corporation and the newly reorganized AT&T, involves treating the corporate compensation function as internal consultants. As such, the pay professionals must market and "sell" their products and services to the operating units. Certain systems such as health and medical plans, pensions, and corporatewide profit sharing remain

---

[21]Fred K. Foulkes, *Personnel Policies in Large Nonunion Companies* (Englewood Cliffs, N.J.: Prentice-Hall, 1980), p. 203.

[22]J. R. Galbraith and D. A. Nathanson, *Strategy Implementation: The Role of Structure and Process* (St. Paul, Minn.: West Publishing, 1978).

under control of the corporate group. But the responsibility for other techniques, such as job analysis and evaluation, surveys, and pay structure design, are delegated to the units. The unit managers may decide to adopt corporate's services, design their own, or even use outside consultants.

Decentralizing certain aspects of pay design and administration has considerable appeal. Pushing these responsibilities (and expenses) closer to the units and managers affected by them may help ensure that decisions are business related. However, decentralization is not without dilemmas. For example, it may be difficult to transfer employees from one business unit to another. Problems adhere to policies which emphasize internal consistency and concerns for potential pay discrimination crop up. So, too, do problems of designing pay systems that support a subunit's objectives but run counter to the overall corporate objectives.

The answer to these and related problems of decentralization can be found in developing a set of corporatewide principles or guidelines which all must meet. These principles probably differ for each major pay technique. For example, a decentralized employer would permit different job evaluation approaches to be adopted by the units, as long as the principles of work relatedness, business relatedness, acceptability to managers and employees, cost effectiveness, and ability to withstand legal challenge were satisfied by the various unit plans.

Keep in mind that the pay system is one of many management systems used in the organization. Consequently, it must be congruent with these other systems. For example, it may be appealing, on paper at least, to decentralize some of the compensation functions. However, if financial data and other management systems are not also decentralized, the pay system will not fit and may even be at odds with other systems.

A final issue related to structuring the responsibility for pay design and administration involves the skills and abilities required in compensation professionals. The grandest strategy and structure may seem well designed, well thought out in the abstract, but could be a disaster if people qualified to carry it out are not part of the staff. Our earlier example in which the business subunits were staffed by personnel generalists who were not trained or prepared to design pay systems tailored to the unit's needs illustrates the point. So all three aspects of management—strategy, structure, and staffing—must be considered.

In view of the importance of a well-trained staff, Appendix A to this chapter discusses the American Compensation Association's professional development program in order to entice readers into the compensation field.

AUDITING AND EVALUATING THE SYSTEM

Evaluating the pay system is the last administrative issue to be discussed. No management system can maintain itself indefinitely. In fact, some argue that management systems need to be regularly destroyed and creatively redesigned.[23] According to this view, absent a built-in mechanism for system destruction, the system becomes bureaucratic turf to be defended. Its existence becomes the end rather than a means to achieving the organization's objectives. Constant monitoring is required to be sure techniques remain goal directed. Throughout the book, we have discussed indexes that may identify problems. Typically, the concerns have been with the pay objectives of equity and efficiency. In this section, we add monitoring the system for legal compliance.

Compliance objectives for the pay system carry with it the requirement that an organization monitor its pay system to ensure legal compliance. As you recall from the previous chapter, two basic standards of discrimination exist: disparate treatment and disparate impact. The disparate treatment standard outlaws the application of different standards to different classes of employees. Disparate impact outlaws practices that may appear to be neutral but have a negative effect on females or minorities, unless those practices can be shown to be business related. We can apply these two standards to our audit, also. Practices can be examined to ascertain any disparate treatment. Results can be examined for disparate impact.

Unequal Treatment

Auditing a pay system for unequal treatment is fairly straightforward. The criteria are outlined in the Equal Pay Act.

Each geographic location constitutes a separate "establishment." Analysis must be done for all protected groups and for all those jobs that the EPA defines as equal. Because disparate treatment affects *individual* employees rather than *classes* of employees, analysis should be done for all females and minorities. Hills and Bergmann recommend cohort analysis: treatment of individual employees who belong to protected groups is compared to treatment of white males hired at the same time into the same jobs.[24] If differences in pay exist, is there a legitimate reason (e.g., differences in seniority, merit, quantity or quality or production) or legally acceptable factors other than sex?

Exhibit 15.12 shows IBM's Salary Equity Analysis, carried out every six months for all minorities and females. While each facility is responsible for its own analysis, each division reviews the facility data, and corporate headquarters reviews division data. The exhibit shows the criteria IBM uses to define a peer for cohort analysis and the various comparisons that are examined (e.g., current salary, percent of last pay increase, and the timing of that increase).

---

[23]Joseph A. Schumpeter, *Capitalism, Socialism and Democracy,* 4th ed. (London: Allen and Unwin, 1954).

[24]Frederick S. Hills and Thomas J. Bergmann, "Conducting an Equal Pay for Equal Work Audit," in *Perspectives on Compensation,* eds. L. Gomez-Mejia and D. Balkin (Englewood Cliffs, N.J.: Prentice-Hall, 1987).

EXHIBIT 15.12
IBM Equity Analysis

Individual Minority/Female Data Sheet

- Minority/female comparison versus peers
    Same EEO job category
    Same IBM salary level
    Same appraisal
    Same time in IBM salary level (six months)
- Primary comparisons
    Current salary comparison
    Percent of last increase
    Timing of increase
- Additional analysis
    Length of service
    Time in previous level
    Level jump factor
    Appraisal history
    Leave of absence in level

Salary Equity Measurement Criteria

When comparing individual minority/female salaries to those of peer groups, we must demonstrate:
1. An equitable relationship—minorities' and females' salary equal to or greater than the average salary of peers.
2. An understanding of the reason(s) for a relationship less than stated in 1 above.
3. Action is taken where warranted.

IBM defines an equitable pay relationship as one in which the salary of minorities and females is *equal to or greater than* the average salary of their peers. If no such equity exists, IBM wants to know why, and what action, if warranted, will be taken to correct the relationship.

Unequal Impact

Elements of a pay system that have unequal impact on protected classes of employees must be business related. Although the notion of disparate impact has been promulgated by the courts in other personnel areas (testing, hiring, etc.), they have been slower to address compensation applications. Cases have tended to focus on job evaluation and have ignored other elements of the pay system. It would seem logical that employers, and perhaps eventually the courts, would examine all aspects of pay setting for any disparate impact. An unresolved difficulty is separating the effects of one pay practice from those of another. While this difficulty may make the disparate impact standards impossible to satisfy in a court of law, the notion of disparate impact can still guide compensation professionals in analyzing the results of their decisions.

Overall Evaluation

Beyond legal compliance, evaluation serves to assess how well the pay system and its policies achieve specified pay objectives. Evaluation also serves to provide feedback by identifying problem areas and directing future development and design efforts. While most professionals and researchers advocate evaluating pay systems, very little attention has been devoted to how to do it.

The effectiveness of the pay system depends on a variety of factors. Perhaps the most obvious are measures of the specific pay objectives such as those suggested in the pay model used in this book. We have already discussed the objective of regulatory compliance. Equity and efficiency are the other two broad objectives in the pay model. Obtaining measures of these two requires developing an information system that generates such indexes as turnover rates of high performers (retention), job acceptance to job offer ratios (attraction), promotion offers to promotion acceptances (willingness to take on more responsibility), unit productivity, unit labor costs, support staff salaries to total sales ratios, and so on. Similarly, it means comparing such indexes as a unit's compa-ratio to the turnover rates of employees rated satisfactory or better, and the rate of change in salaries to the rate of change in earnings, or return on investments.

Another factor to assess in evaluating the pay system is the reactions of the clients or users of the system. In her research on organization effectiveness, Tsui has designed a process for evaluating the personnel function in terms of its various constituencies.[25] Operating managers' appraisals of the various pay techniques as tools to aid their decision making is often revealing feedback. This is done informally in most organizations, although Tsui advocates a more systematic approach.

Another constituency of the pay system is the work force. Employees' acceptance of their pay and the pay system is vital for pay effectiveness. Surveys of employees' work attitudes are common, and usually a few items in the survey are related to pay. However, employers frequently use surveys the way a drunk uses a lamppost: for support, rather than illumination. Most surveys of pay satisfaction miss the mark as diagnostic devices. To be useful, the questions need to focus on specific pay techniques and on perceptions of various aspects of equity rather than satisfaction. Some employers use "sensing sessions" in which small groups of employees are regularly interviewed on a wide range of issues. Pay administrators need to be involved in this process also.

SUMMARY

We have now completed the discussion of the pay administration process. Administration includes control: control of the way managers decide individual employees' pay as well as control of overall costs of labor. As we noted, some controls are designed into the fabric of the pay system (inherent controls, range

---

[25]Ann S. Tsui and Debbie Hirsch, *Research on Personnel/Human Resources Department Effectiveness: A Review and an Approach,* Fuqua School of Business, Duke University, Durham, N.C., working paper, September 1982.

maxima and minima, etc.). The salary budgeting and forecasting processes impose additional controls. The formal budgeting process focuses on controlling labor costs and generating the financial plan for the pay system. The budget sets the limits within which the rest of the system operates.

Other aspects of administration we examined in this chapter included procedural equity, the fair treatment of employees in communications, participation, and appeals processes. Finally we considered the "creative destruction and redesign" of pay systems. The basic point was that pay systems are tools, and like all tools, they need to be evaluated in terms of usefulness in achieving an organization's objectives.

REVIEW QUESTIONS

1. How does the nature of the administration of the pay system affect the pay objectives?
2. What difference does it make how a compensation function is structured?
3. Give some examples of uses of inherent controls.
4. Why is it important to manage labor costs?
5. Who should participate in pay administration? Why?
6. What would you recommend that employees be told about their pay? Under what circumstances would you vary your advice?

Appendix A

Two Compensation Professional Training Programs

AMERICAN COMPENSATION ASSOCIATION CERTIFICATION PROGRAM

ACA is a nonprofit organization for professionals engaged in the design, implementation, and management of employee compensation programs. The certification program is specifically designed to develop professional competencies and qualify participants for designation as a Certified Compensation Professional (CCP).

The program presently includes nine courses, each dealing with a specific body of knowledge associated with compensation practice and theory. Written examinations evaluate an individual's mastery of the content. Certification is earned by scoring 75 percent or better on examinations for courses I through IV, and one additional examination chosen from courses V through IX. These requirements must be completed within a 48-month period.

It is not necessary to enroll in a course to take an examination. Effort has been made to ensure that the examinations test a body of knowledge that does not require a commitment to specific methodologies or philosophies of compensation practice. Participants who fail to pass an examination are required to wait six months before retesting for that particular course.

Each course is offered several times a year in various cities under the direction of practitioners and educators from throughout the country.

Both ACA members and nonmembers are eligible to participate in the certification program. Members, however, receive reduced rates for registration. Schedule and course registration information is available from American Compensation Association, P.O. Box 1176, Scottsdale, Arizona 85252.

ACA's board of directors have approved a statement which presents standards of professional conduct for association members. It states:

> As a member of the American Compensation Association, I will conduct myself in a manner consistent with the following principles while performing professionally related activities:

- To practice the highest standards of integrity in my relationships with my employer, and in my business dealings with other individuals in the field.
- To maintain the highest standards of confidentiality with respect to information entrusted to me and in my dealings with others in the field.
- To recognize the proprietary interest of the Association in the use of its name, symbols, accreditation and copyrights.
- To ensure that my professional affiliations are not used improperly to secure personal advantage or to promote personal business interests.
- To accept my obligation to foster the programs which recognize the individual rights, privileges, contributions, and opportunities without regard to race, religion, creed, national origin, sex, age or nonrelevant physical/mental handicaps.
- To accept my obligation to support the purpose and objectives of ACA as delineated in the Constitution.

This code of standards has been adopted to promote and maintain the highest levels of ethical conduct in the compensation profession. Adherence to these standards is required for membership in ACA.

PERSONNEL ACCREDITATION INSTITUTE

The Institute is a nonprofit organization formed for the purpose of accrediting professionals in the personnel and human resources field.

Accreditation is based on mastery of a body of knowledge as demonstrated by passing a comprehensive written examination, and varying amounts of full-time professional experience in the field as a practitioner, consultant, educator, or researcher. Accreditation is granted at the specialist and generalist roles and at the basic and advanced levels. Individuals must currently be serving in the role appropriate to the type of accreditation they seek. Accreditation can be changed or upgraded as roles change and experience accumulates. Compensation and benefits is listed as a functional area of accreditation for both the specialist and the generalist. A generalist must also pass an examination on five other areas in order to demonstrate broad knowledge, whereas the specialist is expected to possess greater in-depth knowledge. The testing program is administered by the Professional Examinations Division of the Psychological Corporation. Information and application materials are obtained from the Personnel Accreditation Institute, P.O. Box 170, Berea, Ohio 44017.

Appendix B

Salaried Compensation Committee Charter

I. Introduction

This charter provides a guideline for the formulation and operation of the compensation committee.

A. Purpose

The purpose of the salaried compensation committee is to serve as a policy advisory resource to the company and to the personnel committee of the board of directors regarding direct and indirect compensation on a continuous basis.

B. Membership

The committee will consist of six members including: president, vice president human resources, vice president planning and control, vice president international and distributing, vice president equipment group, vice president recreational products group, and vice president irrigation group. The committee will be chaired by the vice president human resources, and the administrative support will be provided by the director, compensation and organizational planning.

C. Administration

The director, compensation and organizational planning, will serve as the administrative resource for the committee by providing internal and external statistics, reports, and recommendations in order to formulate compensation policy recommendations. He will provide the agenda for meetings and will be responsible for preparing and distributing minutes of the meetings.

II. Authority and responsibility

A. Level

The primary responsibility of the salaried compensation committee is to recommend direct and indirect compensation policy applicable to all nonunion employees. It may review and compare internal and external pay relationships, wage and salary structure relationships, policies and

561

internal and external benefit compensation systems, and make appropriate recommendations to the personnel committee of the board of directors or to the human resource department to implement decisions.

  B. Areas

    Major areas of responsibility are:

    1. Management incentive compensation policy.

    2. Perquisite pay policy.

    3. Wage and salary administration policy.

    4. Wage and salary grade and range structure review and recommendation.

    5. Employee benefit policy.

    6. Job evaluation policy.

III. Committee timing and action calendar

  A. April—Annual review of employee benefits. This review will include.

    1. Evaluation of report of cost of employee benefits by benefit category for previous year.

    2. Review of the cost/benefit value of each employee benefit and the competitiveness of each benefit.

    3. Evaluate and recommend possible changes in employee benefits.

  B. June

    1. Set new incentive base and targets for the new fiscal year.

    2. Recommend the final merit budgets for the following year and the merit performance percentage guidelines.

    3. Recommend any changes in the wage and salary structure.

  C. August

    1. Recommend any special incentive compensation awards which are appropriate.

    2. Review a summary report of results of compensation actions for the fiscal year just ended including salary and incentive payouts. The evaluation should include an analysis of the relationship of the payout to performance for both base and bonus compensation.

Chapter *16*

Compensation of Special Groups

After attending a job-enrichment seminar, a sales supervisor decided that some of the suggested techniques could help combat the productivity problem in his sales force. He invited one of his salespeople to his office and told him that he now would be allowed to plan, carry out, and control his own job. The wanted "satisfiers" would be introduced into the man's job.

The salesman asked if he would get more money. The supervisor replied, "No. Money is not a motivator, and you will not be satisfied if I give you more pay."

Once again the employee asked, "Well, if I do what you want, will I get more pay?"

The supervisor answered, "No. You need to understand the motivation theory. Take this book home and read it. Tomorrow we'll get together and I'll explain once again what will really motivate you."

As the man was leaving, he turned back and asked, "Well, if I read this book, will I get more money?"

Ａs the above story suggests, there are some employees for whom "new fangled" sources of job rewards are inappropriate. In contrast to these employees are special groups for whom compensation practices diverge from typical company procedures. In all cases these special practices have been strategically developed to meet unique compensation needs. This does not suggest that the compensation model becomes inoperative, however. Rather, one or more of the internal, external, or individual dimensions stressed in this book must be specially "tuned" for the groups discussed in this section. This chapter is designed to outline the foundations of, and techniques for, compensating these special groups. Exhibit 16.1 identifies the special groups that will be covered and illustrates the compensation challenges which must be met. The following sections discuss compensation practices designed by companies to meet the special needs of these groups.

EXHIBIT 16.1
Compensation Challenges for Special Groups

Group	*Strategic Compensation Challenges*
Supervisors	"In-the-middle" position with often conflicting duties of meeting employee needs and satisfying upper management directives. Exempt status of job may result in no overtime pay. This inequity must be recognized by developing salary differentials with subordinates.
Middle and upper management	Organizational profits presumed to be highly dependent upon quality of performance of these key decision makers. Incentive systems designed to increase motivation viewed as highly important.
Nonsupervisory professional employees	Viewed as highly mobile group with allegiances more to their profession than to any organization. Special emphasis on compensation strategies that will help to retain these employees. Payment also based on special knowledge acquired through extensive education. Compensation relative to that of managers and relative to that of younger peers with more timely (less obsolete) knowledge are particularly important concerns.
Sales personnel	Jobs often unsupervised and especially dependent upon compensation strategies designed to develop and maintain high motivational levels.
Foreign service personnel	Work in foreign countries subject to different cultural, legal, and compensation customs. Geographic distance from domestic operations requires employees capable of exercising greater independence. Equity between foreign and U.S. employees must be balanced against "normal" pay scales in area surrounding foreign subsidiary.

SUPERVISORS

Supervisors, as has been noted many times, are caught in the classic "middle" position. On one hand they must respond to the needs and distinct personalities/skills of their subordinates. In doing this, however, they must satisfy the overriding goals of higher level management. Balancing these (at times) conflicting objectives effectively is essential to any organization.

Compensation of supervisory personnel takes on special importance largely because of a need to preserve equity. Attraction and retention of supervisory personnel depend heavily on a compensation system that recognizes the value differential between a subordinate line position and that of a supervisor. Identifying an appropriate wage differential that rewards workers for assuming supervisory responsibilities, yet does not lead to compression with middle manager salary levels, is the key to this problem.

In a survey of supervisory pay practices for 88 companies, three strategies were used to maintain appropriate supervisor/subordinate differentials.[1] First, the vast majority of companies surveyed (76 of 88) used some form of job evaluation plan to evaluate and place supervisory jobs into pay grades. A major factor in this effort to "slot" supervisory jobs into pay grades is a recognition of the importance of pay differentials. A large majority of the companies ($n = 63$) key base rates of supervisory pay to the base rate of subordinates. The range of differentials reported varied from a low of $+5$ percent to a maximum of $+35$ percent. The most common differential ($n = 29$) was $+15$ percent. The most common target goal was to ensure that the pay of supervisors was 15 percent above the take-home of their highest-paid subordinate.

The second practice to ensure equity of supervisory pay deals with the overtime issue. Approximately 50 percent (47 of 88) of the companies surveyed pay a premium for scheduled overtime.[2] This ensures that the target 15 percent differential is maintained even when subordinates receive legally mandated overtime premiums. (Note: the Fair Labor Standards Act excludes supervisors from the overtime premium provision.)

A third practice targeted at supervisory employees includes incentive and bonus payments. This practice is far less common than the previous two, however, with only 11 percent of the companies reporting bonus and incentive systems directed specifically at supervisory employees.[3]

The key to adequate supervisory compensation appears to be effective monitoring of the differential between supervisors and subordinates. Decreases in

[1]Ernest C. Miller, "Setting Supervisors' Pay and Pay Differentials," *Compensation Review* 11 (Third Quarter 1978), pp. 26–36.

[2]Item, "Supervisory Overtime, Incentive, and Bonus Practices," *Compensation Review* 11 (Fourth Quarter 1978), pp. 12–25.

[3]Miller, "Setting Supervisors' Pay and Pay Differentials."

the historical differential or evidence of declining supervisory morale (e.g., turnover, increased refusal rate for supervisory jobs) should be signals to reevaluate supervisory pay practices.

NONSUPERVISORY PROFESSIONAL EMPLOYEES

Following closely the Fair Labor Standards Act of 1938, a professional is defined here as a person who must have specialized training of a scientific or intellectual nature and whose major duties do not entail the supervision of people. In part, the special distinction of this group is their preference for compensation systems that recognize personal attributes rather than job characteristics. According to a survey of 100 large firms, this leads to two distinct types of compensation systems for professional employees.[4] The first type of system is characterized by relatively few professional employees. The small proportion of professionals precludes a separate compensation mechanism. Rather, professionals are incorporated into the existing job evaluation system for exempt employees. In contrast, slightly less than one half (44 percent) of the surveyed firms reported some use of what is called a dual-track system.

A dual-track system is defined as:[5]

> A distinct framework within the formal compensation policy of a given organization whereby at least two general tracks of ascending compensation steps are available to exempt employees: (1) a "managerial" track to be ascended through increasing responsibility for supervision or direction of people, and (2) a "professional track" to be ascended through increasing contributions of a professional nature which do not mainly entail the supervision or direction of people.

With few exceptions, a dual-track system seems to be confined to organizations that have large numbers of professional employees.[6]

The compensation mechanism in a dual-track system recognizes an inherent distinction in the type of contribution made by professionals versus other exempt employees. For example, consider the rather simple dual-track system shown in Exhibit 16.2. Two distinct career ladders emerge for professionals beyond the second level: a managerial track and a professional track. Efforts are made to continue salary equivalencies across tracks at the same level, but there are apparent limitations on the maximum advancement of a professional without movement into a management position. In fact the maximum salary of a

---

[4]John W. Crim, *Compensating Nonsupervisory Professional Employees* (Ann Arbor, Mich.: UMI Research Press, 1978).

[5]Analog Devices, *Parallel Ladder Program and New Products Bonus Program* (Norwood, Mass.: Analog Devices, 1985); Crim, *Compensating Nonsupervisory Professional Employees.*

[6]Crim's research shows that all but one company with a dual-track system had 800 or more professional employees.

EXHIBIT 16.2
Industrial Research Institute Ladders

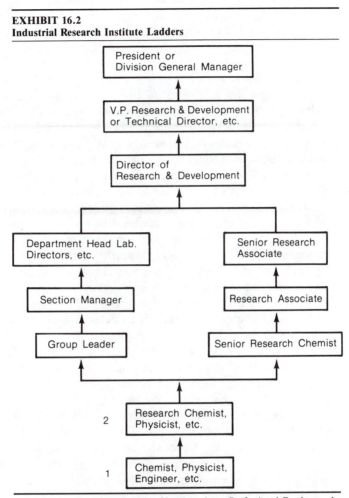

Source: From *Compensating Nonsupervisory Professional Employees,* by John W. Crim. Research for Business Decisions Series No. 8. UMI Research Press, Ann Arbor, MI 48106, 1978.

professional typically peaks at about 30 percent (range: 10 percent to 65 percent) of the chief executive officer's salary.[7]

Up to this point little mention has been made of how professional salaries are actually derived. The answer to this question has two dimensions. First, recognize that engineering, scientific, and technical employees are most likely to be employed in high technology firms. These firms have generated some dis-

---

[7]Crim, *Compensating Nonsupervisory Professional Employees.*

tinctive compensation practices to attract, retain, and motivate the employees whose technical skills are so vital to success in these volatile product markets. One recent survey of these high technology firms indicates that they focus on three reward mechanisms.[8] First, incentive pay has a larger role than in more traditional firms, with a stronger emphasis placed on bonuses, profit sharing, and employee stock ownership plans. Incentives are most often triggered by technological advances and other innovations which impact on the bottom line. Second, special incentives and reward packages are designed specifically for key contributors, recognizing that one significant technological breakthrough can mean millions of dollars to the firm. Finally, as noted earlier, special attention is paid to designing dual-career paths which recognize the separate and distinctive contributions of professional and scientific personnel.

Even in firms which are not in high technology markets, though, there may exist substantial populations of scientific and engineering personnel. Regardless of industry, a common strategy for these groups is to base pay on maturity curves. As Exhibit 16.3 notes, maturity curves plot the empirical relationship between pay and years since a professional has last received a degree (YSLD). Organizations send out salary surveys asking for the current pay and YSLDs of engineers within the responding organizations. The resulting plot of points (or best-fit line) allows organizations to determine a competitive wage level for engineers with varying levels of experience since the last degree was received.

Two points should be noted about these curves (Exhibit 16.3). First, note from the slope of the curve that initial salary increments are quite rapid (typically in the range of 10 to 15 percent/year) and fall off rapidly after 15 to 20 years (0 to 5 percent/year). The differential size of these increases reflects the time it typically takes for obsolescence to occur. Presumably the value of professionals rests largely upon their special expertise. As this expertise becomes more and more dated, the corresponding yearly raises decrease in magnitude. Absent any effort to move into a managerial progression ladder, the salary increments for a professional become smaller over time.

A second point to note is that maturity curves can be designed also to reward merit. Organizations with this objective would seek salary information by YSLD broken down by performance level. Such data might yield separate maturity curves for pricing, by performance level (Exhibit 16.3).

MIDDLE AND TOP MANAGEMENT

Middle and top management employees may be classified as special groups for the purposes of compensation to the extent the organization devises special compensation programs to attract, retain, and motivate this relatively scarce human resource. By this definition, not all managers above the supervisory level

---

[8]David Balkin and Luis Gomez-Mejia, "Compensation Practices in High Technology Industries," *Personnel Administrator* 30 (June 1985), pp. 111–23.

EXHIBIT 16.3
Engineering Employees by Years since Last Degree and Weekly Base Salary

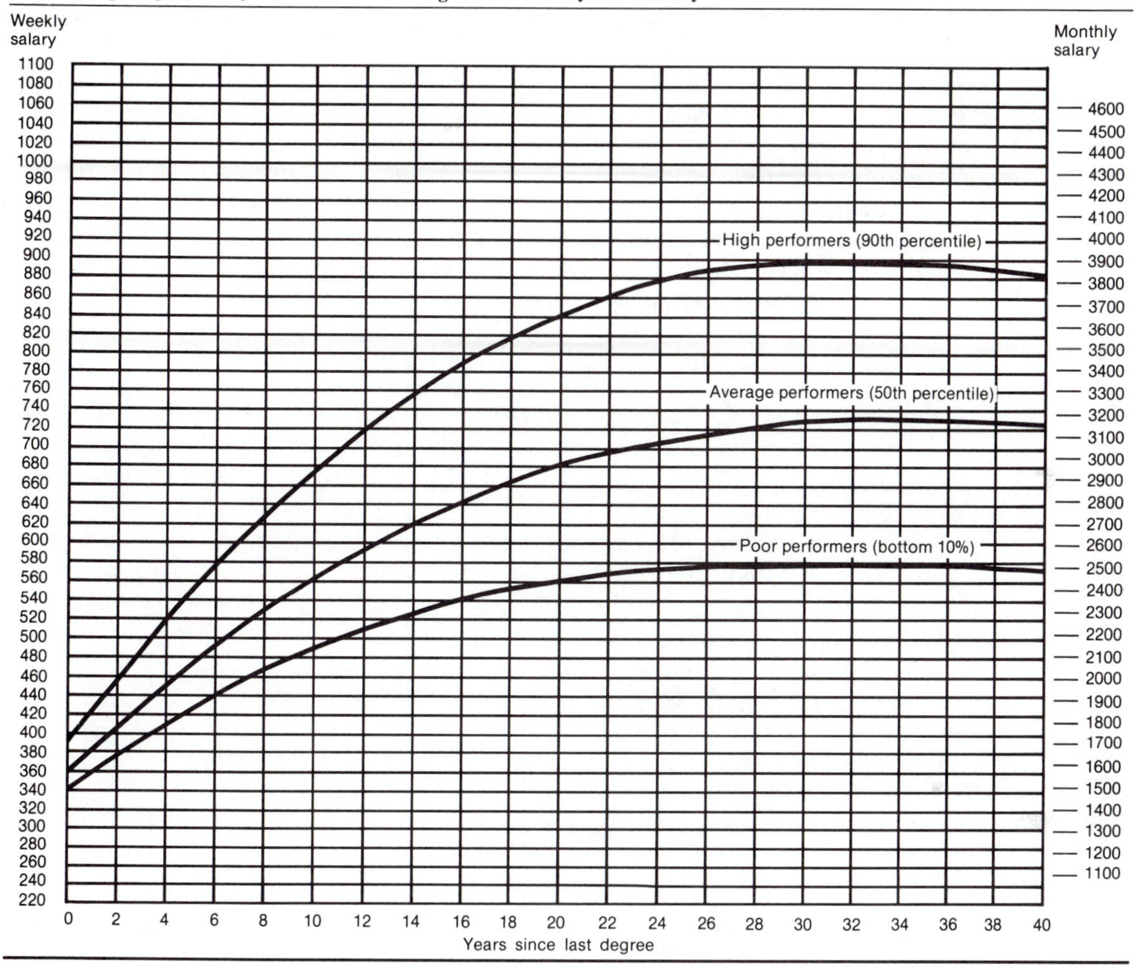

would qualify for consideration as special groups. It is not at all unusual to find middle managers' salaries determined on the basis of a companywide job evaluation system or on the basis of a job evaluation system for all exempt employees. However, at some level in the organization hierarchy pay practices for managers/executives typically deviate from traditional company practices. Generally these special practices incorporate the top 1 to 10 percent of the exempt work force.[9]

---

[9]Thomas H. Patten, Jr., *Pay: Employee Compensation and Incentive Plans* (New York: Free Press, 1977).

The major point of deviation in pay practices for this group is tied to the role of the competitive market.[10] Because the performance of these executives plays a major role in the performance of the organization, retention (avoidance of loss to a competitor being not the least of the retention issues) and motivation become particularly important. One requirement for achieving these goals is a salary that is competitive externally. Consequently many compensation experts agree that executive compensation, in contrast to compensation for lower level jobs, is less likely to be based on maintenance of internal relationships/equity (e.g., based on job evaluation) and more likely to be based on a market competitive rate. It would be foolish, however, to conclude that executive pay should be derived blindly from competitive salary survey data without first understanding the mechanisms and decisions which lead to the final dollar figure.

Conceptual/Empirical Perspectives on Executive Pay

There are at least two dominant theoretical explanations for the level of executive pay, one coming from the sociological literature and the other from neoclassical economic theory. From a sociological perspective, Simon argues that executive salaries can be explained by a unique blending of market forces and company customs regarding appropriate salary differentials between organizational levels.[11] Simon hypothesizes that salaries of low-level executives are determined by competitive market forces. In turn, salaries of higher level executives are "pegged" from these benchmarks, following widespread norms about appropriate salary differentials between organization levels.

In fact, there have been numerous studies documenting Simon's contention that there is a relatively stable relation among the salaries at different organizational levels.[12] Finkin, for example, argues that Exhibit 16.4 illustrates a good rule-of-thumb estimate of subordinate salaries in relation to the chief executive officer (CEO) of industrial corporations.

EXHIBIT 16.4
Pay Relationships in Organizations

Level	Salary as Percentage of CEO Salary
CEO	100
Executive vice president	72
Group vice president	52
Managers	35

[10]Ernest C. Miller, "How Companies Set Top and Middle Management Salaries . . . A Compensation Review Symposium," *Compensation Review* 10 (First Quarter 1977), pp. 15–29.

[11]Herbert A. Simon, *Administrative Behavior,* 2nd. ed. (New York: Macmillan, 1957).

[12]Eugene F. Finkin, "How to Figure Our Executive Compensation," *Personnel Journal* 57 (July 1978), pp. 371–75; Thomas A. Mahoney, "Organizational Hierarchy and Position Worth," *Academy of Management Journal* 22, no. 4 (1979), pp. 726–37.

EXHIBIT 16.5
Ratio of Subordinate Salaries to CEO Salary in Six Industries

	Retail Trade	Manufacturing	Banking	Construction	Gas and Electric	Insurance
CEO salary	100	100	100	100	100	100
Second highest-paid executive	72	68	68	77	58	67
Third highest-paid executive	59	53	52	61	54	54

Note: Chairman of the board and president are separate positions.

A more systematic description of this relationship also appears in The Conference Board's report on executive compensation.[13] Exhibit 16.5 indicates the ratio of subordinate salary to CEO salary for the top three organizational levels in various types of industries.

The second explanation of executive salaries comes from neoclassical economic theory, and actually complements the sociological explanation rather than contradicting it. The focus here is on explaining the level of executive salaries rather than the differential among salaries at different organizational levels. The premise is that the marginal productivity of the chief executive officer varies directly with some measure of company size (e.g., profitability, sales, number of employees).[14] Intuitively, this explanation makes sense. Presumably CEOs in larger companies are paid more because their jobs are more difficult and demanding.

Numerous studies have been done in the past 20 years demonstrating the relationship between company size and the pay of top executives with direct responsibility for organizational effectiveness.[15] (Note: the key here is the prediction of salaries for top executives who have *direct responsibility* for organizational performance, whether it be control of a total organization or an independent profit center.) The approach is not particularly effective for prediction of salaries for lower executives who do not have control over decision making. Hence, the sociological model discussed earlier may be more appropriate for identification of differentials in salaries for subordinates once CEO salaries have been identified. For example, The Conference Board regressed CEO salary against company sales and found between 12 and 15 percent of the variance in

---

[13]Harland Fox and Charles Peck, *Top Executive Compensation: 1986* (New York: The Conference Board, 1985), report no. 875.

[14]D. Roberts, *Executive Compensation* (New York: Free Press, 1958); J. R. Dekcop and T. A. Mahoney, "The Economics of Executive Compensation," Paper presented at the 42nd National Academy of Management Meetings, New York, 1982.

[15]Marc J. Wallace, "Type of Control, Industrial Concentration, and Executive Pay," *Academy of Management Proceedings,* 1976, pp. 284–88; W. Lewellen and B. Huntsman, "Managerial Pay and Corporate Performance," *American Economic Review* 60 (1970), pp. 710–20; CompFlash, "More Proof Positive: Top Executive Pay Is Tied to Performance," *CompFlash* 84–8 (1984), p. 1.

CEO pay accounted for by company size (measured in sales) in different indus-tries.[16]

More recent studies attempting to identify the linkage between executive pay and performance have concluded that the relationship is clouded by other factors.[17] Generally these studies focus on the type of controls and pressures ex-erted on the chief executive. For example, one study distinguished between firms with a dominant stockholder and those with control spread among a large number of investors. Where dominant stockholders prevailed there was signifi-cantly more emphasis on paying for executive performance and less compensa-tion for the scale of operations (e.g., number of employees or dollar sales).[18] Reasoning that dominant stockholders view the firm primarily as an invest-ment, this view suggests that a dominant shareholder commands both the power and incentive to force direct ties of executive compensation and organizational performance.

Current variants on this research suggest that chief executive officers (CEOs) don't always act functionally rational, that political considerations sometimes dominate over purely economic motives. According to this argu-ment, CEOs have a diversity of goals for the firm, some of which conflict with the profit motive.[19] For example, CEOs perform political/symbolic roles in their interactions with the external environment.[20] Managing political coalitions within and outside the organization may have short-term and even long-term ef-fects on traditional performance measures. To the extent political roles of CEOs don't converge with profit maximization responsibilities, though, it may be in-appropriate to measure CEO performance on exclusively economic variables.

The stakes are not small in this effort to document and potentially strengthen the linkage between executive pay and performance. Recent evidence indicates stockholder and general public criticism of executive compensation levels is ris-ing.[21] Some individuals arm their arsenal of complaints with such spectacular data as the salaries of the top paid executives in the United States: T. Boone

---

[16]Fox and Peck, *Top Executive Compensation: 1986.*

[17]M. J. Wallace, "Impact of Type of Control and Industrial Concentration on Size and Profit-ability in Determination of Executive Income," unpublished dissertation, University of Minnesota, 1973; Luis Gomez-Mejia, Henry Tosi, and Timothy Hinkin, "Effect of Managerial Control and Performance on Executive Compensation," working paper, January 1985; K. R. Murphy and M. Salter, "Should CEO Pay Be Linked to Results?" *Harvard Business Review* 53, no. 3 (1975), pp. 66–73.

[18]Gomez-Mejia, Tosi, and Hinkin, "Effect of Managerial Control and Performance on Execu-tive Compensation."

[19]J. Pfeffer, *Power in Organizations* (Marshfield, Mass.: Pitman Publishing, 1981); Gerardo Rivera Ungson and Richard Steers, "Motivation and Politics in Executive Compensation," *Academy of Management Review* 9, no. 2 (1984), pp. 313–23.

[20]Ungson and Steers, "Motivation and Politics in Executive Compensation."

[21]"Big Executive Bonuses Now Come with a Catch: Lots of Criticism," *The Wall Street Jour-nal,* May 15, 1985, p. 35.

EXHIBIT 16.6
Top Executive Salaries by Industry, 1980 and 1984 *(thousands of dollars)**

Industry	1980	1984
Aerospace	$469	$671
Automotive	486	872
Banks	482	641
Chemicals	465	666
Drugs	506	685
Natural resources	563	835
Computers	557	651
Publishing, broadcasting	462	631
Retailing	305	497
Utilities	na†	na†

*Excluding long-term compensation.
†na = Not available.
Source: "Big Executive Bonuses Now Come with a Catch: Lots of Criticism," *The Wall Street Journal,* May 15, 1985, p. 35. Reprinted by permission of *The Wall Street Journal,* © Dow Jones & Company, Inc., May 15, 1985. All rights reserved.

Pickens (total annual compensation equals $22.8 million—Mesa Petroleum) and David Jones (total annual compensation equals $18.2 million—Humana).[22] Less spectacular, but still impressive, are CEO salaries by industry. Exhibit 16.6 illustrates these figures for 1980 and 1984.

It is difficult to determine whether criticisms of CEO salaries are justified. For example, it could be argued that comparably responsible union jobs are paid substantially less. One source estimates that the job of a union president is roughly comparable to that of a human resources vice president at companies with up to $5 billion in annual revenues.[23] Such executives typically earn $90,000 to $140,000 per year. By this standard, the presidents of the autoworkers and the steelworkers are underpaid (e.g., Owen Bieber, president of the UAW, earned $72,704 in 1983).[24]

Whether or not this criticism is justified may be irrelevant. The simple fact is, there have already been ramifications! In early 1985 the Reagan administration lifted import restraints on Japanese cars. The administration reasoned that the large prevailing executive bonuses could be interpreted only as evidence that the auto industry no longer needed special assistance to compete internationally! The next section examines the elements of an executive compensation package, one component of which is the annual bonus.

---

[22]"Executive Pay: Who Made the Most?" *Business Week,* May 6, 1985, pp. 78–103.

[23]CompFlash, "Compared with Business Executives, Union Leaders Underpaid," *AMA CompFlash* 84-8 (1984), p. 4.

[24]Ibid.

Components of an Executive Compensation Package

There are five basic elements of most executive compensation packages: (1) base salary, (2) short-term (annual) incentives or bonuses, (3) long-term incentives and capital appreciation plans, (4) employee benefits, and (5) perquisites.[25] Because of the changing nature of tax legislation, each of these at one time or another has received considerable attention in designing executive compensation packages.[26]

Base salary. As noted earlier, market competitive salary levels become increasingly more important in determining executive base salary at the top levels of the managerial hierarchy in an organization. This does not eliminate the role of formalized job evaluation systems or the importance of maintaining an internally equitable structure, but in reality these inputs become less important.

What becomes more important, at least for the chief executive officer, is the opinion of a compensation committee, comprised usually of the company's board of directors. Frequently this compensation committee will take over some of the data analysis tasks previously performed by the chief personnel officer, even going so far as to analyze salary survey data and performance records for executives of comparably sized firms.[27]

Bonuses. Annual bonuses typically play a major role in executive compensation and are primarily designed to increase performance motivation. For example, 92 percent of all executives in manufacturing, and 81 percent of those in banking, receive bonuses that are a function of their base salary.[28]

There are two constraints on the use of bonuses to compensate executives above base salary levels. First, there are several industries that make relatively little use of bonuses, either because of legal or company policy prohibitions. The types of organizations relying almost exclusively on base salary for total direct compensation typically have one or more of the following characteristics:[29] (1) tight control of stock ownership, (2) not-for-profit institutions, or (3) firms operating in regulated industries.

---

[25]William H. Cash, "Executive Compensation," *Personnel Administrator* 22, no. 7 (1977), pp. 11–19.

[26]Kenneth E. Foster and Gill Kamim-Lovers, "Determinants of Organizational Pay Policy," *Compensation Review* 10 (Third Quarter 1977), pp. 34–41.

[27]Ernest C. Miller, "How Companies Set the Base Salary and Incentive Bonus Opportunity for Chief Executive and Chief Operating Officers . . . A Compensation Review Symposium," *Compensation Review* 9 (Fourth Quarter 1976), pp. 30–44; Monci Jo Williams, "Why Chief Executives' Pay Keeps Rising," *Fortune,* (April 1, 1985), pp. 66–72, 76.

[28]Fox and Peck, *Top Executive Compensation: 1986.*

[29]Cash, "Executive Compensation."

The second constraint on bonus systems is usually tied to organization level of the executives. Eligibility is typically limited to those executives whose performance is judged to have potentially significant impacts on overall company performance.

Over the past decade bonuses have become increasingly more popular as a means of compensation.[30] Typically, executives in companies with bonus plans receive higher total direct compensation (base salary + bonus) than those in nonbonus companies. This is, however, highly dependent upon performance of the particular organization in a particular year. Most companies paying bonuses pay base salaries somewhat lower than nonbonus companies (for example, base pay for bonus-paying companies in the manufacturing sector generally runs about 15 percent below base pay in nonbonus companies). Consequently when a company has an unprofitable year and bonuses are not granted, direct salary will be somewhat lower than in nonbonus companies, and probably considerably lower than in highly profitable years. The increasing tendency toward use of bonus systems and the proportion of salary they entail places a strong financial incentive on executives to perform well.

Long-term incentive and capital appreciation plans (deferred compensation). We discussed some of the more popular forms of deferred compensation in Chapter 12. In recent years long-term incentive plans have become increasingly popular. One survey reports a 5 to 30 percent increase in use of incentive plans, depending on industry.[31] Stock option use varies from a low of 52 percent for compensating executives in construction firms, to a high of 82 percent in manufacturing.[32] This focus on long-term incentives reflects growing concerns by boards of directors for long-term achievements, sometimes even at the expense of short-run profits! One of the more popular long-term incentives is an incentive stock option (ISO), as permitted by the Economic Recovery Tax Act of 1981. Ninety percent of all companies with stock option plans use ISOs.[33] An executive exercising an ISO pays only 20 percent capital gains tax on the first $100,000 of appreciated value. While this compares favorably with the previous tax bite of 50 percent, it still requires a large cash investment by executives to purchase the stock. To eliminate even this cost (and risk!) companies have been experimenting with stock appreciation rights (SARs).[34] A SAR permits an ex-

---

[30]"Big Executive Bonuses Now Come with a Catch: Lots of Criticism" *The Wall Street Journal*; Harland Fox, *Top Executive Compensation: 1978* (New York: The Conference Board, 1980).

[31]Margaret Bentson and Jay Schuster, "Executive Compensation and Employee Benefits," in *Human Resources Management in the 1980s,* eds. Stephen Carroll and Randall Schuler (Washington, D. C.: BNA, 1983), pp. 6. 1–6.33.

[32]Fox and Peck, *Top Executive Compensation: 1986.*

[33]Ibid.

[34]Frederick W. Cook, "Stock Appreciation Rights: A Research Report," *Compensation Review* 9, no. 1 (1977), pp. 63–64.

ecutive all the potential capital gain of a stock option without requiring the purchase of stocks! Payment is provided upon demand for the difference between the stock option price and current market price. The popularity of SARs has fallen recently as firms discover the higher accounting and cash costs associated with their inclusion. Conversely, ISOs blossomed during 1984 and 1985, largely because of the rebirth of the stock market.[35] Other forms of incentives (e.g., performance unit plans), discussed in greater detail in Chapter 12, also have increased in popularity.

Executive benefits. Since many benefits are tied to income level (e.g., life insurance, disability insurance, pension plans), executives typically receive higher benefits than most other exempt employees. Beyond the typical benefits outlined in Chapter 12, however, many executives also receive additional life insurance, exclusions from deductibles for health-related costs, and supplementary pension income exceeding the maximum limits permissible under ERISA guidelines for qualified pension plans.

Other amenities that might normally be classified under executive benefits are included in a special category: executive perquisites.

Executive perquisites. Perquisites, or "perks," probably have the same genesis as the expression "rank has its privileges." Indeed, life at the top has its rewards, designed to satisfy several types of executive needs. One type of perk could be classified as "internal," providing that something extra while the executive is inside the company: luxury offices, executive dining rooms, special parking. A second category also is designed to be company related, but for business conducted externally: company-paid memberships in clubs/associations, payment of hotel, resort, airplane, and auto expenses.

The final category of perquisites should be totally isolated from the first two because of the differential tax status. This category, called "personal perks," includes such things as low-cost loans, personal and legal counseling, free home repairs and improvements, personal use of company property, and expenses for vacation homes.[36] Since 1978 various tax and regulatory agency rulings have slowly been requiring companies to place a value on perks.[37] If this trend continues the taxable income of executives with creative perk packages may increase considerably.

---

[35]Lester Jackson, "Executive Compensation: Where Are We and Where Are We Going?" *Personnel Administrator* 30 (June 1985), pp. 51–57.

[36]Michael F. Klein, "Executive Perquisites," *Compensation Review* 12 (Fourth Quarter, 1979), pp. 46–50.

[37]R. L. VanKirk and L. S. Schenger, "Executive Compensation: The Trend Is Back to Cash," *Financial Executive,* May 1978, pp. 83–91.

SALES FORCE AND SALES EXECUTIVES

As indicated at the beginning of this chapter, sales positions provide special challenges to compensation administrators. Because a large part of a salesperson's job is unsupervised, it becomes essential to use compensation to direct sales activities, thus substituting for the absence of close supervision. Fortunately, most sales positions lend themselves well to some form of incentive system, making a salesperson's compensation highly dependent on units sold (or some measure of quantity). Because of this potential for great variability in compensation based on sales volume, mean salary figures reported in Exhibit 16.7 should be interpreted with caution. It is equally important to look at the variability in compensation paid to good and poor salespersons to determine competitiveness.[38]

Factors Explaining Pay Differences among Salespersons

Over the years a number of factors have been identified to explain pay differentials among salespeople.[39] In large part these factors can be linked to external markets, particularly product markets. These factors include:[40]

1. *The kind of product sold.* In higher sales positions, executives in consumer goods industries earn approximately 10 percent more than their counterparts in industrial goods industries. This trend reverses, however, at the bottom of the organizational hierarchy with field sales personnel in consumer goods industries earning approximately 10 percent more than industrial goods sales personnel.
2. *Sales volume.* Not surprisingly, there is some relationship between sales volume and earnings. Among sales executives, earnings are 40 to 70 percent higher for those with high sales volume in comparison to those with low sales volume. Unfortunately this positive relationship does not hold up for lower level sales positions.
3. *Type of market.* For high-level sales staff, selling a finished good to intermediaries (e.g., wholesalers, retailers) is more often associated with higher earnings than selling either directly to the consumer or selling goods that require further processing or assembly. Again, this relationship is directly reversed at lower organizational levels for sales personnel.
4. *Selling situation.* A distinction can be made between selling of technical goods versus nontechnical goods. The sale of technical goods frequently in-

---

[38]Charles F. Schultz, "Compensating the Sales Professional," unpublished manuscript, Towers, Perrin, Foster and Crosby, 1985.

[39]The Conference Board, *Compensating Salesmen and Sales Executives 1972* (New York: The Conference Board, 1972); Schultz, "Compensating the Sales Professional."

[40]The Conference Board, *Compensating Salesmen and Sales Executives.*

EXHIBIT 16.7
How Salespeople's Total Compensation Is Growing

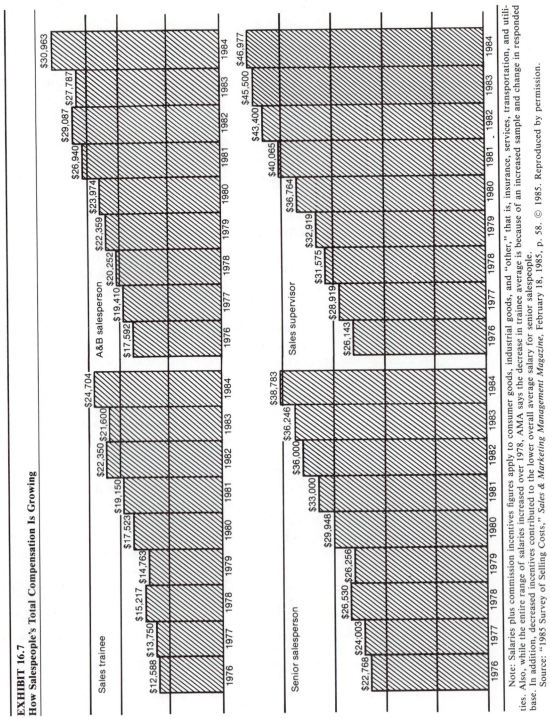

Note: Salaries plus commission incentives figures apply to consumer goods, industrial goods, and "other," that is, insurance, services, transportation, and utilities. Also, while the entire range of salaries increased over 1978, AMA says the decrease in trainee average is because of an increased sample and change in responded base. In addition, decreased incentives contributed to the lower overall average salary for senior salespeople.
Source: "1985 Survey of Selling Costs," *Sales & Marketing Management Magazine*, February 18, 1985, p. 58. © 1985. Reproduced by permission.

volves a team-selling approach, with technical personnel assisting the sales representative in the selling situation. Executive sales personnel in these technical markets earn about 15 percent less than executives in nontechnical fields where a team-selling approach is not necessary. Again, this earnings differential is reversed at lower sales levels, with technical products salespeople earning about 10 percent more than nontechnical sales force.

It probably would be inappropriate for an organization to design a sales compensation plan that conforms to these empirical relationships. No doubt there is a rational foundation for differentiating earnings that would lead to the types of differences just noted. However, the factors to consider in designing a sales compensation plan are much more complex and follow the line of reasoning discussed in the next section.

Factors in Designing a Sales Compensation Plan

The sales environment for many organizations is best characterized as rapidly changing. There are basically five features of this environment to be considered in designing a new sales compensation plan or modifying an existing one.[41]

1. *Customers*
    a. Centralized buying—sales staff may no longer have a direct impact on buying decisions, requiring a compensation plan reflecting this.
    b. Centralized merchandising—if merchandising decisions are not made at the local store level, salespeople may not have much influence on how a product is shelved in the store. This also reduces the control a sales force has over sales volume.
    c. More sophisticated buying decisions—greater awareness of costs, turnover, and profit margins coupled with fewer but more prominent customers leads to a changing sales role and a need for adaptive compensation packages.
2. *Corporate trends*—how the corporation plans to change over time can have important consequences for the sales role. Will the product line become more technical? Will growth come from existing customers and products or expansion along new horizons? These corporate projections must be complemented by a sales compensation package that accounts for desired changes in the sales role.
3. *The sales force*
    a. What are current and projected sales costs if the current compensation package is retained?

---

[41]Gerry Phillips, "Matching the Compensation Plan to the Sales Role," *Canadian Business Review,* Spring 1977, pp. 14–19. For another excellent discussion of issues in designing a sales compensation plan, see Bruce Ellig, "Sales Compensation: A Systematic Approach," *Compensation Review* 15 (First Quarter 1982), pp. 21–45.

b. Will sales jobs become more routine, with increases in the daily routine calls? Or will increased centralization of buying decisions mandate more individualized sales calls at the central office? The nature of this change will have an impact on the sales manager to salesperson ratio (e.g., routine calls can be handled by sales personnel while tailored sales calls at a central office may require more experienced sales personnel).

c. Earnings are often based on some measure of sales volume. Compensation plans are going to have to adopt better performance measures as more sales jobs are typified by centralized buying and fewer but larger customers. These trends make it more difficult to identify a salesperson's performance based on gross sales.

4. *Competition*—quite obviously an important factor in designing your sales compensation plan is the practices of your competition. Data on your competitor's type of compensation package, level of compensation, and degree of success should be obtained. Once your competitor has captured a market or attracted important sales representatives away from your company, it is too late to begin analyzing where your compensation plan has gone awry.

5. *Compensation plan objective*—answers to the previous questions provide the foundation for a set of compensation objectives. For example:

a. What is to be the trade-off between sales volume and customer service?

b. What is the future role of building existing business versus opening new accounts?

c. Do difficulties arise in recruiting new salespeople, or in retaining experienced sales representatives?

d. To what extent should the compensation plan be designed to reduce sales costs as a percentage of sales?

Answers to these questions and others will play a vital role in designing a sales compensation plan.

Designing a Sales Compensation Plan—the Options

Basic sales compensation plans come in one of three forms: salary, commission, and a combination (salary and commission) plan. Each of these three strategies for paying sales personnel is designed to focus pay incentives on one or more sales objectives. Consequently, the type of plan appropriate for an organization depends on what it wants to pay for (i.e., the answers to questions in the last section). Exhibit 16.8 indicates the variations on plans and their relative popularity in industry.

In a salary plan the sales force is paid a fixed income not dependent on sales volume. There is an obvious rationale for this kind of strategy; if the major function of a salesperson is to provide customer service or spend disproportionate amounts of time "prospecting for new accounts under low success conditions," then a straight salary plan is appropriate. Any temporary shifts in

EXHIBIT 16.8
Popularity of Different Sales Compensation Plans

	All Industries	
	---	---
Method	1984 (percent)	1983 (percent)
Straight salary	17.1	20.4
Draw against commission	6.8	5.4
Salary + Commission	29.0	30.9
Salary + Individual bonus	33.6	30.1
Salary + Group bonus	2.3	1.9
Salary + Commission + Bonus	11.2	11.3

Source: Executive Compensation Service, Inc.: *Sales Personnel Report;* Fort Lee: a subsidiary of the Wyatt Company, 1985/1986, 30th edition.

emphasis to increase sales volume typically are handled with a short-term special incentive plan.

Another situation where salary plans are appropriate involves sales jobs where individual sales performance is difficult to measure; either sales volume is based on group effort with individual contributions difficult to separate out, or sales volume in traditional quantified terms is a completely inappropriate index of individual sales effort. An example of a job fitting this latter description would be a position description for a field engineer with an industrial equipment manufacturer. Duties of this job would include:[42]

- Developing and executing sales and product training programs for distributor's sales forces.
- Doing missionary work with selected manufacturers and major oil companies to encourage them to recommend his products to their dealers and mention them in their service and installation manuals.
- Participating in national and local trade shows; conducting occasional training programs for trade groups and associations.
- Suggesting ideas for new products and promotional programs; recommending changes or improvements in existing products.

If you can visualize the anger of someone performing this job and being paid on a commission, you can understand why a salary plan is most appropriate for this type of position.

At the opposite extreme in terms of objectives is a sales compensation plan based on straight commission. Salary based on volume of sales exclusively may be appropriate (1) where the market possibilities are broad and sales boundaries vague, yielding high administrative costs for other types of compensation; (2) where company objectives are strongly geared to motivating sales volume

---

[42]John P. Steinbrink, "How to Pay Your Sales Force," *Harvard Business Review* 56 (July–August 1978), p. 12.

EXHIBIT 16.9
Advantages and Disadvantages of Three Basic Sales Compensation Plans

Straight Salary		Commission		Combination (commission and salary)	
Advantages	*Disadvantages*	*Advantages*	*Disadvantages*	*Advantages*	*Disadvantages*
Assures regular income.	Little financial incentive to increase effort.	Pay tied directly to performance.	High variance in income between salesmen may occur, and income over time (boom versus recession).	Offers benefits of both salary and commission plans. Greater security due to stable base income.	Complex or difficult to communicate.
Develops high degree of company loyalty.	Favors least productive sales personnel.	Easy to communicate and compute.	Generates low loyalty to company.	Allows greater latitude of motivation possibilities.	
Simplifies reassignment of salesmen or territories.	Leads to overemphasis on sales or easiest items to sell.		Emphasis on volume sales rather than profits.		
Ensures performance of nonselling activities.	Increases potential of sales compression between veteran and new recruit.		May lead to neglect of nonselling activities.	Compensates salesmen for all selling activities.	
Facilitates administration.					Sometimes costly to administer.
Provides relatively fixed sales costs.	Typically higher direct selling costs than other plans.	Unit sales costs are proportional to net sales.	Problems arise in changing territories or reassigning salespersons.		

through incentives; or (3) where cost accounting procedures stress the importance of strict controls over sales cost to sales volume ratios.

The final type of plan is a potpourri combination of salary and commission payment schemes. Recognize that most sales jobs do not fit the ideal specifications for either salary or commission payment.[43] In fact, they combine features of both types of jobs in such a way that a straight salary floor permits a salesperson to perform functions with no immediate sales-volume payoff (e.g., customer service), while a commission for sales-volume yields the necessary sales incentive. Exhibit 16.9 outlines some of the advantages and disadvantages of the three basic plans. Consider, as a strategy for selecting a sales compensation plan, the following scenario. First, design of the sales plan must be consistent, indeed must enhance, the strategic plan of the organization. Allocation of sales duties should reinforce this organizational thrust. Second, there should be an evaluation of how important the salesperson's role actually is in a particular product/service line. Some products, because of brand name prominence, literally "sell themselves." When this isn't the case, and the sales effort may play a crucial role, incentive components of pay become increasingly important.[44] Third, an assessment should be made of the skill level required for a particular line of sales. Consider a product which has highly technical components and requires a sales presentation highly steeped in technical detail. The supply of qualified sales personnel in such a situation is likely to be much smaller than, for example, the number of individuals capable of selling shoes in a local mall. The appropriate compensation package suited to this constellation of scarce skills would be more likely to emphasize a large initial salary component to attract the necessary sales talent.[45] The interaction of these latter two factors would yield compensation strategies such as those shown in Exhibit 16.10.

EXHIBIT 16.10
Designing a Sales Compensation Package

		Importance of "Sales" Ability in Closing Sale	
		High	Low
Probability that job has highly technical dimension requiring skills not readily available in population.	*High*	High starting salary to attract, large incentive to motivate.	High salary to attract, no incentive necessary.
	Low	Lower starting salary, but large incentive.	Salary only, and not at high level.

[43]Ibid.

[44]Stephan Motowidlo, "Predicting Sales Turnover from Pay Satisfaction and Expectation," *Journal of Applied Psychology* 68, no. 3 (1983), pp. 484–89.

[45]Schultz, "Compensating the Sales Professional."

EMPLOYEES IN U.S. FOREIGN SUBSIDIARIES

The rapid movement of U.S. corporations into foreign markets over the past 20 years has compounded a serious compensation problem that has probably existed for centuries. The nature of this compensation problem is best hinted at in a somewhat apocryphal story told by Teague:[46]

> Based on excavations at Ur it was determined that at least one foreign subsidiary was located there by the Dilmun Empire some 5,000 to 6,000 years ago. The problems of compensating such employees in a foreign country are suggested by the following fictitious exchange initiated by the employees: "The increase in temple taxes and barbarian incursions on the border has raised the cost of living here by 20 percent. Please adjust my stipend accordingly." And the reply may well have gone: "Thanks for the confirmation of border warfare. Rumors of war here have depreciated Urian currency by 30 percent. This rate of exchange gives you a 10 percent margin neither of us foresaw. Therefore, your allowance is hereby cut by 10 percent."

The problems in compensating foreign service personnel arise out of the need to preserve equity among three distinct employee groups: U.S. expatriates (USEs), local country nationals (LCNs), and third country nationals (TCNs). U.S. expatriates are American citizens working for a U.S. subsidiary in a foreign country. Equity for USEs becomes an issue both in "keeping the expatriates whole" relative to salary of their American-based counterparts and also in providing an incentive wage for accepting employment in an unfamiliar, and perhaps less comfortable, environment. Local country nationals present similar challenges in maintaining equity. As citizens of the country in which the U.S. foreign subsidiary is located, LCNs' compensation could be tied to either local wage rates or to the rates of USEs performing the same job. Either practice brings up equity problems that will be discussed shortly.

Finally, third country nationals are employees of a U.S. foreign subsidiary who maintain citizenship in a country other than the United States or the country housing the U.S. subsidiary (e.g., an Italian working for a U.S. subsidiary located in Germany). For TCNs three different standards could be used to set wages: comparative wages in the United States, the local country, or the country of citizenship. As noted in the following discussion, each standard presents unique equity problems.

Expatriate Compensation

Maintaining equity for expatriates while serving in a foreign country typically translates into a three-component compensation package.[47]

---

[46]Burton W. Teague, *Compensating Key Personnel Overseas* (New York: The Conference Board, 1972), p. 2.

[47]International Compensation, *Expatriate Compensation: An Overview* (Boston: International Compensation, 1978), pp. 2–3.

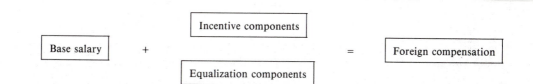

Base salary of expatriates is a function of job worth. Job worth, in turn, is typically determined by using the same job evaluation plan that is applied to domestic employees. Use of the same job evaluation plan for both domestic and foreign employees assumes that job responsibilities are roughly comparable in the two settings and, consequently, that the same compensable factors are appropriate. In many cases this assumption is correct. Granted there may be substantial environmental differences between two (otherwise) identical jobs in different countries, but the incentive and equalization pay components are designed to compensate for these differences. Exhibit 16.11 shows the percentage of firms offering each of four foreign service pay components.

Equalization is one form of equity, in this case designed to "keep the worker whole" (i.e., maintain real income or purchasing power of base pay). This equalization typically comes in the form of four types of allowances:

1. Tax equalization allowance. Income earned in foreign countries has two potential sources of income tax liability. With few exceptions (Saudia Arabia is one) foreign income tax liabilities are incurred on foreign-earned income. In contrast, most home countries do not impose tax liabilities on foreign-earned income. The major exception, of course, is the United States. To counter this double tax liability most major firms—say the Fortune 150—use tax protection or tax equalization programs for U.S. employees assigned abroad. Tax equalization methodologies provide for employer payment of foreign taxes and payment of U.S. income tax requirements on monies paid for cost-of-living differentials, housing allowances, overseas premiums, and so on. In turn, the company uses any available foreign tax credits to help offset these U.S. tax liabilities. The principle of no positive or negative tax impact on base salary compared to a U.S. counterpart underlies this methodology. Hence, employees do not base the decision to accept foreign assignments on such factors as foreign income tax rates or foreign cost-of-living variances.

EXHIBIT 16.11
Popularity of Four Foreign Service Pay Components

Component	1972 (N = 134 firms)	1982 (N = 123 firms)
Foreign service premium	89%	74%
Cost-of-living allowance	96	97
Tax equalization allowance	90	98
Housing plan	86	94

Source: Burton Teague, *Compensating Foreign Service Personnel* (New York: The Conference Board, 1982), no. 818.

Smaller firms are more likely to let employees fend for themselves. If foreign tax rates are high and cannot be translated into foreign tax credits, such companies may make up the difference with incremental salary dollars. Small firms are likely to negotiate the terms of an overseas assignment with individual employees. Larger firms are more likely to proceduralize overseas conditions of employment.

The need to provide tax equalization allowances has been diluted, but not eliminated, by the Economic Recovery Tax Act of 1981. The $95,000 exclusion on foreign earned income allows many USEs to escape U.S. income tax, but they still face heavy foreign tax.[48]

2. Housing allowances. Despite a wide variety of formulas, housing allowances are designed to compensate the expatriate for the difference between U.S. housing costs and comparable foreign housing. In some instances the multinational company will provide housing for the expatriate cadre, thereby eliminating the need for a housing allowance.

3. Education and language training allowance. Many organizations pay for language training of expatriates and their families. They also attempt to ensure educational training for children comparable to U.S. standards. If public schools do not meet these standards the company will typically provide an allowance for private school training.

4. Cost-of-living allowance (COLA). As in the illustration at the beginning of this section, COLA adjustments prove to be the major source of complaints, and hence problems, in expatriate compensation. High quality and readily available goods in the United States may be unavailable in a foreign subsidiary. Problems of this nature make it difficult to compensate expatriates for the differences in "cost of living." Despite the inherent difficulties of comparing apples and oranges, most companies use some index of living costs abroad (e.g., the State Department's index).

The final component of expatriate compensation is an incentive for accepting a foreign assignment that requires the expatriate to (1) work with less supervision than an American counterpart; (2) live and work in strange and, in some cases, uncongenial surroundings; and (3) represent the U.S. employer in the host country.[49] Using what is called a *foreign service premium,* companies either pay a flat percentage (typically 15 percent) of base pay as an incentive, or vary the amount as a function of the perceived hardships in the foreign subsidiary. In the latter case an assignment in Brussels would yield little or no foreign service premium while Nairobi might warrant a considerably larger incentive.

---

[48]Burton Teague, *Compensating Foreign Service Personnel* (New York: The Conference Board, 1982), report no. 818.

[49]Ibid.

Local and Third Country Nationals

If anything, developing a compensation package for LCNs and TCNs that is equitable is an even greater challenge than it is for U.S. expatriates. The problem focuses on determining what the standard for equity should be. As an illustration consider the case where three managers—one a USE, another a TCN, and the third an LCN—all perform essentially the same work for a U.S. foreign subsidiary. If the job performed is used as the basis for judging equitable pay, arguably all three employees should receive the same pay, given essentially similar work. If, however, use is made of an equity standard, such as keeping the worker whole, it is likely that income of the three managers will vary considerably as a function of home country economic conditions and past individual salaries.

Most studies show that companies typically resolve this dilemma in favor of the home country balance-sheet approach (i.e., keeping the worker whole).[50] Between 75 and 80 percent of multinational organizations design compensation packages for foreign-service personnel so that the balance sheet neither favors nor penalizes the employee for employment in the firm.[51] As might be expected, then, these companies who favor keeping the worker whole make more extensive use of allowances designed to equalize the real income effects of employment as foreign-service personnel (e.g., cost-of-living, tax equalization, and housing allowances).

In contrast, companies that prefer an "equal pay for equal work" equity eliminate pay differences. Not surprisingly, these companies tend less frequently to adopt the allowances that are so prevalent under a balance-sheet policy.[52]

Historically, the balance-sheet approach to compensation has been less costly. Salaries were pegged to home country standards rather than to U.S. standards (thus yielding a lower cost as long as salary levels in the United States were among the highest in the world). These cost savings could yield some rather predictable problems, however. If salary differences among these foreign-service personnel became known, complaints about unequal pay for equal work emerged. To minimize this problem, organizations adopted one of two strategies. Either they attempted to make compensation practices secret, or they structured the USE job (typically the source of any large salary differential) as a relatively short-term consulting assignment charged with training LCNs and TCNs and then moving to another assignment before job responsibilities equalized. The USE salary advantage was less noticeable and, perhaps, more justifiable.

---

[50]Teague, *Compensating Key Personnel Overseas;* M. R. Foote, "Controlling the Cost of International Compensation," *Harvard Business Review* 55 (November–December 1977), p. 123; Murphy and Salter, "Should CEO Pay Be Linked to Results?"

[51]Teague, *Compensating Key Personnel Overseas.*

[52]Ibid.

As the trend toward internationalization of business spreads in the 1980s, it would be expected that the compensation of foreign-service personnel will assume a greater importance in strategy sessions. The apparent "fire fighting" and nonsystematic practices currently in vogue are particularly dismaying. Coherent policies and systematic practices must evolve as foreign operations mature and assume greater shares of corporate profits.

SUMMARY

Note that these special groups are special in a second sense, beyond the fact that their compensation has some unique design features. These groups also are special because they are strategically important for organizational success. It is unlikely that such care and attention to system design would arise if the stakes were not so important. As a consequence, the compensation of special groups provides an early forecast of system-wide future compensation changes. Incentive systems, stock ownership plans, and legal insurance, to name but a few compensation components, all originated with one or another special groups. When the special advantages of these "tools" become apparent, organizations begin to assess their value for other employee groups. The end result is more effective compensation systems.

REVIEW QUESTIONS

1. What special compensation issues make pay for supervisors a particular challenge? For middle and upper management employees? For professional employees? For sales personnel? For foreign service personnel?
2. What is the logical explanation for the typical relationship betwen pay increases and years-since-last-degree found in maturity curves for engineering personnel?
3. Why are incentive systems particularly appropriate for paying top executives (consider the nature and objectives of the job)?
4. What are perquisites? Explain their popularity.
5. What factors influence the design of a sales compensation plan?
6. Why is equity such an important concept in the pay of foreign service personnel?

Chapter 17

Union Role in Wage and Salary Administration

Unions are, arguably, facing their most critical challenge of the last 50 years.[1] Unionization has fallen to less than 20 percent of the labor force. Management has taken a harder stand against unions. Domestic and international competition are making it increasingly difficult for unions to extract wage concessions from employers. Indeed, the 1980s have been characterized by an unprecedented number of wage concessions made by unions to preserve employment for their membership. It shouldn't be surprising, then, that a recent survey shows a continued deterioration for unions in the labor-management power relationship. Exhibit 17.1 illustrates this fact.

---

[1]Harry Katz, "Collective Bargaining in 1982: A Turning Point in Industrial Relations?" *Compensation Review* 17 (January 1984), pp. 38–49.

EXHIBIT 17.1
Labor-Management Power: 1983-1984

			Percentage Yes			
		Union			*Management*	
Question	*1983*	*1984*			*1983*	*1984*
1. Does management have the upper hand in negotiations?	82	84			79	83
2. Will management gain more negotiating power in the future?	74	86			89	91
3. Can management force their terms on unions?	84	86			88	90
4. Is there any connection between strikes and layoffs?	63	68			23	26
5. Would union members make wage concessions rather than be laid off?	86	87			83	89
6. In the last three years, has union pressure adversely affected the company?	32	39			88	92
7. Are unions necessary for equitable labor representation?	53	41			3	3
8. Is the current administration against organized labor?	97	97			68	97

		Union Response		*Management Response*		
	Decline	*1983*	*1984*	*Decline*	*1983*	*1984*
9. What percentage decline in union membership do you expect in the next five years?	20	38%	20%	20	4%	2%
	40	33	39	40	26	28
	60	19	31	60	48	51
	80	7	5	80	19	3
	100	3	2	100	3	3

Source: R. Wayne Mondy and Shane Preameaux, "The Labor Management Power Relationship Revisited," *Personnel Administrator,* May 1985, pp. 51–54.

The exhibit indicates that unions and management alike believe that management currently dominates the power relationship between the two groups, and this advantage is only expected to get stronger if estimates of continued membership decline are borne out. Despite these pessimistic statistics, though, it would be a mistake to conclude that the impact of unions on wage and salary administration is minor. Even in a nonunion firm, the actions taken by wage and salary administrators are influenced by external union activity. This chapter is intended to outline compensation issues in unionized firms and then to illustrate the role played by unions in three major areas that have an impact on virtually every facet of compensation administration: (1) impact on general wage level, (2) spillover to nonunion firms, and (3) impact on wage and salary policies and practices in unionized firms. The final discussion focuses on union response to the changing economic environment of the 1980s and the implications for compensation administration.

COMPENSATION ISSUES IN UNIONIZED FIRMS

Some interesting economic realities have made compensation decision making a crucial factor in organizational success for the 1980s. First, it has become increasingly apparent that international competition has a significant impact on the profitability of American enterprises. As our product prices become noncompetitive in the international market, the result, as any executive in the auto industry can attest, can be catastrophic. This noncompetitiveness can further translate into lost jobs and rising unemployment. With a national unemployment rate hovering around double digits and pockets of unemployment exceeding 15 percent (e.g., Alabama, Michigan) in 1983 both workers and management sought relief. Part of this relief came from greater attention to two compensation issues: (1) relative importance of factors affecting wage level and (2) the structure of wage packages.

Factors Affecting Wage Level

Among the most important factors affecting wage determination in unionized organizations are: (1) productivity, (2) changes in the cost of living, (3) ability of an employer to pay, and (4) comparability among wage rates (equity).[2] Not surprisingly, all four of these issues have received considerable attention lately, and the outcome of this attention may well be dramatic changes in compensation of unionized employees.

Productivity. Although the United States has the highest per worker productivity of any country in the world, yearly increases in productivity have lagged far behind most other industrial countries over the past decade. While this decline is undoubtedly due to a host of factors, including slow modernization rates in key manufacturing sectors, a portion of the blame for lower productivity continues to be directed at unions. The sources of these complaints are twofold. First, union contracts establish staffing practices or other work rules that artificially reduce output. Examples of such practices include minimum crew size requirements and provisions limiting subcontracting. Second, union initiated strikes obviously restrict output during the term of the strike.

Alternatively, some experts suggest that output is enhanced by unions. This argument suggests that unions negotiate higher wages and provide an outlet to

---

[2]Daniel Q. Mills, *Labor Management Relations,* 2nd ed. (New York: McGraw-Hill, 1982).

vent grievances against management. By improving satisfaction and lowering turnover the net productivity impact of unions is argued to be positive.[3]

No matter what the outcome of these debates, management is acting as if unions result in lower productivity. The result has been an increasingly tougher stand in negotiations and more agreements to tie wage increases to productivity increases. Incentive systems, profit-sharing plans, and merit-based pay plans are all examples of efforts to make this productivity-wage link stronger.

Cost of living. Unions made a strong drive for wage escalator clauses during the 1970s. Cost-of-living adjustments (COLAs) are designed to increase wages automatically during the life of the contract as a function of changes in the consumer price index. By 1978 COLA clauses had made broad inroads on the labor management scene, despite evidence that such contract clauses fail to keep workers "whole" with respect to inflation.[4] More recently, though, a declining interest in COLAs can be traced to deceleration of the consumer price index. Historically, unions have clamored for COLAs during periods of high inflation and de-emphasized them when inflation rates were more tolerable. Now that the inflation rate has moderated in the past several years, fewer unions consider COLA clauses a vital element of a total package.[5]

Despite the lessened current interest, escalator clauses deserve discussion, if only in anticipation of future bouts with inflation and renewed interest in this contractual safeguard.

All COLAs have two common elements: some measure of change in living costs, and a formula to adjust wages as a function of these changes in living costs. The most common measure of change in living costs is the consumer price index (CPI), prepared by the Bureau of Labor Statistics. Less frequently (about 10 percent of agreements) contracts specify use of a CPI calculated for a particular city. Recall from Chapter 15 that the CPI provides an estimate of the change in cost of a market basket of goods (as many as 4,000 individual items may be priced every month to determine changes in the cost patterns). The cost of this market basket is compared against a base period cost to determine change.

The second element of an escalator clause is the formula for adjusting wages as the CPI changes. The most common formula is to adjust wages 1 cent for each .3 percent rise in the consumer price index.[6]

---

[3]Richard Freeman, "Individual Mobility and Union Voice in the Labor Market," *American Economic Review* 66 (May 1976), pp. 361–68.

[4]Victor J. Sheifer, "Collective Bargaining and the CPI: Escalation v. Catch-up," *Proceedings of the 31st Annual Meeting, Industrial Relations Research Association Series,* 1978, pp. 257–63.

[5]Katz, "Collective Bargaining in 1982: A Turning Point in Industrial Relations?"

[6]Sheifer, "Collective Bargaining and the CPI: Escalation v. Catch-Up."

Ability to pay and wage comparability. The third factor affecting wage levels in unionized organizations is an employer's ability to pay. In profitable years unions reason that part of the profits should accrue to the work force responsible for much of the organization's success. This argument plays a role in the eventual determination of bargained wage levels. What follows then is well known by the American consumer. Product prices are raised, and labor cost increases are cited as a major reason. In the past this has usually worked—consumers continued to purchase what remained a competitively priced product. In large part this phenomenon can be explained by introducing the fourth factor affecting wage levels: comparability among wage rates. As one group of workers received wage increases, product competitors acceded to similar demands of their work force. The result was labor cost and product price increases that rose relatively uniformly. As long as unions were able to control wage increases within an industry (usually by organizing the whole industry) no employer suffered a disproportionate wage increase, resulting in a noncompetitive product price!

Employers were content to go along with this situation as long as they received a reasonable return on investment and their market share remained unaffected. What they failed to realize, and what must be considered in future wage negotiations, is the rapid internationalization of product markets. A classic example is the auto industry. Japanese autoworkers receive compensation worth approximately one half their American counterparts. As long as Japan assumed a small role in the auto market, American auto manufacturers were concerned only about wages relative to other domestic manufacturers. As Japan increased its market share due to competitive price/quality differentials, however, the comparative wage differential loomed larger and larger. This differential played a large role in UAW concessions to both Ford and General Motors in 1982. As an illustration, although UAW workers at General Motors lost no direct wages, they did have COLA increases temporarily suspended.

Increasing product market competition, both domestic (nonunion) and foreign, has had similar impacts in other industries. In 1984 major contract concessions were made in eight industries: air transport, food stores, shoe manufacturing, primary metals, metal cans, transportation equipment, textiles, and trucking.[7] Although discussed in detail later, these concessions have had one interesting impact on wages relative to the ability-to-pay issue. There has been a trend toward coupling wage concessions with profit-sharing plans.[8] Employers reason that profit-sharing plans permit better control over labor costs, with costs varying directly with the ability to pay: Highly profitable years trigger

---

[7]Robert Gay, "Union Contract Concessions and Their Implications for Union Wage Determination," working paper no. 38, Division of Research and Statistics, Board of Governors of the Federal Reserve System, 1984.

[8]Katz, "Collective Bargaining in 1982: A Turning Point in Industrial Relations?"

higher payments to workers and poor years yield correspondingly smaller incentive costs.

The Structure of Wage Packages

The second compensation issue involves the structuring of wage packages. One dimension of this issue concerns the division between direct wages and employee benefits. While there is evidence that unions have an impact on the relative size of the benefits package, particularly for pensions, employers have become increasingly more sophisticated in controlling total package costs.[9] Most organizations now realize that cost control mechanisms must be established from the beginning with any new benefit. It would be far better, for example, to negotiate a dollar contribution by the company. Then, as costs rose in subsequent years, the dollar amount either could be renegotiated or the union could determine if the benefit was sufficiently attractive to justify having employees bear the added cost.

A second dimension of the wage structure issue is a relatively new phenomenon. Along with the concession bargaining movement has come two-tier pay plans. Basically a phenomenon of the union sector, two-tier wage structures differentiate pay based on hiring date. A contract is negotiated which specifies that employees hired after a specified date will receive lower wages than their higher seniority peers working on the same or similar jobs. Two-tier pay plans initially spread because unions viewed them as less painful than wage freezes and staff cuts among existing employees.[10] The trade-off was to bargain away equivalent wage treatment for future employees! Remember, this is a radical departure from the most basic precepts of unionization. Unions evolved and continue to endure, in part, based on the belief that all members are equal. Two-tier plans are obviously at odds with this principle.

The initial reaction of management to two-tier plans was also highly favorable. American Airlines estimated that it saved $100 million in 1984 as a result of its two-tier plan.[11] Indeed, as turnover permitted substitution of low-priced workers for their higher priced predecessors, the wage savings mounted quickly indeed.

Not surprisingly, though, serious reservations about two-tier plans have begun to arise. First, two wage rates for union workers performing the same job in the same location leads to divisiveness. Pressures mount to correct these inequities as the number of "new" workers rises. One supermarket chain, for ex-

---

[9]Augustin Kwasi Fosu, "Impact of Unionism on Pension Fringes," *Industrial Relations* 22, no. 3 (1983), pp. 419–25.

[10]Sanford Jacoby and Daniel Mitchell, "Management Attitudes Toward Two-Tier Pay Plans: An Analysis," UCLA Working Series Paper 87, July 1985, pp. 1–20.

[11]David Wessel, "Two-Tier Pay Spreads, but the Pioneer Firms Encounter Problems," *The Wall Street Journal,* October 14, 1985, pp. 1, 9.

ample, with sufficient time in this dual structure to witness this phenomenon, reports that increasing pressure is being put on the union by newer members to narrow or eliminate the wage gap.[12]

A second concern expressed by unions is that the lower tier will resent the union's role in creating the inequity.[13] In fact, there is even some concern that unions may not be fairly representing all their membership, a direct violation of the Wagner Act.

Some of these concerns have been realized at firms such as Hughes Aircraft, where two-tier plans have been pronounced a failure. New workers didn't stay with the firm, and poor morale amongst remaining workers contributed to a contractual suspension by federal government due to quality control problems.[14] As a result of all these concerns, some sources suspect that two-tier pay plans have peaked and will not be the strategy of choice in future concession bargaining situations.[15]

UNION IMPACT ON GENERAL WAGE LEVEL

Does the presence of a union in an organization raise the level of wages for workers above what they would be if the company was not unionized? The commonly held belief among workers is that unions do have a wage impact. Over 80 percent of the respondents to a quality of employment survey conducted by the Survey Research Center of the University of Michigan believed that unions improved the wages of workers.[16] Efforts to determine if this perception is accurate have been a source of research focus for at least 40 years.

Part of the reason for the continuing interest in this area is that the question of union impact on wages has not been totally resolved. Efforts to determine union impact on wages run into several measurement problems. The ideal situation would compare numerous organizations that were identical except for the presence or absence of a union.[17] Any wage differences among these organizations could then be attributed to unionization. Unfortunately few such situations exist. One alternative strategy adopted has been to identify organizations within the same industry that differ in level of unionization. For example, consider company A, which is unionized, and company B, which is not. It is difficult to argue with assurance that wage differences between the two firms are at-

---

[12]Jane Seaberry, "Two-Tiered Wages: More Jobs v. More Worker Alienation," *Washington Post,* April 7, 1985, pp. G1–G3.

[13]Jacoby and Mitchell, "Management Attitudes Toward Two-Tier Pay Plans: An Analysis."

[14]Wessel, "Two-Tier Pay Spreads, but the Pioneer Firms Encounter Problems."

[15]CompFlash, "Two-Tier Wage Scales: Passe?" *AMA CompFlash* 85-3 (1985), p. 3.

[16]Thomas A. Kochan, "How American Workers View Labor Unions," *Monthly Labor Review,* April 1979, pp. 23–31.

[17]Allan M. Carter and F. Ray Marshall, *Labor Economics* (Homewood, Ill.: Richard D. Irwin, 1982).

tributable to the presence or absence of a union. First, the fact that the union has not organized the entire industry weakens its power base (e.g., strike efforts to shut down the entire industry could be thwarted by nonunion firms). Consequently any union impact in this example might underestimate the role of unions in an industry where percentage of unionization is greater. A second problem in measuring union impact is apparent from this example because company B may grant concessions to employees as a ploy to avoid unionization. These concessions, indirectly attributable to the presence of a union, would lead to underestimation of union impact on wages.

A second strategy in estimating union impact on wages is to compare two different industries that differ dramatically in the level of unionization.[18] This strategy suffers because nonunionized industries (e.g., agriculture, service) are markedly different from unionized industries in the types of labor employed and their general availability. Such differences have a major impact on wages independent of the level of unionization, and make any statements about union impact difficult to substantiate.

Such difficulties make the now classic work of Gregg Lewis even more impressive.[19] In a review and analysis of 12 studies dealing with union impact on wages, Lewis made a number of observations that are still considered valid today.[20]

1. The union impact on wages is dependent on the time period.
2. During recessionary periods, the presence of a union has a larger impact on wages. For example, during the 1932–33 period, union presence may have meant more than 25 percent higher wages for union versus nonunion workers. As the depression receded, union impact reached a low of something less than 5 percent in the late 1940s.
3. Current union impact on wages is estimated somewhere between +10 and +15 percent.[21]

It appears that unions do make a positive difference in wage levels, and this difference is greatest during recessionary periods and least during inflationary periods.[22] Part of the explanation for this time-based phenomenon is related to union resistance to wage cuts during recessions and the relatively slow responses of unions to wage increases during inflationary periods (because of rigidities or lags introduced by the presence of multiyear labor contracts).

---

[18]Ibid.

[19]H. Gregg Lewis, *Unionism and Relative Wages in the United States* (Chicago: University of Chicago Press, 1963).

[20]Ibid.

[21]Orley Ashenfelter, "Union Relative Wage Effects: New Evidence and a Survey of Their Implications for Wage Inflation," in *Econometric Contributions to Public Policy,* ed. R. Stone and W. Peterson (New York: St. Martin's Press, 1979), pp. 82–113.

[22]Robert Flanagan, Robert Smith, and Ronald Ehrenberg, *Labor Economics and Labor Relations* (Glenview, Ill.: Scott, Foresman, 1984).

Corresponding to Lewis's work in the private sector is Lewin's summary of union wage impacts in the public sector.[23] In a summary of 13 public-sector union studies, Lewin concludes that the average wage effect of public-sector unions is approximately +5 percent. As Lewin notes, this wage differential is smaller than typically assumed, and certainly smaller than is estimated for the private sector. Of course, this 5 percent average masks some large variations in wage increases for different occupational groups in the public sector. The largest gains for public-sector employees are reported for fire fighters, with some studies reporting as much as an 18 percent wage differential attributable to the presence of a union. At the other extreme, however, teachers' unions (primarily affiliates of the National Education Association and the American Federation of Teachers) have not fared as well, with reported impacts generally in the range of 1 to 4 percent.[24]

These wage premiums achieved by unions may have come with a very high price tag attached. Wage differentials between union and nonunion sectors continued to widen through 1981.[25] Dating back to 1979, though, and gaining momentum after 1981 has been an increasing trend toward wage concessions by unions. Recent estimates indicate at least 3 million workers have accepted wage concessions (defined as a wage freeze, reduction in wages, or altering of work rules favoring management).[26] Notable concessions have occurred in the automobile, steel, rubber, trucking, meat packing, airline, primary metals, food market, shoe manufacturing, and textiles industries.[27] These wage concessions have not been nearly as prevalent, nor as severe, in the public sector.[28]

Why have these concessions been necessary, and what impact do they have on union roles in compensation? Concessions can be traced to several factors which do not bode well for unions. First, the union-nonunion wage gap continued to widen through 1982. Absent any competition in the product market (or service market) for union goods (services), this may not have presented a serious problem, at least in the short run. However, deregulation, coupled with increased international and domestic nonunion competition, has taken its toll. Lower prices for nonunion goods and services generated pressures on unionized companies to either lower costs or face bankruptcy.

---

[23]David Lewin, "Public Sector Labor Relations: A Review Essay," in *Public Sector Labor Relations: Analysis and Readings,* ed. David Lewin, Peter Feuille, and Thomas Kochan (Glen Ridge, N.J.: Thomas Horton and Daughters, 1977), pp. 116–144.

[24]For a discussion of the reasons for this smaller public-sector union impact see Lewin et al., *Public Sector Labor Relations: An Analysis and Readings.*

[25]Daniel J. B. Mitchell, "Recent Union Contract Concessions," in *Brookings Papers on Economic Activity* (Washington, D.C.: Brookings Institution, 1982), pp. 165–203.

[26]Katz, "Collective Bargaining in 1982: A Turning Point in Industrial Relations?"

[27]Mitchell, "Recent Union Contract Concessions"; Gay, "Union Contract Concessions and Their Implications for Union Wage Determination"; Katz, "Collective Bargaining in 1982: A Turning Point in Industrial Relations?"

[28]Gay, "Union Contract Concessions and Their Implications for Union Wage Determination."

EXHIBIT 17.2
Distribution of Workers by First Year Wage Adjustments in Major Private Sector Collective Bargaining Settlements

Wage Adjustment (percent change)	1980	1981	1982	1983	1984*
Decreases	0†	5	2	15	7
No wage change	0	3	42	22	20
0–4 percent	3	3	9	14	27
4–8 percent	25	9	23	39	43
8 percent and over	71	61	24	10	2

*First six month's data only.
†Percentage of union workers receiving that increase.
Source: Robert Gay, "Union Contract Concessions and Their Implications for Union Wage Determination," Working paper no. 38, Division of Research and Statistics, Board of Governors of the Federal Reserve System, 1984.

Finally, revisions in the bankruptcy code during 1978 provided added impetus for concession bargaining. After 1978 financially troubled organizations found the courts increasingly receptive to setting aside union contracts for financially troubled organizations. This occurred even in situations where the company could not demonstrate that the labor contract would lead imminently to bankruptcy.[29]

The combined impact of these economic and legal forces has weakened the relative bargaining power of unions. For example, the impact on wage adjustments has been predictable, as evidenced in Exhibit 17.2.

The sizes of union wage settlements have declined markedly since 1980. In part, this is obviously due to the declining inflation rate over this period. It also represents a clear signal, though, that unions face grave challenges if they are to survive as an institutional force.[30]

UNION IMPACT: THE SPILLOVER EFFECT

Although union wage settlements have declined in recent years, the impact of unions in general would be understated if only the statistics from Exhibit 17.2 were reported. Unions also have an indirect impact on wages, called the spillover effect, for nonunion employees. Specifically, employers seek to avoid unionization by offering workers the wages, benefits, and working conditions won in rival unionized firms. The nonunion management continues to enjoy the freedom from union "interference" in decision making, and the workers receive the spillover of rewards already obtained by their unionized counterparts. Several studies document the existence and importance of this phenomenon, pro-

---

[29]*NLRB* v. *Bildisco,* 115 LRRM 2805, U.S. Supreme Court, 1984.

[30]Katz, "Collective Bargaining in 1982: A Turning Point in Industrial Relations?"

viding further evidence of the continuing role played by unions in wage determination.[31]

ROLE OF UNIONS IN WAGE AND SALARY ADMINISTRATION

Unions have a positive impact on wage levels in unionized firms relative to non-unionized firms. This tells us little, however, about the specific compensation roles unions play in organizations. The structure of wage demands (i.e., the components of the total wage package that are emphasized most by unions) is largely dependent on a union's evaluation of three factors:[32] (1) equity, (2) ability to pay, and (3) cost of living. The fourth factor mentioned earlier that affects wages—productivity—has traditionally been of greater concern to management than union.

On the equity issue, unions structure wage demands to ensure that workers within an organization are equitably treated relative to each other, and externally relative to the treatment of similar workers in other firms. As a consequence wage and/or benefits changes obtained by nonunion employees in a firm are monitored by the union and form part of the basis for contract demands. Similarly, unions seek to obtain wage packages that can be favorably compared to the settlements received in other industries. For example, the rubber workers may pay particular attention to the terms of a contract worked out between the United Auto Workers and Ford Motor Company. The level of wage increases obtained by the UAW becomes a target for the rubber workers to meet or exceed.

In part, the level of these demands based on the concept of equity is tempered by a second factor: ability to pay. When an organization has highly profitable years, its ability to pay larger wage increases also rises. For example, the United Steel Workers (USW) may feel that equitable or fair treatment requires that they obtain wage concessions equal to those in the auto industry. However, these demands would be tempered somewhat if the steel industry suffered an unprofitable year relative to the auto industry.

Four classic examples of this type of behavior have occurred within the automobile industry during the period 1970–1985. Because of American Motors's profit picture, the UAW agreed to extend the 1973 contract beyond the 1976 expiration date rather than demand a settlement consistent with the Big Three automakers. Operating off an old contract with a considerably lower wage bill gave American Motors the competitive edge it needed to garner a bet-

---

[31]Loren Solnick, "The Effect of Blue Collar Unions on White Collar Wages and Fringe Benefits,"*Industrial and Labor Relations Review* 38, no. 2 (1985), pp. 23–35; Laurence Kahn, "The Effect of Unions on the Earnings of Nonunion Workers," *Industrial and Labor Relations Review* 31, no. 1 (1978), pp. 205–16.

[32]John A. Fossum, *Labor Relations: Development, Structure, Process* (Plano, Tex.: Business Publications, 1982).

ter ability-to-pay position in the subsequent 1979 negotiations. Similarly, the 1979 wage and benefit concessions made by the UAW to avert bankruptcy by Chrysler, and the 1982 concessions for Ford and General Motors, are further examples of wage demands (concessions!) based on ability to pay.

A third factor influential in determining union wage demands centers on the standard of living for union members. Large cost-of-living increases during the 1970s and early 1980s resulted in several years where worker purchasing power (real wages) actually declined. This runs contrary to the union goal of improving member standards of living. Historically, inflation has triggered tougher stands on wage issues at the bargaining table. More recently, the union response has been to negotiate for more liberal cost-of-living adjustment clauses. Currently, though, with union power eroding and inflation rates moderating, standard of living has taken a secondary role for union negotiators to the task of preserving union jobs.

Contractual Wage and Salary Issues

There are basically three characteristics that can be used to describe the role of a union contract in wage and salary administration. The first characteristic is the negotiated magnitude of the economic package. The presence of a union, as already noted, has a +10 to +15 percent impact on the magnitude of the economic package. Unions also play a role in determining two other characteristics of an economic package: (1) form of pay and (2) administration of pay.

Form of pay deals basically with the question of how the economic package is to be allocated between wages and benefits. Whether because of reduced management control, strong union-worker preference for benefits, or other reasons, unionized employees have a greater percentage of their total wage bill allocated to employee benefits.[33] Typically, this shows up in the form of higher pension expenditures or higher insurance benefits.[34] One particularly well-controlled study found unionization associated with 24 percent higher levels of pension expenditures and 46 percent higher insurance expenditures.[35]

Perhaps of the greatest interest to current and future compensation administrators is the role unions play in administering wages. This role is outlined primarily in the contract. The following illustrations of this role are taken from

---

[33]Bevars Mabry, "The Economics of Fringe Benefits," *Industrial Relations* 12 (1973), pp. 95–106.

[34]Robert Rice, "Skill, Earnings and the Growth of Wage Supplements,"*American Economic Review* 56 (1966), pp. 583–93; George Kalamotousakis, "Statistical Analysis of the Determinants of Employee Benefits by Type," *American Economist,* Fall 1972, pp. 139–47; William Bailey and Albert Schwenk, "Employer Expenditures for Private Retirement and Insurance Plans," *Monthly Labor Review* 95 (1972), pp. 15–19; Fosu, "Impact of Unionism on Pension Fringes".

[35]Loren Solnick, "Unionism and Fringe Benefits Expenditures," *Industrial Relations* 17, no. 1 (1978), pp. 102–7.

a summary of 1,711 major (1,000 workers or more) collective bargaining agreements, the majority of which were in effect between 1977 and 1986.[36]

1. Basis of pay. The vast majority of contracts specify that one or more jobs are to be compensated on an hourly basis. Alternatively, agreements may specify a fixed daily, weekly, biweekly, or monthly rate. In addition, agreements often indicate a specific day of the week as payday, and sometimes require payment on or before a certain hour. The following contract clause illustrates this requirement.

> The company will continue to pay wages earned on a weekly basis. The first shift will be paid on/or before 7:30 A.M. Friday; the second shift will be paid on/or before 3:30 P.M. Friday; and the third shift will be paid on/or before 11:30 P.M. Thursday.[37]

Much less frequently, contracts specify some form of incentive system as the basis for pay. The vast majority of clauses specifying incentive pay occur in manufacturing (as opposed to nonmanufacturing) industries. Many of these clauses provide for union-management discussion of incentives:

> It is agreed that all matters pertaining to piece work, incentive pay and bonus are subject to discussion between the company and the union. . . .
>
> All work being performed on incentive basis shall have the allowance established prior to the start of the job; and this allowance and description of the job shall be furnished to the men performing the work at the beginning of the shift or job, except in cases where the allowance for the work to be performed is to be divided between individuals or groups, in which case the allowance shall be given to the individual or group prior to the end of the shift. If the allowance and the description are not furnished as required above, the job shall be considered day work.
>
> Incentive allowance rates will not be reduced after work has been started upon the particular job or after the completion of the particular job covered by the allowance, except when some reduction is made in the quantity of work originally specified or where the method of performing the work has been revised.[38]

2. Occupation-Wage differentials. Most contracts recognize that different occupations should receive different wage rates. Within occupations, though, a single wage rate prevails:[39]

---

[36]U.S. Department of Labor, *Major Collective Bargaining Agreements: Wage Administration Provisions* (Washington, D.C.: Bureau of Labor Statistics, Bulletin 1425–17, 1978); General Motors-UAW, "Agreement between General Motors Corporation and the UAW," September 1984; Bureau of National Affairs, "Wage Patterns and Wage Data," in *Collective Bargaining Negotiations and Contracts, 18.10-18.993* (Washington, D.C.: Bureau of National Affairs, 1984).

[37]General Motors-UAW, "Agreement between General Motors Corporation and the UAW"; Bureau of National Affairs, "Wage Patterns and Wage Data."

[38]Ibid.

[39]Ibid.

	Effective Date of This Agreement
Journeyman brewers and utility men	$7.75
Apprentice brewers	7.75
Brewery workers	7.70
Freight handlers	7.615

Although rare, there are some contracts which do not recognize occupational/skill differentials. These contracts specify a single standard rate for all jobs covered by the agreements. Usually such contracts cover a narrow range of skilled groups.

3. Experience/merit differentials. Single rates are usually specified for workers within a particular job classification. Single-rate agreements do not differentiate wages on the basis of either seniority or merit. Workers with varying years of experience and output receive the same single rate. Alternatively, agreements may specify wage ranges, including all or the top and bottom steps in the range. The following example is fairly typical:[40]

Labor Grade	Minimum							Maximum
A–2	$7.18	$7.23	$7.28	$7.33	$7.38	$7.43	$7.48	$7.53
A–1	6.82	6.87	6.92	6.97	7.02	7.07	7.12	7.17
1	6.45	6.50	6.59	6.60	6.65	6.70	6.75	6.80
2	6.11	6.16	6.21	6.26	6.31	6.36	6.41	6.46
3	5.81	5.86	5.91	5.96	6.01	6.06		6.11
4	5.56	5.61	5.66	5.71	5.76			5.81
5	5.36	5.41	5.46					5.51
6	5.15	5.20						5.25
7	4.87	4.92						4.97
8	4.72							4.77
9	4.56							4.61
10	4.51							4.56

The vast majority of contracts requiring wage ranges specify seniority as the basis for movement through the range. Automatic progression is an appropriate name for this type of movement through the wage range, with the contract frequently specifying the time interval between movements. This type of progression is most appropriate when the necessary job skills are within the grasp of most employees. Denial of a raise is a significant exception, and frequently is accompanied by the right of the union to submit any wage denial to the grievance procedure.

At the other extreme of management intervention, some agreements permit management to shorten the time between automatic progressions for workers with outstanding performance records. For example:

---

[40]Ibid.

Nothing in this provision shall prevent the employer from granting individual increases more frequently than each 16 weeks if, in its judgment, they are merited.[41]

A second strategy for moving employees through wage ranges is based exclusively on merit. Employees who are evaluated more highly receive larger or more rapid increments than average or poor performers. Within these contracts, it is common to specify that disputed merit appraisals may be submitted to grievance. If the right to grieve is not explicitly *excluded,* the union also has the implicit right to grieve.

The third strategy for movement through a range combines automatic and merit progression in some manner. A frequent strategy is to grant automatic increases up to the midpoint of the range and permit subsequent increases only when merited on the basis of performance appraisal.

4. Other differentials. There are a number of remaining contractual provisions that deal with differentials for reasons not yet covered. A first example deals with differentials for new and probationary employees. About one half of major agreements refer to differentials for these employees. The most common rate designation is below or at the minimum of the rate range. For example:

> New employees hired on or after the effective date of this Agreement, who do not hold a seniority date in any General Motors plant and are not covered by the provisions of Paragraph (98b) below, shall be hired at a rate equal to eighty-five (85) percent of the maximum base rate of the job classification. Such employees shall receive an automatic increase to: (1) ninety (90) percent of the job classification at the expiration of one hundred and eighty (180) days, (2) ninety five (95) percent of the maximum base rate of the job classification at the expiration of three hundred and sixty-five (365) days, (3) the maximum base rate of the job classification at the expiration of five hundred and forty-five (545) days.[42]

A second example of contractual differentials deals with different pay to unionized employees who are employed by a firm in different geographic areas. Very few contracts provide for different wages under these circumstances, despite the problems that can arise in paying uniform wages across regions with markedly different costs of living.

A final category where differentials are mentioned in contracts deals with part-time and temporary employees. Few contracts specify special rates for these employees. Those that do, however, are about equally split between giving part-time/temporary employees wages above full-time workers (because they have been excluded from the employee benefits program) or below full-time workers.

5. Wage adjustment provisions. Frequently in multiyear contracts some provision is made for wage adjustment during the term of the contract. There

---

[41]Ibid.

[42]General Motors-UAW, "Agreement between General Motors Corporation and the UAW."

are three major ways these adjustments might be specified: (1) deferred wage increases, (2) cost-of-living adjustments (COLA) or escalator clauses, and (3) reopener clauses. A deferred wage increase is negotiated at the time of initial contract negotiations with the timing and amount specified in the contract. A COLA clause, as noted earlier, involves periodic adjustment based typically on changes in the consumer price index. Finally, a reopener clause specifies that wages, and sometimes such nonwage items as pension/benefits, will be renegotiated at a specified time or under certain conditions.

In recent years, these contractual provisions have frequently specified the schedule for wage concessions agreed to by the union. For example, wage freezes, rollbacks, or lump sum payments instead of general increases were agreed to for the first year in 27 percent of all contracts negotiated in 1984.[43] Subsequent increases negotiated for the second and third year of 1984 contracts averaged 4.0 percent.[44]

UNION RESPONSE TO THE ECONOMIC AND SOCIAL ENVIRONMENT OF THE 1980s

Consider the situation union leadership faces for the 1980s. Domestic and foreign competition and technological innovations play large roles in today's high unemployment levels. Couple this with slow economic recovery and lower profit margins, and it is easily seen that the challenges involved in adapting to a changing economic environment are formidable. Now, on top of this add current interest by the Equal Employment Opportunity Commission (EEOC) in the design and functioning of compensation systems. As social concern about wage discrimination rises, unions must be prepared to cooperate with management in the design of bias-free compensation packages.

Union response to both economic and social change in the 1980s will play a major role in determining the evolution of wage and salary administration. The final two sections cover the probable thrust of union activity.

Union Response to Social Change

One of the biggest challenges compensation administrators and union leaders are likely to face during the 1980s is in the area of wage discrimination. The Equal Employment Opportunity Commission has become increasingly concerned about the failure of minority and female earnings to approach those of their white male counterparts. To correct this problem the EEOC would like to require equal pay for jobs of comparable worth. The key in this battle will be

---

[43]Bureau of National Affairs, "Wage Patterns and Wage Data."

[44]Ibid.

defining the concept "comparable worth." Initial evidence suggests the EEOC will make a major effort to require employers to develop and document sound compensation systems.[45] The foundation of this procedure will be sound job analysis and job evaluation procedures. Herein lies the major challenge to unions.

In the past it has been common for unions to view job analysis and job evaluation with some skepticism. In particular, job evaluation is frequently viewed as a process with almost mystical properties. Derivation of compensable factors, factor weights, and a job hierarchy are viewed by unions as overly complex. A dominant response by unions in the past has been to allow management to develop the system and evaluate jobs. If the end result was not satisfactory, disagreements over evaluated position of jobs were subject to grievance. Unions must take a more active role in jointly determining with management the appropriate components and processes for job evaluation. Such involvement in the process, hopefully, will reduce dissatisfaction with the final job hierarchy, thereby increasing the probability that the job hierarchy will be based on a system that is well-documented and defensible.

Union Response to Economic Change

The economic challenge of the 1980s presents a critical juncture for unions. Union membership has fallen off from a peak of 36 percent during the latter days of the 1930s Depression to approximately 20 percent today. In response, unions have been relatively slow in their efforts to attract workers in geographic areas (e.g., the South) and industries (e.g., service) which historically have been nonunion. It appears now that unions have opportunity under adversity to demonstrate their value to nonunion sectors. This opportunity is dependent upon union responses to the current economic upheavals in the traditional union stronghold: the manufacturing industry. Large segments of the manufacturing sector, most notably the auto and steel industries, have faced unprecedented economic declines and layoffs traceable to our noncompetitive position in the international market. What will be the response of unions? It is unlikely that the spurt of contract reopenings and wage concessions foretells the death of traditional long-term labor contracts. Rather union response is likely to center on ensuring that industries buffeted by deregulation and intense competition are able to control labor costs. This signals continued moderation in annual wage increase demands, increased willingness to consider work rule changes, renewed interest in cooperative labor-management relations, and further experimentation with profit sharing and other wage proposals that increase cost competitiveness. These trends should lessen the union-nonunion wage gap and moderate the decline in union membership.

---

[45]Equal Employment Advisory Council, *Comparable Worth: Issues and Alternatives* (Washington, D.C.: Equal Employment Advisory Council, 1980).

SUMMARY

It is apparent that unions have an impact on compensation administration in both unionized and nonunionized firms. In particular, unions affect general wage levels and the structure of wage packages. If union impact on compensation is to continue as a strong force, though, the unions of tomorrow must evolve to meet new challenges. Increased market competition, the international scope of business, and stiffening resistance to unionization all mandate changes in union tactics and union structures. Included in these changes are sure to be different perceptions toward compensation. Hopefully this will lead to greater cooperation in the design and administration of compensation.

REVIEW QUESTIONS

1. How do COLAs operate? Are they an effective weapon in maintaining the real income of workers?
2. How does the issue of equity affect union compensation demands in the bargaining process?
3. What is the "spillover" effect?
4. What has been the role of ability to pay in recent contract negotiations?
5. Identify strategies unions must adopt to meet future social and economic changes in the United States.

Part 6
Compensation Applications

Case 1 Remtol Corporation: The Reluctant Foreman

Remtol Corporation is the world's largest privately owned construction company. Founded in 1927 by James Remington, Remtol had worldwide revenues last year of $3.5 billion. About 55 percent of this revenue was earned in foreign markets. The largest of these foreign markets is currently Saudi Arabia, where oil revenues finance the construction of an entire modern city designed to support 3 million inhabitants. The budget for Remtol's portion of this project is $8.7 billion over a 15-year period.

Remtol employs 87,000 people worldwide. The breakdown is roughly:

Occupational Group	Employment
Labor	44,000
Clerical	8,800
Semiskilled	1,750
Skilled	2,250
Service (guards, etc.)	1,000
Sales	1,200
Technical	9,000
Professional	13,000
Managerial	6,000

Remtol Corporation has an opening for a new construction foreman to help renovate a Ford Motor Plant in Wixom, Michigan. Because of his past performance as a laborer, Bill Cook has been recommended for the job by the Human Resources Department. Andy White, the general superintendent on the project, has the pleasure of telling Bill about the promotion. Bill is waiting outside Andy's office right now.

Role for Andy White, General Superintendent

Bill Cook has been with Remtol Corporation for six years as a construction laborer. During that time, he has only missed 11 days of work for illness. Your

607

records show he is a hard worker, and you have heard from a number of sources that Bill is a natural leader. The other laborers respect him and his opinions.

You have been asked by the Human Resources Department to inform Bill that he has been chosen as the new laborer foreman in charge of 25 construction laborers. Along with the promotion comes a raise from $10/hour to $12/hour for all hours worked. The opportunity is an excellent one and you are looking forward to telling Bill the good news.

Role for Bill Cook, Construction Laborer

Andy White, General Superintendent of the Wixom Project, has asked you to come into his office. You are a bit leery of going in. After all, no one wants to be caught snuggling up to management. You don't need a razzing from the other guys or from the construction local in Pontiac.

You hope they do not think anything is wrong with your work. You like the hard physical effort; it keeps you in shape. You also like the interactions with the other laborers. They are a good bunch of guys and they seem to respect you. Their friendship and trust is important to you. Almost as important, though, the job really pays. Overtime during the past three years has always been good. That double-time pay for an average of 500 hours a year sure has helped. Things look equally good in the business for the next year. You wonder what the problem is.

Questions

The following questions should be addressed in the meeting between Bill and Andy.

1. Why is Bill Cook reluctant to take the foreman position?
2. What is the wage differential for Bill between the position of laborer and foreman, assuming a 2,000 hour normal work year and continued overtime equaling past averages?
3. What would you recommend as an appropriate differential? What steps should you take to derive that figure?

Case 2 *Remtol Corporation: Compensating Engineers*

You have obtained the following summary information from market competitors for engineers:

N	Years since Last Degree	Performance Level	Monthly Salary
800	2	Bottom 10 percent	$1,640
		Average (50th percentile)	1,770
		Top 10 percent	2,000
325	4	Bottom 10 percent	1,780
		Average	1,960
		Top 10 percent	2,270
525	8	Bottom 10 percent	2,020
		Average	2,300
		Top 10 percent	2,710
460	12	Bottom 10 percent	2,220
		Average	2,580
		Top 10 percent	3,130
280	20	Bottom 10 percent	2,440
		Average	2,960
		Top 10 percent	3,650
240	28	Bottom 10 percent	2,510
		Average	3,130
		Top 10 percent	3,880
200	36	Bottom 10 percent	2,510
		Average	3,130
		Top 10 percent	3,880

Tasks

1. Plot the maturity curves for the three performance levels expressing the relationship between monthly salary and years since last degree.
2. What should be the approximate salary for the 10 Remtol engineers whose pertinent employment data is outlined in Exhibits 1 and 2?
3. What, if any, changes would you recommend in data collection and construction of future maturity curves? Why?

EXHIBIT 1
Employment Data on Ten Engineers

Employee Code Number	Years since Last Degree	Performance Rating
E 7856	6	9
E 4216	2	7
E 13307	8	10
E 5912	12	4
E 6081	15	10
E 2222	4	10
E 1346	28	4
E 5021	12	2
E 9002	16	7
E 8146	30	9

EXHIBIT 2
Distribution of Engineers' Performance Ratings

Overall Evaluation	Position in Performance Distribution
9–10	Top 10 percent
8	Top 25 percent
7	Median
5–6	Top 75 percent
0–4	Bottom 10 percent

Case 3   *Remtol Corporation: Costing Out a Compensation Package for Expatriates*

Remtol has just successfully bid on construction of a hydroelectric power plant in Zimbabwe, Africa. Eventually the project will employ 1,300 expats (expatriates) and 4,000 local nationals. Normally, you would determine expat salaries by surveying other multinational corporations in the local area. Zimbabwe is so underdeveloped, though, that you represent the first foreign corporation of any substance to undertake a major project. To determine what pay is necessary to attract workers to Zimbabwe, you have decided to use Roger Pewter as a test case for costing. Roger is married and has two children in their early teens. Since the project will require four years to complete, and Roger's contract would have to be a two-year minimum, it is likely that he will want to take his family.

Identify the basic components that you think would have to be included in Roger's compensation package. Now determine specific elements for each basic category. Your choices should be guided by the basic philosophy of "keeping the worker whole." A worker should not be punished either financially or psychically for accepting a foreign subsidiary position.

How would you go about determining if the package is equitable?

Glossary of Terms

Ability Refers to the individual's capability to engage in a specific behavior.

Ability to Pay The ability of a firm to meet employee wage demands while remaining profitable; a frequent issue in contract negotiations with unions. A firm's ability to pay is constrained by its ability to compete in its product market.

Access Discrimination Focuses on the staffing and allocation decisions made by employers. It denies particular jobs, promotions, or training opportunities to qualified women or minorities. This type of discrimination is illegal under Title VII of the Civil Rights Act of 1964.

Across-the-Board Increases A general adjustment that provides equal increases to all employees.

Adjective Checklist An individual (or job) rating technique. In its simplest form, a set of adjectives or descriptive statements. If the employee (job) possesses a trait listed, the item is checked. A rating score from the checklist equals the number of statements checked.

Age Discrimination in Employment Act (ADEA) of 1967 (Amended 1978) It makes nonfederal employees between 40 and 70 a protected class relative to their treatment in pay, benefits, and other personnel actions.

All-Salaried Work Force A concept whose objective is to increase employee commitment to the work by adopting a more egalitarian approach to pay practices. It involves equalizing benefits for all employees and converting hourly pay rates to biweekly rates.

Alternation Ranking A job evaluation method that involves ordering the job descriptions alternately at each extreme. All the jobs are considered. Agreement is reached on which is the most valuable, then the least valuable. Evaluators alternate between the next most valued and next least valued and so on until all the jobs have been ordered.

American Compensation Association (ACA) A nonprofit organization for training compensation professionals.

Appeals Procedures Mechanism created to handle pay disagreements. They provide a forum for employees and managers to voice their complaints and receive a hearing.

Base Pay *See* Base Wage.

Base Wage The basic cash compensation that an employer pays for the work performed. Tends to reflect the value of the work itself and ignore differences in contribution attributable to individual employees.

Basic Pay Policies They include decisions on the relative importance of (1) internal consistency, (2) external competitiveness, (3) employee contributions, and (4) the nature of the administration of the pay system. These policies form the foundation on which pay systems are designed and administered and serve as guidelines within which pay is managed to accomplish the system's objectives.

Behaviorally Anchored Rating Scales (BARS) Are a variant on standard rating scales, in which the various scale levels are anchored with behavioral descriptions directly applicable to jobs being evaluated.

Benchmark (or Key) Jobs A prototypical job, or group of jobs, used as reference points for making pay comparisons within or without the organization. Benchmark jobs have well-known and stable contents; their current pay rates are generally acceptable and the pay differentials among them are relatively stable. A group of benchmark jobs, taken together, contains the entire range of compensable factors and is accepted in the external labor market for setting wages.

Bendeaux Plan Individual incentive plan that provides a variation on straight piecework and standard hour plans. Instead of timing an entire task, a Bendeaux plan requires determination of the time required to complete each simple action of a task. Workers receive a wage incentive for completing a task in less than a standard time.

Bennett Amendment Links Title VII of the Civil Rights Act with the Equal Pay Act by providing that it is not unlawful to differentiate on the basis of sex in determining pay if such differentiation is authorized by the Equal Pay Act.

BLS *See* Bureau of Labor Statistics.

Bona Fide Occupational Qualifications (BFOQ) An exception to the restrictions of Title VII of the Civil Rights Act of 1964. Specifies that there are certain jobs for which a specific sex, national origin, or religious affiliation may be legitimate qualifications.

Bonus A bonus is a lump-sum payment to an employee in recognition of goal achievement.

Bootleg Wages Wages paid above the market rate by an employer in a tight labor market to attract and retain qualified workers.

"Bottom Up" Approach to Pay Budgeting   Under this approach individual employees' pay rates for the next plan year are forecasted and summed to create an organization's total budget.

Budget   A plan within which managers operate and a standard against which managers' actual expenditures are evaluated.

Bureau of Labor Statistics   A major source of publicly available pay data. It publishes three basic surveys: area wage studies, industry wage studies, and a National Survey of Professional, Administrative, Technical, and Clerical Pay.

Cafeteria (Flexible) Benefit Programs   A benefit plan in which employees have a choice as to the benefits they receive within some dollar limit. Usually a common core benefit package is required (e.g., specific minimum levels of health, disability, retirement, and death benefit) plus elective programs from which the employee may select a set dollar amount. Additional coverage may be available through employee contributions.

Capital Appreciation Plans   *See* Long-Term Incentive and Capital Appreciation.

Career Paths   Refers to the progression of jobs within an organization.

Central Tendency Error   A rating error that occurs when a rater consistently rates a group of employees at or close to the midpoint of a scale irrespective of true score performance of ratees.

Civil Rights Act   Title VII of the Civil Rights Act of 1964 prohibits discrimination in terms and conditions of employment (including benefits) that is based on race, color, religion, sex, or national origin.

Classification   Job evaluation method that involves slotting job descriptions into a series of classes or grades that cover the range of jobs and that serve as a standard against which the job descriptions are compared.

Commission   Payment tied directly to achievement of performance standards. Commissions are directly tied to a profit index (sales, production level) and employee costs; thus, they rise and fall in line with revenues.

Comparable Worth   A doctrine that maintains that women performing jobs judged to be equal on some measure of inherent worth should be paid the same as men, excepting allowable differences, such as seniority, merit, and production-based pay plans, and other non-sex-related factors.

Compa-Ratio   An index that helps assess how managers actually pay employees in relation to the midpoint of the pay range established for jobs. It estimates how well actual practices correspond to intended policy. Calculated as the following ratio:

$$\text{Compa-Ratio} = \frac{\text{Average rates actually paid}}{\text{Range midpoint}}$$

Compensable Factors Job attributes that provide the basis for evaluating the relative worth of jobs inside an organization. A compensable factor must be work related, business related, and acceptable to the parties involved.

Compensation All forms of financial returns and tangible services and benefits employees receive as part of an employment relationship.

Compensation Budgeting A part of the organization's planning process; helps to ensure that future financial expenditures are coordinated and controlled. It involves forecasting the total expenditures required by the pay system during the next period as well as the amount of the pay increases. "Bottom up" and "top down" are the two typical approaches to the process.

Compensation Committee Usually composed of compensation professionals, operating managers, jobholders, and, less frequently, union representatives. Its purpose is to gain acceptance and understanding of pay decisions. May act in an advisory or sanctioning capacity.

Compensation Differentials Differentials in pay among jobs across and within organizations, and among individuals in the same job in an organization.

Compensation Objectives The desired results of the pay system. The basic pay objectives include efficiency, equity, and compliance with laws and regulations. Objectives shape the design of the pay system and serve as the standard against which the success of the pay system is evaluated.

Compensation System Controls Basic processes that serve to control pay decision making. They include (1) controls inherent in the design of the pay techniques (e.g., increase guidelines, range maximums and minimums), and (2) budgetary controls.

Compliance Pay Objective It involves conforming to various federal and state laws and regulations. To ensure continuous compliance, pay objectives need to be adjusted as these laws and regulations change.

Comprehensive Occupational Data Analysis Program (CODAP) The earliest attempt to quantify job analysis using task-oriented data.

Congruency The degree of consistency or "fit" between the compensation system and other organizational components such as the strategy, product-market stage, culture and values, employee needs, union status.

Consumer Price Index (CPI) Published by the Bureau of Labor Statistics, U.S. Department of Labor, it measures the changes in prices of a fixed market basket of goods and services purchased by a hypothetical average family.

Content Theories Motivation theories that focus on *what* motivates people rather than on *how* people are motivated. Maslow's need hierarchy theory and Herzberg's two-factor theory fall in this category.

Contributory Benefit Financing Plans Costs shared between employer and employee.

Conventional Job Analysis Methods These methods (e.g., functional job analysis) typically involve an analyst using a questionnaire in conjunction with structured interviews of job incumbents and supervisors. They place considerable reliance on analysts' ability to understand the work performed and to accurately describe it.

Cooperative Wage Study (CWS)   A study undertaken by 12 steel companies and the United Steel Workers to design an industrywide point plan (the Steel Plan) for clerical and technical personnel.

Cost of Living   Actual individual expenditures on goods and services. The only way to measure it accurately is to examine the expense budget of each employee.

Cost of Living Adjustments (COLAs)   Across-the-board wage and salary increases or supplemental payments based on changes in some index of prices, usually the consumer price index (CPI). If included in a union contract, COLAs are designed to increase wages automatically during the life of the contract as a function of changes in the consumer price index (CPI).

Cost Saving Plans   Group incentive plans that focus on cost savings rather than on profit increases as the standard of group incentive (e.g., Scanlon, Rucker, Improshare).

CPI   *See* Consumer Price Index.

Davis-Bacon Act of 1931   Requires most federal contractors to pay wage rates prevailing in the area.

Decision-Banding   A single-factor job evaluation system that focuses on measuring the amount of decision making discretion an employee has in a job.

Deferred Compensation Program   Provide income to an employee at some future time as compensation for work performed now. Types of deferred compensation programs include stock option plans and pension plans.

Direct Compensation   Pay received directly in the form of cash (e.g., wages, bonuses, incentives).

Direct Pay   *See* Direct Compensation.

Disparate (Unequal) Impact Standard   Outlaws the application of pay practices that may appear to be neutral but have a negative effect on females or minorities, unless those practices can be shown to be business related.

Disparate (Unequal) Treatment Standard   Outlaws the application of different standards to different classes of employees, unless they can be shown to be business related.

DOLs   Original Department of Labor Methodology of job analysis. It categorized data to be collected as (1) actual work performed and (2) work traits or characteristics. Actual work performed is further refined into three categories: Worker functions (what the worker does), work fields (the methods and techniques employed), and products and services (output).

Double-Track System   A framework for professional employees in an organization whereby at least two general tracks of ascending compensation steps are available: (1) a "managerial" track to be ascended through increasing responsibility for supervision of people and (2) a "professional" track to be ascended through increasing contributions of a professional nature.

Drive Theory A motivational theory that assumes that all behavior is induced by drives (i.e., energizers such as thirst, hunger, sex), and that present behavior is based in large part on the consequences or rewards of past behavior.

Efficiency Pay Objective Involves (1) improving productivity and (2) controlling labor costs.

Employee Benefits That part of the total compensation package, other than pay for time worked, provided to employees in whole or in part by employer payments (e.g., life insurance, pension, workers' compensation, vacation).

Employee Contributions Refers to comparisons among individuals doing the same job for the same organization.

Employee Equity *See* Employee Contributions.

Employee Retirement Income Security Act of 1974 (ERISA) An act regulating private employer pension and welfare programs. The act has provisions that cover eligibility for participation, reporting, and disclosure requirements, establish fiduciary standards for the financial management of retirement funds, set up tax incentives for funding pension plans, and establish the Pension Benefit Guaranty Corporation to insure pension plans against financial failures.

Employee Services and Benefits Programs that include a wide array of alternative pay forms ranging from payments for time not worked (vacations, jury duty), through services (drug counseling, financial planning, cafeteria support) to protection (medical care, life insurance, and pensions).

Entry Jobs Jobs which are filled from the external labor market and whose pay tends to reflect external economic factors rather than organization's culture and traditions.

Equal Employment Opportunity Commission (EEOC) A commission of the federal government charged with enforcing the provisions of the Civil Rights Act of 1964 and the EPA of 1963 as it pertains to sex discrimination in pay.

Equal Pay Act (EPA) of 1963 An amendment to the Fair Labor Standards Act of 1938, prohibiting pay differentials on jobs which are substantially equal in terms of skills, effort, responsibility, and working conditions, except when they are the result of bona fide seniority, merit, or production-based systems, or any other job-related factor other than sex.

Equalization Component As a part of an expatriate compensation package, equalization is one form of equity designed to "keep the worker whole" (i.e., maintain real income or purchasing power of base pay). This equalization typically comes in the form of four types of allowances: tax equalization, housing, education and language training, and cost-of-living (COLA) allowances.

Equity   Absolute or relative justice or "fairness" in an exchange such as the employment contract. Absolute fairness is evaluated against a universally accepted criterion of equity, while relative fairness is assessed against a criterion that may vary according to the individuals involved in the exchange, the nature of what is exchanged, and the context of the exchange.

Equity Pay Objective   Fair pay treatment for all the participants in the employment relationship. Focuses attention on pay systems that recognize employee contributions as well as employee needs.

Equity Theory   A theory proposing that in an exchange relationship (such as employment) the equality of outcome/input ratios between a person and a comparison other (a standard or relevant person/group) will determine fairness or equity. If the ratios diverge from each other, the person will experience reactions of unfairness and inequity.

ESOP (Employee Stock Ownership Plan)   A plan in which a company borrows money from a financial institution using its stock as a collateral for the loan. Principal and interest loan repayment are tax deductible. With each loan repayment, the lending institution releases a certain amount of stock being held as security. The stock is then placed into an Employee Stock Ownership Trust (ESOT) for distribution at no cost to all employees. The employees receive the stock upon retirement or separation from the company. TRASOPs and PAYSOPs are variants of ESOPs.

Essay   An open-ended performance appraisal format. The descriptors used could range from comparisons with other employees through adjectives, behaviors, and goal accomplishment.

Exchange Value   The price of labor (the wage) determined in a competitive market; in other words, labor's worth (the price) is whatever the buyer and seller agree upon.

Executive Perquisites (Perks)   They are special benefits made available to top executives (and sometimes other managerial employees). May be taxable income to the receiver. Company-related perks may include luxury office, special parking, and company-paid membership in clubs/associations, hotels, resorts. Personal perks include such things as low-cost loans, personal and legal counseling, free home repairs and improvements, and so on. Since 1978 various tax and agency rulings have slowly been requiring companies to place a value on perks, thus increasing the taxable income of executives.

Exempt Jobs   Jobs not subject to the provisions of the Fair Labor Standards Act with respect to minimum wage and overtime. Exempt employees include most executives, administrators, professionals, and outside sales representatives.

Expatriates   Employees assigned outside their base country for any period of time in excess of one year.

Expectancies   Beliefs (or subjective probability estimates) individuals have that particular actions on their part will lead to certain outcomes or goals.

Expectancy (VIE) Theory   A motivation theory that proposes that individuals will select an alternative based on how this choice relates to outcomes such as rewards. The choice made is based on the strength or value of the outcome and on the perceived probability that this choice will lead to the desired outcome.

External Competitiveness   Refers to the pay relationships *among* organizations and focuses attention on the competitive positions reflected in these relationships.

Extrinsic Rewards   Rewards that a person receives from sources other than the job itself. They include compensation, supervision, promotions, vacations, friendships, and all other important outcomes apart from the job itself.

Face Validity   The determination of the relevance of a measuring device on "appearance" only.

Factor Comparison   A job evaluation method in which jobs are assessed on the bases of two criteria: (1) a set of compensable factors and (2) wages for a selected set of jobs.

Factor Scales   Reflect different degrees within each compensable factor. Most commonly five to seven degrees are defined. Each degree may also be anchored by the typical skills, tasks and behaviors, or key job titles.

Factor Weights   Indicate the importance of each compensable factor in a job evaluation system. Weights can be derived either through committee judgment or statistical analysis.

Fair Labor Standards Act of 1938 (FLSA)   A federal law governing minimum wage, overtime pay, equal pay for men and women in the same types of jobs, child labor, and recordkeeping requirements.

Federal Insurance Contributions Act (FICA)   The source of Social Security contribution withholding requirements. The FICA deduction is paid by both employer and employee.

Flexible Benefits   *See* Cafeteria (Flexible) Benefit Programs.

Flexible Occupational Analysis System (FOCAS)   A task-based quantitative job analysis inventory. It differs from other job analysis techniques in that separate questionnaires have been developed for different occupations. All these questionnaires have a common core of task-based items, and unique items are added to the core for each unique occupation.

Forms of Compensation   Pay may be received directly in the form of cash (e.g., wages, bonuses, incentives) or indirectly through services and benefits (e.g., pensions, health insurance, vacations). This definition excludes other forms of rewards or returns that employees may receive, such as promotion, recognition for outstanding work behavior, and the like.

Forms of Pay   *See* Forms of Compensation.

Functional Job Analysis (FJA)   A conventional approach to job analysis which is followed by the U.S. Department of Labor. Five categories of data are collected: what the worker does; the methodologies and techniques employed; the machines, tools, and equipment used; the products and services that result; and the traits required of the worker. FJA constitutes a modification of the DOLs methodology and is widely used in the public sector.

Gain-Sharing or Group Incentive Plans   Incentive plans that are based on some measure of group performance rather than individual performance. Taking data on a past year as a base, group incentive plans may focus on cost savings (e.g., the Scanlon, Rucker, and Improshare plans) or on profit increases (profit-sharing plans) as the standard to distribute a portion of the accrued funds among relevant employees.

Gantt Plan   Individual incentive plan that provides for variable incentives as a function of a standard expressed as time period per unit of production. Under this plan a standard time for a task is purposely set at a level requiring high effort to complete.

General Schedule (GS)   A job evaluation plan used by the U.S. Office of Personnel Management for white collar employees. It has 18 "grades" (classes). Most jobs are in 15 grades; the top three are combined into a "supergrade" which covers senior executives.

Green Circle Rates   Pay rates that are below the minimum rate for a job or pay range for a grade.

Group Incentive Plans   *See* Gain-Sharing or Group Incentive Plans.

Halo Error   A positive or negative rating error in which rating in one performance dimension strongly influences ratings on other performance dimensions, irrespective of true score relationship across dimensions.

Halsey 50-50 Method   Individual incentive plan that provides for variable incentives as a function of a standard expressed as time period per unit of production. This plan derives its name from the shared split between worker and employer of any savings in direct costs.

Hay System   A point factor system that evaluates jobs with respect to know-how, problem solving, and accountability. It is used primarily for exempt (managerial/ professional) jobs.

Health Maintenance Organization (HMO)   A nontraditional health care delivery system. HMOs offer comprehensive benefits, outpatient services as well as hospital coverages, for a fixed monthly prepaid fee.

Hierarchies (or job structures)   Jobs ordered according to their relative content and/or value.

Hit Rate   The ability of a job evaluation plan to replicate a predetermined, agreed-upon job structure.

Human Capital Theory A branch of labor economics proposing that the investment one is willing to make to enter an occupation is related to the returns one expects to earn over time in the form of compensation.

Improshare (IMproved PROductivity through SHARing) A gain-sharing plan in which a standard is developed which identifies the expected hours required to produce an acceptable level of output. Any savings arising from production of agreed upon output in fewer than expected hours are shared by the firm and the worker.

Incentive Inducement offered in advance to influence future performance (e.g., sales commissions).

Incentive Stock Options (ISOs) A form of deferred compensation designed to influence long-term performance. Gives an executive a right to pay today's market price for a block of shares in the company at a future time. No tax is due until the shares are sold.

Increase Guidelines Inherent compensation system controls. They specify amount and timing of pay increases on an organization-wide basis.

Indirect Compensation Pay received through services and benefits (e.g., pensions, health insurance, vacations).

Individual-Based Systems They focus on employee rather than job characteristics. Pay is based on the highest work-related skills employees possess rather than on the specific job performed.

Instrumentality The perceived contingency that an outcome (performing well) has for another outcome (a reward such as pay).

Internal Consistency Refers to the pay relationships among jobs or skill levels within a single organization and focuses attention on employee and management acceptance of those relationships. It involves establishing equal pay for jobs of equal worth and acceptable pay differentials for jobs of unequal worth.

Internal Equity *See* Internal Consistency.

Internal Labor Markets The rules or procedures that serve to regulate the allocation of employees among different jobs within a single organization.

Internal Pricing Pricing jobs in relationship to what other jobs within the organization are paid.

Interrater Reliability The extent of agreement among raters rating the same individual, group, or phenomena.

Inventories Questionnaires in which tasks, behaviors, and abilities are listed. The core of all quantitative job analysis.

Job Analysis The systematic process of collecting and making certain judgments about all of the important information related to the nature of a specific job. It provides the knowledge needed to define jobs and conduct job evaluation.

Job Based Systems Focus on jobs as the basic unit of analysis to determine the pay structure; hence, job analysis is required.

Job Classes or Grades Each represents a grouping of jobs which are considered substantially similar for pay purposes.

Job Cluster A series of jobs grouped for job evaluation and wage and salary administration purposes on the basis of common skills, occupational qualifications, technology, licensing, working conditions, union jurisdiction, workplace, career paths, and organizational tradition.

Job Competition A model which asserts that workers do not compete for pay in labor markets. Rather, pay for jobs is "quoted" or established and workers compete through their qualifications for the job opportunities (Thurow).

Job Content Information that describes a job. May include responsibility assumed and/or the tasks performed.

Job Description A summary of the most important features of the job as it is performed. It identifies the job and describes the general nature of the work, specific task responsibilities, outcomes, and employee characteristics required to perform the job.

Job Evaluation A systematic procedure designed to aid in establishing pay differentials among jobs within a single employer. It includes classification, comparison of the relative worth of jobs, blending internal and external market forces, measurement, negotiation, and judgment.

Job Evaluation Committee Usually having a membership representing all important constituencies within the organization. It may be charged with the responsibility of (1) selecting a job evaluation system, (2) carrying out or at least supervising the process of job evaluation, and (3) evaluating the success with which the job evaluation has been conducted. Its role may vary among organizations.

Job Evaluation Manual Contains information on the job evaluation plan and is used as a "yardstick" to evaluate jobs. It includes a description of the job evaluation method used, descriptions of all jobs, and if relevant, a description of compensable factors, numerical degree scales, and weights. May also contain a description of available review or appeals procedure.

Job Evaluation Methods Four fundamental JE methods are in use: ranking, classification, factor comparison, and point plan. They can be distinguished by looking at (1) whether the evaluation is based on the whole job or specific factors, (2) whether jobs are evaluated against some standard or against each other, and (3) whether the evaluation is qualitative or quantitative.

Job Family Jobs involving work of the same nature but requiring different skill and responsibility levels (e.g., computing and account-recording is a job family; bookkeeper, accounting clerk, teller are jobs within that family).

Job Grade *See* Pay Grade.

Job Hierarchy A grouping of jobs based on their job-related similarities and differences, and on their value to the organization's objectives.

Job Structure Relationships among jobs inside an organization, based on work content and the job's relative contribution to achieving organization's objectives.

Job Value Approach to Pay Survey Under this approach the employer uses its internal job evaluation plan to assess the benchmark jobs provided in the survey.

Just Wage Doctrine A theory of job value that posited a "just" or equitable wage for any occupation based on that occupation's place in the larger social hierarchy. According to this doctrine, pay structures should be designed and justified on the basis of societal norms, custom, and tradition, not on the basis of economic and market forces.

Key Jobs *See* Benchmark (or Key) Jobs.

Knowledge-Based Pay Systems Under this approach employees are paid for the highest work-related skills they possess rather than the specific job they are performing. That is, the wage is assigned to an employee regardless of the job performed.

Labor Demand In economic models the demand of labor is a curve that indicates how the desired level of employment varies with changes in the price of labor when other factors are held constant. The shape of the labor demand curve is downward sloping. Thus, an increase in the wage rate will reduce the demand for labor in both the short and long run.

Labor Supply In economic models the supply of labor is a curve or schedule representing the average pay required to attract different numbers of employees. The shape of the labor supply curve varies depending on the assumptions. In perfectly competitive markets, an individual firm faces a horizontal (elastic) supply of labor curve.

Lag Pay Level Policy Setting a wage structure to match market rates at beginning of plan year only. The rest of the plan year, internal rates will lag behind market rates. Its objective is to offset labor costs, but it may hinder a firm's ability to attract and retain quality employees.

Lead Pay Level Policy Setting a wage structure to lead the market throughout the plan year. Its aim is to maximize a firm's ability to attract and retain quality employees and to minimize employee dissatisfaction with pay.

Least Squares Line In regression analysis, the line fitted to a scatterplot of coordinates that minimizes the squared deviations of coordinates around the line. This line is known as the "best fit" line.

Legally Required Benefits Benefits that are required by statutory law: workers' compensation, social security, and unemployment compensation.

Leniency Error A rating error in which rated performance consistently exceeds true score performance of ratees.

Level of Aggregation The size of the work unit for which performance is measured (e.g., individual, work group, department, plant, organization) and to which rewards are distributed.

Level Rise The percentage increase in the average wage rate paid.

$$\text{Percent level rise} = 100 \times \frac{\text{Average pay year end} - \text{Average pay year beginning}}{\text{Average pay at the beginning of the year}}$$

Linear Regression A statistical technique which allows an analyst to build a model of a relationship between variables that are assumed to be linearly related.

Local Country Nationals (LCNs) Citizens of a country in which a U.S. foreign subsidiary is located. LCNs' compensation is tied either to local wage rates or to the rates of U.S. expatriates performing the same job. Each practice has different equity implications.

Long-Term Disability (LTD) Plans An insurance plan that provides payments to replace income lost through an inability to work that is not covered by other legally required disability income plans.

Long-Term Incentives Inducements offered in advance to influence longer range (multiyear) results. Usually offered to top managers and professionals to focus on long-term organizational objectives.

Management by Objectives (MBO) An employee planning, development, and appraisal procedure in which a supervisor and a subordinate, or group of subordinates, jointly identify and establish common performance goals. Employee performance on the absolute standards is evaluated at the end of the specified period.

Marginal Product of Labor The additional output associated with the employment of one additional human resources unit, with other factors held constant.

Marginal Productivity Theory (MPT) By contrast with Marxist "surplus value" theory, MPT focuses on labor demand rather than supply and argues that employers will pay a wage to a unit of labor that equals that unit's use (not exchange) value. That is, work is compensated in proportion to its contribution to the organization's production objectives.

Marginal Revenue of Labor The additional revenue generated when the firm employs one additional unit of human resources, with other factors held constant.

Market Pay Lines Summarize the distributions of market rates for the benchmark jobs under consideration. Several methods to construct the lines can be used: a single line connecting the distributions' midpoints (means or medians), or the 25th, 50th, and 75th percentiles. Often the lines are fitted to the data through a statistical procedure, such as regression analysis.

Market Pricing Pricing jobs so that the job worth and the pay structure are almost exclusively determined through reliance on external data.

Maturity Curves   A plot of the empirical relationship between current pay and years since a professional has last received a degree (YSLD), thus allowing organizations to determine a competitive wage level for specific professional employees with varying levels of experience.

Merit Pay   A reward that recognizes outstanding past performance. It can be given in the form of lump-sum payments or as increments to the base pay. Merit programs are commonly designed to pay different amounts (often at different times) depending on the level of performance.

Merit Pay Increase Guidelines   Ties pay increases to performance. They may take one of two forms: The simplest version specifies pay increases permissible for different levels of performance. More complex guidelines tie pay not only to performance but also to position in the pay range.

Merrick Plan   Individual incentive plan that provides for variable incentives as a function of units of production per time period. It works like the Taylor plan, but three piecework rates are set: (1) high—for production exceeding 100 percent of standard; (2) medium—for production between 83 percent and 100 percent of standard; and (3) low—for production less than 83 percent of standard.

Middle and Top Management   Employees, above the supervisory level, who have technical and administrative training and whose major duties entail the direction of people and the organization. They can be classified as special groups to the extent the organization devises special compensation programs to attract and retain these relatively scarce human resources. By this definition, not all managers above the supervisory level qualify for consideration as a special group.

Minimum Wage   A minimum wage level for most Americans established by Congress as part of the FLSA of 1938. As of January 1981 it was established at $3.35 per hour. Forty-seven states also have minimum wage laws which cover employees exempt from FLSA.

Motivation   An individual's willingness to engage in some behavior. Primarily concerned with: (1) what energizes human behavior; (2) what directs or channels such behavior; and (3) how this behavior is maintained or sustained.

National Electrical Manufacturing Association (NEMA)   A point factor job evaluation system that evolved into the National Position Evaluation Plan sponsored by NMTA associates.

National Metal Trades Association Plan (NMTA)   A point factor job evaluation plan for production, maintenance, and service personnel.

National Position Evaluation Plan   A point factor job evaluation system that evolved from the former NEMA plan. Today, the plan is sponsored by 11 management/manufacturing associations and is offered under the umbrella group known as NMTA associates.

Need Theories Motivation theories that focus on internally generated needs which induce behaviors designed to reduce these needs.

Nonexempt Employees Employees who are subject to the provisions of the Fair Labor Standards Act.

Nonqualified Deferred Compensation Plans A plan does not qualify for tax exemption if an employer who pays high levels of deferred compensation to executives does not make proportionate contributions to lower level employees.

Objective Performance-Based Pay Systems Focus on objective performance standards (e.g., counting output) derived from organizational objectives and a thorough analysis of the job (e.g., incentive and gain-sharing plans).

Organizational Culture The composite of shared values, symbols, and cognitive schemes which ties people together in the organization.

Organizational Values Shared norms and beliefs regarding what is socially, organizationally, and individually right, worthy, or desirable. The composite of values contributes to form a common organizational culture.

Paired Comparison A ranking job evaluation method that involves comparing all possible pairs of jobs under study.

Participation Rate The total number of employees anticipated to receive pay increases in the plan year divided by the total number of employees eligible to receive pay increases.

Pay Discrimination It is usually defined to include: (1) access discrimination which occurs when qualified women and minorities are denied access to particular jobs, promotions, or training opportunities; and (2) valuation discrimination which takes place when minorities or women are paid less than white males for performing substantially equal work. Both types of discrimination are illegal under Title VII of the Civil Rights Act of 1964. Others argue that valuation discrimination can also occur when men and women hold entirely different jobs (in content or results) which are of comparable worth to the employer. Existing federal laws do not support the "equal pay for work of comparable worth" standard.

Pay Grade One of the classes, levels, or groups into which jobs of the same or similar values are grouped for compensation purposes. All jobs in a pay grade have the same pay range—maximum, minimum, and midpoint.

Pay Increase Guidelines The mechanism through which performance levels are translated into pay increases and, therefore, dictate the size and time of the pay reward for good performance.

Pay Level An average of the array of rates paid by an employer.

Pay Level Policies Decisions concerning a firm's level of pay vis-`a-vis product and labor market competitors. There are three classes of pay level policies: to lead, to meet, or to follow competition.

Pay Mix   Relative emphasis among compensation components such as base pay, merit, incentives, and benefits.

Pay Objectives   *See* Compensation Objectives.

Pay Plan Design   A process to identify pay levels, components, and timing which best match individual needs and organizational requirements.

Pay Policy Line   Represents the organization's pay level policy relative to what competitors pay for similar jobs.

Pay Ranges   The range of pay rates from minimum to maximum set for a pay grade or class. They put limits on the rates an employer will pay for a particular job.

Pay Satisfaction   A function of the discrepancy between employee perceptions of how much pay they *should* receive and how much pay they *do* receive. If these perceptions are equal an employee is said to experience pay satisfaction.

Pay Structures   The array of pay rates for different jobs within a single organization; they focus attention on differential compensation paid for work of unequal worth.

Pay Techniques   Mechanisms or technologies of compensation management, such as job analysis, job descriptions, market surveys, job evaluation, and the like, that tie the four basic pay policies to the pay objectives.

Pay with Competition Policy   This policy tries to ensure that a firm's labor costs are approximately equal to those of its competitors. It seeks to avoid placing an employer at a disadvantage in pricing products or in maintaining a qualified work force.

PAYSOPs (Payroll-Based Tax Credit Employee Stock Ownership Plans)   A new form of TRASOPs beginning in 1983 in which the tax credit allotted to plan sponsors who permit and match voluntary employee contributions is payroll based, not investment based.

Pension Plan   A form of deferred compensation. All pension plans usually have four common characteristics: (1) they involve deferred payments to a former employee (or surviving spouse) for past services rendered; and they all specify (2) a normal retirement age at which time benefits begin to accrue to the employee; (3) the formula employed to calculate benefits; and (4) integration with social security benefits.

Percentage Pay Range Overlap   The degree to which adjacent pay ranges in a structure overlap is usually calculated in terms of the following percentage:

$$\text{Percentage overlap} = 100 \times \frac{\text{Maximum rate for lower pay grade} - \text{Minimum rate for higher pay grade}}{\text{Maximum rate for lower pay grade} - \text{Minimum rate for lower pay grade}}$$

Performance Evaluation (or performance appraisal) A process to determine the correspondence between worker behavior/task outcomes and employer expectations (performance standards).

Performance Ranking The simplest, fastest, easiest to understand, and least expensive performance appraisal technique. Orders employees from highest to lowest in performance.

Planned Compa-Ratio Budgeting A form of top down budgeting in which a planned compa-ratio rather than a planned level rise is established to control pay costs.

Planned Level Rise The percentage increase in average pay that is planned to occur after considering such factors as anticipated rates of change in market data, changes in cost of living, the employer's ability to pay, and the effects of turnover and promotions. This index may be used in top down budgeting to control compensation costs.

Planned Level Rise Budgeting A form of top down budgeting under which a planned level rise rather than a planned compa-ratio is established as the target to control pay costs.

Point (Factor) Method A job evaluation method that employs (1) compensable factors, (2) factor degrees numerically scaled, and (3) weights reflecting the relative importance of each factor. Once scaled degrees and weights are established for each factor, each job is measured against each compensable factor and a total score is calculated for each job. The total points assigned to a job determine the job's relative value and hence its location in the pay structure.

Policy Capturing Approach to Factor Selection *See* Statistical Approach to Factor Selection.

Portability Transferability of pension benefits for employees moving to a new organization; ERISA does not require mandatory portability of private pensions. On a voluntary basis, the employer may agree to let an employee's pension benefits transfer to an individual retirement account (IRA) or, in a reciprocating arrangement, to the new employer.

Portal-to-Portal Act of 1947 Defines compensable working time to include only the "principal activity" unless the custom is otherwise.

Position Analysis Questionnaire (PAQ) A structured job analysis technique that classifies job information into seven basic factors: information input, mental processes, work output, relationships with other persons, job context, other job characteristics, and general dimensions. The PAQ analyzes jobs in terms of worker-oriented data.

Position Description Questionnaire (PDQ) A quantitative job analysis technique.

Pregnancy Discrimination Act of 1978 An amendment to Title VII of the Civil Rights Act. It requires employers to extend to pregnant employees or spouses of employees the same disability and medical benefits provided other employees or spouses of employees.

Prevailing Wage Laws A government-defined prevailing wage is the minimum wage that must be paid for work done on covered government projects or purchases. In practice these prevailing rates have been union rates paid in various geographic areas. The main prevailing wage laws are: (1) Davis-Bacon (1931), (2) Walsh-Healey Public Contracts Act (1936), and (3) McNamara-O'Hara Service Contract Act of 1965.

Procedural Equity Concerned with the process used to make and implement decisions about pay. It suggests that the way pay decisions are made and implemented may be as important to employees as the results of the decisions.

Process Theories Motivation theories that focus on *how* people are motivated rather than on what motivates people (e.g., drive, expectancy and equity theories).

Product Market The market (or market segments) in which a firm competes to sell products or services.

Professional Employee An employee who has specialized training of a scientific or intellectual nature and whose major duties do not entail the supervision of people.

Profit-Sharing Plans Focus on profitability as the standard for group incentive. These plans typically can be found in one of three distributions: (1) cash or current distribution plans provide full payment to participants soon after profits have been determined (quarterly or annually); (2) deferred plans have a portion of current profits credited to employee accounts, with cash payment made at time of retirement, disability, severance, or death; and (3) combination plans incorporate aspects of both current and deferred options.

Progression through the Pay Ranges There are three strategies to move employees through the pay ranges: (1) automatic or seniority-based progression, which is most appropriate when the necessary job skills are within the grasp of most employees; (2) merit progression, which is more appropriate when jobs allow variations in performance; and (3) a combination of automatic and merit progression. For example, employers may grant automatic increases up to the midpoint of the range and permit subsequent increases only when merited on the basis of performance appraisal.

Qualified Deferred Compensation Plan To qualify for tax exemption, a deferred compensation program must provide contributions or benefits for employees other than executives that are proportionate in compensation terms to contributions provided to executives.

Quantitative Job Analysis (QJA) Job analysis method that relies on scaled questionnaires and inventories that produce job-related data which are documentable, can be statistically analyzed, and may be more objective.

Range Maximums   The maximum values to be paid for a job grade, representing the top value the organization places on the output of the work.

Range Midpoint   The salary midway between the minimum and maximum rates of a salary range. The midpoint rate for each range is usually set to correspond to the pay policy line and represents the rate paid for satisfactory performance on the job.

Range Minimums   The minimum values to be paid for a job grade, representing the minimum value the organization places on the work. Often rates below the minimum are used for trainees.

Range Overlap   The degree of overlap between adjoining grade ranges is determined by the differences in midpoints among ranges and the range spread. A high degree of overlap and narrow midpoint differentials indicate small differences in the value of jobs in the adjoining grades, and permit promotions without much change in the rates paid. By contrast, a small degree of overlap and wide midpoint differentials allow the manager to reinforce a promotion with a large salary increase.

Range Width or Spread   The range maximum and minimum are usually based on what other employers are doing and some judgment about how the range spread fits the organization, including the amount of individual discretion in the work.

Ranges   *See* Pay Ranges.

Ranking   A simple job evaluation method that involves ordering the job descriptions from highest to lowest in value.

Rating Errors   Errors in judgment that occur in a systematic manner when an individual observes and evaluates a person, group, or phenomenon. The most frequently described rating errors include halo, leniency, severity, and central tendency errors.

Red Circle Rates   Pay rates that are above the maximum rate for a job or pay range for a grade.

Reinforcement Theories   Such as expectancy and operant conditioning theory grant a prominent role to rewards (e.g., compensation) in motivating behavior. They argue that pay motivates behavior to the extent merit increases and other work-related rewards are allocated on the basis of performance.

Relative Value of Jobs   Refers to their relative contribution to organizational goals, to their external market rates, or to some other agreed upon rates.

Relevant Markets   Those employers with whom an organization competes for skills and products/services. Three factors commonly used to determine the relevant markets are: the occupation or skills required, the geography (willingness to relocate and/or commute), and the other employers involved (particularly those who compete in the product market).

Reliability   The consistency of the results obtained. That is, the extent to which any measuring procedure yields the same results on repeated trials. Reliable job information does not mean that it is accurate (valid), comprehensive, or free from bias.

Reopener Clause   A provision in an employment contract that specifies that wages, and sometimes such nonwage items as pension/benefits, will be renegotiated under certain conditions (changes in cost of living, organization profitability, and so on).

Revenue Act of 1978   It primarily simplified pension plans, added tax incentives for individual retirement accounts (IRAs), and adjusted requirements for ESOPs. The act also provided that cafeteria benefit plans need not be included in gross income, and reaffirmed the legality of deferring compensation and taxes due on it for an employee. In addition, the act permits savings programs for which employee contributions avoid federal, state, and FICA taxes.

Reward System   The composite of all organizational mechanisms and strategies used to formally acknowledge employee behaviors and performance. It includes all forms of compensation, promotions, and assignments; nonmonetary awards and recognitions; training opportunities; job design and analysis; organizational design and working conditions; the supervisor; social networks; performance standards and reward criteria; performance evaluation; and the like.

Rowan Plan   Individual incentive plan that provides for variable incentives as a function of a standard expressed as time period per unit of production. It is similar to the Halsey plan, but in this plan a worker's bonus increases as the time required to complete the task decreases.

Rucker Plan   A group cost savings plan in which cost reductions due to employee efforts are shared with the employees. It involves a somewhat more complex formula than a Scanlon plan for determining employee incentive bonuses.

Salary   Pay given to employees who are exempt from regulations of the Fair Labor Standards Act, and hence do not receive overtime pay (e.g., managers and professionals). "Exempts" pay is calculated at an annual or monthly rate rather than hourly.

Salary Continuation Plans   Benefit options that provide some form of protection for disability. Some are legally required, such as workers' compensation provisions for work-related disability, and Social Security disability income provisions for those who qualify.

Salary Sales Compensation Plan   Under this plan the sales force is paid a fixed income not dependent on sales volume.

Sales Compensation   Any form of compensation paid to sales representatives. Sales compensation formulas usually attempt to establish direct incentives for sales outcomes.

Scanlon Plan A group cost savings plan designed to lower labor costs without lowering the level of a firm's activity. Incentives are derived as the ratio between labor costs and sales values of production (SVOP).

Seniority Increases These tie pay increases to a progression pattern based on seniority. To the extent performance improves with time on the job, this method has the rudiments of paying for performance.

Severity Error A rating error in which rated performance is consistently lower than the true score performance of ratees.

Short-Term Disability *See* Workers' Compensation.

Short-Term Incentives Inducements offered in advance to influence future short-range (annual) results. Usually very specific performance standards are established.

Short-Term Income Protection *See* Unemployment Insurance.

Sick Leave Paid time when not working due to illness or injury.

Simplified Employee Pension (SEP) A retirement income arrangement intended to markedly reduce the paperwork for regular pension plans.

Single Rate Pay System A compensation policy under which all employees in a given job are paid at the same rate instead of being placed in a pay grade. Generally applies to situations in which there is little room for variation in job performance, such as an assembly line.

Skill-Based/Global Approach to Wage Survey This approach does not emphasize comparison of pay for specific jobs. Instead, it recognizes that employers usually tailor jobs to the organization or individual employee. Therefore, the rates paid to every individual employee in an entire skill group or function are included in the salary survey and become the reference point to design pay levels and structures.

Skill Requirement Includes experience, training, and ability as measured by the performance requirements of a particular job.

Social Information Processing Theory (SIP) Counters need theory by focusing on external factors that motivate performance. According to SIP theorists, workers pay attention to environmental cues (e.g., inputs/outputs of co-workers) and process this information in a way that may alter personal work goals, expectancies, and perceptions of equity. In turn this influences job attitudes, behavior, and performance.

Social Security The Social Security Act of 1935 established what has become the federal old-age, survivors, disability, and health insurance system. The beneficiaries are workers that participate in the Social Security program, their spouses, dependent parents, and dependent children. Benefits vary according to: (1) earnings of the worker, (2) length of time in the program, (3) age when benefits start, (4) age and number of recipients other than the worker, and (5) state of health of recipients other than the worker.

Special Groups Employee groups for whom compensation practices diverge from typical company procedures (e.g., supervisors, middle and upper management, nonsupervisory professionals, sales, and foreign service personnel).

Spillover Effect This phenomenon refers to the fact that improvements obtained in unionized firms "spill over" to nonunion firms seeking ways to lessen workers' incentives for organizing a union.

Standard Hour Plan Individual incentive plan in which rate determination is based on time period per unit of production, and wages vary directly as a constant function of production level. In this context, the incentive rate in standard hour plans is set based on completion of a task in some expected time period.

Standard Metropolitan Statistical Area (SMSA) Geographical division used by the Bureau of the Census and the Social and Economic Statistics Administration of the Department of Commerce. Each SMSA consists of one or more counties that meet standards pertaining to population and metropolitan character.

Standard Rating Scales Characterized by: (1) one or more performance standards being developed and defined for the appraiser; and (2) each performance standard having a measurement scale indicating varying levels of performance on that dimension. Appraisers rate the appraisee by checking the point on the scale that best represents the appraisee's performance level. Rating scales vary in the extent to which anchors along the scale are defined.

Statistical Approach to Factor Selection This method uses a variety of statistical procedures to derive factors from data collected through quantitative job analysis from a sample of jobs that represent the range of the work employees (or an employee group) perform in the company. It is often labeled as "policy capturing" to contrast it with the committee judgment approach.

Stock Appreciation Rights (SARs) An SAR permits an executive all the potential capital gain of a stock incentive option (ISO) without requiring the purchase of stock and, thus, reduces an executive's cash commitment. Payment is provided on demand for the difference between the stock option price and current market price.

Stock Purchase Plan (Nonqualified) A plan that is, in effect, a management stock purchase plan. It allows senior management or other key personnel to buy stock in the business. This plan has certain restrictions: (1) the stockholder must be employed for a certain period of time; (2) the business has the right to buy back the stock; and (3) stockholders cannot sell the stock for a defined period.

Stock Purchase Plan (Qualified) A program under which employees buy shares in the company's stock, with the company contributing a specific amount for each unit of employee contribution. Also, stock may be offered at a fixed price (usually below market) and paid for in full by the employees.

Straight Piecework System Individual incentive plan in which rate determination is based on units of production per time period, and wages vary directly as a constant function of production level.

Strategic Issues Critical considerations in compensation design such as congruency between the pay system and the strategy, the organization's culture and values, employee needs, and the nature of the union relationships.

Strategy The fundamental direction of the organization. It guides the deployment of all resources, including compensation.

Subjective Performance-Based Pay Systems Focus on subjective performance standards (e.g., achievement of agreed upon objectives) derived from organizational objectives and a thorough analysis of the job.

Substantive Equity In contrast with procedural equity, substantive equity refers to the equity of the outcomes (results such as pay level, structure, and employee differentials) of the pay system.

Supplemental Unemployment Benefits (SUB) Plan Employer-funded plan which supplements state unemployment insurance payments to workers during temporary periods of layoffs. Largely concentrated in the automobile, steel, and related industries.

Surplus Value The difference between labor's use and exchange value. According to Marx, under capitalism wages are based on labor's exchange value—which is lower than its use value—and, thus, provide only a subsistent wage.

SVOP (Sales Value of Production) This concept includes sales revenue and the value of goods in inventory.

Tax Equalization Allowances A method whereby an expatriate pays neither more nor less tax than the assumed home-country tax on base remuneration. The employer usually deducts the assumed home-country tax from monthly salary and reimburses the employee for all taxes paid in the country of assignment and any actual home-country tax on company remuneration only.

Taylor Plan Individual incentive plan that provides for variable incentives as a function of units of production per time period. It provides two piecework rates that are established for production above (or below) standard, and these rates are higher (or lower) than the regular wage incentive level.

Third Country Nationals (TCNs) Employees of a U.S. foreign subsidiary who maintain citizenship in a country other than the United States or the host country. TCNs' compensation is tied to comparative wages in the local country, the United States, or the country of citizenship. Each approach has different equity implications.

Thrift Savings Plans The typical thrift plan is designed to help American workers in meeting savings goals. The most common plan involves a 50 percent employer match on employee contributions up to a maximum of 6 percent of pay.

Time Span of Discretion (TSD)   A single-factor job evaluation system that focuses on measuring the amount of discretion an employee has in a job. Under this method jobs are comprised of tasks, and each task has an implicit or explicit time before its consequences become evident. TSD designs the longest period of time in completing an assigned task that employees are expected to exercise discretion with regard to the pace and quality of the work without managerial review.

Title VII of the Civil Rights Act of 1964   A major piece of legislation prohibiting pay discrimination. It is much broader in intent than the EPA, forbidding discrimination on the basis of race, color, religion, sex, pregnancy, or national origin.

"Top Down" Approach to Pay Budgeting   Also known as unit-level budgeting. Under this approach a total pay budget for the organization (or unit) is determined and allocated "down" to individual employees during the plan year. There are many approaches to unit-level budgeting. They differ in the type of financial index used as a control measure. Controlling to planned level rise and controlling to a planned compa-ratio are two typical approaches.

Total Compensation   The complete pay package for employees including all forms of money, benefits, services, and in-kind payments.

TRASOP (Tax Reduction Act Employee Stock Ownership Plan)   A form of Employee Stock Ownership Plan (ESOP) that meets specific requirements of the Tax Reform Act of 1975, as amended.

TSD   *See* Time Span of Discretion.

Two-Tier Pay Plans   Wage structures that differentiate pay for the same jobs based on hiring date. A contract is negotiated that specifies that employees hired after a specified date will receive lower wages than their higher seniority peers working on the same or similar jobs.

Unemployment Benefits   *See* Unemployment Insurance.

Unemployment Compensation   *See* Unemployment Insurance.

Unemployment Insurance (UI)   State-administered programs that provide financial security for workers during periods of joblessness. These plans are wholly financed by employers except in Alabama, Alaska, and New Jersey, where there are provisions for relatively small employee contributions.

Unequal Impact   *See* Disparate (Unequal) Impact Standard.

Unequal Treatment   *See* Disparate (Unequal) Treatment Standard.

United States Expatriates (USEs)   American citizens working for a U.S. subsidiary in a foreign country. Main compensation concerns are "to keep the expatriates whole" relative to American-based counterparts and, also, to provide them with an incentive wage for accepting the assignment in a foreign country.

Universal Job Factors Factors that could theoretically be used to evaluate all jobs in all organizations.

Use Value The value or price ascribed to the use or consumption of labor in the production of goods or services.

Valence The amount of positive or negative value placed on specific outcomes by an individual.

Validity The accuracy of the results obtained. That is, the extent to which any measuring device measures what it purports to measure.

Valuation Discrimination Focuses on the pay women and minorities receive for the work they perform. Discrimination occurs when members of these groups are paid less than white males for performing substantially equal work. This definition of pay discrimination is based on the standard of "equal pay for equal work." Many believe that this definition is limited. In their view, valuation discrimination can also occur when men and women hold entirely different jobs (in content or results) which are of comparable worth to the employer. Existing federal laws do not support the "equal pay for work of comparable worth" standard.

Vesting A benefit plan provision that guarantees that participants will, after meeting certain requirements, retain a right to the benefits they have accrued, or some portion of them, even if employment under the plan terminates before retirement.

VIE Theory *See* Expectancy Theory.

Wage Pay given to employees who are covered by overtime and reporting provisions of the Fair Labor Standards Act. "Nonexempts" usually have their pay calculated at an hourly rate rather than a monthly or annual rate.

Wage Adjustment Provisions Clauses in a multiyear union contract which specify the types of wage adjustments that have to be implemented during the life of the contract. These adjustments might be specified in three major ways: (1) deferred wage increases—negotiated at the time of contract negotiation with the time and amount specified in the contract; (2) cost-of-living adjustments (COLAs) or escalator clauses; and (3) reopener clauses.

Wage and Price Controls Government regulations that aim at maintaining low inflation and low levels of unemployment. They frequently focus on "cost push" inflation, limiting the size of the pay raises and the rate of increases in the prices charged for goods and services. Used for limited time periods only.

Wage Survey The systematic process of collecting information and making judgments about the compensation paid by other employers. Wage survey data are useful to design pay levels and structures.

Walsh-Healey Public Contracts Act of 1936 A federal law requiring certain employers holding federal contracts for the manufacture or provision of materials, supplies, and equipment to pay industry-prevailing wage rates.

Work or Task Data   Involve the elemental units of work (tasks), with emphasis on the purpose of each task, collected for job analysis. Work data describe the job in terms of actual tasks performed and their output.

Worker or Behavioral Data   Include the behaviors required by the job. Used in job analysis.

Workers' Compensation   An insurance program, paid for by the employer, designed to protect employees from expenses incurred for a work-related injury or disease. Each state has its own workers' compensation law.

YSLD   Years since a professional has last received a degree.

Name Index

Subject Index

This book has been set Linotron 202 in 10 and 9 point
Times Roman leaded 2 points. Part and chapter numbers
are 48 point Times Bold Italic; part and chapter titles are
30 point Times Bold Italic. The size of the type page is 35
by 48 picas.

Req, of a good pay structure:
1. The mkt. line is in the center of the box on the graph
2. The structure has an up-going step progression.
3. all minimums are below the previous pay grade max. by a reasonable amt
4. The range spread is increasing as the pay grade increases and the change is consistent.

1. Defined benefit vs defined contribution:

Def. Contribution

ex. "my co. will put 10% of your salary into the plan."
- Co.'s contribution is fixed
- Benefit varies (Benefit = what employee gets out of the plan)
- Co. likes this because they know exactly what they'll have to put in.

Defined Benefit

ex. "at retirement you will get $25,000."
- Benefit to employee is fixed
- contribution varies (NPV analysis)
- Employees like this because they know exactly what they'll get out of the plan (regardless of interest rates etc.)

Cafeteria Plans (P 405-406)
↳ ① Growing trend toward Flexible benefit plans (P 406)

Vesting (P 433-434)

2. Gov't mandated benefits (P 472, 412-423)

3. Salary Survey (Pg. 221-245)
- How do you define your labor mkt?

nuclear Desi. Eng. (or manager)	Carpender (or welder)
- can't look local because there aren't enough	- local lab. mkt
- The type of co is import here (knowledge of the specific topic or product is important!)	- Type of co. not important (cutting & nailing is the same no matter where you go).
- The sz of the co. would not matter.	- sz of co. might matter here in terms of how much they pay the carpender.
- Toss out odd ball co's	
- make sure that the job is a gd. match	

→ what are the things that would cause you to react differently in terms of the lab. mkt.

4. Bench Mark Jobs (P 231) work on this

5. motivation → perf. oriented   satisfaction → happy
   → focus on performance   → survey peoples wants & attitudes
   → look at output

   output vs. turnover.

   Think of situations where turnover is more important than output....

        Turnover impt when:
        long training process

          ↑ satis. → ↓ absenteeism, ↓ turnover

6.

⑦ Growing Trend Toward Flexible Benefit Plans. (Pg 405-406)
- Look at ①

⑧ Justice - Perceived sense of equity
Procedural ⇒ outcome doesn't matter
A. Can focus on the appeals process
→ Does your appeals plan focus on process or outcome.
- outcome oriented process
~ employee must state why they feel the outcome was not just
- process oriented
~ employee must state what was unjust about the process.
B. Can look at the design of the system itself
- In MRI we used a combo:
1. Set up structure
2. Compared to jobs in the external labor market.

⑨ ↑ in the minimum wage (458-460)

⑩ Comparable Worth vs. Equal Pay Act.
what is fair?
Equal Pay? Comparable Pay?
→ what is equal pay?

— Difficult to implement because it is very difficult to make
meaningful comparisons between jobs from totally unrelated
job classifications
— Equal Pay Act says that males + females should be paid the same
for equal - ie. identical work ⇒ same job.
— Comparable worth doctrine says than men & women should
be paid the same for comparable work.

- Two major approaches for achieving equal pay:
1. EEO + affirmative action say should move more
females into job classifications traditionally occupied
by males.
2. Comparable worth approach says should increase the
wage scales of the predominantly female classifications
to match those of the predominantly male classifications.
Ideally we'd like to achieve equity but if we overturn
the traditional system of job evaluation how will we price
jobs in the future.

⑪ Lincoln Electric
* employee acceptance
1. involvement
2. gd track record plan paid off
3. fair sys. of perf evaluations
- spread out over the course of a yr.
4. socialized ⇒ self selection
5. elements of the ec. ⇒ co. does one thing + does it well
~ easier to measure.
6. simple

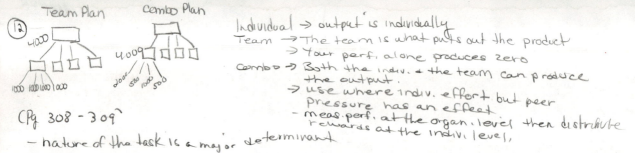

(12)

Team Plan

Combo Plan

Individual → output is individually
Team → The team is what puts out the product
→ Your perf. alone produces zero
Combo → Both the indiv. & the team can produce
the output.
→ use where indiv. effort but peer
pressure has an effect
- meas. perf. at the organ. level then distribute
rewards at the indiv. level,

(Pg 308 - 309)

- nature of the task is a major determinant